THE RISE OF THE KOREAN SOCIALIST MOVEMENT

Nationalist Activities in Russia and China, 1905-1921

이 도서의 국립중앙도서관 출판예정도서목록(CIP)은 서지정보유통지원시스템 홈페이지(http://seoji.nl.go.kr)와
국가자료공동목록시스템(http://www.nl.go.kr/kolisnet)에서 이용하실 수 있습니다.
CIP제어번호: CIP2016006159(양장), CIP2016006160(반양장)

THE RISE OF THE KOREAN SOCIALIST MOVEMENT

Nationalist Activities in Russia and China, 1905-1921

Byung Yool Ban

Hanul
Academy

In Memory of My Eldest Brother,

Mr. Byong-ho Ban

This book is intended to be a study of the Korean revolutionary exiles in China and Russia, who strove to attain the independence of their country from Japanese colonial rule in the early twentieth century. This study covers the period from approximately 1905 (the establishment of a Japanese Protectorate) to 1921 (the foundation of the Korean Communist Party, Koryŏ Kongsandang). The author believes that Korean nationalists dominated the Korean resistance movement against Japanese colonial rule until 1921; but after 1921, the newly emerged Korean Communists attempted to win the hegemony of the anti-Japanese movement from non-Communists.

This work is an examination of the political thoughts and activities of the Korean nationalists. It offers an analysis of how they adjusted their political thoughts and strategies as the circumstance surrounding Korea changed. At the same time, this research paid attention to the international situation, especially events such as the Russo-Japanese War (1904-1905), the Japanese annexation of Korea (1910), the revolution in China (1911), World War I (1914-1918), the Russian

Revolution (1917), the intervention in Siberia (1918-1922) and the Paris Peace Conference (1919).

Previous works on the Korean nationalistic activities for independence have demonstrated two main problems. First of all, most of them have focused on the period after the March First Movement in 1919. They have paid less attention to the period from 1910 to 1919. Accordingly, they have failed to explain effectively the continuity and changes which had occurred during the period between the Koreans' desperate struggles against the Japanese in the period before annexation and the outbreak of rejuvenating revolutionary movements after the March First Movement. For example, previous works on the Korean independence movements after the March First Movement have failed to explain why the majority of Korean nationalists arrived at an early consensus as to the form of government for a future independent Korean state without serious controversies among themselves. A study shows that, as early as 1917, Korean nationalists in Shanghai discarded the idea of monarchism and adopted republicanism for the future Korean provisional government system. Although the study implies that World War I and the Russian (February) Revolution influenced their adoption of republicanism, it did not clearly explain how the Korean nationalists came to discard the idea of monarchism which they had held until the time shortly after the outbreak of the World War I.[1]

The author believes that without understanding the revolutionary movement in the 1910s, it is difficult to explain such questions as how the main leaders of the pre-annexation anti-Japanese movements (both military and cultural) developed their political ideas in the 1910s; how the conflicts between the advocates for peaceful educational and cultural methods and militant Righteous Armies [Ŭibyŏng] leaders came to be united in some places and to persist with previous contests in other places; how Korean nationalists adopted republicanism in 1917; and how and at whose direction the Korean Communist movement began. In sum, the author hopes that, in terms of political ideas and strategies, his work will contribute to building a bridge between the pre-annexation and the post-March First Movement periods.

What led previous scholars to disregard the 1910s? First of all, the relatively declining activities of Korean nationalists in the period have made it a less popular area of study for historians. As a result of the intensified suppression of the people of Korea by the Japanese colonial authorities since the Russo-Japanese War, particularly with the Japanese annexation of Korea, Korean resistance against Japanese colonial rule tended temporarily to wane. Japan's entry into the war (WWI), whereby it became Russia's ally, made it extremely difficult for Korean nationalists in the Russian Maritime Province to continue their struggle. In addition, Japan's increasing pressure against the Chinese government also undermined the political situation of Korean nationalists in China, particularly in Manchuria. Accordingly, the Korean revolutionary movement in Russia and China was in an extremely difficult situation during the period from 1914 (the outbreak of the World War I) to February 1917 (the Russian Revolution). The World War I period is one of the main parts of this book.

Secondly, the relative insufficiencies of primary sources such as newspapers and magazines have made it difficult for historians to study the Korean revolutionary movement of the 1910s. Suppression by the Chinese and Russian authorities made it difficult for Korean nationalists to retain for storage the primary materials which usually enable historians to improve their understanding of any period. Compared with the number of newspapers and magazines available for the 1900s, a much smaller number of newspapers and magazines were published in the 1910s by the Koreans. There are a very limited number of primary sources written in the 1910s by Korean nationalists themselves. For example, the *Kwŏnŏp Sinmun* (Work Promotion Gazette), published by Koreans in Vladivostok since 1912, was in 1914 forced by the Russian authorities to cease publishing. Only the *Sinhan Minbo* (The New Korea) could continue to be published through the 1910s, mainly because it was based in the United States. *The Sinhan Minbo* is one of the very few primary sources that inform us about the situation of the Korean nationalist movement during the 1910s, particularly of the World War I period.

The author tried to resolve this problem by exploiting scattered materials written in a number of languages: Korean, Japanese, Russian, Chinese, German and English. For example, the official and private documents written in Japanese and Russian will be useful as supplemental sources for the study of the Korean revolutionary movement of the 1910s.

The second problem is that previous works have paid less attention to the relationship between the Korean revolutionary movements, the international situation and the revolutionary movements in Korea's neighboring countries (Russia, Japan and China). Considering the fact that Korean revolutionary exiles were influenced by the political situations of the countries where they resided and that they continuously tried to take advantage of the international situation to attain their goals, it is most important to observe carefully how international political conditions brought new political conditions to bear on Korean nationalists. The author is also concerned to answer the question: How, and in what aspects, the revolutionary movements in Russia, China and Japan influenced Korean nationalists in terms of their determining their political ideologies and strategies?

According to the changing international political environment in Russia and China, the countries where they resided, Korean nationalists moved frequently from one country to another. For example, they frequently crossed the Sino-Russian border areas between Manchuria and the Russian Maritime Province in order to find a more favorable place to continue their struggle. Therefore, it is necessary to trace the movement of Korean nationalists as decided by their judgments and perspective of the political situations in Russia and China. Although some works succeeded in analyzing the Korean revolutionary movements in the context of the political situations and revolutionary development in the respective countries where Korean nationalists resided, they have failed to analyze revolutionary movements in one country in the context of Korean revolutionary activities in other countries. For example, although some prominent works succeeded in describing the Korean revolutionary movement in the political context of Russia, they failed to describe and analyze those movements in the whole context of the Korean revolutionary movements in China, Korea, Japan and America. The author tried to overcome an approach which tends to confine Korean revolutionary movement to respective countries by taking into consideration the Korean revolutionary movements in a broader transnational perspective. In this way, this study tried to view the Korean revolutionary movement in the context of the general revolutionary situation in East Asia.

The establishment of "unified" political leadership was the major concern of Korean patriots through the whole period of the Japanese colonial rule. The March First Movement in 1919 provided one of the best chances for Korean revolutionary forces to achieve a "united front" — unified political leadership over the various Korean anti-Japanese political forces. Although some Korean nationalist groups and leaders refused to join, the "unified" Shanghai Provisional Government established in November 1919 had the potential authority and power to bring under its leadership the various Korean anti-Japanese revolutionary forces which had risen through the first decade of Japanese colonial rule.

However, in 1921, this "united front" between the nationalists and socialists in the "unified" Shanghai Provisional Government collapsed when the Korean Socialist Party withdrew from the Government. The breakdown of the "united front" was followed by factional struggles between the two Korean Communist groups — the Korean Socialist Party (Shanghai Group)[2] and the "Irkutsk Group" — over the political and military leadership of suddenly proliferating Korean Communist organizations and military forces in Russia and China.

The Korean Socialist Party (Shanghai Group) during this crucial period of 1919-1920 both in the Korean nationalist and Communist movement played a central role. Because of this, key leaders of this group such as Yi Tong-hwi, Kim Rip and Pak Chin-sun [Ivan Pyotrovich] were targets of criticism by both nationalist opponents and the "Irkutsk Group." These attitudes of the opponents of the Korean Socialist Party (Shanghai Group) have consistently influenced the academic perspectives of the scholars who used the various sorts of records which they left.

Putting aside the question of responsibility for failure in establishing "unified" leadership, it is the basic belief of this study that the leaders of the Korean Socialist Party (Shanghai Group) were also the key leaders of the Korean nationalist movement in the 1910s in the North Chientao and the Primorye (Russian Maritime Province). What activities and political perspectives did the leaders of the Korean Socialist Party (Shanghai Group) have in the nationalist movement in North Chientao and the Primorye in the 1910s? What positions did these leaders take in the Korean nationalist movement in North Chientao and the Primorye, particularly in comparison with other groups or leaders? How and what internal and external contexts did they come to create the first pro-Bolshevik Korean revolutionary party? These are the main questions of this study.

In a decision issued on November 15, 1921, the Commission on the Korean Question of the Comintern in Moscow[3] concluded that the factional struggles between the two Korean Communist groups — the "Shanghai Group" and the "Irkutsk Group" were the continuation of conflict between the two "national revolutionary organizations" — the Korean Provisional Government in Shanghai and the Korean National Council in Vladivostok. In addition, the decision stated that the "Irkutsk Group" mainly united the Korean emigrated people (in Russia) and the "Shanghai Group" had "intimate connection with the Korean nationalist movement."[4]

The competition between the Shanghai Provisional Government and the Korean National Council started in the fall of 1919 when the Council reversed its previous decision to join the "unified" Shanghai Provisional Government, arguing that the Government had "violated" the agreement which the two sides had reached in August 1919. In this split, the Korean Socialist Party decided to join the "unified" Shanghai Provisional Government and separated from the Korean National Council, with whose key members they had worked through the 1910s in the Primorye and North Chientao. In January 1921, fourteen months later, the Korean Socialist Party — the "Shanghai Group" — decided to separate itself from the "unified" Shanghai Provisional Government and came to compete with another Korean Communist Group, called the "Irkutsk Group" in which members of the Korean National Council occupied key positions. Thus the conflict between the Shanghai Provisional Government and the Korean National Council was in fact the competition between the Korean Socialist Party and the Council. Most leaders of these two organizations had worked together in the Korean nationalist movement in the Russian Far East and North Chientao, and their competition, therefore, had its roots in the nationalist movement of the previous years. The main concern of this study is to analyze the Korean nationalist movement from 1905 to early 1921 with concentration on Korean nationalist group led by Yi Tong-hwi and Kim Rip who also established the Korean Socialist Party in May 1918.

Because of the repressive policies of the Japanese government, it was almost impossible to establish the political leadership of Koreans inside Korea during the whole period of the Japanese colonial rule. In the 1920s under the "cultural policy" of the Japanese colonial regime (which was the result of the response to the popular uprising of the March First Movement and the influence of the Taishō democracy in Japan), colonial Korea experienced explosive growth of social, cultural and political activities, but the main stages for anti-Japanese movement of Koreans were still outside Korea.

Manchuria and the Russian Far East, which Koreans called *Wŏndong* (the Far East) in comparison with *Naeji* (inside Korea) or *Haeoe* (abroad-America, Hawaii and Mexico), had been regarded as the most appropriate bases for anti-Japanese activities, mainly because of geographical proximity to Korea and the existence of a large Korean population. Throughout the whole Japanese colonial period, the *Wŏndong* region had been the central stage for the anti-Japanese movement of Koreans.

The geographical adjacency of these regions to Korea made Korean patriots, whether nationalists or communists, consider the regions as staging areas for the full-scale military attack on northern part of Korea which would provoke the response of the Korean people from inside Korea. The frequent military attacks on northern part of Korea throughout the Japanese colonial period were the reflection of these strategies. Secondly, the large size of the Korean communities in these regions enabled them to provide manpower and resources for the anti-Japanese movement. The favorable attitudes of the local authorities toward the Korean nationalist movement also attracted a lot of Korean patriots to these regions. In addition, because Manchuria and the Primorye had once been territory of ancient Korean people, Korean nationalists felt a strong sense of historical franchise toward these regions. Especially, in the 1910s and early 1920s, the Russian Far East was the center of anti-Japanese movement except for a short period under White Russian rule (1918-1920). Chapter 1 examines the historical background of Korean emigration to North Chientao and the Primorye and the policies of the local authorities of China and Russia.

The establishment of the Japanese Protectorate rule in Korea and subsequent annexation caused anti-Japanese Korean patriots to move to North Chientao and the Primorye. These Korean nationalists contributed to the development of the nationalist movement in the North Chientao and the Primorye. Chapter 2 deals with the Korean nationalist movement from 1905 to 1917 shortly before the Russian

February Revolution. Chapter 2 is divided into two parts, the first dealing with from 1905 to 1910 and the second with from 1911 to early 1917. The first part describes the diplomatic and military activities of the Korean patriots loyal to King Kojong and educational and cultural activities of the Kungminhoe nationalists (led by An Ch'ang-ho) who employed gradualist strategies for independence of Korea and republican political ideas. The main concern of the first section is what attitude the Korean population, particularly the wealthy *wŏnhoin* (old settlers) had toward those nationalists who had moved to the Primorye from Korea.

The second part of Chapter 2 deals with major Korean nationalist organizations in North Chientao and the Primorye — Kanmin Kyoyukhoe (Educational Association in North Chientao), Kanminhoe (Korean Association in North Chientao) in North Chientao and the Kwŏnŏphoe (Work Promotion Association) in the Primorye. Here, the study is concerned with the goals of the nationalist organizations, particularly their strategies and internal and external problems such as opposition from other Korean groups, regional factionalism among Korean patriots, the policies of local Chinese and Russian authorities toward Korean nationalists, and tactics and policies of the Japanese authorities toward Korean nationalists.

After 1917, the Russian Far East was dragged into the complicated process of the Russian Revolution. Chapter 3 examines the process of reshaping of Korean anti-Japanese activists into two competing camps — the Association of Koreans in All Russia [Chŏllo Hanjokhoe] and the Korean Socialist Party — each of which gradually came to consolidate conflicting political ideologies within their own groups. Chapter 3 will also attempt to answer the question of who started the socialist (pro-Bolshevik) movement.

After the 1919 March First Movement, competition between the two major Korean organizations in the Primorye escalated to the Korean nationalist movement. The Association of Koreans in All Russia [Chŏllo Hanjokhoe] reorganized itself into the Korean National Council and attempted to claim itself as the central organ of all Koreans and accordingly carried out "power struggles" with the Provisional Government in Shanghai. The Korean Socialist Party also endeavored to intensify its pro-Bolshevik stance after its 2nd Congress in April 1919. Chapter 4 analyzes the policies and activities of the Korean National Council and the Korean Socialist Party and deals with the process of how the Korean National Council and the Korean Provisional Government in Shanghai reached a unification agreement after their political struggles.

Under its weakened authority and influence, the Korean National Council declared its dissolution in August 1919, but then reversed its decision, arguing that the Shanghai Provisional Government had "violated" the agreement to dissolve together. With the political stalemate caused by different interpretations of the agreement for unification, the Korean Socialist Party decided to join the "unified" Shanghai Provisional Government. As a result, the relationship between the Korean Socialist Party and the Korean National Council deteriorated from competition to hostility. Chapter 5 deals with the questions of why the Korean Socialist Party joined the "unified" Shanghai Provisional Government; the difference between the political stance of the Korean Socialist Party and other groups within the "unified" Shanghai Provisional Government; and why the Korean Socialist Party finally decided to withdraw from the Shanghai Provisional Government. Chapter 5 also deals with the diplomatic activities of the Korean Socialist Party to the Soviet government and the Comintern. The last part of Chapter 6 describes how the competitions between the two groups of Korean Communist Party [Koryŏ Kongsandang] led to the bloody suppression of the "Shanghai Group" by the Far Eastern Secretariat of the Comintern and its Korean section, "Irkutsk Group," in the Svobodnyi Gorod (Free City) in June 1921.

This book is based on my doctoral dissertation, "Korean Nationalist Activities in the Russian Far East and North Chientao (1905-1921)," submitted to the University of Hawaii at Manoa, in 1996. Finding that the basic contents and problems addressed by the dissertation are still academically relevant today, I decided to publish this work in its original form with minor corrections and revisions.

Note on transliteration

The Romanization of Korean words follows the McCune-Reishauer system. For Chinese the generally Pinyin system is used; for Japanese, modified Hepburn system of Kenkyusha's New Japanese-English Dictionary (Tokyo: Kenkyusha, 1974). Russian words are transliterated by the Library of Congress system. Korean, Chinese and Japanese surnames precede given names. Names of places, newspapers, magazines and organizations (in Korean, Chinese, Japanese and Russian) are translated whenever possible.

Acknowledgements

In preparing and writing this book, I got various kinds of support and help from many persons and institutions. First of all, I am grateful to my advisor, Professor Yong-ho Ch'oe for his consistent support and encouragement at every stage of my academic progress. I also thank Professors John Stephan, Sharon Minichiello, Daniel Kwok and Dae-sook Suh who provided outstanding direction as members of my dissertation committee. Professor Stephan, in particular, inspired my interest in Siberia and the Russian Far East through his constant intellectual and personal example. I also appreciate Professors Hugh H. W. Kang and Ho-min Sohn of the University of Hawaii and Dr. Lee-jay Cho of the East — West Center for their repeated demonstrations of encouragement and support.

In addition to my dissertation committee and other members of the UH and EWC faculty members, I received assistance from fellow graduate students, Korean Professors, and several Russian colleagues.

I want to thank Dr. Robert Fahs, Ms. Sandy Davis, Dr. Joni Keohn and Mr. Allen McDlermaid for their careful reading and editing of my dissertation draft. Special thanks must be delivered to my close friend, Dr. Fahs who encouraged me by providing academic and personal advices. My history department colleagues, Dr. Kevin Daley, Professor Michael Seth, Professor Kenneth Robinson, Mrs. Masako Kobayashi, Ms. Sumie Ota and Professor Dong-fang Shao also helped me in many ways. For collecting materials and sources, I appreciate the help provided by librarians of the University of Hawaii Hamilton Library, Mr. Sam-suk Hahn, Ms. Patricia Polansky, the late Dr. Matsui Masato, Ms. Kyungmi Chun and Mrs. Sun-young Chang as well as the helpful staff of the Interlibrary Loan Office, Wilma Wilkie, Pat Sexton and Sally Drake.

Professor Yun Pyŏng-sŏk, the late Professor Kang Woo-chul, Professor Cho Tong-gŏl, Professor Pak Hyŏn-sŏ, Professor Lew Young Ick, Professor Im Kye-sun, Professor Kim Yong-dŏk, Professor Yu

Hyo-jong, the late Professor Chŏng Ch'ang-ryŏl and the late Professor Yi Kyun-yŏng generously provided academic and personal support over many years from the genesis of my research through the completion of my dissertation. Professor Yun Hae-dong, Professor Chang Sŏk-hŭng, Professor Yun Chŏng-wook, Professor Chŏn Hyŏn-su, Professor Pak Hwan, Ms. Song U-hye, Dr. Kim Kwang-je, and Professor Chŏng Ŭn-sang also shared valuable historical documents related to my research.

The late Professor Boris Pak in Irkutsk, Ms. Yulia Borisovna Nah, Mr. Ichenko Vlad, Professor Amir Khisamutdinov and Ms. Nina Semenovna Ivantsova in Vladivostok all greatly enriched my field research in Russia. The Korean Russians, the late Professor Mikhail Pak, Professor Mun Yŏng-gil, Mr. Pak Chae-uk, Mr. Pyotr Davidovich Pak, Mr. Tel'mir Afanas'evich Kim, Mr. Filipp Pak in the Russian Far East, Mr. Kye Hak-nim and Mrs. Liudmilla Davidovna Lee in Kazakhstan patiently agreed to interviews that expanded my perspective on many issues related to the dissertation topic.

I received various kinds of scholarly grants at crucial points of my study and research. I am grateful for financial support from the East-West Center, the School for Hawaiian, Asia and Pacific Studies of the University of Hawaii, Northeast Asia Council of the Association for Asian Studies, the Joint Committee on Korean Studies of the Social Science Research Council and the American Council of Learned Societies.

Finally, I wish to express my deep love and appreciation for my family. The late Mr. Ban Byong-Ho, my eldest brother, enabled me to get a higher education and my father-in-law, the late Dr. Gim Sheon-gi, encouraged my transition to a new career as a scholar. Mr. Gim Du Shun, my brother-in-law, also gave me warm encouragement and support. My lovely sons, Dr. Han Yong Ban and Hong Yong Ban, patiently awaited my academic progress, sacrificed their joyful childhood by sharing various hardships with their parents. I also want specifically acknowledge Han Yong for his edits along with very critical and helpful suggestions which led to many improvements in the final version of the book. Above all, I gratefully acknowledge my wife, Dr. Bohi Gim Ban, who has always stood by me while pursuing her own academic career and shouldering every family burden. Her steadfast encouragement and sacrifice make everything possible.

■ LIST OF TABLES

■ LIST OF MAPS AND ILLUSTRATIONS

Maps

Illustrations

Chapter One

KOREAN EMIGRATION TO NORTH CHIENTAO AND THE RUSSIAN FAR EAST

A. Historical Background

In ancient times, Manchuria and the Primorye (Russian Maritime Province) were populated by the people of Puyŏ (Chin. Fuyu) to whom Koreans trace their origins. This kingdom of the Puyŏ people was centered on the basin of the Sungari River. Puyŏ's historical existence is indicated today by the city named "Fuyu," north of Zhangchun city in Jilin Province. A branch kingdom of Puyŏ, Koguryŏ (B. C. 37-A. D. 668), arose north of the middle stream of the Yalu River (Kor. Apnok River). By subjugating various Manchurian peoples, included the Puyŏ, Kidan, Xienbei, and Mohe, Koguryŏ at the peak of her power dominated a vast territory stretching from the central Korean Peninsula to the Sungari River and from the Liaodong Peninsula to the Primorye. Koguryŏ's rule over such vast stretches of Manchuria and the Primorye provided historical justification for the Korean claims of jurisdiction over those regions.

After Koguryŏ, Parhae (699-926, Chin. Bohai) rose in this region. Although there is scholarly controversy concerning the ethnicity of its ruling class, Parhae extended its dominance to the mouth of the Amur River, in addition to most of the territory held by Koguryŏ. With the defeat of Parhae by the Kidan in 926, however, Manchuria was lost as a "homeland" for the Korean people and their political domain became limited to the Korean Peninsula, although part of the northern peninsula remained under the control of nomadic peoples such as the Kidan, Mongols and Nüzhen [Jurchen].

Koryŏ ruled the Korean Peninsula from 918 untill 1392, claiming to be the successor to Koguryŏ. Although some Koryŏ kings pursued an expansionist policy, seeking to recover the former territory of Koguryŏ, Koryŏ's northern border remained below a line stretching from the mouth of the Yalu River to the present Wŏnsan Bay, including the southern part of today's Southern Hamgyŏng Province. It was King Sejong (r. 1418-1450) of the Chosŏn dynasty (1392-1910) who established six garrison settlements [*yukchin*] in the Tumen River (Kor. Tuman River) region and four frontier districts [*sagun*] along the Yalu River with the purpose of consolidating the northern frontier against intrusions by the Nüzhen. From that time on, the Yalu-Tumen line has remained Korea's northern border.

After the Manchus established their rule in China as Qing, the Manchu government prohibited any migration into Manchuria in order to protect and preserve its homeland. Responding to the policy of the Qing government, the Korean government strictly punished persons who committed the crime of crossing the river [*wŏlgangjoe*]. Watchful border guards implemented this policy, even imposing the

Map 1. 1

Russian Far East and Northeast Asia

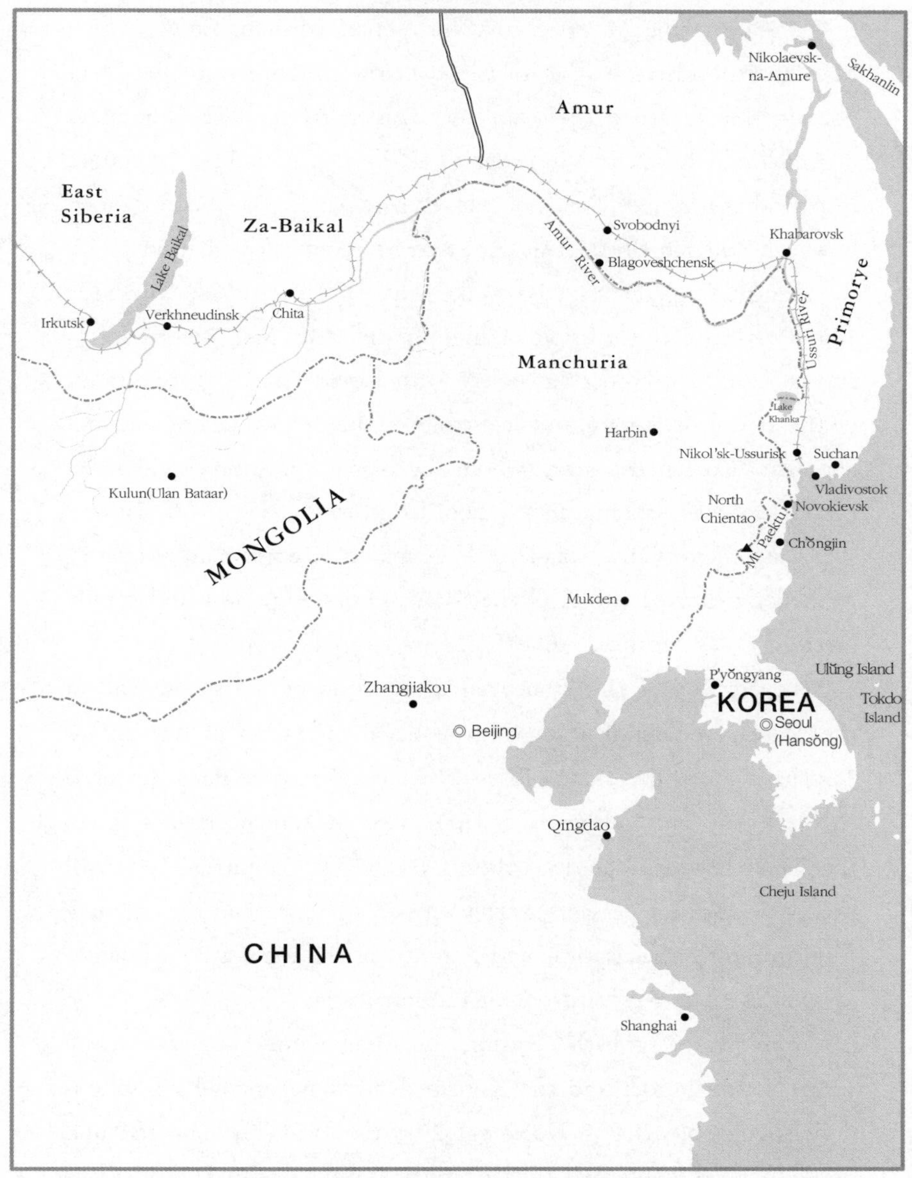

death penalty.[1]

The Kangxi Emperor (r. 1662-1722) of the Qing dynasty decided to incorporate the Mt. Paektu (Chin. Zhangbaishan) range, which Manchus considered as the holy land of their origins, into the Qing domain. He regarded the Yalu and Tumen rivers as the boundary of China and Korea and in order to clarify this boundary, he sought to extend the frontier along the Mt. Paektu range. The precise border, however, still remained unclear due to its remote location. In 1712, the Kangxi Emperor assigned Mukedeng, governor of Ula (presently Jilin Province), the mission of investigating the Mt. Paektu range and concluding a border agreement with Korea. As the representative of the powerful empire and its strong emperor, Mukedeng did not allow the Korean delegates (whom the Korean government had dispatched for the territorial negotiation) to go to the top of Mt. Paektu. Replacing them with a couple of low-ranking Korean military officers, Mukedeng himself surveyed the Mt. Paektu range and unilaterally erected a demarcation stone [*chŏnggyebi*] on its summit.[2]

The erection of this stone was a reflection of the strong will of the Manchu government to control illegal migration of Koreans to Manchuria across the Tumen River. However, Korean peasants continued to sneak into and cultivate border regions in Manchuria in spite of the harsh laws and border controls of the two countries.[3] A small number of Korean peasants usually crossed the border in the morning to farm during the daytime and returned in the evening — a practice known as "one-day return cultivation" ["*ilgwi kyŏngjak*"].[4]

From the early 19th century, the Qing dynasty began to lose control of its border and the Korean dynasty began to have serious domestic problems. As Korea's tax system was mismanaged and abused, the discontented peasants increasingly revolted against the government. In the Hong Kyŏng-nae Rebellion of 1811, dissident local *yangban*, disgruntled with the dynasty's policy of discrimination against the people of P'yŏngan Province, succeeded in mobilizing the peasants. The northern border region below the Yalu River was in turmoil for some months. Thereafter, there were many rebellions and the rural turbulence culminated in 1862 in the uprising in Chinju in southern Korea. Unable to bear this hardship, Korean peasants increasingly migrated into Manchuria by crossing the border.

B. Korean Emigration to North Chientao

1. Early Korean Emigration, 1860-1905

The permanent emigration of Korean peasants to Chientao generally began in the 1860s. There are many explanations for the origins of the Chinese name, "Chientao" (Kor. "*Kando*"), but it was widely accepted by Koreans and later by the Japanese as indicating the land between the two rivers — called 土門 ("T'omun" in Korean, "Tumen" in Chinese), and the other called 豆滿 ("Tuman" in Korean, "Douman" in Chinese) or 圖們 ("Tomun" in Korean, "Tumen" in Chinese). There are two ways of writing "*Kando*" in Chinese characters. One is 間島, which means "in-between island" and another is 墾島, which means "cultivated island."[5] Chientao, in the narrowest usage, included three prefectures: Yanji, Helong, Wangqing and usually Hunchun Prefecture bordering China, Korea and Russia. In order to distinguish it from regions north of the Yalu River which Koreans called "*Sŏgando*" ("West Chientao"), they called the original Chientao "*Pukkando*" ("North Chientao") or "*Tonggando*" ("Eastern Chientao").[6]

It is popularly believed that supposed Yi Kwi-in and Yi Kwi-son, supposed peasant brothers from Musan, in North Hamgyŏng Province, were the first permanent emigrants to Chientao in the early 1860s.[7] As a result of consecutive poor harvests from 1866 to 1869, northern Korea experienced an unprecedentedly severe famine. Poor communications and horrible administrative mismanagement by the government aggravated the situation. Although there are no exact statistics, it is believed that as many as 500,000 persons died from hunger. Seeking relief, a large number of Korean families migrated to Manchuria and the Primorye.[8] Kyŏngwŏn and Kyŏnghŭng, two frontier towns on the southern side of the Tumen River became almost deserted. Koreans in Manchuria and Russia later called the famine in 1869, "*kisa hyungnyŏn*" ("famine in the year of *kisa*") and the mass crossing in 1870, "*kyŏngo togang*" ("river-crossing in the year of *kyŏngo*"). Contemporary records describe horrible scenes of people wandering in hunger, roadways scattered with corpses, and even incidents of cannibalism.[9] To escape such misfortune, many Korean peasants left their homes and crossed the border into Manchuria to the promises of fertile lands in Chientao.[10]

Although the Qing and Korean governments still considered the border-crossing illegal, local government officials could not prevent the Korean migration to North Chientao. In 1880, Hong Nam-ju, magistrate of the border town Hoeryŏng on the southern bank of the Tumen River, even encouraged Korean farmers to cultivate lands on the Chinese shore of the River. Following the example of Hoeryŏng, people of neighboring border counties began to cultivate the riverside areas in Chientao. Soon the northern side of the Tumen River was cultivated for a length of 500 *li* and width of 40-50 *li* (ten *li* is 4 km).

The newly cultivated area did not seem foreign to Koreans, who frequently crossed the Tumen River. Local authorities of the Korean government dispatched land surveyors to investigate the cultivated lands and to make land registers. The land documents were called "*Kando yach'o*" ("Field Register of Chientao") from which, one Korean contended, the "*Kando*" in Korean originated. As a result, Koreans in the area were subjected to taxation and compulsory labor just as in the homeland. Koreans later called this development of Chientao "*kyŏngjin kaech'ŏk*" ("colonization in 1880").[11] At this time, the Koreans gave names to these newly cultivated regions in Chientao, such as *Onsŏng Kando*, *Chongsŏng Kando*, *Hoeryŏng Kando*, *Musan Kando*, following the names of border towns on the opposite side of the Tumen River.[12]

From the 1860s Qing China gradually opened Manchuria to Chinese settlers. In response to Russia's acquisition of the Priamur (Amur and Primorye) following the Treaty of Aihun (1858) and the Treaty of Beijing (1860), Qing China encouraged Chinese emigration to northern Manchuria. The Qing government opened the Hulan River plains and northwest Jilin in 1860 and 1861, respectively.[13]

The Qing government's lift of its prohibition policy in Manchuria to encourage Chinese migration after concession of the Primorye to Russia enhanced the strategic importance of the fertile delta region between the Tumen (土門) and Tuman (豆滿) Rivers. In 1875 it decided to legalize cultivation of land in Manchuria and established government offices north of the Yalu River.[14] Subsequently, in 1881, the Qing government decided to apply the same policy to the region north of the Tumen River. It decided to colonize Chientao and established the Bureau for Encouraging Cultivation in 1881.[15] Chinese officials, who were dispatched by the Qing government with the mission of investigating the Chientao region in 1881, were surprised at the fact that Chientao was already cultivated and occupied by Koreans.[16]

Despite encouragement by the Qing government, the rate and numbers of Chinese migration to Chientao, were far below those of the Korean immigrants, mainly due to the difficulty of crossing the Mt. Paektu range as well as the availability of land in other areas of Manchuria. Compared to obstacles for the Chinese, it was very easy for Koreans to cross the Tumen River.[17] By the early 1880s, the proportion of Korean peasants in Chientao reached eighty percent of the total populace, while the remaining 20 percent were Chinese. The Korean peasants also occupied 80 percent of the land in Chientao. With support of the Qing officials, however, Chinese attempted to occupy the land which Koreans had already cultivated. As a result, frequent conflicts occurred between Chinese and Korean peasants.[18]

Utilizing her military presence in Korea after the Soldiers' Riot of 1882 [*Imo Kullan*], Qing China declared that Chientao was Chinese territory and that the Chinese government would enforce taxation, census registration and judicial authority on the Koreans in Chientao under the administration of Hunchun and Dunhua Prefectures. Instead of immediately expelling Korean settlers from Chientao, however, Qing China, with the obvious intention of utilizing the economic achievement of Koreans, allowed them to stay in Chientao as long as they became Chinese citizens and accepted Chinese administration. The Korean government, which did not want Korean peasants become Chinese citizens, hesitantly promised to make Korean peasants in Chientao return to Korea within one year.[19] In the winter of 1882, the Military-Governor of Jilin notified the Korean government to recall Korean peasants and in 1883,

Dunhua Prefecture also notified magistrates of Chongsŏng and Hoeryŏng to recall all Koreans.[20]

Korean residents in Chientao and the China-Korea border regions were surprised at the news that the Korean government planned to call them back to Korea. The Korean people in the border regions, however, were familiar with a demarcation stone on Mt. Paektu which said that the regions south of the Tumen (土門) River belonged to the territory of Korea. This information might legitimize Korean settlement in Chientao. Not wanting to go back to Korea, they appealed to Yi Chŏng-rae, magistrate of Chongsŏng, and Ŏ Yun-jung, Commissioner of North-West Region Management, who was at that time staying in Kyŏngwŏn.[21] The latter reported to his government that it was impossible to execute all criminals who crossed the river. Influenced by his report, the Korean government at last lifted the law prohibiting border-crossing of the Koreans in 1883.[22]

Ŏ Yun-jung dispatched an agent (Kim U-sik) twice in May and June 1883, to investigate the demarcation stone on the top of Mt. Paektu and the source streams of the Tumen (土門) and Tuman (豆滿) Rivers which originated from the Dragon King Pool (*Yongwangdam* in Korean, *Longwangdan* in Chinese)[23], a pool also located atop Mt. Paektu. Based on these investigations, the magistrate Yi Chŏng-rae sent a report to the local Chinese official in Dunhua district. In his report, Yi Chŏng-rae argued that "Tumen" (土門) in the inscription of the boundary stone in fact meant the Tumen (土門) River which originated from the boundary stone and a source and tributary of the Sungari River, and accordingly was completely different from the Tuman (豆滿) River, which the Qing called the Tumen (圖們) River. Accordingly, Yi Chŏng-rae argued that it would be unnecessary to recall the Koreans in Chientao. This was how the territorial dispute between Korea and China occurred. Yi Chŏng-rae's report corroborated assertions of the Korean commissioners during the three futile territorial negotiations between China and Korea in 1885 and 1887.[24]

Utilizing its suzerain status and strengthened position after the 1882 incident in Korea, the Qing government was not willing to compromise with Korea and even tried to nullify the authenticity of the boundary stone at the top of Mt. Paektu. They argued that Koreans had falsified the stone, that Koreans had moved it from the source of the Tumen River, and that the demarcation stone did not have any Manchu characters.[25] Awed by the superior status and power of Qing, the Korean government withdrew its original claim that the Tumen (土門) River formed the border. Accordingly, the dispute between the two countries narrowed to disagreement over which source stream of the Tumen River formed the border. China at first contended the Sŏdusu (Chin. Xidaoshui), the southernmost tributary, did. Faced with the strong opposition of the Korean delegate, Yi Chung-ha who insisted it was the Hongt'osu (Chin. Hongtushui), the northernmost tributary, China suggested the Sŏgŭlsu (Chin. Shiyishui), tributary between the Sŏdusu and the Hongt'osu.[26] Although the parties could not agree on this border, the territorial dispute over the Chientao was dropped, and it became Chinese territory.[27]

The failure of the territorial negotiations must have propelled the local Qing authorities to take strong positions against Koreans in Chientao. In 1890, the Military-General of Jilin decreed that only Koreans who adopted the Manchu hair-style (pigtail hair or pheasant hair) and clothing would have privileges such as landownership equal to the Chinese. Before 1890, local Qing authorities had allowed Koreans to form their own communities and schools using only Korean language and even remanded Korean criminals to the local Korean officials in border areas of Korea.[28] According to the decree, Koreans who would not accept Chinese authority were deprived of their lands and were expelled to Korea.[29] In order to control Korean peasants who did not follow the decree, a Chinese cavalry composed of more than 100 horsemen from Hunchun raided and burned Korean houses in Chientao. Koreans were at last forced to accept the Manchu hair-style and clothing.[30]

The Qing government began its administration over Korean immigrants by appointing district administrators responsible for the Korean communities, and by destroying all land registers and documents which the local Korean officials of the border regions had previously made and distributed to Koreans in the early 1880s. Without any help from their government, the Koreans suddenly lost their vested interests in Chientao. Koreans later called this incident "*kyŏngin ch'ibal nan*" ("pheasant hair disturbance of the year of 1890").[31] Escaping suppression after 1890, a number of Koreans in Chientao emigrated to the Primorye in Russia.[32]

In this way, the Qing government forced Korean owners of the cultivated lands to become Chinese citizens. Additionally, the Qing government also encouraged colonization of the uncultivated lands in remote regions of Chientao by the Chinese. Chinese landowners, who got vast uncultivated lands from the Qing government without payment, employed Korean tenants for the cultivation of those lands. In order to promote land cultivation, the Qing government did not force those Korean tenants to accept the Manchu hair style and clothing or Chinese citizenship. Most Korean peasants did not like "pheasant-tail hair and Manchu clothing." Accordingly the Koreans who did not have land or had migrated recently from Korea chose to be tenants of the Chinese landowners.[33] The differential policy of the Qing government at this time determined great disparity in the socio-economic status of Korean peasants compared to the Chinese.[34]

Exploiting the weakened position of Qing China as a result of China's defeat in the Sino-Japanese War in 1895, the Korean government attempted to raise the territorial issue, and Koreans in Chientao also dared to ignore the authority of the Qing administration.[35] Furthermore, Russia occupied various strategic points in Manchuria during the Boxer Rebellion in 1900, and the Korean government attempted to establish its influence in Chientao by reclaiming territorial rights over Chientao. Hearing the news of the invasion by the Russian army into Hunchun from Vladivostok, most Chinese people in Chientao escaped to the Jilin region.[36] At first, many Koreans also escaped to Korea in order to avoid being plundered by the fleeing Manchu soldiers. When the Russian army occupied Chientao, however, the Koreans returned to Chientao.[37] A completely new situation arose in Chientao as many Koreans abandoned pheasant-tail hair and Manchu clothes and resumed their own hair styles and white Korean clothes. Some Koreans, relying on the Russian authorities, resisted abuses by Qing officials.[38]

In 1901, the Korean government also established a border area police station [*pyŏngye kyŏngmusŏ*] in Hoeryŏng with branch detachments in Musan and Chongsŏng. The police station dealt with administrative and judicial affairs of the Koreans in Chientao.[39] In 1902, the Korean government for the first time responded to appeals by Koreans in Chientao to protect them from the abuses of the local Qing authorities by dispatching Yi Pŏm-yun with the mission of investigating the conditions of the Koreans in Chientao. Yi Pŏm-yun arrived in Chientao on June 23, 1902, announced his mission to the Koreans, and witnessed the terrible oppression of Manchu officials over Koreans throughout the area. Yi Pŏm-yun felt strongly the need for armed forces to protect Koreans from the Manchu officials. In July 1903, he was again appointed by the Korean government to the position of Administrator of Northern Border and Chientao [*Pukpyŏn Kando Kwanrisa*].[40]

His appointment clearly demonstrated the will of the Korean government to realize its territorial claims over Chientao, asserted since early 1880s: land between Tumen (土門) River and the Tuman (豆滿) River belonged to Korea as inscribed on the boundary stone atop Mt. Paektu.

Yi Pŏm-yun, without any financial and military support from the Korean government, organized a corps of young Korean gunmen [*sap'odae*] and began to collect taxes from Koreans in Chientao. In addition, he arrested local Chinese community leaders (*xiangyue* in Chinese) who were appointed by the local Qing authorities, and declared that Koreans did not have any duty to pay Qing government taxes. Although the Qing government asked the Korean government to recall and punish Yi Pŏm-yun, Yi continued to challenge the Manchu authorities by establishing offices in major Korean villages and building military camps.[41] After defeat in military clashes with the superior Manchu army, Yi Pŏm-yun's corps retreated to Korean territory and waited until the outbreak of the Russo-Japanese War in January 1904,[42] during which Yi Pŏm-yun joined the Russian armies with a reorganized corps of gunmen and resumed his previous military and administrative activities in Chientao. The Qing government repeatedly asked the Korean government to recall Yi Pŏm-yun and attempted to retaliate against Koreans by prohibiting them from exporting grain back to Korea.[43] With the defeat of Russia in the Russo-Japanese War, however, Yi Pŏm-yun and his soldiers were exiled to Pos'et in the Primorye with the retreating Russian army.[44] At a later time, he and his armed force will come to form one of the anti-Japanese partisan units.

2. Koreans in North Chientao under the Japanese Protectorate Rule of Korea, 1905-1909

As a result of the Protectorate Treaty imposed on Korea in November 1905, Japan came to possess full authority over all aspects of Korean foreign relations. Accordingly, the long-pending Chientao question regarding the status of Korean immigrants was also handed over to the new Japanese authorities. Based on the 1905 Protectorate Treaty, Japan tried to return the Koreans to their side away from Chinese influence. After 1905, after the establishment of the branch office of the Residency-General of Korea in 1907, competition between China and Japan over the Koreans continued.[45]

In August 1907, after several years of preparation, the Japanese government established a branch office of the Residency-General of Korea in Longjingcun (Kor. Yongjŏngch'on).[46] The branch office was assigned all powers concerning the Koreans in Chientao by the Korean government — that is, the Japanese Residency-General — and ordered to have the same power with the local Chinese authority in charge of the Chientao region [*lishiting*].[47] At first Japan dispatched 91 personnel including 53 military policemen to Chientao, but by the time of withdrawal of the branch office in 1909, the number had increased more than threefold to 305.[48] Detachments of military police boxes were established in seven key points of Chientao and seven more detachments were established by 1909.[49] Saitō Suejirō, chief of the branch office of the Residency-General, gathered thousands of Koreans from various places in Chientao and held a ceremony to celebrate the opening of the branch office in Longjingcun. At this gathering, Saitō tried to win over Koreans by stating that Chientao, ancient territory of Koguryŏ kingdom, was cultivated by the "bloody sweat" of Koreans. He also declared that the branch office would try to make Chientao a territory of Korea and would "protect lives and property of the Koreans in Chientao."[50]

The policies regarding Chientao and Koreans in Chientao were clearly demonstrated by Saitō at the conference of detachment chiefs in December 1908.

1) To regard Chientao as Korean territory.
2) Not to require Koreans to observe the judicial judgement of the Qing.
3) To recognize the taxation of the Qing on Koreans, but not to allow other forced collections of money from Koreans.
4) Not to recognize all laws issued by the Qing.
5) To treat the Korean *xiang* (village) chiefs and head *xiang* chiefs in general in the same way as other general Koreans.[51]

Realistically the Japanese branch office could not collect taxes from the Koreans, thus it recognized Qing authority to do so. By claiming Chientao as Korean territory, however, the branch office rejected the laws of the Qing and requested that the Koreans submit to judicial Qing authority. It is notable that the branch office decided to consider Koreans who had Chinese citizenship as Korean subjects. Furthermore, the Japanese branch office denied the Chinese citizen of Korean community leaders such as village chiefs (Chin. *cunzhang*), local community leaders (Chin. *xiangyue*) and head of local community leaders (Chin. *duxiangyue*) appointed in 1903 by the local Qing authorities.[52]

In order to reinforce its control over the Koreans in Chientao, the branch office appointed 335 local Korean officials in Korean villages and rural districts — 4 *tosajang*, 41 *sajang*, 290 *ch'onjang* — in exact parallel to Korean community leaders appointed by the Qing authorities.[53] From Korea, Japan also brought numerous members of the Ilchinhoe (One Advancement Association),[54] a pro-Japanese Korean political organization to Chientao to support the rule of the branch office. The Ilchinhoe organized a chapter in Longjingcun with Yun Kap-pyŏng as its leader, and at the same time, its district branches were established in various regions of Chientao.[55] Ilchinhoe's religious organization, the Sich'ŏngyo (Religion of Serving the Heaven) also came to enjoy prosperity in Chientao thanks to the support of the Japanese. At its peak, the number of the Sich'ŏngyo reached 7,500 in this region.[56] The Japanese also encouraged and supported the establishment of schools for the purpose of spreading pro-Japanese political ideas.

Relying on the power of the branch office, the members of the Ilchinhoe maintained that Chientao would be a territory of Korea soon and that Koreans should reject paying taxes to the Qing government. Encouraged by the incitement of the Ilchinhoe, pro-Japanese Koreans even set up wooden marks indicating their ownership on the lands of the Chinese and proceeded to occupy uncultivated lands.[57] Members of the Ilchinhoe could be considered one of the first examples of a "vanguard of Japanese imperialism" from the Chinese view of Koreans.

In response, the Qing government made strong effort to counteract the infiltration of Japanese into Chientao. First, it did not recognize the branch office of the Japanese Residency-General, requesting several times that the Japanese withdraw the branch office. In addition, it also appointed new administrative and military officials in Yanji and afterwards strengthened her military presence there. Chen Zhao-chang and Wu Lü-cheng were the frontier director general and the assistant frontier director general respectively, whose offices were stationed in Juzijie of Yanji.[58] The Qing also refused territorial negotiation on Chientao with Japan. The Qing authorities were also determined to keep full judicial authority over those Koreans in the region.[59] In response to the establishment of Korean schools by the Japanese, Chinese authorities began encouraging Korean education, even while ignoring the education of Chinese children. The competition between Japan and China for Koreans frequently led to confrontation.[60]

Although a small number of Koreans such as the members of the Ilchinhoe sided with Japan, almost all Koreans sided with China.[61] In particular, Korean Confucian scholars were critical of the activities of the branch office of the Residency-General and the Ilchinhoe and in reaction organized Yŏnŭihoe (Performance of Righteousness Association). At the end of 1907, the Confucian scholars sent their representative to the Military-General of Jilin with a letter signed by their members. Contending that the Chientao was Chinese territory, they asked the Chinese authorities for protection of Koreans from the Japanese. The rumor spread that members of the Yŏnŭihoe were planning to cooperate with Yi Pŏm-yun in Pos'et when Yi's troop came to Chientao. Another group of Korean Confucian scholars also submitted an application to the Military-Governor of Jilin at the end of January 1908 for the establishment of a shrine for Confucius and a school. In March 1908, they submitted a statement criticizing the policies of the branch of the Residency-General and asked for protection from the Japanese. In the statement, complaints that "the whole Korean territory was being oppressed by Japan and as far as the Chientao question is concerned, Japan does not care about the Koreans, but is only concerned about their interests in Manchuria were made." In order to preclude possible anti-Japanese political activities, Japanese officials arrested the leaders of the Confucian scholars. Under the threats of the Japanese, the Yŏnŭihoe was forced to dissolve and one of the Confucian scholar leaders, Sŏ Sang-ŭn, was imprisoned in Hamhŭng, in Southern Hamgyŏng Province, on charges of conspiring against Japanese political interests.[62]

The Japanese, on December 12, 1907, also arrested Hyŏn Tŏksŭng, one of the four head rural district chiefs (*duxiangyue* in Chinese) appointed by the Qing authorities under the charge of spreading anti-Japanese rumors and extorting money from the pro-Japanese Koreans. At the promise of the Qing authority to discharge Hyŏn, he was released. However, contending that the Qing officials did not keep promises, Japanese policemen, two years later, again arrested and brought Hyŏn to Chongsŏng, a border town in Northern Hamgyŏng Province, and sentenced him to fifteen years imprisonment.[63]

The case of Hyŏn clearly demonstrate Japanese intentions to seize jurisdiction over all the Koreans, including even those with Chinese citizenship. Japan claimed legal jurisdiction over Koreans on the precedent that the judicial affairs of the Koreans in Chientao were under the responsibility of magistrates at the Six Garrison Settlements (before 1890) and the border area police station (after 1901). In addition,

Japan referred to provisions in the Sino-Korean Treaty of 1899 which admitted the extraterritorial rights of the Korean government over Koreans in China. Chinese authorities argued that traditionally Chinese authorities dealt with the judicial affairs of the Koreans in Chientao and that Koreans living north of the Tumen River, as river-crossed people, took Chinese citizenship. China also retorted that the extraterritorial rights defined in the Sino-Korean Treaty of 1899 were supposed to be applied only to Koreans in commercial regions, not to those in Chientao.[64] Regardless of the arguments between Japan and China, as the case of Hyŏn Tŏk-sŭng clearly shows, in the face of Japan's superior power, the local Qing authorities could not protect Koreans who had Qing citizenship and local Chinese administrative posts from the Japanese police.

In addition to legal jurisdiction over the Koreans in Chientao, additional conflicts between the officials, civilians and soldiers of China and Japan worsened relations between the two countries.[65] The diplomatic negotiations which started after the establishment of the branch office of the Residency-General in 1907 came to a deadlock in mid-1909. A military conflict between Japan and China seemed imminent. The branch office of the Residency-General declared that they would regard Chientao as Korean territory and take every action with the risk of confronting the Chinese. The Japanese government also notified China that Japan would proceed with reconstruction of the Andong-Fengtien line.[66] Japanese military forces in Chientao attacked the Chinese military force. Two hundred Japanese military police also attacked Koreans who joined the Chinese. The branch office asked the Residency-General in Korea to dispatch additional military forces to the region.[67]

In the middle of 1909, the Qing government took a firm attitude concerning the Chientao question and promoted Wu Lü-cheng, a graduate of the Japanese Military Academy, to the position of frontier director general. In June 1909, Wu came to Juzijie in Yanji county.[68] It was also rumored that the Qing government would dispatch an additional regiment force from Fengtien in August.[69] In the middle of intensified tensions which might have led to a large-scale war, Japan and China reached a compromise on September 4, 1909. In an agreement concerning mines and railways in Manchuria, Japan obtained the rights of construction of new railroads (Hsinmint'un-Mukden Railway, Jilin-Zhangchun Railway and reconstruction of Andong-Mukden Railway) and mining concessions from China which it had earlier opposed. In exchange, Japan agreed to recognize Chientao as Chinese territory in the so-called Chientao Agreement.[70]

By this agreement, Chientao became indisputably Chinese territory — with the Tumen River being recognized as the border. Regarding the source of the Tumen River atop Mt. Paektu, which had been the focus of disagreement between China and Korea during territorial negotiations in the late 1880s, the stream Shiyishui (Kor. Sŏgŭlsu) was agreed to as a borderline (Article 1). Japan promised to withdraw the branch office of the Residency-General from Chientao within two months (Article 7). Japan, however, also obtained agreement from China to open up the four towns of Longjingcun, Doudaogou, Juzijie and Baicaogou as residence and trade centers for foreigners, and to allow the Japanese government to establish a consulate-general in Longjingcun with branch offices in other towns (Article 2). Japan also obtained the right to construct the Ji-Hui Railroad which would connect Jilin to Hoeryŏng (Article 6). The Qing government allowed Korean residency on the demarcated regions of agricultural lands lying north of the Tumen River (Article 3) and acknowledged the ownership of lands and buildings of Koreans in Chientao. Koreans were also given the right to cross the Tumen River freely in either direction (Article 5). Korean subjects residing on agricultural lands within the mixed residence district to the north of the Tumen River were put under the jurisdiction of the Chinese authorities and on an equal footing with Chinese subjects in matters of taxation and all other administrative measures. All legal cases of Korean subjects on agricultural lands within the mixed residence district would be decided by the local Chinese courts. Japanese Consulate officials, however, had the right to attend all cases relating to such Korean subjects with the right to ask the Qing court to review "unfair" decisions of serious cases (Article 4).

In historical context, the Chientao Agreement was a victory for Japan, mainly resulting from her superior political and military power. The territorial issue had been in fact resolved at the time of border negotiations between China and Korea in the late 1880s. The only unsolved issue at that time was disagreement over which one of the three sources of the Tumen River, located at the demarcation stone near the Dragon King Pool on the top of Mt. Paektu, formed the borderline. Japan agreed to China's claim and accordingly failed to keep even the border which Korean negotiator Yi Chung-ha had maintained in 1887. Furthermore, it is notable that after the establishment of the Japanese protectorate in Korea, anti-Japanese Korean scholars chose to cooperate with the Chinese authorities by recognizing Chientao as China's territory. Inspired by the Japanese, it was pro-Japanese Koreans such as members of the Ilchinhoe who revived the territorial claims over Chientao.

Secondly, although Japanese contended that the protocol enhanced the judicial and economic rights of Koreans in Chientao by establishing construction rights and land ownership prohibited to foreigners,[71] the Koreans in Chientao who had Chinese citizenship were already allowed to own land and buildings. Any Korean could buy land or buildings simply by obtaining Chinese citizenship. This was encouraged by local Chinese authorities who wanted Koreans to become naturalized Chinese citizens. In this context, the provision concerning such rights might be seen as a device for economic infiltration of Japanese authorities who could now obtain real estate in the name of their Korean collaborators.

Finally, although it was argued that the judicial concessions benefited Koreans, Japanese consular officials would effectively use the consular jurisdiction and the right to intervene in Chinese courts as a means to persecute anti-Japanese Koreans.[72] This practice intensified after Japan's annexation of Korea in 1910.

One of the most important things is that Japan and China did not specify the legal status of Koreans who obtained Chinese citizenship. This remained a major dispute between Japan and China until 1945, even after it was resolved in 1931 in Manchuria. Qing authorities had contended that all Koreans in Chientao who crossed the river to live in Chientao should be considered Chinese citizens. However, after establishing the Residency-General branch office, Japan had decided not to recognize Koreans with Chinese citizenship as Chinese subjects. By the Chientao Agreement, China abandoned its earlier position by allowing Koreans to live in Chientao as aliens. China, nevertheless, still considered naturalized Koreans in Chientao as Chinese subjects, while the Japanese Resident-General and Korean government-General [Chōsen Sōtokufu] established in 1910, did not allow Koreans to abandon their own nationality, and in effect their Japanese citizenship. After the agreement, it was quite impossible for Koreans to obtain Chinese citizenship[73] as the Japanese denied the right of China to naturalize Koreans; the best Koreans could hope for was double citizenship.[74] Japan would not abandon this position until its defeat in the Second World War. If anti-Japanese Koreans, particularly in Chientao, were allowed to give up Japanese nationality, it would have been completely impossible for the Japanese authorities to supervise and control them both inside and outside Korea.[75] Koreans in China, particularly the nationalist Koreans in Manchuria, struggled to obtain Chinese citizenship in order to escape Japanese jurisdiction. Even those who were naturalized did not succeed in their goals as Japan continued to insist on their Japanese nationality.[76]

3. Korean Emigration to North Chientao after 1905

Korean emigrants to Chientao were mainly peasants who had suffered economic misfortune due to famines and exploitation by the local Korean officials. As Japan established the Residency-General in Korea and increased its repressive control over Korea after its victory in the Russo-Japanese War, a new type of mass Korean emigration occurred. Economic penetration of the Japanese into agricultural lands with the political and legal support of the Japanese Residency-General in Korea also accelerated the emigration of Koreans to Manchuria and the Primorye. Although illegal, Japanese were purchasing fertile lands in the name of Koreans around the time of the Russo-Japanese War. After the conclusion of the so-called Protectorate Treaty in 1905, the Residency-General gradually removed the political and legal obstacles to Japanese acquisition of land anywhere in Korea. The Oriental Development Company, a government-financed agricultural company which was established in December 1908 after the model of colonial companies such as the Dutch and the English East India Company, bought fertile lands concentrated in Chŏlla, Kyŏngsang and Hwanghae Provinces. More importantly, the Oriental Development Company simultaneously encouraged Japanese emigration to Korea.[77] The land survey carried out from August 1912 to November 1918 caused many Korean peasants to lose their lands. For those who remained on the land, tenancy and various new taxes on the tenants increased economic burden.[78] For these reasons, Korean farmers during this period increasingly left their homeland for Manchuria and the Primorye. The report of the central office of the Tokōkai (Same Light Society) of February 1923, summed up the situation well:

> Since the rule of Japan, paddy fields and dry fields were turned to the hands of the special company of Japanese capitalists. Once land was turned to the hands of the Japanese, Koreans were expelled from the land. . . . Japanese ignored the customs and habits of the Koreans and expelled the original tenants and replaced them with the Japanese tenants. . . . When one Japanese household comes, five Korean households cannot help but leave. When five Japanese households come, then twenty-five Korean households come to lose their occupation. The person who was expelled this way deserted the land of his ancestors' homes to which he had been accustomed for a long time, bearing limitless resentment in mind and left for other regions within the country or beyond the frontier.[79]

Map 1. 2

Provinces of Korea in the 1910s

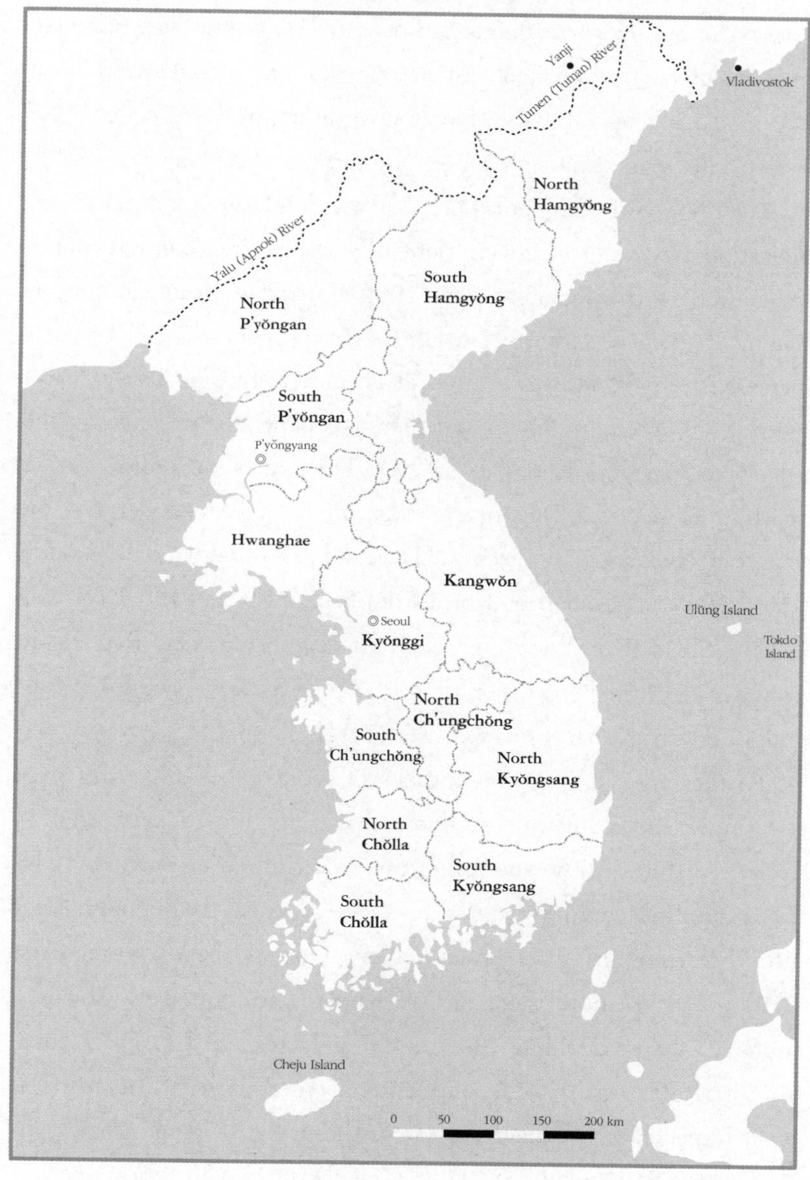

In addition to peasants, the increasing number of anti-Japanese *ŭibyŏng* (Righteous Army) and intellectual activists, escaping the suppression of the Japanese military, moved to Manchuria and Primorye. In particular, the so-called "Great Suppression in southern Korea" ["*namhan taet'obŏl*"] by the Japanese military in October of 1909 caused the mass exile of *ŭibyŏng* fighters to these sanctuaries.[80]

Together with frequent poor harvests and on-going harsh exploitation by the local government officials, political and economic infiltration of the Japanese after 1905 spurred Korean emigration. During the period from 1894 to 1907, Korean population in Chientao increased from 34,000 to 71,000 at an annual rate of nearly 3,000. From 1907 through 1910, more than 10,000 Koreans per year emigrated to Chientao (see Table 1. 1). The repressive policies in all areas of Korea after Japan's annexation of Korea accelerated the tempo of emigration to Chientao. For example, during the 16 months after Japan's annexation of Korea from September 1910 to December 1911, 28,816 Koreans emigrated to foreign countries, that is, an average of 1,800 people per month. About 62% of these Koreans emigrated to North Chientao (see Table 1. 2).

Furthermore, a growing number of Korean peasants who were put under the increasing economic hardship due to expropriation by the Japanese chose to emigrate to Manchuria. It was very easy for the political and economic refugees to cross the Tumen River into the neighboring Chientao region. During the six years from 1910 to 1916, more than 15,000 Koreans emigrated to Chientao annually, almost doubling the number of Korean settlers in Chientao from 109,500 to 203,426. The annual emigration of the Koreans again leaped by more than 20,000 in the next five years. Total population again doubled to 307,806 in 1921. In Chientao, Koreans

TABLE 1. 1

Population of Korean and Chinese in Chientao, 1881-1926

Year	Korean	Chinese	Total	Koreans in Manchuria*
1881				10,000
1894	34,000			65,000
1904				78,000
1907	71,000 (75.1)	23,500 (24.9)	94,500	
1908	89,000 (76.2)	27,800 (23.8)	116,800	
1909	98,000 (75.4)	31,900 (24.6)	129,900	
1910	109,500 (76.6)	33,500 (23.4)	143,000	202,070
1911	126,000 (78.2)	35,200 (21.8)	161.200	
1912	163,000 (76.9)	49,000 (23.1)	212,000	238,403**
1915	198,492**			282,070**
1916	203,426 (77.0)	60,896 (23.0)	264,322	328,298**
	211,362**			
1917	212,381**			337,461**
1918	253,961 (77.8)	72,602 (22.2)	326,563	
1920				459,427
1921	307,806 (80.7)	73,748 (19.3)	381,554	
1922	323,806 (82.1)	70,698 (17.9)	394,504	
1923	323,011 (80.6)	77,709 (19.4)	400,720	
1924	329,391 (79.9)	82,730 (20.1)	412,121	
1925	346,194 (80.8)	82,472 (19.2)	428,666	531,973
1926	356,016 (80.1)	86,349 (19.5)	442,365	

Notes * Korean population in Manchuria is from Ki-hoon Kim "Japanese Policy for Korean Rural Immigration," Unpublished Ph. D., Diss. U. of Hawaii (1992), p. 43.
** "Chosŏn oe esŏ ŭi Chosŏnin sanghwang ilban," pp. 476-77.

Source Hyŏn Kyu-hwan, *Hanguk yuiminsa,* pp. 161, 174.

comprised more than 75% of the total population through the 1910s, and the percentage rose to more than 80% in the 1920s. The Koreans in North Chientao comprised from 55% to 65% of the total Korean population in Manchuria (see Table 1. 1). In 1910, these Koreans

TABLE 1. 2

New Korean Emigration (Sep. 1910–Dec. 1911)

	N. HG	S. HG	N. PA	S. PA	Other	Total
North Chientao	17,253 (97)	402	8	25	65	17,753
West Chientao	5,546 (75)	102	1,166	64	508	7,386
Primorye	2,967 (89)	329	9	10	11	3,326
Others	314 (89)	2	1	2	32	351
Total	26,080 (91)	835	1,184	101	616	28,816

Note N. HG: North Hamgyŏng Province, S. HG: South: Hamgyŏng Province, N. PA: North Pyŏngan Province, S. PA: South Pyŏngan Province

Source "Sŏnin oeguk iju" [Korean Emigration to Foreign Countries], Kuksa P'yŏnch'an Wiwŏnhoe (Korean History Compilation Committee) ed., *Hanguk tongnip undongsa* [History of Korean Independence Movement], vol. 2, 1968 (Seoul: Chŏngŭm Munhwasa, 1983), pp. 553-54.

(202,070) constituted over 1% of the total population in Manchuria (18 million). In 1930, the percentage of the Korean population increased to about 3%, constituting the largest minority group in Manchuria, excluding Han Chinese.[81] In general, this distribution of the Korean population in Chientao and Manchuria endured until the end of Japanese colonial rule.[82]

We do not have any statistics about the composition of the Korean population in Chientao according to their native origins. However, the overwhelming majority of the Korean immigrants in Manchuria were from Hamgyŏng and P'yŏngan Provinces, the border areas south of the Tumen River and the Yalu River respectively (see Table 1. 3). In 1894 and 1904, about 50% of them were from Hamgyŏng and 40% were from P'yŏngan Province. During the period from 1910 to 1918, among the total number of 161,320 Koreans who emigrated to Manchuria and the Primorye, 58.4% were from Hamgyŏng

TABLE 1. 3

Native Place of Koreans in Manchuria, 1894 and 1904

Native Place	1894	1904
North Hamgyŏng	31,500 (48.5)	32,00 (41.0)
South Hamgyŏng	3,200 (4.9)	4,800 (6.2)
North P'yŏngan	14,400 (22.2)	23,500 (30.1)
South P'yŏngan	9,200 (14.2)	8,500 (10.9)
Hwanghae	3,100 (4.8)	3,000 (3.8)
North Kyŏngsang	1,300 (2.0)	1,800 (2.3)
South Kyŏngsang	1,200 (1.8)	1,700 (2.2)
Kangwŏn	- (0.0)	- (0.0)
Other	1,100 (1.7)	2,700 (3.5)
Total	65,000 (100.0)	78,000 (100.0)

Source Hyŏn Kyu-hwan, *Hanguk yuiminsa,* pp. 143.

Province and 22. 2% were from P'yŏngan Province (see Table 1. 4). New emigrants from Hamgyŏng Provinces, particularly from North Hamgyŏng Province, were the majority of the total emigrants to (North) Chientao as well as to the Primorye. During the period shortly after Japan's annexation of Korea from September 1910 to December 1911, among 28,816 of total new emigrants, the new emigrants from North Hamgyŏng Province (26,808) were the overwhelming majority of emigrants to North Chientao (97%), the Primorye (89%), West Chientao (75%) (see Table 1. 2).

This trend basically continued during the early period of the Japanese colonial rule. As we can see in Table 1. 4, during the period from 1910 to 1918, shortly before the outbreak of the March First Movement, the number of new emigrants from Hamgyŏng Provinces to North Chientao (61,144) and the Primorye (19,040) constituted about 90% and 72% of the total emigrants to those

TABLE 1. 4

New Emigration after the Japanese Annexation of Korea, 1910-1921

(1) 1910-1918

	HG	PA	HH	KG	CC	KW	KS	CL	Total
N	61,144 (89.0)	3,505 (5.1)	774 (1.1)	233 (0.3)	174 (0.2)	1,201 (1.7)	1,016 (1.5)	42 (0.0)	68,729 (100.0)
W	13,557 (20.5)	26,926 (40.8)	582 (0.9)	363 (0.5)	462 (0.7)	4,094 (6.2)	20,047 (30.4)	19 (0.0)	66,050 (100.0)
O	19,040 (71.7)	5,371 (20.2)	252 (0.9)	452 (1.7)	115 (0.4)	279 (1.1)	794 (3.0)	238 (0.9)	26,541 (100.0)
T	94,281 (58.4)	35,792 (22.2)	1,608 (1.0)	1,048 (0.6)	751 (0.5)	5,574 (3.5)	21,857 (13.5)	299 (0.2)	161,320 (100.0)

(2) 1910-1921

	HG	PA	HH	KG	CC	KW	KS	CL	Total
N	71,520 (76.2)	9,053 (9.6)	3,821 (4.1)	797 (0.8)	425 (0.5)	5,352 (5.7)	2,765 (2.9)	150 (0.2)	93,883 (100.0) (39.0)
W	16,195 (16.0)	16,195 (41.5)	1,382 (1.4)	409 (0.4)	569 (0.6)	5,172 (5.1)	35,312 (34.9)	53 (0.1)	101,080 (100.0)
O	28,533 (61.9)	12,163 (26.4)	1,091 (2.4)	1,032 (2.2)	272 (0.6)	739 (1.6)	1,686 (3.7)	548 (1.2)	46,064 (100.0)
T	116,248 (48.2)	63,204 (26.2)	6,294 (2.6)	2,238 (0.9)	1,266 (0.5)	11,263 (4.7)	39,763 (16.5)	751 (0.3)	241,027 (100.0)

Note N: North Chientao, W: West Chientao, O: Other Regions (mainly, Primorye), T: Total, HG: Hamgyŏng Provinces, PA: P'yŏngan Provinces, HH: Hwanghae Province, KG: Kyŏnggi Province, CC: Ch'ungch'ŏng Provinces, KW: Kangwŏn Province, KS: Kyŏngsang Provinces, CL: Chŏlla Provinces

Sources Japanese Government-General Office of Korea, *Manshūkyū Shiberia jihō ni okeru Chōsenjin jijō*, pp. 11-14; Hyŏn Kyu-hwan, *Hanguk yuiminsa*, pp. 166-68.

regions. Accordingly, people from Hamgyŏng Provinces maintained their overwhelming majority among the Korean settlers in North Chientao and the Primorye in the 1910s as during the previous years. Despite the increase of emigrants from other provinces such as P'yŏngan Provinces and Kyŏngsang Provinces in the late 1910s, this trend continued in the 1920s. In 1929, of the total population of Koreans in Chientao (381,507), the percentage of the people from Hamgyŏng Provinces was 79% (301,454) — North: 71% (270,446) and South: 8% (31,008).[83]

Table 1. 4 shows a sharp increase in Korean emigration after 1919 following the completion of the Land Survey and the March First Movement; more people in P'yŏngan Provinces and Kyŏngsang Provinces emigrated to Manchuria and the Primorye. The increase of the emigrants from these provinces dropped the percentages of the number of new emigrants from Hamgyŏng Province to North Chientao and the Primorye by about 10%: North Chientao, from 89% (1910-1918) to 76% (1910-1921), Primorye, from 71.7% to 61. 9% (Table 1. 4). In particular, the emigrants from Kyŏngsang Provinces, the south-eastern part of the Korean peninsula, which, in 1904, composed less than 5% of the Korean population in Manchuria (Table 1. 3), drastically increased to 16. 5% of the total Korean immigrants during the period from 1910 to 1921. In West Chientao, the number of new emigrants from Kyŏngsang Provinces, during the period from 1910 to 1921, composed about 35% of the total emigrants, the second position following P'yŏngan Provinces (42%) (see Table 1. 4). This significant rise in the emigration from Kyŏngsang Provinces may be due to the Japanese infiltration into Kyŏngsang Provinces, which had fertile lands and were nearest to Japan.

C. Korean Emigration to the Russian Far East

1. Korean Emigration before the Establishment of Diplomatic Relations, 1863-1884

Koreans first had contact with Russians in the middle of the seventeenth century when the Manchu government asked the Korean government to dispatch military troops against Russians in the Amur region. The Korean government twice dispatched military forces of 150 soldiers in 1654 and 200 soldiers in 1658. The Korean soldiers equipped with "bird-shaped firearms" ["*choch'ong*"] similar to those used by Japanese at the time of the Hideyoshi invasion, contributed to frustrating Russian territorial ambitions.[84] Koreans call these brief encounters with the Russians the "*Nasŏsn Chŏngbŏl*" ("Expedition against Russia").

Since then, it was almost two hundred years before Koreans and Russians had another encounter. In 1854, Russian admiral Efimy Vasilevich Putiatin visited the Wŏnsan Bay in northeastern Korea, hoping for trade and treaty, but had no result. Four years later when China was at war with England and France, Russia obtained the upper Amur River from the weakened Qing government in 1858. Lands east of the Ussuri River followed in 1860. Russia now shared the Tumen River as a border line with Korea. During the period shortly after incorporating the Primorye, a few thousand natives, Chinese, and Russian pioneers lived in this area together with the Ussuri Cossacks who formed part of the Amur Cossack Host in 1858.[85]

During this time, a few unmarried Koreans went to Vladivostok and other southern Ussurisk *krai* (the Russian Maritime Province) for summertime works such in ports, fortress, and road construction. In 1863, about sixty Koreans from thirteen North Hamgyŏng Province families settled without permission of the Russian authorities on the government lands in the valley of Tizinkhe River, five *versta* (a little more than 5 km) north from Pos'et beside Novogorod Bay. These Koreans are considered as the first permanent Korean emigrants to Russia.[86] A band of Russian Cossacks were stationed at that time in the regions near the Pos'et Bay, and a few more than ten Chinese households were engaged in saltworks and agriculture.[87] These Koreans appealed to the Russian Lieutenant Rezanov to allow them to settle in the Tizinkhe region and requested a dispatch of at least five soldiers to protect them from Manchu bandits, presumably *honghuzi* (Kor. *honghojŏk*) which means "red bearded bandits." Russian authorities not only allowed the Koreans to cultivate these lands, but also provided seed and foodstuffs.[88]

The first group of Korean immigrants founded a village called Tizinkhe or Rezanovo which the military governor of the Primorye Province officially named after the Russian Lieutenant Rezanov, who had reported first to the Military-Governor about the new first Korean immigrants on November 30, 1863.[89] In order to protect their village from attack of the *honghuzi*, these immigrants organized a private arsenal [*sap'oyŏng*]. Wanting to have more Koreans, twenty-five members of the arsenal secretly entered the Six Garrison Towns in Korea and gathered those Koreans who wanted to emigrate to Russia. Riding on more than sixty oxcarts and thirty horses, this group succeeded in crossing the border after an armed conflict with the local soldiers of Kyŏng-hŭng.[90] In 1865, three local Russian officials with more than ten soldiers and an Korean interpreter, Ch'oe Un-bo, visited the local office in Kyŏnghŭng and requested permission for commercial trade, but local Korean officials stubbornly refused.[91]

Accordingly, the news of these first Korean immigrants spread infectiously among Korean peasants in the border regions of North Hamgyŏng Province and triggered the flow of Korean peasants to the Pos'et region. The number of Korean emigrants to southern Ussurisk *krai* increased annually in subsequent years.[92] During the period from 1863 to 1869, about 1,400 Koreans settled in southern

Ussurisk *krai*.[93] Avoiding exploitation by corrupt and suppressive Korean government officials and the famine which resulted from repeated poor harvests, Korean peasants dared to emigrate to Ussurisk *krai* risking the death penalty promulgated by the Korean government which strictly prohibited their subjects from crossing the Tumen River.[94]

In addition to Tizinkhe, already settled in 1864, Korean settlements later arose in Ianchikhe, Sidimi, Adimi, Chapigou, Krabbe and Fuduvai along the rivers of Ianchikhe, Adimi, Sidimi, Tizinkhe and the Krabbe Peninsula in southern Ussurisk *krai*.[95] The first mass emigration of the Koreans to Ussurisk *krai* began in 1869. That year, Korean farmers in the border regions of northern Korea, particularly in the Six Garrisons Towns, experienced such an "unprecedented, terrible draught caused by a long-standing duststorm, that there was not a grain to be gathered in the fields."[96] The number of peasants who risked their lives by crossing the river to Chientao and the Ussurisk *krai* drastically increased.[97] During the six months from June to December 1869, about 6,500 Koreans emigrated to the Tizinkhe region.[98] Among these people, 4,500 Koreans arrived at Tizinkhe at the beginning of December. Of this group, 300-400 families brought a few of cattle and a small amount of food, while the remaining 700 families came with nothing.[99] It was not easy to support these large number of new immigrants. The scarcely populated wild land was also suffering a bad harvest.[100] The Koreans who had settled earlier in Tizinkhe could not fully provide enough food for the new immigrants, who outnumbered established settlers by five to one. Hundreds of people starved to death each day. Fewer than half survived, in part due to grain provided by the Russian authorities.[101]

Troubled by the unanticipated influx of so many starving Korean immigrants, the military governor of the Priamur, I. V. Furugel'm (1865-1871), dispatched Trubetskoi to Kyŏnghŭng and concluded an agreement with its magistrate of Kyŏnghŭng concerning the return of the immigrants to Korea. Both Russian and Korean local authorities agreed to facilitate their return. However, Furugel'm failed to persuade the Korean immigrants in Tizinkhe to cooperate. They refused to follow Furugel'm's order for Koreans without means for survival to leave their Russian settlements. The Koreans announced that they would rather die from starvation in Russian territory than return to Korea. They also did not believe the promise of the magistrate of Kyŏnghŭng. In the end, Furugel'm decided to allow the 6,500 Korean immigrants to settle on Russian territory, while taking measures to provide for their sustenance.[102]

The stubborn attitude of these Korean immigrants does not seem to have been the key factor in changing local Russian policies. More importantly, it was the conclusion of Furugel'm that the Korean immigrants in southern Ussurisk *krai* would be of substantial benefit to the Russian population "providing good and cheap laborers."[103] He therefore proceeded to utilize the Korean immigrants in colonizing and developing southern Ussurisk *krai*. First of all, Furugel'm mobilized them to work at the construction of military facilities in Novokievsk and the dock in Vladivostok port, as well as roads throughout the Daubikhe region. Korean settlers in Razdol'noe and Astrakhan were ordered to supply firewood for steamers floating in the Ussuri and Suifen Rivers and Lake Khanka.[104] At the same time, Furugel'm relocated a large number of recently arrived Korean immigrants to the valleys of the Suifen, Shufan, and Lef Rivers originating from Lake Khanka, and later even to the valley of the Suchan River in the south-eastern part of Primorye Province.[105]

By the order of N. P. Sinel'nikov (the Governor-General of Eastern Siberia who had travelled to inspect the Korean settlement in southern Ussurisk in 1870), the local Russian authorities of Priamur Province relocated 431 Koreans from 103 families in the Pos'et area to Amur Province. A New Korean village was called Blagoslovennoe (Kor. Samalli) at the mouth of the Samara River, a tributary of the Amur River, 547 *verst*s (about 547 km) from Blagoveshchensk. The Russian government spent 16,570 rubles for the relocation of these Koreans. According to the Migration Promotion Law of 1861, these Koreans were forever exempted from the poll tax, and for twenty years from the land tax; they obtained Russian citizenship and 100 *desiatin*s of land (one *desiatin* is about 2. 7 acres) per household.[106]

The Russian government's relocation of Korean immigrants to regions far from the frontier region had already begun in 1867.[107] This policy clearly reflected the uneasiness of local Russian authorities regarding the settlement of so many Koreans near the Korean frontier.[108] As a result of the relocation policy all 3,473 Koreans founded 13 Korean villages in the southern Ussurisk *krai* — 5 in Suifen district, 6 in Khanka district and 2 in Suchan district — in 1872. Korean settlements in southern Ussurisk *krai* continued to increase through the 1870s, and in 1878, 6,142 Koreans were living in 20 villages — 9 in Suifen district, 8 in Khanka district and 3 in Suchan district.[109]

Korean immigrants in southern Ussurisk *krai* were hospitably accepted by the Russian authorities, which provided food, seed, cattle and lands. Although the local Russian authorities felt uncomfortable with starving Korean immigrants, their wish to colonize the *krai* led them to accept emigrés from Korea with sympathy. The Ussurisk

TABLE 1. 5

Russian Migration to the Priamur

Period	Increase of Peasant Migrants					
	Amur (1)		Primorye (2)		Priamur (1) + (2)	
	Period	Yearly	Period	Yearly	Period	Yearly
1859-1882	8,709	363	5,705	238	14,414	601
1883-1899	24,089	1,417	45,196	2,659	69,285	4,076
1900-1908	42,106	4,678	130,356	14,484	172,462	19,161
1859-1908	74,904	1,498	181,257	3,625	256,161	5,123

Source Derber Petr Iakovlevich and Sher M. L., *Ocherki Khazaistvennoi Zhizni Dal'nego Vostoka* [Essays on Agricultural Life of the Far East] (Moscow and Leningrad: Gosudarstvennoe Izdatel'stvo, 1927), p. 30.

krai, which Russia had recently obtained from China, was sparsely populated. It was unrealistic for the Russian authorities to hope for colonization of the newly-obtained territory by Russian settlers.[110] Transportation difficulties, lack of facilities necessary for settlement, severe climate, remoteness from central Russia discouraged the migration of Russians to the Far East. The Russian government's effort to induce Russian settlers to the Far East had not led to satisfactory results. Even the majority of the new migrants who crossed the Urals preferred to settle in other parts of Siberia, instead of moving further east.[111]

As we can see in Table 1. 5, the number of Russian settlers in Ussurisk *krai* is smaller than that in the Amur Province. Furthermore, the rate of the Russian migration to the Ussuri region dropped sharply from 1871, obviously influenced by the "Manza War" in 1868,[112] when the *honghuzi* attacked Russian settlements.[113] As of 1882, the number of Korean settlers equalled 10.9% of the whole population in the Primorye *oblast* and outnumbered that of the ethnic Russian settlers (see Table 1. 6).

TABLE 1. 6

Population in the Primorye — Koreans and Russians, 1882-1908

Year	Korean			Russian	Total
	Russian	Alien	Total		
1882	-	10,137 (10.9)	10,137 (10.9)	8,385 (9.0)	92,708 (100.0)
1892	12,940 (78.1)	3,624 (21.9)	16,564 (11.2) (100.0)	57,000 (38.6)	147,517 (100.0)
1902	16,140 (49.8)	16,270 (50.2)	32,410 (10.4) (100.0)	66,320 (21.2)	312,541 (100.0)
1908	16,190 (35.7)	29,207 (64.3)	45,397 (8.6) (100.0)	383,083 (72.9)	525,353 (100.0)

Source V. V. Grave, *Kitaitsy, Koreitsy i Iapontsy v Priamur'e*, pp. 129-30.

Furthermore, Koreans proved themselves to be much more efficient farmers than Russians. Koreans diligently cultivated the vast undeveloped land which Russian cossacks and peasant settlers leased to them.[114] Russian cossacks and migrants obtained foodstuffs, cheap labor, and agricultural skills from Koreans. In short, Koreans played a major role in the economic growth of the Primorye.[115] In this context, it was natural for the local Russian authorities to welcome Korean immigrants to Ussurisk *krai*.

2. Korean Emigration to Russia under Diplomatic Relations, 1884-1905

In the 1880s (for the purpose of remedying its weak position in the Far East, in contrast to the growing colonization and military presence of China in Manchuria) the Russian government began to implement some active policies based on the principle of "Russia for the Russians."[116] First, in order to populate the Ussurisk *krai*, the Russian government issued an edict in 1882 prohibiting all but Russian subjects from acquiring land in Siberia. The Governor-General would lease land to foreigners only in exceptional circumstances.[117] For the effective administration of the Far East, the Russian government in 1884 separated Za-Baikal, Amur, and Primorye and Sakhalin Island from the governor-generalship of Eastern Siberia and put them under the newly created Priamur Governor-General centered in Khabarovsk.[118]

The Russian government experimented with financing the transport of Russian migrants from Odessa to the Far East by means of the Russian Volunteer Fleet beginning in 1879. In 1882 the first party of 250 families was transported to Vladivostok at government cost.[119] In order to attract migrants from the southern Russian provinces to Ussurisk *krai*, the government established the South Ussuri Resettlement Law under the Governor-General of Eastern Siberia, Dmitry Anuchin. In addition to land-allotment (15 *desiatin*s per person, with a maximum of 100 *desiatin*s per household), the law granted various privileges such as tax exemption for five years, food supplies for eighteen months, construction materials and agricultural tools to the migrants.[120]

The growth of Russian colonization thus increased after 1883. As Table 1. 5 indicates, during the first 24 years from 1859 to 1882, migration proceeded slowly, mainly to the Amur. However, during the next seventeen years (1883-1899), the colonization increased almost seven times faster than during the previous period. In particular, the number of migrants to the Primorye became twice as large as that to the Amur, which is explained by arrivals by sea.[121]

The Russian population in 1882, 8,385, was only 9% of the total population in the Primorye and was even less than that of the Koreans. After 10 years, it leaped to 57,000 in 1892, composing 38.6% of the entire Primorye population, becoming the largest single ethnic group. At the beginning of 1898, the Russian population was the largest ethnic group in all parts of the Primorye region (see Table 1. 7), and continuously increased thanks to supportive government policies. In 1908, it reached 383,083, 72.9% of the entire population.[122] In 1886, the first Governor-General of the Priamur, Baron A. N. Korf (1884-1893) convened a conference of governors and other high officials in Khabarovsk to discuss the question of Korean and Chinese settlers in the Priamur. The conference decided to expel the Chinese immigrants living more than fifty *verst*s from the Chinese border.[123] After the conference, the Russian authorities took restrictive measures against Koreans.[124] For example, when the frontier between Manchuria and the southern Ussuri region was agreed on by Russia and China in 1886, a Korean village called Nasŏn-dong (Sabyolovka in Russian) located near the mouth of the Tumen River, became Chinese territory, and Russian police proceeded to destroy it by force.[125]

On November 22, 1886, after conferring with the Governor-General of the Priamur the Russian government promulgated a law which allowed the Minister of Internal Affairs to relocate Koreans to the interior regions far from border areas. This policy, however, could not be enforced for two reasons: 1) relocation of Koreans was too expensive; 2) it might have caused difficulties in food supply for Russian military and government officials. Accordingly Baron Korf decided to allow Koreans to stay in the Pos'et region.[126]

The Russian government also addressed issues of Korean emigration through diplomacy. Twenty-five years after Korea and Russia

TABLE 1. 7

Population in the Primorye (Jan. 1, 1898)

	Rus.	Indig.	Kor.	Chin.	Jap.	Other.	Total
Cities							
Vladivostok	15,918	-	1,361	10,181	961	464	29,185
Khabarovsk	11,067	33	127	3,641	187	27	15,082
Nikolaevsk	4,353	8	131	1,109	94	31	5,726
Petropavlosk	376	7	7	4	-	4	398
Okhotsk	173	26	-	-	-	-	199
Districts							
S. Ussurisk	67,947	459	20,087	9,949	246	23	98,711
Uss. Cossack	15,650	1,261	845	3,081	69	11	20,917
Ud	2,559	6,931	34	348	154	6	10,032
Khabarovsk	5,483	5,728	539	914	18	10	12,692
Petropavlovsk	2,244	5,766	-	-	-	-	8,010
Okhotsk	341	4,270	-	-	-	4	4,615
Gizhinsk	624	6,947	-	-	-	-	7,571
Komandorsk	46	606	-	1	-	-	653
Anandysk	129	12,296	-	-	-	-	12,425
Mining Dist.	2,036	367	148	56	1	-	2,608
Total	128,946	44,705	23,279	29,284	2,030	580	228,824

Notes **Rus.**: Russians, **Indig.**: Indigenous Non-Russians, **Kor.**: Koreans, **Chin.**: Chinese, **Jap.**: Japanese, **Other**: Other Foreigners

Source P. F. Unterberger, *Primorskaya Oblast'. 1856-1898 gg.* [Primorye Oblast, 1856-1898] (St. Petersburg: V. F. Kirshbauma, 1900), Appendix, pp. 1-a.

had shared the border, diplomatic relations with Korea were formalized when the two countries signed a "Treaty of Friendship and Commerce" on July 7, 1884. Together with the Korean government's removal of the ban on border-crossing in the previous year, the treaty made it much more convenient for Koreans to cross the Tumen River into Russian territory.[127]

After conclusion of this treaty, local Russian authorities also allowed local self-rule for Koreans in Ussurisk *krai*. In 1884, local Russian authorities appointed Ch'oe Chae-hyŏng as the first Korean headman (Kor. *tohŏn*), a kind of magistrate, in Pos'et where the majority of the Korean immigrants had settled.[128] The headman was in charge of collecting taxes, enforcing orders of the Russian authorities, minor legal decisions, and police activities.[129] Below the headman were unofficial village district leaders called *p'ungjon* (custom leader) or *noya* (elderman). *P'ungjon* were usually elected in rural areas and *noya* in urban areas. Several unofficial village leaders were called *p'ungsok* (village custom leaders). Headmen, *p'ungjon* and *noya* were good at foreign languages such as Russian and Chinese, and usually mediated in affairs with foreigners.[130]

Soon after the establishment of diplomatic relations, the Russian government, seriously concerned about Korean emigration, attempted to resolve the issue through diplomatic negotiation. The first Russian ambassador to Korea, Karl I. Weber, who arrived in Seoul in October 1885, immediately started negotiations of the rules governing commercial intercourse on the Russo-Korean border at the Tumen River. In order to achieve his government's policy of checking Korean emigration and promoting naturalization, Weber proposed to grant rights equivalent to those of other Russian subjects to Koreans who had emigrated to Russia before the 1884 Treaty. President of the Board of Foreign Affairs of Korea Kim Yun-sik agreed and promised to issue an order to local Korean authorities in the frontier region. However, hesitating to allow the Koreans in Russia to become Russian citizens, the Korean government did not document the agreement either in the order to its local authorities in the frontier region or in the convention on frontier trade at the Tumen River, which was signed between Russia and Korea on August 20, 1888.[131] The convention of 1888 included the opening of Kyŏnghŭng to Russia; any Korean without a Russian passport was not allowed to emigrate to Russia.[132]

Although Russia and Korea agreed that Koreans who had emigrated to Russia before 1884 must obtain Russian citizenship, local Russian authorities did not put the agreement into practice immediately after the conclusion of the convention of 1888. Priamur Governor-General, Baron Korf at first considered Koreans politically useless for the colonization of the *krai* and accordingly did not hurry to grant citizenship to those who had emigrated before the 1884 Treaty.[133] Pavel Fyodorovich Unterberger (1888-1897), Primorye Military-Governor, was also "a decisive opponent to the acceptance of the Koreans to Russian citizenship, worrying that the position of the Koreans would be durable once they were given the land allotment."[134] Baron Korf and General Unterberger clearly considered it advantageous to keep the status of Koreans uncertain in order to expel unfavorable elements from among Koreans, to promote Russification of the Koreans, and to collect taxes from the Koreans who came before 1884 as other Koreans and Chinese of non-Russian subjects.[135]

In 1890, however, the strong Chinese policy toward Koreans in Chientao, by which Koreans were either forced to obtain Chinese citizenship for landownership or expelled, clearly influenced local Russian authorities in the Far East.[136] Baron Korf issued an order prepared by General Unterberger on July 21, 1891. According to the decree, all Koreans living in Russia fell into three categories.[137] The first category identified Koreans who had already settled and were farming in Russia before the treaty of 1884. They were promised Russian citizenship and 15 *desiatins* (40.5 acres) of land with an obligation not to rent to transient Koreans. The second category covered Koreans who had settled after 1884. They were given two years to liquidate their businesses. During this two year grace period, they had to follow the natural and monetary duties of the first category. After two years, however, they would be treated like Koreans of the third category, Koreans who came temporarily to Russia as foreigners and they were required to hold passports issued both by the Korean and Russian governments.[138] The negative attitudes of the local Russian authorities such as Baron Korf and General Unterberger towards Koreans culminated in the 1891 decree by which the landownership of foreigners was prohibited and the land allotment of 100 *desiatin*s was allowed only to Russians.[139] Furthermore, the conference which Baron Korf convened between governors and representatives of the local businesses in 1893 resolved that Koreans were "unnecessary" to the Ussurisk *krai*.[140]

Baron Korf died in 1893 leaving the enforcement of his order to his successors S. M. Dukhovskoi (1893-1898) and N. I. Grodekov (1898-1902), both of whom had radically different views on the Korean question.[141] Unlike his predecessor, Governor-General Dukhovskoi was an advocate of liberal policies toward Korean immigrants: 1) utilization of the Koreans for the colonization of the Ussurisk *krai*; 2) welcoming them to Russian citizenship with allotments of land; 3) and Russification.[142] Russian authorities investigated population and the number of the households in September 1895 for Koreans in the Primorye. For the first time, about 1,500 families among those belonging to the first category obtained Russian citizenship by oath in 1896.[143] They received land allotments of fifteen *desiatin*s per household and like other Russian subjects were exempted from the poll tax and land tax for twenty years.[144] Governor-General

Dukhovskoi extended the term of the stay of the Koreans who immigrated after 1884 (second category) and ordered a review of their rights to obtain Russian citizenship.[145] Continuing the policies of Dukhovskoi, Governor-General Grodekov went even further. In 1898, he accepted Koreans of the first category who were not yet naturalized and promised to give Russian citizenship even to the Koreans of the second category if they continued to settle in Russia for more than 5 years.[146] According to this order, Koreans of the second category were encouraged in 1898-1899 to migrate and to rent government lands located deep in the interior. As a result, New Korean villages arose in the northern part of the Primorye along the Iman, Khora, and Kiya Rivers between Khabarovsk and Nikol'sk as well as along the Amur River. Within five years, these Koreans became Russian subjects.[147]

In general, thanks to the policies of Dukhovskoi and Grodekov, the number of the new Korean immigrants steadily increased. The Korean population in the Primorye doubled from 16,564 to 32,410 during the period from 1892 to 1902, mainly due to the increase in newcomers (see Table 1. 6). At the beginning of 1898, Koreans composed the fourth largest ethnic group after Russians, indigenous peoples, and Chinese. 86% of the Koreans had settled in the southern Ussurisk *krai*, where they composed about 20% of the entire population, the second largest ethnic group after the Russians (see Table 1. 7).

Korean immigrants who received Russian citizenship and land allotments during the period from 1895 to 1901 enjoyed equal rights with the Russians. After this period, in fact, the Russian government never allotted land to Koreans.[148] Together with Koreans who were relocated by the Russian authorities to the Samara River valley, Blagoslovennoe village (1871) and the Taubikhe region (1886), they were very wealthy. They received Russian educations, and their life-style was almost the same as that of Russian settlers.[149]

These early-naturalized Koreans came to be called *wŏnhoin* (原戶人 or 元戶人, old immigrants), in comparison with *yŏhoin* (餘戶人, new immigrants) or *yuhoin* (流戶人, drifting immigrants) who were not naturalized people, and mainly farmed for the cossacks or the *wŏnhoin* Koreans.[150] Also, there were temporary laborers, called *oep'umsari*, presumably a dialetic derived from *oep'umsari* (wage-earners in foreign land) who came to Russia for wages and returned to their homes after making money. The *wŏnhoin* usually rented their land called *wŏnhoji* (land of the *wŏnhoin*) to the *yŏhoin* [*yuhoin*] or hired *oep'umjari* as workers.[151] The *wŏnhoin* lived in their own villages called *wŏnhoch'on* (village of the *wŏnhoin*)[152] which were separated from the villages of the *yŏhoin* Koreans called *yŏhoch'on* or *yuhoch'on*.[153] The villages of the *wŏnhoin* Koreans, as Mrs. Bishop who had visited the Korean villages in southern Ussurisk *krai* in 1897 described vividly in detail, were good examples of the successful transformation of Korean immigrants from "starving folk [who] fled from famine" into "energetic, thriving, peasant farmers."[154]

Among the *wŏnhoin* was a group of the most wealthy Koreans who successfully accumulated wealth by providing military supplies such as beef or constructing military facilities for the Russian armies. These Korean *podriadchik* (contractors) were good at the Russian language and usually hired tens of thousands of Korean and Chinese workers for businesses contracted with the local Russian authorities in which they made money by exploiting the margin of their terms. One or two wealthy Korean *podriadchik* already appeared early in the 1880s, but it was late in the 1890s that a couple of successful Korean *podriadchik* came to get more business opportunities in projects related to the construction of the Trans-Siberian and Chinese Eastern Railroads and increased Russian military activities during the Boxer Rebellion and the Russo-Japanese War.[155]

From the second half of the 1890s, with their enhanced legal status as Russian subjects and improved economic position in Russia, some of the *wŏnhoin* began to increase their role as leaders of the Ussurisk *krai* Koreans in their new and old countries, Russia and Korea. After Queen Min was brutally murdered by the Japanese in August 1895, King Kojong escaped to the Russian legation in Seoul in February 1896 [*Agwan P'ach'ŏn*]. The new pro-Russia cabinet of Korea asked Russia to support Korea. Thanks to the increased influence of Russians within the Korean government, many Koreans were recruited from regions such as Pos'et and Suifen as interpreters for the consulate officials and military instructors whom Russian government dispatched to Korea. Fortunately, some of them were appointed government officials of Korea.[156] In 1896, Ch'oe Chae-hyŏng [Pyotr Semyonovich], the first district headman of Korean communities in the Pos'et area, was dispatched, together with Kim To-il, to St. Petersburg as a representative of the Koreans in Russia at the coronation ceremony for Russian Tsar Nicholas II.[157]

Immediately after the outbreak of the Boxer Rebellion in 1900, restrictive policies on Chinese and Korean immigrants were suggested again. A special committee was established with the director of mining as its chairman. Sentiment in favor of expelling Chinese laborers from gold mines in the Far East was strong in the committee, but the feeling against Korean laborers was not. The committee decided to expel Chinese from the gold mines, but it encouraged Korean immigration to the Russian Far East and Russification of them.[158] After the beginning of Japanese domination in 1905, another massive influx of Korean emigration to the Primorye occurred.

3. Korean Immigrants in Russia during the Protectorate and Colonial Rule Period

a. Russian Policies on Korean Immigrants

Local Russian authorities basically welcomed Korean emigration to the sparsely populated Ussurisk *krai* soon after its acquisition from Qing China, although initially Russians were perplexed by its increasing volume. As the number of Russian emigrants from European Russia to Ussuri *krai* and other parts of Siberia increased, however, restrictions on Chinese and Korean emigration were frequently suggested. The urgent need to colonize the region, to use Koreans as cheap and capable laborers for the gold mines and supply food for the Russians in the Primorye by cultivating the poor quality agricultural land in the Primorye all made restriction on Koreans unpopular.[159] The rapid increase of Russian migration to the Far East later on changed this calculation. Table 1. 6 shows the rate of migration during the period from 1900 to 1908 surpassed that of the previous period by more than four and a half times. Three times more Russians migrated to the Primorye than to the Amur, related to the opening of the Za-Baikal Railroad in 1900, and later in 1902, of the Chinese Eastern Railroad which had facilitated the migration.[160] The Russian migration to the Priamur continued to increase from 1909 to 1914 with annually almost one and a half times more than that of the previous period — 27,135 persons compared to 19,161 persons during the period from 1900 to 1908.[161]

In this situation, many Russians felt that it was necessary to

TABLE 1. 8

Korean Population in the Primorye, 1906-1923

	Russian-Koreans (1)	Foreign-Koreans (2)	Total (1) + (2)	Whole Population
1882a	-	10,137	10,137	92,708*
1892a	12,940	3,624	16,564	147,517*
1902a	16,140	16,270	32,410	312,541*
1906b	16,195	17,434	34,399	377,129
1907b	16,007	29,907	45,914	503,191
1908b	16,190	29,307	45,497	562,755
1909b	14,799	36,755	51,554	523,361
1910	17,080	36,996	54,076	523,840b
1911	17,476	39,813	57,280	
1912	16,263	43,452	59,715	
1913	19,277	38,163	57,440	
1914	20,109	44,200	64,309	
1923	34,559	72,258	106,817	

Notes a: V. V. Grave, *Kitaitsy, Koreitsy i Iapontsy v Priamur'e*, pp. 129-30,
b: P. F. Unterberger, *Priamurskii Krai*, 1906-1910 gg., Appendix, pp. 2-3.
* V. V. Grave, *Kitaitsy, Koreitsy i Iapontsy v Priamur'e*, pp. 19-130.

Source Semen Davidovich Anosov, *Koreitsy v Ussuriiskom krae*, p. 27, p. 29.

expel foreigners in order to protect their interests. Support for employing only Russians and expelling the yellow foreigners, mainly Chinese and Korean laborers in the Priamur regions, grew after November 1907, when the conservative third Duma was established, from the Russian central government to the local officials in the Far East.[162]

It was P. F. Unterberger who represented the opinion of "Russia for the Russians" in the Far East. In his first book, *Primorskaia oblast' 1856-1898* (Primorye Oblast, 1856-1898) published in 1900, two years after his resignation from the military-governorship of the Primorye (1888-1897), Unterberger concluded that Koreans "clarified to us [Russians] their uselessness as colonizing elements in parts of

TABLE 1. 9

Governor-General of the Eastern Siberia

N. N. Murav'ev-Amursky	1847-1861
M. S. Korsakov	1861-1871
N. P. Sinel'nikov	1871-1875
P. A. Frederiks	1875-1880
D. G. Anuchin	1880-1898

the Primorye *oblast*," and "were entirely alien to us (Russians)" in all respects.[163] General Unterberger's skepticism on Korean immigrants as "unreliable elements" might have influenced the local Russian authorities in the 1900s.

It is noteworthy that after the governor-generalship of Grodekov (1898-1902), the Russian government hesitated to allow Koreans to become Russian citizens, although a land allotment of fifteen *desiatins* was promised according to the decree of June 22, 1900. We can confirm this in Table 1. 8 by the fact that the number of naturalized Koreans did not substantially increase at all until 1913, when Governor-General Nikolai Lvovich Gondatti (1911-1917) allowed Koreans to obtain Russian citizenship, but with no land allotment.

Under the governor-generalship of General Unterberger (1905-1910), the Russian government initiated a campaign against emigration of Koreans to Russia. During his tenure, Unterberger represented himself as an advocate of the theory of "Russia for the pure Russians" — to protect Russian laborers and peasants in the Far East — and that of the Yellow Peril, assuming that yellow races would invade the Maritime Province and then Siberia. In his report of 1908 to the Minister of Internal Affairs, Governor-General Unterberger identified the Koreans as those who would be "an extraordinarily favorable foundation for broad organization of espionage by our enemies" in case of war with Japanese or Chinese.[164] Again in a 1910 talk with V. V. Grave, while criticizing his predecessors (who had believed that the uninhabited *krai* must be settled, even if by the Koreans), Unterberger threatened to take harsh measures against Koreans as well as against the Chinese and Japanese, and to gradually oust them from the Ussurisk *krai*.[165]

With the support of popular opinion both in center and in the Far East advocating restriction on Chinese and Korean immigration, the Russian government promulgated a law prohibiting Koreans and Chinese from working in the Priamur on June 14, 1909.[166] According to the law, non-naturalized Koreans were prohibited from settling in the area of public lands, contracting public delivery and working at the public expense.[167] Immigrants worried about the imminent firing and expulsion of Koreans working at gold mines began a petition to the Russian government. A delegation representing 50,000 Koreans went to St. Petersburg and turned in the petition signed by Korean workers to the Ministry of Internal affairs, and visited members of the Duma.[168] Korean representatives said that if the Russian government allowed Koreans to stay, they would adopt the Russian orthodox religion, perform military service and other duties, not ask for any government assistance, and that they would build facilities needed for allotted lands by investing in their own private property.[169] Despite the appeal, the Russian government passed a law on July 4, 1910[170] placing economic burden on the Russian gold miners who benefitted from Korean workers.[171]

However, the Russian government soon recognized the problems caused by expelling Koreans from the workplace. The appointment of N. L. Gondatti as the new governor-General of Priamur reflected that change of mood in the Russian Government. Governor-General Gondatti had served as the Director of the South Ussuri Resettlement Office (1899-1902) and had recently headed the Amur Expedition (1909-1910).[172] The Expedition's favorable and more realistic opinion on Korean immigrants was articulated in its report by V. V. Grave to the Ministry of Internal Affairs, *Kitaitsy, Koreitsy i Iapontsy v Priamur'* (Chinese, Koreans, and Japanese in the Priamur) (1912). Governor-General Gondatti and his predecessor, General Unterberger were well-known "representatives of the two different points of view on the Korean question."[173] Governor-General Gondatti continued the policy of Governor-Generals Dukhovskoi and Grodekov. As we will see in Chapter 2, Governor-General Gondatti was very sympathetic with the Koreans and accordingly welcomed by the Koreans in the Russian Far East as the "patron of the Koreans."[174]

Governor-General Gondatti attended the conference which was held in St. Petersburg on March 20, 1911, to discuss the question of colonization of the Far East. While the conference discussed not only encouraging Russian migration to the Far East, but also the appeal of the gold miners concerning non-naturalized Korean laborers. Instead of allowing the non-naturalized Koreans to work at gold mines, the conference decided to welcome Korean applications for Russian citizenship.[175] The conference also authorized Gondatti, pending final approval of the Tsar, to allow Koreans who applied for Russian citizenship to work at gold mines. Gondatti accepted Koreans' application for Russian citizenship.[176] At the same time, officials of the office of naturalization in Vladivostok were dispatched to various regions to investigate the situation of Korean settlers and to encourage non-naturalized Koreans to apply for citizenship.[177] The Korean laborers were permitted to obtain Russian citizenship without land allotments,[178] and accordingly could work at gold mines in various regions. As a result, an unusual number of Koreans were going to the gold mines.[179]

On March 23, 1911, the Russian government finally decided to abolish the nominal law prohibiting non-naturalized Koreans from working at gold mines.[180] The cabinet meeting held on May 4, 1911 confirmed those decisions made at the conference on the Far East.[181] The adoption of the policy encouraging naturalization and the appointment of Gondatti as the Governor-General of the Priamur seem to have been closely related to the Japanese annexation of Korea. The Russian government must have understood that the existence of a number of non-naturalized Koreans would provide room for Japanese interference in the affairs of Koreans in Russia. The Russian government rejected the claim of the Japanese government that Koreans in Russia had become Japanese subjects after Japan's annexation of Korea, and that the Koreans did not have the right to discard Japanese citizenship by obtaining the citizenship of another country — although the weak Chinese Government had to accept this claim.[182] Although the Japanese government succeeded in enforcing this claim during the Siberian Intervention (1918-1922), this firm policy of the Russian government made the position of naturalized Koreans in Russia fundamentally different from that of the Koreans in China, particularly in Chientao.

However, the situation of non-naturalized Koreans was quite different. Although the Russian government clarified that it would consider Koreans as Korean subjects, not as Japanese subjects, the Secret Declaration of June 1, 1911, and more importantly, the increasing rapprochement between Russia and Japan, made the legal position of non-naturalized Koreans very insecure.[183] In this context, as we will see in Chapter 2, Korean nationalists in the Priamur, particularly members of the Kwŏnŏphoe, organized a campaign for the naturalization of the Koreans as the Korean nationalists did in Chientao. The Koreans who obtained Russian citizenship thanks to this campaign during the period of Gondatti were called "Gondatti products." In terms of economic status and political attitude, they were by and large quite different from the *wŏnhoin*, who had obtained Russian citizenship during the governor-generalships of Dukhovskoi and Grodekov.[184]

On the other hand, the Russian authorities needed to strengthen their control over non-naturalized Koreans and Chinese who did not have passports (*billet*). On November 27, 1911, the Russian police of Vladivostok arrested 24 Koreans without passports, released twelve and expelled the other twelve to Korea. Three hundred Chinese were also arrested and among them sixty-six were expelled to China.[185] Governor-General Gondatti ordered the local officials to expel non-naturalized Koreans from the Pos'et immigration district — an area from Pos'et area to the north of the Tumen River below Mongugai (currently Barabash) village, where only naturalized Koreans were allowed to work.[186] In July 1912, Gondatti also ordered the expulsion of all yellow people in Egershel'da in Vladivostok and the employment of only Russian workers after August.[187]

b. Korean Immigrants in the Primorye after 1905

The establishment of the Japanese protectorate rule in Korea in 1905 and Japanese annexation of Korea in 1910 created a new type of Korean emigrant to Russia. A number of politically-oriented patriots, who were dissatisfied with Japanese dominance in Korea after the Russo-Japanese War, concluded that it was no longer possible to continue their anti-Japanese activities within Korea. The Korean emigrants chose Russian territory as a proper base for their anti-Japanese activities because the Russian Far East was geographically adjacent to their homeland and more importantly, hoped that Russia, having been defeated by Japan, would be sympathetic with the anti-Japanese aspirations of the Korean patriots.

Participation of a number of the Koreans in Ussurisk *krai* on the Russian side during the Russo-Japanese War obviously inspired pro-Russian feelings among the Korean patriots. Koreans in Ussurisk *krai* participated in transportation of military supplies for the Russian army. Koreans, mostly *wŏnhoin* such as Kim In-su, Kim To-il, Kim Sang-hŏn, Yu Chin-yul, Yun Il-byŏng, Ku Tŏk-sŏng, Hwang Pyŏng-gil, and Ŏm In-sŏp, accompanied Russians as interpreters when Russian military troops entered Hamgyŏng Provinces. Well-known Korean *podriadchik*s, Ch'oe Pong-jun [Alexander Ch'oe] and Han Ik-sŏng, made big money by providing supplies to the Russian troops. We will see later in Chapter 2, most of these Koreans became leaders of anti-Japanese activities in Russia as was the case of Yi Pŏm-yun in Chientao.[188] Most of the pro-Russian Koreans retreated to Vladivostok before and after Japan's annexation of Korea[189] and had a base in Vladivostok when they communicated with colleagues in other regions.[190] As we saw earlier, increasing economic infiltration of the Japanese in Korea also forced a lot of Korean peasants to emigrate to Manchuria and the Primorye.

During the period from 1906 to 1912, the Korean population in the Primorye increased by 74% from 34,399 to 59,715, mainly due to a 150% increase in the number of non-naturalized Koreans — from 17,434 to 43,452. The number of non-naturalized Koreans would be much larger if we include the unreported Koreans who

TABLE 1. 10

Governor-General and Commander of the Priamur Krai Army

A. N. Korf	1884-1893
S. M. Dukhovskoi	1893-1898
N. I. Grodekov	1898-1902
D. I. Subbotich	1902-1903
N. P. Linevich	1903-1904
R. V. Khreshchatitskii	1904-1905
P. F. Unterberger	1905-1910
N. L. Gondatti	1910-1917

Sources Unterberger, *Primorskaia Oblast'. 1856-1898 gg.*, Appendix, p. 12; Unterberger, *Priamurskii Krai, 1906-1910 gg.*, pp. 37-38.

did not have passports, which was estimated to be 30% of the entire Korean population.[191] Accordingly, it was estimated that the unofficial number of the Korean population in the Ussurisk *krai* in 1910 was 80,000[192] or more than 100,000, a larger number than official statistics.[193] Very small number of Koreans were also in Amur and Za-Baikal regions — in 1910, 1,538 in Amur and 378 in Za-Baikal.[194] This trend continued during the early period of the Japanese colonial rule of Korea, the total Korean population, reaching 64,309 in 1914 (see Table 1. 8). During World War I, the Korean population temporarily decreased because of the migration of Koreans to Manchuria in order to escape the depression caused by war, and mobilization by the Russian government.[195] Thousands of Korean workers also migrated to the Ural areas and European Russian areas. According to the Japanese report, at the end of 1917 there were more than 7,000 Koreans, mostly workers in European Russia.[196] However, the outbreak of the Russian February Revolution in 1917 and the March First Movement in Korea in 1919 induced a number of Koreans to leave Korea and Manchuria for the Russian Far East.

Once more, thousands of Koreans, mainly members of the Korean anti-Japanese partisan units, came to the Priamur region from Manchuria to escape the indiscriminate attacks of the Japanese military against the Korean communities in October 1920. However, the consolidation of Soviet power in Siberia after 1923 made the number of the Koreans in the Russian Far East a stable figure. According to the census of 1926, the Korean population was 168,009 — half of them were naturalized Koreans who made up 9.7% of the whole population in the Russian Far East.[197] During the Soviet period, there was no noticeable immigration of the Koreans from oustside to the Russian Far East. According to G. A. Tkachev, the number of Koreans in the Russian Far East varied from 160,000 to 180,000, during the 1930s, shortly before the forced relocation to Central Asia.[198]

Chapter Two

KOREAN NATIONALIST MOVEMENT IN THE RUSSIAN FAR EAST AND NORTH CHIENTAO, 1905-1916

A. Loyalists Urge Patriotism

1. Diplomatic Activities

In the face of encroaching Western powers and Japan, Korean patriots had endeavored to revitalize their weakening country in the latter half of the 19th century. There have been various theories concerning when the Korean nationalist movement began. A prominent nationalist historian and activist Pak Ŭn-sik, in his book, *Hanguk tongnip undong chi hyŏlsa* (Bloody History of the Korean Independence Movement) published in 1920 in Shanghai, regarded the Kapsin Coup of 1884 as the starting point of the Korean independence movement.[1] Chong-sik Lee posited the Tonghak peasant rebellion of 1894 as a "harbinger of revolution in Korea."[2] Some historians paid attention to the Confucian scholars' anti-foreign movements after later 1870s and the anti-Japanese *ŭibyŏng* movement of 1895 which was triggered by the murder of Queen Min by the Japanese and the decree of "anti-top knot" issued by the government. Their common goal to save their country, however, did not necessarily promote cooperation between Korean nationalists. Rather, their different political perspectives and strategies made it difficult for them to cooperate and conflicts arose.[3]

The Russo-Japanese War and the establishment of Japanese protectorate rule in Korea 1905, however, drastically changed the situation. Through the successful establishment of her supremacy in Korea after desperate showdowns with China in the first Sino-Japanese War (1894-1895) and with Russia in the Russo-Japanese War (1904-1905), Japan emerged as a common target of the Korean nationalist movement and ironically created a favorable situation in which diverse Korean nationalist forces desperately united to recover the independence of their country. A milestone in the Korean nationalist movement, the establishment of the Japanese protectorate over Korea in 1905, inspired a wave of national patriotism, which is best summarized by the author of *Sunjong kukchannok* (Record of the National Funeral for King Sunjong):

> After those who had been unenlightened were awakened, they turned their attention to seeking a variety of knowledge and producing talented people. As a result, they established schools around the country, and associations for guiding and promoting education were organized representing each region. Patriots who grasped the situation came forward lifting their shoulders and encouraged the spirit of patriotism by forming associations, publishing newspapers and magazines, delivering addresses, or writing

books. They fostered an advanced movement for rescuing the fatherland by introducing a new culture. As a result an anti-Japanese spirit prevailed.[4]

Although Korean patriotism gained momentum after 1905, the very fact that Japan, rather than indigenous Korean forces, subjugated and finally overthrew the Korean monarchy, impeded political debates over monarchy and republicanism. Furthermore, the different political environments of foreign countries, China, Russia and America, where Korean patriots pursued anti-Japanese activities, provided fewer opportunities for Korean patriots to develop political ideas. The Korean nationalist movement in North Chientao and the Russian Far East exemplifies this intricate process.

Japan's suppressive policies against the Korean patriots involved in political anti-Japanese activities and the *ŭibyŏng* movement produced a number of political exiles. Korean nationalists referred to West and North Chientao and the Primorye as "*Wŏndong*" ("Far East") rather than *Haeoe* (Overseas) which meant America, Hawaii and Mexico. Both regions offered a sanctuary because of the large Korean population, the geographical proximity to Korea, and a relatively favorable political environment. Korean nationalists considered the Russian Far East and North Chientao as the most suitable base for a future Korean independence movement.[5]

In North Chientao, however, because of the presence of the Japanese Residency-General branch office (1907-1909), there was a lack of conspicuous anti-Japanese activities prior to 1910. As a result, the Primorye became a proper sanctuary for anti-Japanese Korean nationalists during the period from 1905 to 1910. During this period, loyal monarchists, former bureaucrats, and Confucian scholars propagated anti-Japanese patriotism among Koreans in the Russian Far

East. Among these loyalists, Yi Yong-ik and Yi Pŏm-yun played the most important roles during the early stage of the anti-Japanese movement.

Yi Yong-ik was a former mining businessman from Myŏngch'ŏn, North Hamgyŏng Province, who had accumulated wealth in gold mines in Kapsan, South Hamgyŏng Province and eventually rose to ministerial posts for the Royal Treasury and Military Affairs by obtaining the trust of King Kojong and Queen Min.[6] Yi Yong-ik was a well-known loyalist politician who had played a key role in initiating various economic reform which was intended to enhance King Kojong's political power by reinforcing the financial power of the royal family during the period of the *Kwangmu* Reform (1897-1904). Just before the outbreak of the Russo-Japanese War, Yi Yong-ik and other "neutral factions" succeeded in declaring the neutrality of Korea. In February 1904, due to his stubborn anti-Japanese position, the Residency-General abducted Yi Yong-ik and put him under surveillance in Japan. It was not until October 1904 that he could return to Korea after promising under duress not to militate against Japan.[7]

After his return from Japan, Yi Yong-ik established many cultural and educational institutions including Posŏng College whose students were mostly from Hamgyŏng Provinces. Yi Yong-ik also established sister schools of Posŏng College in various regions which aimed to instill anti-Japanese patriotism in the students.[8] These Posŏng schools, together with the Poch'ang schools and Pogwang schools which were established by Yi Tong-hwi and Yi Chun respectively were called "*Sambo*" ("Three Treasures") for education by Koreans.[9] Yi Yong-ik was the political and financial patron for leading nationalist leaders from Hamgyŏng Provinces including Yi Tong-hwi, Yi Chong-ho,

Kim Rip, Kim Ha-gu and Yun Hae. Yi Chong-ho was Yi Yong-ik's grandson and became a prominent nationalist leader with properties inherited from his grandfather. Yi Tong-hwi entered officers's training school on Yi Yong-ik's recommendation and his nationalist activities were financially supported by Yi Yong-ik and Yi Chong-ho. Kim Rip and Yun Hae, graduates of Posŏng College, became well-known nationalist leaders and came to work as close associates of Yi Tong-hwi and Yi Chong-ho. Kim Ha-gu served in a government position on Yi Yong-ik's recommendation and went to study economics at Waseda University in Japan with Yi Chong-ho's financial support.[10]

In August 1905, under the increasing dominance of Japan in Korea, Yi Yong-ik secretly went to Shanghai and from where he travelled to St. Petersburg via Paris and Berlin. With an assignment from King Kojong, Yi Yong-ik intended to undertake activities abroad to secure help from the Western Powers including America, France, and Russia. In St. Petersburg, Yi Yong-ik met Yi Pŏm-jin, who was also a prominent pro-Russian politician and a key player in the *Agwan P'ach'ŏn* (whereby the King Kojong sought refuge in the Russian legation) in 1896 and was the former Minister to America and Russia. Yi Pŏm-jin was in exile after Japan established protectorate rule in Korea. Yi Yong-ik also met the Russian Minister of Foreign Affairs and Evgenii Fedorovich Shtein, the former secretary of Russian legation in Seoul. Surviving a murder attempt by his interpreter, Kim Hyŏn-t'o, in St. Petersburg, he finally arrived at Vladivostok in the middle of 1906.[11]

In Vladivostok, Yi Yong-ik met his close associates and pro-Russian Koreans such as Yi Pŏm-yun, Yi Hyŏn-jae (Yi Chong-ho's father), Yi Yun-jae, Kim In-su, Kim To-hyŏn.[12] In addition to these former government officials, who worked for the Russian army during the

Russo-Japanese War, Yi also met local Russian officials including the Military-Governor of the Primorye.[13] Yi enjoyed his authority over Koreans as a former pro-Russian politician and King Kojong's close associate. The news that King Kojong sent Yi Yong-ik 40,000 rubles also enhanced his authority. Expecting Yi's comeback to a powerful political position if Russia resumed its influence in Korea, Koreans presented gifts to Yi Yong-ik and even bought government posts from him. It was in that context that some Korean *wŏnhoin* grew to dislike Yi Yong-ik.[14]

Yi Yong-ik's most noticeable activities in Vladivostok were his involvement in dispatching a secret delegation to the Second World Peace Conference in the Hague, a plan initiated by the Russian Tsar Nicholas II. In the winter of 1905-1906, Yi Chun and Yi Sang-sŏl initiated the plan and received King Kojong's agreement. The delegation would be assigned to deliver an appeal that the Protectorate Treaty of 1905 was concluded by force without King Kojong's agreement and, as a result, it was illegitimate. Yi Yong-ik helped Yi Chun recruit Yi Wi-jong, son of Yi Pŏm-jin and the former secretary of the Korean Ministry in St. Petersburg, who was fluent in English, French and Russian. Yi Wi-jong and Yi Pŏm-jin were staying in St. Petersburg when the Korean Ministry in Russia was closed as a result of the "Protectorate Treaty."[15] According to the memoirs of General Ŏ Dam, King Kojong asked Yi Yong-ik in Vladivostok to recommend members of the delegation and Yi Yong-ik recommended four. In January 1907, King Kojong also informed Nicholas II of his appointment of Yi Yong-ik as the head of the Korean plenipotentiary delegation in charge of the question of Korean independence.[16] Yi Yong-ik would have headed the secret delegation to the Hague. However, Yi died suddenly in February 1907 and could not accomplish the mission which King Kojong had assigned to him. King Kojong then appointed Yi Sang-sŏl as the head of the delegation and Yi Chun and Yi Wi-jong as his deputies.[17]

Yi Sang-sŏl had resigned his post as chief secretary of the cabinet to protest the conclusion of the Protectorate Treaty in 1905, and moved to North Chientao and established the first modern Korean school, Sŏjŏn Sŏsuk, in the fall of 1906.[18] Faithful to the will of his grandfather Yi Yong-ik, Yi Chong-ho funded the trip of the secret delegation.[19] Yi Sang-sŏl came from Chientao, and met Yi Chun who came to Vladivostok from Seoul with Yi Chong-ho at the end of April 1907. Yi Chun was from Pukch'ŏng, North Hamgyŏng Province, and worked as a prosecutor after he studied at Waseda University in Japan. Yi Chun was a key leader of various patriotic, cultural, and educational activities. Koreans in Vladivostok held a welcoming meeting at Kim Hak-man's house.[20] The appearance of three prominent patriots aroused Koreans in Vladivostok. In Vladivostok, Koreans raised 20,000 rubles for the delegation.[21] Yi Sang-sŏl and Yi Chun were joined by Yi Wi-jong in St. Petersburg. After meeting with the Russian Tsar Nicholas II as arranged by Yi Pŏm-jin, they went to the Hague.

The delegation, however, failed to accomplish its original mission which resulted in political turmoil in Korea. After news of King Kojong's secret delegation spread in early July 1907, the Japanese government first pressed King Kojong to abdicate for his impotent son and then dissolved the Korean army. Not content with the abdication of Kojong, on July 24, the Japanese government imposed a new agreement (the Korean-Japanese Treaty of 1907) giving the Japanese Resident-General formal authority to interfere in all Korean domestic affairs.[22] At the same time, Japan forced the Korean government to pass a law concerning the press and Public Security Law, which was intended to prohibit any anti-Japanese activities by Koreans. Japan forced the Korean government to sentence Yi Sang-sŏl to death and Yi Chun and Yi Wi-jong received a life sentence.[23]

Koreans desperately resisted Japanese repression. Demonstrators in Seoul clashed with Japanese police on July 19 and 20. Korean soldiers who refused to accept the "order of dissolution" also rose against the Japanese in Seoul, Wŏnju and on Kanghwa Island. The nationwide uprisings of Korean soldiers opened a third wave of anti-Japanese *ŭibyŏng*, which Korean historians call the *Chŏngmi Ŭibyŏng* (Righteous Army's Uprising of 1907). This *Chŏngmi Ŭibyŏng* sparked patriotic anti-Japanese feelings among Koreans in the Primorye and escalated to the mobilization of *ŭibyŏng* soldiers there.

2. *Ŭibyŏng* Movement

Yi Pŏm-yun's corps of gunmen [*sap'odae*] were the main force of the first *ŭibyŏng* movement in the Primorye. During the Russo-Japanese War, Yi Pŏm-yun, on King Kojong's order, reorganized a corps of gunmen of 1,000 Koreans called *ch'ungŭibyŏng* (loyal righteous soldiers) and helped the Russian army in Hamgyŏng Provinces commanded by General Anisimov, by hampering the Japanese army in border areas.[24] After the war, Yi's troops, however, retreated to Hunchun, but General Ansimov disarmed them. In early 1906, the local Chinese authorities in Hunchun ordered Yi Pŏm-yun and his soldiers to leave Manchuria. Some soldiers returned to Korea; Yi Pŏm-yun and other 700 soldiers crossed the border to Novokievsk.[25] The Russian government awarded Yi a medal for his wartime contribution.[26]

Ch'oe Chae-hyŏng provided facilities for Yi Pŏm-yun and his followers in Novokievsk.[27] Born in Kyŏngwŏn, North Hamgyŏng Province, Ch'oe emigrated with his parents to a Korean village, Tizinkhe, during the big famine and mass river-crossing of 1869-1870. After the age of 18, Ch'oe served first as an interpreter for the Russian army, then as a second-lieutenant in the Russian Navy, and inspector-general in the Russian police. After resigning from these offices, late in the 1880s, Ch'oe worked as the first Pos'et area headman [*tohŏn*] for fifteen years. One of several well-known *podriadchik*s who provided beef to the Russian army in Pos'et, Koreans honored him with the names "Ch'oe *tohŏn*" or "Ch'oe *pijikkae*."[28] Ch'oe Chae-hyŏng provided *ŭibyŏng* soldiers with credentials bearing his stamp which read: "This person [holder of the credential] is my follower working actively for Korea. Therefore, I ask you to supply him with every convenience such as clothing and food."[29]

Backed by Ch'oe Chae-hyŏng, Yi Pŏm-yun dispatched agents to Korean villages with the mission of inspiring patriotism and raising funds for the reorganization of his anti-Japanese militia. Koreans in the Primorye donated tens of thousands of rubles and voluntarily participated in the *ŭibyŏng* militia of Yi Pŏm-yun.[30] In raising funds and mobilizing *ŭibyŏng* soldiers, Yi Pŏm-yun utilized the authority given by King Kojong while he had been dispatched to North Chientao. Yi continued to use his previous title, "Administrator of Northern Border and Chientao" ["*Pukpyŏn Kando Kwanrisa*"]. Yi Pŏm-yun also used the *map'ae* (horse medal) which the Korean King traditionally gave to his plenipotentiary officials as a sign of his full authorization.[31] Accordingly, Koreans called his soldiers the *kwanribyŏng* (Soldiers of the Administrator).

The news of Yi Chun's death in the Hague incited anger and

patriotism among Koreans in the Primorye.[32] Yi Pŏm-yun and Ch'oe Chae-hyŏng established the *ŭibyŏng* headquarters in Novokievsk at the height of this elevated patriotism among Koreans.[33] In the spring of 1908, Korean political exiles came to Novokievsk in order to join the *ŭibyŏng* under the leadership of Yi Pŏm-yun and Ch'oe Chae-hyŏng. An Chung-gŭn, Ŏm In-sŏp and Kim Ki-ryong, who were known as sworn brothers, had organized an eighty-seven-member secret society for raising funds and gathering *ŭibyŏng* fighters, joined Ch'oe Chae-hyŏng's camp together with their colleagues.[34] Popular among Koreans thanks to his activities in the Hague as a member of the secret delegation, Yi Wi-jong came to Novokievsk from St. Petersburg with 10,000 rubles on orders of his father, Yi Pŏm-jin.[35] Through Yi Wi-jong's initiative, Korean leaders established a patriotic organization called the Tongŭihoe (Comrades' Association) in Novokievsk.[36] The Tongŭihoe, although publicly for patriotic education and mutual aid, covertly supported the *ŭibyŏng* movement.[37]

The most prominent and influential patriotic leader in the Primorye[38], Ch'oe Chae-hyŏng headed the association, and Yi Pŏm-yun served as Vice-President. Yi Wi-jong, Ch'oe Chae-hyŏng's sworn brother,[39] became chief-executive and with Ch'oe' Chae-hyŏng's nephew (sister's son), Ŏm In-sŏp,[40] as his deputy.[41] Ch'oe Chae-hyŏng reputedly donated 13,000 rubles for Tongŭihoe activities.[42] Novokievsk served as headquarters and branch offices were established in Vladivostok and Suchan.[43] The number of the Tongŭihoe membership approached two or three thousand,[44] but the active members numbered 30 to 40, most of whom were living in exiles.[45]

At the end of March 1908, Kim In-su, former commander of the Korean battalion in Pukch'ŏng in North Hamgyŏng Province,[46] met E. Smirnov, border commissioner in southern Ussurisk *krai* and requested the return of guns which Russian authorities retrieved from the Korean soldiers after the Russo-Japanese War.[47] Yi Pŏm-yun dispatched seven agents to the Chinese authorities in Hunchun to receive 300 guns which Yi Pŏm-yun had mortgaged by borrowing funds from Chinese authorities at the end of November 1905.[48] Both the Russian and Chinese authorities rejected these requests.

In order to avoid unnecessary diplomatic trouble with Japan, local Russian authorities including the border commissioner in southern Ussurisk *krai*, the Military Governor of the Primorye and the Priamur Governor-General adopted the policy of "no official support" and "no impediment" as long as their activities did not violate Russian law.[49] Although Yi Pŏm-yun failed in recruiting discharged Russian soldiers sympathetic to the Korean *ŭibyŏng* movement, he bought many weapons from them.[50] In the middle of 1908, Yi Pŏm-yun was at the height of his influence. Under his command, there were about 2,500 *ŭibyŏng* soldiers and fifteen guards always followed Yi Pŏm-yun when he rode a two-horse-cart.[51]

At the end of June 1908, hoping to instigate nationwide uprisings against the Japanese with support from *ŭibyŏng* units and the population in Manchuria and North Korea, the *ŭibyŏng* units in Novokievsk advanced to Northern part of Korea.[52] In early July 1908, the Tongŭi-hoe band, composed of 100 *ŭibyŏng* commanded by Chŏn Che-ik, An Chung-gŭn and Ŏm In-sŏp, crossed the Tumen River by ship to Kyŏnghŭng and defeated the Japanese garrison at Hongŭi-doxng. Simultaneously, another band composed of 100 *ŭibyŏng* soldiers belonging to Yi Pŏm-yun's *ŭibyŏng* corps arrived at Kyŏng-hŭng and defeated the Japanese garrison at Sinasan. These two *ŭibyŏng* bands separately advanced to Hoeryŏng, obviously hoping for the support of other

TABLE 2. 1

Collisions between Korean *ŭibyŏng* Fighters and Japanese Forces

		Times		Number of Fighters	
Period		1908	1909	1908	1909
Area	N. Hamgyŏng	11	-	283	-
	S. Hamgyŏng	99	14	6,438	270
	Other Areas	1,866	1,724	76,046	38,323
	Total	1,976	1,738	82,767	38,593

Source Kuksa P'yŏnch'an Wiwŏnhoe, *Hanguk tongnip undongsa* [Korean Independence Movement], vol. 1, pp. 295-96.

ŭibyŏng units in North Korea and North Chientao. These two bands gathered at Hoeryŏng and fought together against the Japanese army at Hoeryŏng. Four Korean soldiers died in this battle along with eight officers and 40 soldiers of Japanese army.[53] Unable to overcome the superiority of the Japanese army both in terms of firepower and the number of soldiers, some *ŭibyŏng* soldiers retreated to North Chientao, and the others to Novokievsk.[54]

The other 600 *ŭibyŏng* troops, which belonged to Yi Pŏm-yun's band, arrived at a region between Sŏngjin and Ch'ŏngjin in August and attacked Myŏngch'ŏn in September 1908, eliminating 60 officers and soldiers of the Japanese army. Other *ŭibyŏng* bands organized in Kyŏngsŏng joined this attack.[55] These attacks of the *ŭibyŏng* in north Hamgyŏng Province forced the Japanese to keep Hamgyŏng Province in a state of siege for three months (from July to September).[56]

Since the fall of 1908, the *ŭibyŏng* movement in the Primorye was at the low tide and no fighting occurred in North Hamgyŏng Province in 1909 (see Table 2. 1). The fighting in the border areas and the Ch'ŏngjin region in 1908 was the last major campaign accomplished by the Korean patriots in Russia until the March First Movement in 1919.

There were several reasons for the subsidence of the *ŭibyŏng* movement in the Primorye. First of all, since the fall of 1908, local Russian authorities discarded their previous policy of "non-support" and "non-prohibition" and began to prevent any *ŭibyŏng* activities in the Primorye. Responding to Japanese protests, the Russian government ordered the Priamur Governor-General to immediately arrest Yi Pŏm-yun if Yi mobilized the *ŭibyŏng* again.[57] The Russian authorities stationed military units along the Tumen River in order to prevent any possible passage by the *ŭibyŏng* fighters. Furthermore, the Russian authorities began to prohibit any gathering, training, or holding of weapons.[58] On January 1, 1909, at the request of the Chinese authorities, the Russian sixth regiment stationed in Pos'et confiscated all weapons of the *ŭibyŏng* and ordered their dissolution at the *ŭibyŏng* headquarters as it was suspected that two Chinese soldiers were killed by the *ŭibyŏng*.[59]

Secondly, the *ŭibyŏng* leaders experienced internal conflict. Ch'oe Chae-hyŏng and Yi Wi-jong criticized the authoritative attitude of Yi Pŏm-yun, who attempted to put the whole *ŭibyŏng* movement under his control.[60] Since the establishment of the Tongŭihoe, discord reigned between the followers of Yi Pŏm-yun and those of Ch'oe Chae-hyŏng and Yi Pŏm-yun's associates even attempted to kill Ch'oe Chae-hyŏng's close associate, Kim Ki-ryong.[61] Disgruntled with Yi Pŏm-yun, Yi Wi-jong left for St. Petersburg in the summer of 1908.[62] As a result, the campaigns were not fully coordinated. After the unsuccessful summer campaigns, conflicts between Ch'oe Chae-hyŏng and Yi Pŏm-yun even deepened and Ch'oe withdrew his support of Yi Pŏm-yun as well as of the *ŭibyŏng* movement in general.[63]

Yi Pŏm-yun's popularity declined drastically in the fall of 1908. Yi Pŏm-yun's loss of popularity among Koreans in the Primorye resulted primarily from his authoritarian demeanor and extravagant life style. Twenty-six *wŏnhoin* Koreans criticized him in 1910:

> Yi [Pŏm-yun] utilized the humane and patriotic feelings of Korean people and received tens of thousands of rubles. Everybody thought that by using these funds, Yi Pŏm-yun would set out to Korea with his already-organized troops for anti-Japanese activities. . . . [However] Yi spent all these funds, exclusively on his pleasure, residing at a first-class hotel and paying tens of rubles a day. Yi answered to the association [Korean Association] that with the funds, he acquired weapons from the Russian government and carried out activities against the Japanese, but his troops suffered defeat in Korea because of the exhaustion of funds. It is obvious to every Korean that Yi Pŏm-yun did not dispatch his troops to Korea.[64]

Furthermore, ill feelings toward the Korean government were common among all Koreans in the Primorye. Most had arrived from the Hamgyŏng and P'yŏngan Provinces, people who long suffered under political and social discriminative policies and economic exploitation of the government officials. Wealthy and influential *wŏnhoin* merchants such as Ch'oe Pong-jun and Kim Hak-man began to raise their anti-*ŭibyŏng* voices in response to increasing anti-Yi Pŏm-yun sentiment.[65] Primorye Koreans called Ch'oe Pong-jun and Kim Hak-man, together with Ch'oe Chae-hyŏng, the "three great heroes" ["*samgŏl*"].[66] Born in Kyŏnghŭng in 1863, Ch'oe Pong-jun emigrated during the big famine and mass river-crossing of 1869-1870. As seen in Chapter 1, Ch'oe became a wealthy Korean merchant by providing military supplies and beef to the Russian army during the Boxer Rebellion and the Russo-Japanese War.[67] Ch'oe bought a ship called Chunch'angho from a Japanese and managed a commercial and shipping company with branches in Vladivostok, Wŏnsan, Sŏngjin and Osaka. Ch'oe established the first Korean newspaper in Russia, the *Haejo Sinmun* (Vladivostok Korean Gazette), on February 26, 1908, but on May 26, after three months, he suspended its publication under duress of the Japanese.[68]

Ch'oe Pong-jun also opposed military measures, arguing that the *ŭibyŏng* inhibited Korean industry and blockaded commerce with Russia.[69] In the fall of 1908, Ch'oe Pong-jun discussed measures for suppressing the *ŭibyŏng* movement in the Primorye with an agent dispatched by the Japanese Residency-General and the Korean Minister of Internal Affairs.[70] After this, Ch'oe Pong-jun asked the Russian authorities not to respond to Ch'oe Chae-hyŏng's request for help, and in early December 1908, Ch'oe Pong-jun went to Pos'et to criticize both Ch'oe Chae-hyŏng and Yi Pŏm-yun.[71] Ch'oe Pong-jun advised his sworn brother, Ch'oe Chae-hyŏng, to dissolve his *ŭibyŏng* units.[72] Ch'oe Pong-jun, together with Kim Hak-man, Ch'a Sŏk-po, Yi Yŏng-ch'un, wealthy *wŏnhoin* merchants in Vladivostok, published advertisements in the *Taedong Kongbo* (The Great East Gazette) requesting Koreans not to respond to the demands of the *ŭibyŏng* leaders, obviously targeting Yi Pŏm-yun.[73] The conflict between Yi Pŏm-yun and Ch'oe Pong-jun escalated to the point that Ch'oe physically assaulted Yi in Vladivostok and Yi reported Ch'oe to the Russian authorities as a Japanese spy.[74]

In January 1909, Yi Pŏm-yun's followers also clashed with Korean residents in Novokievsk. Robbed of 20 rubles by Yi Pŏm-yun's followers, a Korean merchant appealed to a Korean village leader [*sajang*].

When the village leader summoned Yi's followers, they refused to respond, boasting of the authority of Yi Pŏm-yun's title as the *Kwanrisa* (Administrator). In response, Korean residents recruited by the village leader arrested and imprisoned thirty-one followers of Yi Pŏm-yun in Vladivostok.[75]

Eventually Ch'oe Chae-hyŏng's declaration of the withdrawal of his support of the *ŭibyŏng* activities delivered a fatal blow to the *ŭibyŏng* movement in the Primorye. Ch'oe severely criticized the abusive behavior of *ŭibyŏng* activists in the Primorye in the Vladivostok newspaper *Taedong Kongbo* on January 20, 1909:

> I heard the news from every region that a number of scoundrels calling themselves *ŭibyŏng* who are extorting a lot of money from Koreans by disguising their love of fatherland and are taking advantage of well-known figures in our region and are distributing a number of falsified letters to every region using my name without permission. They spent all the money using the excuse of miscellaneous expenses and are involved in matters of life and death to Koreans in order to demonstrate their authority. . . . I hope from now on you do not donate aid money to those who are utilizing falsified letters and boasting patriotism and will watchfully reject their abuses and punish them.[76]

Korean anti-*ŭibyŏng* feelings must have influenced Ch'oe Chae-hyŏng's declaration, but the pressure by the Russian authorities directly forced Ch'oe Chae-hyŏng to denounce the *ŭibyŏng* activists. Under diplomatic pressure from England and America and also obviously requested by the Japanese government, the local Russian authorities in Vladivostok recalled Ch'oe Chae-hyŏng on February 15, 1909, and urged him to dissociate from *ŭibyŏng* activities.[77]

Stockholders elected Ch'oe Chae-hyŏng as the President of the *Taedong Kongbo* at a special meeting on January 31 shortly after his declaration.[78]

A report of a Japanese official on February 13, 1909, precisely reflected the declining situation of the *ŭibyŏng* movement in the Primorye:

> According to reports from every place on the opposite side of the [Tumen River], there is no going-and-coming of the bandits at all and it is almost a closed situation. It is said that there is no talk about bandits in the 3 *li* [12 km] area on the left side of Tumen River.[79]

Thus, the *ŭibyŏng* activities, which had been on the rise from 1906 to 1908, "degenerated already to the point that [Japanese authorities] did not worry about them any more."[80] This situation continued until the summer of 1910 when another high tide of anti-Japanese feeling came when Japan annexed Korea.

With the decline of the *ŭibyŏng* movement which sought to restore the independence of Korea through armed struggle (*kŭpchin undong* or the immediate advancement movement) since the fall of 1908, the focus of the Korean nationalist movement in the Primorye gradually moved toward educational and cultural activities (*wanjin undong* or gradual advancement). The publication of the *Taedong Kongbo* from November 1908[81] and Ch'oe Chae-hyŏng's joining the *Taedong Kongbo* in January 1909 signaled the change.

B. Nationalism Develops

1. Kungminhoe Spreads Nationalism

a. Kongnip Hyŏphoe (United Korean Association)

Loyalist patriots played key roles in diplomatic activities and the armed struggle to recover Korean independence. Loyalty to the monarch inspired their anti-Japanese activities. Most loyalists including Yi Yong-ik, Yi Sang-sŏl and Yi Pŏm-yun, were former officials of the Korean government. Other figures such as Ch'oe Chae-hyŏng and Hong Pŏm-do who were not former government officials can also be included in this category of loyalist patriots. If we use the term nationalism limitedly as a political ideology which includes national independence as well as the people's sovereignty and the equal rights of people, Korean nationalists in America played major roles in the early stages of the Korean nationalist movement in the Primorye.

The most influential figure among Korean nationalists in America was An Ch'ang-ho (1878-1938). Born the son of a farmer in 1878, in Kangsŏ, South P'yŏngan Province, An Ch'ang-ho studied English, Western knowledge and the fundamentals of Christianity in a Christian school founded by Horace Grant Underwood, the American Presbyterian missionary in Seoul, as a teenager. In 1897, An Ch'ang-ho joined the Independence Club [Tongnip Hyŏphoe], an active political organization which Sŏ Chae-p'il [Philip Jaisohn], leader of the unsuccessful 1884 coup and a George Washington University graduate in medicine, established to reinforce Korean sovereignty through Western-style mass gatherings and publications. Through impressive addresses and strong criticism of the government in mass gatherings,

TABLE 2. 2

Korean Organizations in America

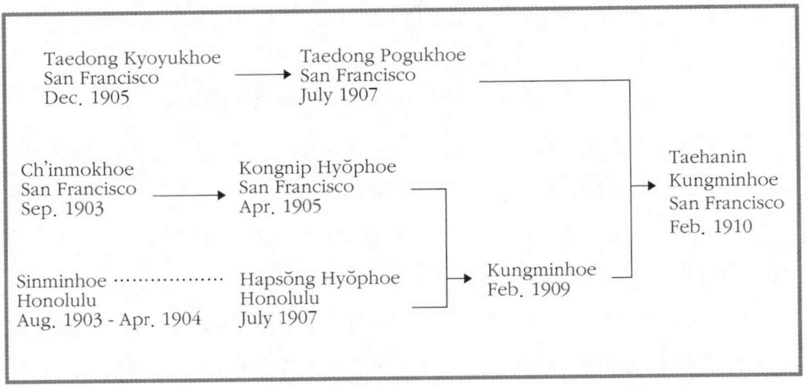

Sources Hong Ŏn, "Kungminhoe yŏksa" [History of the Kungminhoe], *Sinhan Minbo*, Feb. 5, 1914, p. 1: Feb. 26, 1914, pp. 1-2; Kim Wŏn-yong [Warren Y. Kim], *Chaemi hanin osimnyŏnsa* [Fifty Year History of Koreans in America] (Reedley: 1959), pp. 83-111.

An Ch'ang-ho became a well-known public speaker both in P'yŏngan Province and Seoul. An Ch'ang-ho's regional social background and his experience in political activities in the 1890s greatly influenced the formation of his characteristic political ideas which focused on long-term and gradual preparation through education and industry.[82]

In 1902, An Ch'ang-ho went to San Francisco to study, but he changed his mind and helped Korean immigrant workers improve their life-styles and promoted labor opportunities, fellowship and mutual assistance. The Ch'inmokhoe (Friendship Association) which An Ch'ang-ho organized in San Francisco in 1903 with eight other Koreans was the first fruit of his efforts.[83] In order to extend the scope of their activities to new immigrants from Hawaii and Korea, An Ch'ang-ho reorganized the Ch'inmokhoe into the Kongnip Hyŏphoe (United Korean Association) with 49 other Koreans on

April 5, 1905, with the goal of the "unity of compatriots and mutual assistance." As anti-Japanese patriotic feelings rose high among Koreans with the news of the conclusion of the "Protectorate Treaty" (November 17, 1905), the Kongnip Hyŏphoe moved toward a more political platform, including the restoration of complete independence in Korea and anti-Japanese propaganda. At the same time, the Kongnip Hyŏphoe began to publish its official organ *Kongnip Sinbo* (The United Korean) on November 20, 1905, three days after the conclusion of the Protectorate Treaty.[84] In December 1905, the Kongnip Hyŏphoe established its position as the central organization of Korean communities in America by setting up its central executive committee in San Francisco which controlled the recently established-branches in Los Angeles, Redlands, Riverside, Oakland, and Rock Springs in California.[85] At the first annual conference on April 5, 1906, one year after its establishment, the enrolled membership of the Kongnip Hyŏphoe reached about 500.[86]

In order to broaden its influence beyond America, the Kongnip Hyŏphoe decided to dispatch its organizers to the Far East. Worried about the increasing Japanese encroachment on Korea after the Protectorate Treaty, An Ch'ang-ho decided to go to Korea himself. Before he left for Korea in January 1907, An Ch'ang-ho and his associates initiated in Riverside, California, the Taehan Sinminhoe (Korean New People's Association), a secret anti-Japanese organization with the purpose of "establishing a new nation after building a new organization and awakening a new spirit."[87] In Korea, An Ch'ang-ho succeeded in organizing the Sinminhoe together with nationalist "enlightenment" movement leaders including Yang Ki-t'ak, Yi Kap, Yi Tong-hwi, Chŏn Tŏk-ki, Yi Tong-nyŏng and Yu Tongyŏl.[88] Thanks to the activities of these leaders, the membership of the Sinminhoe reached 300 in 1910.[89]

In September 1907, Korean nationalists of the Kongnip Hyŏphoe established connections with Koreans in Vladivostok. Ch'oe Man-hak [Lev Petrovich], Chairman of the Korean Association in Vladivostok sent a letter and his subscription fee to the Kongnip Hyŏphoe with his Vice-Chairman Yang Sŏng-ch'un.[90] After this, copies of the *Kongnip Sinbo* began to be distributed to Koreans in Russia through its branch office in Vladivostok and thereby contributed to the spread of ideas of Korean nationalists in America.[91] According to the resolution made at the general meeting on February 20, 1908 to expand branches in Vladivostok and Hawaii,[92] the Kongnip Hyŏphoe dispatched Yi Kang to Vladivostok and raised funds for his activities.[93] Soon after his arrival on March 24, Yi Kang worked as an editor of the *Haejo Sinmun* (February 26-May 26, 1908)[94] published by Ch'oe Man-hak, nephew and manager of Ch'oe Pong-jun's business company.[95] Because of the high tide of the *ŭibyŏng* activities through the summer of 1908, Korean nationalists began to join the Kongnip Hyŏphoe after the fall of 1908. The eventual decline of the *ŭibyŏng* movement contributed to the expansion of the influence of the Kongnip Hyŏphoe, which emphasized gradual preparation by means of education and industry.

Thanks to the activities of Yi Kang and Kim Sŏng-mu, the latter also arrived at Vladivostok from America on December 13, 1908,[96] branches of the Kongnip Hyŏphoe and its organ, the *Kongnip Sinbo*, were established in Suchan, Vladivostok, Harbin and Khabarovsk.[97] In a Korean village called Sinyŏng-dong (currently Nikolaevka) in the Suchan region, 38 Koreans, mostly *wŏnhoin* Koreans organized the first branch of the Kongnip Hyŏphoe in Russia on September 25, 1908.[98] Through the leadership of Yi Kang and Kim Sŏng-mu,

30 Korean nationalists established Vladivostok branch on January 7, 1909.[99] Active members of the Vladivostok branch such as Yi Kang, Kim Sŏng-mu, O Chu-hyŏk, Chŏng Sun-man, Yun Il-byŏng and Han Hyŏng-gwŏn established night schools and held speech meetings.[100] The branches of the Kongnip Hyŏphoe in the Primorye played an important role in presenting adults as well as children with more educational and cultural activities which emphasized self-reliance, the improvement of one's life-style, unity among compatriots, the moral essence of Christianity, and patriotism.[101]

The Kongnip Hyŏphoe members in Vladivostok joined the *Taedong Kongbo* when it began publication in November 1908; Yi Kang was chief-editor,[102] Ham Tong-ch'ŏl, Chŏng Sun-man and An Chung-gŭn were field reporters,[103] and Yun Il-byŏng was the Russian translator.[104] At the end of January 1909, the *Taedong Kongbo* could not solve its financial difficulties until the general meeting of stock-holders elected Ch'oe Chae-hyŏng, who had been a strong patron of *ŭibyŏng* activities, as President of the *Taedong Kongbo*.[105] Throughout 1909, full-scale Japanese suppression forced armed resistance both inside and outside Korea into the last desperate stage. Such dire situation in Korea also created favorable soil for more moderate activities such as "enlightenment" and the religious (Christianity) movement. As a result, 1909 was the best year for the Kongnip Hyŏphoe and its successor, the Kungminhoe.

b. Kungminhoe [Korean National Association]

Thanks to the continuous efforts of the Kongnip Hyŏphoe's key leaders in unifying all Korean nationalists both inside and outside Korea since 1907, Chŏng Chae-gwan, Chairman of the Kongnip Hyŏphoe and Chŏng Wŏn-myŏng, Chairman of the Hapsŏng

Hyŏphoe (United Korean Association) in Hawaii, declared the merger of two associations and created a new unified organization, the Kungminhoe (Korean National Association) on November 30, 1908.[106] On February 1, 1909, the two organizations were officially unified and the two official organs, the *Kongnip Sinbo* and the *Hapsŏng Sinbo* (The United Korean News) changed their titles to the *Sinhan Minbo* and the *Sinhan Kukpo* (The New Korea National Herald), respectively.[107] The Kungminhoe announced its four goals: to promote education and industry, to advocate freedom and equality, to enhance the esteem of the compatriots, and to restore the independence of Korea.[108]

With the words, "*kungmin*" ("national people") and "*sinhan*" ("new Korea"), this unification had a great political significance beyond the simple merger of two organizations. The Kungminhoe adopted federal constitution modelled on the United States. In its platform, the Kungminhoe posited its status as the "qualified provisional government" which succeeded the decayed government in Korea. They also adopted republican federalism for the political structure of their central and regional organizations: the Central Executive Committee [*chungang ch'onghoe*] assigns the power of supervision over the local branches [*chibanghoe*] to the regional central executive committee [*chibang ch'onghoe*].[109]

Both editorials and articles published in its official organ, the *Sinhan Minbo* clearly demonstrated the republicanism of the Kungminhoe. Shortly after the establishment of the Kungminhoe, the *Sinhan Minbo* declared its own goal "to promote the people's spirit of self-independence, preserve and protect the glory and dignity of the people."[110] Another article published on February 10, 1910, also severely criticized the monarchy and aristocracy as follows:

In countries which are ruled by the dictatorship of a monarch and the dominance of aristocrats, the spirit of people becomes dispersed, politics corrupt and are certainly inclined to ruin.[111]

The *Sinhan Minbo* article dated May 25, 1910 even criticized Yi Pŏm-yun and Yi Pŏm-jin, Korean aristocrats who had been involved in anti-Japanese activities:

Mr. Yi Pŏm-yun, former Administrator of Chientao, is a person who has been using its seal until now to extend the authority of the Administrator over Koreans in every part of Russia. Yi Pŏm-yun is one who has fattened himself by threatening and extorting money from innocent people. Yi Pŏm-yun keeps close contact with Yi Pŏm-jin who disgraced the national polity [of Korea] by playing chuck-farthing with students and hiding packages of sugar, as well as other unspeakable behavior while working in Washington as the Minister of Korea to America.[112]

Pak Yong-man, one of the key leaders of the Kungminhoe, severely criticized both King Kojong and King Sunjong in his poems published on April 26, 1911, in the *Sinhan Minbo*. King Kojong in particular, Pak criticized, had ruled Korea for fifty years by dictatorship, had harmed good loyal officials, wasted funds, and ruined the nation.[113]

In order to realize its goal of achieving a position as the "qualified provisional government" over the regional central committees in the Far East, which Korean nationalists had regarded as the central base for the independence movement, the Kungminhoe decided to dispatch two prominent nationalists, Yi Sang-sŏl and Chŏng Chae-gwan. Yi Sang-sŏl was well-known to Koreans thanks to his activities as the head of King Kojong's secret delegation to the Hague. After he

Map 2. 1

Major Cities in Siberia

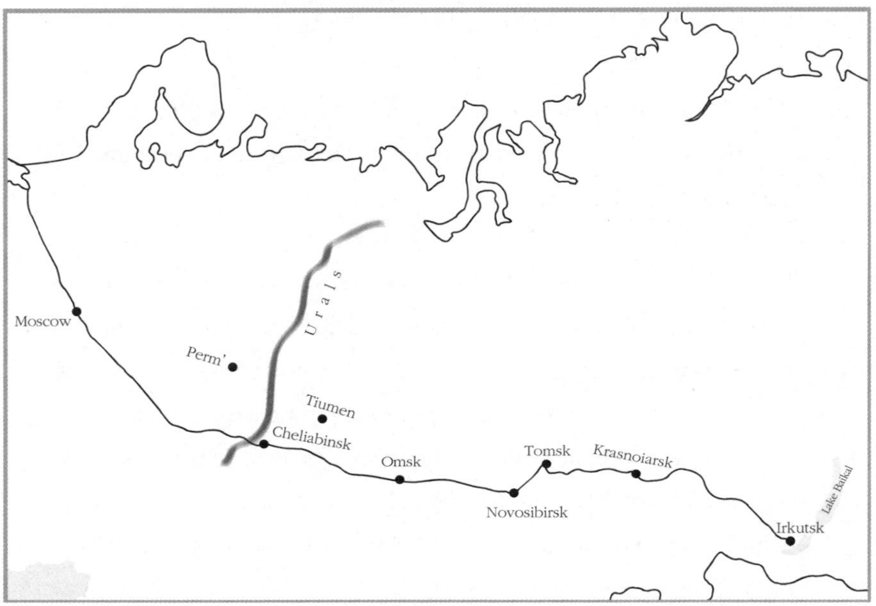

went to America in February 1908, Yi Sang-sŏl together with Homer B. Hulbert, a foreign member of the Korean secret delegation to the Hague, travelled around New York, Chicago and Los Angeles criticizing the Japanese encroachment into Korea and the illegitimate conclusion of the 1905 Protectorate Treaty.[114] Yi Sang-sŏl joined the Kungminhoe in February 1909[115] and was appointed as the plenipotentiary with "full power in all affairs related to the Far East" ["*Wŏndong taep'yo*"] by the Kungminhoe.[116] Chŏng Chae-gwan, who now resigned the chairmanship of the Kongnip Hyŏphoe and chief-editor of the *Kongnip Sinbo* in order to unify Koreans in Vladivostok, accompanied Yi Sang-sŏl.[117] Koreans welcomed Yi Sang-sŏl and

TABLE 2. 3

Structure of the Kungminhoe Organization

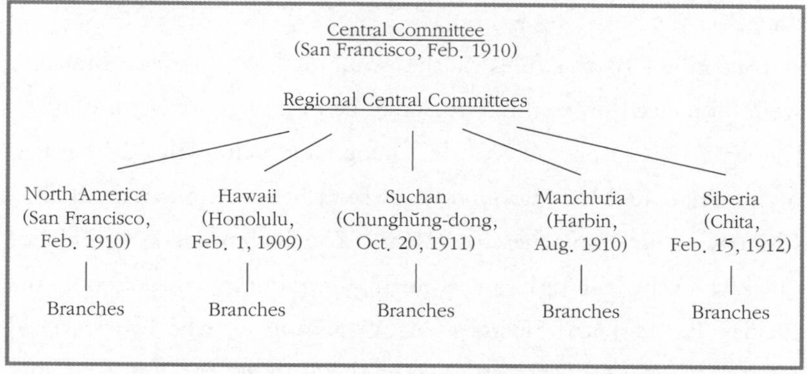

Chŏng Chae-gwan, who arrived at Vladivostok on July 14, 1909, via Europe. [118]

Thanks to the efforts of members such as Yi Kang, Kim Sŏng-mu, Chŏng Chae-gwan in Vladivostok, Yi In-sŏp and Hong Nam-gu in North Manchuria, the Kungminhoe spread its influence fast in the Far East.[119] Until the end of 1909, working from Kongnip Hyŏphoe branches or creating new ones, all thirteen branches [*chibanghoe*] of the Kungminhoe were established in urban areas such as Vladivostok, Novokievsk, Nikol'sk-Ussurisk, Khabarovsk, Iman, Chita and Harbin and in various Korean villages including Sinyŏng-dong, Manch'un-dong, Hongsŏk-tong, Udimi, Tonggaet'ŏ, Sipyŏch'on in the Suchan region.[120]

Throughout 1910-1911, the Kungminhoe continued to spread its influence by establishing branches through the Russian Far East, Siberia and along the Chinese Eastern Railroad: Suifen, Blagoveshchensk, Verkhneudinsk, Cheliabinsk, Krasnoiarsk, Tomsk, Tiumen, Perm', and nine branches in Korean villages in Suchan regions such as Hwanggu-dong, Samyŏng-dong, Sŏkt'an-dong, Sinp'ung-dong, Korike, Chinyŏng-dong, Sŭngji-dong, Chunghŭng-dong, Tongho-dong.[121]

According to the rules of the Kungminhoe, all these branches were organized into three regional central executive committees [*chibang ch'onghoe*]: Suchan RCE in Chunghŭng-dong with 12 branches, Manchurian RCE in Harbin with 8 branches, and Siberian RCE in Chita with nine branches in 1912.[122] The Kungminhoe's influence quickly swept through all Korean communities throughout the Russian Far East and Siberia.[123] As Yi Kwang-su, who had travelled around the Korean communities in the Russian Far East and met many prominent Korean nationalists in 1913, recollected, "the Kungminhoe had unified all Korean communities in Siberia (and the Russian Far East) under its influence."[124] Based on the report of O Chu-hyŏk on February 14, 1909, the Kungminhoe recognized the Kongnip Hyŏphoe Vladivostok branch which had been organized on January 7, 1909 as part of its organization.[125]

On June 4, 1909, the Vladivostok branch submitted an application for recognition of the Kungminhoe to the Military-Governor of the Primorye. The Military-Governor did not approve the application on the grounds that some portions of Kungminhoe regulations were not translated into Russian and that it aimed to realize political goals.[126] The failure to obtain recognition of the Russian authorities clearly showed that the Russian government suspected its political purposes, particularly in regard to the Kungminhoe's republicanism and American influence.

The incident of An Chung-gŭn's assassination of Ito Hirobumi, the former Resident-General of Korea, in Harbin on October 26, 1909, illustrates how the Russian government dealt with Korean nationalists involved in anti-Japanese activities. Key Kungminhoe Vladivostok branch members such as Chŏng Chae-gwan, Yi Kang, Chŏng Sun-man and Yun Il-byŏng together with Yi Chin-yul and Konstantin Petrovich Mikhailov planned the incident. These were all key members of the *Taedong Kongbo*.[127] In planning the incident, they expected that the Russian court would put An Chung-gŭn and his accomplices on trial on the ground that Harbin was a leased territory of Russia.[128]

An article published on November 1, 1909, in the *Taedong Kongbo* also contended that An Chung-gŭn and his accomplices must be tried by Russia because, according to the Sino-Russian Treaty of 1896, any judicial case occurred in the Chinese Eastern Railroad zone would be tried by the Russian court.[129] However, as the Russian government was more concerned about the relations with Japan, it immediately turned An Chung-gŭn and his comrades over to the Japanese authorities. Furthermore, the defending attorneys, including Konstantin Mikhailov Petrovich who resigned the presidency of the *Taedong Kongbo* in order to defend An Chung-gŭn, were excluded from the Japanese court.[130]

Although the Harbin incident greatly fueled patriotism among Koreans, the Japanese authorities used the incident to justify their suppression of anti-Japanese Koreans both in and outside Korea and to hasten its preparations to annex Korea. In Korea, hundreds of Koreans including An Ch'ang-ho, Yi Kap, Yi Chong-ho and Yu Tong-yŏl, key leaders of the New People's Association, were arrested shortly after the incident.[131] At the same time, the Japanese government dispatched 13 agents, 27 members of the Ilchinhoe and six assassins to Vladivostok in order to get information and arrest Koreans involved in the incident.[132] As a result of the activities of these agents,

TABLE 2. 4

Two Groups Involved in the Yang Sŏng-ch'un Incident

Group A	(1)	(2)	(3)	(4)	Group B	(1)	(2)	(3)	(4)
Chŏng Sun-man	K	S	T	*yŏho*	Yang Sŏng-ch'un	K			*wŏnhoin*
Yun Il-byŏng	K	S	T	*yŏho*	Chŏng Chae-gwan	K	W	T	*yŏhoin*
Kim Hyŏn-t'o		S	T	*yŏho*	Yi Kang	K	W	T	*yŏhoin*
Yi Ch'i-gwŏn	K	S		*yŏho*	Kim Sŏng-mu	K	W		*yŏhoin*
An Han-ju		S		*yŏho*	Ham Tong-ch'ŏl	K	W	T	*yŏhoin*
Kang Sun-gi		S		*yŏho*	Yu Chin-yul		W	T	*wŏnhoin*
Kwŏn Yu-sang		S		*yŏho*	Ch'a Sŏk-po		W	T	*wŏnhoin*
Yi Min-bok		S		*yŏho*					

Notes (1) **K**: Kungminhoe members.
(2) Regional Backgrounds
S: Kyŏnggi and Ch'ungch'ŏng Provinces (Seoul faction), **W**: P'yŏngan and Hwanghae Provinces (Western faction)
(3) **T**: *Taedong Kongbo* members.
(4) *wŏnhoin* (old settler) / *yŏhoin* (new settler).

Sources *Taedong Kongbo*, 24 Apr. 1910, p. 3; *Sinhan Minbo*, 17 Feb. 1909, p. 1; Kuksa P'yŏnch'an Wiwŏnhoe, *Hanguk tongnip undongsa*, vol. 1, pp. 978-86; Ibid., vol. 7, pp. 223-24, 248, 254, 266-69, 282, 403, 466; Pak Hwan, *Rsia Hanin minjok undongsa*, pp. 80-85.

the Japanese government gathered comprehensive and detailed information of anti-Japanese Korean nationalists in the Primorye.[133]

Internecine conflicts among the Korean nationalists, mostly Kungminhoe members in Vladivostok soon shattered the enhanced spirit of unity among the Korean nationalists that the Harbin incident had fostered. In January 1910, Chŏng Sun-man, Vice-President of the Kungminhoe Vladivostok branch, shot Yang Sŏng-ch'un to death.[134] Yang Sŏng-ch'un served as an executive member of the Kungminhoe Vladivostok branch[135] and the President of the Korean Residents' Association.[136] The Russian authorities arrested eight Koreans including Chŏng Sun-man, Yi Ch'i-gwŏn, Yi Min-bok, Yi Ki and An Han-ju.[137]

The incident reflected a conflict between two regional factions. Table 2. 4 is a list of the Koreans involved. Group A, *Kihop'a* or Seoul faction members who had origins in the central parts of Korea (Kyŏnggi and Ch'ungchŏng Provinces); Group B, *Sŏdop'a* or Western faction members who had origins in the northwestern parts of Korea (P'yŏngan and Hwanghae Provinces). Chŏng Sun-man was said to have organized a death band [*kyŏlsadae*] with An Han-ju, Kang Sun-gi and Kwŏn Yu-sang at Yi Ch'i-gwŏn's house for the purpose of killing members of the Western faction. According to reports in the *Taedong Kongbo*, Chŏng Sun-man insulted Ch'a Sŏk-po, Yu Chin-yul, Yang Sŏng-ch'un and Chŏng Chae-gwan and accused Kim Sŏng-mu of personally spending Kungminhoe's money from San Francisco for the *Taedong Kongbo*. Yun Il-byŏng also reproached Chŏng Chae-gwan for wasting funds for the T'aedong Industry Company which the Kungminhoe organized in order to assist Koreans emigrate and cultivate land in Fengmisan in the Sino-Russian border region. Kim Hyŏn-t'o, who attempted to kill Yi Yong-ik in St. Petersburg in 1906, criticized Chŏng Chae-gwan, Kim Sŏng-mu, Yi Kang and Ham Tong-ch'ŏl, arguing that the Western faction was guilty of discriminatory behavior.[138]

Factional conflict among Korean nationalists in Vladivostok originated from the fact that the Kungminhoe dispatched two prominent leaders, Yi Sang-sŏl and Chŏng Chae-gwan, who had conflicting political ideas, careers and regional backgrounds, to Vladivostok. According to the recollection of Yi In-sŏp, who worked during the first half of the 1910s as an organizer for the Kungminhoe in North Manchuria and the Chita region, Yi Sang-sŏl and Chŏng Chae-gwan "had a conflict of opinions in Paris on the way to Vladivostok from America."[139] Yi Kwang-su who was a close associate of An

Ch'ang-ho, Chŏng Chae-gwan and Yi Kang and stayed in Vladivostok in early 1913, provided a more detailed explanation:

> As soon as Yi Sang-sŏl arrived at Vladivostok, he betrayed and repudiated the Kungminhoe claiming the Kungminhoe was an organization conspiring treason. This brought in Chŏng Sun-man's killing of Yang Sŏng-ch'un. . . . only Chŏng [Chae-gwan], Yi [Kang] and Kim [Sŏng-mu] . . . were working to carry out the activities of the Kungminhoe in Siberia and Manchuria. The reason why Yi Sang-sŏl and Chŏng Sun-man accused the Kungminhoe of treason was as follows: The use of two characters "Sin" and "Han" in the titles of the official organs, "the *Sinhan Minbo*" in San Francisco and "the *Sinhan Kukpo*" in Hawaii, is treasonous against "Taehan" ("Great Korean Empire"). This means that An Ch'ang-ho will be the President [*Taet'ong-nyŏng*] and Chŏng Chae-gwan will be the Emperor [*Hwangje*]. (This is the address which Chŏng Sun-man delivered at the meeting of the Korean Residents.)[140]

Although we have to keep in mind that Yi Kwang-su, as a close associate of An Ch'ang-ho, Chŏng Chae-gwan and Yi Kang, was partial to the Western faction, his description seems very reliable. From Yi Kwang-su's recollection, we can see that the conflicts of the two sides, Yi Sang-sŏl and Chŏng Sun-man on one side and An Ch'ang-ho and Chŏng Chae-gwan (1871-1921) on the other side, originated from the combination of both aspects: regionalism and political ideology. An Ch'ang-ho and Chŏng Chae-gwan were respectively from South P'yŏngan Province and Hwanghae Province, the region which had been discriminated against by the Korean government in procuring government jobs.[141] In childhood, An and Chŏng studied the basic fundamentals of Chinese classics in private local village schools [*sŏdang*], but devotion to the Confucian classics was not strong enough to call them Confucians. Their loyalty to King Kojong was also much weaker than that of Yi Sang-sŏl and Chŏng Sun-man. Both An Ch'ang-ho and Chŏng Chae-gwan went to San Francisco to study, but they instead became the key architects of the Kongnip Hyŏphoe and the Kungminhoe, which advocated and adopted American-style republicanism.[142]

Yi Sang-sŏl (1871-1917) and Chŏng Sun-man (1876-1911) were all from North Ch'ungch'ŏng Province, which together with Kyŏnggi Province was called the *Kiho* region and there were relatively more *yangban* families who produced more government officials. Yi Sang-sŏl was a well-known Confucian who had a broad knowledge in Western sciences and worked as the Chief-Secretary of the cabinet until 1905. King Kojong dispatched Yi to the Hague as imperial plenipotentiary to the Western Powers in 1907.[143] Chŏng Sun-man was a student of Chŏn U, one of the most prominent Korean Confucicanist scholars. After Chŏng participated in the *ŭibyŏng* uprising in 1895, he had been involved in patriotic activities. King Kojong appointed Chŏng later together with Yi Pŏm-sŏk and Yu In-hyŏk as a member of secret mission to recruit soldiers. In April 1907, Chŏng Sun-man went to North Chientao together with Yi Sang-sŏl and established a Korean school called Sŏjŏn Sŏsuk. Chŏng worked as the chief secretary of the *Haejo Sinmun* and acted as chief editor of the *Taedong Kongbo*.[144]

In conclusion, the two sides contrasted sharply in their regional backgrounds and political ideas. After the Chŏng Sun-man incident, Yi Sang-sŏl and his followers left themselves from the Kungminhoe and began to consolidate their own faction. Factional struggles intensified after the Chŏng Sun-man incident caused the *Taedong Kongbo* to be suspended. Thirty-six young Koreans,[145] mostly *wŏnhoin* Koreans, gathered and resolved to pacify factional struggles and promote friendship among Koreans and to take over the management of the *Taedong Kongbo*. Thanks to their efforts to raise capital and recruit employees, the meeting of stockholders resolved to republish the *Taedong Kongbo* on March 17, 1910. Regional factionalism, however, arose again over the issue of the appointment of the new chief editor.[146]

In this situation, the struggles between the Seoul faction and the Western faction aroused resentment among *wŏnhoin* Koreans, the majority of whom came from Hamgyŏng Provinces. On April 28, 1910, in an article titled "Fellow Patriots, Quickly Pacify the Factional Struggles," a reporter of the *Taedong Kongbo*, obviously a *wŏnhoin* Korean, severely criticized the those patriots who came recently from Korea:

> Originally northern people [people from Hamgyŏng Provinces] were in a lower place, and do not struggle based on clan and power, and our compatriots in the Russian territory are merely simple and humble and live by cultivating fields and drinking water by digging wells, wear clothing by themselves. As a result, there was no internal strife and they formed a unique society like a paradise. A couple of years ago, the so-called patriots who had come from the East, West and South spread harmful habits from Korea to compete against each other and this has brought about terrible results.[147]

Although a *Taedong Kongbo* article dated April 28 reported that factional struggles had calmed down,[148] it seems to have been reflecting hope rather than reality. Ch'oe Chae-hyŏng, President of the *Taedong Kongbo*, became disgusted with the factional struggle and declared that he would cancel his promise to provide 100 rubles a month to the newspaper. He then severely criticized those who came from Korea:

> A couple of years ago, I welcomed all patriots who had come from Korea and agreed eagerly to the development of society. Now these so-called patriotic figures formed their factions and are making it a part of daily life to attack one another. They do not have any principle of peace. When my thoughts reach this point, I cannot help deploring it. Please be aware that I will not send the 100 rubles I have provided to the newspaper (*Taedong Kongbo*).[149]

Around this time, Ch'oe Chae-hyŏng experienced growing conflict with Yi Sang-sŏl,[150] who according to a Japanese report, went to Vladivostok at the invitation of Ch'oe.[151] In the middle of 1910, loyalists and former high-ranking officials represented by Yi Sang-sŏl lost the confidence of the *wŏnhoin* society represented by Ch'oe Chae-hyŏng, as had Yi Pŏm-yun in 1908.[152]

2. Anti-Annexation Movement

As stated earlier, the anti-Japanese *ŭibyŏng* movement in the Primorye declined after the summer attack of 1908. The assassination of Ito Hirobumi, whom Koreans had widely regarded as the "mastermind of the Japanese invasion of Korea," inspired loyalist *ŭibyŏng* leaders in the Primorye. Yu In-sŏk, a prominent *ŭibyŏng* leader who had a broad following among Confucian scholars and had come to the Primorye in the summer of 1908,[153] sent letters to Yi Pŏm-yun and Ch'oe Chae-hyŏng requesting that the *ŭibyŏng* movement be launched again.[154] However, Yi Pŏm-yun had faced strong opposition from the Korean communities since the fall of 1908, particularly the *wŏnhoin* Koreans who included Ch'oe Chae-hyŏng and Ch'oe Pong-jun. Ch'oe Chae-hyŏng had already turned away from his *ŭibyŏng* activities and joined the *Taedong Kongbo*.

Utilizing the rising tide of anti-Japanese sentiment after the Harbin incident, Yi Pŏm-yun began to prepare for a military attack on northern Korea. Yi Pŏm-yun, with his follower Yi Sŭng-ho, established the "General Staff Office of the Righteous Army" ["Simu Ch'ongmuso"] in Novokievsk. They set up branch offices in eight locations and began to raise funds and purchase weapons.[155] Yi Pŏm-yun distributed copies of an announcement [*t'onggo*] to Koreans both in and outside Korea and urged the people to participate in his military activities. In the announcement, Yi claimed to be the "Administrator and General Director of All Mountain Hunters' Corps" ["*Kwanrisa gyŏmim kakkun sanp'osajang*"]. In order to demonstrate his authority, Yi Pŏm-yun sealed the announcement with a stamp given by King Kojong.[156]

Yi Pŏm-yun's resumption of military activities must have provoked fiery disputes among Korean patriots over what measures would be most effective in the face of the imminent downfall of Korea. In an editorial dated May 26, 1910, titled "Immediate Advancement and Gradual Advancement" ["*kŭpchin kwa wanjin*"], the *Taedong Kongbo* urged the two conflicting camps, the "immediate advancement party" ["*kŭpchindang*"] and the "gradual advancement party" ["*wanjindang*"], to unite and cooperate:

> Now there are two parties, one is the party of the *kŭpchin* and the other is the party of the *wanjin*. The belief of the *kŭpchin* is that today [our] nation is ruined and people have reached the point of extermination, so regardless

of the opportunity or situation, every person must go to his death and not wait for preparation. The party of the *wanjin* argues that today the enemy is strong and we are weak; the enemy is light and we are dark. As a result, if we act carelessly in the morning and fail, it will certainly be regretted for a thousand years. It is appropriate that when we unify the spirit of the people by organizing societies, enlighten the people by encouraging education, and prepare financially by expanding industry, we carry out a grand plan. We can not advance with our bare hands, isolated army and weak soldiers. I think both of these beliefs are correct. I suggest that by agreeing with each other's belief, the *kŭpchin* can be the vanguard, and the *wanjin* can be the supporting force.[157]

Although the *Taedong Kongbo* editor, presumably Chŏng Chaegwan, was careful not to arouse opposition from the "immediate advancement party," the *Sinhan Minbo* in San Francisco which was in close communication with the Kungminhoe members in Vladivostok severely criticized Yi Pŏm-yun's plan by recalling his previous behavior:

All thoughtful people among Koreans in various places in the Russian territory are opposed to Yi Pŏm-yun's plan of mobilizing soldiers. If Yi Pŏmyun is not the Yi Pŏm-yun of the past, but a new-born Yi Pŏm-yun, then we can not but appreciate and respond to his call. However, if Yi Pŏm-yun has not repented, there will be a great [bad] effect on our people. . . . If Yi Pŏmyun corrects his previous bad practices, really feels pity for his compatriots, and works considering the independence [of Korea] as most important, these [previous] faults will be gone. We hope that Yi Pŏm-yun will pay attention [to this].[158]

TABLE 2. 5

Members of the Sipsamdo Ŭigun

Toch'ongjae, Chief President	Yu In-sŏk
Ch'angŭi Ch'ongjae	Yi Pŏm-yun
Changŭi Ch'ongjae	Yi Nam-gi
Chief of Foreign Affairs	Yi Sang-sŏl
General Staff Members	Yi Pŏm-yun, Yi Sang-sŏl, Hong Pŏm-do, Yi Chin-yong, Kim Chwa-du, An Han-ju, Yi Kyu-p'ung, Yi Pŏm-sŏk, Kwŏn Yu-sang, Yi Ki, Yi Ch'i-gwŏn, Yi Chong-ho, Kim Hŭi-sŏn, An Ch'ang-ho, Yi Kap

Sources Yun Pyŏng-sŏk *Kugoe Hanin sahoe wa minjok undong*, pp. 177-78; Boris Pak, *Osvoboditel'naia Koreiskogo naroda nakanune pervoi mirovoi voiny* [The Liberation Struggle of the Koreans on the Eve of the First World War] (Moskva: Nauka), p. 181; S. S. Grigortsevich, "Uchastie koreitsev russkogo Dal'nevo Vostoka v antiiaponskoi natsional'noosvoboditel'noi bor'be, 1906-1916" [Participation of Koreans in the Russian Far East in the Anti-Japanese National Liberation Struggle], p. 146; Pak Min-yŏng, "Kuhanmal sŏbuk pyŏngyŏng chiyŏk ŭi ŭibyŏng yŏngu," pp. 329-34.

More harmful criticisms of the *ŭibyŏng* leaders came from the *wŏnhoin* Koreans. Twenty Koreans in Pokrovka and Borisovka in the Primorye sent an appeal to the magistrate of Nikol'sk-Ussurisk district Kegel'man on July 20, 1910. They requested the expulsion of Yi Pŏm-yun and his followers "as elements who are producing certain harm to the [Russian] government and also to ensure freedom from violence and extortion for the peaceful Korean population."[159] Hong Pŏm-do, one of the most popular *ŭibyŏng* leaders due to his previous legendary *ŭibyŏng* activities in northern Korea,[160] was also preparing for a military attack on northern Korea. Although Hong did not have any direct relations with Yi Pŏm-yun, the *wŏnhoin* Koreans widely regarded him as an associate of Yi Pŏm-yun. When Hong Pŏm-do found out that his treasurer, Pak Ki-man, had wasted all the funds which Hong had collected for the military attack on northern Korea scheduled for March 6, 1910, he killed Pak. At the news of Hong's execution of Pak Ki-man, a close associate of Mun

Ch'ang-bŏm [Vasilii Andreevich], who was a wealthy *podriadchik* in Suifen, Mun Ch'ang-bŏm, An Chun-hyŏn and Ch'oe Sun-gyŏng dispatched a band of 250 Koreans to arrest Hong Pŏm-do. They tortured Hong for two weeks until eight cossacks dispatched by the commander of the Russian army in Nikol'sk-Ussurisk, saved him.[161]

In July 1910, Koreans got the news of the Japanese plan to annex Korea. The *Sinhan Minbo* reported that in order to thwart the American government's proposal of the neutralization of all railroads in Manchuria, Japan hurried to conclude the second Russo-Japanese Agreement. Russia recognized the Japanese annexation of Korea and furthermore, the two governments planned to include an article concerning the extradition of Korean nationalists from Russia to Japan.[162] In this imperative situation, Yu In-sŏk tried to scheme a way in which both the "immediate advancement party" and the "gradual advancement party" could participate.[163] Yu In-sŏk sent a letter dated July 1, 1910, to Yi Sang-sŏl and immediately dispatched his close associates to Yi. While mentioning Japan's "conspiracy" to annex Korea and the conclusion of the second Russo-Japanese Agreement, Yu suggested to Yi that they discuss "a plan which could bring about the restoration" of Korea.[164] On June 21, 1910, Korean loyalists including Yu In-sŏk, Yi Pŏm-yun, Yi Sang-sŏl and Yi Nam-gi organized the Sipsamdo Ŭigun (Righteous Army of All Korea) at Ambambi, across the Amur Bay from Vladivostok in order to launch anti-Japanese military activities in northern Korea.[165] The Sipsamdo Ŭigun planned to broaden its organization throughout all thirteen provinces of Korea.[166]

The leaders of the "gradual advancement party," such as An Ch'ang-ho, Yi Chong-ho and Yi Kap, who came recently from Korea through Qingdao in China, joined the Sipsamdo Ŭigun. But loyal monarchists represented by Yu In-sŏk and Yi Sang-sŏl played key roles and the majority of the executive members were from the central parts of Korea. The Sipsamdo Ŭigun sent a memorial dated July 28 to King Kojong in the name of Yu In-sŏk and Yi Sang-sŏl. They asked King Kojong to provide funds for military activities, to seek exile in the Primorye and to head a movement for the restoration of independence by establishing a government-in-exile.[167] The Sipsamdo Ŭigun member visited the Japanese Consulate General in Vladivostok and asked him to deliver a letter to the Japanese emperor with the signatures of 500 Koreans, in which they protested the illegitimacy of the annexation and requested that the Japanese emperor reconsider the annexation.[168]

When a telegram announcing the Japanese annexation of Korea reached a Vladivostok newspaper, *the Dalekaia Okraina* (Far Outskirts) on August 23, 200 Koreans gathered at a Korean school and organized the Sŏngmyŏnghoe (聲明會, Manifesto Association). The purpose of the organization is explained in its name: "sŏng (聲)" and "myŏng (明)" were borrowed from the words "sŏng-p'i-ji-joe, myŏng-a-ji-wŏn" ("聲彼之罪 明我之寃," denounce their crime, clarify our resentment).[169] The Sŏngmyŏnghoe distributed copies of its prospectus in the name of its leaders, Yu In-sŏk, Yi Pŏm-yun, Kim Hak-man, Ch'a Sŏk-po, Kim Chwa-du and Kim Ch'i-bo, to Koreans in Russia and China. They also gathered signatures for a protest criticizing the illegitimate annexation of Korea by Japan to be distributed to foreign countries.[170] That night, young Koreans organized a death squad composed of 50 Koreans and began to attack Japanese residences. The next day, the membership of the death squad increased to a thousand.[171] The Sŏngmyŏnghoe immediately sent telegrams to foreign countries in which it claimed the Japanese annexation of Korea to be invalid.[172] The leaders of the Sŏngmyŏnghoe also sent a protest written in French and English to the governments of Austro-Hungary, Britain, Germany, Netherlands, Italy, China, Russia and America. The protest was signed by 8,624 Koreans in Russia and China.[173] On August 24, the Japanese ambassador to Russia in St. Petersburg visited the Russian Vice-Minister of Foreign Affairs and requested that he deliver an order to protect the Japanese from Korean attacks.[174] At the same time, the Japanese government handed the Russian authorities and the Chinese government a list of anti-Japanese Koreans and requested their expulsion from Russian and Chinese territories.[175]

The Russian government ordered Governor-General Unterberger to take preventive measures against any anti-Japanese activities.[176] On September 13, the Vladivostok police and *gendarme* surrounded the Korean Village [Kaech'ŏngni] and arrested forty-two Koreans, but Yi Pŏm-yun, Hong Pŏm-do, and Ŏm In-sŏp escaped.[177] Among those arrested, seven Koreans, Kim Chwa-du, An Han-ju, Yi Kyu-p'ung, Yi Pŏm-sŏk, Kwŏn Yu-sang, Yi Ki and Yi Ch'i-gwŏn, were expelled to Irkutsk on October 10, 1910.[178] On September 9, 1910, the Governor-General of the Priamur also suspended the *Taedong Sinbo*, which was the newly-titled successor of the *Taedong Kongbo* as of August 14, 1910, on charges of publishing an article opposing the Japanese annexation of Korea.[179]

In addition to the traditional way of requesting the Russian government to check on the anti-Japanese Koreans, the Japanese government began to apply a new strategy. The Japanese Consul-General, on orders from Tokyo, distributed a note to Korean merchants in Vladivostok and Nikol'sk-Ussurisk stating that "your cattle trade from Korea will be liquidated if your compatriots develop an active participation in the anti-annexation of Korea."[180] In response, Mun Ch'ang-bŏm issued a "circulated order" using the falsified name of Yi Pŏm-yun. The order urged Koreans to participate in the *ŭibyŏng* movement and donate funds. The order threatened to punish Koreans if they did not respond to the request. This order, however, was discovered by Shcherbakov, the head of the Ussurisk Railroad Administrative *gendarme*, as false.[181] Mun again falsified the names of Hong Pŏm-do and his two associates in whose names Mun wrote a letter to another associate of Hong's. The letter explained their plan to kill Kegel'man, the magistrate of Nikol'sk-Ussurisk. Because of this letter, Hong's three associates and 86 other naturalized Koreans were arrested on October 20, 1910. However, Hong again succeeded in avoiding arrest.[182]

At last, on October 24, 1910, the Russian authorities arrested Yi Pŏm-yun in Nikol'sk-Ussurisk following information provided by associates of Mun Ch'ang-bŏm and expelled him to Irkutsk.[183] Once more, in early 1911, the Japanese authorities in Vladivostok attempted to use the hands of the Russian authorities to arrest Ch'oe Chae-hyŏng. They falsified an information report stating that Ch'oe Chae-hyŏng had maintained secret relations with the Japanese government. At first, the head of the Primorye military district decided to expel Ch'oe Chae-hyŏng, but Ch'oe just barely avoided expulsion thanks to the strong opposition of the local Russian administrator who was familiar with Ch'oe's loyalty to Russia and his anti-Japanese career.[184]

C. The Nationalist Movement Advances

1. In North Chientao

a. Korean Educational Association in Chientao [Hanmin Kyoyukhoe, Kanmin Kyoyukhoe]

The forerunner of modern nationalistic education in North Chientao was the Sŏjŏn Sŏsuk established by Yi Sang-sŏl, Yi Tong-nyŏng, Chŏng Sun-man and Pak Mu-rim in the fall of 1906 in Longjingcun.[185] Those nationalists taught new Western educational courses including politics, history, geography, mathematics and law to young Koreans.[186] However, under political pressure from the Japanese and due to financial difficulties resulting from Yi Sang-sŏl's involvement in the Hague secret delegation, the Sŏjŏn Sŏsuk sold its assets to the Ilchinhoe in the fall of 1907, shortly after the establishment of the Residency-General branch office.[187] Despite its short life of eight months, the students of the Sŏjŏn Sŏsuk taught at Korean schools in North Chientao and thereby contributed to the development of modern education in North Chientao.[188]

Together with the founders of traditional private schools [*sŏjae* or *sasuk*] in Longjingcun, including Kim Yak-yŏn, Kim Ha-gyu, and Nam Wi-yŏn, Pak Mu-rim, a former teacher of the Sŏjŏn Sŏsuk, established the Myŏngdong Sŏsuk in 1908. The Myŏngdong Sŏsuk soon transformed itself into a Christian school, with the new name Myŏngdong School, as suggested by Chŏng Chae-myŏn, a Christian who had arrived in Longjingcun in May 1909.[189] Chŏng Chae-myŏn was dispatched by the Pukkando Kyoyuktan (North Chientao Education Group) organized by Christian nationalists including Yi Tong-hwi and Yi Tong-nyŏng in order to support education in North Chientao.[190]

The conclusion of the Chientao Agreement between China and Japan in September 1909, which defined the border of Chientao, intensified both China's and Japan's desire to win Koreans to their side. The Japanese Consulate-General established schools for Koreans in every resident district and the Chinese authorities also endeavored to establish schools for Koreans [Hanmin Hakkyo] in order to protect "the rights of Koreans" from the Japanese.[191]

Despite the withdrawal of the Japanese Residency-General branch office from North Chientao at the conclusion of the Chientao Agreement, as recounted in Chapter 1, Japanese consular officials were able to intervene in the Chinese courts and persecute anti-Japanese Koreans. Furthermore, the Japanese Residency-General (and the Japanese Government-General after 1910) did not allow Koreans to discard their Korean nationality even if they obtained Chinese citizenship. Such precarious status for Koreans propelled Korean nationalists to hurriedly organize Korean associations which could protect them from the possibility of arbitrary Japanese interference.

Shortly after the conclusion of the Chientao Agreement, Pak Mu-rim established the Korean Self-Administrative Association [Hanmin Chach'ihoe] with its residence in Juzijie, Yanji Prefecture with the assistance of Yi Tong-ch'un, who at that time worked as an interpreter for Tao Bin, the magistrate of Yanji Prefecture.[192] The Korean Self-Administrative Association was "able enough to get the confidence of Koreans in North Chientao thanks to its tight structural make-up and system."[193] The Japanese, however, protested that this association was in fact an organization for anti-Japanese activities, and Chinese authorities, who were worried about expansion in the self-autonomous capacity of Koreans, used this as an excuse to dissolve the organization.[194]

In March 1910, Tao Bin persuaded Yun Hae and Yi Pong-u to organize the Korean Educational Association [Hanmin Kyoyukhoe] with the goal of broadening educational opportunities for Koreans in North Chientao.[195] Tao Bin reported the establishment of the Korean Educational Association in North Chientao and received official recognition from Guo Zong-xi, the governor of the Jilin Dongnanlu (Yanji, Wangqing, Helong). Governor Guo was also very supportive of the association and donated 1,500 *diao*.[196]

The Korean Educational Association was the product of the first cooperative and compromising effort between anti-Japanese Korean nationalists and the local Chinese authorities, both of whom had a common political purpose in frustrating the expansion of Japanese influence in North Chientao. In this context, Japanese officials believed that the Korean Educational Association was a surrogate of the Korean Self-Administrative Association.[197]

The Korean Educational Association began first by raising funds needed for establishing Korean schools: one elementary school in each of 20 districts in Yanji Prefecture. In order to strengthen cooperative relations with local Chinese authorities, the Korean Educational Association set up the Research Association [Yŏnguhoe] in June 1910. While the Educational Association concentrated on education with the goal of training and educating pro-Chinese Koreans, the Research Association, as "one section of the Chinese administration," was responsible for investigating and reporting various suggestions and information related to the Chinese rule of Koreans. Yi Tong-ch'un and Yun Hae served as the President and Vice-President of the Korean Educational Association respectively, and Yi Pong-u became President of the Research Association. Yi Tong-ch'un had emigrated from Korea twenty years before and his credibility among the local Chinese officials was quite high. Yun Hae and Yi Pong-u, on the other hand, had recently come from Korea in order to continue their anti-Japanese activities.[198]

The Japanese annexation of Korea in August 1910 accelerated cooperation between the Educational Association and the local Chinese authorities. In September 1910, shortly after the Japanese annexation of Korea, the Korean Educational Association in Chientao [Hanmin Kyoyukhoe] hurried to change its name to the Kanmin Kyoyukhoe by replacing the first character, "*Han*" (韓, Korean) with "*Kan*" (墾, Chientao). As a result, the new name was literally the Educational Association of Chientao People.[199] The change of name clearly illustrates the political considerations of Korean nationalists who wished to counter the Japanese claim that all Koreans residing in Chientao are Japanese subjects with the annexation of Korea. The Educational Association in Chiento also adopted a policy of encouraging Koreans to achieve Chinese citizenship in order to continue legitimate and open anti-Japanese activities with Chinese support. The Chinese authorities welcomed and encouraged this policy. By promoting naturalization, the Chinese hoped to "break up the solidarity of the Korean communities and facilitate their assimilation with the Chinese."[200]

Two agreements, the "General Agreement" ["*pot'ong choyak*"] and the "Secret Agreement" ["*pimil choyak*"], between the Chinese magistrate of Yanji [Tao Bin] and the Korean Educational Association clearly demonstrate such a political compromise. In the General Agreement, the local Chinese administrator would control the Educational Association, but they promised to grant the executive members of the association the same status as the local Chinese officials. The Chinese authorities also allowed the Educational Association to set up a special department for self-administration and to manage

TABLE 2. 6

Major Korean Organizations in North Chientao, 1909-1914

"New Knowledge Clique" ["Sinp'a"]			
Hanmin Chach'ihoe → (Fall 1909)	Hanmin Kyoyukhoe → (Mar. 1910)	Kanmin Kyoyukhoe → (Sep. 1910)	Kanminhoe (Apr. 1913)
"Old Knowledge Clique" ["Kup'a"]			
		Saugye ——————→ (Sep. 1912)	Konggyohoe (Nov. 1913)
			Nongmugye (June 1913)

all Korean schools which the Chinese authorities had already established. In addition, Chinese authorities allowed the Educational Association the power to abolish all traditional private schools [*sasuk*] established by Korean Confucians. The Chinese authorities also granted the Educational Association the right to put the common property of the Korean communities under its control. In the Secret Agreement, the Educational Association agreed to encourage naturalization of Koreans into Chinese citizens and the Chinese authorities agreed to allow the Koreans self-administration after all Koreans become Chinese citizens. In addition, the Educational Association also promised to investigate and report on secret affairs (certainly related to Japan) to the Chinese authorities.[201] As Japanese officials soon discovered, the Educational Association was recognized by local Chinese authorities as a kind of self-administrative organization for Koreans in North Chientao.[202]

At the same time, with the recognition and support of Tao Bin and Guo Zong-xi, the Educational Association established Mobŏm Haktang (Chin. Mufan Xuetang, Model School) in Juzijie as the model of all Korean schools in North Chientao. The Chinese authorities provided funds to pay two Korean teachers and allowed the Educational Association to gather funds for annual expenses from every Korean household. The Mobŏm Haktang established two classes, one for elementary students and the other to train teachers for Korean schools.[203]

Thanks to donations from 72 "most influential" key members,[204] the Educational Association built its own office building in Juzijie on September 10, 1910, and began to publish its official organ, the *Wŏlbo* (Monthly Report), which was distributed not only in North Chientao, but also in other Korean communities, even in America.[205] From September 1910, shortly after the annexation of Korea, in response to the orders of the Tao Bin, the members of the Research Association, who had already been secretly dispatched to Korean villages since June 1910, actively fomented anti-Japanese sentiment among the villagers and launched the movement to adopt Chinese citizenship and Manchu hair-style and clothing.[206]

The Educational Association strengthened its membership and activities with the addition of anti-Japanese progressive intellectuals who had come from Korea from the end of 1909 to early 1911. By February 1911, the membership of the Educational Association had already reached 200 in North Chientao.[207] Most of the Educational Association members were Protestants, obtained or received Chinese citizenship, and adopted Manchu or Western hair-style and clothing.[208] In the Educational Association, there were some believers of the Taejonggyo (Religion of Tangun Worship) such as Pak Ch'an-ik, Paek Sun, and Hyŏn Ch'ŏn-muk, but the majority of Educational Association members were Christians.[209] And, they were not only educators, but also Christian evangelists.[210]

Because of their activities in promoting modern education and Christianity and their appearance, the members of the Educational Association were called "reformers" ["*yusinp'a*"],[211] the "new education clique" ["*sinhakp'ae*"] or the "new faction" ["*sinbae*"]. By their opponents, they were cynically known as the "pheasant-hair clique" ["*ch'ibalp'ae*"].[212] These "Westernized" Koreans came from the Hamgyŏng Provinces and were close followers of Yi Tong-hwi (1873-1935).

Yi Tong-hwi was born in 1873, the son of low-level local official [*ajŏn*] and farmer in Tanch'ŏn, South Hamgyŏng Province. On Yi Yong-ik's recommendation, Yi Tong-hwi entered an military officers' training school in Seoul in 1896, which Russians managed after King Kojong's escape to the Russian legation in Seoul [*Agwan P'ach'ŏn*]. Yi had served in the Palace Guard of King Kojong for six years and was promoted to Major, holding the commandership of a local battalion on Kanghwa Island. While serving as an officer in the regular Korean army, Yi Tong-hwi got involved in anti-Japanese activities led by Min Yŏng-hwan, Yi Yong-ik, and Yi Chun, who were highranking officials renowned for their loyalty to King Kojong.

In early 1905 during the Russo-Japanese War, Yi Tong-hwi resigned from the Korean army in resentment over increasing Japanese encroachment in Korea. He then started an educational movement. At the same time, Yi became a Christian (Methodist) with a belief that "only Christianity can save the declining nation and people" of Korea. With increasing political restrictions, Christian churches were the only places where anti-Japanese Koreans could inspire patriotism and enjoy freedom of assembly and speech.[213] In August 1907, shortly after King Kojong's abdication and the dissolution of the Korean army, the Japanese police arrested Yi on charges of his involvement in the Hague secret mission and in an armed uprising of soldiers and people on Kanghwa Island. Upon released in December 1907 four months after his arrest, Yi Tong-hwi together with other anti-Japanese nationalists including An Ch'ang-ho, Yi Kap and Yu Tong-yŏl organized the underground New People's Association [Sinminhoe] and the legal educational organization, the Sŏbuk Hakhoe (Northwestern Educational Association) whose members were drawn mainly from the western and northern parts of Korea (P'yŏngan, Hwanghae and Hamgyŏng Provinces). Unaware of the existence of the secret New People's Association, Japanese officials called the Sŏbuk Hakhoe a "hotbed of the anti-Japanese party" ["*paeildang ŭi sogul*"].

In 1909, Yi Tong-hwi volunteered to assist Robert Grierson, a missionary in charge of the Canadian Presbyterian missionary organization based in Sŏngjin, North Hamgyŏng Province. From that time on, Yi Tong-hwi worked in the missionary organization organized by Grierson with the purpose of spreading Christianity among Koreans in north Korea, North Chientao and the Primorye. In his memoirs, Robert Grierson wrote his recollections about Yi Tong-hwi:

> At about this time, I had a visitor, a Korean, whose name was Lee Tong Hee [Yi Tong-hwi]. He was a native of this [Sungjin] area and a long-standing Christian. He was well-known in our area as a great Korean nationalist. He was not only a Major in the Korean army, but actually had been in His Majesty's own Body-Guard. On account of his known opposition to their manoeuvre, the Japanese had kept him in prison for several years [several months]. . . offered him high position if he would discontinue his opposition to them. This he refused. . . . His visit to me was based on his desire to work for the advancement of the Church of

> Christ. He had based on a great hope, like others, in the educational uplift of the nation, but now felt that only Divine Grace and Divine aid could save his country. He asked me to give him an appointment as a preacher in our field. . . . Everywhere he went, crowds gathered to hear him preach, and the Japanese police kept close watch on his movements and utterance.[214]

The Japanese, who worried about Yi Tong-hwi's possible anti-annexation activities, arrested Yi once again in early August 1910. Yi Tong-hwi was only released shortly after the official declaration of the Japanese annexation of Korea. Before and after the annexation, Yi Tong-hwi dispatched about thirty of his followers, whom the Japanese officials called "Yi Tong-hwi's disciples," to North Chientao with the declared purpose of missionary work.[215] Yi Tong-hwi himself visited North Chientao from the end of January through February 1911, on a mission assigned by the Canadian Presbyterian Mission. Yi Tong-hwi travelled around Korean communities in North Chientao to promote patriotism, Protestantism and the unity of Koreans. Yi's visit to North Chientao, to a great extent, encouraged the activities of the Educational Association and Protestants in North Chientao came to outnumber Catholics.[216]

In addition to his religious activities, Yi Tong-hwi secretly convened a congress of representatives from various anti-Japanese nationalist groups of whom most were his followers. These representatives organized the Restoration Union [Kwangboktan] as "the steering center" of anti-Japanese activities.[217] Because of the lack of sources, we cannot determine in detail the membership and activities of the Union, but the limited material that is available clearly show that members of the Restoration Union played key roles not only in the

Korean nationalist movement, but also in the socialist and communist movements in the 1910s and 1920s. The Japanese arrested Yi Tong-hwi once again in March 1911 shortly after his return to Sŏngjin on charges of involvement in the case of An Myŏng-gŭn and Yang Ki-t'ak who had been falsely charged with planning the assassination of Terauchi Masatake, the first Governor-General of Korea. He was banished for one year to Taemuŭi Island, near Inch'ŏn. Yi Tong-hwi was later released in July 1912 and moved to North Chientao again in June 1913.[218]

Backed by the "harmonious support" of the local Chinese authorities, members of the Educational Association established modern schools and Christian churches in almost every Korean community. They also organized mutual financial associations and cooperatives for purchase and sale of basic necessities. About forty to fifty Korean schools were also established in North Chientao.[219] The Educational Association organized a textbook compilation committee with Kye Pong-u, Chŏng Chae-myŏn and Nam Kong-sŏn as members with each individual members asked to author textbooks designed to inspire patriotism. Beginning in the higher grades of elementary schools, students were required to receive military training.[220] Educational Association members communicated with Korean nationalists in Russia and America, particularly with those in Vladivostok. The association distributed its official organ, the *Wŏlbo*, to Vladivostok and San Francisco while also distributing both the *Kwŏnŏp Sinmun* (Work Promotion Gazette) and the *Sinhan Minbo* to Koreans in North Chientao through its branches.[221]

A good example of a Korean school under the management of the Educational Association was the Kwangsŏng School, which was established in March 1911 in Xiaoyingzi, 5 km southeast of Juzijie.[222]

Korean nationalists considered the Kwangsŏng School as the "best school in the educational world in North Chientao."[223] In early 1911, Kim Rip came from Vladivostok with Yi Chong-ho's financial support and a plan for the school. Thirteen key members of the association including Yi Tong-ch'un, Kim Rip, Yun Hae, Yi Pong-u, Chang Ki-yŏng, Kye Pong-u and Kim Ha-sŏk worked as teachers and administrators.[224]

The activities and goals of the Educational Association, however, were not fully welcomed by the Koreans of North Chientao. The Educational Association members were often expelled from the villages by Korean peasants who regarded modern education to be completely useless and with suspicion. Some conservative Koreans even beat members or tried to hand them over to the Japanese Consulate in Longjingcun by force.[225]

The strongest opposition, however, came from the loyalist Confucian scholars including Kim Chŏng-gyu, Chi Chang-hoe and Ch'a Ho-gyun who had led the anti-Japanese *ŭibyŏng* struggles in 1908 in Kyŏngsŏng, North Hamgyŏng Province, together with Yi Nam-gi, a close associate of Yu In-sŏk and leader of the anti-annexation movement in the Primorye. After their defeat in the summer of 1908, these Confucian *ŭibyŏng* leaders emigrated to North Chientao during the period from the end of 1908 to the middle of 1909.[226] They strongly opposed the policies of the local Chinese authorities and the Educational Association. Upset with the compulsory policy of the Chinese government, Kim Chŏng-gyu (1881-1953) attempted to protest directly to Wu Lü-cheng, the Frontier Director-General, at the end of 1909 (October 11, 1909, lunar calendar), but he failed to see Wu in person.[227] Instead, Kim left a letter to Wu:

> Recently [public] schools [for Koreans] are recruiting students. They are enrolling students by compelling the private village schools by tiger's threats. I do not know whether this is really what the great man [Wu Lü-cheng] did. It is difficult for today's new knowledge to change the old custom of previous days as well. . . . When transformed gradually, then it will be renewed by itself. Although [you] can establish a school by threatening and [people] will come to obey, it does not mean that their minds will obey. They can not resist by force, but they will certainly have revenge. If revengeful minds revolt against each other, how can we be peaceful in the future? I heard that people are feeling disturbed, are wrinkling their foreheads, are shedding tears looking to the East, and spilling tears toward the hill.[228]

Although Kim Chŏng-gyu's criticism focused on abusive measures taken by the Chinese authorities, Confucian scholars, in fact, were in a state of crisis due to the activities of the "new education clique" who had the power to abolish private village schools [*sasuk*]. Twenty-four Confucian scholars, including Chŏng An-rip, Kim Chŏng-gyu, Ch'a Ho-gyun and Chi Chang-hoe, took the initiative to organize the Sasuk Kaeryanghoe (Association for Private Village School Reform). In its prospectus, the Sasuk Kaeryanghoe declared three main goals: to avoid the "suppression of the 'new clique' by reforming the private village school; to uphold Confucian principles by reading mostly Chinese books, and; to prepare for the future by unifying "the minds of the people."[229]

In September 1912, 155 Confucian scholars held a general meeting at Chŏng An-rip's house.[230] The temporary Chairman, Nam Ch'ŏl-bung, declared that the goal of the Sasuk Kaeryanghoe was to oppose modern education and to defend the old private schools. Nam also urged the participants to make every effort to take the hegemony of education in North Chientao away from the "new knowledge clique" ["*sinhakp'ae*"]. The meeting, however, failed to receive official permission in advance from Chinese authorities. Furthermore, the Educational Association criticized Nam Ch'ŏl-bung and other leaders of being members of the pro-Japanese Ilchinhoe. As a result, the local Chinese authorities, who also suspected a political motive and Japanese influence, considered the goals of the Sasuk Kaeryanghoe harmful to the Chinese and forced the Sasuk Kaeryanghoe to dissolve itself.[231]

A week later, in reaction to the unfavorable policy of the local Chinese authorities, twenty-two Confucian scholars who had initiated the Sasuk Kaeryanghoe, created a secret organization called the Saugye (Confucian Scholars' Compact), with the goal of upholding Confucian principles based on the *Lushi Xiangyao* (Kor. *Yŏssi Hyangyak*).[232] The Saugye secretly recruited members and in the fall of 1913, had already reached a membership of more than 100.[233]

A more systematic and stronger interference in the activities of the Educational Association came from the Japanese authorities. In order to counteract the activities of the Educational Association, Yi Hŭi-dŏk and Ch'oe Nam-gi, who were members of the Ilchinhoe and acting on the advice and support from the Government-General of Korea and the Japanese Consulate General, organized the Korean Association [Chosŏninhoe] with the goal of opposing Korean reliance on the Chinese government and "protecting the lives and property of Koreans and aiding people in misery." The Korean Association made accusations that the Educational Association would bring trouble to Koreans in North Chientao. The Japanese Consulate General also attempted to win favor of Koreans by providing funds for elementary schools, local Confucian schools, associations for seniors, Buddhist temples, and churches of the Sich'ŏngyo, the religious wing of the Ilchinhoe.[234]

There is currently no available material by which we can evaluate when and how the Educational Association was dissolved. Although the Educational Association experienced internal factional struggles based on regionalism,[235] ultimately it was Japanese diplomatic pressure which caused Chinese authorities to decide to dissolve the Educational Association.[236]

b. Kanminhoe [Korean Association in Chientao]

On January 13, 1913, twenty former members of the Educational Association initiated the Kanminhoe (Korean Association in Chientao) and invited the heads of 100 households [*paekhojang*] and local influential Koreans in Yanji, Helong, Wangqing and Hunchun to attend the organizational general meeting scheduled on February 26, 1913. In its notice, the initiators clarified the goals of the Kanminhoe: to promote the welfare of Koreans within the limits of Chinese law and to achieve status as an "administrative unit" of the Chinese government which would enjoy authority over all affairs related to the lives and property of Koreans in North Chientao. In contrast to the Educational Association [Kanmin Kyoyukhoe], the Kanminhoe was granted political status as a self-administrative organization of Koreans in North Chientao under the supervision of the local Chinese authorities. Furthermore, the Kanminhoe expanded its scope of activities beyond Yanji to the whole of North Chientao: Yanji, Wangqing, and Helong Prefectures. Tao Bin, the former magistrate of Yanji Prefecture and the Governor of the East-South Route [Jilin Dongnanlu] recognized the initiative of the Kanminhoe in advance.[237]

TABLE 2. 7

Executive Members of the Kanminhoe (Apr. 26, 1913)

	Position	Age	Birthplace (Province)	Years of Residence	Address
Kim Yak-yŏn	Pres.	49	Hoeryŏng (N. H.)	20	Helong
Paek Ok-po	Vice-Pres.	33	P'yŏngyang (S. P.)	?	Yanji
Kim Rip	Census	33	Myŏngch'ŏn (N. H.)	3	Yanji
Yi Tong-ch'un	Industry	39	Hoeryŏng (N. H.)	20	Yanji
To Sŏng	Gen. Secr.	28	Hamhŭng (S. H.)	3	Yanji
Nam Kong-sŏn	Law	28	Wŏnsan (S. H.)	3	Yanji
Chang Ki-yŏng	Education	26	Changdan (K.)	3	Yanji
Cho Yŏng-ha	Finance	33	P'yŏngyang (S. P.)	3	Yanji
Kim Pyŏng-hŭp	Council	33	Wŏnsan (S. H.)	3	Yanji
Pak Ch'ang-ik	Secretary				
Council Members (20)					
Yanji (12)	Kim Yŏng-hak, Cho Kŭk, Wang Kŭm-bung, Hyŏn Yŏng-ju, Chŏng Chae-myŏn, Yi Chung-jip, Kang Ku-wu, Ch'oe Yang, Kim Cha-ch'ŏn, Cho Hŭi-rim, Wang Sŏng-sŏ, Yi Yong				
Helong (4)	Cho Yŏl, Sim Kŭn, Kim Si-hyŏng, Nam Kun-p'il				
Wangqing (4)	Hong Pŏm-t'ae, Chŏn Ŭi-gŭn, Chŏn Yŏ-un, O Ki-yŏn				

Note Birthplaces
N. H.: North Hamgyŏng Province, **S. H.**: South Hamgyŏng Province, **S. P.**: South P'yŏngan Province, **K**: Kyŏnggi Province

Sources "Baogaoshu dierhao" [Report no. 2, to Tao Bin], KIHA, Document no. 6393-37, 30 Apr. 1913; "Kanminhoe t'ongjisŏ" [Notice of the Kanminhoe], KIHA, Document no. 6393-39, 1 May 1913.

Those attending the preparatory general meeting of February 26, organized the Kanminhoe and passed a draft of the regulations which would be attached to the application for the recognition of Chinese authorities. On March 30, Chinese authorities officially recognized the application of the Kanminhoe.[238] The General Executive Committee was located at the former office building of the Educational Association in Juzijie, Yanji Prefecture.[239] Kanminhoe regulations limited the membership to male Koreans residing in the mixed residential district at least three years. The president reported the official affairs of the Association to the Governor.[240] The Kanminhoe held its first official general meeting on April 26, 1913, in Juzijie and elected members of the Central Executive Committee [*Chungang Ch'onghoe*] (see Table 2. 7).

President Kim Yak-yŏn was one of the most respected Christian leaders among Koreans in North Chientao and at that time served as the superintendent of the Myŏngdong School in Longjingcun. Yi Tong-ch'un was a former President of the Educational Association and superintendent of the Kwangsŏng School and the Kilsin Women's School and had worked as an interpreter for the local Chinese administration since the 1890s. As a result, he had close connections with the local Chinese officials including Tao Bin. Most of the executive members were young intellectuals who had emigrated around the time of the Japanese annexation of Korea in order to continue their anti-Japanese activities in North Chientao. Two thirds came from Hamgyŏng Provinces. The regional ratio of the council members seemed to have reflected the population of Koreans in each prefecture,[241] and council members were mostly the influential "big landowners."[242] Soon the Kanminhoe dispatched organizers to Korean villages and organized branches in three prefectures, Yanji, Wangqing, and Helong, and chapters for every 50 houses during May 1913.[243]

On July 11, 1913, the Kanminhoe applied for a census to the Governor of North Chientao with the purpose of investigating the population of Koreans and receiving the recognition of Chinese authorities. According to the application, the Kanminhoe members would take the census in close cooperation with Chinese police.[244] On July 20, 1913, the Kanminhoe held an opening ceremony for

TABLE 2. 8

Executive Members of the Nongmugye (Nov. 1913)

	Position	Age
Ch'oe Nam-gi	President	64
Yi Wŏn-hyŏk	Vice-Pres.	50
Kang Wi-ch'ŏn	Branch (P'yŏnggang, Yanji)	68
Nam Ch'ŏl-bung	Branch (Changsŏk, Yanji)	68
Hyŏn Un-ho	Branch (P'alp'ogang, Yanji)	65
Kim Hong-gu	Branch (Taehŏmun, Yanji)	84
Ch'oe Pyŏng-yong	Branch (Helong)	?
Han Chin-dong	Secretary-General	?
Hong Cha-mun	Inspirator and Organizer	?

Sources KIHA, Document No. 5437-1; KIHA, Document no. 5437-3 (Nov. 13, 1913).

its new office building in Juzijie with the participation of 700 Koreans and about 10 local Chinese officials. The Governor of North Chientao, Tao Bin, attended and delivered a complimentary address emphasizing the close solidarity of Chinese and Koreans and the importance of education and industry for Koreans.[245] In order to solve its budget problem, the Kanminhoe decided to collect 30 *qian* from every household in an extraordinary general meeting held on July 21.[246]

The Kanminhoe members also organized two partner youth organizations, the Taedong Hyŏpsinhoe (Association for Cooperation and Renewal of Great East) and the Youth Friendship Association [Ch'ŏngnyŏn Ch'inmokhoe]. The former published the monthly magazine the *Taejin* (Great Lightening) with Kye Pong-u as its chief editor. The latter was united with the Youth Club [Ch'ŏngnyŏn Kurakpu] and Nam Kong-sŏn and Chŏng Chae-myŏn served as its key executive members and published a monthly organ, the *Ch'ŏngnyŏn* (The Youth).[247]

With the purpose of establishing cooperation with the Chinese, both Korean and Chinese Christians organized the Chinese-Korean Joint Christian Mission [Chung-Han Yŏnhap Chŏndohoe] in August 1913 and elected a Chinese, Jing Tou-ji, and a Korean, Yi Tong-hwi[248] as its President and Vice-President respectively. The other executive member posts were also equally shared by both Chinese and Koreans. They decided to establish close communications with churches in various places in North Chientao,[249] with the intention of attaching Korean churches officially to the Chinese Christian mission in order to prevent Japanese interference.[250] At the same time, the Kanminhoe dispatched its representatives, Yi Tong-hwi, Yi Tong-ch'un, Chŏng Chae-myŏn, and Pak Ch'an-ik, to Beijing. They congratulated the Chinese on the establishment of the Chinese Republic and requested President Yuan Shi-kai to support Koreans by enhancing their autonomous status in China.[251] Around this time, in mid 1913, about 250,000 Koreans in China applied for Chinese citizenship.[252]

As was the case with the Educational Association, Confucians, especially members of the Saugye (Confucian Scholars' Compact), severely criticized the "assimilation" policies of the Kanminhoe which included naturalization and the adoption of the Chinese hair-styles and clothing. From the diary of Kim Chŏng-gyu, a key member of the Saugye, we can see how those Confucian patriots viewed the policies of the Kanminhoe:

> I and Chi Chang-hoe lamented and said. "The pheasant clique is trying to destroy our people." They dare to say loudly: "to protect our people, to restore our national sovereignty in the future. Therefore, [we] establish this, the Kanminhoe. . . . The Kanminhoe. . . aims to transform Koreans into Chinese. What does it mean? It is our custom to tie our hair and wear white

clothes. In addition to pheasant-hair and black clothes, now [they are encouraging the adoption of] the same language and same customs. . . . Then, how can we find Korean thoughts? To speak of restoring our sovereignty without Korean thoughts is an extreme act of deception. Is the clothing of the Chinese Republic really an old custom of China? It is a Western style. [They] are following the Western style and at the same time, admiring China. If a learned person hears this, he will surely laugh. . . . [They] are saying that because this region is occupied by the Chinese Republic, it is proper to get Chinese citizenship. . . . It is as extreme as the Ilchinhoe encouraging naturalization. The Ilchinhoe has only dedicated the land [to the enemy, but] the Kanminhoe nowadays is binding the people to a domain where precedent was forgotten and the following is disconnected. It is a truly lamentable."[253]

Kim Chŏng-gyu based his criticism on the long-standing ideology of Korean Confucians called "*Sojunghwa* (小中華)," which stated that Korea became the true successor of the "Middle Kingdom" when the Manchu "barbarian" destroyed Ming Dynasty and established the Qing. Like the "new clique," they welcomed the 1911 Revolution, not because it established a republican state, but because it overthrew the Manchu dynasty. On the other hand, Kim Chŏng-gyu's criticism demonstrates how clearly Korean Confucians in North Chientao misunderstood the political goals of the Kanminhoe. Members of the Kanminhoe considered the policies of "assimilation" only as a means for obtaining the protection of Chinese authorities by which Koreans could thwart Japanese interference. The Kanminhoe's eventual objective was to achieve the independence of Korea.[254]

The leaders of the Kanminhoe were aware of the Confucians' misconceptions and felt it necessary to communicate with them.

According to Kim Chŏng-gyu, Yi Tong-hwi, "the head of the Christians," sent a letter on August 10 to Kim and suggested they meet six days later at the Kilsin Women's School to discuss plans for cooperation toward common goal: the restoration of the fatherland. The meeting, however, was not realized, because Kim did not respond.[255]

Additional and in some cases more serious opposition came from old settled landowners. In opposition to the ambitious policies of the Kanminhoe to embrace all Koreans in North Chientao, Ch'oe Nam-gi, Han Chin-dong, Hong Cha-mun and Wi Yŏng-in organized the Nongmu-gye (Agricultural Community Compact) on June 29, 1913, in Zhirenhsiang district, Yanji Prefecture, with the participation of 300 members. The Nongmugye declared its main purpose to be the "destruction of the Kanminhoe" and recruited members mostly from old settlers and Confucian scholars who accused the Kanminhoe of being an organization harmful to Koreans in North Chientao.[256]

President of the Nongmugye, Ch'oe Nam-gi, expressed its purpose in his address at the foundation meeting of the Nongmugye:

> We came here about thirty years ago and as a result, we are old landowners. However, the key members of the Kanminhoe came to Chientao only a few years ago. How can we endure being despised by them? I heard that they are planning to force us to pay 30 *qian*. . . . I am hoping all members will reject their extortion and will organize at today's meeting. Let's strive together with a unified spirit.[257]

While the Confucians opposed the assimilation policies and new education of the Kanminhoe, the Nongmugye challenged the political status of the Kanminhoe as a self-administrative association of Koreans

TABLE 2. 9

Major Differences between Kanminhoe and Nongmugye

	Kanminhoe	Nongmugye
Key leaders	Anti-Japanese activists	Earlier and Wealthy Land Owners
Policies	Naturalization Patriotism Republicanism	Non-naturalization No Patriotism Monarchism
Outward Appearances	Short Hair Black Clothing (Manchu or Western Style)	Long and Tied Hair White Clothing (Korean Style)
Religion	Christianity (mostly)	Confucianism
	yusinp'a (reformists)	sugup'a (conservatists)

Source KIHA, Document no. 6393-57.

in North Chientao. Guan Yun-cong, the magistrate of Yanji Prefecture, well summed up the characteristics of the Nongmugye members:

> Ch'oe Nam-gi and Hong Cha-mun. . . . united Koreans in Yanji, Helong and Wangqing who had immigrated to China, cultivated land and resided there for a long time. All of them have lands and properties and their lives have no relation to the ruined fate of Korea. Although they are not seemingly naturalized, they already assimilated internally long time ago. . . . They do not change their clothes and hats and their customs are still the same as in the past. As a result, they were called "*sugup'a* (conservatives)".[258]

The Nongmugye was in many ways in conflict with the Kanminhoe as in Table 2. 9, which was based on the reports of local Chinese authorities in North Chientao.

Both the Chinese authorities and the Kanminhoe, however, suspected Nongmugye's key leaders, Ch'oe Nam-gi, Hong Cha-mun, Nam Ch'ŏl-bung and Han Chin-dong as Japanese agents.[259] The efforts of the Japanese to utilize the anti-Kanminhoe policies of the Nongmugye corroborated the suspicion. The Japanese Consulate General in Doudaogou attempted to provide funds of 300 *yen* to the Nongmugye through Han Chin-dong, a Japanese agent and Secretary-General of the Nongmugye. At a general meeting held in August 1913, an executive member boasted that the Japanese Consulate General would provide all expenses for their organization. Surprised by the Japanese involvement, more than two thirds of the members were said to have withdrawn from the Nongmugye.[260]

In their report to Chinese authorities, they boasted the numbers of its membership was 15,000 (8,000 in Yanji, 2,400 in Helong and 100 in Wangqing),[261] but its member, in fact, numbered only 3,000 as of November 1913.[262] As Yi Tong-ch'un, a key leader of the Kanminhoe, analyzed it, the majority of the Nongmugye members were not pro-Japanese, but most of the farmers were "obstinate and illiterate." As a result, the Chinese authorities and the Kanminhoe worried there was always a possibility that the Japanese could utilize the Nongmugye for their goals.[263]

Encouraged by the activities of the Kongjiaohui (Kor. Konggyohoe, Association of Confucians) led by Kang Yu-wei in Beijing, Korean Confucian members of the Saugye, a secret organization which was established in the fall of 1912, and a long-time opponent of the "new knowledge clique," organized the Yanji branch of the Konggyohoe (Chin. Kongjiaohui) on November 29, 1913. Declaring their opposition to the new education and policies of the Kanminhoe, 386 Confucians gathered in Juzijie, Yanji and elected their executive members. In its leaflets, the Konggyohoe tried to undermine the authority of the Kanminhoe by emphasizing the fact that it was recognized by the Chinese government, while the Kanminhoe was recognized only by the Jilin Civil-Administrator.[264]

The Kanminhoe considered the Association of Confucians to have a similar purpose as the Nongmugye. Also, in spite of official government recognition, Chinese authorities themselves worried about the Association of Confucians. Shan Yuan, the magistrate of Helong Prefecture, in his report to Tao Bin, suggested that in order to prevent possible harm to future education, it would be necessary to "prohibit and punish" the Konggyohoe members who were restoring old-style Korean private schools and disrupting the new schools.[265] Furthermore, the Konggyohoe branch in Lonjingcun was a well-known pro-Japanese Korean organization under the control of the Japanese Consulate General,[266] and because of the leading role played by Chŏng An-rip and Pak Ŭi-p'ung in the Konggyohoe Yanji branch, the Kanminhoe leaders suspected Japanese involvement in the Konggyohoe. Pak Ŭi-p'ung was a well-known pro-Japanese Korean and Chŏng An-rip, because of his strong opposition to the Kanminhoe, was at first suspected by the Kanminhoe leaders to be a pro-Japanese agent as well.[267]

When its first public lecture meeting [*kanghak*] was held at the Kilsin Women's School in Juzilie, Kanminhoe members went to the school and criticized Chŏng An-rip, who was the vice-superintendent of the school, for changing his religion too frequently (first Taoism, Christianity, then Confucianism), and for making arrangements to use the school without consulting with the members of the Kanminhoe, in particular, Yi Tong-ch'un, its superintendent.[268] Born in Kimp'o, Kyŏnggi Province, Chŏng An-rip served as magistrate of the Korean government and the Chancellor of Posŏng College in Seoul. Chŏng

An-rip maintained close relations with Yi Sang-sŏl, Yi Pŏm-yun and Chŏng Sun-man, leaders of the Seoul faction in Vladivostok. At first, Chŏng An-rip cooperated with Kanminhoe members as one of the Kanminhoe initiators by January 1913. In addition, he served as vice-superintendent of the Kilsin Women's School in Juzijie established by Korean Christians in early 1913. Chŏng was also a member of the Chinese-Korean Joint Christian Mission which Yi Tong-hwi organized in August 1913.[269] However, by the fall of 1913, Chŏng An-rip had publicly opposed the Kanminhoe, the majority of whose members were from Hamgyŏng Provinces, arguing that the Kanminhoe should be in the control of peasants, and not of anti-Japanese activists.[270]

From the fall of 1913, the Japanese utilized the conflicts among Koreans to their benefit and began to organize the Peasant Association [Nongminhoe]. This association recruited Korean peasants with the purpose of opposing the Kanminhoe. Under the Chientao Agreement, Koreans could purchase and own land. As a result, the Chinese authorities considered the Peasant Association under Japanese control as an imminent threat.[271] In this context, the Chinese local council [*defang yishihui*] decided to prohibit Koreans from selling and purchasing land.[272]

At the end of October 1913, the Kanminhoe dispatched members to every Korean village and took a census. They also collected 30 *qian* from every household with Chinese policemen accompanying the Kanminhoe members.[273] At this period, the Nongmugye and the Konggyohoe agreed to unite in opposition to the Kanminhoe. In particular, the incident at the Kilsin Women's School led Kim Chŏng-gyu and Chi Chang-hoe of the Konggyohoe and Hong Cha-mun of the Nongmugye to agree to submit petitions and accusations against the Kanminhoe to the Chinese authorities.[274] In December 1913, members of the Nongmugye and the Konggyohoe criticized the Kanminhoe, particularly, Yi Tong-ch'un, Kim Rip and To Sŏng [Yu Ch'an-hŭi] who were key members, in their sporadic appeals to the various levels of the local Chinese authorities in Yanji and Jilin. Accusations leveled against Kanminhoe members included: the dissolution of the Sasuk Kaeryanghoe (September 1912) and the "beatings" of its members; misappropriation of funds by Yi Tong-ch'un, the President of the Educational Association; "threatening farmers who did not want to join the Kanminhoe with expulsion from Chinese territory"; "forced extortion of 30 *qian* from Koreans at the time of the census"; "dissolution of the Konggyohoe meeting and the beatings of its members (November 1913)."[275]

The behavior of local Chinese officials and land proprietors who extorted money from Korean farmers in the name of the Kanminhoe, also worsened the anti-Kanminhoe mood among Korean peasants, who were easily manipulated and inspired by the Nongmugye leaders for anti-Kanminhoe purposes.[276] At last, the Nongmugye leaders including Ch'oe Nam-gi and Hong Cha-mun distributed leaflets criticizing the Kanminhoe and requested a gathering in Juzijie with the purpose of protesting to the Chinese authorities. On January 7, 1914, more than 2,000 farmers, who were inspired by the leaders of the Nongmugye, gathered in Jiawanzi, Yanji Prefecture, and boasted they would kill key members of the Kanminhoe and set fire to its office building. They requested the magistrate of Yanji to prohibit the Kanminhoe from collecting 30 *qian* as well. Most of them, however, dispersed immediately when 60 Chinese policemen and 100 soldiers came and 300 Koreans were arrested. According to the investigation of the Chinese authorities, most of the Korean farmers (except for

TABLE 2. 10

Executive Members of the Kanminhoe (Feb. 4, 1914)

	Position	Age	Birthplace (Province)	Years of Residence	Address
Paek Sun	Pres.	51	Seoul (K)	4	Helong
Cho Hŭi-rim	Vice-Pres.	43	Hamhŭng (S. H.)	?	Yanji
Kim Ha-sŏk	Gen. Sec.	29	Kilchu (N. H.)	4	Yanji
Pak Ch'ang-ik	Secretary	22	Puryŏng (N. H.)	?	Yanji
Pak Hak-rin	Finance	30	?	?	Yanji
Chang Ki-yŏng	Census	28	Changdan (K)	4	Yanji
Yi Pyŏng-hwi	Education	31	Hoeryŏng (N. H.)	4	Helong
Im Sang-ch'o	Law	35	Hamhŭng (S. H.)	?	Yanji
Hyŏn Yŏng-ju	Council	25	Seoul (K)	?	?
Council Members: Yi Tong-ch'un, Yi Sŭng-gyo and other 28 members.					
External Affairs: Pak Tong-wŏn, Pak Se-ho					

Notes Birthplaces
N. H.: North Hamgyŏng Province, **S. H.**: South Hamgyŏng Province, **K**: Kyŏnggi Province

Sources "Baogao disihao" [Report no. 4], KIHA, Document no. 6393-11 (Feb. 2, 1914); *Kwŏnŏp Sinmun*, 8 Mar. 1914, p. 2.

a few) came with no exact purpose and did not have any complaints about the Kanminhoe's collection of 30 *qian*. Hong Cha-mun also failed to provide evidence regarding the Kanminhoe's extortion to the Chinese investigators. Nevertheless, the demonstration forced the Chinese authorities to prohibit the Kanminhoe from collecting 30 *qian* from Korean peasants.[277]

On February 4, 1914, 700 Kanminhoe members held a general meeting in response to the Nongmugye Incident on January 7. At the meeting, it was decided that the qualifications of new members will be examined (whereas previously any Korean resident could join) in order to prevent pro-Japanese "elements" from infiltrating the association and causing problems. Yi Tong-ch'un, Kim Rip and To

Sŏng, who had been the main targets of accusations leveled by the Nongmugye and Konggyohoe, were excluded from the newly-elected executive members, although they remained council members. Like previous executive members, most of the new executive members were anti-Japanese activists who had recently immigrated from Korea (see Table 2. 10).[278]

Shortly after the general meeting, the Kanminhoe organized a public meeting where about 10,000 Koreans gathered in Juzijie in order to discuss the issue of naturalization. The meeting elected Yi Tong-ch'un and Kim Rip as Korean representatives to Beijing. Yi and Kim went to Beijing and met President Yuan Shi-kai. Yuan ordered the Ministry of Internal Affairs to support Koreans in obtaining Chinese citizenship. Yi and Kim returned to North Chientao and began to prepare for the naturalization of all Koreans in China.[279] However, the project was soon frustrated by the dissolution of the Kanminhoe. On March 14, 1914, Tao Bin, the Governor of North Chientao ordered both the Kanminhoe and the Nongmugye to be dissolved following orders from President Yuan Shi-kai that all autonomous organizations be dissolved.[280]

This policy of dissolution came about as a result of the diplomatic pressure by the Japanese. After the Nongmugye incident of January 7, 1914, it was reported in a Japanese newspaper that the Kanminhoe, in cooperation with the Korean *ŭibyŏng* forces and with the support of Chinese and Russian authorities, was planning to attack the Japanese Consulate General in Lonjingcun and kill all Japanese and pro-Japanese Koreans before advancing to north Korea in February or March. In an article dated February 15, the *Kwŏnŏp Sinmun*, a Korean newspaper in Vladivostok, rebutted the report as fabrication by the Japanese who wanted justification for action against the Kanminhoe.[281]

Korean fears became a reality within a month of the article. Stating that the Kanminhoe and the Nongmugye would bring about "bad influence to the Japanese administration in Korea," Japanese Consul General in Longjingcun strongly requested that Tao Bin dissolve the two organizations.[282]

Even after the order of dissolution, however, the Kanminhoe and the Nongmugye factions continued to raise accusations of legal misconducts against each other to the Chinese authorities. The local branches of the two Korean organizations also continued with their local activities.[283] On March 26, 1914, one hundred and forty-two former leaders of the Kanminhoe submitted an appeal to Tao Bin to investigate the accusations made by the Nongmugye leaders. In the appeal, the Kanminhoe leaders refuted the accusations listed in the petitions of the Nongmugye in detail and requested the Chinese government to punish the leaders of the Nongmugye, including Hong Cha-mun, Ch'oe Nam-hun, and Kim U-jong for slander.[284] The Nongmugye also repeatedly appealed to the Chinese authorities to fire Yi Tong-ch'un and Pak Tong-wŏn, who as key Kanminhoe members worked as interpreters for the local Chinese officials, and also asked that Kim Rip and To Sŏng be expelled from Chinese territory and to change the perception of the Nongmugye as pro-Japanese.[285]

In order to resolve the conflicts between the two Korean organizations, Tao Bin ordered an investigation of the accusations submitted by the Nongmugye members and to interview representatives of the two associations.[286] Based on the reports submitted by three magistrates of Yanji, Helong and Wangqing, Tao Bin concluded in a report to the Military-Governor in Jilin that the accusations made by the Nongmugye members were completely groundless and while also rejecting rumors of the Nongmugye cooperating with the Japanese.[287]

2. In the Russian Far East

a. Kwŏnŏhoe [Work Promotion Association] in Vladivostok

The anti-annexation movement was the last significant undertaking led by conservative loyalists including Yu In-sŏk and Yi Sang-sŏl, most of whom were from the central regions of Korea. In their struggle, they tried to combine two major avenus upon which conservative loyalists had relied since 1907: the armed attacks on north Korea and gaining the diplomatic support of the Western Powers. The collapse of the Chosŏn dynasty, however, contributed to the eventual weakening of their leadership within the anti-Japanese movement. Furthermore, the increasing political rapprochement between Russia and Japan after the second Russo-Japanese Agreement in July 1910 removed opportunities for the *ŭibyŏng* leaders to utilize the Russian territory as the base for their armed conflict. In particular, the Russo-Japanese Treaty of Extradition (June 1, 1911) included a secret agreement whereby Russia and Japan agreed to extradite political criminals.[288] As a result, the Russian authorities were not in the position to tolerate any open hostile activities by Korean patriots in Russia against Japan. Gondatti, the Governor-General of the Primorye, pointed out that the Russo-Japanese Treaty of Extradition gave Japan a "serious measure in its struggle against the Korean insurgents" and eliminated "the threat of conflict with Japan in the near future."[289] It became apparent that unless Russia came into direct military conflict with Japan, there would be no tolerance for Koreans to engage in military activities against Japan from Russian territory.

In addition, the Korean population, (in particular, the wealthy and influential *wŏnhoin* Koreans) eventually came to distrust the *ŭibyŏng* movement as represented by Yi Pŏm-yun. These factors resulted in naturalized Koreans in Russia not being able to be easily utilized and mobilized by the leaders of the "immediate advancement party." Non-naturalized Koreans, who were more insecure in their legal status, were even more difficult to mobilize. Governor-General Gondatti had encouraged Koreans to get Russian citizenship, but at the same time, took a strict policy against non-naturalized foreign laborers. In addition, by the time of Japan's annexation of Korea, non-naturalized Koreans had to overcome the Japanese claims that those who were Koreans now became Japanese subjects after the annexation. Over time as the strategies of the "immediate advance party" who advocated an immediate and decisive military showdown became more and more unrealistic. The methods proposed by the "gradual advancement party" or "new knowledge clique," who advocated a long-term plan emphasizing educational, cultural and industrious activities until an opportune time in the future, came to be seen as more convincing and pragmatic. The campaign for naturalization eventually became accepted as an effective way for Koreans to protect themselves from the Japanese interference by obtaining legal protection from Russia.[290]

In light of these developments, the Kungminhoe, which had advocated and implemented the strategy of the "gradual advancement," seemed to be in position to take over the leadership of the Korean nationalist movement in the Primorye. The leadership of the Kungminhoe was also further reinforced when An Ch'ang-ho, Yi Kap and Yi Kang came to Vladivostok by way of Qingdao, China in the summer of 1910. However, due to their republicanism and close connection with Americans, particularly Presbyterian missionaries, put the leaders of the Kungminhoe at odds with Russian authorities. The increasing rivalry between Russia and America with regards to interests in Manchuria, particularly after the second Russo-Japanese Agreement (July 1910), which was expedited largely because of the American Secretary of State Knox's proposals for the neutralization of all railroads in Manchuria,[291] further intensified suspicion of Kungminhoe leaders by the Russian authority. Local Russian authorities worried Kungminhoe leaders might carry out pro-American propaganda among Koreans in the Primorye. According to Yi Kang, shortly after their arrival in the summer of 1910, An Ch'ang-ho and Kungminhoe leaders met the head of the Russian *gendarme* in order to resolve this issue.[292]

The attitude of the Russian authorities toward the Kungminhoe leaders is summarized in a report dated February 26, 1911 (Russian calendar), by R. P. Sherbakov, the head of the Ussurisk Railroad *gendarme*-police to the Military-Governor of the Primorye, Svechin:

> At the present time, the association [Kungminhoe] is quickly growing to the detriment of Russian influence over the minds of Koreans. Obviously, a certain strong hand is directing the activities of this association, certainly not to the favor of Russia. Only through the permission by the Russian authorities of the legal Korean association, which they [Koreans] repeatedly requested, can we rescue our Koreans from the influence of the Japanese or Americans and win them over permanently to the Russian side.[293]

The report makes clear that the Kungminhoe was losing favor with the local Russian authorities. It implies the existence of other groups which were vying with the Russian authorities for recognition as the official "Korean association" in the region. There were in fact three major groups of Korean nationalists who were competing for leadership among Koreans in 1911. The first group was the *Kihop'a* or *Kyŏngp'a* (Seoul faction)[294] which was formed after Yi Sang-sŏl came to Vladivostok from America in the fall of 1909. Its unity was well demonstrated at the time of Chŏng Sun-man's killing of Yang Sŏng-ch'un in early 1910. Most members of the Seoul faction were sons of high-ranking officials who had gone to St. Petersburg to study at Russian military schools or various other schools at the time of Russia's supremacy in Korea. During the Russo-Japanese War, about forty to fifty of those students served in the Russian military as interpreters or officers and after the war, they were employed by the Russian *gendarme*, police and administrative agencies in the Primorye.[295] Yi Sang-sŏl, the leader of the Seoul faction was working as a part-time advisor at a Russian information agency in Khabarovsk and had helped members of his faction get hired as information agents.[296] In Vladivostok, there were more than 10 members of the Seoul faction get including Yun Il-byŏng and Ku Tŏk-sŏng (also Ku Tŏk-sŭng) who worked as agents or interpreters at the Russian *gendarme*.[297] Chang To-bin, who came to Vladivostok in 1912, had commented that the Seoul faction's spirit of solidarity was too strong to be broken.[298]

The second group was the Ch'ŏngnyŏn Kŭnŏphoe (Youth Association for Diligence and Industry)[299] which was organized at the latest around early 1911 by young Korean nationalists including Han Hyŏng-gwŏn, Yu Chin-yul [Nikolai Petrovich Yugai] and Vasilii Kim. Most of these numbers were born in Russia or had come to Russia long before the recent immigrants. Although they lacked knowledge about Korea, they were heavily influenced by anti-Japanese nationalist activities since 1905 and were not susceptible to regional factionalism. These young Koreans had demonstrated their patriotism and solidarity in February 1910 when they worked to pacify factional struggles and rose to take over the management of the *Taedong Kongbo* after its suspension due to internecine disputes after the Chŏng Sun-man incident. About ten months after the suspension of the *Taedong Kongbo*, they obtained permission from the Military-Governor of the Primorye to start publishing their bi-weekly newspaper, the *Taeyangbo* (Ocean Gazette) on June 18, 1911,[300] with Yu Chin-yul and Sin Ch'ae-ho as its publisher and chief editor respectively.[301] Some key members including Han Hyŏng-gwŏn and Ham Tong-ch'ŏl were Kungminhoe members and as a result of the support of An Ch'ang-ho as well as their cooperation with other Kungminhoe members including Chŏng Chae-gwan and Yi Kang in the *Taedong Kongbo*, these young Koreans were favorably inclined toward the Kungminhoe.

The third group was the *Pukp'a* or Northern faction led by Yi Chong-ho. Yi Chong-ho was born in 1886 in Myŏngch'ŏn, North Hamgyŏng Province, a grandson of Yi Yong-ik, a prominent anti-Japanese minister. Thanks to his grandfather, Yi Chong-ho became a chamberlain of King Kojong at the age of 15 and served in this position about two or three years. Helping his grandfather, Yi Chong-ho became involved in dispatching the secret delegation to the Hague and provided financial assistance to the Sŏbuk Hakhoe (Northwestern Educational Association) and various schools including Posŏng College. He was arrested on a charge of involvement in An Chung-gŭn's assassination of Ito Hirobumi at the end of 1909, before being released in February 1910. After his release, he made his way to Vladivostok by way of Qingdao in August 1910 together with An Ch'ang-ho and Yi Kap.[302] Yi Chong-ho began to strengthen his own group relying on the Hambuk Ch'ŏng-nyŏnhoe (North

Hamgyŏng Province Youth Association), which had been organized in June 1910, probably in response to the intensification of regional factionalism between the Seoul and Western factions.[303] According to Yi Kang, key leaders of the New People's Association including An Ch'ang-ho, Yi Chong-ho and Yi Kap, agreed in Qingdao to purchase land in Fengmishan in the eastern part of Manchuria, about 200 miles north of Vladivostok, and develop the region as a future base for self-sufficient Korean communities and a military training school. After they arrived at Vladivostok, however, Yi Chong-ho withdrew his promise to provide funds for the plan. According to Yi Kang, it was Kim Rip and Yun Hae who persuaded Yi Chong-ho not to go to Fengmishan and instead work together with people from Hamgyŏng Province in Vladivostok. An Ch'ang-ho was greatly disappointed at the failure of the plan and returned to San Francisco in the spring of 1911.[304] At around that time, Yi Chong-ho was said to have 200,000 *yen* (about 100,000 dollars) which his grandfather, Yi Yong-ik, had saved in the Hollinger Bank in order to buy rice from Vietnam.[305]

From March 1911, Yi Chong-ho, with the permission of the Russian authorities, began to expand the North Hamgyŏng Youth Association into a mass Korean organization.[306] Yi Chong-ho called his close associate Kim Rip from North Chientao to Vladivostok,[307] and dispatched his close associates to Korean villages in various regions to gain supporters.

Yi Chong-ho also succeeded in obtaining support from Ch'oe Chae-hyŏng, Hong Pŏm-do and Sin Ch'ae-ho.[308] Finally, on June 1, 1911, Yi Chong-ho's group established an initiating committee for the Kwŏnŏphoe, with Ch'oe Chae-hyŏng and Hong Pŏm-do as its President and Vice-President, and Kim Rip as the Chief of

TABLE 2. 11

Initiating Committee of the Kwŏnŏphoe and Kŭnŏphoe

Kwŏnŏphoe (June 1, 1911)		Kŭnŏphoe (July 16, 1911)
Pres.	Ch'oe Chae-hyŏng	Ch'oe Chae-hyŏng
Vice-Pres.	Hong Pŏm-do	-
General Affairs	Kim Rip	Kim Rip
Secretary	Cho Ch'ang-ho	Yi Kŭn-yong
Finance	Hŏ T'ae-hwa	Vasilii Kim
Council Members		
Gregory Kim, Ŏm In-sŏp, Yu Ki-ch'an, O Ch'ang-hwan, Cho Chang-wŏn, Kim Ki-ryong, Kim T'ae-bong		Kim Kyu-sŏp, Kim Hyŏng-gwŏn, Han Hyŏng-gwŏn, Yi Hyŏng-uk, Kim Ch'i-bo, Cho Ch'ang-ho,
		Newspaper: Yi Chong-ho, Yu Chin-yul

Source *Kwŏnŏp Sinmun*, 19 Dec. 1912, p. 3.

General Affairs (see Table 2. 11). The Kŭnŏphoe group which was facing financial difficulties in publishing the *Taeyangbo*, finally agreed to unite with Yi Chong-ho's group and joined the new initiating committee for the Kŭnŏphoe on July 16, 1911 (see Table 2. 11).[309] Yi Chong-ho also received the support of wealthy *wŏnhoin prodriadchik*s including Mun Ch'ang-bŏm in Nikol'sk-Ussurisk and Kim Hak-man and Kim Pyŏng-hak [Nikolai Ivanovich], the former and present Chairman respectively of the Korean Residents' Association in Vladivostok. Through Kim Hak-man and Kim Pyŏng-hak, who were in close contact with Yi Sang-sŏl, Yi Chong-ho sought the cooperation of the Seoul faction as well. Yi Chong-ho also established his own commercial shop at Cho Ch'ang-ho's house, the main office of the Kŭnŏphoe, in order to secure financial stability.[310] Yi Chong-ho also provided 5,000 rubles to the construction of the building of the Korean People's School [Hanmin Hakkyo], the biggest Korean school in the New Korean Village. This school was managed by the Korean Residents' Association.[311] In the middle of 1911, thanks to the support of Koreans from Hamgyŏng Provinces (an overwhelming majority of the Korean population in the Primorye) and his own financial power, Yi Chong-ho and his group consolidated the leadership among Koreans by increasing their influence in activities such as newspapers, education and commerce.[312]

Yi Chong-ho's increasing influence was concurrent with the internecine struggles among other Korean groups. The main targets were Kungminhoe leaders including Chŏng Chae-gwan, Yi Kang, Kim Sŏng-mu, Paek Wŏn-bo and Hwang Kong-do. Yi Sang-sŏl's Seoul faction made accusations to the Russian police four Kungminhoe leaders (An Ch'ang-ho, Chŏng Chae-gwan, Yi Kang and Kim Sŏng-mu) of instigating the murder of Chŏng Sun-man.[313] Chŏng Sun-man, the leader of the Seoul faction, had been imprisoned after he had killed Yang Sŏng-ch'un. He was released after eight months on February 7, 1910.[314] Upset with the lenient punishment of Chŏng, Yang Sŏng-ch'un's brother and wife killed Chŏng on June 13, 1911.[315] Based on accusations made by the Seoul faction, the Russian police issued a warrant for the arrest of Yi Kang and Chŏng Chae-gwan.[316] Paek Wŏn-bo was arrested by the Russian *gendarme* on the charge of being a "wandering and beggaring unfavorable person" on June 13 and was released after 15 days.[317] Furthermore, seven Koreans including Yi Pŏm-yun from Irkutsk who had been exiled by the Russian authorities in the fall of 1910 were Seoul faction members and some were involved in the Chŏng Sun-man incident, and had returned to Vladivostok in July 1911.[318] They were said to have been preparing "dangerous acts" against the Kungminhoe leaders.[319]

Yi Chong-ho's Northern faction joined the Seoul faction in "suppressing" the Kungminhoe leaders (Western faction). Yi Chong-ho accused Chŏng Chae-gwan, Yi Kang, Kim Sŏng-mu and Hwang

Kong-do of being "meddlers in Yi Chong-ho's activities." Kim Sŏng-mu was threatened by the *honghuzi* hired by Yi Chong-ho. Paek Wŏn-bo was even beaten by Ŏm In-sŏp, a close associate of Yi Chong-ho. The two factions led by Yi Chong-ho and Yi Sang-sŏl formed a loose-kint alliance in attacking Kungminhoe leaders in the summer of 1911. During this time Kungminhoe members lamented that "we are surrounded by foes on all sides [*samyŏn ch'oga*]."[320] Many letters sent from Kungminhoe leaders in Vladivostok to An Ch'ang-ho in San Francisco were filled with criticism of Yi Chong-ho and Yi Sang-sŏl and requested financial support necessary to hide themselves from and protect themselves from the hostile environment. Avoiding arrest by Russian authorities, Chŏng Chae-gwan and Yi Kang managed to leave for Chita, while Kim Sŏng-mu was forced to return to Fengmishan in Manchuria. Only Paek Wŏn-bo was able to hide in Vladivostok.[321]

The process of acquiring recognition by the Kwŏnŏphoe initiating committee was not without obstacles. First, Yu Chin-yul, a key member of the *Taeyangbo* was in conflict with Yi Chong-ho and Kim Rip regarding the management of the newspaper resulting in his resignation from the initiating committee.[322] To worsen matters, the printing types of the *Taeyangbo* were stolen and all printing was suspended.[323] Kim Kyu-sŏp, Ch'a Sŏk-po and Ch'oe Pong-jun who had a relationship with the *Taeyangbo* also joined Yu Chin-yul in rejecting the initiating committee.[324]

More serious opposition to the initiating committee of the Kŭnŏphoe came from Yi Sang-sŏl's Seoul faction. Yi Sang-sŏl separately applied to the Russian authorities for recognition as the "Korean association" with the name of the Kwŏnŏphoe.[325] At the same time, Yi Sang-sŏl interfered with the application of the initiating committee of the Kŭnŏphoe by utilizing his faction's close connection with the Russian authorities. In this situation, the Military-Governor of the Primorye and the head of Vladivostok *gendarme* summoned and advised Yi Chong-ho and Yi Sang-sŏl, who were also feeling the necessity of compromise, to create a unified "Korean Association."[326]

On November 24, 1911, the Kwŏnŏphoe received official recognition from the Russian authorities[327] under the name of five naturalized Koreans: Viktor Sergeevich Hong [Hong Pyŏng-hwan], Yakov Ivanovich Kim, Roman Ivanovich An, Pavel Pavlovich Hong, and Inokentii Ivanovich Kim.[328] In order to secure and demonstrate its status as "the representative organization of all Koreans in Russia," Yi Sang-sŏl and Kim Rip sought unity and reconciliation with the leaders of the Western faction. In particular, Yi Sang-sŏl sent a letter to Chŏng Chae-gwan in Chita to come to Vladivostok appealing for "unity and solidarity." Hwang Kong-do and Paek Wŏn-bo in Vladivostok joined the Kwŏnŏphoe as well. As a result, a coalition of the three main factions was formed.[329]

The Kwŏnŏphoe was officially founded at the first general meeting held at the Korean People's School in the New Korean Village on December 19, 1911, and elected executive members (See Table 2. 12).[330] The declared purpose of the Kwŏnŏphoe was to "teach Koreans to observe economy in life, to impart education, to elevate ideas, consciousness and faithfulness to Great Russia."[331] According to the recognized regulations of the association, its membership was limited to naturalized Koreans and to elementary and intermediate students. The military and navy employees were not allowed to become members. The scope of its activities was confined only to the Primorye. The Russian authorities reserve the power to dissolve the association at any time.[332]

The composition of the executive membership, for the most part, balanced the three main factions, Northern, Seoul, Western. The key organ of the Kwŏnŏphoe structure was the council, which acted as the actual decision making body when the general meeting was out of session. The council was headed by Yi Sang-sŏl and Yi Chong-ho as its Chair and Vice-Chair respectively. The other members were shared equally by the Northern and Seoul factions (see Table 2. 12).

The declared purpose and name of the association "*Kwŏnŏp*" ("work promotion") were intended to avoid possible interference from the Japanese. The Kwŏnŏphoe was a self-administrative organization of Koreans in the Primorye under the control of Russian authorities, but was also an organization for anti-Japanese activities of Korean nationalists. This political consideration was also understood by the local Russian officials including Governor-General Gondatti.[333] As we can see in Table 2. 12, the majority of the executive members were non-naturalized Korean nationalists. Although this was obviously contrary to the recognized regulation, the Russian authorities allowed this.

In particular, Governor-General Gondatti considered Koreans immigrants as reliable elements and useful for the political and economic interests of Russia. Because of their potential usefulness at the time of conflict with Japan, he encouraged the naturalization of Koreans and patronized their activities.[334] Koreans greatly welcomed the appointment of Gondatti as the Governor-General of the Priamur. In reporting such policies of Gondatti as permission for Koreans to work in gold-mines, railroad construction and building the New Korean Village, the *Taeyangbo*, in 1911, even praised Gondatti as the "Living Buddha."[335] Gondatti visited the New Korean Village on February 23, 1912, and more than 3,000 Koreans held a big welcoming meeting. In his address to the Koreans, Gondatti praised the moralistic and modest characteristics of Korean immigrants and encouraged the social,

TABLE 2. 12

Executive Members of the Kwŏnŏphoe (Dec. 19, 1911)

	(a) Position	(b) yŏho / wŏnho	(c) Group
Presidium (4)			
(1) Yu In-sŏk	Head Pres.	*yŏho*	S
(2) Yi Pŏm-yun	President	*yŏho*	S
(3) Kim Hak-man	President	*wŏnho*	P
(4) Ch'oe Chae-hyŏng	President	*wŏnho*	P
Council (9)			
(5) Yi Sang-sŏl	Chairman	*yŏho*	S
(6) Yi Chong-ho	Vice-Chairman	*yŏho*	P
(7) Kim Rip	Gen. Affairs	*yŏho*	P
(8) Han Hyŏng-gwŏn	Gen. Affairs	*yŏho*	T (W)
(9) Kim Ki-ryong	Finance	*wŏnho*	W
(10) Yi Min-bok	Secretary	*yŏho*	S
(11) Yi Pŏm-sŏk	Member	*yŏho*	S
(12) Hong Pyŏng-hwan	Member	*wŏnho*	P
(13) Kim Man-song	Member	*yŏho*	W
Executives (11)			
(14) Chŏng Chae-gwan	Education	*yŏho*	W
(15) Ch'oe Man-hak	Work Arrangement	*wŏnho*	P
(16) Cho Ch'ang-ho	Economy	*yŏho*	P
(17) Hwang Kong-do	Religion	*wŏnho*	W
(18) Sin Ch'ae-ho	Publication	*yŏho*	T (W)
(19) Yun Il-byŏng	Inspection	*wŏnho*	S
(20) Kim Ch'i-bo	Communication	*yŏho*	W
(21) Kim Pyŏng-hak	Reception	*wŏnho*	P
(22) Yi Nam-gi	Record	*yŏho*	S
(23) Hong Pŏm-do	Police	*yŏho*	P
(24) Ko Sang-jun	Relief	*yŏho*	W

Notes (b) *wŏnho*: Russian citizens (8). Among eight *wŏnhoin*, Kim Ki-ryong, Hwang Kong-do and Yun Il-byŏng had Russian citizenship, but these three recently immigrated to Russia.

yŏho: Non-naturalized Koreans (16)

(c) Group

S: Seoul faction represented by Yi Sang-sŏl and mostly loyalist conservatives from central Korea (7), **P**: Northern faction represented by Yi Chong-ho and mostly liberalists from Northeastern Korea (9), **W**: Western faction represented by Chŏng Chae-gwan and mostly liberalists from Northwestern Korea (P'yŏngan and Hwanghae Province) (6), **T**: *Taeyangbo*. Kŭnŏphoe group (2). Favorable toward Western faction

Sources *Kwŏnŏp Sinmun*, 19 Dec. 1912, p. 3; Paek Wŏn-bo, letter to An Ch'ang-ho, 29 Nov. 1912, *Tosan An Ch'ang-ho charyojip*, vol. 1, pp. 172-73; Boris Dmitrievich Pak, *Koreitsy v Rossiiskoi imperii*, p. 210.

educational and cultural activities of Koreans.[336] Gondatti's statement, "Korean who does not love Korea will not be welcomed in Russia either" in his address to Koreans at the office building of the Kwŏnŏphoe, was enough to impress nationalist Koreans in Russia.[337]

On February 29, Yi Sang-sŏl, Yi Chong-ho, Chŏng Chae-gwan, and Han Hyŏng-gwŏn visited Gondatti in order to show their appreciation for his approval of the establishment of the Kwŏnŏphoe. During this visit, Gondatti agreed, at their invitation, to become an honorable member of the Kwŏnŏphoe. On that day, three other Russians, G. V. Podstavin (Korean language professor at the Eastern Institute in Vladivostok), B. M. Polianovsky (secretary of Vladivostok Theological Consistorial) and I. F. Diukov (member of the Vladivostok City Council) were also made honorable members.[338] On December 11, 1912, M. M. Manakin, Military-Governor of the Primorye, and Redin, Police Inspector-General, were additionally added to the list of honorary members.[339] Gondatti expressed his support for the group by delivering a telegram through Podstavin congratulating the Kwŏnŏphoe on its first anniversary on December 20, 1912.[340]

Due to generous policies of the Russian authorities, the Kwŏnŏphoe was able to strengthen its activities in the region. First, the Kwŏnŏphoe obtained the permission of the Military-Governor to publish its weekly organ, the *Kwŏnŏp Sinmun* on March 31, 1912 and began publication on May 5, 1912. The editor was I. F. Diukov, an honorary member of the Kwŏnŏphoe and former publisher of the *Taedong Kongbo*[341] while Sin Ch'ae-ho became the chief editor until his resignation on September 1912. Afterwards, Kim Ha-gu and Yi Sang-sŏl succeeded to the position and other nationalists including Yun Hae and Kye Pong-u worked as reporters. The *Kwŏnŏp Sinmun* continued publication without interruption until August 1914 when it was suspended by the Russian authorities after a total of 126 issues. Its circulation number was around 930 copies in 1912, but this increased to 1,400 by August 1914.[342] Copies were distributed not only to Korean villages in Russia, but also in Korea, China and America. The *Kwŏnŏp Sinmun*, as the successor of the Korean newspapers the *Haejo Sinmun*, *Taedong Kongbo*, and *Taeyangbo*, played a key role in supporting the activities of the Kwŏnŏphoe by spreading new knowledge, informing Koreans on international politics, promoting naturalization, and inspiring patriotism among Koreans in Russia. In the first half of the 1910s, the *Kwŏnŏp Sinmun* was well-known as one of the three major anti-Japanese Korean newspapers together with the publications of the Kungminhoe, the *Sinhan Minbo* (San Francisco), and the *Sinhan Kukpo* (Honolulu).[343]

By the second half of 1912, the Kwŏnŏphoe started to establish its branches and chapters in various Korean communities in the Primorye. In September 29, 1912, the Kwŏnŏphoe appointed Yi Chong-ho, Pak Yŏng-bin and Ŏm In-sŏp as its branch organizers.[344] From the second half of 1912 to August 1914, branches were established in more than 10 major Korean communities such as Nikolaevsk-na-Amure, Khabarovsk, Sinel'nikovo (in Suifen), Iman (Dal'nerechensk), Nikol'sk-Ussurisk (Ussurisk), Novokievsk (Kraskino), Daubikhe (Auchino), Grodekovo (Pogranichinyi), Taudemi (in Suchan), K'ŭnyŏng (Vladimiro-Akexandrovskoe in Suchan), Sinyŏng-dong (Nikolaevka in Suchan), Lavliu (Luk'yanovka), Mongugai (Barabash).[345] The membership increased from the original 300 members to more than 10,000 by July 1914.[346] At the end of 1913, in response to the request of the Kwŏnŏphoe leaders to establish a branch in Blagoveshchensk in the Amur Province, Gondatti favorably advised them to apply to the Military-Governor of the Amur Province.[347]

The Kwŏnŏphoe strove to support and encourage educational activities. As a result of these efforts, by February 1914, about 10 schools and 1,000 students were under the direct management of the Kwŏnŏphoe.[348] The Kwŏnŏphoe also established Sunday reading and lecture programs in the New Korean Village with the purpose of "satisfying and developing the theological requirements" necessary for the naturalization of Koreans.[349] The educational department of the Kwŏnŏphoe also took over the management of the Korean People's School [Hanmin Hakkyo] in the New Korean Village when the Korean Residents' Association merged into the Kwŏnŏphoe on March 15, 1914.[350]

The Kwŏnŏphoe functioned as a central the administrative agency for Russian authorities. The Military-Governor's office requested the Kwŏnŏphoe to work as proxy agency to help non-naturalized Koreans get Russian citizenship. In early December 1912, the Kwŏnŏphoe immediately appointed its member Pak Yŏng-bin as chief-executive for naturalization.[351] As a direct result of the activities of the Kwŏnŏphoe, about 4,000 Koreans obtained Russian citizenship during this period (see Table 1. 8 in Chapter 1). The Kwŏnŏphoe was also assigned by the Russian Military-Governor's office to take a census of Korean residents in Vladivostok in March 1913.[352]

One of the most ambitious projects the Kwŏnŏphoe undertook was to build a Korean agricultural complex for newly naturalized Koreans in Lavliu [Luk'yanovka] which was located north of the Iman River (currently Bolshaya Ussurka River). On August 7, 1912, the Kwŏnŏphoe dispatched Chŏn Che-ak and Pak Tong-wŏn to the Iman region to find land suitable for the complex. On September 14, based on their report, the Kwŏnŏphoe applied to the immigration department of the Governor-General Office in Khabarovsk for an allotment of unoccupied lands along the Iman River and received permission on December 1, 1912. The Kwŏnŏphoe immediately established a special agricultural committee with Yi Chong-ho as its Chairman and began to gather stockholders.[353] At the same time, the Kwŏnŏphoe applied for detailed plans such as the establishment of agricultural schools, organizing a self-defence corps, and stationing village policemen.[354] Throughout 1914, the Kwŏnŏphoe endeavored to promote the project by dispatching its members and making arrangements for settlements, but less than 100 households settled in Lavliu.[355]

The official support of Russian authorities was the single most crucial factor for the existence and activities of the Kwŏnŏphoe. As a result, the Kwŏnŏphoe made every effort to satisfy Russian authorities. In January 1913, by the request of the Minister of Internal Affairs, the Military-Governor of the Primorye asked the Kwŏnŏphoe to dispatch representatives of Koreans to a ceremony for the 300th anniversary of the Romanov dynasty. The Kwŏnŏphoe and the Korean Residents' Association jointly organized a fundraising committee for the delegation of 42 members with Kim To-yŏ as its Chairman and elected Yi Chong-ho, Pak Yŏng-bin and Diukov as "representatives of Koreans in the Far East."[356] Obviously concerned about possible trouble with the Japanese, the Russian authorities, however, changed their mind and did not allow the Korean delegation to go to St. Petersburg.[357] Instead, they allowed the Korean delegation to participate in a local ceremony held in March 1913 in Vladivostok.[358]

After June 1913, Koreans in the Primorye began to discuss a plan for the fiftieth anniversary ceremony of Korean immigration to Russia.[359] At the end of 1913, four *wŏnhoin* leaders, Ch'oe Chaehyŏng (President of the Kwŏnŏphoe), Ch'oe Pong-jun, Ch'ae Tu-sŏng and Pak Yŏng-hwi, organized an initiating committee for the ceremony. The committee asked Korean communities in the Primorye to dispatch representatives (one or two from every *p'ungsok*) to Vladivostok. From February 3 to 7, 1914, 25 representatives from eight places, Suifen, Novokievsk, Nikol'sk-Ussurisk, Suchan, Daubikhe, Rip'o (currently Osinovka), and the Kwŏnŏphoe, the Korean Residents' Association in New Korean Village and three Russian honorary members (Podstavin, Diukov, Polianovsky) held a meeting and decided to hold the ceremony in Vladivostok on October 4, the date which Lieutenant Rezanov reported the existence of the first group of Korean immigrants to the Russian authorities. The meeting also decided to build a monument in Pos'et (Koreans called Mokhŏu or Mokhŏwi') and to publish a history of Korean immigration both in Korean and Russian.[360] The initiating committee was also able to obtain official permission for the ceremony from Gondatti.[361] On April 7, 1914, more than 30 representatives from various Korean communities held the second meeting of the initiating committee in Nikol'sk-Ussurisk. They organized a committee with Ch'oe Chae-hyŏng as its President for a celebration of Korean immigration to the Primorsk with 22 members, mostly *wŏnhoin* Koreans. A plan finalizing a detailed plan including the budget and fundraising measures for the ceremony was also worked out at this meeting.[362] Results from the meeting were published in the *Kwŏnŏp Sinmun* in the name of the committee on April 26, 1914.[363]

1914 was also the 10th anniversary of the outbreak of the Russo-Japanese War. The Amur Railroad was supposed to be completed at the end of 1914 and rumors of a second Russo-Japanese War spread among Russians, particularly among low-rank soldiers.[364] War between Russia and Japan was exactly what Korean nationalists had been anticipating for a long time as they believed it would provide a crucial opportunity for the restoration of an independent Korea.

After the end of 1913, the expectation of a war of retribution by Russia against Japan escalated among Korean nationalists.[365] In his letter to An Ch'ang-ho in America, Yi Tong-hwi, who had come from North Chientao in early October 1913, also wrote: "Entering this year [1914], regardless of inside or outside Korea [everybody] is voicing "*kabin* (the year of 1914)" "*kabin*" and preparing for *kabin* and as a result, this year will not pass without any event."[366] In another letter, Yi Tong-hwi maintained that it would be inevitable to take the strategy of "immediate advancenment" [*kŭpchinjuŭi*] and Korean nationalists both in Russia and China were cooperating in this way.[367]

Through the initiative of Yi Tong-hwi, the Korean nationalists, both in the Primorye and Manchuria, including Yi Chong-ho, Yi Sang-sŏl, Chŏng Chae-gwan and Yi Tong-nyŏng, organized a secret military organization, the Korean Restoration Military Government [Taehan Kwangbokkun Chŏngbu] with the purpose of preparing for the "second Russo-Japanese war"; training soldiers, purchasing weapons and organizing military troops. Yi Sang-sŏl was appointed as the *Chŏngdoryŏng* (President) and Kye Pong-u, Yi Tong-hwi's sworn brother and reporter for the *Kwŏnŏp Sinmun*, worked as the chief-secretary.[368] The title '*Chŏngdoryŏng*' was borrowed from the Korean traditional book of prophecy, *Chŏnggamnok*, which foretold the demise of the Chosŏn (Yi) dynasty which would be succeeded by the Chŏng dynasty.[369] The organizers utilized the prophecy of the *Chŏnggamnok*, whose story was widely known and believed among Korean peasants in the Primorye,[370] in order to inspire hope for the restoration of Korea.[371]

The Military Government divided Russia and Manchuria into three military districts: 1st district (the Primorye), 2nd district (North Chientao) and 3rd district (West Chientao).[372] After Yi Sang-sŏl withdrew from both the Kwŏnŏphoe and the Restoration Military Government at the end of 1913, Yi Tong-hwi became the *Chŏngdoryŏng* of the Military Government.[373] Yi Tong-hwi himself composed an anti-Japanese song called "*Kabinga*" ("Song of the year of 1914") and distributed it to Korean schools in the Primorye for use during physical training.[374] The leaders of the Korean Restoration Military Government planned to raise military funds at the time of the ceremony for the fiftieth anniversary of Korean immigration to Russia.[375]

Although Korean nationalists in the Primorye enjoyed some freedom in their activities, these military activities in particular, were strictly monitored by the Russian authorities who wanted to avoid unnecessary trouble with Japan.[376] As a result, the activities of the Kwŏnŏphoe were curbed to focus on education, culture and industry. However, even such legal and peaceful activities were constant targets of diplomatic pressure from Japanese government. The Japanese repeatedly requested that the Russian authorities check on Korean nationalists and dissolve the Kwŏnŏphoe. As soon as one month after the establishment of the Kwŏnŏphoe, in February 1912, Otori Fujitarō, the Japanese Consul General in Vladivostok, requested that Gondatti restrict the activities of the Kwŏnŏphoe, anti-Japanese Koreans and the distribution of Korean newspapers. Fujitarō eventually got Gondatti to agree.[377] In early 1914, the Japanese authorities delivered materials related to the anti-Japanese activities of the Kwŏnŏphoe and again requested the dissolution of the association.[378]

A prime example of how Russian and Japanese authorities dealt with the anti-Japanese Korean was the mass arrest of anti-Japanese Korean nationalists when former Japanese Prime Minister, Katsura Tarō, visited Russia in July and August 1912. The Japanese government, which vividly remembered the assassination of Ito Hirobumi by the Korean patriot An Chung-gŭn in Harbin (1909), requested that Russian authorities take proper measures to prevent any attempts by anti-Japanese Koreans to assassinate Katsura. At the end of June 1912, the Japanese delivered to Malevskii-Malevich, the Russian ambassador to Tokyo, a list of 61 anti-Japanese Koreans in Russia and the Chinese Eastern Railroad regions. Malevskii-Malevich in turn forwarded the request of the Japanese government to the Vladivostok military governor, the Irkutsk Governor-General, the Directorate of the Chinese Eastern Railroad and General Martynov.[379]

Upon the receipt of this request, the Russian authorities in Vladivostok, Harbin, and Chita arrested anti-Japanese Koreans on charges of an assassination conspiracy against Katsura. In Vladivostok, the Russian police arrested five Korean nationalists, Yun Hae, Cho Chang-wŏn, Cho Yŏng-jin, Yi Pŏm-sŏk and Yi Ch'un-sik, on June 25 and 26, all of whom were incarcerated until July 18.[380] In Chita, Russian police arrested Yi Kang and several Korean students and released them only after a whole week of confinement.[381] In Harbin, based on the secret Russo-Japanese Treaty of Extradition, Japanese Consul General Honda Ryūhei strongly requested to Dmitry Leonidovich Horvath, the Directorate of the Chinese Eastern Railroad, that he take strict measures against anti-Japanese Koreans. In response on July 11, the Russian police stormed the houses of Korean suspects in 16 places and arrested 88 Koreans, most of whom were attending worship services at church. The Russian authorities ordered the dissolution of Korean nationalist organizations including the Kungminhoe, the Korean Youth Association, and the Mutual Assistance Association [Kongjehoe]. Among those arrested, 18 Koreans, including Chŏng Tae-ho (An Chung-gŭn's close friend), Son Chŏng-do, Chang Su-myŏng and Kim Sŏng-ok, were handed over to the Japanese

Governor-General through the Japanese Consulate General in Harbin.[382]

Even after Katsura's return to Tokyo from St. Petersburg, the Japanese Consulate General, again with the help of Chinese police, arrested seven Korean nationalists and transferred four Koreans including Cho Sŏng-hwan to Seoul.[383] The Japanese police in Seoul failed to find evidence for an assassination conspiracy and instead exiled those 22 Koreans to isolated islands for one year and placed a three-year residence restriction on charges of violation of the Security Law.[384]

In the case of Vladivostok and Chita, the Russian authorities did not directly hand over Korean nationalists to Japanese authorities. In Harbin, however, as noted by Wada Haruki, the Japanese experienced the most effective success from the secret Russo-Japanese Treaty of Extradition.[385] From 1911 to 1917, as Boris Pak has correctly pointed out, Russian authorities in the Primorye did not transfer any anti-Japanese Koreans in response to Japanese requests as agreed in the Russo-Japanese Treaty of Extradition.[386] Attempts by Japanese authorities to use the Russians via the treaty to expel Korean nationalists had mixed results. In March 1913, the Priamur military district staff obtained a secret report which was skillfully falsified by the Japanese. The false report showed Yi Chong-ho taking a census of Koreans in the Primorye at the request of the Japanese Consulate General in Vladivostok, disguising the census as being created internally only for his organization, Kwŏnŏphoe. As a result of the report, Yi Chong-ho was immediately arrested, only to be released soon after the Russians found him innocent.[387]

These types of tactics used by the Japanese authorities were only intensified by the internecine regionalistic factional struggles among Korean nationalists. After the establishment of the Kwŏnŏphoe, the Seoul faction, whose members were working in the Russian *gendarme*, frequently utilized those connections to mollify rival Koreans. In August 1912, Kim Ch'i-gwan, Chŏng Chae-gwan's close associate who was from Yonggang, South P'yŏngan Province, and had taught at the Myŏngdong School in Longjingcun was arrested by the Russian *gendarme* because of accusations by the Seoul faction that he was a Japanese spy.[388] In September 1912, Pak Yŏng-gap, a Kungminhoe leader who had established and managed the Korean Teachers' College in Suchan, was also arrested by the Russian *gendarme* on the same charges. Paek Wŏn-bo (alias Paek Kun-bo), a Kungminhoe leader in Vladivostok, somehow got the Russian officials not transfer Kim and Pak to the Japanese Government-General in Korea.[389]

In November 1913, the Russian *gendarme* also stormed Yi Chong-ho's house and confiscated all the documents of the Kwŏnŏphoe. When the Russian *gendarme* investigated Kim Ha-gu regarding the case of Yi Chong-ho, Koreans came to realize that it was in fact Ku Tŏk-sŏng who accused Yi Chong-ho. As a result of this episode, the Seoul faction lost its credibility among Korean patriots.[390] In early December 1913, it was reported in a Russian newspaper that Yi Sang-sŏl resigned as chief editor in order to provide secret information about Russia and Koreans to the Japanese. Believing that the source of the report was Yi Chong-ho, Yi Sang-sŏl left for Khabarovsk severing all relations with the Kwŏnŏphoe and the Korean Restoration Military Government.[391]

b. Kungminhoe [Korean National Association] in Chita

By the summer of 1911, the Kungminhoe leaders were facing difficulties in the Primorye. However, subversive activities of the Seoul faction were not the only factor that forced Chŏng Chae-gwan and Yi Kang to move to Chita. Unfavorable political attitude of the local Russian authorities during this time in the Primorye was a more crucial factor for their exodus from Vladivostok to Chita. In the second half of 1911, Kungminhoe leaders in Russia came to bitterly understand their failure in the past to obtain the confidence of the local Russian authorities in the Primorye. In a letter to key leaders of the Kungminhoe in America from Muling, North Manchuria, Yi Kap, a close associate of An Ch'ang-ho wrote:

> Is the Far East not really absolutely crucial in our future activities? Nevertheless, there are various reasons why our activities in the Far East has not gone well, but the biggest cause is that [our] diplomacy with the Russian authorities these years have not been satisfactory. . . . Why? Russia is in fact an autocratic state and freedom of assembly and publication is not allowed. As a result, if we do not get the permission of government officials, it is difficult to proceed with any activity. . . . The personal opinion of the [Russian] authorities is no other than law. Until today, this has been an obstacle to our activities, but if we utilize it well, on the contrary, it will be favorable means to our activities.[392]

With this in mind, Yi Kap advised An Ch'ang-ho in America not to publish articles unfavorable toward Russia and to express friendship by praising the policies of Russia if possible in the *Sinhan Minbo*.[393] Yi Kap also emphasized the importance of getting the confidence of Russian authorities in order to get official permission for the activities of the Kungminhoe in Russia.

At the same time, it was also necessary for the Kungminhoe branches in Russia to have different rules in the Kungminhoe constitution based on American style republicanism, which was obviously in conflict with Tsarist political system of Russia. As a result, the Central

Committee of the Kungminhoe in America in November 1912 eventually allowed their branches in Russia to have their own regulations which were not in conflict with the Russian political system.[394]

Yi Kap's analysis was shared widely by Kungminhoe leaders in Russia in general. They had concluded that in the current political climate, it would be impossible to get official approval for the Kungminhoe in the Primorye. Yu Chin-yul, a strong opponent of the Kwŏnŏphoe, advised Paek Wŏn-bo, a Kungminhoe leader in Vladivostok, to apply for an organization in other provinces including the Amur or Za-Baikal, under a different name such as the "Hangugin Kongjehoe" ("Korean Mutual Assistance Association"), which An Ch'ang-ho had tried to organize when he was in Vladivostok at the end of 1910.[395]

Chŏng Chae-gwan and Yi Kang arrived at Chita in September 10, 1911 through Khabarovsk and Blagoveshchensk. Two days later, in a letter to An Ch'ang-ho, Chŏng Chae-gwan and Yi Kang emphasized the necessity of launching the activities of the Kungminhoe immediately in Amur and Za-Baikal in order not to "repeat the experience in Vladivostok" where other people had spread their influence to these regions beforehand.[396] Noticing the existence of about 100,000 Korean workers in the gold mines in these regions, they were very optimistic about their plans to establish churches, schools, and publish a magazine in Za-Baikal, Amur, and Siberia.[397] As far as these activities were concerned, Chŏng Chae-gwan and Yi Kang also had the same conclusions as Yi Kap and Yu Chin-yul. To improve their chances of obtaining legal permission for their activities, they decided to convert to the Russian Orthodox church from the Presbyterian church. Both Chŏng and Yi became god-children of the Deputy-Bishop of the Russian Orthodox Church in Chita,

Kuznetsov Efrem and got Russian names Mikhail Efremov Chŏng and Avraam Efremov Yi respectively. Through Efrem, Chŏng and Yi succeeded in getting permission to publish the *Taehanin Chŏnggyobo* (Bulletin of the Russian Orthodoxy for Koreans), a monthly religious magazine. The Deputy-Bishop, Efrem himself, drafted the purposes of the magazine in which it would be flexible enough to publish articles about Korean nationalist activities and information about relevant geopolitical situations.[398]

As stated earlier, the Kungminhoe branches were organized in various places in Amur, Za-Baikal and even in Siberia (in Chita, Verkhneudinsk, Blagoveshchensk, Irkutsk, Tomsk, Tiumen and Cheliabinsk). The Kungminhoe branches in Chita and Blagoveshchensk had a large memberships compared to other branches and as a result, Chŏng Chae-gwan and Yi Kang considered the two cities as a suitable residence for the Regional Central Committee of Siberia.[399] The Chita branch was organized on October 16, 1910, by 85 members and Nam Ch'ang-sŏk (President), Kwŏn Hwa-sun (Vice-President) and Ko Sŏng-sam (Chief of General Affairs) were elected executive members. 60 members of 85 were from the Hamgyŏng Provinces.[400] Kwŏn Hwa-sun and Ko Sŏng-sam were members of the New People's Association which An Ch'ang-ho had organized in Seoul.[401] The Blagoveshchensk branch was established on November 20, 1911, by 144 people of whom the prominent figures were Kim Su-yŏ (President), Kim To-hyŏn (Vice-President), Kim To-yŏ and Yi Wŏn-hae.[402] Kim Man-sik, former secretary of the *Taeyangbo* in Vladivostok, came to Chita and joined Chŏng and Yi.[403] All these people were active members of the Kungminhoe in Chita.

During this time, the Kungminhoe branch in Chita faced internal factional struggles. The struggle originated when the Chita

Kungminhoe branch expelled Nam Ch'ang-sŏk, the President of the branch from Chita, because of his violation of Kungminhoe rules: inflicting damage on the property of compatriots, hindering education, and threatening the lives of other people.[404] Chŏng and Yi succeeded in persuading the two sides to compromise.[405] Although this peace did not last, this temporary unity of Kungminhoe leaders in Chita succeeded in publishing the *Taehanin Chŏnggyobo* in which Nam Ch'ang-sŏk rejoined and began publication on January 2, 1912. Mun Yun-ham, President of the Chita branch, was made the publisher and Yi Kang the chief editor.[406]

The declared purpose of the *Taehanin Chŏnggyobo* was to spread fundamentals of the Russian orthodox faith, new knowledge, news of political and economic situation of Koreans inside and outside of Korea and geopolitical news.[407] The main Korean nationalists in Nikol'sk-Ussurisk, Novokievsk, Vladivostok, Khabarovsk, Blagoveshchensk, Nikolaevsk-na-Amure, Irkutsk, St. Petersburg, Harbin, Muling (Kor. Mongnŭng), North Chientao, San Francisco, Hawaii, Tokyo, and Mexico, became the supporters of the *Taehanin Chŏnggyobo*.[408] Although the *Taehanin Chŏnggyobo* took the form of a religious magazine for Koreans, it published articles inspiring patriotism and criticizing the suppressive rule of the Japanese. Kungminhoe leaders such as Paek Wŏn-bo (Vladivostok), Hwang Kong-do (Suchan) and Pak Yŏng-gap (Hunchun) frequently contributed articles to the magazine. Because of protests by the Japanese Foreign Ministry in August 1912, the *Taehanin Chŏnggyobo* was suspended for one year before restarting publication in February 1914. Until the outbreak of the World War I, the Kungminhoe published four more editions of the *Taehanin Chŏnggyobo*.[409]

At about the same time, Chŏng Chae-gwan and Yi Kang requested that An Ch'ang-ho send the credentials of the Central Executive

Committee of the Kungminhoe to authorize Chŏng and Yi as plenipotentiaries in the Russian Far East.[410] Chŏng Chae-gwan and Yi Kang decided to establish the Siberian Regional Central Committee (Siberia Chibang Ch'onghoe) in Chita in order to control the 10 branches in Russia with the exception of 12 branches in Suchan where another regional central committee was already established (November 11, 1911).[411] Responding to the request of Chŏng and Yi, the Central Committee of the Kungminhoe appointed Chŏng and Yi as plenipotentiaries with the assignment of organizing the Siberian Regional Central Committee. As a result, Chŏng and Yi immediately set up a temporary office for the Siberian Regional Central Committee in Chita, under whose control nine branches in Khabarovsk, Blagoveshchensk, Chita, Verkhneudinsk, Irkutsk, Krasnoiarsk, Tomsk, Cheliabinsk, and Nikolaevsk-na-Amure (Kor. Miyong) were organized.[412] After Chŏng Chae-gwan left for Vladivostok on December 28, 1911, to join the Kwŏnŏphoe on the invitation of Yi Sang-sŏl, Yi Kang led the activities of the Kungminhoe in Chita.[413]

The Siberian Regional Central Committee held two congresses in Chita before the outbreak of the World War I: the first with 19 branches from May 28 through June 7, 1913, and the second with 16 branches from June 15, 1914, through June 20, 1914.[414] The first congress decided to make the *Taehanin Chŏnggyobo* its official organ and appointed 25 supporters to collect fees from Kungminhoe members.[415] The second congress in June 1914 resolved to dispatch representatives to the ceremony for the fiftieth anniversary of Korean immigration to Russia for which Koreans in the Primorye were preparing.[416] At the second congress, representatives were dispatched from nineteen branches in major cities along the Trans Siberian Railroad from Amur to western Siberia including Blagoveshchensk,

Verkhneudinsk, Chita, Irkutsk, Krasnoiarsk, Tomsk, Novosibirsk, Omsk, Tiumen, Perm', Alexandrovsk and Cheliabinsk.[417] The third congress was supposed to be held in December of 1915, but because of the World War, the Kungminhoe could not continue its activities until the February Revolution.[418]

In July 1912, the Manchurian Regional Central Committee and eight branches had been dissolved by Russian authorities when Katsura visited Harbin on the way to St. Petersburg. The Kungminhoe branches in the Primorye were also replaced by those of the Kwŏnŏphoe. At last, the Kwŏnŏphoe organized its branches in April 1914 in Taudemi, Sinyŏng-dong and K'ŭnyŏng [Vladimiro-Aleksandrovskoe] in Suchan, which used to be one of the strongest base for the Kungminhoe in the Primorye. Although Kungminhoe members could continue their influence by keeping secret connections in the Primorye,[419] the Siberian Regional Central Committee remained the only base of the Kungminhoe in the Far East. Because of their geographical location, the members of these Kungminhoe branches had earlier contacts with Russian revolutionaries and played important roles in early Communist movement in Korean communities not only in Siberia, but also in the Russian Far East.

D. The World War I and the Korean Nationalists

As World War I broke out, martial law was declared in Vladivostok on August 1, 1914. Immediately, the Kwŏnŏphoe and the *Kwŏnŏp Sinmun* expressed strong support for the war efforts of the Russian government and started a movement to support the Russian government. On August 6, the Kwŏnŏphoe branch in Khabarovsk held a prayer meeting for the victory of Russia and gathered donations. On August 16, the *Kwŏnŏp Sinmun* published an article "Uri tongp'o ŭi ŭihyŏpsim" ("Righteousness and Heroism of Our Compatriots") and contended that Koreans should support Russia in all its efforts:

> Considering the fact that we Korean compatriots have lived for fifty years thanks to the benevolence of the Russian government, in the event of this war, it is right to help [the Russian government] by devoting our bodies and property. Hearing that [Koreans] held prayer meetings and gathered donations in Khabarovsk, we agreed to their acts. From now on, let all compatriots in all places pray and donate as much as we can. That is the way to express our faithfulness and appreciation and save our honor. . . . When opportunity and reality allow, it will be pleasant for men to go to the war fields shouldering guns and try our courage. Our loving compatriots![420]

In Vladivostok, the Kwŏnŏphoe notified Koreans to participate in a prayer meeting in the New Korean Village on the request of Vasilii O [O Yŏng-jun], a Korean Russian Orthodox priest. At the meeting, Koreans gathered donation and resolved to collect money to support the Russian government's war efforts.[421]

All these efforts of Koreans, however, could not overcome the adverse tide created by the war in which Russia and Japan cooperated as allies. All nationalist activities led by the Kwŏnŏphoe since the end of 1911 were forced to stop. Firstly, Governor-General Gondatti ordered the postponement of the ceremony for the fiftieth anniversary of Korean immigration, which was supposed to be held on October 9, to the following year (1915).[422] On August 20, the Military-Governor of the Primorye issued an order to dissolve the Kwŏnŏphoe. 36 Korean nationalists were ordered to leave Russian territory within 48 hours.[423]

The *Kwŏnŏp Sinmun* was also suspended in early September with the 126th edition dated August 29, 1914, as the last edition.[424]

These immediate actions of the local Russian authorities did not satisfy the Japanese government. On September 2, 1914, Nomura Motonobu, the acting Japanese Consul General in Vladivostok, sent a secret letter to the Military-Governor of the Primorye. In the letter, he pointed out that anti-Japanese Koreans in the Primorye were plotting to achieve independence of Korea during a war between Japan and Germany, Nomura requested the Military-Governor to "take appropriate measures not only for the sake of preventing the realization of the conspiracy [of anti-Japanese Koreans], but also for absolute eradication of the anti-Japanese mood among Koreans." By mentioning the precedent set by the dissolution of the Russian revolutionary newspaper and expulsion of Russian revolutionaries in Nagasaki in 1905, Nomura requested the Governor to order: 1) the suspension of the *Kwŏnŏp Sinmun* and dissolution of the Kwŏnŏphoe and Hapsŏng Hoesa, a Korean trade company; 2) banishment of 21 (in fact 20) anti-Japanese Korean leaders from the territory of Russia appended to the letter (see Table 2. 13).[425]

Most of these Korean nationalists were key leaders of the Kwŏnŏphoe and the *Kwŏnŏp Sinmun* with some exceptions: Yi Chong-man (Yi Chong-ho's younger brother), Yi Hyŏn-jae, Yi Pŏm-yun (former *ŭibyŏng* leader), Kang Sun-gi (An Chung-gŭn's sworn brother and *ŭibyŏng* leader), An Chŏng-gŭn and An Kong-gŭn (An Chung-gŭn's younger brothers). Of the people on the list only Cho Ch'ang-ho and Kim To-yŏ had Russian citizenship; the other eighteen people did not.

Perceiving the new suppressive policies, the key Korean nationalists immediately left Vladivostok. Yi Chong-ho escaped to Khabarovsk and visited Yi Sang-sŏl in order to discuss anti-Japanese activities.[426]

TABLE 2. 13

List of Anti-Japanese Koreans Whom the Japanese Consul General in Vladivostok Requested to be Expelled (Aug. 1914)

	Age	Birthplace
1. Yi Chong-ho	28	Myŏngch'ŏn (N. H.)
2. Yi Chong-man	23	Myŏngch'ŏn (N. H.)
3. Yi Hyŏn-jae	58	Myŏngch'ŏn (N. H.)
4. Yi Tong-hwi	41	Tanch'ŏn (S. H.)
5. Yi Tong-nyŏng	52	Mokch'ŏn (S. C.)
6. Yi Pyŏng-hwi	33	Hoeryŏng (N. H.)
7. Yun Hae	30	Yŏnghŭng (S. H.)
8. Cho Ch'ang-ho*	38	Tanch'ŏn (S. H.)
9. Cho Yŏng-jin*	38	Tanch'ŏn (S. H.)
10. Cho Chang-wŏn	34	Yŏnghŭng (S. H.)
11. Chŏng Chae-gwan	37	Chaeryŏng (H.)
12. Kim Ha-gu	30	Myŏngch'ŏn (N. H.)
13. O Chu-hyŏk	48	Tanch'ŏn (S. H.)
14. Kye Pong-u	35	Yŏnghŭng (S. H.)
15. Kim To-yŏ	47	?
16. Hŏ Kŭn	51	Musan (N. H.)
17. Yi Pŏm-yun	59	Changdan (K.)
18. Kang Sun-gi	45	Seoul (K.)
19. An Chŏng-gŭn	35	Haeju (H.)
20. An Kong-gŭn	27	Haeju (H.)
21. Yi Kap	37	Sukch'ŏn (S. P.)

Notes Birthplace
N. H.: North Hamgyŏng Province, **S. H.**: South Hamgyŏng Province, **S. C.**: South Ch'ungch'ŏng Province, **H.**: Hwanghae Province, K: Kyŏnggi Province, **S. P.**: South P'yŏngan Province.
* Cho Ch'ang-ho is the pen name of Cho Yŏng-jin.

Sources Nomura (Japanese Consul General in Vladivostok), letter to the Military-Governor of the Primorye, 20 Aug. 1914 (Far Eastern Central State Archives in Tomsk, F. 1, O. 12, E. 581); Birthplace were from "Zaigai hainichi Senjin yuryokusha meibo," ms. (1919) and other sources.

Yi Pyŏng-hwi [Yi Sŏng] and Kye Pong-u moved to North Chientao and other Koreans hid in Vladivostok, Nikol'sk-Ussurisk or other rural areas.[427] In September, Yi Chong-ho dispatched Yun Hae to Vladivostok with a plan to republish the *Kwŏnŏp Sinmun*.[428] It is likely that Yun Hae worked with Vasilii O in this effort as it was Vasilii O who applied to the new Military-Governor of the Primorye, Stashevsk to allow the publication of a new Korean newspaper. The application was ultimately rejected.[429]

Chŏng Chae-gwan went to Blagoveshchensk, but was arrested as a Japanese agent by the Russian *gendarme* based on the accusation of a pro-Japanese Korean.[430] Chŏng was released after two weeks and went to Chita. In Chita, the *Taehanin Chŏnggyobo* was already suspended by order of the Russian authorities.[431] In Chita, Chŏng Chae-gwan and Yi Kang attempted to revive the activities of the Kungminhoe by delivering nationalistic addresses to Koreans. However, the Kungminhoe leaders faced accusations from an opposition group led by Nam Ch'ang-sŏk, who had been expelled in 1911 from the Kungminhoe because of his violation of the rules of the Kungminhoe. Nam Ch'ang-sŏk and five other Koreans accused Kungminhoe leaders, including Chŏng Chae-gwan and Yi Kang, of "extorting annual fees from Koreans," "establishment of police department" and "exerting private punishment" to the Russian *gendarme* and requested their transfer to Korea. Because of the accusations, the seven Koreans were arrested for ten days before they were released on bail.[432] The news of the arrest created unfavorable circumstances for the activities of the Kungminhoe in Za-Baikal and Amur Provinces.[433] Yi Kang tried to distribute the copies of the *Sinhan Minbo*[434] and Chŏng Chae-gwan left for Suchan. At the end of 1915, Chŏng volunteered for the battlefront as a Russian soldier in order to help "the host country."[435]

Japanese diplomatic pressure on anti-Japanese Koreans were constant during the war period. As *quid pro quo* for suppressive policies of the Japanese government toward Russian revolutionaries in Nagasaki after 1905 and the secret Russo-Japanese Treaty of Extradition, Motono Ichirō [Tarō], Japanese Ambassador in St. Petersburg, made a request to Russian authorities in October "to dissolve all Korean organizations, all Korean newspapers and expel those Korean leaders who had led those activities from Russia." Sergei Dmitrievich Sazonov, Minister of Foreign Affairs, asked the Governor-General of the Priamur and Irkutsk Provinces to follow the request of the Japanese government.[436] Gondatti, Governor-General of the Priamur, however, viewed the request of the Japanese government unfavorably. Gondatti believed that the expulsion of the anti-Japanese Koreans was undesirable as repressive measures against Korean nationalist leaders might arouse disturbances among Koreans in the Priamur and accordingly, lead to difficulties handling them under conditions of the war. However, Sazonov firmly rejected Gondatti's argument responding that "in the present political moment, it is very important for us to consider the mood of the Japanese over those of Koreans."[437]

In December 1915, Gondatti telegrammed Sazonov, that he took all measures and that "in Priamur *krai*, there is no anti-Japanese propaganda: the Korean association was closed, the single Korean newspaper was closed, the agitator Yi Chong-ho was expelled." "In my jurisdiction. . . there is now absolutely no existing evidence of anti-Japanese propaganda in the *krai*."[438] In August 1915, Motono again delivered an oral note concerning the question of expulsion from the territory of Russia and the transferring to the Japanese authorities of 28 Koreans who were involved in anti-Japanese propagan-

TABLE 2. 14

List of Anti-Japanese Koreans Delivered by the Japanese Government to the Russian Government (Aug. 1915)

1. Yi Tong-hwi	11. Yi Kang	21. Ŏm In-sŏp
2. Yi Pyŏng-hwi	12. Yi Pŏm-yun	22. Yi Sang-sŏl
3. Kang Sun-gi	13. Yi Tong-nyŏng	23. Hong Pŏm-do
4. Cho Yŏng-jin	14. Yi Chong-ho	24. Yu Sang-don
5. Cho Chang-wŏn	15. Yi Chong-man	25. Kim Sŏng-mu
6. Yun Hae	16. Kim To-yŏ	26. Ch'oe Chae-hyŏng
7. Hŏ Kŭn	17. An Chŏng-gŭn	27. Kim Sŏng-yŏp
8. Kye Pong-u	18. An Kong-gŭn	28. Kim Sŏng-baek
9. O Chu-hyŏk	19. Chŏng Chae-gwan	
10. Kim Ha-gu	20. Yi Wi-jong	

Source Boris Dmitrievich Pak, *Koreitsy v Rossiiskoi imperii*, pp. 228-32.

da in Priamur, Irkutsk and Chinese Eastern Railroad region (see Table 2. 14). The Korean nationalists listed were labelled as "irreconcilable enemies of Japan." Motono suggested the Russian government expel them from the territory of Russia and hand over to Japan (non-Russian citizens) or to exile them to inner part of Siberia (Russian citizens).[439]

At the end of 1914 and early 1915, most Korean nationalists escaped to Manchuria. Yi Chong-ho and Yun Hae moved to Sanchakou, in Dongning Prefecture, Manchuria and Yi Tong-hwi and Kye Pong-u moved to a Korean village in Hamatang, Wangqing Prefecture, where Korean nationalists such as Ku Ch'un-sŏn, Kim Hak-kyu, Yim Pyŏng-gŭk were living. Yi Tong-hwi's family, including his father Yi Sŭng-gyo [Yi Pal], also moved here from Juzijie.[440] Yi Tong-hwi reinforced the Restoration Union, which he had organized in early 1911 in North Chientao, and established a military officers' training school [Mugwan Hakkyo] with Yi Chong-ho's financial support at a Korean village in Luozigou, Wangqing Prefecture, North Chientao.[441] The military officers' training school had about 80 students and Kim Rip, Chang Ki-yŏng, Kim Ha-sŏk, O Yŏng-sŏn,

Hong U-man, Han Hong, former members of the Kanminhoe, worked as teachers.[442] Two or three German officers were supposedly hired as training teachers.[443]

In early 1915, the diplomatic tension escalated between Japan and China over the so-called Twenty-One Demands. Expecting that the North Chientao region would be a battlefield when war between Japan and China broke out in the event of diplomatic rupture, Korean nationalists, former members of the Kanminhoe in North Chientao, prepared for the war in cooperation with China. Yi Tong-hwi and Yi Tong-ch'un established connections with Korean nationalists in the Primorye and Yi Pong-u and Yun Hae began activities in Juzijie. In early April, Yu Chin-gu [Yi Hae-sa] was dispatched to get the support of Yi Chong-ho in Sanchakou who would provide financial aid. Rumors of military cooperation between Chinese military troops and Korean armed forces spread in Hunchun and secret meetings of anti-Japanese Koreans and Christians were held in Juzijie with the purpose of recruiting *ŭibyŏng* fighters and raising military funds. The expectation of war by Korean nationalists reached a climax when Japan presented an ultimatum to China on May 7, but military action was not realized by the conclusion of the Twenty-One Demands on May 25, 1915.[444]

Responding to strong pressure from the Japanese government, the Chinese authorities launched a large-scale suppression of Korean nationalists in North Chientao. Yi Tong-hwi, Chŏn Il, Paek Ok-po, Ch'oe Pin and Kim Kang escaped to the inner part of North Manchuria, the Chinese Eastern Railroad regions and the Primorye. Kim Yak-yŏn, Cho Hŭi-rim, Yi Tong-ch'un, Pak Tong-wŏn, Hwang Pyŏng-gil and Yang Ha-gu, who had close connections with local Chinese authorities, were restrained from any official activities.[445] The reversed situation of the Korean nationalist movement in North Chientao is well reflected in a Japanese report:

> Regardless of whether they are Christians or non-Christians, any anti-Japanese Koreans in North Chientao conceal their voice and are not speaking any anti-Japanese words. The figures who feared possible danger all escaped to the deep inner parts of Chientao or other regions. In Chientao, recently within a year, we came to see a quite different mood from the old days.[446]

In this context, the Chinese authorities ordered the Korean military officers' training school in Luozigou to close in response to the protests of the Japanese Consulate General at the end of 1915.[447] About 40 students pledged to raise funds to reopen the school by accumulating their wages at Russian factories in the Urals and went to Perm' in order to work as laborers.[448]

By the second half of 1916, the Japanese authorities began to see the fruit of their efforts to incapacitate the Korean nationalist movement. In November 1916, the Japanese Consulate General received information that Yi Tong-hwi would visit his family in Hamatang, Wangqing Prefecture, to celebrate his wife's birthday and immediately dispatched secret policemen to arrest Yi Tong-hwi. They surrounded the Korean village and raided Yi Tong-hwi's house, but failed to arrest Yi Tong-hwi, who ran away, resisting with gun in hand. The Japanese policemen, instead, arrested Kye Pong-u, who was a member of the Educational Association, Kanminhoe, Kwŏnŏphoe, the chief-secretary of the Korean Restoration Military Government and a reporter of the *Kwŏnŏp Sinmun*.[449] At that time, Kye Pong-u was writing a biography of An Chung-gŭn, which he had published in the *Kwŏnŏp Sinmun* in 10 series (June 28-August 29, 1914) based on materials An Chŏng-gŭn, An Chung-gŭn's brother, had provided.[450] Kye Pong-u was transferred to Korea and sentenced to one-year banishment on Yŏng-jong Island, Chŏlla Province, and a three-year residence restriction in Yŏnghŭng, his hometown, on charges of violating the Security Law.[451] The arrest of Kye Pong-u became an issue among local Chinese authorities. On November 30, 1916, Zhao Zhen, new magistrate of Wangqing prefecture, expressed regret for not preventing the arrest of the "pro-Chinese influential Korean, Kye Pong-u," and ordered Chinese officials to take immediate and firm measures to protect pro-Chinese Koreans when Koreans asked for protection from the Japanese.[452]

In Russia, the Japanese utilized their traditional measures of using the Russian authorities to debilitate anti-Japanese Korean nationalists. Before the war, the Japanese authorities used falsified document and arranged for its availability to the Russian authorities resulting in painting targeted Korean nationalists as being "Japanese agents." During the war, Japanese officials used rumors of secret contacts between German officials and Koreans to charge Korean nationalists as "German agents." In 1915, rumors spread that German diplomats in Beijing, in cooperation with Chinese and Koreans, organized the Staunch Defense Union (Chin. Gongweituan, Kor. Kongwidan) with the purpose of destroying railroads (including the Chinese Eastern Railroad), bridges, and buildings, and were collecting information for Germany in China, Manchuria, Mongolia and preparing the publication of an anti-Russian and anti-Japanese newspaper.[453] Russian and Japanese authorities exchanged this information and sought to reinforce cooperation to frustrate these plans.[454]

In 1916, unconfirmed reports that German and Austro-Hungarian

Consulate General officials were planning with Korean nationalists in Beijing and Shanghai to create disturbances in the Chinese Eastern Railroad region, attack armories in Harbin and Vladivostok and raise riots in the Primorye together with German and Austro-Hungarian POWs who were at that time imprisoned in Nikol'sk-Ussurisk. In return, Germans were said to have promised to help the independence movement of Koreans and provide funds.[455] Although no evidence exists to confirm these plots, the Japanese authorities utilized these rumors to turn Russian authorities against Korean nationalists. The Japanese officials also spread rumors that Yi Tong-hwi and Yi Chong-ho concluded a secret agreement with German agents and in particular that Yi Chong-ho had agreed with the German minister in Beijing to organize military units composed of the *honghuzi* and Koreans with the purpose of attacking Russians in border areas. The *Manchurian Daily News*, published in Dairen by the Japanese-owned South Manchurian Railroad Company, in its article in December 1916, reported that Korean nationalists led by Yi Tong-hwi established a plan to destroy the Chinese Eastern Railroad.[456]

By utilizing more consolidated relations with Russia, particularly after the conclusion of the Russo-Japanese Treaties of July 3, 1916, the Japanese government requested the arrest of anti-Japanese Koreans in Vladivostok. In August 1916, the Russian *gendarme* arrested Kim Rip, Yi Hyŏn-jae and Ch'oe Chae-hyŏng and stormed the houses of Yi Chong-ho and Kim To-yŏ.[457] Although Yi Hyŏn-jae and Ch'oe Chae-hyŏng were released soon, Kim Rip was imprisoned on the charge of being a "German agent." Korean agents at the Russian *gendarme* provided the information that German officers were working at the military officers' training school in Luozigou which Yi Tong-hwi, Kim Rip and Yi Chong-ho had established in 1914.[458] The *Sinhan*

Minbo lamented that "presently, there is no trace of Korean nationalists in Vladivostok just as if they were swept away."[459]

At the end of 1916 and in early 1917, the main Korean leaders of Korean nationalist movement in the Primorye passed away or were imprisoned by the Russian or the Japanese authorities.[460] Kim To-yŏ, former President of the Kwŏnŏphoe, died on December 28, 1916[461] and Yi Sang-sŏl and Yi Kap died in April and in May respectively shortly after the Russian February Revolution.[462]

Yi Tong-hwi, who was travelling around the Korean communities along the Amur River preaching Christianity and inspiring patriotism, was once arrested by the Russian authorities with the charge of being a "German agent," but fortunately was released.[463] However, hearing the news of the establishment of the Russian Provisional Government, Yi Tong-hwi hurried to Vladivostok from North Manchuria in order to resume his nationalist movement in Russia, but was immediately arrested by Ku Tŏk-sŏng, a Seoul faction member and Korean agent working at the Russian *gendarme* in Vladivostok on April 17, 1917.[464]

Yi Chong-ho, a financial supporter and key leader of the Korean nationalist movement in North Chientao and the Primorye, escaped from Vladivostok to Shanghai, only to be arrested in Shanghai by the Japanese on charges of being a "jobless vagabond" and then was placed under three-year house arrest at his hometown, Kilchu, in Southern Hamgyŏng Province.[465]

Chŏng Chae-gwan, a Kungminhoe leader, was on the battlefront in Europe. The revolutionary period created by the Russian February Revolution came to the Korean communities when the Korean nationalist movement both in North Chientao and the Russian Far East was at low tide.

Members of the Korean Provisional Government in Shanghai, China at a New Year's Day Ceremony on January 1, 1920
In the second row, seventh from the left, are Son Chŏng-do, Sin Kyu-sik, Yi Tong-nyŏng, Yi Tong-hwi, Yi Si-yŏng, An Ch'ang-ho, Kim Chŏl, Kim Rip, Chang Kŏng-sang, Yun Hyŏn-jin, Sin Ik-hŭi, Yi Kyu-hong, Yi Ch'un-suk, and Chŏng In-gwa (left to right).

Members of the Provisional Government and Provisional Legislative Assembly at a New Year's Day Ceremony on January 1, 1921
In the second row, from the left are Yi Kyu-hong, Kim Chŏl, Sin Ik-hŭi, Sin Kyu-sik, Yi Si-yŏng, Yi Tong-hwi, Yi Sŭng-man [Syngman Rhee], Son Chŏng-do, Yi Tong-nyŏng, Nam Hyŏng-u, An Ch'ang-ho, O Yŏng-sŏn, Yun Hyŏn-jin, Sŏ Pyŏng-ho, Cho Wan-gu (left to right).

…ourrier de la Conférence

DE LA PAIX

Rédigé par WILLIAM T. STEAD

…nnement par semaine:
… la Hollande fl. 0.65
… l'Etranger fl. 0.75
…ix du numéro:
fl. 0.15.

Collaborateurs:
Mme la Baronne BERTHA VON SUTTNER,
M. ALFRED H. FRIED,
M. FRÉD. PASSY,
M. FELIX MOSCHELES.

Publié sous les auspices de la FONDATION POUR L'INTERNATIONALISME à La Haye.

Directeurs-Editeurs: MAAS & VAN SUCHTELEN

…X: Princessegracht 6A, La Haye. — Téléphone No. 287. — Adr. Télégr. MAASSUCHTELEN.

…VIS.

…International.

…liscours, pour les thés …rences, les cartes d'in…sentes sont valables, …y aura de la place. …retenir des places contre …0,25 par personne et …adresser au Bureau,

…uillet à 4 heures after… du Dr. D. S. van Emden …mbardement." (en alle…

…llet à 8 heures du soir …rs de S. A. R. le Prince …ar: „L'Etat actuel de … et actes commis par …rée".

Le Bureau.

…te de la fête.

…Prince Coréen Yi.

…aient coutume de placer … table de festin, pour …ux convives la vanité …s. La Conférence de La …pécisle des Dieux im…ge de posséder un aide… Aujourd'hui, assis à …Ritterzaal, se trouve …

Tjoune. Yi-Sang-Sul. Prince Tjjong-Oui-Yi.

Et pourtant c'est par suite de ce document illégal et sans valeur que la Corée est exclue de la Conférence."

— „Mais que voulez-vous donc?"

— „Présenter notre appel à l'autel du Dieu du Droit et de la Justice, à La Haye; demander si le Traité est valide en Droit International. Où est donc votre Haute Cour d'Arbitrage? Où …

pas? Eh bien, voyez en moi la négation suprême de toute votre foi. La Corée était un pays sans armements. La Corée n'avait pas d'ambitions agressives. La Corée ne demandait que la permission de vivre en paix et en solitude. Nous pratiquions ce que vous prêchez, vous, Pacifistes. Où en sommes-nous maintenant?

Non, non, continue-t-il …

Qu'est-ce que la Contrebande de Guerre?

La Définition de l'Allemagne.

Voici la Proposition de la délégation Allemande, concernant la Contrebande de Guerre en réponse au Questionaire: (Questions VI, VII).

Art. 1. Ne pourront être considérés comme contrebande de guerre que les objets suivants:

a. les armes, y compris les armes de chasse, ainsi que les matériaux qui ne sont susceptibles que d'un usage de guerre, (contrebande absolue.);

b. les autres matériaux et objets pouvant servir à la guerre et destinés à la force armée de l'ennemi (contrebande relative);

s'ils forment le chargement d'un batiment qui a mis le cap directement sur un port ennemi ou occupé par l'ennemi, ou sur la force armée de l'ennemi et que ces matériaux et objets aient été expressément déclarés contrebande de guerre.

Art. 2. Il y a présomption péremptoire que les matériaux et objets désignés à l'article 1b sont destinés à la force armée de l'ennemi, quand l'envoi en question est adressé aux autorités ou à un fournisseur militaire de la puissance ennemie ou quand il est à destination d'une place fortifiée du pays ennemi ou d'une autre

Emperor Kojong's Secret Special Delegation to the Hague From left to right: Yi Chun, Yi Sang-sŏl, Yi Wi-jong.

Choe Chae-hyŏng Right. President of the Comrades' Association [Tongŭihoe] — anti-Japanese Righteous Army Organization in the Russian Maritime Province.

An Chung-gŭn who shot and killed Ito Hirobumi in 1909 in Harbin, Manchuria.

Yi Chong-ho Leader of the Kwŏnŏphoe (Work Promotion Association). He sponsored the Korean Nationalist activities in the Russian Far East and North Chientao.

Yi Sang-sŏl Leader of the Kwŏnŏphoe (Work Promotion Association) and the first President of the Korean Restoration Military Government [Taehan Kwangbokkun Chŏngbu].

Yi Sŭng-man [Syngman Rhee] President of the "Unified" Korean Provisional Government in Shanghai.

An Ch'ang-ho Organizer of the "Unified" Korean Provisional Government in Shanghai and Head of Labor Bureau.

Mun Ch'ang-bŏm Chairman of the Korean National Council in Vladivostok, Russia. He did not take the Korean Provisional Government's Ministership of Communication.

Kim Kyu-myŏn Leader of the New People's Union [Sinmindan] and his comrades in Vladivostok, Russia (1920). Kim Kyu-myŏn is on the far left.

Alexandra Stankevich Petrovna Kim First Korean Bolshevik and founder of the Korean Socialist Party.

Pak Chin-sun Beside Lenin at the Colonial and Semi-Colonial Questions Committee, the Second Congress of the Comintern (July – Aug., 1920)

Delegates of the Korean Socialist Party to the Comintern Left photo — From left to right: Pak Chin-sun, Pak Ae, Yi Han-yŏng and an unidentified Russian Bolshevik. ; Right photo — From left to right: an unidentified Russian Bolshevik, Pak Ae, Pak Chin-sun and Yi Han-yŏng.

Leaders of the Korean Community Party (Shanghai Group) Seated from the left in the front row are Hyŏn Chŏng-gŏn, Yi Tong-hwi, Pak Chin-sun and Kim Rip. Standing in the second row from the left are Kim Chŏl-su, Kye Pong-u and an unidentified person. Kim Rip was a key leader of the Korean Socialist Party and a close associate of Yi Tong-hwi.

Yi Tong-hwi Premier of the "Unified" Korean Provisional Government in Shanghai and founder of the Korean Socialist Party.

Alexandr M. Krasnoshchekov 1920. He was the first President of the Far Eastern Republic and supported the Korean Socialist Party (Shanghai Group).

Boris Shumiatsky 1930s. Head of the Far Eastern Secretariat of the Comintern. He suppressed the Korean Socialist Party (Shanghai Group) and supported the "Irkutsk Group" of the Korean Communist Party.

Nestor Alexandrovich Kalandarishchvilli Commander-in-chief of the Korean Revolutionary Military Council at the time of the Sbovodnyi (Free City) Incident.

Chapter Three

THE RUSSIAN REVOLUTION AND THE RISE OF THE KOREAN SOCIALIST MOVEMENT

A. Korean Communities under the Russian Provisional Government

1. Koryŏjok Chungang Ch'onghoe

The Russian Provisional Government, created as a result of the February Revolution in 1917, promised to establish the democratic freedoms of assembly, speech, religion and, association. In this sense, the Russian Provisional Government broke with the political tradition of Tsarist Russia. Diplomatically, however, the new regime continued Tsarist policies by upholding treaty commitments and promising to remain loyal to the Western Powers in the war. This ambivalence was complicated by the so-called "dual power" shared by both the Provisional Government and the Soviets. Conflicts among various

Russian political forces over the political agenda and positions on key issues — the structure of political power; continuation of the war or immediate truce; and agrarian reform — gradually intensified the complexity of the Russian political landscape. The Provisional Government found itself in an awkward position between the Allies and the Soviets. As time progressed, the relationship between the Provisional Government and the Soviets shifted from tense coexistence to conflict. The April Crisis, the July Incident, and particularly the Kornilov Affair in August accelerated the process by which the Bolsheviks, who advocated the immediate transfer of power to the Soviets, increased their influence in the Soviets, particularly at St. Petrograd.

The political mood of the Korean communities also reflected this situation in Russia, particularly in the Russian Far East. As we saw in Chapter 2, at the time of the outbreak of the February Revolution, anti-Japanese nationalist activities of the Koreans in Russia were at their lowest ebb. In a letter dated July 13, 1917, to An Ch'ang-ho in San Francisco, Paek Wŏn-bo, a Korean nationalist in the Russian Far East, reported what he had experienced in Niko'lsk-Ussurisk during the second half of 1916, a couple of months before the February Revolution:

> I returned to Sowangnyŏng [Niko'lsk-Ussurisk] in September (lunar calendar) [of 1916]. . . . Upon arriving at Sowangnyŏng, I saw that even Sŏgo [Yi Tong-nyŏng] lost hope like ash and all other people do not have any concern about national public interest and are only in despair.[1]

Such a difficult situation of the Korean nationalist movement in Russia is also confirmed by the report of Japanese General Tachibana Koichirŏ, who had been appointed commander of the newly-established 19th Division in 1916 after serving for five years as commander of the *gendarmerie* in Korea. Tachibana, in his press interview, said:

> I may say that there are still in the country a large number of conservative persons who harbor anti-Japanese feelings, while other anti-Japanese Koreans are scattered about in Russian territory and Hawaii. The Koreans in Hawaii have their own schools and are clamoring for the independence of Korea. Sometimes, they send anti-Japanese literature to Korea, but owing to the strict control of the authorities, they can do nothing. As to the Korean refugees in the Russian territory, there was a time when they were welcomed by Russia, but in the existing relationship between Japan and Russia, the anti-Japanese ideas of the Koreans, of course, find no sympathy among the Russians. Consequently, anti-Japanese agitations among the Koreans at Vladivostok, Nikolaevsk, and Harbin seem to have practically stopped.[2]

As mentioned in Chapter 2, the outbreak of World War I resulted in Tsarist Russia and Japan becoming allies, and accordingly, any political and cultural activities of Koreans in Russian territory were severely suppressed by the Tsarist government. Shortly after the outbreak of World War I, the Russian authorities forced every Korean organization to be dissolved and prohibited all public activities. In September 1914, local Russian authorities ordered the Kwŏnŏphoe (Work Promotion Association), the central unified organization of the Korean people in the Primorye, as well as its organ *Kwŏnŏp Sinmun* to shut down. At the same time, thirty-six major Korean leaders were ordered to leave Russian territory within 24 hours.

As a result of suffering under these conditions, it was understandable that most Koreans in Russia, welcomed the February Revolution with great delight.[3] To them the overthrow of the Tsarist regime represented the end of the discriminative and suppressive policy against the Koreans, and opened an avenue for a Korean national movement to develop politically and economically inside Russia.[4] For Koreans in Russia, the February Revolution was like the coming of spring after a long winter. On the other hand, the revolution meant that the Korean communities in Russia were to be transformed according to their class backgrounds, occupations, citizenship status, regional origins, and the background activity of their constituents.

The February Revolution provided "a great upsurge of social and political activities" among Koreans in the Russian Far East.[5] Shortly after the February Revolution, the *wŏnhoin* Koreans in Suchan, Nikol'sk-Ussurisk, and Vladivostok organized Korean communities under the names of Hanin Chach'ihoe (Self-Rule Association of the Koreans), Hanin Hyŏphoe (Korean Association) or Hanin Minhoe (Korean People's Association). In organizing these associations, *wŏnhoin* Koreans including Ch'oe Ko-ryŏ and Kang Chu-mun in the Suchan region and Ch'oe Pong-jun, Mun Ch'ang-bŏm, Ch'oe Man-hak [Lev Petrovich], and Han Yong-hŏn [Andrei Konstantinovich] in the Nikol'sk-Ussurisk region played leading roles. Koreans in Vladivostok and Nikol'sk-Ussurisk also decided to publish their own newspapers in the Korean language.[6] The *yŏhoin* Koreans also revived branches of the Kungminhoe which had been dissolved shortly after the outbreak of the World War I[7] while Korean peasants began organizing peasant leagues.[8]

For several months after the February Revolution, it was the *wŏnhoin* Koreans who initiated and dominated political opinions of Korean communities in the Russian Far East. For the first time among the

Koreans in Russia, the *wŏnhoin* Koreans in Vladivostok expressed publicly their political support for the Provisional Government. On March 20, 1917, the Koreans in Vladivostok held a meeting which elected five delegates to the city executive committee: Kim Ch'i-bo, L. I. Kim, N. I. Kim, Ia. P. Kim, and P. I. Ŏm. The meeting also telegraphed the Chairman of the National Duma declaring "Priamur Koreans, together with the Russians, are happy with the renovation of Russia." Simultaneously, they sent out letters appealing to Korean workers and soldiers in Russia to be faithful to the Provisional Government. The delegates also sent a telegram to the Supreme Commander in Chief stating that "Korean soldiers will serve the new government with faith and truth and protect the motherland until the last drop of blood."[9]

Attempts to unify Koreans under one organization was initiated by the *wŏnhoin* Koreans in response to discriminative acts of Russians in the Primorye. In April 1917, the Russians held a congress in Nikol'sk-Ussurisk in order to organize county and village *zemstvo*s, and many *wŏnhoin* Koreans who also participated were elected members of the *zemstvo*. Furthermore, some of the *wŏnhoin* Koreans rose to influential positions in the public security committees for the region from the north of Tumen River to Nikol'sk-Ussurisk where Koreans made up the majority of the population. In fear of the increasing influence of these Koreans, ethnic Russian members worked to expel Korean members from the *zemstvo*s and the public security committees. Argument by ethnic Korean Russians that they were entitled to equal rights were rejected by the ethnic Russians. As efforts to achieve equality in Russian organizations such as the *zemstvo*s and the committees of public safety failed, angered *wŏnhoin* Koreans initiated a separate congress for Koreans in the Russian Far East.[10]

From June 4 to June 12, 1917, ninety-six delegates from the regions from the Russian Far East to Za-Baikal, east of Irkutsk, held the Congress of the Delegates of Koreans in Russia [Chŏllo Hanjok Taep'yojahoe] in Nikol'sk-Ussurisk. The purpose of the congress was to achieve Korean autonomy in Russia by forming an independent organization.[11] In invitation letters and telegrams sent to Koreans in various regions of the Russian Far East, the organizers of the congress declared that they would form "the largest and unified organization of all Koreans in Russia," and that it would work to "increase cooperation and coordination between newspapers and the various Korean organizations." The organizers called for two delegates from each region. About seventy *wŏnhoin*s and 30 *yŏhoin*s[12] attended, mainly comprised of members from the public safety committees, the leagues of the peasants, and the Kungminhoe.[13]

The congress was led by teachers primarily made up of members of the Socialist Revolutionary Party (SRs).[14] Ch'oe Man-hak, a second generation Korean and a nephew of Ch'oe Chae-hyŏng, was congress chairman.[15] The congress did not give voting rights to the delegates of the *yŏhoin* Korean tenants and of the Kungminhoe.[16] One example, was the case of the well-known Kungminhoe leader, Yi Kang who was not allowed to participate in the congress. Fearful of his anti-Japanese tendency, the congress argued that he had only received citizenship in the previous year.[17]

Congress delegates discussed the following issues: the political attitude of Koreans in Russia toward the Provisional Government; Korean cultural autonomy; and Korean representation at the Constituent Assembly.[18] Delegates of the anti-Japanese national revolutionary groups who supported Soviet Power left the congress after they failed to get a majority.[19] The remaining delegates of the congress decided to support the Provisional Government policy of "war until a victorious end," and sent a welcoming telegram to the government. The congress passed resolutions to allow one seat for the Korean representative at the future Constituent Assembly, to organize the Association of the Representatives of the Koreans [Hanjok Taep'yohoe], to demand land for agriculture, to appeal for the separation of schools from the church, to publish weekly newspapers in Korean (the *Ch'ŏnggu Sinbo* in Nikol'sk-Ussurisk, the *Hanin Sinbo* in Vladivostok), and to organize the Korean village *zemstvo*s [*ch'onchach'ihoe*] following the Russian model, with reference to a Korean system.[20]

The resolutions of the congress generally focused on autonomy and enhancing the rights of the *wŏnhoin* Koreans, but did not include any resolutions regarding anti-Japanese activities. The majority of the congress did not want to raise anti-Japanese issues. This was clearly indicated by the fact that the congress gave no attention to the question of releasing Korean nationalist prisoners such as Yi Tong-hwi who had been imprisoned because of his anti-Japanese nationalistic activities.[21] The majority of the congress did not want to challenge the Provisional Government, which in turn did not want to provoke its ally, Japan.

Dominated by *wŏnhoin* Koreans, the congress established the Central Executive Committee of the Korean Associations in All Russia [Chŏllo Koryŏjok Chungang Ch'onghoe, hereafter cited as the Koryŏjok Ch'onghoe] consisting of only *wŏnhoin* Koreans with residence in Nikol'sk-Ussurisk.[22] As a result, the congress failed to organize "the largest and most unified organization of all Koreans in Russia," one of the main goals of the congress.[23]

Policies of the Provisional Government (such as the continuation of the war and faithfulness to the Russo-Japanese alliance, as well as the pro-Provisional Government political positions of *wŏnhoin* Korean intellectuals dominant in the Korean communities) explain why Korean national revolutionaries failed to voice their anti-Japanese agenda.[24] The absence of influential anti-Japanese Korean nationalist leaders at such a critical time made worsened the matters. Shortly before and after the February Revolution, most main anti-Japanese nationalist leaders had died or were imprisoned. Anti-Japanese leaders who had organized and led the Kwŏnŏphoe (such as Kim To-yŏ, Yi Sang-sŏl and Yi Kap) died shortly before and after the February Revolution. Yi Chong-ho, a financial supporter and organizer of the anti-Japanese movement of Koreans in Russia and Manchuria, escaped from Russian captivity, only to be arrested in Shanghai by the Japanese with the charge of "jobless vagabond" and placed in house arrest at his hometown, Kilchu, in Southern Hamgyŏng Province.[25]

Kim Rip and Yi Hyŏn-jae were also arrested with suspicion of "German espionage" by the Russian authorities in August 1916.[26] Yi Tong-hwi, who had heard the news of the establishment of the Russian Provisional Government, hurried from Northern Manchuria to Vladivostok to resume anti-Japanese activities in Russia, but was arrested on April 17, 1917, as a "German agent" by Ku Tŏk-sŏng, a Korean agent working for the Russian *gendarme* in Vladivostok.[27]

Korean soldiers who returned from the European war front also declared their support for the Provisional Government policy of continuation of the war. At the time of the founding meeting of the Korean Soldiers' Association [Hanin Kuninhoe] in Vladivostok on July 17, 1917, they resolved: 1) to dispatch Korean representatives to the city citizens' council of Vladivostok; and 2) to take special action against Koreans, who were called upon to mobilize by the government as soldiers but hid to avoid military services.[28]

2. The Question of Yi Tong-hwi

The exclusion of the *yŏhoin* Koreans and abandonment of the anti-Japanese agenda at the June Congress brought about opposition from the dissatisfied *yŏhoin* Koreans and returning Korean soldiers. Shortly after the June congress at Nikol'sk-Ussurisk, the *yŏhoin* Koreans from the New Korean Village in Vladivostok tried to organize their own association. Embarrassed with this development, the *wŏnhoin* Koreans initiated discussions with the *yŏhoin* Koreans and came to an agreement to organize a single unified association of Koreans at the New Korean Village [Sinhanch'on Hanin Minhoe].[29]

In early September 1917, the Korean Soldiers' Association also attempted to control the Association of the Koreans in the New Korean Village in Vladivostok.[30] This bold attempt obviously demonstrated the fact that the political mood among the returned Korean soldiers had changed drastically within two months. This change in the political mood among returned Korean soldiers was parallel to that of the Russian soldiers and workers, who began to turn away from the Russian Provisional Government in favor of the Bolshevik party after the failure of Kerensky's "Great Attack" in June and General Kornilov's Coup in August, and, in particular, the increase of Bolshevik influence in Vladivostok during the summer of 1917.[31]

A prime example of this changing political viewpoint among Koreans was the movement for the release of Yi Tong-hwi. As stated in Chapter 2, Japanese agents tried to arrest Yi Tong-hwi ever since his move to Manchuria, and Yi had escaped arrest several times. His arrest was the result of continuous efforts by the Japanese intelligence agencies and also demonstrated the fundamental political reality of cooperation by the Provisional Government. Even though the charge of "German espionage" for Yi Tong-hwi proved to be invalid after several interrogations,[32] the Provisional Government did not release him on the ground that "the original charge of [German espionage] was raised by the previous government," and the new government "is just executing it."[33] In addition to the activities of the Japanese intelligence agencies and suppressive policies of the Russian authorities, factional struggles among Koreans also brought about the arrest of their leaders. Korean agents who were from the capital area [*Kiho*] and hired by the Russian military police accused Yi Tong-hwi before the Russian authorities. In order to prevent Yi Tong-hwi from launching new activities in Russia, they utilized an article appearing in the Japanese newspaper, the *Manchurian Daily News*, which claimed that the goal of Korean nationalists such as Yi Tong-hwi was to destroy the Chinese Eastern Railroad.[34]

In September 1917, the Korean Soldiers' Association of New Korean Village in Vladivostok elected Ch'oe Ko-ryŏ and Semyon Pak as delegates, and they visited Vladivostok Soldiers' Soviet and other Russian authorities and strongly defended Yi Tong-hwi's innocence requesting his immediate release. At the same time, Koreans in Vladivostok, Khabarovsk, and Chita sent appeals and telegrams requesting Yi Tong-hwi's release and decided to dispatch delegates representing all Koreans and to appoint lawyers in his support.[35] In his letter to An Ch'ang-ho dated September 23, 1917, Paek Wŏnbo reported; "telegrams and petitions arrived from all sides" in Russia.[36]

In response to the enthusiastic support of Koreans, Russian authorities transferred Yi Tong-hwi to the military prison of Khabarovsk.[37]

The Korean Soldiers' Association of Vladivostok again dispatched Semyon Pak and Ivan Pak (assumably Pak Chin-sun) and the Association of the Koreans in Vladivostok sent Han Yong-hŏn to Khabarovsk. In Khabarovsk, Stephan Yu, a Russian military officer, and Chŏn T'ae-guk, chairman of the Korean Association in Khabarovsk, led the movement for the release of Yi Tong-hwi. Vasilii O visited Yi Tong-hwi in prison and provided clothes. Even elementary students in Khabarovsk participated in the movement. Koreans in Suchan also collected and sent money to Yi Tong-hwi's family.[38]

Upon the request of the Japanese government to hand over Yi Tong-hwi to Tokyo for trial, the Russian authorities prepared to cooperate by again relocating Yi Tong-hwi to a military prison in Alekseyevsk [Svobodnyi].[39] The most influential Korean Bolshevik in Khabarovsk, Alexandra Kim, who had been dispatched by the Ekaterinburg Bolshevik party to organize pro-Bolshevik activities among Korean communities in the Russian Far East, heard from her husband, Vasilii O, that Yi Tong-hwi was in prison at Alekseyevsk and was on the point of being sent to Japan for trial. As a result, she worked to support the movement of the Koreans in Khabarovsk for the release of Yi Tong-hwi.[40]

Yi Tong-hwi was finally released in November 1917, after the October Revolution. In spite of the opposition of Alexander Rusanov, the *krai* commissar of the Kerensky government, General Khgondokov, the commander of the Priamur military district ordered the release of Yi Tong-hwi. The release of Yi Tong-hwi was the result of the active help of the Soviet leaders, A. Y. Neibut, K. V. Sukhanov and Utkin, and the enthusiastic support of Koreans.[41] As soon as he was released from the prison, Yi Tong-hwi went to Khabarovsk. He visited Alexandra Kim and other Russian Bolsheviks who had assisted in his release and expressed deep appreciation for their help.[42]

3. Alexandra Petrovna Kim in the Urals

The first pro-Bolshevik organization of Koreans was formed in the Urals during the summer of 1917 by Alexandra Petrovna Kim Stankevich. Alexandra Kim was a second-generation Korean and the first Korean Bolshevik to have participated in "three Russian Revolutions."[43] Alexandra Kim's father Kim Tu-sŏ [Pyotr Semyonovich Kim] was among the 96 poor families who had emigrated from Kyŏnghŭng in the winter of 1869.[44] She was born on February 22, 1885 in Sinel'nikovo (Kor. Taejŏnja), a Korean village in Pokrovskii, Suifen, not far from Nikol'sk-Ussurisk.[45] Kim Tu-sŏ was one of the well-known Korean *podriadchik*s (contractors), who earned much money gathering Korean and Chinese laborers for the construction of the Chinese Eastern Railroad.[46]

In 1893, Alexandra Kim went to Harbin where her father was working as a *perevodchik* (translator or *t'ongsa* in Korean) for Korean and Chinese workers at the construction fields of the Chinese Eastern Railroad.[47] She spent her childhood among the Korean, Chinese and Russian workers, and learnt to speak Chinese.[48] Kim Tu-sŏ died in 1897, when Alexandra Kim was a twelve-year-old elementary school student in Harbin[49], and she was put in the care of her father's close Polish friend, Mark Iosipovich Stankevich. Stankevich had her enter a municipal high school in Vladivostok. During this time, she came into contact with the literature of Russian revolutionaries such as Gertsen, Dobroliubov, Pisarev, Chernyshevsky and Plekhanov, and began to pay attention to social problems.[50] Around this time, she began to learn foreign languages such as English, French and Japanese, which proved to be a useful asset for her revolutionary career.[51]

In 1904, she married in Harbin the son of M. I. Stankevich, her father's friend who had raised and educated her.[52] Their married life was not a happy one, and they divorced in 1908. Alexandra Kim moved from Harbin to Vladivostok with her first son, Viyacheslav Markovich, who was born in 1908. In 1909, she married Vasilii Vasile'vich O [O Yŏng-jun], a second-generation Korean-Russian who was a Russian Orthodox missionary (later priest) and taught Russian language to Koreans in Vladivostok.[53] Vasilii O relieved Alexandra Kim from housework, enabling her to participate in revolutionary activities.[54]

When World War I broke out in 1914, Alexandra Kim went as a *perevodchik* to timber factories at Perm'.[55] In the Urals there were many government-owned factories producing war materials or lumber for the Russian military. The factories employed a great number of Korean and Chinese laborers through *podriadchik*s from the Russian Far East in 1914.[56] The *podriadchik* who gathered Korean and Chinese laborers in Vladivostok was a notorious Korean named Kim Pyŏng-hak, who accumulated wealth by constructing military facilities and houses in Vladivostok.[57]

Kim Pyŏng-hak — once an executive member of the Kwŏnŏphoe in charge of reception — gathered Korean workers in Vladivostok, took thousands of Korean laborers to the Ural area, using falsified contract documents before running away from authorities.[58] The Korean laborers in the Urals faced difficult working conditions. It was common for their working term became protracted, from one year to two years, and for them to work longer per day for lower wages than had been originally promised. When the term ended, their Russian employers generally did not release them. There are many instances where the Russian managers treated the workers very cruelly. They were not allowed to go out of the factories, or to send and receive letters. Security guards recruited from Chinese mercenaries kept watch over the workers. When they went on strike, the factory authorities stopped all supplies of food and clothing in response, and some workers were murdered.[59]

Among Korean laborers there were students of the Korean Military Academy from Luozigou in North Chientao, which established in April 1914 by Yi Tong-hwi, Yi Chong-ho, Kim Rip, Chang Ki-yŏng, Kim Ha-sŏk and O Yŏng-sŏn. The Academy was forced to close in May of 1915 due to financial problems and the suppressive policy of the Chinese government which was forced to agree to Japan's Twenty-one Demands.[60] After the closing of the academy, some of the students promised to each other that they would work as laborers in order to acquire the funds needed to reopen the academy. One of the students, Yi Chae-hyŏng, became a member of the first pro-Bolshevik Korean labor union, the Workers' Union in the Urals [Ural Nodongja Tongmaeng].

Alexandra Kim's concern for these students was said to have been extremely deep and strong.[61] While Alexandra Kim fought for the Korean laborers she came in contact with the Ekaterinburg Committee of the Russian Social Democratic Party which was controlled by the famous Bolshevik, Iakov Mikhailovich Sverdlov.[62] After the Russian February Revolution, she worked to legalize all underground activities and organized party cells within factories, becoming even more popular after the Russian February Revolution. She was so popular that more than 5,000 Korean and Chinese workers, who could not understand Russian cast their ballots for her in various elections of the local soviets and party organizations.[63]

The terrible situation of Korean workers in the Urals became an urgent issue among Koreans in the Russian Far East. In May 1917, the Korean Association in Vladivostok appointed Alexandra Kim to negotiate the question of Korean laborers with the Kerensky government.[64] The Koryŏjok Ch'onghoe also provided funding for the negotiations.[65] Alexandra Kim went to Petrograd and succeeded in getting the Kerensky government to take responsibility for releasing Korean workers. It was at this time that she joined the Russian Social Democratic (Bolshevik) Party.[66] Yi In-sŏp, who first met Alexandra Kim in Omsk in the spring of 1917, claimed Alexandra Kim had visited Moscow and St. Petersburg twice in 1917 in order to meet with Bolshevik leaders, including Lenin.[67] As a direct result of her activities, Korean and Chinese laborers in the Urals were released from their condition of virtual slavery.[68]

Alexandra Kim believed that it was too early for young Korean patriots who hated the rule of Japan to become Bolshevik party members, but it was proper for them to form a political organization.[69] In June 1917, she organized the first Korean pro-Bolshevik labor union, the Workers' Union in the Urals with Korean and Chinese laborers as members.[70] Most of Korean members were Korean patriotic emigrés born in Korea who had been deeply involved in nationalist activities in Manchuria and the Primorye. Due to limited sources, the identity of only eight Korean members of the Union is known. They were Yi In-sŏp, An Kyŏng-ŏk, O Sŏng-muk, Sim Paek-wŏn [Sim Ch'an-ho], Kim Yong-hwan [Kim T'ae-jun], Ch'oe Yŏng-hun, Yim Ch'i-hak, Yi Chae-hyŏng.[71] Members of the Workers' Union in the Urals (including Yi In-sŏp, An Kyŏng-ŏk, O Sŏng-muk, Kim Yong-hwan and Sim Paek-wŏn) were also the main leaders of the Korean Association in Omsk.[72] As we will see later, the members of the Union, under the leadership of Alexandra Kim, played a key role in spreading Bolshevism among the Koreans in Siberia and the Russian Far East and particularly in creating the Korean Socialist Party.

Yi In-sŏp, the chairman of the Union, was born in 1888 in P'yŏngyang and participated in the *ŭibyŏng* struggle (anti-Japanese partisan movement) from 1907 to 1910. At the time of Japan's annexation of Korea, he led his troops into Manchuria. Yi worked as an organizer of the Kungminhoe in Northern Manchuria, Za-Baikal, and Eastern Siberia. In early 1917, Yi went to the Urals as a laborer and met many Russian Bolsheviks, including Alexandra Kim in June 1917. She led Yi to work in the Bolshevik organizations and to translate regulations and programs of the Russian Social Democratic Labor Party as well as the Communist Manifesto into Korean, and to continue to organize socialist groups at several cities in Eastern Siberia. Yi was elected chairman of the Workers' Union in the Urals when it was organized. After Alexandra Kim left for the Russian Far East, he organized socialist organizations among the Koreans in western Siberia and became a member of the Bolshevik Party in November 1919.[73]

O Sŏng-muk was born in 1886 in Myŏngch'ŏn, Hamgyŏng Province, and emigrated to Manchuria in 1892 at the age of six. In 1913, he was one of the key members of the Korean Association in Chientao [Kanminhoe] in Manchuria with other Korean nationalistic patriots. Escaping the suppressive policies of the Chinese authorities in 1915, O Sŏng-muk moved to Nikol'sk-Ussurisk and finally went to the Urals as a laborer in the timber-cutting fields. Experiencing harsh conditions as a laborer in the Urals, he sympathized with Bolshevik ideas. Then, O Sŏng-muk went to Omsk and joined the Workers' Union in the Urals in 1917. While staying in the Omsk region, he collected funds from Koreans for the *Hanin Sinbo*, a Korean newspaper published in Vladivostok. After the October Revolution, he conferred with Alexandra Kim and other Korean revolutionaries in Khabarovsk spreading Bolshevism among the Koreans.[74]

Yi Chae-hyŏng was born in Kyŏngsang Province and emigrated to Chientao. He was one of forty students of the Korean Military Academy at Luozigou who went to the Urals to work as a laborer pledging to reopen the academy with the wages they would earn and was released from the factories thanks to Alexandra Kim.[75]

At the end of July, the Ekaterinburg city committee of the Russian Social Democratic Party (B) dispatched Alexandra Kim to the Far East with the responsibility of carrying out propaganda and party organization, particularly among the Korean communities.[76] The news that Alexandra Kim had liberated all Korean workers, who had been sold by the notorious *podriadchik*, Kim Pyŏng-hak, to Russian factories in the Urals, spread widely among the Korean communities in the Russian Far East. She arrived at Vladivostok in the summer of 1917. The *Hanin Sinbo* reported the visit of Alexandra Kim to its editor's office:

> Alexandra Kim, who has liberated thousands of Korean and Chinese laborers from the terribly suffering at the wood-cutting factories, has come back from the Urals and visited our editors' office. She is a Korean Bolshevik and braver than any man, and she is urging the Korean liberation movement to move forward to the socialist stage of political development.[77]

It was not long before Alexandra Kim soon became one of the major Bolshevik leaders in the Russian Far East. As a representative of the Muraviev Amurskii region, she participated in the Second Russian Social Democratic Party Conference of the Far Eastern Regional Representatives held from October 18 to 20, 1917, in Vladivostok.[78]

B. October among the Koreans

1. Hanjok Chungang Ch'onghoe

After the Bolshevik Revolution occurred in Petrograd, the Workers' and Soldiers' Soviet of Vladivostok declared on December 12 that it supported the Soviet government and that it would assume power in Vladivostok. From December 25, 1917, through January 2, 1918, in Khabarovsk, all supporters of the October Revolution of the Russian Far East (Primorye, Amur, Sakhalin, and Harbin) gathered and held the third Soviet Conference of the Far Eastern Region in order to establish Soviet authority in the Russian Far East.[79]

On January 18, 1918, according to the resolution of the Conference, Dalsovnarkom (Far East Regional Executive Committee of Soviets of Workers', Soldiers', and Peasants' Deputies and Self-Administrations — in June 1918, this organization changed its name into the Far Eastern People's Committee) was organized as a regional power of the Russian Far East. The Bolshevik leader Alexandr Mikhailovich Krasnoshchekov,[80] who played an important role in solving the dispute between hard-liners and moderates on whether Soviet power in the Far East would include the *zemstvo* forces or not, was elected as the chairman of the committee.[81] Hereafter, together with Vladivostok, Khabarovsk became the center of revolutionary activity in the Russian Far East, and it therefore became necessary to strengthen its Bolshevik Party organization in the region. For this purpose, Alexandra Kim, L. E. Gerasimov, and M. E. Popko moved to Khabarovsk.[82]

Dispatched by the Ekaterinburg committee of the RSDP (B) to the Russian Far East, Yi In-sŏp recollected the activities of Alexandra Kim and the members of the Workers' Union in the Urals in Khabarovsk as follows:

> Arriving at Khabarovsk, we met local Bolshevik comrade Malyshev and Bolsheviks who had returned from banishment, penal labor, and political emigration, comrades M. E. Popko, L. E. Gerasimov and others. Together with them, we created a separate Bolshevik organization under the slogan, "For the Soviet Power," and began to fight against the SRs, and Mensheviks in the local Provisional Government.[83]

Alexandra Kim became secretary and treasurer of the Khabarovsk city organization and a Commissar for the Foreign Affairs of the Khabarovsk Soviet.[84] Her duty as a commissar was to solve the various problems of the POWs of Germany, Austria, Hungary and Czechoslovakian who were gathered at the military camps in Khabarovsk. Her proficiency in several foreign languages was useful in these works.[85]

While the Bolsheviks were strengthening their power in the main cities of the Russian Far East such as Vladivostok and Khabarovsk after the October Revolution, the Koryŏjok Chungang Ch'onghoe (organized in Nikol'sk-Ussurisk congress in June 1917 and mainly composed of *wŏnhoin* Koreans) adopted the policy of supporting the Constituent Assembly and the Siberian *zemstvo*. Before and after the October Revolution leading *wŏnhoin* Koreans were elected at every level of the *zemstvo*s. At the two canton *zemstvo*s in Nikol'sk-Ussurisk, Koreans were elected as chairmen. Ch'oe Chae-hyŏng was elected a *zemstvo* member of Nikol'sk-Ussurisk county. Han Yong-hŏn was elected a member of Public Security Executive Committee and became the member of the Primorye Zemstvo representing Koreans.[86]

Following the resolution of the Nikol'sk-Ussurisk congress, the Koryŏjok Ch'onghoe requested that the committee on apportionment of the forthcoming Constituent Assembly grant one seat to a Korean deputy, but the request was not granted, presumably due to a shortage of Korean population.[87] All seven seats for the Constituent Assembly were allotted to the Russian Far East region; four for the Primorye, two for the Amur, and one for Sakhalin.[88] In this situation, the Koryŏjok Ch'onghoe tried to choose a Russian candidate who could represent Koreans at the Constituent Assembly. At the election on November 25-27, 1917, it decided to vote for the candidate of the Primorye Soviet of the Peasant Deputies[89] who accepted three Koryŏjok Ch'onghoe conditions: 1) Korean agreement with the independence of the Siberian government, 2) that two seats would be given to Korean deputies when Siberia becomes independent, and that 3) Koreans who had lived more than five years in Russia, could own land, regardless of citizenship.[90]

The *Ch'ŏnggu Sinbo*, the newspaper of the Koryŏjok Ch'onghoe listed the candidate of the Primorye Soviet of the Peasant Deputies as the most favorable candidate, pointing him out with the slogan "vote for no. 2 slate candidate." The candidate of the Bolshevik party was listed the least favorable among six candidates who had "relations with" the Koreans.[91] The *Hanin Sinbo* also published the election advertisement of the Primorye Soviet of the Peasant Deputies,[92] and he was elected.[93]

After the election to the Constituent Assembly, the Koryŏjok Ch'onghoe, in the name of Trofim Pak (temporary chairman), Chuprov Nikolai Kim (vice-chairman), Han Yong-hŏn (member of the Primorye *zemstvo*) and Ch'oe Chae-hyŏng (member of the Nikol'sk-Ussurisk county *zemstvo*), delivered the "mandate" ["*nakaz* "] of the Koreans to the elected Constituent Assembly members who were representing the Primorye Soviet of the Peasant Deputies.

In the mandate, the Koryŏjok Ch'onghoe which claimed to represent all Koreans in Russia, presented demands on seven questions: the form and organization of the government; the rights of the people; the land; education; religion; war; and the political and legal status of the Koreans in Russia. The Koryŏjok Ch'onghoe requested the Constituent Assembly members of the Primorye Soviet of the Peasant Deputies "to realize the demands and thereby not to make any correction on those demands even in the face of any opponents with all your efforts." In the mandate, the Koryŏjok Ch'onghoe advocated the republican form of government system and autonomy of all nationalities which would allow equal rights for all nationals in Russia, as well as land distribution to the cultivators without requirement of compensation or payment.[94] The mandate of the Koryŏjok Ch'onghoe obviously demonstrated its support for the Constituent Assembly and the idea of the establishment of the Siberian independent republic.

One interesting development during this time was that the *wŏnhoin* Koreans who once had supported the Provisional Government policy of "war until a victorious end" at the Nikol'sk-Ussurisk congress in June 1917, now came to support the armistice.[95] This change

TABLE 3. 1

Major Korean Organizations, 1917-1918 in the Primorye

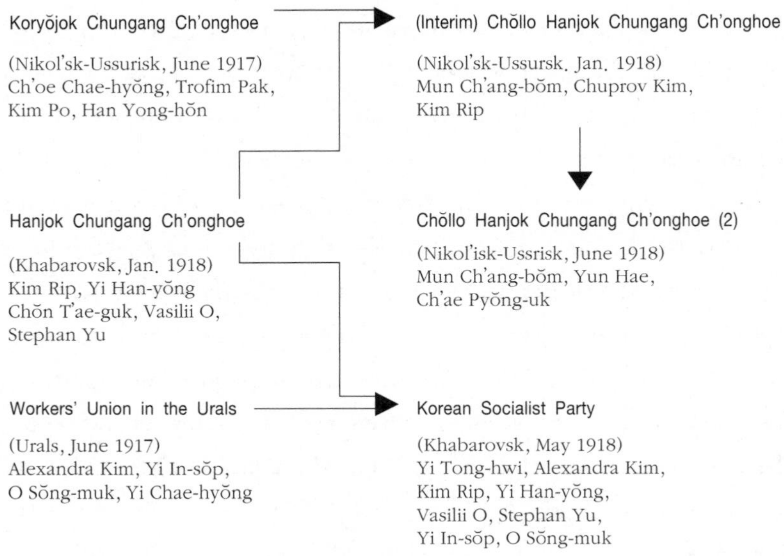

reflected the general change in the political mood of Russia which had occurred during the latter half of 1917.

The pro-Siberian Congress was realized on January 11, 1918, when the Koryŏjok Ch'onghoe resolved to dispatch two Korean deputies, including Ch'oe Chae-hyŏng, the respectful leader and member of the Niskol'sk-Ussurisk county council, to the Siberian Regional Congress.[96] This was in response to the appeal to the minority nationalities of the Siberian Regional Congress which was created at the Provisional Congress of All Siberia held from January 6 to 15, 1918, to dispatch two deputies.[97] These policies of the Koryŏjok Ch'onghoe were also in accordance with the political attitude of the majority of the Korean population in Russia.[98]

These series of actions taken by the Koryŏjok Ch'onghoe, however, brought opposition from pro-Bolshevik Koreans in Khabarovsk, such as Kim Rip, Ch'ae Sŏng-o, Yi Han-yŏng, Chŏn T'ae-guk, Stephan Yu and Vasilii O.[99] Shortly after the October Revolution, they organized another Central Executive Committee of the Korean Associations in Russia [Hanjok Chungang Ch'onghoe, hereafter cited as Hanjok Ch'onghoe].

Kim Rip, who had been a key leader of the Kwŏnŏphoe in Vladivostok and the Kanminhoe in Chientao, was arrested on suspicion of "[German] espionage" by Russian authorities in the spring of 1916. After being released in May 1917, Kim Rip moved to Khabarovsk and started cultural and educational activities with the goal of inspiring nationalistic patriotism. In September, Kim Rip established the Korean publishing company, Pomunsa (Spreading Literature Company) with Yi Han-yŏng, Ch'ae Sŏng-o, Chang Ho-mun, Cho Hyŏn and published school textbooks on Korean history, literature and geography.[100] Kim Rip and Yi Han-yŏng also reestablished Mundŏk Middle School which was originally established in 1909 by Korean nationalists such as Yi Tae-yu, Kim Chong, Nam Pyŏng-gyu, and Yun Ch'ang-sŏn.[101] When Alexandra Kim came to Khabarovsk, Kim Rip became involved in Bolshevik activities.[102] Some of the Hanjok Ch'onghoe organizers such as Chŏn T'ae-guk, Stephan Yu and Vasilii O had participated in the movement for the release of Yi Tong-hwi and particularly, Kim Rip and Vasilii O were under the strong influence of Alexandra Kim. Furthermore, some of them were main leaders of cultural and educational activities in Khabarovsk — Kim Rip, Ch'ae Sŏng-o, Yi Han-yŏng, Chŏn T'ae-guk.

In its prospectus of establishment of a separate organization of Koreans, the Hanjok Ch'onghoe criticized the Nikol'sk-Ussurisk

TABLE 3. 2

Interim Executive Committee of the Korean Associations in All Russia [Chŏllo Hanjokhoe Chungang Ch'onghoe] (Jan. 1918)

Chairman	Mun Ch'ang-bŏm (KCC)
Vice Chairman	Kim Rip (HCC)
Section of Educational Affair	Kim Rip (HCC)
Section of General Affair	Chang Ki-yŏng (HCC, HS)
Secretary	Chang Ki-yŏng (HCC, HS)
Section of Financial Affair:	Sŏ Yun-ch'ŏl (KCC)
Constitution Drafting Committee	Han Yong-hŏn (KCC, HS), Kim Rip (HCC), Chang Ki-yŏng (HCC, HS), Kim Ha-gu (HCC, HS)

Notes **KCC**: Koryŏjok Chungang Ch'onghoe, **HCC**: Hanjok Chungang Ch'onghoe, **HS**: *Hanin Sinbo*.
Source Yu Hyo-jong, "Kyokutō Roshia ni okeru jiūgatsu kakumei to Chōsenjin shyakai," pp. 26-28.

Congress (June 1917) organizing the Koryŏjok Ch'onghoe that embraced only Koreans with Russian citizenship. They also declared that the Hanjok Ch'onghoe "would include all male and female Koreans living on the Russian Territory from the age of 18 years regardless of citizenship, develop the colonization of Koreans, and aim to extend education and encourage industry" necessary for the future of nation." They suggested discussion on January 14, 1918, of the questions concerning the unification of regional Korean organizations, stabilization of occupations, extension of education, establishment of stores, finance unions, organizations of labor unions, and opening of bookstores and publishing companies.[103] In short, the declared goals of the Hanjok Ch'onghoe were the enhancement of the political, social and economic status of the Koreans in Russia, and were not in conflict with those of the Koryŏjok Ch'onghoe.[104]

Immediately responding to the idea of the "great unity" of all Koreans in Russia regardless of citizenship, the Koryŏjok Ch'onghoe decided to seek unification of the two associations on January 11,

1918.[105] Accordingly, Kim Po, the chairman of the Koryŏjok Ch'onghoe was dispatched to attend the inaugural congress of the Hanjok Ch'onghoe which was held from January 14 to 21, 1918. Both sides finally agreed to a unified organization, the Chŏllo Hanjokhoe (Association of the Koreans in All Russia). The two sides also agreed to hold a Constituent Congress for establishing the Chŏllo Hanjokhoe within five months. Both sides appointed the members of the interim Central Executive Committee of the Chŏllo Hanjokhoe as in Table 3. 2.

The two sides sought balance in the ratio of the committee. Mun Ch'ang-bŏm, Han Yong-hŏn [Andrei Konstanotinvich], Sŏ Yun-ch'ŏl were *wŏnhoin* Koreans, and Kim Rip, Chang Ki-yŏng, and Kim Ha-gu, were *yŏhoin* Koreans. Kim Rip, Chang Ki-yŏng, and Kim Ha-gu were all long-time comrades in anti-Japanese activities both in Korea, Chientao (Southeast Manchuria) and the Primorye. Mun Ch'ang-bŏm was a key member of the Koryŏjok Ch'onghoe and a famous Korean *podriadchik* in Suifen region, who had accumulated wealth by providing beef to the Russian military in Nikol'sk-Ussurisk.[106] Han Yong-hŏn was a member of the Primorye *zemstvo* and publisher of the *Hanin Sinbo* in Vladivostok. Kim Rip, was key organizer of the Hanjok Ch'onghoe and chief editor of the Pomunsa, a Korean publishing company in Khabarovsk. Chang Ki-yŏng was the first chief editor of the *Hanin Sinbo*, and Kim Ha-gu was its current chief editor. It is notable that three of the committee members — Han Yong-hŏn, Chang Ki-yŏng, and Kim Ha-gu — were from the *Hanin Sinbo*, the organ of the Korean Association of Vladivostok, the association which both *wŏnhoin* and *yŏhoin* Koreans supported.[107]

Although the two sides agreed to unite their organizations, this did not remove the fundamental difference in their respective political standpoints. While the Koryŏjok Ch'onghoe in Nikol'sk-Ussurisk, under the influence of the SRs, supported the anti-Bolshevik Siberian Congress, the Hanjok Ch'onghoe in Khabarovsk, newly emerged as the center of the Bolshevik political force after the October Revolution, supported the Soviet government.[108]

The increasing influence of the Hanjok Ch'onghoe in Khabarovsk, backed by the Bolsheviks, forced the Koryŏjok Ch'onghoe in Nikol'sk-Ussurisk to make a large concession allowing "equal rights" to the Hanjok Ch'onghoe.[109] The Hanjok Ch'onghoe also had to consider the situation that the Bolsheviks had not yet consolidated their dominance in the Russian Far East, a traditional stronghold of the SRs. Furthermore, the Hanjok Ch'onghoe had to notice the fact that even after the October Revolution, the majority of the Korean population in the Russian Far East, sympathetic with the Siberian *zemstvo*, took a "wait-and-see-attitude."[110]

The unification of the two groups may be called, in some sense, a political victory for the Nikol'sk-Ussurisk group. It succeeded in keeping its power base, Nikol'sk-Ussurisk as the headquarters of the unified Association of the Koreans in All Russia in exchange for allowing the "Hanjok" of the Khabarovsk group as the name for the new unified organization, instead of "Koryŏjok." In addition, by allying with the *yŏhoin* Korean leaders such as Kim Rip, Chang Ki-yŏng, and Kim Ha-gu, the Nikol'sk-Ussurisk group succeeded in weakening the influence of the pro-Bolshevik *wŏnhoin* Koreans such as Chŏn T'ae-guk, Stephan Yu, Vasilii O and Yi Han-yŏng, who traditionally had the power base in Khabarovsk.[111]

2. Korean Socialists Form a Party

Ever since Alexandra Kim came to the Russian Far East in the summer of 1917 from the Urals, she had worked to redirect the Korean nationalist movement toward Bolshevism. She and members of the Workers' Union in the Urals had tried to establish a Korean Bolshevik organization in the Far East. In order to fulfill this plan, she had sought the release of Yi Tong-hwi who had great influence among the anti-Japanese Korean revolutionaries in Russia and Manchuria.[112]

The October Revolution and consequent deterioration of Russo-Japanese relations contributed to strengthening the anti-Japanese mood among Koreans in Russia. Dispatch of the Japanese military ships the *Iwami* and the *Asahi* to Vladivostok on January 12 and 18, 1918 respectively, raised the prospect of Japanese military intervention in Russia. This military demonstration alarmed both Russian Bolsheviks and Koreans in the Russian Far East. The Japanese military threat resulted in producing an environment favorable to cooperation between the Bolsheviks and anti-Japanese Korean activists in Russia. The outlook of Yi Tong-hwi clearly shows the revival of the anti-Japanese issue among Koreans long after the outbreak of World War I:

> At the present time, it becomes obvious that Japan will send troops to Russia and Manchuria. On the day when it [Japanese expedition] comes true, then we have to say that it will be the favorable opportunity which we have long awaited. Now, there are a number of Koreans who were relieved from the military service and returned from the European warfronts. Every one of them is receiving guns and ammunition. Will we hesitate again, encountering this chance of a lifetime? We estimate that the number of the

TABLE 3. 3

Participants of the Congress of the Korean Political Exiles (Feb. 1918)

Regions: Participants	(a)	(b)	(c)	(d)
Khabarovsk (11)				
A. Krasnoshchekov		RB		1, 2, 3
Alexandra Kim	*wŏnho*	RB, WUU	+	1, 2, 3, 4
Yi Tong-hwi	*yŏho*	NPA, RU	+	1, 2, 3, 4
Kim Rip	*yŏho*	NPA, RU	+	1, 2, 3, 4
Pak Ae	*wŏnho*	RB	+	2, 3
Yi Han-yŏng	*wŏnho*		+	2, 3
Stephan Yu	*wŏnho*	RB	+	2, 3
Vasili O	*wŏnho*		+	2, 3
Im Ho	*yŏho*		+	2
Chŏn Il	*yŏho*	NPA, RU	+	2
Pak Wŏn-sŏp	*wŏnho*		+	3
Kim Chong	*wŏnho*		+	4
Nikol'sk-Ussurisk (1)				
Yi Tong-nyŏng	*yŏho*	NPA, RU	-	1, 2, 4
Vladivostok (1)				
Kim Ha-gu	*yŏho*	NPA, RU	+	1
Suchan (2)				
Chang Ki-yŏng	*yŏho*	NPA, RU	+	1
Ch'oe T'ae-yŏl	*yŏho*		+	1
Chita (1)				
Ko Sŏng-sam	*yŏho*	NPA, KM	0	1
Amur (2)				
Yi Wŏn-hae	*wŏnho* (?)		0	1
Han Cha-mun	*wŏnho* (?)		0	1
Omsk (4)				
Yi In-sŏp	*yŏho*	KM, WUU, RB	+	2
Kim Yong-hwan	*yŏho*	NPA, WUU	+	1
Sim Paek-wŏn	*yŏho*	WUU	+	1
O Sŏng-muk	*yŏho*	RU, WUU	+	2
Northern Manchuria (2)				
Hong Pŏm-do	*yŏho*		0	1
Kim Sŏng-mu	*yŏho*	NPA, KM	-	1

Southern Manchuria (1)				
Yang Ki-t'ak	*yŏho*	NPA, RU	0	1, 2, 4
Hunchun Southeastern Manchuria (1)				
Kim Kyu-myŏn	*yŏho*	NPA	+	1
Beijing (1)				
Yu Tong-yŏl	*yŏho*	NPA	+	1, 2, 4
Others (3)				
An Chŏng-gŭn	*yŏho*	NPA, RU	-	5
Cho Sŏng-hwan	*yŏho*	NPA, RU	-	5
O Ha-muk	*wŏnho*		+	2

Notes (a) *wŏnhoin* (old settler) / *yŏhoin* (new settler).

(b) Organizations

RB: Russian Bolshevik Party, **WUU**: Workers' Union in the Urals, **NPA**: New People's Association, **RU**: Restoration Union, **KM**: Kungminhoe

(c) +: Left Wing, -: Right Wing, 0: neutral or unclear

(d) 1. Yi Yŏng-il, "Yi Tong-hwi Sŏngjae sŏnsaeng," pp. 212-16; 2. *Sipwŏl hyŏngmyŏng sipchunyŏn kwa Ssovet Koryŏ minjok*, p. 46; 3. Kim Kyu-myŏn, *Nobyŏng Kim Kyu-myŏn ŭi pimangnok esŏ* [Memorandum of Old Soldier, Kim Kyu-myŏn], ms., pp. 2-3; 4. Yi In-sŏp, "Aleksandra Kim ŭi chŏngi (1)," p. 76; 5. *Purgŭn Kunsa*, 24 Dec. 1921.

Korean soldiers, who had gone to the war amount to 20,000 at least. . . . If we gather them and rise up [against Japan], it will be easier to strike a blow to Japan. Our real hope will not stop here.[113]

With the support and guidance of Alexandr Krasnoshchekov and Alexandra Kim, the initiators of the Hanjok Ch'onghoe in Khabarovsk in early 1918 organized a preparatory committee for the congress of the Korean political exiles [Chosŏn Chŏngch'i Mangmyŏngja Hoeŭi]. Yi Tong-hwi became the committee chairman and his close associate, Kim Rip, took the role of secretary-general. The preparatory committee sent invitation letters asking the anti-Japanese Korean, patriotic organizations in Russia and Manchuria to dispatch deputies to the congress.[114]

In February 1918, about forty Korean anti-Japanese activists gathered in Khabarovsk. Table 3. 3 shows the participants in the conference. The congress discussed the revolutionary politics in Russia and the future tasks of Korean revolutionaries. Alexandra Kim provided reports on international issues and urgent tasks of Korean revolutionaries in the current international situation.[115] Relying on the beliefs of Marxism and Leninism, she also criticized deep-seated regional factionalism among Korean revolutionaries which had exerted negative effects on the Korean liberation movement and Korean communities in Russia.[116] Although delegates pledged to curtail regional disputes,[117] they were divided into two groups disagreeing over what kind of relationship the Korean anti-Japanese revolutionary movement should have to the Russian Bolsheviks. A right wing group composed of national democrats and constitutional monarchists stressed the independent standpoint of the Korean independence movement, and proposed to organize the Kwangŭidan (the Union of Restoration and Righteousness) with the purpose of achieving only the independence of Korea. Opposed to this group was a left wing group contending that Korean liberation from Japanese rule could be achieved only by the success of social revolution in Russia, and a close friendship between Korean and Russian laborers. The result was that the conference failed to agree upon a unified resolution due to deep unresolved disagreements.[118]

As illustrated in Table 3. 3, the members of the Sinminhoe (New People's Association), an influential underground anti-Japanese organization established in 1907, were split at the congress. Some key members of the New People's Association (including Yang Ki-t'ak, Yi Tong-nyŏng, Cho Sŏng-hwan, and An Chŏng-gŭn) refused to agree to the proposal of Alexandra Kim and Yi Tong-hwi. Accordingly, Yi Tong-hwi's plan to unite the members of the New People's Association and to bring those key members into a new organization with close and cooperative ties with Russian Bolsheviks failed. Later, at the end of 1921, Yi Tong-hwi recollected this development as follows:

> The Socialist Party was established in Khabarovsk in 1918. Since the revolutionary organization, the New People's Association, was established, I have communicated with many people on Russian territory. In 1918, I had a conference with the members of the New People's Association, Yu Tong-yŏl, Yang Ki-t'ak, Cho Sŏng-hwan, Yi Tong-nyŏng and An Chŏng-gŭn, but our opinions were not in accord, so I withdrew from the Association. Then, I launched into organizing the Socialist Party and dealt with the party works with tens of people such as Vasilii O, Kim Rip, Yi Han-yŏng, O Sŏng-muk, O Ha-muk, Kim Chong, and Mrs. Stankevich.[119]

We can see that the Khabarovsk congress brought about Yi Tong-hwi's final and official disconnection with the New People's Association which he had organized with other nationalists including An Ch'ang-ho, Yang Ki-t'ak, Yu Tong-yŏl, and Yi Tong-nyŏng in 1907.

As we see in Table 3. 3, the members of the Restoration Union which Yi Tong-hwi organized in 1911 in North Chientao and which a number of the Korean nationalists in Manchuria and the Primorye joined, were also split at the congress. In his report to the Comintern, "the Socialist Movement in Korea," Pak Chin-sun [Ivan Pyotrovich], who was dispatched to the Comintern by the April Congress of the Korean Socialist Party in 1919, reported that "the ever-increasing dissent within the Union of Liberation (Restoration Union, Kwang-boktan), ended in the inevitable split. The Khabarovsk conference of 1918 ascertained the split as a *fait accompli*."[120] Han Hyŏng-gwŏn, a plenipotentiary to Moscow of the Korean Provisional Government in Shanghai in April 1920, wrote of "the Union of Serene Liberation (Union of Iron and Blood Restoration, Ch'ŏlhyŏl Kwangboktan) out of whose left wing the Korean Socialist Party was formed" in his article "The Situation in East Asia."[121]

The left wing group which had followed the advice of Alexandra Kim and Yi Tong-hwi at the congress — Kim Rip, Yu Tong-yŏl, Pak Ae [Matvei], Yi Han-yŏng, O Sŏng-muk, O Ha-muk, Yi In-sŏp, Stephan Yu, Vasilii O, Im Ho, Chŏn Il, Kim Chong and Pak Wŏn-sŏp — began to organize a pro-Bolshevik Korean revolutionary party after the failure of the Khabarovsk Conference.[122] The instigators were members of the Workers' Union in the Urals (Omsk group) led by Alexandra Kim: Yi In-sŏp, O Sŏng-muk, Kim Yong-hwan and Sim Paek-wŏn; and the organizers of the Central Executive Committee of the Korean Associations [Hanjok Chungang Ch'onghoe] (Khabarovsk group): Kim Rip, Yi Han-yŏng, Stephan Yu, Vasilii O, Kim Chong and Pak Wŏn-sŏp.

The landing of Japanese marines from the *Iwami* and the *Asahi* at Vladivostok on April 5, 1918, in response to the killing of two Japanese in Vladivostok, made Bolshevik leaders and Koreans feel an urgent need to prepare for additional Japanese military actions.[123] During the period from the end of April to early May, Alexandr Krasnoshchekov, who had returned from Blagoveshchensk[124] to Khabarovsk, met anti-Japanese Koreans including Yi Tong-hwi, Yu Tong-yŏl, Yang Ki-t'ak and Vasilii O. These Korean leaders also met German POW officers through Alexandr Krasnoshchekov and discussed countermeasures for the forthcoming Japanese expedition to Siberia. Yi Tong-hwi also met Meng Si-yan, the Chinese military commander in Jilin, who was known as "pro-German and anti-Japanese," to discuss cooperation against Japan.[125]

In this climate, the expanded general meeting of the preparatory committee was held in Khabarovsk on May 13, 1918.[126] Eighteen Korean socialists attended this meeting including Alexandra Kim, Yi Tong-hwi, Kim Rip, Yi Han-yŏng, Vasilii O, Stephan Yu, Pak Ae, Sim Paek-wŏn, O Sŏng-muk, Yi In-sŏp, Yu Tong-yŏl, Kim Yong-hwan [T'ae-jun], An Hong-gŭn, and O Ha-muk. Alexandra Kim opened the meeting by suggesting the necessity to form a Korean revolutionary party.[127]

The need for a Korean Socialist Party was agreed to by the majority of participants beforehand, so the meeting mainly consisted of discussion on what to name the party. Alexandra Kim proposed the "Korean Social-Democratic Workers' Party." Following this, Kim Rip asked for a definition of "Bolshevik." After hearing her explanation of the term's origin, the meeting accepted Kim Rip's proposal: since there is neither a majority nor a minority in the Korean party, "Bolshevik" would not be included in the name. Then Yu Tong-yŏl pointed out that "today's situation of Koreans is different from the situation of Russia. Among the Korean population, the peasants compose the absolute majority. If the party is called the workers' party, then there is a danger of losing the peasants. Therefore, I propose to call the party not 'of workers', but 'of peasants'." After further discussion, Kim Rip proposed to use neither "workers" nor "peasants" in the name of the party and to call the party "the Korean Socialist Party" ["Hanin Sahoedang"].[128]

The discussion of the name of the party clearly demonstrated that many of the participants of the meeting had not theoretically understood the political differences among Russian socialist parties, particularly the difference between Bolsheviks and Mensheviks. However, instead of directly adopting the name of the Russian

Bolshevik party, they worked to come up with a name more suitable to the political reality of the Korean society they claimed to represent.

The general meeting adopted the program of the Korean Socialist Party, key contents of which were socialistic, anti-Japanese, and anti-imperialistic, and new members of the Central Committee were elected. Three sections were set up: Organization, Military, and Propaganda. The central committee also decided to publish its organ, the *Chayujong* (Freedom Bell, *Kolokol* in Russian). The meeting elected the members of the Central Committee as follows:

Chairman	Yi Tong-hwi
Vice-Chairman	Vasilii O
Head, Military Section	Yu Tong-yŏl
Superintendent, Party Military Academy	Yu Tong-yŏl
Chairman, Youth Committee	O Sŏng-muk
Chief, Finance Section	Yi In-sŏp
Chief, Propaganda Section	Yi In-sŏp, Chŏn Il (member)
Chief Editor, The *Chayujong*	Kim Rip
Secretary, Korean Language	Kim Rip
Secretary, Russian Language	Vasilii O[129]

According to Yi In-sŏp, who attended the meeting, Alexandra Kim did not accept Yi Tong-hwi's recommendation of her to one of the executive positions, but she refused it by saying:

> Anybody must be a member of one party, not of two parties at the same time. I am a member of the Russian Social Democratic Party (B) and the chief secretary of the city party. In order to be an executive member of the

Korean Socialist Party, I have to leave the RSDP and work with you. However, considering the present situation, I should not do so. It is better for me to work at the Russian Party. I suggest, instead, that Yi In-sŏp, who has worked with me at the RSDP, leave the RSDP and work among the Koreans as a member of the Korean Socialist Party. I recommend Yi In-sŏp to continue the propaganda work, which he has done until now in the Korean Socialist Party.

Yi Tong-hwi added that Yi In-sŏp should be in charge of finance. He consequently withdrew from the RSDP and became the chief of the finance and propaganda sections.[130]

Members of the Korean Socialist Party were mainly political exiles, who lacked a close relationship with the peasantry. The party, therefore, spared no effort to expand its influence among Korean peasants by establishing regional branches in various areas with the support of Bolshevik organizations in Khabarovsk.[131]

The first issue of the *Chayujong* was published on May 14, 1918. The *Chayujong* was the first literature printed in Korean to promote Bolshevism.[132] In order to support the publishing activity of the Korean Socialist Party, A. M. Krasnoshchekov contributed a lithographic machine, printing funds amounting to five thousand rubles, and paper worth more than one thousand rubles. Yu Tong-yŏl and Kim Rip were in charge of Korean translation, and Kim Chin-bo and Vasilii O were in charge of Russian translation.[133]

3. The Second Special Congress of the Delegates of the Koreans in Russia

From June 13-23, 1918, about one month after the establishment of the Korean Socialist Party, the Second Special Congress of the Delegates of the Koreans in All Russia was held in Nikol'sk-Ussurisk in accordance with the agreement reached at the beginning of January 1918, between the Koryŏjok Ch'onghoe (Nikol'sk-Ussurisk group) and the Hanjok Ch'onghoe (Khabarovsk group).

In early May 1918, the Interim Executive Committee of the Korean Assoications in All Russia had an extraordinary meeting and decided to hold the Second Special Congress of the Delegates of the Koreans in All Russia. The committee also passed rules and agenda for the Congress.

When the congress was held, Czech troops were already in revolt against the Bolsheviks at key junctures along the Trans-Siberian Railroad. According to the agreement with the Soviet government, in May 1918 Czech troops began to move from western Siberia to the Far East in order to return to Europe by ship from Vladivostok. They clashed, however, with Bolsheviks in major cities, overthrowing the Bolshevik regional governments. As a result of this, anti-Bolshevik regional authorities were set up in their place. At the same time, the Allies were preparing military intervention, and anti-Bolshevik Russians, encouraged by this situation, also reinforced their own positions. Accordingly, the Bolsheviks faced internal and external threats.

One hundred and twenty-nine delegates representing various regions and "democratic" organizations, were recognized as voting delegates, including Ch'oe Chae-hyŏng, Kim Ch'ang-wŏn and Kim Ha-gu, who were invited by the Interim Central Executive Committee to deliver reports. Thirteen delegates, who came later, were also recognized as voting delegates.

Bolshevik interest in the congress was indicated by the fact that they dispatched delegates of Dalsovnarkom including Alexandr Krasnoshchekov, Alexandra Kim, Stephan Yu and a delegate from the Red Guard Army in Nikol'sk-Ussurisk. Dalsovnarkom, Commissar for Foreign Affairs of the Dalsovnarkom in Khabarovsk, and the Red Guard Army in Nikol'sk-Ussurisk were recognized as non-voting delegates. Key members of the Korean Socialist Party, such as Yi Tong-hwi, Kim Rip, Vasilii O, also attended.

On the second day (June 14), immediately after the chairman Kim Ch'ang-wŏn's opening address, Stephan Yu, representing the Dalsovnarkom, delivered a congratulatory address. The delegates elected the following officials to the Congress.

Mandate Committee: Nam Kong-sŏn, Alexandr Andreevich Li,
Ivan Pyotrovich Pak [Pak Chin-sun]
Temporary Security Guards: Vasilii O [O Yŏng-jun], Yi Wŏn-hae
Chairman: Kim Ch'ang-wŏn [Roman Ivanovich]
Vice-Chairmen: Han Yong-hŏn [Andrei Konstantinovich], Yun Hae
Secretaries: Ch'ae Pyŏng-uk [Andrei Alekseevich] (Russian Language),
Sŏ O-sŏng, O Ch'ang-hwan (Korean Language)
Honorable Chairmen: Yi Tong-hwi, Ch'oe Chae-hyŏng[134]

Six committees on land, labor, education, legislation, budget, and companies for the public welfare were set up and were assigned to prepare the drafts for the resolutions concerning respective questions.

On the third day of the Congress (June 15), Alexandr Krasnoshchekov, who was accompanied by his Korean secretary Pak (Matvei), delivered an address to the delegates on that day. He urged the Koreans to support and cooperate with the Bolsheviks:[135]

> What our party proposes to do is to relieve the poor and workers at the lower strata of society and to seize political power through their hands, to remove the oppression of the propertied and to eradicate imperialism. I think that among of the Korean Associations present here, there are some of the propertied class. However, if it is the case that Koreans, in general, are suffering under the oppression of the capitalists and imperialism, I believe firmly and do not doubt that Koreans will support the ism of our party. Now, in the Orient, only Japan is advocating imperialism and is committing tyranny. When Koreans support our principle and cooperate with us, it will not be difficult to overthrow Japanese imperialism and restore the independence of Korea.[136]

The representatives responded to Krasnoshchekov's address with a big applause. According to Mun Ch'ang-bŏm, who was elected at the congress as the chairman of the newly organized Central Executive Committee of the Korean Associations in All Russia, the big applause "came out from the respect for the present status of Krasnoshchekov, but was not necessarily the expression of supporting Bolshevism."[137]

Then discussions on the current politics followed. Representatives were split on the question concerning the "revolutionary tasks of Korea in general and Korean emigrants in particular," with discussions involving the participation of forty-one speakers. The resulting discussions caused apparent conflict between the *wŏnhoin* and the *yŏhoin*. Concerning current events, three resolutions were submitted. One by the majority of *wŏnhoin* Koreans supported the Constituent Assembly and the Siberian Regional Congress and advocated the revival of all levels of the local *zemstvo*s and self-administrative bodies. They worried that the Soviet government would solve the land issue by sacrificing their land ownership. On the other side, the *yŏhoin*

Koreans believed that only Soviet power could solve the question of land and enhance their status. They believed that they should seek the support and recognition from the Soviet government.[138] According to Ivan Gozhenskii, members of the Korean Socialist Party emphasized "the international character of the Russian Revolution which assaulted the stronghold of international capital, with the aim of liberation of all working masses from the dual yoke of native and foreign exploiters, urging the congress to take its initiative of organizing the Korean revolutionary masses in Russia for the joint struggle for the idea of the proletariat."[139]

Finally, the following resolution compromising the two conflicting resolutions was adopted by sixty eight votes (among seventy-eight votes):

> The second congress of the delegates of the Koreans in All Russia declares with unified mind that what the Great Russian Revolution has achieved should be advocated as the slogan to achieve our national independent life on the basis of freedom, equality, and fraternity. Long live our freedom. Long live the Russian Revolution. Long live socialism.[140]

The resolution took a position of "neutrality." The majority of representatives were still influenced by the Russian Socialist Revolutionary Party (SRs), but, instead of carelessly declaring themselves pro-Constituent Assembly and pro-Siberian Regional Congress, they chose not to directly oppose Soviet power. The careful choice of general, but not specific words such as "Russian revolution" and "socialism" reflect the realistic difficulty which the majority of the Koreans faced.

How to interpret the meaning of the resolution on the current events of that period has raised academic controversies concerning the political standpoint of the congress. Criticizing Walter Kolarz who argued that the congress took the standpoint of neutrality, Hara Teruyuki contended that the congress "took a definite and realistic step toward siding with and pledging loyalty to the Soviet regime," and "sought national autonomy under the Soviet guidance." However, this argument cannot explain why the Bolshevik writers such as Ivan Gozhenskii and Semyonov Anosov pointed out that the majority of the representatives of the congress opposed the proposals of the Korean Socialist Party members who had contended to have close relationship with the Soviet Power and their eventual departure from the congress.[141]

The congress gave the Executive Committee of the Korean Associations in All Russia rein to observe "the most strict neutrality."[142] However, the congress also resolved that personal affiliation with Russian political forces would be left up to individuals.[143] Therefore, Ivan Gozhenskii, who must have attended the congress, criticized the resolution by saying, "they stood for neutrality, hoping finally to side with the winning side, while subjugating themselves to the existing power."[144]

The most dramatic moment occurred on the fourth day (June 16) when delegates discussed the question of land. On the point of accepting the report of the committee on land, a written statement of opinion was submitted and the chairman of the session, Han Yong-hŏn, read the statement to the delegates without asking whether the congress would accept it for discussion or not. After that, Kim Rip criticized Han Yong-hŏn, arguing that "the content of the statement, in general, was unfavorable to the present situation. The chairman dared to read the statement by himself and intended to deal with it unilaterally using his authority." In response, Han Yong-hŏn announced his resignation from the chairman's seat. "The whole audience was thrown into a turmoil and the disputes reached an extreme for several hours." The audience was so out of control that Han Yong-hŏn eventually brandished a gun shouting, "I will kill anybody who attempts to destroy this conference and kill myself as well."[145]

Although on the next day, the congress adopted the resolution to solve the land issue by relying on the "Russian Law of the Land" and "socialism." Discussion of the land issue continued for three days until the sixth day, June 18.[146] Based on reports by the land committee, the congress passed a resolution requesting the Russian authorities to open new offices for naturalization in Vladivostok, Nikol'sk-Ussurisk, Khabarovsk, Olga, Iman, Nikolaevsk-na-Amure, and Blago-veshchensk. These offices would be responsible for getting support for new immigrants. They also decided to dispatch deputies to those offices. The congress also authorized the Central Executive Committee to appeal to local Russian governments for present damage compensation. However, while the land resolution described in detail how to provide financial support for the immigrants in general, it excluded non-naturalized Korean immigrants from participating in the land distribution.[147]

It seems that during the discussion on the land question, "many delegates from the poor section of the Korean population, particularly from tenants," and members of the Korean Socialist Party left the congress. The tenant delegates could not stay until the end of the congress, first, "because of cost," but also because there was no expectation for a "positive result." When they left the congress, the tenant delegates proposed that the fraction of the Korean Socialist Party convene a "business-like congress" in Khabarovsk promising every support for the programs of the party.[148] At the same time, many

TABLE 3. 4

New Central Executive Committee of the Korean Associations in All Russia [Chŏllo Hanjok Chungang Ch'onghoe] (June 1918)

Central Committee
(1) Executive Committee
Chairman: Mun Ch'ang-bŏm Vice-chairmen: Yun Hae, Ch'ae Pyŏng-uk
(2) Standing Committee
Members: Nikolai Chuprov Kim, Iagov Andreevich Kim, Wŏn Se-hun, Han Kun-myŏng Candidates: Kang Yang-o, Kim I-jik, Pyotr Stephanovich Yŏm
Probation Committee
Members: Matvei Stephanovich Ch'ae, Ŏm Chu-p'il, Mikhail Nikolaevich Han Candidates: Kim Ki-ryong, Kim Ch'ŏl-hun, Mikhail Mikhailovich Kim
Honorable Chairman
Yi Tong-hwi, Ch'oe Chae-hyŏng
Deputies to the Commissariat for International Affair of the Dalsovnarkom
Han Yong-hŏn, Pak Chin-sun

yŏhoin Korean revolutionaries and key members of the Korean Socialist Party also left the congress.[149] As a result, the congress became a field for "conflict between naturalized and non-naturalized Koreans."[150] Non-participation by the tenants reduced Korean Socialist Party's influence on the congress.[151] For example, in regards to the education question, the proposal to introduce the Korean language as a major subject in schools, which was probably advanced by the Korean Socialist Party, was rejected. Furthermore, the congress decided to stop providing funds for the two middle schools, Mundŏk and Taegwang from June 1918, the fund which the Hanjok Ch'onghoe based in Khabarovsk had decided to provide in January 1918.[152]

The Korean Socialist Party failed to accomplish both its goals of moving the headquarters of the Central Executive Committee of its Koreans from Nikol'sk-Ussurisk to Khabarovsk, its stronghold, and to transform the composition of the Central Executive Committee in favor of the Korean Socialist Party.[153] The members of the Korean Socialist Party including Kim Rip, the vice-chairman of the interim Central Executive Committee of the Koreans, were excluded from the reorganized and newly elected Central Executive Committee [Chŏllo Hanjok Chungang Ch'onghoe] (see Table 3. 4). Furthermore, the majority of key members were the *wŏnhoin* Koreans influenced by the Socialist Revolutionary Party members (SRs) and even pro-White Koreans.[154]

Nevertheless, the congress tried to take a very realistic approach to Soviet Power. In one example, it decided to dispatch two deputies — Han Yong-hŏn and Pak Chin-sun — to the Commissariat for International Affair of the Dalsovnarkom. However, it failed to include members of the Korean Socialist Party in the composition of the Chŏllo Hanjok Chungang Ch'onghoe and unify the various Korean factions. The Korean Socialist Party criticized its lack of representation and that the "naturalized (Koreans) came to hold the full power of the Central Executive Committee of the Korean Associations in All Russia."[155]

The congress of Korean youth was also held in Nikol's-Ussurisk at the same time and attempted to unify the two organizations; one of the Russianized Koreans, mainly composed of the intelligentsia, and the other of non-Russianized, mainly poor peasants. This attempt at unification also ended in failure.[156]

C. Korean Socialists under the Intervention

On June 28, 1918, Czech troops in Vladivostok rose to overthrow the Bolshevik authorities. This event radically changed the situation in the Russian Far East. The Czech revolt at Vladivostok provided the opportunity for military intervention by the Allies, composed of thirteen countries including the U. S., Japan, Britain and France. At the beginning of August 1918, the Allies intervened militarily in Siberia, ostensibly to save the Czechs. The Chŏllo Hanjok Ch'onghoe was also "bogged down in the general stream of the democratic counter-revolution."

Regardless of the resolution of the second congress to observe "the most strict neutrality," the Chŏllo Hanjok Ch'onghoe after the Czechoslovakian coup suddenly gave up the idea of neutrality which it had so ardently defended under Soviet power. It published in Korean and Russian a newspaper of Socialist Revolutionary Party-orientation where anti-Bolshevik feuilletons appeared. The supreme political organ of the Korean population in Russia clung to nationalism by welcoming Czechs and the "Siberian People's Army" which had attacked the Soviets, jointly with the Japanese expeditionary troops.[157]

In this context, the Chŏllo Hanjok Ch'onghoe decided to work "in any direction which it gives benefit to the independence movement" of Korea. Shortly after the uprising of the Czechs, the Chŏllo Hanjok Ch'onghoe held a welcoming meeting for the Czechs.[158] It revived the SR organizations, and even helped the Russian Whites. The Chŏllo Hanjok Ch'onghoe dispatched Pyotr Stephanovich Yŏm [Yŏm Ha-ik] as the delegate to the SR organization in Vladivostok and expressed its support. After the beginning of the military intervention of the Allies, the Chŏllo Hanjok Ch'onghoe dispatched vice-chairman Yun

Hae and Yi Hŭng-sam, the reporter of the *Hanjok Kongbo* (new name of the *Ch'ŏnggu Sinbo*, organ of the Koryŏjok Ch'onghoe) to its branches and Korean schools and told the Koreans not to engage in "rash and thoughtless action," but to wait until the arrival of a favorable day.[159] Due to such cautious approach in its favorable policies toward the Whites, the Chŏllo Hanjok Ch'onghoe was able to keep its legal status until March 1919, when it was dissolved by the Russian authority because of its leadership in the anti-Japanese demonstration.[160]

When Vladivostok came under the occupation of Whites and the Allies, and the Czech and Japanese troops advanced to Khabarovsk, leaders of the Korean Socialist Party in Khabarovsk discussed countermeasures and decided to organize the Korean Red Guards. With the support of the Bolsheviks, the Central Executive Committee members of the Korean Socialist Party were dispatched to Korean villages in the Primorye and Manchuria and gathered Korean volunteers: Kim Rip, Yi Han-yŏng, Yu Tong-yŏl, Yi In-sŏp and Chŏn Il in Khabarovsk, and Yi Tong-hwi in Sino-Russian border areas in Northern Manchuria. They discussed plans with the key members of the Chŏllo Hanjok Ch'onghoe such as Mun Ch'ang-bŏm and Kim Po, chairman of the Association of the Koreans in Alekseyevsk.[161]

As the commissar for foreign affairs of the Khabarovsk soviet, Alexandra Kim was actively involved in organizing an international Red Guards composed of Austro-Hungarian POWs and other minority nationals such as Chinese, Koreans, Serbians, and Latvians who sympathized with the Soviet Power.[162] Most of the Korean volunteers for the Red Guards were recruited from the recent immigrants who expected improvements in their material and legal conditions from the Soviet government.[163] Pak No-sun was born in Tŏgwŏn, Southern Hamgyŏng Province, North Korea, and had participated in the labor strike in his hometown. He emigrated to Vladivostok and worked at the port. Pak moved to Khabarovsk in spring of 1918 and worked as a laborer. Pak recalled his experience in the Khabarovsk region during the middle of 1918:

> The employer said "today" or "tomorrow" and did not pay wages for what our work during the whole summer. We, therefore, became restless and argued about the measures [for getting the wages]. Someone said that we could go to Alexandra Kim, the aide of Krasnoshchekov, the chairman of the Dalsvonarkom, and she could help us get the wages. Kim was a commissar at that time, and we, laborers, saw her carry two short guns. It was widely said that she was the woman who had liberated Korean and Chinese laborers who were on the way to be sold to the far inside place [Urals] Siberia. It was around August [of 1918]. The rumor was that America, England, Japan and other capitalist invading armies came to Vladivostok, joined with the Russian old Parties [Whites], and attacked the new party [Bolshevik] with the war beginning accordingly. At that time, the role of the Korean Socialist Party in Khabarovsk was great. The propagandists came and said frequently, "Koreans also joined the Russian Red faction-new party and went to the Ussuri war field and are fighting against the Russian old faction-white and Japanese. If the Russian red factions and the Koreans fight together to destroy the Japanese, Korea will be liberated." At that time, we six men who had worked together — Andrei Pak, Ch'oe In-uk, Pak Yŏng-sik, Pak Ki-su, Kim Ung-ryong, and Pak No-sun — gathered, and agreed that we, like others, should join the Russian red faction and participate in the war for eradicating the Japanese army and white faction. First, we departed to see Alexandra Kim, and arrived at the city [Khabarovsk].

On the way to the office of Alexandra Kim, Pak No-sun and other Korean laborers met the Russian army officers and joined the Red Guards.[164]

The swift advance of the military forces composed of the Japanese, Czechs, and Russian Cossacks and the formation of Ussuri front prohibited communication between "north and south" of the Primorye and did not allow the Korean Socialist Party to form larger units of the Korean Red Guards. About one hundred Koreans, led by Ch'oe Pang-jŏn [Nikolai] joined the combat at Iman, Vyazemka and Krasnaya Rechka. In fighting against Kalmykov's Whites and "interventionists," more than half of the Koreans died.[165] Yi In-sŏp, one of the leaders of the Korean Red Guards units, recollected, "when we were forced to retreat with the Russian Red Guards to Krasnaya Rechka, only ten Koreans were alive."[166] These units of the Korean volunteers organized by the Korean Socialist Party were the first Korean Red Guard in the history of the Korean liberation movement.[167]

On August 25, 1918, the Fifth Emergency Regional Congress of the Soviet of the Far East, held in Khabarovsk, acknowledged the necessity of preparing for a partisan system. On August 28, party and Soviet workers and commanders of the Red Guards of Za-Baikal gathered at Urulga near Nerchinsk and decided to switch the regular front system into partisan warfare at the end of August and to move into the Amur region. All organizations of the Bolshevik party and Soviet had to leave Khabarovsk.[168] They decided to retreat from Khabarovsk in different routes. The first group was supposed to escape by land to the Amur region in order to regain communication with Moscow. The second group was to go to the Amur region and Mongolia to resume contact with Moscow. Alexandra Kim decided to join the second group in order to take charge of the final arrangements and act as a rear guard.[169]

On the last ship to leave Khabarovsk, the Baron Korf, there were "International Red Guards troops" composed of about four hundred soldiers, including leaders of the Korean Socialist Party and about twenty Korean partisans under the leadership of Alexandra Kim. However, they were captured by Whites at the Russian cossack village called Ekaterino-Nikol'sk by the Amur River and handed over to Ataman Kalmykov in Khabarovsk.[170] It was Trofim Pak, former temporary chairman of the Central Executive Committee of the Korean Associations [Koryŏjok Chungang Ch'onghoe] in Nikol'sk-Ussurisk, who came as the representative of a neighboring Korean village called Samalli (Blagoslovennoe), and helped the soldiers of Kalmykov disarm the arrested members of the Korean Socialist Party.[171] Twelve Koreans including the leaders of the Korean Socialist Party, Yu Tong-yŏl, Yi In-sŏp and Chŏn Il were released. At that time, Kim Rip was released, but was arrested together with Sŏ Yŏng-ch'an later on October 2 at Pak Yŏng-sun's house in Evgenevka (near Khabarovsk). Kim and Sŏ were held without evidence in a Japanese prison in Khabrovsk where they were beaten, kicked and tortured. Kim was sent by train to Nikol'sk-Ussurisk for investigation, but escaped dramatically from the train. However, Alexandra Kim was shot along with other eighteen Bolshevik leaders.[172] After Alexandra Kim was executed, Vasilii O, her husband, was arrested and tortured brutally by the Japanese *gendarme*. He later suffered and died from heart disease caused by the torture.[173] The Czech Uprising and subsequent military intervention by the Allies dealt a fatal blow to the Korean Socialist Party and key members had to scatter to Manchuria and the countryside of the Primorye.

As we will see in Chapter 4, at the end of 1918, the members of the Korean Socialist Party who had been scattered into various regions, resumed their communication, and worked to restore the organization and its propaganda. Korean Red Army units retreated to the Taban and Anban regions to try to reinforce their members.[174]

Chapter Four

KOREAN SOCIALISTS AND THE MARCH FIRST MOVEMENT

A. Developing a Strategy

1. The March First Movement in the Primorye

The Japanese Siberian expedition and the establishment of White regimes in the Russian Far East deteriorated the social and political conditions for Korean activities in the Primorye. Under these conditions, however, news of the end of World War I and the upcoming Versailles Peace Conference greatly inspired Korean nationalists both within Korea and abroad. The majority of Korean social and political organizations hoped to achieve the independence of Korea with the help of the Allied powers. They were particularly inspired by the American President Woodrow Wilson's principle of national self-determination. The Korean nationalists in the Russian Far East had witnessed friction between American and Japanese military forces over intervention policy and knew that the Allies, especially the United States, supported Czechoslovakian independence. It was natural for Korean nationalists in the Russian Far East to compare the case of Korea with that of Czechoslovakia and expect similar views from the United States.[1]

Under the Kolchak government in Omsk, the Central Executive Committee of the Korean Associations in All Russia [Chŏllo Hanjok Chungang Ch'onghoe, hereafter cited as the Chŏllo Hanjok Ch'onghoe] was the only legal Korean organization in the Russian Far East.[2] At the end of 1918, the Chŏllo Hanjok Ch'onghoe began to discuss the issue of dispatching a delegation to Paris and planned for a mass demonstration to express the desire of the Korean people for independence from Japan.[3] This was certainly stimulated by the news that Korean nationalists in America were planning to dispatch a delegation to Paris. At first, the "three great leaders" of Koreans in Russia — Yi Tong-hwi, Ch'oe Chae-hyŏng and Mun Ch'angbŏm — were considered for delegates.[4]

At the end of January 1919, Yŏ Un-hyŏng, dispatched by the New Korea Youth Party [Sinhan Ch'ŏngnyŏndang] in Shanghai, came to Russia through Manchuria and met Korean leaders in Vladivostok and Nikol'sk-Ussurisk. When Yŏ Un-hyŏng told them that Kim Kyu-sik in Shanghai had already been dispatched to Paris as the delegate of the New Korean Youth Party,[5] the Chŏllo Hanjok Ch'onghoe changed its original plan and instead, dispatched Yun Hae and Ko Ch'ang-il, who were "familiar with foreign languages such as English and French and who had knowledge about the international politics."[6] Yun Hae and Ko Ch'ang-il left Nikol'sk-Ussurisk on February 5, 1919 with certificates written in Russian and French designating them "representative of all Koreans."[7]

On February 25, 1919, shortly before the outbreak of the March First Movement in Korea, the Chŏllo Hanjok Ch'onghoe convened the Congress of the Koreans in All Russia [Chŏlloguk nae Hanin Hoeŭi] in Nikol'sk-Ussurisk. About eighty delegates came not only from Russia, but also from North Chientao, West Chientao and even Korea itself. The conference was originally intended to prepare a manifesto for Korean independence[8] and continued until early March 1919.[9] The invitation letters to various regions of Russia were sent in the name of Kim Chin.[10]

By the initiative of Mun Ch'ang-bŏm, Kim Ch'i-bo, Kim Ha-sŏk, Chang Ki-yŏng and Kim Chin,[11] it was decided at the conference to transform the Chŏllo Hanjok Ch'onghoe into the Korean National Council [Taehan Kungmin Ŭihoe], following the example of the Czechoslovakian National Council.[12] The Korean National Council adopted the soviet system and accordingly had three functions of parliament, administration and legislature. The standing committee composed of 30 members was responsible for the important decisions needed during the period of recession of the Council's annual general meetings. All Korean associations in various regions of Russia inhabited by Koreans were allowed to function as the regional branches of the Korean National Council. Additional branches were also organized in Northern Chientao and Hunchun in Manchuria and even in Korea. Unlike the Chŏllo Hanjok Ch'onghoe which was the central body only of Koreans in the regions of the Russian Far East, the Korean National Council claimed itself to be the central organization of Koreans in general.[13]

Mun Ch'ang-bŏm, the Chairman of the Central Executive Committee of the Chŏllo Chungang Ch'onghoe, was elected Chairman of the Korean National Council, and Kim Ch'ŏl-hun and O Ch'ang-hwan were elected as Vice-Chairman and Secretary, respectively. In addition to these offices, there were executive ministries in charge of war, finance, internal affairs and foreign affairs. Yi Tong-hwi, the Chairman of the Korean Socialist Party, was elected "Minister of War Declaration" (later, changed to Minister of Military Affairs) without his knowledge,[14] and his close associate, Kim Rip was appointed his chief staff member.[15] Because Yi Tong-hwi did not take the post, Kim Ha-sŏk was appointed acting Minister in his place.[16]

According to the suggestion of Kim Ha-sŏk, who was known to have participated in the March First Movement in Korea and came to Nikol'sk-Ussurisk from Korea,[17] the Korean National Council increased the number of members on the standing council [*sangsŏl wiwŏnhoe*] of the Korean National Council from fifteen to thirty by adding fifteen members, five from the Western faction [*Sŏp'a*, P'yŏngan Province] and five from the Seoul faction [*Kyŏngp'a* or *Kihop'a*, Kyŏnggi and Ch'ungch'ŏng Provinces].[18] This increase was definitely intended to overcome the one-sided composition of the Chŏllo Hanjok Ch'onghoe in which the people from the Northern faction (*Pukp'a*, Hamgyŏng Province) composed the majority and thereby to enhance the authority of the Korean National Council as the representative organization of all Korean people.

The conference worked out a plan in three stages to realize the independence of Korea. For the first stage, they planned a peaceful movement mainly focusing on the distribution of the Declaration of Independence of Korea, hoisting the Korean national flag at every Korean house, and staging mass street demonstrations. In the second stage, all armed forces both inside and outside Korea would advance to fight the Japanese in Korea. In the last stage, simultaneously with the start of the war with Japan, the Korean delegation would submit an appeal to the Allied Powers requesting them to press Japan to allow independence for Korea.[19]

The leaders of the Korean National Council realized that they could not achieve the independence of Korea simply by means of peaceful demonstrations and diplomatic activities in Paris. They also understood that the Western Powers could not provoke a war against Japan to accomplish the independence of Korea. Accordingly, they concluded that it was necessary to make all Korean armed forces in Manchuria and Russia attack Japan militarily in Korea. Only then, they hoped, would the Allies recognize the Korean armed forces as "a belligerent" and discuss the question of Korea at the Paris Peace Conference.[20]

The Korean National Council applied to Russian authorities to allow a mass demonstration in Vladivostok on March 15, 1919. However, the White regime did not accept this application, and, on March 14, ordered the Korean National Council and the Korean Association in the New Korean Village in Vladivostok to be dissolved, and not to commit actions which might harm the Russo-Japanese relationship.[21] The Korean National Council decided to defy the order of the Russian authorities and postponed the date to March 17. On the morning of March 17, the Korean National Council issued "the Declaration of Independence of Korea," written in Russian, English, Chinese and Korean in Nikol'sk-Ussurisk in the name of Mun Ch'ang-bŏm (Chairman), Kim Ch'ŏl-hun (Vice-Chairman) and O Ch'ang-hwan (Secretary). The copies of "the Declaration of Independence of Korea" were distributed to the Russian government office and eleven foreign general consulates including Japan. While every Korean house hoisted the Korean national flag, Mun Ch'ang-bŏm and Kim Ch'ŏl-hun presided over the ceremony for Korean independence with 20,000 Koreans in the New Korean Village. After the ceremony, Mun led the mass demonstration to the center of Vladivostok where they then distributed copies of the Declaration to people on the street.[22]

Following a request of the Japanese Consulate General to stop the demonstrations, Russian officials arrested two Korean students, and ordered the removal of all Korean national flags.[23] Unhappy with the Russians, the Korean National Council ordered Korean workers to go on a strike. On March 18, a large number of the Korean workers left their workplaces, and gathered in the New Korean Village to protest the Russian authorities' prohibition of the Korean demonstration on the previous day.[24] It was the members of the Korean Socialist Party who prepared and initiated the demonstration of the Korean workers in Vladivostok, and O Sŏng-muk and Afanasii Arsentievich Kim [Kim Sŏng-u], members of the Korean Socialist Party, drafted and issued a proclamation written in Korean, Russian, Chinese and English. The proclamation criticized mass arrests of Koreans and terror exercised within Korea by the Japanese during the March First Movement.[25] Demonstrations by Koreans continued until the middle of April in the main cities of the Primorye, such as Nikol'sk-Ussurisk, Spassk, Razdol'noye (Hamat'ang in Korean), Khabarovsk and Pos'et.[26]

From the end of March, the Koreans in the Primorye and Manchuria shifted their emphasis from peaceful demonstrations to preparation for armed struggle against the Japanese, organizing partisan units and military training of young Koreans. Acting Minister of War Declaration of the Korean National Council, Kim Ha-sŏk, was in charge of the armed struggle efforts with the Japanese as outlined by the three-stage plan. With the support of the Korean National Council, Kim Ha-sŏk organized the Korean Association for Achieving Independence [Hanjok Tongnip Kisŏnghoe], which planned to build up a force of about 10,000 Korean soldiers to wage an armed conflict against the Japanese. Their offensive against the Japanese was to be coordinated with guerilla (partisan) units from within Korea. The Korean National Council and the Korean Association for Achieving Independence eventually sought to declare a Korean Provisional Government in Northern Chientao or in Northern Hamgyŏng Province the moment the Korean armed forces entered Korean territory.[27]

At the same time, the Korean National Council supported the plan of Kim Ha-sŏk who concluded a contract with General Dmitry Leonidovich Horvath, former governor of the Chinese Eastern Railroad and presently "High Plenipotentiary" in the Far East appointed by Admiral Kolchak's Omsk government,[28] to send three thousand persons to Yehho as garrison guards for the Chinese Eastern Railroad.[29] Horvath promised that he would provide the young Koreans with weapons and support their independence movement at the time of victory over the Soviets.[30] Attracted by the slogan of the Korean National Council, "train officers!" and "learn military tactics!," many young Koreans, particularly, members of the Union of Iron and Blood Restoration [Ch'ŏlhyŏl Kwangboktan], a strong patriotic nationalist organization whose members were working in Manchuria and Primorye, responded to the call of the Korean National Council.[31] The Korean National Council gathered and sent more than six hundred young Koreans to the Independent Special Korean National Battalion under the command of Pyotr Ivanovich Kim, supervised by General Horvath, and located at Yehho near the Chinese Eastern Railroad.[32]

Due to suppressive measures taken by the White regime established under the Allies' military intervention, key members of the Korean Socialist Party hid in the rural areas of the Primorye or in Manchuria. As a result, only a few members such as Chang Ki-yŏng, Kim Chin and Chŏn Il were able to get involved in organizing the Korean National Council and its main activities such as dispatching a delegation to Paris, peaceful demonstrations for the "independence of Korea," and military cooperation with General Horvath in Harbin.

Yi Tong-hwi, for example, was in Luozigou (Najagu in Korean), Russo-Chinese border area in Manchuria.[33] Later in 1922, in a letter to the Comintern, the Irkutsk faction, which included key members of the Korean National Council including Kim Ha-sŏk, Kim Ch'ŏl-hun and Han Myŏng-se, criticized Yi Tong-hwi's non-involvement in the programs of the Korean National Council:

> His [=Yi Tong-hwi's] activities, rather inactivity, while he was in Siberia prior to the March First Movement in 1919 (when he really knew nothing about the whole project until after the mission was sent to Paris, after the outbreak took place in Korea, and after the Provisional Government was formed) have classed him as only a passive and not an initiative element.[34]

Yi Tong-hwi returned from Manchuria at the end of March, 1919 and began to establish contacts with Russian Bolsheviks who were involved in underground activities. Yi Tong-hwi met Russian Bolshevik leaders such as A. Y. Neibut and S. V. Stankov with Pak Chin-sun [Ivan Pyotrovich] as interpreter and discussed plans of organizing Bolshevik party cells within the Korean villages in the Primorye and establishing contacts between Korean and Russian partisan units.[35] A Japanese intelligence agent also got information

TABLE 4. 1

Executive Members of the Korean Independence Army Headquarters

Commander-in-Chief	Hong Pŏm-do
Commander	Yi Yong
Military Supplies	Ch'oe Pyŏng-jun, Hwang Wŏn-ho
Military Fund	O Chu-hyŏk, Pak Kun-bu
Chief Staff Members	Kim Rip, Yi Chung-jip

Source Twibabo, "Aryŏng silgi (12)," *Tongnip Sinmun*, 8 Apr. 1920, p. 3.

about the return of Yi Tong-hwi from Manchuria:

> "A discontented Korean," Hong Pŏm-do came to Vladivostok on [March] 22 and Yi Tong-hwi, together with Cho Sŏng-hwan, appeared at Nikol'sk-Ussurisk, and accordingly the situation in that place became agitated.[36]

While not taking the office of the Minister of War Declaration appointed by the Korean National Council, Yi Tong-hwi secretly and separately organized the Korean Independence Army Headquarters [Tongnipkunbu] in Vladivostok.[37] He then appointed the key positions of the Korean Independence Army Headquarters (see Table 4. 1).

The military camps were set up in Korean villages in the valley called Sidaogangzi located between Tumenzi and Sanchakou in Hunchun on the Sino-Russian border area near Suifun. In this region, there were a large number of Koreans who had received Russian citizenship without land allotments during the early period of the governor-generalship of Gondatti. They moved there to escape Russian mobilization after the outbreak of Word War I. They had recently migrated to Russia, around the time of the Japanese annexation of Korea. Accordingly, unlike the *wŏnhoin* Koreans, they did not feel a strong responsibility to or appreciation of the Russian government. In general, they held more anti-Japanese feelings and were more supportive of the independence movement.[38]

Koreans with "anti-Japanese" attitudes, and also those influenced by socialism — particularly Bolshevism — avoided the military conscription by the White Russian regime in order to join Yi Tong-hwi's camp, stating that: "We would rather fight against the Japanese for the liberation of Korea than respond to the military call of the Whites and fight against the Bolsheviks."[39]

The graduates of the Korean Military Academy at Luozigou, which had been established in Manchuria by Yi Tong-hwi, Kim Rip, and Chang Ki-yŏng, joined as officers and trained the soldiers. The soldiers were recruited from Russia, China and even from Korea. Also Hong Pŏm-do, who was active in Northern Chientao, and Hwang Pyŏng-gil, Yi Myŏng-sun, and Ch'oe Kyŏng-ch'ŏn, who were active in Hunchun, sent some of their detachments.[40] Kikuji Girō, the Japanese consul general in Vladivostok, reported stories told by two Koreans who had visited the Korean camps in a Korean village, Tajiagou (Kor. Tangŏjaegol), run by Yi Tong-hwi in April 1919:

> Hŏ Kŭn, who returned from Tajiagou (Kor. Tangŏjaegol) on May 3, had worked as a carpenter for several months in the station of Manchuria, but recently he heard the news about the intensification of the Korean independence movement. He could not keep silent, left Manchuria, . . . visited Tajiagou, met Yi Tong-hwi and returned to Vladivostok. According to Hŏ, a considerable number of young men gathered under Yi Tong-hwi from every direction and all of them have been accommodated within

> Korean villages and are now being trained by the instructors. They have a lot of weapons as well.
>
> In addition, Maria Yi, a Korean woman residing in Suifen (Kor. Ch'up'ung), told our spy that she recently went to Tajiagou in order to buy opium and saw that Korean houses in every place were filled with the Korean soldiers and that every house was accommodating seventy persons. They were being trained regularly and worked very hard in agriculture or other work while not in training.[41]

The Japanese information agents evaluated that Yi Tong-hwi had gathered enough military funds and weapons for training and housing soldiers, as well as a number of weapons. The rise of the anti-Japanese mood among the Koreans after the March First Movement contributed greatly to the military activities of Yi Tong-hwi. He and his associates bought weapons from Bolsheviks and ex-soldiers, also insisting every volunteer come with at least a gun. In the Primorye, it was not difficult to buy weapons from dismissed soldiers who kept weapons and bullets.[42]

Political positions and activities of the Korean Socialist Party and the Korean National Council during the period of the March First Movement were controversial points between the Shanghai and Irkutsk Groups into which the Korean Socialist Party and the Korean National Council developed. One problem of the Korean National Council was in that it expected to obtain independence for Korea by gaining sympathy and help from the Allies intervening in Russia in cooperation with Japan and the Russian Whites. How could the Koreans get their independence by getting the sympathy of their enemy's friends? Furthermore, the Korean National Council seeking help and cooperation from the military forces of General Horvath in Harbin was seen as problematic.

These activities of Korean National Council members, such as the dispatch of the delegation to the Versailles Peace Conference and military cooperation with "anti-revolutionary" White General Horvath contributed to their eventual purge from the Russian Communist Party in the late 1920s. In November 1929, Kim Ha-sŏk — a key member of the Korean National Council — tried to defend himself by contending that his cooperation with Horvath was "a temporary measure for Korean revolution" and more importantly that he had consulted with Yi Tong-hwi, Kim Rip and other comrades. Yi Tong-hwi, in a report to the Korean newspaper *Sŏnbong* (The Vanguard), rejected the contention of Kim Ha-sŏk:

> On last November 11, [1929] when party member, comrade Kim Ha-sŏk, faced the purge of the party, he was known to have said in defense that "when he gathered and sent Korean soldiers to the army of the White Guard, Horvath in the spring of 1919, it was a temporary means for the Korean revolution, and he discussed the matter with comrade Yi Tong-hwi and other comrades. And he dealt with all matters related to this in the capacity of the acting Minister of Military Affairs." The fact is not so. The executive members of the Korean National Council including Kim Ha-sŏk already put the project of gathering and sending Korean soldiers to the army of Horvath into practice when I was in Louzigou in Chinese territory. It was after the project was already completed that I arrived at Sibeichang (Kor. Sŏbukch'ang). I never consulted with [Kim Ha-sŏk] and Mun Ch'ang-bŏm. I was in a mountain village called Isunhŏ of Raohe-xuan in China when Mun Ch'ang-bŏm and other persons organized the Korean National Council and appointed me as the Minister of Military Affairs. Therefore, I am saying here

that there was not anything like notice or consultation, or agreement.[43]

Kim Ha-sŏk again published his argument in the *Sŏnbong* providing a different explanation which refuted the argument of Yi Tong-hwi:

> I participated in the March First Movement in Korea, was exiled and arrived at Sowangnyŏng [Nikol'sk-Ussurisk] on 12 March. After several days, I was appointed a member of the Ministry of Military Affairs and took the position of acting Minister of Military Affairs. . . . After the March First Movement, independence activists, both inside and outside Korea, with no exception, felt urgent need for the military action. The [Restoration] Union established a project in Yehho [to send Korean soldiers to the Horvath army in Yehho] and made the Korean National Council support this project. In April in that year (1919), Yi Tong-hwi and Kim Rip in Northern Sibeichang (Kor. Sŏbukch'ang) called me. Accordingly, I met [them] and discussed the strategies for the independence movement. . . . As a result, I put the decision into practice working as the acting Minister of Military Affairs. As a result, ... I concluded a contract to send three thousand young Koreans to Yehho as garrison guards and in May of that year, dispatched more than six hundreds soldiers.[44]

At this point, it is difficult to determine who is telling the truth based on available sources. However, it is clear the conflict between the Korean Socialist Party and the Korean National Council did not start quite the way as many recollections describe. As Yi Tong-hwi himself contended, he was not in a position to be consulted about his appointment as the Minister of Military Affairs of the Korean National Council. However, it does not mean that Yi refused to accept the position.[45] More importantly, however, is that although

Yi Tong-hwi and Kim Rip were proceeding with their own plan, the key members of the Korean National Council, such as Mun Ch'ang-bŏm, Kim Ha-sŏk, Ch'oe Chae-hyŏng, O Ch'ang-hwan and Kim Hak-man, considered Yi Tong-hwi and Kim Rip as the persons in charge of the military affairs of the Korean National Council.[46] It is certain that the key members of the Korean National Council at that time did not know the existence of the Korean Socialist Party.

That is why the Korean National Council tried to support the military activities of Yi Tong-hwi. For the Korean National Council, the military activities of Yi Tong-hwi were the most important steps in its three-stage plan for achieving the independence of Korea. In addition, the Korean National Council energetically supported the military activities of Yi Tong-hwi, because it had to compete with the Korean Provisional Government in Shanghai [Sanghae Imsi Chŏngbu] which was organized on April 13, 1919.[47]

Most of the key figures of the Korean National Council (Mun Ch'ang-bŏm, Kim Ch'i-bo, Kim Ha-sŏk, Kim Chin, and Chŏn Il) travelled around the Korean villages in the Primorye and tried to gather funds and young volunteers for the military activities being led by Yi Tong-hwi. In particular, Mun Ch'ang-bŏm was so energetic for supporting the Korean independence movement that he was criticized by Ch'oe Chae-hyŏng for spending the funds originally gathered by Ch'oe for supporting the Korean Teachers' College.[48] It was in this context that Japanese officials came to regard the Korean National Council as the supporting organization for Yi Tong-hwi.[49] At the same time, Japanese officials in Vladivostok strongly urged their government "to negotiate with Chinese officials and to seek measures for arresting Yi Tong-hwi and dissolving all his support groups and to confiscate all the weapons of the Koreans."[50]

Until its April Congress, the Korean Socialist Party did not take a firm position toward the policies of the Korean National Council. Some key members of the Korean Socialist Party, such as Chang Ki-yŏng and Kim Chin, had played key roles in organizing the Korean National Council, and many members of the Korean Socialist Party were appointed to responsible positions on the Korean National Council. Yi Tong-hwi and Kim Rip were appointed as the Minister of War Affairs and its chief staff member, and Chŏn Il was chosen as a member of the Ministry of Internal Affairs.[51] Kim Chin, Chŏn Il and O Yŏng-sŏn were key members in gathering and training of young Koreans for armed struggle planned by the Korean National Council.[52] In this context, Pak Chin-sun, a member of the Korean Socialist Party delegation to the Comintern, pointed out in his Comintern report that "in parts, elements of the right wing of our union [Korean Socialist Party] built their illusions" on "the Versailles Peace Conference and the League of Nations."[53]

2. The Socialist Party Congress

At the end of April 1919, the Congress of the Delegates of the Korean Socialist Party was held in a forest located in the suburbs of Vladivostok.[54] In his report to the Comintern, Pak Chin-sun, the member of the delegation dispatched by the Congress to Moscow, described the background of the congress as follows:

> The "Rice Riots" in Japan; the end of the world war with its results — the Versailles Peace Conference and the League of Nations, on which our national patriots and, in part, elements of the right wing of our union built

their illusions; the defeats of the Socialists in the newly-created states and the March Uprisings in Korea — all this gave a new meaning to our life, whose wheel turning with dizzying speed gave birth to new events and new questions, which demanded of society conscious answers.[55]

The leaders of the Korean Socialist Party must have been impressed by the explosive forces of the masses demonstrated in the March First Movement in Korea, the Rice Riot in Japan and the uprisings led by the Communists in Germany, Lithuania, and Hungary. More importantly, the Korean Socialist Party leaders, with great uneasiness, noticed that those uprisings had faced terrible defeats because of the lack of correct leadership. Particularly, they considered that the uprising in Korea which was "being led by national-patriots and directed by them towards a false path of national antagonism, would not, under such conditions, lead to desirable results."[56] Therefore, it was an urgent task for them to reinforce the Korean Socialist Party and to prepare their own strategies based on an analysis of the current situation. The ambivalent attitude of some key members of the Korean Socialist Party, who were participating in the activities of the Korean National Council whose policies were in conflict with traditional policies of the Korean Socialist Party, also must have raised the urgent necessity to convene the party congress.

According to Pak Chin-sun, forty-nine delegates representing 30,000 members, one third from the Korean Socialist Party and the other two thirds from the New People's Union [Sinmindan], attended the Congress.[57] The leaders of the two revolutionary groups agreed to unite the two organizations into one, "Korean Socialist Party." Kim Rip was the main figure who had initiated the idea of the unification of the two organizations and accepted members of the New People's Union into the Socialist Party.[58]

The leader of the New People's Union was Kim Kyu-myŏn (alias Kim Paek-ch'u), who was born at Kyŏnghŭng in North Hamgyŏng Province, studied at the National Teachers' School and a short-course military school in Seoul. He became a Baptist, and participated in the "new educational movement" as a member of the New People's Association [Sinminhoe]. In 1914, when the Baptists in Korea were split over the issue of who would succeed Malcom C. Fenwick, a Baptist missionary from Canada, Kim Kyu-myŏn declared "independence from abroad (foreign missionaries)" and established his own Independent Church [*tongnip kyohoe*] called "Sŏngnigyo (Holy Truth Religion)" with about 300 churches and 30,000 followers. Kim Kyu-myŏn united Christians in Northern Korea, Manchuria, and the Primorye by starting a radical movement in the churches, which contended that Korean Christians should depart from their habit of subservience to foreign missionaries. Kim Kyu-myŏn himself became the bishop of the Independent Church and exercised the highest authority. When "the Rules for Religious Activities" ["*p'ogyo kyuch'ik*"] were promulgated by the Japanese Government-General Office in August 16, 1915, Kim Kyu-myŏn refused to register his church with the Japanese Government-General Office. In Hunchun, Manchuria, just before the outbreak of the March First Uprising, with the goal of achieving the independence of Korea, he organized a secret underground organization, the New People's Union, whose name was borrowed from the New People's Association [Sinminhoe]. The New People's Union was composed of two or three hundred faithful Independence Church members.[59]

Under its constitution and platform dated March 12, 1919, the New People's Union pledged to fight for the "complete independence of the fatherland" and "great unity" by "destroying regional factions and unfair ambitions" and to establish an independent Korea based on a democratic system.[60] After its establishment, the New People's Union began to raise soldiers and funds for military activities against Japanese rule, and organized its own partisan units in Hunchun, North Chientao, and the Primorye. At the time of the Congress, after the discussion with Yi Tong-hwi, the New People's Union moved its headquarters from Hunchun to Vladivostok, keeping branches in Hunchun and Northern Chientao.[61]

In an article submitted to the *Communist International* (August 1920), Han Hyŏng-gwŏn, an envoy to Moscow dispatched by the Korean Provisional Government in Shanghai, listed the New People's Union along with the United National Block, the Korean Socialist Party, the Union of Iron and Blood Restoration, and the Union of Terrorists, as the five strong "political parties" which had members in Russia, China and America as of April 1919.[62] A Japanese informer also reported that, "compared with other organizations of the independent movement, the New People's Union increasingly consolidates its foundation, is said to be capable of accomplishing its programs, and has a good reputation among the public. It achieved good results in recruiting members and collecting funds, the number of members has already reached thirty thousands and the unity is firm."[63]

The congress approved the proposal to unify the Korean Socialist Party and the New People's Union under the name of "Korean Socialist Party." The unification was easily achieved, for the members of the two organizations even earlier "had manifested a unanimous accord on almost all questions and had acted with comradely solidarity."[64] Regardless of the unification, the congress decided to preserve the New People's Union as the nationalistic mass organization. We will see later that the unification of the Korean Socialist Party and the New People's Union, to a great extent, contributed to the strength of the Korean Socialist Party in terms of its finance and membership.

As a result of the unification, the Korean Socialist Party succeeded in overcoming its weakness as a body composed mainly of exiled revolutionaries and intellectuals. This reinforcement of the Korean Socialist Party in 1919 was also possible thanks to the March First Movement, which produced thousands of anti-Japanese activists and sympathizers. While the creation of the Korean Socialist Party in 1918 was supervised and supported by the Russian Bolsheviks, the April Congress and the reinforcement of the Korean Socialist Party were the products of Korean socialists without any direct support from Russian Bolsheviks. It clearly shows that the March First Movement brought about an explosive surge of Korean anti-Japanese activities among Koreans.

At the Congress, disputes between the left and right factions were ever present. Based on a "purely class principle," the left argued that activities of the Korean Socialist Party should have close ties with the proletarian movement of the whole world. The right contended that the Korean Socialist Party should have close contacts with the native bourgeoisie and nobility, considering them to also be "revolutionary" nationalists. The right pointed out chauvinistic tendencies among the Japanese proletariat. The left contended that Korean liberation should be carried out with the support of the working class people in Japan and other countries. That the struggle of Koreans should not be a national chauvinistic movement against Japan, but merely a movement against Japanese imperialism. Over the duration of the congress, the left ultimately won out.[65]

Currently we are not able to identify the exact composition of these two factions. However, one can guess that the majority of the right segment came from the New People's Union whose platform suggested "complete independence of the fatherland" and national "great unity." Furthermore, some members of the old Korean Socialist Party might have joined the right. Eventually, with the exception of five delegates, the right agreed to the arguments of the left.[66]

The "purely class principle" of the left was reflected in the "basic theses" adopted by the congress. The Korean Socialist Party viewed Korea as entering the "capitalistic stage." Accordingly, the "basic theses" suggested the importance of the party's struggle both against Japanese imperialism and capitalist exploitation. To advance their goals in these struggles, the close cooperation between the revolutionary organizations in Korea and Japan was emphasized. The thesis also called for the organization and education of proletariat and agricultural laborers "in the spirit of revolutionary Marxism" and to lead them in their daily struggle with capitalism. The congress found that the Soviet system was "the most expedient form of government" and "the most proper to the vital interests of the working classes of Korea."[67]

These "basic theses" were also applied to the Korean Socialist Party programs by the congress. The congress concluded that the March First Movement had been directed by national patriots "toward a false path of national antagonism" and the Korean Socialist Party ought to "direct the movement into the channel of class struggle" by establishing close ties with Japanese Socialists.[68]

Concerning the international political stage, the congress resolved to conduct intensified agitation and propaganda among the masses against the authority of the Peace Conference, which the congress feared, would not give any attention to the Korean question. Concurrently, the congress resolved to carry on agitation and propaganda among the masses for the recall of Korean delegates from the Versailles Peace Conference.[69]

In order to carry out the program of the Korean Socialist Party, the congress resolved to dispatch party members to the New People's Union and the Union of Iron and Blood Restoration,[70] two mass organizations to which many of the party members belonged. For propaganda purposes, the congress decided to utilize newspapers and magazines, such as *Chayujong* (Freedom Bell, the organ of the Korean Socialist Party), the *Sinminbo* (the organ of the New People's Union), the *Tongnip Sinmun* (The Independence Newspaper), published by the members of the Korean Socialist Party, Chang Ki-yŏng and Kim Chong-hyŏn, and the *Hanin Sinbo*, the organ of the the Korean Association in Vladivostok.[71]

The Congress elected five members of the Central Executive Committee composed of Chairman (Yi Tong-hwi), heads of three committees (organization, propaganda, and military) and Secretary-General (Kim Rip). Kim Kyu-myŏn was elected one of two vice-chairmen and head of military committee.[72] The Congress also decided to join the Comintern, which was established in early March 1919, in Moscow, and to dispatch a delegation composed of Pak Chin-sun, Pak Ae and Yi Han-yŏng, three key members of the Korean Socialist Party who spoke Russian fluently, to the Third Communist International.[73] The congress resolved to establish close connections with Bolsheviks and partisan units in the Far East.[74]

The Moscow-oriented policy of the Korean Socialist Party contrasted sharply with the Paris-oriented policy of other influential social and political organizations, such as the Ch'ŏndogyo (Religion of

Heavenly Way), Christian communities, the Union of Iron and Blood Restoration, United National Block, and the Union of Terrorists, which composed the majority of Korean nationalist revolutionary forces.[75] The two competing "emigrant centers," the Korean National Council and the Shanghai Provisional Government, were also "under the influence of Entente diplomacy," believing that the Peace Conference and the League of Nations would do something crucial for Korean independence. Based on this belief, the two organizations dispatched their own respective delegations to Paris.[76]

The congress discussed the question about the relationship with the Korean National Council, in which some members of the Korean Socialist Party such as Chang Ki-yŏng, Kim Chin and Chŏn Il were deeply involved. Although Yi Tong-hwi, the Chairman of the Korean Socialist Party, was not involved directly in the projects and activities of the Korean National Council, he had once been mentioned as a member of the Paris delegation together with Ch'oe Chae-hyŏng and Mun Ch'ang-bŏm, and was also designated the Minister of War Declaration of the Korean National Council.

The congress resolved to propose that the members of the Korean Socialist Party give up their responsible positions within the Korean National Council when it pursued policies in conflict with those of the Korean Socialist Party. It also decided to authorize the Central Executive Committee of the Korean Socialist Party to decide the question of a final recall of party members from the Korean National Council.[77] This resolution expressed the critical attitude of the Korean Socialist Party toward the Korean National Council, whose policies were anti-Bolshevik and oriented toward the Paris Peace Conference.[78]

The Congress also resolved to reinforce the influence of the Korean Socialist Party within nationalist organizations and partisan troops of Koreans in Manchuria and the Primorye. Accordingly, the Congress decided to strengthen the influence of the Socialist Party within the Korean National Council and the New People's Union and to dispatch party agents to Chientao and Shanghai for the purpose of establishing relations with the national revolutionary organizations there.[79]

The Congress also resolved to convene the Conference of the People for unifying the Korean National Council in Vladivostok, the Provisional Government in Shanghai and the Military Government in Jilin [Kilim Kunjŏngsa][80] which were contending to be the sole Korean government.[81] This resolution implies that the Korean Socialist Party would remain neutral until these three governmental organizations were unified and the Korean Socialist Party would allow its members to participate when the unification was accomplished.

In general, the left dominated the mood of the congress. However, it should be noted that although the congress adopted the "pure principle of class struggle," it allowed the possibility of accepting arguments of the right in resolutions related to current questions. First of all, while the congress criticized national patriots who led the March First Movement "towards a false path of national antagonism," it also considered it "inexpedient to oppose the revolutionary movement."[82] Accordingly, it means that the congress chose not to boycott all the activities of the "national patriots." That the congress resolved to convene the Conference of the People for unifying the three provisional "governments" demonstrated the strong will of the Korean Socialist Party toward the establishment of a central national revolutionary organ for Koreans.

Furthermore, the congress advised members of the Korean Socialist Party to resign from their positions in the Korean National Council on the condition that "if the Korean National Council continues its policies" and designated the final decision of the resignation to the Central Executive Committee. In short, the congress was an obvious victory of the left, but opinions of the right were also reflected in resolutions concerning specific issues related to current events.

B. The Korean National Council in Vladivostok and the Korean Provisional Government in Shanghai

Six different "provisional governments" were declared or organized by Korean nationalists after the March First Movement in 1919. Of these, the Korean National Council in Russia, the Korean Provisional Government in Shanghai, and the Hansŏng Government in Seoul attracted the attention of Korean nationalists in terms of authority or actual activities.[83]

The Korean Provisional Government was organized by twenty-nine Korean leaders at a meeting held on April 10-11, 1919 in Shanghai. The participants transformed the meeting into the Korean Provisional Assembly which would organize the Korean Provisional Government. It is notable that Yi Tong-nyŏng, Cho Wan-gu, and Cho Sŏng-hwan, all from Nikol'sk-Ussurisk, played a key role in organizing the Korean Provisional Government.[84] Although they represented the Seoul faction [*Kihop'a*] in the Korean National Council, they opposed the establishment of the Korean National Council as the central organization of Koreans and left for Shanghai to work for the Korean Provisional Government.[85] Yi Sŭng-man [Syngman Rhee], a well-known champion of diplomatic means to regain independence, and favored by Christians, people from Kyŏnggi and Ch'ungch'ŏng Provinces as well as by Koreans in America, was elected as Premier in the Korean Provisional

TABLE 4. 2

Cabinet Members of the Shanghai Provisional Government
(Apr. 12, 1919)

Premier (Kungmu ch'ongni)	Yi Sŭng-man	
Minister of Home Affairs	An Ch'ang-ho	Vice Sin Ik-hŭi
Minister of Foreign Affairs	Kim Kyu-sik	Vice Hyŏn Sun
Minister of Finance	Ch'oe Chae-hyŏng	Vice Yi Ch'un-suk
Minister of Military Affairs	Yi Tong-hwi	Vice Cho Sŏng-hwan
Minister of Communication	Mun Ch'ang-bŏm	Vice Sŏnu Hyŏk
Minister of Justice	Yi Si-yŏng	Vice Nam Hyŏng-u

Source "Che ilhoe imsi uijongwon hoeŭirok" [The Minutes of the First Session of the Provisional Assembly], *Kukp'yŏn charyo*, vol. 2, pp. 386-88.

Government. The members of the cabinet were as in Table 4. 2. The appointment of Yi Tong-hwi, Mun Ch'ang-bŏm, and Ch'oe Chae-hyŏng, three key Korean leaders in Russia, may be said to reflect the intentions of Korean nationalists in Shanghai to draw the support of their compatriots from the Korean National Council.

On April 15, four days after the establishment of the Shanghai Provisional Government, the Korean National Council dispatched Wŏn Se-hun, the Chairman of its standing committee to Shanghai and suggested uniting the Korean National Council with the Provisional Assembly in Shanghai and relocating the Korean Provisional Government in Russia. This proposal caused arguments among the Korean nationalists in Shanghai concerning the future of the Provisional Government.[86]

On April 29, 1919, the Korean National Council held a meeting in Vladivostok to decide its official policy toward the Shanghai Provisional Government. The meeting was presided over by Vice-Chairman, Kim Ch'ŏl-hun. Twenty-three leaders of the Korean

National Council including Mun Ch'ang-bŏm and Ch'oe Chae-hyŏng discussed the question concerning the Shanghai Provisional Government.[87] The reason why Kim Ch'ŏl-hun presided at the meeting seems to have been that Chairman, Mun Ch'ang-bŏm was appointed Minister of Communication by the Shanghai Provisional Government. At this meeting, the Korean National Council decided to temporarily approve the establishment of the Shanghai Provisional Government. However, the Korean National Council decided to defer complete cooperation with the Shanghai Provisional Government until the Provisional Government was moved to Russian territory. The Korean National Council also decided to relocate the Provisional Government from Shanghai to Russian territory after the withdrawal of Japanese military forces from Siberia.[88]

At this meeting, the Korean National Council also decided to concentrate all efforts on strengthening its own position. Concurrently, the Council dismissed Yi Tong-nyŏng and Cho Wan-gu as standing committee members for going to Shanghai without consulting Council leaders and playing key roles in the organization of the Shanghai Provisional Government. These actions reflected the anti-Shanghai Provisional Government mood which dominated the first official meeting of the Korean National Council. The temporary "approval" of the Shanghai Provisional Government was no more than a nominal gesture and, in fact, suggested the opposite

The conflict of power between the Korean National Council and the Shanghai Provisional Government proceeded to a new phase with the formation of the Hansŏng Government in Seoul at the end of April. The Hansŏng Government was initiated and designed in the middle of March by leaders of the various public and religious organizations within Korea.[89] On April 17, after more than a month's

Table 4. 3

Cabinet Members of the Hansŏng Government (Apr. 23, 1919)

Chief Executive [Chipchŏnggwan ch'ongjae]	Yi Sŭng-man
Premier (Kungmu ch'ongni ch'ongjae)	Yi Tong-hwi
Minister of Home Affairs	Yi Tong-nyŏng
Minister of Foreign Affairs	Pak Yong-man
Minister of Finance	Yi Si-yŏng, Vice Han Nam-su
Minister of Justice	Sin Kyu-sik
Minister of Military Affairs	No Paek-rin
Minister of Communication	Mun Ch'ang-bŏm
Minister of Education	Kim Kyu-sik
Director of the Bureau of Labor	An Ch'ang-ho
Minister of the General Staff	Yu Tong-yŏl, Vice Yi Se-yŏng
Delegates to the Paris Peace Conference	Yi Sŭng-man, Min Ch'an-ho, No Paek-rin, An Ch'ang-ho, Pak Yong-man, Yi Tong-hwi, Kim Kyu-sik

Source Kim Chŏng-myŏng [Kin Seimei] ed., *Chōsen dokuritsu undō*, vol. 2, pp. 17-20.

preparation, the organizers drafted a manifesto for the People's Rally [*Kungmin Taehoe*], drew up a provisional constitution, and appointed cabinet members to the Hansŏng Government. While the principle organizers of the provisional government had already been arrested by the Japanese police, thousands of copies of the constitution and cabinet appointments were signed by twenty-five representatives of the thirteen provinces of Korea, and distributed in Seoul on April 23.[90] The cabinet members were as in Table 4. 3.

Through these actions, the organizers of the Hansŏng Government worked to form a collective body from the representatives of all the political parties, all of whom were abroad. They proposed that this body undertake temporary leadership of the whole anti-Japanese movement until the formal assembly convened.[91] The organizers of the Hansŏng Government dispatched some to Shanghai in order to ask the Koreans there to establish government and to lead the independence movement.

In the middle of April, Han Nam-su, Yi Ch'un-suk, Hong To, Yi Pong-su, Yi Kyu-gap and Chang Pung, the organizers of the Hansŏng Government, came to Shanghai and announced that the government was organized in Seoul, but organizers of the Shanghai Provisional Government decided not to recognize the Hansŏng Government. Instead, they distributed the list of the cabinet members of their own Shanghai Provisional Government.[92] It could be argued that the Hansŏng Government was in a more authoritative and legitimate position than the Shanghai Provisional Government or the Korean National Council, as the Hansŏng Government based its legitimacy on the ground that it had been organized by the representatives of the thirteen provinces of Korea. Although the "People's Rally" was not successfully carried out, more than two hundred seventy people were imprisoned because of their involvement in the project.[93]

However, the Hansŏng Government was in a weaker position as all the appointed cabinet members were abroad, and accordingly, its activities and maintenance depended on nationalists abroad (and not the organizers themselves). This was also complicated by the fact that some organizers of the Hansŏng Government, who went out to Shanghai, joined the Shanghai Provisional Government itself.[94] Ironically it will not be due to the organizers of the Hansŏng Government, but rather the power struggle between the two "governments" in Shanghai and Vladivostok, that would bring the authority and legitimacy of the Hansŏng Government to the forefront.

On May 13, at the suggestion of six members the legislature of the Provisional Government in Shanghai — the Provisional Assembly — discussed the question of where to locate the Provisional Government. The Provisional Assembly resolved to make efforts to unify the Korean National Council into the Provisional Assembly, based on the argument that the Assembly had a close relationship with the Shanghai Provisional Government and it would be difficult to separate them. The Provisional Assembly also resolved to make the Shanghai Provisional Government dispatch deputies to the Primorye.[95]

It was An Ch'ang-ho, arriving at Shanghai from America on May 25, who took responsibility for negotiating unification with the Korean National Council. Dispatched by Koreans in America to help the establishment of the Provisional Government, An Ch'ang-ho was appointed as the Minister of Home Affairs by the Shanghai Provisional Government. Most of the young Koreans in Shanghai including Vice-Ministers of the Provisional Government turned to An Ch'ang-ho as the leader. Most of those who were appointed as Ministers of the Provisional Government did not come to Shanghai and hence they were regarded as not being sincere or as having other intentions. So the young Koreans looked to An Ch'ang-ho to lead the government while the young Vice-Ministers administered the day to day operations of the government. On June 28, one month after his arrival in Shanghai, An Ch'ang-ho, following the persistent persuasion by the Vice-Ministers, decided to take the office of Home Minister and acting Premier of the Shanghai Provisional Government. However, as a condition for his taking these offices, An Ch'ang-ho proposed that the Provisional Government in Shanghai should make every effort to gather leaders from all regions.[96] An Ch'ang-ho was particularly enthusiastic about uniting with the Korean National Council in Russia. The rumor that An Ch'ang-ho went to Russia in order to negotiate with Yi Tong-hwi and Mun Ch'ang-bŏm was the reflection of the strong will of An Ch'ang-ho.[97]

Under the leadership of An Ch'ang-ho, members of the Shanghai Provisional Government followed the Provisional Assembly resolution of May 13 to meet and negotiate with Wŏn Se-hun, who had been dispatched to Shanghai by the Korean National Council to negotiate with the Shanghai Provisional Government. On June 17, the Shanghai Provisional Government submitted to the Provisional Assembly a proposal which its envoys would take to Vladivostok. The Provisional Assembly passed the following proposal:

1) To locate the Provisional Government in Shanghai.
2) To organize the Assembly by unifying the Provisional Assembly and the National Council to be located in Shanghai. When the National Council refuses and insists that the Assembly should be located in Russian territory, this would be allowed (with the condition that no more than six legislature members from the Russian territory).
3) New Assembly would function as a *bona fide* Assembly. Reason: the National Council in Russia has three functions [administration, legislature, and judicial].[98]

Based on this proposal, members of the Shanghai Provisional Government negotiated with Wŏn Se-hun representing the Korean National Council. The arguments in negotiations between the two sides focused on where to locate the Provisional Government. Members of the Provisional Government in Shanghai stressed the importance of security for the existence of the Provisional Government, and the necessity of communication with other regions. Although Shanghai was not sufficiently safe, it was safer than other regions, for Japanese influence there was limited. They also pointed out that despite large communities of Koreans in Manchuria and the Primorye, a majority of them were from Hamgyŏng Province, so it would be difficult to govern all Koreans. Furthermore, the members believed that Manchuria and the Primorye were still under the influence of Japanese officials. As the Russian regime in the Primorye only existed with Japanese help, it was deemed to be an inappropriate base for the Provisional Government.

In contrast, the Korean National Council emphasized that the Primorye had a large Korean population near China and Korea, which facilitated communication and many other benefits for projecting authority over Koreans. They pointed out that as the French Leased Territory, Shanghai was generally inconvenient and that the Provisional Government in Shanghai had the existed these in name only as many designated cabinet members were not even in Shanghai at the time.[99]

Despite the competition, either side failed to realize their claims as the sole Korean government. As far as the Shanghai Provisional Government was concerned, its reputation among the Koreans within and outside Korea increased, mainly thanks to the geographical advantage which Shanghai had in terms of safety and communications over other areas, such as Manchuria, the Primorye and America. Furthermore, its popularity gradually strengthened as many Korean nationalists from various regions as well as from Korea gathered in Shanghai to join the Shanghai Provisional Government.[100]

Even so, the Shanghai Provisional Government failed to build itself up as an authoritative government over Koreans in every region. An Ch'ang-ho, who was as the most influential figure in the early period of the government, acknowledged such problems:

> It is true that they did not work satisfactorily in establishing the Assembly and Government here. They did not ask the opinions of [Koreans in] Western Chientao, Northern Chientao, Russia or America. Furthermore, they did not let the persons who were elected as the Ministers know of the organization [of the Provisional Government in Shanghai]. . . . It was true that as a result of the unsatisfactory effort at the beginning, although the sides of Russia and North Chientao recognized the existence of our central body, they did not submit to our central body and cooperate with us.[101]

Firstly, many Korean leaders who were appointed as members of the cabinet were absent from Shanghai or refused to fill their positions. In early May, Yi Tong-nyŏng (the Speaker and acting Premier), Yi Si-yŏng (Minister of Justice) and Cho Sŏng-hwan (Vice-Minister of Military Affairs) resigned from the Provisional Government mainly because of conflicts with the younger Korean nationalists active in the Provisional Government, eventually leaving Shanghai.[102] Yi Tong-hwi (Minister of Military Affairs) was in Russia and did not join the Provisional Government apparently because of the resolution of the Korean Socialist Party's April Congress. Mun Ch'ang-bŏm (Minister of Communication) and Ch'oe Chae-hyŏng (Minister of Finance), two main leaders in the Korean National Council, also refused to participate. Kim Kyu-sik (Minister of Foreign Affairs) was occupied in Paris working to obtain Allied sympathy.

Yi Sŭng-man in America, who was appointed Premier [*Kungmu ch'ongni*] of the Provisional Government in Shanghai, wanted to recognize the authority and legitimacy of the Hansŏng Government, and did not recognize the Shanghai Provisional Government. Hearing news of the establishment of the Hansŏng Government which appointed him as the Chief Executive, Yi Sŭng-man set up the office of the Chief Executive [*Chipchŏnggwan Ch'ongjae*] of the Hansŏng Government in Washington D. C, and began to use the title of "Chief Executive" rather than that of "Premier," the title of the Shanghai Provisional Government. On his own initiative, Yi Sŭng-man began to use the title of "President" in the documents and newspapers distributed to foreigners.[103] Among the cabinet members of the Shanghai Provisional Government, only An Ch'ang-ho (Minister of Home Affairs), who was dispatched by the Korean National Association in America [Taehanin Kungminhoe], took up his position.[104]

The condition of the Korean National Council in Russia was worse than that of the Shanghai Provisional Government. It was gradually forced into the losing side due to several factors. First, the Council failed to demonstrate any accomplishments at the Paris Peace Conference, which concluded at the end of June 1919. Yun Hae and Ko Ch'ang-il were dispatched by the Council, but because of the fighting between Reds and Whites in Western Siberia, they could not reach Paris until September 26, 1919, almost three months after the Peace Conference adjourned. By contrast, Kim Kyu-sik, the Minister of Foreign Affairs of the Shanghai Provisional Government, arrived at Paris and conducted propaganda activities against Japanese rule. Kim Kyu-sik promoted the case for Korean independence in Paris, although ultimately he failed to include the Korean question in the Peace Conference agenda. As a result, the activities of the Shanghai delegation were widely known to Koreans both within Korea and abroad.

To worsen matters, the Korean National Council was outlawed by the Russian authorities because of its leading role in demonstrations in the Primorye. This added to its difficulties in carrying out its programs. Moreover, Korean revolutionary organizations in Manchuria gradually withdrew their support from the Korean National Council. This support was crucial for the Council to legitimize itself as the "representative central body of all Koreans." Chang To-jŏng, the founder of the One World Party [Ilsedang] and a key member of the "Shanghai Group," pointed out the two reasons why the Council came to lose the support of Korean revolutionary organizations in Manchuria in the middle of 1919:

> [The Korean National Council], in the spring of 1919, was more or less powerful thanks to the joining of the organizations in China, but increasingly declined in the middle of 1919. The causes were: first, the National Council arbitrarily spent the 5,000 *yuan* [rubles] which organizations in China had assigned to buy weapons. Second, in Yehho (near the Chinese Eastern Railroad), Horvath, a head of the White party, and the Korean National Council negotiated together, organized the Korean military unit and gathered young Koreans living in China with the intention of training officers. However, it failed and all Koreans were scattered.[105]

In the middle of 1919, the relationship of the Korean National Council and the Korean Socialist Party also deteriorated. As mentioned earlier, the Korean National Council strongly supported the military activities of Yi Tong-hwi, because Yi came from Hamgyŏng Provinces just as the majority of the Council members (whereas the majority of the leaders of the Shanghai Provisional Government came from Seoul area and P'yŏngan Provinces).

After the April Congress of the Korean Socialist Party, however, the Council and the Korean Socialist Party competed to persuade young Koreans from Korea, Manchuria, and Russia to their respective sides. The Korean National Council dispatched key members to Vladivostok, Nikol'sk-Ussurisk, Suchan, Olga and other regions in the Primorye, agitating that "Yun Hae and Ko Ch'ang-il, delegates of the Korean National Council, are submitting the issue of Korean independence [to the Paris Conference], so that to fight in opposition to the Allied armies in Russia would be politically harmful for Korean partisans." At the same time, the delegates said, "young Koreans must not be shot innocently by the American, Japanese, English, other Allied Armies, or White Russians while helping and fighting for the Russian Reds and instead, must go to the Korean Military Academy located at the Chinese Eastern Railroad and study." Influenced by the agitations of the Korean National Council, young Koreans went to the Chinese Eastern Railroad or returned to their hometowns, so some Korean partisan units which had close relations with the Korean Socialist Party dissolved as a consequence.[106]

The Korean Socialist Party, on the other hand, planned to move independence armies in Manchuria to the Primorye and to organize them into Korean partisan armies under the command of Hong Pŏm-do to fight in defense of Soviet Power.[107] According to this plan, the Korean Socialist Party was also to strengthen its activities against the programs of the Korean National Council. The Korean Socialist Party dispatched responsible members to the Korean villages and sent two agitators to Harbin where Korean National Council troops were under Horvath. Thanks to those activities, the Korean Socialist Party "was welcomed among Koreans with remarkable sympathy." It was around this time (at the end of July) that the Japanese first obtained information about the existence and activities of the Korean Socialist Party.[108]

The prime example of conflicts between the Korean Socialist Party and the Korean National Council was an intense struggle for securing "bare hands troops" ["*tosu pudae*"], which were organized and sent to Russia by the Independence Union [Tongniptan] located in Western Chientao. The Independence Union gathered patriotic young Koreans who came from Korea in order to participate in the independence armies [*tongnipkun*] after the March First Movement. The number of young Koreans reached more than one thousand, so the Independence Union could not afford to provide enough training, equipment and weapons.[109] Cho Maeng-sŏn, Yang Ki-t'ak, and Ch'oe Yŏng-ho, leaders of the Independence Union, sent Yun Ch'ŏl-gyu to Russia. Yun met Hong Pŏm-do in Tajiagou [Tangŏjaegol] in Suifen and Yi Tong-hwi in Vladivostok, and agreed to move the young Koreans to Suifun to organize the Korean partisan troops under the command of Hong Pŏm-do, and they were then to join the Russian partisans.[110] Yun Ch'ŏl-gyu returned to Western Chientao and led the first "bare hands troop" of 400 young Koreans to Grodekovo (currently Pogranichinyi), handing them over to Ch'oe T'ae-yŏl, a member of the Korean Socialist Party and the Chairman of the Korean Association in Grodekovo.

After Yun Ch'ŏl-gyu returned to Manchuria, Ch'oe Yŏng-ho, the Commander-in-Chief of the Independence Union, went to Grodekovo and began to organize partisan units, composed of Independence Union members. However, strong supporters of the Korean National Council and the members of the Union of the Righteous Army Corps [Ŭigundan], such as Ch'oe Ŭi-jun, Sin U-gyŏng, and Ma Chung-ch'ŏl in cooperation with local Russian landlords, killed Ch'oe Yŏng-ho and more than ten other Independence Union members. As a result, the first "bare hands troop" dispatched from Manchuria to Russia was dissolved. When the second "bare hands troop" of

300 young Koreans led by Yun Ch'ŏl-gyu arrived at Yehho on the way to Suifen, the soldiers under the influence of Kim Ha-sŏk, a key figure in charge of military affairs for the Korean National Council, detained them by force. The third "bare hands troop" of 300 was also detained in Harbin by Korean troops under the command of Mikhail Wŏn, a Horvath's officer.[111] However, in early July, these members of the Independence Union escaped together with the members of the Union of Iron and Blood Restoration.[112]

The Korean National Council was gradually losing its once prominent position as the united front of the Koreans in Russia, Northern Chientao, and Hunchun after the New People's Union resolved to work with the Korean Socialist Party at the end of April. The New People's Union strengthened its influence among Koreans with the help of Kim Rip and other members of the Korean Socialist Party, who had been dispatched to the Union according to the resolution of the April Congress.[113] The New People's Union also received vigorous support from Christians in Russia and Manchuria.[114]

At a meeting of the Korean National Council on July 14, 1919, Mun Ch'ang-bŏm, harshly criticized Kim Rip, for ignoring the Korean National Council and working instead for the New People's Union.[115] As members of the Korean National Council such as Kim Rip and others worked primarily for the New People's Union, the relationship between the Korean National Council and the New People's Union deteriorated to the point that common activities became impossible. This was, in fact, a direct result of anti-Korean National Council activities carried out by the Korean Socialist Party.

The Korean National Council could not avoid the financial burden resulting from the dispatch of the delegation to the Paris Peace Conference. The financial difficulty only worsened with the conclusion of the Peace Conference, which brought about the decline of enthusiasm for the independence movement among Koreans. This in turn led to decrease in the funds donated to the Korean National Council.[116] The financial difficulty became so serious that the Council was even unable to take financial responsibility for the Korean Teachers' College in Nikol'sk-Ussurisk. Rumors arose that the Korean National Council would be dissolved and merged with the Shanghai Government. The Japanese official made following report on extremely difficult position the Korean National Council:

> These days, people state that the National Council is going to be dissolved. Rumors are as follows. The Council gathered originally donations of about 150,000 rubles as the fund for the independence movement. Among them, 50,000 rubles and 20,000 rubles were given to the two delegates to Paris as travel fair and expenses for their clothes and the rest was spent for travel and other expenses. These days, the number of donors are very few and all financial sources are dried up and it comes to the situation in which [the National Council] can not do anything and can not help being dissolved inevitably. . . . It is not plausible for [the National Council] to be dissolved right now, but it seems that the last day of the Council is not far. There is argument that the Korean National Council intends to be unified into the Shanghai Government, but it is estimated that in the context of the factional relationship, the National Council is not likely to voluntarily apply for the unification by itself. However, if the Shanghai Government adopts the policy of utilizing Mun Ch'ang-bŏm and Ch'oe Chae-hyŏng appointed in its cabinet members and thereby controls the force of the Koreans in Russia, it is not an impossible thing.[117]

C. The Dissolution of the Korean National Council

Although the Korean delegation to the Paris Peace Conference led by Kim Kyu-sik was unsuccessful in achieving its goal, the Shanghai Provisional Government became the winning side in the competition of broadening support among Korean nationalists. Shortly after the Paris Conference, the Korean Socialist Party decided to recognize the Shanghai Provisional Government. Key members of the Korean Socialist Party including Yi Tong-hwi, Kim Kyu-myŏn, Kim Rip, Pak Chin-sun, Pak Ae, Yi Han-yŏng, Ch'oe T'ae-yŏl, Chang Ki-yŏng, Kim Ha-gu, Kim Chin, and Afanasii Kim held a meeting and discussed the issue of whether the party should join the Shanghai Government or not. At the meeting, the Korean Socialist Party decided to join the Shanghai Government in recognition of the increasing influence of the Provisional Government. The meeting also resolved to dispatch Yi Tong-hwi and Kim Rip to Shanghai as well as Pak Chin-sun, Pak Ae, and Yi Han-yŏng to Moscow.[118]

Yi Tong-hwi, who was appointed as Premier of the Hansŏng Government and Minister of Military Affairs of the Shanghai Provisional Government, was at first opposed personally to participation in the Shanghai Provisional Government, but was finally persuaded by party members, who advised Yi to "fight against imperialism by entering the nationalist body."[119]

Pak Chin-sun, Pak Ae and Yi Han-yŏng left for Moscow shortly after the meeting in July according to the resolution of the April Congress.[120] It seems that the Korean Socialist Party had suspended the departure of its delegation to Moscow in order to wait and see the results of the Paris Peace Conference. Kim Kyu-myŏn, the Chairman of the New People's Union and a Vice-Chairman of the

Socialist Party, provided the travel expenses for the delegation.[121] It was around this time that Yi Tong-hwi started using the title of Minister of Military Affairs, apparently the title of the Shanghai Provisional Government, in the credentials given to his fundraisers in Korea.[122]

The decision of the Korean Socialist Party to support the Provisional Government in Shanghai was indirectly declared through the manifesto of the New People's Union dated July 6, 1919 in the *Sinmindanbo* (the New People's Union Report). The New People's Union declared its decision to recognize and support the Provisional Government in Shanghai. It explained that although it had wanted to recognize the Shanghai Provisional Government after its establishment and to support the diplomatic activities of Kim Kyu-sik, it was restrained from doing so in order not to damage the "great unity of national people," and not to hinder the "achievement of our independence." The New People's Union declared its two point resolutions: 1) to carry out the task of recognizing and supporting the Shanghai Government in cooperation with the general nationalist people; 2) to send the funds for the independence movement to the delegation in Paris as much as possible.[123] Considering the fact that the New People's Union was united with the Korean Socialist Party at the April Congress, and Kim Rip, a key member of the Korean Socialist Party and Yi Tong-hwi's close associate, was expending all his efforts in the New People's Union, this policy of the New People's Union could transitively be considered as the official policy of the Korean Socialist Party at that time.

The policy of the Korean Socialist Party and the New People's Union was widely followed by the main organizations of Koreans in Manchuria. Kim Sun-yak, who came to Shanghai in early July as a delegate of the Union of Elderly Men (Noindan), one of the major mass organizations together with the Korean National Council, the New People's Union, and the Union of Iron and Blood Restoration in Vladivostok,[124] reported that "the Koreans in Russia have whole-hearted confidence in the Shanghai Government." After early August, the Korean National Council also took a cooperative attitude toward the Shanghai Provisional Government by sending travel expenses for the Korean delegate, Kim Kyu-sik, and getting the signatures of one million persons necessary for credentials, which the Korean delegation would submit to the upcoming League of Nations.[125] On August 5, the Military Government in Jilin [Kilim Kunjŏngsa], which was headed by Yu Tong-yŏl, a former key member of the Korean Socialist Party, also dispatched Wang Sam-dŏk, to submit a copy of the constitution, and a report on the activities of the Military Government. The Korean National Association [Taehan Kungminhoe], the most influential mass organization among Koreans in Northern Chientao, also reported its organization and activities in the name of its Chairman, Ku Ch'un-sŏn, an anti-Japanese Christian leader and Yi Tong-hwi's long-time associate.[126]

The Korean nationalists who were dispatched from inside Korea, America, and Manchuria to Shanghai, communicated and gathered information of their regions. In early August, by the initiative of the Shanghai Provisional Government, the Conference of the Representatives of Korean People [Kungmin Taeri Taehoe] was held and passed a five-point resolution on establishing a unified Provisional Government. The resolution emphasized that the Hansŏng Government created in Seoul was the only legitimate Korean government and that the location of the Government should be in Shanghai.[127] The resolution declared:

1) To dissolve all the governments established in Shanghai and Russia and to uphold the Hansŏng Government, established within Korea by the representatives of thirteen provinces of Korea, by acknowledging that the representatives of thirteen provinces of Korea are the representatives of the whole people.
2) The site of the Government would be Shanghai, for Shanghai is comparatively convenient for communication with every region.
3) The system and the selection [of the cabinet members] of the Government established in Shanghai would be dissolved and then the Chief Executive [*Chipchŏnggwan*] system and the selection of the Hansŏng Government would be adopted. However, the administration in Shanghai would be acknowledged since its establishment.
4) The name of the Government would be the Provisional Government of the Republic of Korea [Provisional Government in Shanghai]. It is for the purpose of keeping the historical significance that [the Shanghai Government] was established after the declaration of the independence satisfactorily representing every region.
5) The current cabinet members of the Government would resign all together and hand the Government to the cabinet members selected by the Hansŏng Government.[128]

The resolution reflects, on the one hand, that neither of the Korean National Council nor the Shanghai Government was successful in its claim to be the "highest body" of the Koreans, and, on the other hand, that the Shanghai Government was in a comparatively stronger position than the Korean National Council. It was natural for the Provisional Government in Shanghai to take the initiative in working out the plan for establishing a unified government. Under the leadership of An Ch'ang-ho, it passed the resolution and got the agreement of

Korean National Council envoy Wŏn Se-hun.[129] An Ch'ang-ho and Wŏn Se-hun agreed to take responsibility for dissolving the Shanghai Government and the Korean National Council, respectively.[130]

The resolution for unification was announced to Koreans in the name of all the cabinet members of the Hansŏng Government,[131] and seems to have been widely accepted by Koreans. Based on this optimism, An Ch'ang-ho could report at the session of the Provisional Assembly in Shanghai as follows:

> At present, patriotism and demand for unification among the whole people are on the rise and letters from persons and organizations in various regions delivering their loyalty to the Shanghai Government arrive everyday, so it is the best time for a great unification.[132]

It was urgent for the Shanghai Government to obtain recognition and support from Koreans in Northern Chientao and Russia who had been under the influence of the Korean National Council. First of all, the Shanghai Government dispatched Pae Hyŏng-sik and Sŏ Sŏng-gwŏn as delegates to Chientao on August 9 and again Chŏng Chae-myŏn on August 23 to the Korean National Association in North Chientao.[133]

In parallel, the Shanghai Provisional Government dispatched Hyŏn Sun and Kim Sŏng-gyŏm as the special delegates to Vladivostok. Their mission was to get the agreement of the Korean National Council and to bring Yi Tong-hwi, who had been appointed Premier of the Hansŏng Government to join the "unified" Shanghai Government.[134] In a letter to his long-time follower Yi Kang in Vladivostok, An Ch'ang-ho ordered him to exert every effort to "dissolve the National Council in Vladivostok, which has government function and to merge it with the Provisional Government in Shanghai. In the case that the National Council would not dissolve, you should at least bring Yi Tong-hwi on board and send him to this place [Shanghai]."[135]

In the middle of August, Hyŏn Sun and Kim Sŏng-gyŏm left for Vladivostok with Wŏn Se-hun and arrived in Vladivostok from Manchuria on about August 30.[136] On August 30, the official conference of the Korean National Council was held in Vladivostok. Thirty-five leaders including standing committee members attended. At the conference, the Korean National Council agreed with proposals which Hyŏn Sun and Kim Sŏng-gyŏm brought from Shanghai and proposed to make the Hansŏng Government the sole legitimate Korean government. The conference unanimously accepted the proposal and declared the dissolution of the Korean National Council. An Ch'ang-ho's plan was successfully achieved. On September 2, Hyŏn Sun and Kim Sŏng-gyŏm reported to Shanghai that their mission in Russia was successful.[137]

What were the main contents of the agreement which made the Korean National Council decide its self-dissolution? The official declaration of the Korean National Council, dated February 15, 1920, describes the conference as follows:

> The Shanghai Government dispatched two men, Vice-Minister of Home Affairs Hyŏn Sun and Kim Sŏng-gyŏm, to the Council and concluded an agreement at the conference of the Council held on August 30 of last year [1919]. It was already obvious in the written declaration that both the Korean National Council and the Shanghai Provisional Assembly would dissolve together and uphold the Provisional Government which was organized and declared to the whole world by the representatives of the

thirteen provinces, who gathered in Seoul in the name of the People's Rally in Seoul and that the Council would deal with the remaining affairs until cabinet members of the Hansŏng Government could take the offices and the legitimate new assembly could be convened.[138]

It is in accord with the resolutions adopted in Shanghai that they would uphold the Hansŏng Government. There was, however, one crucial point — that is, the Korean National Council understood that after the dissolution of the Council and the Provisional Assembly, the cabinet member of the Hansŏng Government would take offices and "legitimate new Assembly" would be convened. As we will see in chapter 5, this became the key point of the dispute between the Shanghai Provisional Government and the Korean National Council.

The following entry in the memoirs of Yi Kang, who attended the conference, tells another story:

On the day when the National Council was held, I went there as a Council member together with two persons [Hyŏn Sun and Kim Sŏng-gyŏm]. Pastor Hyŏn and Yi Tong-hwi held each other's hands and cried. All saw the two crying and their minds were touched. Then the conference proceeded, and at any rate, the National Council was dissolved that evening. The proposed condition was that four fifths of the members of the National Council would enter the [new] Shanghai Provisional Assembly. Once Yi Tong-hwi agreed to that, the National Council was unanimously dissolved.[139]

Two points from the story of Yi Kang are noticeable. First, Yi Tong-hwi played a key role at the conference in making the Korean National Council declare its dissolution. Second, one of the conditions for the dissolution was that four fifths of the Council members would become members of the new Provisional Assembly in Shanghai. Considering the fact that the Korean National Council numbered thirty, twenty-four members were supposed to enter the new Assembly. It is not clear how many members would be in the new Assembly, but the Korean National Council was at least determined to form the most powerful group in the new Assembly, and to continue its influence in the new Assembly and Government.

Two records, however, demonstrate that misunderstanding had already occurred between Shanghai and Vladivostok about conditions for the dissolution of the Korean National Council and about the plan establishing the "unified" Shanghai Government. Shortly after dissolving the Korean National Council, the Shanghai Provisional Assembly passed the draft of the Provisional Constitution [*Imsi Hŏnpŏp*] proposed by the Shanghai Provisional Government on September 8, 1919, in which the total number of the Assembly members would be fifty-seven of which only six seats were allotted to Koreans in Russia.[140] The seed for a revived power struggle and the "rebuilding" of the Korean National Council had been planted.

As soon as the Korean National Council dissolved, the political bureau of the central executive committee of the Korean Socialist Party sent instructions to members of the Party to resign from responsible positions on the Council.[141] At the adamant suggestion of Yi Kang, Yi Tong-hwi, Kim Rip and Nam Kong-sŏn hurried to leave for Shanghai with Hyŏn Sun and Kim Sŏng-gyŏm.[142] Yi Tong-hwi assigned Kim Kyu-myŏn to take charge of all remaining affairs of the Party in the Primorye.[143] On September 18, Yi Tong-hwi and others arrived in Shanghai.[144]

Chapter Five

FAILED UNITED FRONT: THE KOREAN SOCIALIST PARTY AND THE SHANGHAI PROVISIONAL GOVERNMENT

A. Between Shanghai and Vladivostok

1. Dispute between Vladivostok "Recognition" and Shanghai "Restructuring"

Although An Ch'ang-ho succeeded in obtaining the agreement of Wŏn Se-hun, the envoy from the Korean National Council, on the five-point resolution concerning the unification of Shanghai and Vladivostok, he had to solve a problem caused by Yi Sŭng-man [Syngman Rhee], the Chief Executive-designate of the Hansŏng Government. Before August 1919, Yi Sŭng-man had resisted accepting the Premiership [*Kungmu Ch'ongni*] of the Shanghai Provisional Govern- ment and used the title of Chief Executive [Chipchŏnggwan ch'ongjae] of the Hansŏng Government. After Shanghai and Vladivostok agreed to be merged into the Hansŏng Government, Yi Sŭng-man had been using the title of President, instead of the title of Chief-Executive, in his documents delivered to foreign countries and articles in newspapers.[1]

An Ch'ang-ho and the leaders of the Shanghai Provisional Government were annoyed by this behavior. An Ch'ang-ho, the acting Premier of the Shanghai Provisional Government, sent a telegram on August 25, 1919, to Yi Sŭng-man in Washington D. C. and requested Yi not to use the title of President:

> At first the [Shanghai] Provisional Government took the Premiership [*Kungmu ch'ongni*] system and the Hansŏng Government took the Chief Executive [*Chipchŏnggwan*] system. In both governments, there is no title of President [*Taet'ongnyŏng*], so Your Excellency is not the President. Now you have to represent the Government with the title of Chief Executive [*Chipchŏnggwan*]. If you act as President without revising the constitution, you are violating the constitution and betraying the spirit of unifying governments. So do not act in the name of President.[2]

Yi Sŭng-man, however, did not accept An Ch'ang-ho's warning. Rather, in response to the telegram, on August 28, he sent a telegram to the Provisional Government and insisted that he would not stop using the title of President and that Korean leaders in Shanghai should take responsibility for dealing with all future opposition within the Korean independence movement to his using the title "President":

> We are making all effort to obtain the recognition of our government [from foreign countries] and I, in the name of the President, sent official letters to every country and published [articles] about Korea. Therefore, I cannot change the title of President. If we argue with each other and the rumor

that we are in conflict spreads to the world, it will be a great hindrance to the independence movement, and the whole responsibility will be on you. So do not argue.[3]

Facing this opposition from Yi Sŭng-man, An Ch'ang-ho and leaders of the Shanghai Provisional Government decided to discard the title of "Chief Executive" ["*Chipchŏnggwan ch'ongjae*"] of the Hansŏng Government and to adopt the title "President" ["*Taet'ongnyŏng*"]. Furthermore, instead of waiting until the new Assembly convened, An Ch'ang-ho decided that the Provisional Government and Assembly would be in charge of restructuring the Shanghai Provisional Government based on the list of the cabinet members of the Hansŏng Government. The main purpose of these decisions was to make Yi Sŭng-man President of the Provisional Government.[4] Leaders of the Shanghai Provisional Government led by An Ch'ang-ho thought that this revision represented only change in the title of the head of the Provisional Government from Chief Executive [*Chipchŏnggwan ch'ongjae*] to President [*Taet'ongnyŏng*] and that there would be no significant difference among the terms "Premier," "Chief Executive," and "President." They also believed that the title of "President" would be better in issuing government bonds. Kim Kyu-sik, head of the Korean delegation to the Paris Peace Conference, also advised An Ch'ang-ho to elect Yi Sŭng-man as "President" arguing that the title of "President" would be convenient for diplomacy as well. An Ch'ang-ho expected that Koreans in North Chientao and the Primorye would welcome the restructuring of the Provisional Government.[5]

Accordingly, the Provisional Assembly passed the new constitution on September 6 and officially elected Yi Sŭng-man as President and other cabinet members listed in the Hansŏng Government unanim-

Table 5. 1

Cabinet Members of the Shanghai Provisional Government
(Nov. 23, 1919)

	Ministry	(1)	(2)	(3)
Yi Sŭng-man	President	Seoul (Hwanghae)*	America	+
Yi Tong-hwi	Premier	Hamgyŏng	Russia / North Chientao	+
Yi Tong-nyŏng	Internal	Ch'ungch'ŏng	Russia/Manchuria	+
Pak Yong-man	Foreign	Kangwŏn	America	-
Yi Si-yŏng	Finance	Seoul	Manchuria	+
Sin Kyu-sik	Justice	Ch'ungch'ŏng	China	+
No Paek-rin	Military	Hwanghae	America	+
Mun Ch'ang-bŏm	Communication	Hamgyŏng	Russia	-
Kim Kyu-sik	Education	Seoul (Kyŏngsang)*	China	+
An Ch'ang-ho	Labor (Bureau)	P'yŏngan	America	+
Yu Tong-yŏl	General Staff	P'yŏngan	Russia / Manchuria	+

Notes (1) Birthplace, (2) Regions for main Activities, (3) + : Joined the Government, - : Refused to join the Government

* Yi Sŭng-man and Kim Kuy-sik left their birthplaces at the age of three and four respectively.

Sources *Tongnip Sinmun*, 2 Sep. 1919, p. 1; "Taehan Minguk Imsi Chŏngbu kwanryŏn yosich'alin myŏngbu" [List of the Persons Related to the Korean Provisional Government Who Need to be Observed] (Seoul: Kukka Pohuncho', 1996), pp. 56, 68, 92, 36, 112.

ously (see Table 5. 1).[6]

So why did Korean nationalists in Shanghai decide to change the title of the Provisional Government and revise the Constitution only for one person, Yi Sŭng-man? First, Yi Sŭng-man's record as leader of the Independence Club, long-time political prisoner (1897-1904), well-known Christian leader, as well as his successful academic achievement in America (M. A. from Harvard and Ph. D. degree at Princeton — the first Korean ever to have earned a Ph. D. in America) all increased Koreans' expectations of him.[7]

More importantly, Korean nationalists in Shanghai valued highly Yi Sŭng-man's relationship with the American President, Woodrow Wilson even though the relationship was somewhat exaggerated. Yi was known to be a former student of Wilson at Princeton. The majority of the Shanghai Provisional Government expected that President Wilson's fourteen point principle of "self-determination of the peoples" applied to Korea and that Yi Sŭng-man's diplomacy based on his relationship with Wilson would contribute greatly to the cause of Korean independence. The following recollection of a Korean activist in Shanghai explains the reason why leaders of the Shanghai Provisional Government chose Yi Sŭng-man in spite of the strong opposition, particularly of the Korean National Council in Vladivostok:

> Both the Korean National Council and Yi Sŭng-man were equally stubborn. The authorities of both the Provisional Government and the Provisional Assembly fell into an extremely difficult position. If they chose to secure the National Council, it would lead to losing Yi Sŭng-man who was regarded as the head of the Koreans in America; the effect on Koreans in America was obvious. If they chose Yi Sŭng-man, they would lose the National Council and accordingly, alienate the Koreans in Russia. Therefore, they tried in every way to appease both sides, but to no avail. The public at that time was fascinated with Mr. Wilson's principle of fourteen points, considering the Versailles Conference one of righteous gods who restrain the strong and prop up the weak. They inaccurately considered Yi Sŭng-man politically great. As a result, they tragically erred by separating themselves from the Koreans in Russia.[8]

It soon became clear that An Ch'ang-ho's expectation was too optimistic when leaders of the Korean National Council came to Shanghai from Vladivostok. As we saw in Chapter 4, the Korean National Council in Vladivostok dissolved itself and was ready to join the "unified" Shanghai Provisional Government on August 30, 1919. To carry out this purpose, Yi Tong-hwi and Kim Rip arrived at Shanghai together with Hyŏn Sun and Kim Sŏng-gyŏm, delegates from Shanghai, on September 18, 1919. Mun Ch'ang-bŏm, Chairman of the Korean National Council, together with Wŏn Se-hun, envoy of the Korean National Council to Shanghai, who had negotiated and reached agreement of unification with An Ch'ang-ho, also came to Shanghai in order to assume the ministership of communication of the "unified" Korean Provisional Government about October 20, 1919.[9]

Mun Ch'ang-bŏm and Wŏn Se-hun, however, came to criticize An Ch'ang-ho and leaders of the Shanghai Provisional Government.[10] They pointed out that the Shanghai Provisional Government violated the agreement between Shanghai and Vladivostok by which both sides resolved to "recognize" the Hansŏng Government. According to the understanding of the Korean National Council, the Shanghai Provisional Assembly should have already been dissolved together with the Korean National Council. Furthermore, neither the Shanghai Provisional Government nor the Provisional Assembly had any power to restructure the government or prepare the new constitution.[11] They also argued that the Shanghai Provisional Government had discarded the chief executive system and adopted the presidential system for only one person, Yi Sŭng-man, ignoring the opinions of Koreans in the Primorye and Manchuria. This blemished the spirit of upholding [*pongdae*] the Hansŏng Government.[12] In short, leaders of the Korean National Council were extremely upset with the leaders of the Shanghai Provisional Government led by An Ch'ang-ho arguing that the Shanghai Provisional Assembly treacherously "deceived" the Korean National Council.[13]

The hard-line leaders of the Korean National Council, particularly the *wŏnhoin* Koreans such as Mun Ch'ang-bŏm and Ch'oe Chae-hyŏng, from the beginning, did not want the Council to be merged with the Shanghai Provisional Government.[14] In fact, we can say that the Shanghai Provisional Government's "violation" of the agreement by adopting the presidential system and "restructuring" the Provisional Government provided an opportune excuse for the Korean National Council to declare its "rebuilding." While the majority of the Korean nationalists in the Shanghai Provisional Government were from the central parts of Korea (Kyŏnggi, Ch'ungch'ŏng, and Hwanghae), most of the Korean National Council members were from the northeastern part of Korea, Hamgyŏng Provinces.[15] In addition, Yi Sŭng-man was widely discredited among Korean nationalists in the Primorye because of what they called "pro-Japanese" articles in his *T'aep'yŏngyang Chapchi* (Pacific Magazine) in Honolulu, Hawaii,[16] his image as the leader of the Seoul faction in America, and especially the notorious internecine factional struggles with Pak Yong-man in Hawaii. In short, Yi Sŭng-man's popularity in Vladivostok was not as high as in Shanghai. Furthermore, Yi Sŭng-man was criticized by many Korean nationalists, such as Sin Ch'ae-ho, for his petition in February 1919 to President Woodrow to accept the mandatory rule of Korea by America.

The most important factor for the decision of the Korean National Council, however, was the drastic political change in Siberia, created by the growing influence of the Bolsheviks and imminent downfall of the Kolchak regime. Key leaders of the Korean National Council including Mun Ch'ang-bŏm were also expecting that political change in Siberia and the Russian Far East would provide favorable opportunities for Korean political forces in Russia:

> The Omsk government will be exterminated and the influence of the maximalists will expand. The reasons are as follows: In order to establish his power, Kolchak tried to destroy the maximalists, same race by utilizing the army of the Japanese, different race. . . . Siberian people try to overthrow the Omsk government and shake hands with the maximalists and expel the Japanese army. . . . In the near future, the Japanese army will lose its power in Siberia and will have inflicted enormous harm. We Koreans these days are suffering under the limitless abuses. However, when the Omsk government is changed, the situation will be favorable for [our] activities in the North Continent.[17]

As many Koreans including Mun Ch'ang-bŏm expected, the Kolchak regime retreated to Irkutsk from Omsk in the middle of November 1919, but the Red Army finally occupied Irkutsk and overthrew the Kolchak Regime in early January 1920. Kolchak, who had controlled Siberia in defiance of the Bolshevik regime in Moscow for more than a year, was at last arrested and executed by the Bolshevik on February 7, 1920.[18]

Finally, in November 1919, Mun Ch'ang-bŏm refused to join the Shanghai Provisional Government stating that "it is not right to take a position in the cabinet of the [Provisional] Government which does not correspond to the will of the people."[19] The hardliners of the Korean National Council led by Kim Ha-sŏk, who had been seeking the chance to revive the Council by utilizing the Union of Iron and Blood Restoration,[20] held a special general meeting on

December 15, 1919, to resume its activities and strengthen its organization.[21] Two months later, on February 14, 1920, the Korean National Council held a general meeting and decided to rebuild its organization. The next day, the Korean National Council declared its official rebuilding and distributed manifestos which officially revoked the previous declaration of its dissolution and severely criticized the "unfaithfulness" of the Shanghai Provisional Government.[22]

2. The Second Best Choice

In the political turmoil caused by the unexpected disputes between Vladivostok and Shanghai with regard to the agreement concerning unification, Yi Tong-hwi did not take the Premiership of the Provisional Government for more than one month after his arrival in Shanghai. During that time, An Ch'ang-ho and Yun Hyŏn-jin (Vice-Minister of Finance) urged him to assume the position immediately. On October 28, Yi Tong-hwi had the first meeting with three Ministers, Yi Tong-nyŏng (Internal Affairs), Sin Kyu-sik (Justice) and Yi Si-yŏng (Finance).[23] At a "meeting of people" held at the Korean Residents's Association in Shanghai on November 1, 1919, Kim Rip, close associate of Yi Tong-hwi and Secretary-General of the Korean Socialist Party, stated that Yi Tong-hwi was not taking office just to achieve unification of the two sides.[24] At this meeting, while Wŏn Se-hun severely criticized the leaders of the Shanghai Provisional Government,[25] the supporters of that government urged Yi Tong-hwi to join them.[26]

On November 3, an official ceremony for the inauguration of Yi Tong-hwi, Yi Tong-nyŏng, Sin Kyu-sik, Yi Si-yŏng and An Ch'ang-ho (Director of Labor) was finally held.[27] This time also officially marked the first day of the "new" Provisional Government. Kim Rip was appointed Chief Secretary of the cabinet and Director of General Affairs[28] and a "well-known" writer and member of the Korean Socialist Party became the editor of the official organ of the Provisional Government, the position which the Korean Socialist Party had suggested as one of the conditions for joining the Provisional Government.[29]

We can see the underlying reasons that the Socialist Party had for joining the Provisional Government through a letter which Yi Tong-hwi sent on November 27, 1919, to key leaders of the Korean nationalist movement in North Chientao. North Chientao, as we saw in Chapter 2, was the long-time base for the nationalistic activities of Yi Tong-hwi and his followers. In the letter, Yi Tong-hwi explained the reasons for his decision to join the Provisional Government and requested the leaders to support him and the Provisional Government:

> Regardless of the [two opposing arguments], one of the Korean National Council in Russian territory which contends that we should recognize the Hansŏng Government and the other one of the Shanghai Provisional Assembly which contends that we should restructure the Hansŏng Government, I will try humbly to do my best for 20 million Koreans. Although comrades are saying that Yi Tong-hwi's taking the post of the "restructured" government is in great conflict with the "recognition" of comrades. . . based on my conscience which does not divide 20 million into "we" and "they,". . . . I cannot stand with the prejudices of the comrades. . . . Today when the Japanese are trying to utilize our dissension, I cannot open a political war with leaders of the Shanghai Provisional Government by insisting on the contention of the Korean National Coun-

cil. . . . I would rather be Yi Tong-hwi who makes a concession in this conflict of opinions among us comrades, but I can not be Yi Tong-hwi who destroys the achievement by stubbornly insisting on my opinion. . . . Comrades, if you perceive my difficulties and understand my faithfulness, help me in holding together the government which I am wholly in charge of. . . .[30]

We can understand Yi Tong-hwi's personal reasons for participation in the Provisional Government, but this does not explain the strategic and ideological reasons why the Korean Socialist Party decided to choose the Shanghai Provisional Government while dissociating itself from the Korean National Council. As we saw in Chapter 4, the April Congress of the Korean Socialist Party adopted party programs which were critical of the "native national bourgeoisie" which had organized both the Korean National Council and the Shanghai Provisional Government. What made the Korean Socialist Party decide to join the Shanghai Government which was dominated by the "national bourgeoisie?"

Han Hyŏng-gwŏn, the member of the Korean Socialist Party and delegate of the Shanghai Provisional Government to Moscow, in an article contributed to the *Communist International*, the organ of the Comintern, pointed to three reasons for the Korean Socialist Party's decision to join the Shanghai Provisional Government. First, the Korean Socialist Party revised its program of "pure class struggle" adopted at the party congress in April 1919, and recognized the progressive aspect of the native Korean national bourgeoisie. At the April Congress, the Korean Socialist Party declared that the task of the Korean Socialists was anti-capitalist class struggle against the national bourgeoisie and nobility who, like the Japanese imperialists, were the exploiters of the Korean working class. Now the Korean Socialist Party came to differentiate the nature of the nobility and national bourgeoisie (the former as anti-revolutionary and the latter as revolutionary):

> The country is passing through a period of growth of capitalism, which is replacing the dying feudalism, and, the very revolutionary bourgeoisie, is moving hand in hand with the poorer popular masses. Therefore, the central point of our propaganda is not the struggle against the bourgeoisie, but an agrarian revolution.[31]

Thus, as a result of its change in attitude toward the Korean national bourgeoisie, the Korean Socialist Party laid the theoretical basis necessary for its joining the Shanghai Provisional Government.

Secondly, the Korean Socialist Party was optimistic about its activities in the Shanghai Provisional Government. According to Han Hyŏng-gwŏn, the position of the Korean Socialist Party in the Shanghai Provisional Government would not necessarily be weak, for the "liberals," the majority of the Shanghai Provisional Government, were favorable toward Socialism and the Soviet government:

> Our Liberals are not averse to boasting of enjoying Socialist rights, the word Socialism having become a kind of fashion among the educated classes in the East. . . . the Korean Provisional Government, notwithstanding all its bourgeois qualities, is awaiting the approach of the Red Army with impatience.[32]

This optimism was closely related to the confidence of key leaders of the Korean Socialist Party in Yi Tong-hwi's leadership within the Provisional Government as the Premier, which was a much more authoritative and influential position than that of Minister of War in the Korean National Council. Furthermore, if the Korean Socialist Party did not join the Provisional Government as did the Korean National Council, they feared that the leadership of the anti-Provisional Government movement, particularly in the Primorye and North Chientao, would side with the National Council. Han Hyŏng-gwŏn's following explanation reflects that Korean Socialist Party perspective:

> What would the attitude of the wider popular masses be towards us, the Korean Socialist Party, if we were to refuse to take part in the Provisional Revolutionary Government in defiance of the April Congress?. . . . At the given moment, our task lies in directing the national liberation movement along the course of an agrarian revolution, and in the external — a complete rupture with the "League of Nations" and adhesion to the Third Communist International. But the masses would not have understood our conduct, they would have identified us with the intriguers out of the camp of the Korean National Council, who are hoping to revive the latter. Our Party would have been in the position of a commander of an army without soldiers. The Union of Serene Liberation (Union of Iron and Blood Restoration or Ch'ŏlhyŏl Kwangboktan) out of whose Left Wing, the Korean Socialist Party was formed, would have taken advantage of the antipathy against us evinced by the masses and have tried to attract all those who had followed our lead.[33]

The joining of the Korean Socialist Party to the Shanghai Provisional Government was significant in that Korean socialists adopted the united front strategy already in 1919, one year before the second Comintern Congress where Lenin's famous thesis of united front with national bourgeoisie was officially adopted.

The joining of Yi Tong-hwi greatly contributed to enhancing the authority and influence of the Shanghai Provisional Government among Koreans, particularly, in nationalist organizations in North Chientao and the Primorye which were Yi Tong-hwi's long-time base and until that time had refused to recognize the Shanghai Provisional Government as the central political body of Koreans. That was why An Ch'ang-ho gave a secret order to Yi Kang in Vladivostok, "in case the National Council would not dissolve," at least to "take Yi Tong-hwi" to Shanghai.[34] In this sense, Yi Tong-hwi's joining was a great political victory for the Shanghai Provisional Government. Leading anti-Japanese nationalist organizations such as the Korean National Association [Taehan Kungminhoe], Military Government in North Chienato [Pungno Kunjŏngsŏ] and Hong Pŏm-do's Korean Independence Army [Taehan Tongnipkun] in North Chientao, the Korean People's Association [Hanjokhoe], the Military Government in West Chienato [Sŏro Kunjŏngsŏ] in Western Chientao and the Military Government in Jilin [Kilim Kunjŏngsa] expressed their support and promised to follow the order of the Provisional Government.[35]

In the Primorye, stubborn leaders of the Korean National Council such as Ch'oe Chae-hyŏng and Kim Ha-sŏk revived its activities with the support of right-wing of the Union of Iron and Blood Restoration [Ch'ŏlhyŏl Kwangboktan],[36] but did not succeed in increasing influence among Koreans. In contrast, Chŏng Chae-gwan and Kim Kyu-myŏn, key leaders of the Korean Socialist Party who had organized movement for advocating the Shanghai Provisional Government, were successfully expanding support from Koreans.[37]

Accordingly, as of the end of 1919, there were in all 45 major Korean organizations both inside and outside Korea which supported and followed the orders of the Shanghai Provisional Government.[38] As we can see in Table 5. 1, all Ministers except two (Mun Ch'ang-bŏm, Pak Yong-man) agreed to take their posts.

The Korean Socialist Party enjoyed the "big authority" of the Provisional Government and Yi Tong-hwi's premiership in the Shanghai Provisional Government. However, the geographical distance caused by the relocation of the party leadership under Yi Tong-hwi and Kim Rip to Shanghai made it difficult for the party members to communicate efficiently with each other. This difficulty was in many ways worsened by the hostile opposition of the Korean National Council.[39]

The Korean Socialist Party's break-up with the Korean National Council, much more than the leaders of the Party had expected, was a catalyst which would deepen and intensify the confrontation and conflicts with the Korean National Council. The National Council became an uncompromising and hostile rival in the Russian Far East. The Korean National Council criticized Yi Tong-hwi and Kim Rip, arguing that they betrayed the faithfulness of the comrades who had "shared suffering and happiness for more than ten years" and took the offices of the government "without any principle, without any political opinion and without any faithfulness."[40] The conflicts originating from the issue of participation in the Shanghai Provisional Government became a prelude to the deep-seated internecine factional struggles between the Shanghai Group and Irkutsk Group in the Korean Communist movement.

The dispute concerning "recognition" and "restructuring" [*sŭngin kaejo punjaeng*] also provided a chance for various anti-Shanghai

Provisional Government groups to form a strong coalition. On the way back to Vladivostok, Mun Ch'ang-bŏm went to Beijing and met Pak Yong-man and Sin Ch'ae-ho, stubborn opponents of the Shanghai Provisional Government, particularly, of Yi Sŭng-man, and discussed cooperative strategies in opposing the Shanghai Provisional Government. This gathering signified the formation of an anti-Shanghai Provisional Government block which would become the Congress of Military Organizations in 1921 and the "Creation Faction" ["*Ch'angjop'a*"] at the Congress of People's Representatives [Kungmin Taep'yohoeŭi] in 1923.[41]

B. Disputes In Diplomacy

1. Yŏ Un-hyŏng's Visit to Tokyo

Shortly after the establishment of the "unified" Shanghai Provisional Government, the leaders of the government demonstrated differences in their perspectives and strategies for an independence movement with regard to the issue of Yŏ Un-hyŏng's visit to Tokyo. Yŏ Un-hyŏng (1885-1947) was from Yangp'yŏng, Kyŏnggi Province, and studied at the Paejae School (whose superintendent was a American missionary, Henry Gerhart Apenzeller) and the Hŭnghwa School established by Min Yŏng-hwan who committed suicide protesting the "Protectorate Treaty" in 1905. Yŏ Un-hyŏng was well-known as a young Christian and educational leader. He went to China in 1914 and studied at Jinlin College in Nanjing. He then moved to Shanghai and shortly after the conclusion of the World War I, with Kim Kyu-sik, Kim Ch'ŏl and Sŏnu Hyŏk, organized the New Korea

Youth Party in November 1918. The New Korea Youth Party dispatched Kim Kyu-sik to Paris, Chang Tŏk-su to Japan and Korea, and Yŏ Un-hyŏng to Manchuria and the Primorye.

In February 1919, Yŏ Un-hyŏng visited Korean nationalists in Manchuria and the Primorye with the purpose of gathering Korean leaders at Shanghai. Thanks to Yŏ Un-hyŏng's efforts, thirty Korean patriots came to Shanghai from Manchuria and the Primorye: Yi Tong-nyŏng, Cho Wan-gu, Cho Sŏng-hwan and Cho Yŏng-jin from the Primorye, and Kim Tong-sam, Yi Si-yŏng and Cho So-ang from Manchuria. Yŏ Un-hyŏng and other members of the New Korea Youth Party played a key role in establishing the Shanghai Provisional Government in April 1919, together with other Korean nationalists who had come from Manchuria, Russia, Japan and America. In the Provisional Government, Yŏ Un-hyŏng worked as a member of the committee for foreign affairs.[42]

Influenced by the people's uprising in the March First Movement, the Japanese authorities came to realize the problems of the severe militaristic rule in Korea during the 1910s and began to seek so-called "cultural politics" ["*bunka seiji*"] or "reform policy" in Korea to placate the angry Koreans. This new policy would be effective in increasing more pro-Japanese Koreans and dividing Korean nationalists from within. The plan to invite Yŏ Un-hyŏng to Tokyo was a result of this new policy. The Japanese authorities proceeded to invite one of the most influential Korean nationalist leaders and Yŏ Un-hyŏng was finally chosen. Yŏ Un-hyŏng was considered by the Japanese authorities such as Koga Renzō, Minister of Colonial Affairs, as a moderate or even mistaken as an advocate of self-rule.[43]

With the financial and political support of the Japanese authorities, particularly Koga Renzō, Tanaka Giichi (Minister of Army), Murakami

Yukichi of the Japanese Union Church [Nihon Kumiai Kyokai] and Fujita Kyūko (executive secretary of the Japanese YMCA in Shanghai) proceeded from July 1919 to plan Yŏ Un-hyŏng's visit to Tokyo. Four months later, in October, Koga sent a letter to Yŏ Un-hyŏng inviting him to come to Tokyo to exchange opinions concerning Korean political matters. At the same time, Yamazaki, the Japanese Consul General asked Wildon, French Consul General in Shanghai, to advise Yŏ Un-hyŏng to go to Japan and promised to guarantee his safe trip and free action. Yŏ Un-hyŏng, after consulting with George Feech, Shanghai YMCA Director, and members of the Provisional Government such as An Ch'ang-ho, Yun Hyŏn-jin (Vice-Minister of Finance) and Yi Kwang-su, publisher and chief editor of the *Tongnip Sinmun* (Independence Gazette), Korean nationalist newspaper in Shanghai, decided to go to Japan.[44]

However, Yŏ insisted that the Japanese government release his close comrade, Chang Tŏk-su, who was in exile in Kohaŭi Island in South Chŏlla Province as a condition of his visit, and that he be allowed to accompany Yŏ as an interpreter.[45] Chang Tŏk-su was a graduate of Waseda University and was dispatched by the New Korea Youth Party in Shanghai early 1919 to Japan and Korea with the mission of secretly discussing plans for the independence movement. Chang went to Korea through Japan, but he was arrested in Inch'ŏn [Chemulp'o] in March 1919.[46]

On November 14, Yŏ Un-hyŏng left for Japan together with Ch'oe Kŭn-u, a close associate of Yŏ and a director of the Korean YMCA in Shanghai, and Sin Sang-wan, all of whom were presumably chosen by An Ch'ang-ho. They arrived at Nagasaki and met Chang Tŏk-su at Shimonoseki on November 16. The day after Yŏ's departure, on November 15, the *Tongnip Sinmun* began publication of reports on Yŏ Un-hyŏng's four-weeks' visit to Japan. The articles intended to clarify and advocate the purpose of his visit and more importantly to preclude unnecessary misunderstandings and accusations. His purpose was stated as communicating the opinions of Koreans regarding the independence movement, that is, the will for complete independence of Korea [*chŏltae tongnip*]. The article also made a point of stating that Yŏ Un-hyŏng's visit was made as an individual and had no relations with the Provisional Government or any other Korean organizations. The *Tongnip Sinmun* also published the list of Japanese high-ranking officials whom Yŏ would meet, including Hara Takashi (Kei, Prime Minister), Tanaka Giichi (Minister of Army), Koga Renzō (Minister of Colonial Affairs), Saitō Makoto (Japanese Governor-General of Korea) and Mizuno Rentarō (General Director of Administration, Japanese Government-General of Korea).[47]

During the visit, Yŏ Un-hyŏng was officially treated as an honored guest and met Tanaka Giichi, Koga Renzō, Mizuno Rentarō and other high ranking officials of the Japanese government. He had several meetings with Koga and debated key issues related to Japanese rule of Korea.[48] He also had a meeting with the Korean Students Association in Tokyo and the Sinjinkai (New People's Association) led by Yoshino Sakuzo, law professor of Tokyo Imperial University.[49]

On November 27, Yŏ Un-hyŏng held a press conference at the Imperial Hotel at which more than fifty Japanese, foreign reporters and members of the Peace Association [Heiwa Kyokai] attended. Reiterating what he had said in talks with Koga, Yŏ Un-hyŏng freely appraised the awakening of the Korean people and strongly advocated the independence movement which corresponded to the new "restructuring" trend of the world and was indispensable for peace in East Asia. Yŏ also criticized the Japanese justification of their rule over Korea as protection from the threat of Russia stating that Russia was no longer a threat to Korea and Japan.[50]

As Japanese authorities allowed newspapers to report about Yŏ Un-hyŏng for the first time,[51] Yŏ Un-hyŏng's address at the press interview was published both in Japanese and English newspapers. The Japanese newspaper *Jiji Shinpo* (Current Affair Gazette) reprimanded the Japanese authorities for inviting Yŏ Un-hyŏng in its comments: "We heard that a Korean from Shanghai is shouting at the center of the Imperial Capital. . . . If we may say so directly, this violates state law." The newspaper also called for the Japanese government to punish the persons who made arrangements for Yŏ Un-hyŏng's visit to Japan.[52]

It became clear that the political goal of the Japanese government to persuade a leading Korean nationalists to take a pro-Japanese stance and thereby strengthen the validity of the Japanese colonial rule of Korea, had completely failed.[53] The Japanese government canceled its original plan to have Yŏ's meeting with Hara Takashi [Kei] and the Japanese Emperor. Furthermore, the Japanese Government-General, disturbed by the rumors that Yŏ Un-hyŏng's visit to Korea would incite anti-Japanese demonstrations, prohibited his visit to Korea which the Japanese authorities had originally promised to arrange.[54] As a result, Yŏ Un-hyŏng, Ch'oe Kŭn-u and Sin Sang-wan returned to Shanghai on December 10, 1919, while Chang Tŏk-su went to Korea.[55]

Yŏ Un-hyŏng's visit to Japan aroused polemics and mutual accusations among Korean nationalists in Shanghai. The leaders of the Shanghai Provisional Government were divided in their attitude towards Yŏ Un-hyŏng's visit to Tokyo. When Yŏ Un-hyŏng met with the cabinet members, Yi Tong-hwi had strongly urged him not to go to Japan arguing that armed struggle was the only way to achieve independence and that it was unnecessary to have dialogue with the Japanese.[56] He warned that Yŏ Un-hyŏng would only be used in a political scheme of the Japanese.[57] Yi Tong-hwi also reminded Yŏ Un-hyŏng of the public support for "complete independence,"[58] obviously targeting the movement for self-administration under the Japanese rule led by pro-Japanese journalist, Min Wŏn-sik, and the appeal for American mandatory rule of Yi Sŭng-man. Yi Tong-hwi even held suspicions that Yŏ Un-hyŏng might have been bribed by the Japanese government.[59]

On November 16, after Yŏ Un-hyŏng left for Japan, Yi Tong-hwi issued a government decree severely criticizing him for defying the government's order not to go to Japan.[60] Together with a brief summary of Yi Tong-hwi's decree, the *Tongnip Sinmun* (under the control of An Ch'ang-ho and Yi Kwang-su),[61] published interviews with An Ch'ang-ho and Yi Tong-nyŏng which advocated for Yŏ Un-hyŏng's visit to Tokyo. Yi Tong-nyŏng, Minister of Internal Affairs, criticized Yi Tong-hwi stating that although Yŏ Un-hyŏng's visit to Tokyo was not a problem, Yi Tong-hwi issued the "government decree" unilaterally and without any consultation with the Cabinet Council. An Ch'ang-ho, the Director of the Labor Department, did not directly criticize Yi Tong-hwi, but instead stressed his "absolute confidence in Yŏ Un-hyŏng's pure and passionate patriotism for the nation" and cautioned the readers not to confuse Yŏ's "sincere patriotic" purpose with that of the "unrighteous" Min Wŏn-sik.[62] Supported by the interviews with Yi Tong-nyŏng and An Ch'ang-ho, the *Tongnip Sinmun* severely criticized Yi Tong-hwi and his decree by pointing out that he "had thoughtlessly attacked a comrade of achievement and capability and accordingly damaged his public esteem for him and his future."[63]

The political polemics were not limited to the leaders of the Provisional Government. Korean nationalists in Shanghai began to argue for or against the visit of Yŏ Un-hyŏng to Japan. The Korean Residents' Association in Shanghai initiated a public meeting on November 17, 1919 and resolved to publicize a declaration clarifying that Yŏ Un-hyŏng's visit to Japan was Yŏ's personally and had no relation with the Provisional Government or any other organization.[64] Five members who were assigned to draft the declaration were, however, split in interpreting the contents of the resolution. Three members, Sin Ch'ae-ho, Han Wi-gŏn and Wŏn Se-hun wanted to include an "aggressive message" in the declaration based on the words in the resolution that "the behaviors of Yŏ and the other three persons are against the people's will." The other two members, Ok Kwan-bin and Sin Kuk-kwŏn were opposed to this and instead wanted to simply declare that Yŏ's visit to Japan was personal.[65] Regardless of the opposition, Sin Ch'ae-ho, Han Wi-gŏn and Wŏn Se-hun distributed a declaration accusing Yŏ Un-hyŏng of promoting "self-rule" ["*chach'i*"] under the Japanese or assimilation [*tonghwa*]. At the second and third public meetings on November 25-26 and 29-30, fierce arguments were exchanged, but a majority of the participants, who were in favor of Yŏ Un-hyŏng, published an additional declaration nullifying the declaration issued by Sin Ch'ae-ho, Han Wi-gŏn and Wŏn Se-hun. The meeting also resolved to seek an apology from the three persons to which the three rejected and responded with justifications.[66]

Arguments at the third meeting clearly demonstrated the deep mistrust and misunderstanding amongst Korean nationalists in

Shanghai.[67] The Korean nationalists (Sin Ch'ae-ho, Han Wi-gŏn, Wŏn Se-hun, Nam Kong-sŏn, Pak Kŏn-byŏng, Chŏng Hae-ri), who had criticized Yŏ Un-hyŏng, were mostly persons who had been opposed to the Shanghai Provisional Government or members of the Korean National Council. In addition, they typically came from the northern parts of Korea and had worked in North Chientao or in the Primorye. The other Korean nationalists (Ok Kwan-bin, Sin Kuk-kwŏn, Yi Kwang-su, Chu Yo-han, Son Tu-hwan, Kim T'ae-yŏn), who advocated Yŏ Un-hyŏng, were persons who had contributed to the establishment of the Shanghai Provisional Government, and were mainly from the central or western part of Korea, Shanghai and America.

The two groups were deeply divided in their strategies for the independence of Korea. The first group prioritized armed struggle and were very suspicious of any diplomatic approach to independence, particularly with Japan. Yi Sŭng-man's appeal for a mandated rule of Korea by America and Min Wŏn-sik's movement for self-administration were used as examples supporting the arguments of this group. On the other hand, the second group advocated for diplomacy or a peaceful approaching for achieving independence. This conflict was the first public political confrontation among Korean nationalists after the establishment of the "unified" Provisional Government, but its roots went back to the first group's censure of Yŏ Un-hyŏng's visit to Japan. The suspicion and mistrust of the first group had also been increased by the previous dispute over the "recognition" or "restructuring."

Through the reports in the *Tongnip Sinmun*, especially the detailed report of Yŏ Un-hyŏng's activities recorded by Ch'oe Kŭn-u who had accompanied him to Japan, polemics among the Korean nationalists in Shanghai calmed down.[68] In his "second decree" dated December 29, 1919, Yi Tong-hwi declared that he had investigated the facts, but did not find any violation of the position of absolute "independence," and that he "granted special forgiveness" to Yŏ Un-hyŏng.[69]

One of the most significant factors in the dispute over Yŏ Un-hyŏng's visit to Tokyo was the cabinet members' failure to express a unified voice over the issue. Yi Tong-hwi issued his "government decree" without discussion with other cabinet members, to which Yi Tong-nyŏng and An Ch'ang-ho publically voiced their disapproval. Furthermore, the *Tongnip Sinmun* and the *Sin Taehan* (New Great Korea), the two major Korean nationalist newspapers published in Shanghai, were also divided in support. The *Tongnip Sinmun* under control of Yi Kwang-su, An Ch'ang-ho's close associate, was to attack the Premier. Sin Ch'ae-ho, a stubborn opponent of the Provisional Government (mainly due to his distate Yi Sŭng-man, its President), began to intensify his criticism in his articles in the *Sin Taehan*,[70] which Korean nationalists (mainly from Kyŏng-sang Provinces led by Nam Hyŏng-u) had begun to publish on October 28, 1919.[71]

2. Diplomacy in Moscow — Pak Chin-sun and Han Hyŏng-gwŏn

The Korean Socialist Party had pursued pro-Soviet policies after its establishment in May 1918. As we saw in Chapter 4, the Korean Socialist Party dispatched a delegation of three members, Pak Chin-sun, Pak Ae and Yi Han-yŏng, to Moscow at its Congress in April 1919. The delegation carried a congratulatory letter to the Soviet government and a party report to the Comintern. The delegation had to pass through Siberia which was still under the control of the Whites. Yi Tong-hwi told the delegation to get help from Yi In-sŏp, who was founding member of the party and had been dispatched to Omsk in early 1919, when they would pass the war front between the Whites and the Reds.[72] However, Pak Ae and Yi Han-yŏng were struck with typhoid fever in Omsk and hospitalized in a medical unit attached to the fifth corps of the Red Army. Only Pak Chin-sun continued his travel and arrived at Moscow with the help of Vladimir Dmitrievich Vilenskii-Sibiryakov, plenipotentiary of the Soviet government's Ministry of Foreign Affairs to the Far Eastern Republic.[73] The *Tongnip Sinmun*, based on a telegram from the Reuter in London, reported that the delegate of the Korean Socialist Party arrived in Cheliabinsk on November 15, 1919, and would attend the Congress of the Workers' and Soldiers' Soviets in Moscow, quoting the announcement issued by the delegation in Cheliabinsk:

> The Korean Socialist Party recently held a congress in a place in East Siberia. As the left wing prevailed, [the congress] resolved to eliminate the propertied classes and to cooperate with the Russian Party of the Workers and Soldiers. [The congress] also immediately elected the General Executive and declared martial law over the whole of Korea.[74]

From this public announcement, the existence of the Korean Socialist Party was made known to the public for the first time. In Moscow, Pak Chin-sun visited the executive committee of the Comintern and submitted a list of party members and a report on the April Party Congress titled "the Socialist Movement in Korea."[75] The joining of the Korean Socialist Party to the Comintern was publicized by a declaration of the Soviet government dated December

7, 1919, which began to frequently be quoted in the Soviet government's literatures for propaganda among Koreans.[76]

The news about Pak Chin-sun's arrival at Moscow was also known to the Korean partisan units in the Primorye through the Chinese-Korean joint newspaper *Yuandongbao* (Kor. *Wŏndongbo*, The Far Eastern Gazette) in Harbin and aroused cheers among Koreans.[77] The *Tongnip Sinmun* also reported that Pak Chin-sun, as representative of the "Korean revolutionary party," together with a member of the central executive committee of the "Korean Labor Party in Russia," member of the central executive committee of "Chinese Labor Party in Russia," and Nakahira, representative of the "Japanese Revolutionary Party," sent a letter to Lenin celebrating his fiftieth birthday. In the letter, those East Asians "celebrate the birthday of Lenin, a respectful revolutionary socialist fighter, wish him to be the leader of the future East Asian people's liberation movement." The *Tongnip Sinmun* based its report on a report in the Chinese newspaper, the *Dalubao* (The Continental Gazette) which was also based on a telegram from A. Voznesenskii, the former deputy-ambassador to China and then director of the Eastern Department of the Soviet government. Shortly thereafter, the *Tongnip Sinmun* also introduced Pak Chin-sun: "Mr. Pak Chin-sun is, this year, 25 years old young man who graduated from the Teachers' College in Blagoveshchensk and is now staying in Moscow. He is renowned among young men and his personality and knowledge are elegant."[78]

In December 1919, as declared in his statement in Cheliabinsk, Pak Chin-sun attended the Congress of the Workers' and Soldiers' Soviets in Moscow and delivered an address stressing the new socialistic and communistic stage in the Korean revolutionary movement and the hegemony of the Korean Socialist Party:

The Koreans believed that the declaration of Wilson would save Korea and have fought against Japan over the past 17 months, but they failed because they misled the masses. As a result, every party lost its power. It is difficult to achieve the liberation of Korea by the national movement. Japan made it impossible for even middle-class Koreans to secure their living. The fight against Japan can not but be social and communistic. [We] can not but carry on propaganda in Japan and among the Japanese army. Even now, the only party which has power in Korea is the Communist Revolutionary Party [Korean Socialist Party], but the party belongs to the Third International and has the same political principle and means with the Russian Communist Party.[79]

According to a Japanese report, in December 1919, a representative of "the Korean Labor Party" (obviously Pak Chin-sun) had a meeting with Han Tong-wŏn (Korean student from America), Nikolai Li (Korean Russian), Xia Ji-feng (representative of the Chinese workers), and Tanaka (Japanese student from America), and discussed future plans to spread Bolshevism in the Far East.[80] Starting with his report on the April Congress of the Korean Socialist Party ("Socialist Movement in Korea" published in the *Communist International* in December 1919),[81] Pak Chin-sun published all eight articles in newspapers and magazines of the Bolsheviks (such as the *Izvestiia*, the *Communist International* and *Zhizn' Natsionalostei*) until he left Moscow for Shanghai in September 1920. Those articles dealt with various topics related to the Korean revolutionary movement: "Reform in Korea and the Korean Socialist Party,"[82] "Liberation Movement of the Peoples of the East in Soviet Russia,"[83] "Awakening of Korea,"[84] "Korean Emigration to Russia,"[85] "Revolutionary East and the Next Task of the Communist International,"[86] "Revolutionary Movement in

Korea,"[87] and "Women's Movement in Korea."[88]

These articles of Pak Chin-sun provided valuable inside information about Korea and the Korean revolution to Russian Bolsheviks who were not familiar with Korea at that time. In this context, E. H. Carr commented that Pak Chin-sun "became for a time the recognized spokesman on Korean affairs in Moscow."[89] It is no doubt that these articles have contributed to Pak Chin-sun's election to the position of the executive member in charge of the Far East at the second Congress of the Comintern (July-August 1920). In early 1920, the Korean Socialist Party planned to dispatch the delegation of the Shanghai Provisional Government to Moscow. The recognition of the independence of Korea and the Shanghai Provisional Government by the Soviet government in July 1919 must have encouraged the leaders of the Provisional Government as well.[90]

Various Korean materials all record Aleksei Potapov, a Russian General, as the person who had advised Korean patriots in Shanghai to dispatch a delegation to Moscow. According to an interview article in the *Tongnip Sinmun*, Potapov was born in 1872 in Kronshtadt and graduated from a Russian Military Academy and Military Staff College. He had been in Seoul as military attaché at the Russian Ministry from 1903 until the outbreak of the Russo-Japanese War. Potapov was awarded the highest medal by the Tsar for his military accomplishments in the Russo-Japanese War and World War I. At the time of the February Revolution, he had contributed to the collapse of the Romanov dynasty by mobilizing his First Royal Guard Regiment. Because of his involvement in democratic movements after the Revolution, Potapov became so famous that "there was nobody who did not know his name." Potapov was expelled by the Kolchak in February 1919 with the accusation of "big enemy" and went to Japan. The Japanese government again expelled Potapov on the charge of "interfering with the public security" in December 1919.[91]

According to Han Hyŏng-gwŏn, a member of the Korean Socialist Party, the idea of dispatching an official delegation to Moscow came from Potapov. As we saw in Chapter 2, Han Hyŏng-gwŏn had worked as a leader of the Kwŏpŏphoe and the *Kwŏnŏp Sinmun* in Vladivostok. Han moved to Harbin after the Siberian Intervention in 1918 escaping the Japanese army in the Primorye. There he established the *Yuandongbao*. In Harbin, he learned from a Russian newspaper that Potapov would come to Shanghai with "a very important mission." He then came to Shanghai and worked as an executive member of the *Sin Taehan*. Han Hyŏng-gwŏn was very critical of the diplomatic activities focused only on the Western Powers, particularly on America and Britain as were Kim Kyu-sik, Yun Hae, Ko Ch'ang-il and Yi Sŭng-man. He felt a strong necessity to obtain funds from the Soviet government for carrying out the "nation-wide movement in all areas of politics, industry, culture, diplomacy and military."[92]

Han Hyŏng-gwŏn met Potapov and submitted his plan for a Korean revolutionary movement. Han asked financial support and training for a military force. After several meetings, Potapov advised Han to get the Shanghai Provisional Government to dispatch an official delegation to Moscow.[93] Han Hyŏng-gwŏn immediately reported to Yi Tong-hwi his discussions with Potapov. By the initiative of Yi Tong-hwi, the Cabinet Council appointed Han Hyŏng-gwŏn, Yŏ Un-hyŏng and An Kong-gŭn as members of the delegation.[94] Han Hyŏng-gwŏn wanted to go to Moscow as early as possible and decided to go through Mongolia and Siberia before other rival groups in Russia dispatched delegations to Moscow. However, according to Han Hyŏng-gwŏn, Yŏ Un-hyŏng was opposed to Han's proposal arguing that the way was too dangerous. Yŏ suggested waiting until a way through Europe, which was blocked at that time, was open. Others suggested waiting until another delegate from Siberia An Kong-gŭn, arrived Shanghai before departing. However, Han Hyŏng-gwŏn who felt the mission was urgent, ultimately decided to travel to Moscow alone.[95]

Han was further delayed for a period of three months, however, because of a dispute between Yi Tong-hwi and An Ch'ang-ho as well as financial issues. Yi Tong-hwi strongly opposed to the dispatch of Yŏ Un-hyŏng, arguing that if the government sent Yŏ to Moscow, it would be difficult to get support from Koreans in Russia.[96] The main reason why Yŏ Un-hyŏng was discredited by Koreans in Russia was that Yŏ had visited the Primorye in February 1919 shortly before the outbreak of the March First Movement. There he asked Korean nationalists to come to Shanghai. Accordingly, Yi Tong-nyŏng, Cho Wan-gu and Cho Sŏng-hwan, members of the Korean National Council went to Shanghai and played a key role in establishing the Shanghai Provisional Government. In addition, as we saw earlier, Yi Tong-hwi had strongly opposed Yŏ Un-hyŏng's visit to Japan as did most Korean patriots in the Primorye. Although Yi Tong-hwi cleared suspicion about Yŏ Un-hyŏng after Yŏ's return, he did not forget Yŏ Un-hyŏng's defiance.[97]

An Ch'ang-ho, who had agreed to the plan of the Moscow delegation and met Potapov by the invitation of Yi Tong-hwi,[98] soon came to be critical of Yi Tong-hwi after he refused to dispatch Yŏ Un-hyŏng to Moscow.[99] In addition, An Ch'ang-ho rejected the request of Kim Rip and Yun Hyŏn-jin to fund Yi Tong-hwi, possibly for the travel expense of Han Hyŏng-gwŏn, by utilizing a portion of the funds which Koreans in America had sent to An Ch'ang-ho.[100]

Later on, An Ch'ang-ho would come to wholly oppose the idea of dispatching the delegation to Moscow itself.[101]

On the issue of sending a delegation to Moscow, Yi Tong-hwi received support from the four Vice-Ministers, Kim Rip (cabinet chief-secretary), Yun Hyŏn-jin (finance), Kim Ch'ŏl (communication) and Yi Kyu-hong (internal affairs), who were called "the foursome [*sainjo*]" within the government, and succeeded in secretly dispatching Han Hyŏng-gwŏn to Moscow by the end of April 1920.[102] Yi Tong-hwi gave Han Hyŏng-gwŏn the credential of the Provisional Government as a special envoy, a secret report to the Soviet government, and his personal letter to Alexandr Krasnoshchekov, the President of the Far Eastern Republic in Verkhneudinsk.[103] Han Hyŏng-gwŏn succeeded in reaching Verkhneudinsk, the capital of the Far Eastern Republic, by way of Beijing, Zhangjiakou and Mongolia where he was welcomed by a special military unit composed of 200 Koreans. In the Soviet territory from Irkutsk to Moscow, the Russian authorities prepared a special train exclusively for Han Hyŏng-gwŏn and welcomed him as a national guest. In major cities along the Trans-Siberian Railroad, local governors held official welcoming ceremonies and parades of the Red Armies for Han Hyŏng-gwŏn. In Moscow, Lev Mikhailovich Karakhan, Vice-Minister of Foreign Affairs welcomed Han Hyŏng-gwŏn, who then had meetings with Karakhan and Georgy Vasilyevich Chicherin, Minister of Foreign Affairs.[104]

With the help of Pak Chin-sun, Han Hyŏng-gwŏn met Lenin as well.[105] He presented the following four-points proposal to Lenin and stated that Korea and Soviet Russia should cooperate in fighting the common enemy, Japan. According to Han Hyŏng-gwŏn, Lenin agreed to his proposals and said:

I know well that without destroying imperialistic and militaristic Japan, there will be no freedom and happiness for the Asian peoples. And in Korea, a proletarian social revolution is not necessary at this time. It is the time for only national liberation, that is, an independence movement. Therefore, we will support the Korean independence movement with all of our strength.[106]

Lenin also accepted the four-point proposal of Han Hyŏng-gwŏn: 1) to recognize the Korean Provisional Government; 2) to furnish the Korean Independence Army with sufficient arms and facilities comparable to those of the Red Army; 3) to establish a Korean Military Academy in some designated place in Siberia for the training of military officers; 4) to provide a large sum of funds to the Shanghai Provisional Government.[107] The Soviet government promised to provide 2 million gold rubles to the Shanghai Provisional Government.[108] Considering the dangerous situation in Siberia which was in control of the Kolchak government, the Soviet government gave 400,000 rubles as a first installment. Although Han Hyŏng-gwŏn, in his recollection, completely ignored the role of Pak Chin-sun and the Korean Socialist Party, the Soviet government, in fact, assigned control of funds directly to the Central Executive Committee of the Korean Socialist Party which at that time had joined with the Shanghai Provisional Government.[109]

In Moscow, Han Hyŏng-gwŏn also attended the Third All Russian Congress of Chinese Workmen living in Russia and Turkestan held on June 18, 1920. In response to the welcoming address of Liu Shaozhou, Chairman of the congress, Han Hyŏng-gwŏn delivered an address in Chinese on behalf of the Korean revolutionaries who attended the congress. Han's address was interpreted into Russian by Liu.[110]

In addition to Pak Chin-sun and Han Hyŏng-gwŏn, other members of the Korean Socialist Party were in Moscow in the first half of 1920. Pak Ae and Yi Han-yŏng, who had been hospitalized in Omsk because of typhoid fever, came to Moscow later. In order to communicate with other party members, Pak and Yi left Moscow with some funds and mission from the Comintern in the middle of April 1920, before the opening of the second Congress of the Comintern.[111] Kim Kyu-myŏn, vice-chairman of the Korean Socialist Party and chairman of the party military committee, came to Moscow in order to attend the Second Congress of the Comintern.[112] Another member of the Korean Socialist Party, Yi In-sŏp also came from Omsk in order to attend the congress as a member of the Chinese delegation.[113]

The Second Congress of the Comintern was held from July 19 to August 7, 1920, in Moscow. Grigory Eveseevich Zinoviev, the Chairman of the Comintern, would later report at the third congress of the Comintern in 1921 that the First Congress of the Comintern was "merely a meeting of a very number of representatives of various groups." In fact, it was the Second Congress that was the "actual constituent Congress of the Communist International."[114] Pak Chin-sun attended the congress with a voting right representing the "Korean Communist Party" [Korean Socialist Party]. An Yong-hak, a former Kungminhoe member in Tiumen, attended the congress together with Liu Shao-zhou representing China. The Russian Communist Party demonstrated its deep interest in the congress by dispatching all 64 delegates including Lenin, Trotsky, Bukharin, and Zinoviev. Alexandr Krasnoshchekov, the head of the Far Eastern Republic and long-time patron of the Korean Socialist Party, also attended the congress as a delegate of the Russian Communist Party.[115]

Pak Chin-sun belonged to two committees of the ten congress committees: the committee for international situation and the Comintern's main tasks and the committee for national and colonial questions.[116] In particular, Pak Chin-sun worked actively at the committee for national and colonial questions to which Lenin also belonged. A picture of Pak Chin-sun seated beside Lenin was published in various literature of the Comintern and Bolshevik press and frequently quoted as evidence of Lenin's confidence in Pak Chin-sun, encouraging the members of the Korean Socialist Party, and later the "Shanghai Group" of the Korean Communist Party.[117] At the congress, Pak Chin-sun reported on the revolutionary movement in Korea,[118] and delivered an address and participated in debates at the fifth session on the national and colonial questions.[119] During the congress, Pak Chin-sun's article, "Revolutionary East and the Next Task of the Communist International," was published both in the *Petrograd Pravda* on July 27 and the *Communist International*.[120] Due to these activities, Pak Chin-sun was elected as one of 19 members of the Comintern Executive Committee, in charge of the Far East regions.[121] Pak Chin-sun, along with Kim Kyu-myŏn, was also a signatory of the report of the Congress, "Capitalist World and the Communist International" (issued on August 6), as a representative of the Korean Socialist Party and Korean partisan units in the Far East.[122]

Han Hyŏng-gwŏn recollected that the Korean Socialist Party's "diplomacy toward the Soviet was a great success," and he felt that "the [Korean] independence movement was certain to succeed."[123] As a result of these efforts, Pak Chin-sun attained an influential position as an executive member of the Comintern responsible for the Far East. In addition, the Soviet government promised to provide enough funds (2 million gold rubles), military academy, and arms and facilities for the independence army. In early September 1920, after the Second Congress of the Comintern, Pak Chin-sun and Han Hyŏng-gwŏn left Moscow for Shanghai with the 400,000 rubles in gold packed in seven boxes.[124]

C. Growing Schism

1. Frustrated Insurgence — Unsuccessful Attempt to Expel Yi Sŭng-man [Syngman Rhee]

Yi Sŭng-man, President of the Shanghai Provisional Government, was a main target for the activities of anti-Provisional Government groups. As we saw earlier, his petition to the American President Wilson for America's "mandated rule" ["*wiim t'ongch'i*"] of Korea was utilized by his opponents to accuse Yi of lacking the spirit for the "complete independence" ["*chŏltae tongnip*"] of Korea. Furthermore, Yi Sŭng-man's uncompromising insistence on changing the title of the government from "Chief Executive" ["*Chipchŏnggwan*"] to "President" [*Taet'ongnyŏng*] heightened the "recognition" and "restructuring" disputes between the Shanghai Provisional Government and the Korean National Council.

An Ch'ang-ho, the driving force in the early period of the Shanghai Provisional Government and for the establishment of the "unified" Shanghai Provisional Government, had been mainly criticized for his support of Yi Sŭng-man. First, An Ch'ang-ho was the President of the Korean National Association in America when the Association appointed Yi Sŭng-man as a member of the delegation to the Paris

Peace Conference, and more importantly it was during his tenure that Yi submitted the petition for America's mandated rule of Korea in the name of the Korean National Association. Secondly, in order to make Yi Sŭng-man the "President" of the Provisional Government, he led the process of revising the constitution of the Provisional Government to change the title of the government head from "Chief Executive" [*Chipchŏnggwan*] of the Hansŏng Government, which Shanghai and Vladivostok had agreed as the only "unified" and "legitimate" government of Korea, to "President [*Taet'ongnyŏng*], which arose out of Yi Sŭng-man's arbitrary usage of the title.

In addition to the Korean National Council (led by Mun Ch'ang-bŏm and Wŏn Se-hun), Pak Yong-man's group in Beijing and the *Sin Taehan* group (led by Nam Hyŏng-u, Sin Ch'ae-ho and Kim Tu-bong) joined the anti-Provisional Government camp.[125] The main argument of these anti-government groups was that Yi Sŭng-man, who had demonstrated his "lack of spirit for independence" by his petition for American mandated rule, "was not qualified for the Provisional Government whose objective was the 'complete independence' of Korea and accordingly, all other cabinet members did not deserve the confidence [of the people]."[126] The leaders of the Shanghai Provisional Government, who had revealed political disharmony over the issues of Yŏ Un-hyŏng's visit to Tokyo and the delegation to Moscow, were also experiencing internal conflicts which resulted from their different political ideas of the independence movement and regionalism.[127]

Even after the establishment of the "unified" Provisional Government, Yi Sŭng-man continued in his arbitrary and dictatorial acts unilaterally in America thereby further agitating external and internal problems of the "unified" Provisional Government. In August 1919,

Yi Sŭng-man established the Korean Commission in America and Europe [Kumi Chuch'a Hanguk Wiwŏnbu] on his own without any prior consultation or post recognition from the Provisional Government. The Korean Commission in America and Europe was not simply an organization for diplomacy with America and European powers. It was, in fact, a super-constitutional organization under Yi Sŭng-man's direct control in charge of diplomacy, finance, and administration of the Korean Provisional Government in America and Europe. In an operational sense, the Korean Commission was hierarchically not lower than the Cabinet in Shanghai and functioned virtually as Yi Sŭng-man's "separate government." Through the Korean Commission, Yi Sŭng-man attempted to monopolize financial donations. He began to collect donations from Korean communities in America by floating "government bonds" ["*kongch'ae*"] through the Commission and going as far as prohibiting the Korean National Association from collecting "patriotic funds" ["*aekukkŭm*"].[128]

The main financial source for the Provisional Government had been from the Korean National Association in America, which collected "patriotic funds" to be sent to the Shanghai Provisional Government. In 1919, the Korean National Association provided 30,000 dollars with which An Ch'ang-ho could maintain the Provisional Government. In this context, the "unified" Shanghai Provisional Government also expected to be maintained by financial support from Koreans in America. As a result, Yi Sŭng-man's monopoly of financial source from Koreans in America led to conflicts with the Korean National Association over these donations and created serious confusion and discord among Korean communities in America.[129]

During the first crucial period for enhancing the authority and influence of the Provisional Government (from September 1919 to

May 1920) Yi Sŭng-man monopolized all funds from Koreans in America and did not send any money to the Shanghai Provisional Government.[130] Only after criticism against him heightened in the middle of 1920, did he begin to send a small portion of the funds to appease the leaders of the Provisional Government.[131] In addition, Yi Sŭng-man issued government orders without any consultation with cabinet members in Shanghai.[132] The urgent necessity to control various Korean military and political organizations, which sprang up in Manchuria particularly after the March First Movement and after the Bolshevik victory in Siberia in Russia, under one command of the Provisional Government also increased Korean nationalists' dissatisfaction with Yi Sŭng-man who did not have any intention to come to Shanghai and lead that government.

Among the cabinet members, it was Yi Tong-hwi who most severely criticized Yi Sŭng-man. Although both Yi Sŭng-man and Yi Tong-hwi were Christians and well-known educators, their manner and thinking was sharply contrasted and often came in conflict more than any other members in the cabinet. While Yi Sŭng-man was from the central part of Korea and descended from the Yi royal clan, which he often boasted about, Yi Tong-hwi was from the northern part of Korea (long discriminated against by the Chosŏn dynasty government) and came from a low social-economic class. While Yi Sŭng-man carried out his activities mainly in Hawaii and America, Yi Tong-hwi's activities concentrated in North Chientao and Russia. At the same time, while Yi Sŭng-man had never been to China and Russia, Yi Tong-hwi had never been to America. As far as strategies and tactics for achieving the independence of Korea, Yi Sŭng-man emphasized diplomatic activities with Western Powers, particularly with America, which Yi Tong-hwi had high hope of an armed struggle with Japan as the ultimate means for achieving independence of Korea in close cooperation with Soviet Russia. Yi Sŭng-man's strong negative attitudes toward Soviet Russia was mirrored by Yi Tong-hwi's attitude toward America. The style of their activities also contrasted: while Yi Sŭng-man was a elitist and authoritative, Yi Tong-hwi was a populist who stressed the importance of organizing the masses. More importantly, except for a short period of participation in two patriotic organizations in the Poanhoe (Association for Protection Land) and Hyŏptonghoe (Association for Cooperation) in 1904,[133] they did not share any substantial comradeship in nationalistic activities after 1905.

As Yi Sŭng-man was monopolizing all funds from Koreans in America, the financial difficulties of the Shanghai Provisional Government came to be so serious that the government could not manage funds for daily operational expenses. Accordingly, after February 1920, the leaders of the Shanghai Provisional Government began to feel a need to take urgent measures for revitalizing the activities of the government. In the spring of 1920, the outspoken critics within the government were Premier Yi Tong-hwi and Yun Hyŏn-jin, Vice-Minister of finance. Pointing out that the main problems originated from Yi Sŭng-man, Yi Tong-hwi asked An Ch'ang-ho to help in his efforts to replace Yi Sŭng-man and reform the government.[134]

An Ch'ang-ho, Yi Tong-hiw's long-time comrade since the days of the New People's Association [Sinminhoe], had strong influence over Koreans in America and was a leader of the Provisional Government with financial support from the Korean National Association. An Ch'ang-ho was thus crucial to Yi Tong-hwi in his plan to expel Yi Sŭng-man. Yun Hyŏn-jin, Vice-Minister of Finance, supported

Yi Tong-hwi's idea and from February to April 1920, repeatedly suggested to An Ch'ang-ho that he reorganize the government by replacing Yi Sŭng-man with Yi Tong-hwi and appointing himself as the Premier. Yun Hyŏn-jin's proposal was to establish a Cabinet composed of young leaders [*ch'ŏngnyŏn chŏngbu*] under the leadership of Yi Tong-hwi and An Ch'ang-ho.[135] On March 19, 1920, Yun Hyŏn-jin, together with other 16 Assembly members, submitted a resolution to the Provisional Assembly requesting Yi Sŭng-man to come to Shanghai within two months.[136] The resolution passed the Assembly on March 22 and was sent to Yi Sŭng-man immediately.[137]

An Ch'ang-ho also felt that Yi Sŭng-man, like the anti-government groups outside the government, was hindering the activities of the Provisional Government.[138] However, he strongly opposed the proposals of Yi Tong-hwi and Yun Hyŏn-jin to replace Yi Sŭng-man arguing that even a small change in the status quo of the Provisional Government would lead to the complete collapse of the government, and advised Yi and Yun to seek harmony and unity among the Cabinet members.[139] At the same time, An Ch'ang-ho wanted to resolve misunderstandings among the cabinet members, and persuade Korean leaders to support his own idea of creating "revolutionary central organization" in which all members of the Provisional Government and Korean patriots in Shanghai would participate. He thought that unity among the cabinet members would solve the problems of regional factionalism on the one hand, and overcome opposition from outside the government on the other hand.[140]

He succeeded in obtaining verbal agreement from all cabinet members to his suggestion, but it soon became clear that the agreement could not be the fundamental solution. Yi Tong-hwi and all Vice-

Ministers would eventually launch a full-scale non-confidence movement against Yi Sŭng-man. In early May 1920, Yi Tong-hwi declared that he did not have any intention to work together with Yi Sŭng-man and three other ministers in the cabinet (Yi Tong-nyŏng, Yi Si-yŏng, and Sin Kyu-sik). He also expressed his intention to go to West Chientao.[141] Yun Hyŏn-jin also began to heighten his criticism against Yi Sŭng-man and the three ministers, arguing that they favored regionalism.[142]

At last in early May 1920, Yi Sŭng-man's notice to Yi Si-yŏng, that he had appointed Hyŏn Sun as a member of the Korean Commission in America and sent money for Hyŏn's travel, ignited a non-confidence movement of all Vice-Ministers against Yi Sŭng-man. Yi Sŭng-man made the decision without any prior consultation, while this was the first time money was ever sent from America. On May 15, all six Vice-Ministers, Kim Rip, Yun Hyŏn-jin, Yi Kyu-hong, Kim Ch'ŏl, Kim Hŭi-sŏn and Chŏng In-gwa, threatened to resign from the Provisional Government, demanding the discharge of Yi Sŭng-man. They maintained that unless Yi Sŭng-man resigned, they all would resign from the government.[143] In his talks with An Ch'ang-ho, Yi Tong-hwi also supported the anti-Yi Sŭng-man movement of the six Vice-Ministers and stated that he would not work with Yi Sŭng-man even though the Vice-Ministers changed their attitudes.[144] Yi Tong-hwi also urged An Ch'ang-ho to join the anti-Yi Sŭng-man movement and expressed his strong dissatisfaction with An Ch'ang-ho by saying, "why are you so worried about overthrowing one person," Yi Sŭng-man.[145]

In this situation, An Ch'ang-ho actively tried to dissuade the Vice-Ministers from simultaneous resignation.[146] He finally succeeded in dissociating Kim Hŭi-sŏn and Chŏng In-gwa, who, like him, were from P'yŏngan Provinces from the other four Vice-Ministers.[147] On June 7, 1920, however, the other four Vice-Ministers, Kim Rip, Yun Hyŏn-jin, Yi Kyu-hong and Kim Ch'ŏl,[148] who had postponed wholesale resignation due to An Ch'ang-ho's persuasion, finally submitted their requests to the Cabinet Council: 1) to dissolve the Korean Commission in Washington under Yi Sŭng-man; 2) to establish the committee for diplomacy in America and European countries; 3) to establish an office for financial plenipotentiary under the Provisional Government; 4) to prohibit Yi Sŭng-man from issuing arbitrary decrees without any prior consultation with the Cabinet. They also declared that unless their requests were accepted, they would resign immediately.[149] The core of their requests was to remove Yi Sŭng-man from the Provisional Government.[150] However, An Ch'ang-ho persuaded these four to delay their resignations in order to prepare for the visit of the inspection team of American congressmen to China and Korea.[151]

The Provisional Government was also criticized from outside. On June 9, 1920, members of the Union of Iron and Blood [Ch'ŏlhyŏltan], an anti-Provisional Government group, distributed documents advocating the overthrow of the government and the assassination of some leaders. The Union of Iron and Blood even stormed the Ministry of Internal Affairs and greatly damaged the authority of the Provisional Government among Koreans in Shanghai.[152]

The rumor that Yi Tong-hwi was involved in organizing a "workers-peasants' government" in Russia, however, was spread among the leaders of the Provisional Government and greatly weakened the base of Yi Tong-hwi's anti-Yi Sŭng-man movement. In response to Yi Tong-hwi's movement for replacing Yi Sŭng-man, Yi Tong-nyŏng, Yi Si-yŏng, and Sin Kyu-sik, strong supporters of Yi Sŭng-

Table 5. 2

Ministers and Vice-Ministers of the Shanghai Provisional Government (May 1920)

	Minister	Regions	Vice-Minister	Regions
President	(Yi Sŭng-man)	Hwanghae (Seoul)		
Premier	**Yi Tong-hwi**	Hamgyŏng	**Kim Rip**	Hamgyŏng
Internal	**Yi Tong-nyŏng**	Ch'ungch'ŏng	-	
Foreign	-		**Chŏng In-gwa**	P'yŏngan
Finance	**Yi Si-yŏng**	Seoul	**Yun Hyŏn-jin**	Kyŏngsang
Justice	**Sin Kyu-sik**	Ch'ungch'ŏng	-	
Military	(No Paek-rin)	Hwanghae	**Kim Hŭi-sŏn**	P'yŏngan
Communication	-		**Kim Ch'ŏl**	Chŏlla
Education	(Kim Kyu-sik)	Kyŏngsang (Seoul)	**Yi Kyu-hong**	Kyŏngsang
Labor (Bureau General Staff)	**An Ch'ang-ho**	P'yŏngan	-	

Notes A) Advocates for the replacement Yi Sŭng-man: Yi Tong-hwi, Kim Rip, Yun Hyŏn-jin, Kim Ch'ŏl, Yi Kyu-hong.
B) Supporters of Yi Sŭng-man: Yi Tong-nyŏng, Yi Si-yŏng, Sin Kyu-sik.
C) Not Supporting Yi Sŭng-man, but opposing to replace Yi Sŭng-man: An Ch'ang-ho, Chŏng In-gwa, Kim Hŭi-sŏn.
* Bolded persons were in Shanghai.

Sources Kim Hu-gyŏng, *Taehan Minguk tongnip undong konghunsa* [History of the Meritous Figures Who Contributed to the Independence of the Republic of Korea] (Seoul: Kwangbok Ch'ulp'ansa, 1983); Sin Tonga P'yŏnjipsil, *Hanguk kŭndae inmul paeginsŏn* [Selected One Hundred Persons of Modern Korea] (Seoul: Tonga Ilbosa, 1985).

man, counterproposed to remove both Yi Sŭng-man and Yi Tong-hwi from the government simultaneously.[153] On June 16, 1920, Yi Sŭng-man sent a telegram asking who had dispatched "a secret delegate" to Moscow without prior consultation with him and warned not to advance any diplomacy toward America and European countries without his knowledge. An Ch'ang-ho also told Yi Tong-hwi to report on the Moscow delegation to Yi Sŭng-man and to seek cooperation with Yi Sŭng-man.[154] At this time, An Ch'ang-ho clarified his strong opposition to the cooperative relationship with Soviet Russia, arguing that it would result in loss of support from the Western Powers and would be a big hindrance to unifying people.[155] By June, Yi Tong-hwi completely lost confidence in An Ch'ang-ho. He, who had once expected that "if he cooperated with An Ch'ang-ho, there would be nothing impossible to deal with under the heaven," now told Kim Rip that he had less confidence in An Ch'ang-ho than in Yi Sŭng-man, and other Ministers.[156] On June 18, Yi Tong-hwi at last distributed his letter of resignation explaining the reasons for his nonconfidence in Yi Sŭng-man, and left for Weihaiwei on June 22.[157]

It is noteworthy that, as we can see in Table 5. 2, regionalism still strongly influenced the attitude of the leaders of the Shanghai Provisional Government with regard to the issue of replacing Yi Sŭng-man. Yi Tong-nyŏng, Yi Si-yŏng and Sin Kyu-sik who were from the central part of Korea absolutely supported Yi Sŭng-man. Although An Ch'ang-ho and other Vice-Ministers, Kim Hŭi-sŏn and Chŏng In-gwa did not support Yi Sŭng-man, they also opposed Yi Tong-hwi's move to replace Yi Sŭng-man.

2. Korean Communist Party [Hanin Kongsandang] in Shanghai

At the end of 1919, when the Bolsheviks got the upper hand in Siberia and the Russian Far East it elevated the hope of pro-Soviet Koreans for the increased Soviet activity in the region,[158] The Soviet government began to dispatch Korean agents with the mission of spreading Bolshevism among Koreans in the Far East. In particular, after the overthrow of the Rozanov government in Vladivostok, the Soviet government selected Vladivostok as a proper base for Communist activities in the Far East. At first, the Eastern Department of the Ministry of Foreign Affairs was in charge of propaganda and organizing Communist organizations among Koreans in Siberia and the Far East. It recruited influential Koreans and Chinese who had resided in the Soviet Russia.

Yi Wi-jong, a widely known figure among the Koreans for his anti-Japanese activities as member of the secret delegation to the Hague and leader of the *ŭibyŏng* organization based in Novokievsk in the Primorye in 1908, represented Korea at the Eastern department.[159] He was also famous for his activities in seizing Ufa and in 1919 headed the machine-gun brigade and rifle regiment.[160] At a meeting in Moscow, held on the occasion of the March First Movement on August 12, 1919, about 200 Korean patriots resolved to establish the Central Executive Committee of the Korean National Associations in Russia [Taehan Kungminhoe Chungang Ch'onghoe] with the purpose of organizing Korean military units under the Russian Red Army to fight against the Japanese in Siberia and Korea.[161] According to a Japanese report, Yi Wi-jong organized a Korean military government under the Red Army and began to mobilize Koreans younger than forty year old living in the regions under the control of the Soviet Russia between Moscow and Irkutsk.[162]

The Eastern Department dispatched Sŏnu Chŏng, U Si-ha and Kim Chŏng-hae (three key members of the Central Executive Committee of the Korean National Associations and a Korean cell of the Russian Communist Party in Moscow which was organized shortly after the meeting of August 12, 1919) to Korean communities in the Primorye with the mission of establishing ties and spreading Bolshevism among the Koreans.[163] Sŏnu Chŏng was the Chairman of the Central Executive Committee of the Korean National Association[164], and U Si-ha and Kim Chŏng-hae had worked as members of the Kungminhoe in Western Siberia, and played a key role in establishing the Central Executive Committee of the Korean National Associations in Moscow. In particular, Sŏnu Chŏng came to the Primorye accompanying Vilensky, the plenipotentiary representative of the Soviet government in Vladivostok, and tried to organize party cells among Korean partisan units.[165]

In Irkutsk, the Propaganda Bureau of Chinese, Mongolia, Korea and Japan was established under the leadership of Yakov Davidovich Yanson, who had been working in Omsk in early 1920, shortly after the overthrow of the Kolchak Regime. The Propaganda Bureau was in charge of carrying out propaganda of Communism and organizing Communist organizations in the Far East until the end of July 1920, when the Bureau for the Eastern Peoples (later known as the Asian Bureau) under the Siberian Bureau of the Russian Communist Party took over the mission.[166] Yi In-sŏp and Ch'ae Sŏng-yong, who had been publishing a Korean newspaper called the *Saebyŏkbuk* (Dawn Drum), organ of the Korean Communist cell within the Siberian Bureau of the Russian Communist Party in Omsk, moved to Irkutsk in order to work at the Propaganda Bureau in the spring 1920.[167]

Sŏnu Chŏng, Kim Chŏng-hae and U Si-ha met Korean nationalists in Vladivostok such as Kim Man-gyŏm, Kim Chin, Kim Ha-gu, Kim Ha-sŏk and Chin Hak-sin. They obtained the nationalists' agreement to establish revolutionary organizations and spread Bolshevism with the funds provided by the Soviet government. However, their mission could not be realized due to the Japanese military attack on the Russian revolutionaries and Koreans on April 4-5, 1920.[168]

In major cities in the Primorye such as Vladivostok, Olga, Nikol'sk-Ussurisk, Khabarovsk, Shkotovo and Spassk, the Japanese military forces occupied major government offices and institutions, disarmed Russian police and revolutionary forces, and arrested government and Party leaders who could not escape. At the same time, the Japanese military forces, stormed the New Korean Village in Vladivostok, and arrested Korean leaders. This was after brutal killings, plundering, and setting fire to houses, churches, school, as well as the building of the *Hanin Sinbo*.[169] According to Canfield F. Smith, about three hundred Koreans were killed and about one hundred were arrested.[170] Japanese reports indicates that Japanese military forces arrested 54 Koreans in Vladivostok and 76 Koreans in Nikol'sk-Ussurisk.[171]

In Nikol'sk-Ussurisk, the Japanese shot to death the most prominent Korean leader Ch'oe Chae-hyŏng along with three other Korean leaders, Kim I-jik, Hwang Kyŏng-sŏp and Ŏm Chu-p'il without any legal procedures.[172] All anti-Japanese Korean organizations including the Korean National Council, the Korean Socialist Party, the Union of Elderly Men, Women's Union for Independence (Puin Tongniptan), were dissolved and accordingly hundreds of Korean patriots were forced to escape to regions such as Blagoveshchensk in the Amur, Suchan and North Chientao away from Japanese forces.[173] As a result of the incident, which Koreans later called the *Sawŏl Ch'ambyŏn* (The April Disaster), Koreans lost their long-time anti-Japanese base in Vladivostok. The Japanese military police stationed at the New Korean Village, and Japanese authorities in Vladivostok and Nikol'sk-Ussurisk began to establish Korean Residents' Associations, Korean schools, hospitals, and newspapers under their control.[174]

It became clear to the Soviet government that Vladivostok could not be a proper base for Bolshevik propaganda any longer. The Soviet government, instead, chose Shanghai as an alternative base for propaganda of Communism in the Far East.[175] Vilensky in Vladivostok decided to dispatch Kim Man-gyŏm [Ivan Stepanovich Serebriakov], Vice-Chairman of the Korean National Council to Shanghai. On May 3, Kim Man-gyŏm and Kang Han-t'aek left Vladivostok with Soviet funds of 40,000 rubles and arrived at Shanghai in early May 1920.[176] Gregory N. Voitinsky and another agent, who were dispatched from Irkutsk with the mission of organizing the Chinese Communist Party, accompanied Kim Man-gyŏm.[177]

Voitinsky and Kim Man-gyŏm were not the first agents dispatched by the Soviet government to Shanghai. According to a Japanese report, as early as March 1920, a Russian agent came to Shanghai together with two Koreans (Han Tong-wŏn and Nikolai Li) and Xia Ji-feng who had met with Pak Chin-sun in Moscow in December 1919, and visited the Shanghai Provisional Government.[178] This report is confirmed by a letter dated May 11, 1920, from three key members of the Korean Socialist Party in Shanghai (Yi Tong-hwi, Kim Rip and Kye Pong-u)[179] to Ku Ch'un-sŏn, Chairman of the Korean National Association in North Chientao. In the letter, Yi, Kim and Kye wrote to Ku that they had concluded a secret agreement with "important figures, that is, Russian diplomats dispatched to Shanghai and Tianjin," with the following key plans: 1) to establish a base for training military officers and preparing planes and weapons such as cannons in the west of Irkutsk; 2) to plan for the final military campaign against the Japanese in cooperation with the Red Army.[180]

Voitinsky and another Russian Bolshevik agent, together with Kim Man-gyŏm, visited the Shanghai Provisional Government on May 13, and delivered two official letters from the Soviet government.[181] In the first letter, the Soviet government expressed great sympathy with the Korean Provisional Government in Shanghai and promised "enough support" and "recognition" of the Provisional Government. The second letter took the form of an official and public document delivered to the general Korean population offering the sympathy of the Soviet government promising to support Koreans "until the end" while urging the Koreans to spread Bolshevism.[182]

It is noteworthy that key members of the Korean Socialist Party, Yi Tong-hwi and Kim Rip, kept their contacts with Russian agents a secret from An Ch'ang-ho and other leaders of the Shanghai Provisional Government. An Ch'ang-ho's diary, in which he recorded daily affairs in detail, did not include any information about these contacts with Russian agents. With the help and encouragement from Russian and Korean agents, Yi Tong-hwi, together with Kim Rip, concentrated his efforts on recruiting members of the Korean Socialist Party and on party activities.[183] Together with Kim Man-gyŏm, Yi Tong-hwi and Kim Rip, who had been boycotting the Provisional Government and requesting the expulsion of Yi Sŭng-man from the government, began to publish a socialist magazine, the *Sin Taehan Tongnippo* (New Great Korea Independence Report) and established the Institute for Study of Socialism [Sahoejuŭi Yŏnguso] with the purpose of spreading Bolshevism among Korean nationalists in Shanghai.[184] Kye Pong-u took the chief-editorship of the *Chayujong* (Freedom Bell), the official organ of the Korean Socialist Party.[185] Around this time, these activities of the Korean Socialist Party began to be known to An Ch'ang-ho and other leaders of the Shanghai Provisional Government.[186]

While staying in Weihaiwei from the end of June to the end of July 1920, Yi Tong-hwi pressed the leaders of the Shanghai Provisional Government to replace Yi Sŭng-man.[187] Yi Tong-hwi's ultimate purpose was to go to Moscow and to organize another "Workers' and Peasants' Government" which would have focus on military activities with support from the Soviet government.[188] However, Yi Tong-hwi had to return to Shanghai at the end of July when detailed plans of Kim Rip's secret "conspiracy" became known to An Ch'ang-ho and his followers. In a letter, which was intercepted by a follower of An Ch'ang-ho, Kim Rip talked about the movement for obtaining loan from the Soviet government, and advised Yi Tong-hwi to withdraw from the Provisional Government and go to Moscow.[189] An Ch'ang-ho, Yi Kwang-su and An's other followers decided not to publicize Kim Rip's secret letter and obtained Kim Rip's apology.[190] The affair of Kim Rip's secret letter functioned as a decisive factor in losing support from key members of the anti-Yi Sŭng-man movement such as Yun Hyŏn-jin and Yi Kyu-hong. Yi Tong-hwi's position and claims in the anti-Yi Sŭng-man movement drastically weakened, and he returned to Shanghai and resumed the Premiership,[191] persuaded to return by Yi Kyu-hong who had been dispatched to Weihaiwei by the Provisional Government.[192] Accordingly, the anti-Yi Sŭng-man movement which Yi Tong-hwi had led since February 1920 ended in failure.

Another factor which caused Yi Tong-hwi's urgency to return to Shanghai was the return of Yi Han-yŏng, a member of the Korean Socialist Party delegation, from Moscow. Yi Han-yŏng, who had been dispatched as a member of together with Pak Chin-sun and Pak Ae, came to Shanghai with some funds from the Comintern in Moscow.[193] The situation of the Korean Socialist Party in the middle of 1920 is well summarized in Kye Pong-u's recollection:

The founder and head of the Korean Socialist Party, Sŏngjae [Yi Tong-hwi] and Ilse [Kim Rip] took positions in the Cabinet of the Provisional Government as Premier and Chief-Secretary of the Cabinet respectively. . . . Then when confidence in the Paris Peace Conference and the League of Nation disappeared completely — in spring of 1920 — they resigned from those positions and concentrated their efforts only on the activities of the Party. At the very time, Voitinsky, an agent from the Comintern came to Shanghai and was leading the parties of Korea, Japan and China. It was at this time when the Korean Socialist Party changed its name into the [Korean] Communist Party, that I became the party member and chief-editor of the *Chayujong*, and that Yi Han-yŏng came [to Shanghai] with some funds for propaganda [for Communism] dispatched from the Comintern.[194]

Yi Han-yŏng left Moscow in the middle of April 1920 with Pak Ae[195] and, on his way to Shanghai, attended the Congress of the Representatives from the Korean Communist Sections within the Russian Communist Parties [Rŏsia Kongsandang nae Koryŏ Kongsan Tanch'e Taep'yojahoe]. All 12 representatives from Korean sections within the Russian Communist Parties and military organizations in Irkutsk, Omsk and Verkhneudinsk attended the congress which had been held from July 7 to July 15, 1920, in Irkutsk under the leadership of Niuma Burtman, Director of the Bureau for the Eastern Peoples. Pak Ae and Yi Han-yŏng attended the congress in order to "establish close communications between the Socialist Party and Communist Party" with a voting right and a consultative right respectively.[196] Yi Han-yŏng delivered celebration address as a representative of the Korean Socialist Party.[197] The congress organized the Central Executive Committee of the Korean Communist Organizations within the Russian Communist Parties [Koryŏ Kongsan Tanch'e Chungang Kanbu] which took the role of the Korean Section within the Bureau for the Eastern Peoples. Its members later became the core group of the so-called "Irkutsk Group." Yi Han-yŏng discussed with the leaders of the "Irkutsk Group" how to unify the two groups in Shanghai. The "Irkutsk Group" dispatched Yi Kwal together with Yi Han-yŏng to Shanghai with the mission of communicating with Korean Communists in Shanghai.[198]

In early September 1920, the Korean Socialist Party held a congress and decided to change its name into the Korean Communist Party [Hanin Kongsandang].[199] Although Voitinsky suggested the change of the party name,[200] the adoption of the name "Communist Party" was a requirement for a membership in the Comintern.[201] Pak Chin-sun in Moscow also was already using "Korean Communist Party" in his address at the second congress of the Comintern,[202] and was registered as a delegate of the Korean "Communist Party" in the list of the participants of the Congress.[203] The Korean Communist Party strengthened its membership by recruiting many Korean patriots in Shanghai. According to Yŏ Un-hyŏng, influential Korean leaders in Shanghai including Yŏ Un-hyŏng, An Pyŏng-ch'an, Cho Tong-ho, Ch'oe Ch'ang-sik, Yi Ch'un-suk, Sin Ch'ae-ho, Kim Tu-bong, Yang Hŏn, Sŏnu Hyŏk, Yun Ki-sŏp and Cho Wan-gu joined the Party.[204] The congress elected seven new members of its Central Executive Committee: Yi Tong-hwi (Chairman), Kim Man-gyŏm, Kim Rip, Yi Han-yŏng, An Pyŏng-ch'an, Yŏ Un-hyŏng (Translation) and Cho Tong-ho (Publication).[205]

According to the report to the Constituent Congress of the Korean Communist Party in Irkutsk in May 1921, the Party in Shanghai established three departments: Agitation and Publication, Culture and Education, and Labor. The Agitation and Publication department had a Korean printing house and published a newspaper *Sin Saenghwal*

(New Life), a successor to *Sin Taehan Tongnippo*, and a magazine *Kongsan* (Communism), a successor to *Chayujong*, official organ of the Korean Socialist Party since 1918. The Party published about 5,000 copies of the *Sin Saenghwal* (three editions) and the *Kongsan* (three editions), and translated and distributed communist literature such as the *Communist Manifesto* (3,000 copies), *Spider and Fly* (5,000 copies), and the platform of the Russian Communist Party (3,000 copies).[206] Five agitators, who belonged to the agitation and publication department, were in charge of three regions (one for Korea, one for Japan and three for China). The Party had a big library for members of the labor organizations. The labor department organized a labor union with membership of 200, for whom the members of the culture and educational department provided weekly lectures on labor and the international communist movement.[207] We can easily see that the Korean Communist Party in Shanghai focused on propaganda and publication for communism, which was appropriate in view of the location of Shanghai.

Considering the fact that many key members of the Korean Socialist Party in Russia could not attend the congress, the Korean Communist Party in Shanghai can not be considered as the complete successor of the Korean Socialist Party. It was an organization of only Korean Communists in Shanghai. The congress also resolved to endeavor to build an "All-Korea Communist Party" ["Chŏnhan Kongsandang"] by uniting other Korean Communist groups including the "Irkutsk Group" (the Central Executive Committee of the Korean Communist Organizations within the Russian Communist Parties), which had been established two months earlier in July 1920 in Irkutsk.[208]

The Central Executive Committee of the Party decided to dispatch

Kim Rip and Kye Pong-u to the Comintern in Moscow. According to Kim Rip's suggestion, Yi Han-yŏng, who was born in Russia and spoke Russian, accompanied Kim and Kye. Their main mission was to report about the organization of the Korean Communist Party in Shanghai, but they also had other purposes: to study the theory and strategies of Bolshevism;[209] to discuss with the "Irkutsk Group" the plan for a unified Korean Communist Party;[210] to check the result of the diplomatic activities of Pak Chin-sun and Han Hyŏng-gwŏn;[211] to establish connection with Alexandr Krasnoshchekov, President of the Far Eastern Republic; and to get information on the developing political situation after the Japanese government's declaration to withdraw Japanese military forces from Za-Baikal.[212]

In order to go to Russia, Kim Rip resigned as Chief-Secretary of the Cabinet on September 15, 1920, and O Yŏng-sŏn, the second son-in-law of Yi Tong-hwi, took the post.[213] The resignation of Kim Rip clearly demonstrated that Yi Tong-hwi and other key leaders of the former Korean Socialist Party would divert more attention to the activities of the Party rather than to the Provisional Government. Kim Rip and Yi Han-yŏng left for Siberia on September 22 and Kye Pong-u left on September 23 with secret letters from Voitinsky to Russian Bolsheviks in Irkutsk.[214] Because the Central Executive Committee of the Party in Shanghai recalled Yi Han-yŏng in Beijing to Shanghai,[215] only Kim Rip and Kye Pong-u arrived at Verkhneudinsk at the end of October (or early November) in Siberia via Beijing, Zhangjiakou, and Kulun [Ulan Bataar] in Mongolia.[216]

D. Defeat at Two Fronts

1. Withdrawal from the Provisional Government

The Japanese military offenses against the Korean revolutionary forces in the Primorye and Chientao in April 1920 were greatly detrimental to the activities of the Shanghai Provisional Government as well. As we saw earlier, in April 4-5, 1920, the Japanese military forces attacked Korean communities and carried out mass arrests and killings of Koreans in the Primorye in order to undermine the Korean independence movement, which had been increasingly reinforcing its military and political activities in cooperation with the Russian revolutionary forces [*Sawŏl Ch'ambyŏn*]. Although the Korean National Council criticized the Shanghai Provisional Government at the time of its rebuilding in February 1920, it soon came to take a cooperative stance toward the Shanghai Provisional Government. At the ceremony for the second anniversary of the March First Movement on March 1, 1920, Han Kun-myŏng [Egor], acting Chairman of the Korean National Council, declared that the Council would follow orders from the Shanghai Provisional Government.[217] At that time, the Korean National Council was under the strong influence of the Korean Socialist Party, which was organized as the successor to the One World Party [Ilsedang] led by Chang To-jŏng, Mikhail Mikhailovich Kim [Kim In] and Kim Chin and was also taking a cooperative stance toward the Shanghai Provisional Government.

However, in Blagoveshchensk, Amur Province, Mun Ch'ang-bŏm, Kim Ha-sŏk and Wŏn Se-hun, stubborn opponents of the Shanghai Provisional Government, resumed leadership of the Korean National

Council and began to make strong anti-Shanghai Provisional Government policies.[218] Furthermore, on September 15, 1920, the Korean National Council declared itself as "the government" with executive ministers in charge of internal affairs, military, justice, foreign affairs, education, finance and labor, and expressed a strong will to establish military troops and carry out "state powers."[219]

In spite of its internal conflicts, until the summer of 1920, the Shanghai Provisional Government succeeded, to a certain degree, in extending its influence in North Chientao. Thanks to the mediation of Yi Yong, An Chŏng-gŭn and Wang Sam-dŏk, who had been dispatched by the Shanghai Provisional Government in the spring of 1920, major Korean military forces in North Chientao established the Korean Military Command in North Chientao [Pungno Tokkunbu] there with Ch'oe Chin-dong (President), Hong Pŏm-do (Commander-in-Chief) and An Mu (Adjutant) as its key leaders. As a Japanese information report pointed out, the successful achievement of the unified military organization among the major Korean military forces in North Chientao was the result of the efforts of Yi Tong-hwi, the Premier of the Shanghai Provisional Government, who was familiar with the leaders and condition of the region.[220]

In the middle of 1920, however, the Japanese military forces launched counter-attacks on the Korean communities in North and West Chientao in order to destroy the bases of the Korean military forces which had attacked North Korea from the end of 1919 to the first half of 1920.[221] In Fengwudong (Kor. Pongodong) in North Chientao in early June 1920, the Japanese military forces attacked the military headquarters of the Korean Military Command in North Chientao, but was defeated by the cooperative campaigns among the military forces led by Korean commanders such as Hong Pŏm-do,

Ch'oe Chin-dong, and An Mu.[222]

Retaliating for assaults of Chinese horse-riding bandits on the Japanese consulate branch office in Hunchun (Hunchun Incident) on September 12 and October 2, 1920, the Japanese government dispatched two divisions to Chientao regions — the 19th division from the Primorye and the 21st division from Nanam, Korea — "to complete the security and remove threats to the border regions by eradicating the evil roots of invasions of the ominous Koreans and horse bandits." [*Kanto Shuppei* in Japanese][223] From the middle of October 1920, Japanese military forces attacked Korean independence armies, and at the same time, fired on the houses and churches of Koreans, destroying Korean villages and killing civilian Koreans.[224] According to a report of November 30, 1920, sent from a correspondent of the Shanghai Provisional Government in Chientao, the Japanese military attack, which Koreans called the *Kyŏngsin Ch'ambyŏn* (Disaster of the year of 1920), inflicted enormous damage on Korean communities in West and North Chientao: 3,469 killed, 170 arrested, 71 raped with 3,209 houses, 36 schools, and 14 churches burnt.[225] This disaster is also known as the Kando Incident [Kando Ch'ampyŏn]. In spite of this disaster, the Korean independence armies won a military victory in Qingshanli (Kor. Ch'ŏngsanni), a successful result of the combined campaigns by the Korean Independence Army led by Hong Pŏm-do and the Military Government in North Chientao led by Kim Chwa-jin.[226] Regardless of this military victory, the superior Japanese army succeeded in destroying the bases of the Korean forces in Manchuria, and forced them to relocate to the Russian Far East.

Both the April Incident and the Chientao Incident destroyed the bases of the Korean independence movement in the border regions in the Primorye and Chientao. At the same time, the two incidents shattered what the Shanghai Provisional Government had accomplished since the establishment of the "unified" government — the unification of the various military and political organizations in both regions and broadening support for the Shanghai Provisional Government. In particular, the Kando Incident, aroused great shock and rage among Koreans and provoked explosive criticism against the Shanghai Provisional Government from both inside and outside: what did the government, which had claimed itself to be the highest central headquarters of Korean independence movement, do while innocent Koreans were being killed by the enemy? While the anti-government groups resumed their attacks on the government, the leaders of the Shanghai Provisional Government demonstrated conflicting strategies for achieving the independence of Korea, particularly with disagreement over how to respond to the Japanese massacre of Koreans in Manchuria.

According to Yi Kwang-su, chief editor of the *Tongnip Sinmun*, it was Yi Tong-hwi who strongly advocated the immediate declaration of war against Japan.[227] At the end of November 1920, Yi Tong-hwi convened several meetings such as the Cabinet meeting and Assembly members' meeting, and representatives of Korean organizations in Shanghai in order to discuss countermeasures against the Japanese military attacks on Korean communities in Chientao. According to Yi Kwang-su, the advocates of "the immediate advancement strategy" ["*kŭpchinnon*"] outnumbered the advocates of "the gradual advancement strategy" ["*wanjinnon*"].[228] As Kim San [Chang Chi-rak] recollected in his interview with Nym Wales, Yi Tong-hwi, at this time, was anxious to organize various Korean military forces in Manchuria and the Russian Far East under the unified command of the Provisional Government and to start a war against the Japanese.[229]

Table 5. 3

The Korean Military Troops in Svobodnyi City as of March 1921
From Primorye, Priamur and Amur

From Primorye, Priamur and Amur
1) Troop from Nikolaevsk (Ilia Pak, Im Ho, Ko Myŏng-su)
2) Troop from Taban (Nikolai Ch'oe)
3) Tongniptan Kundae (Independence Army Troop) [Gregory Pak, Pavel Ch'oe]
4) Free Battallion (Troop in Svobodnyi City) [O Ha-muk, Ch'oe Ko-ryŏ, Hwang Ha-il]
From Manchuria (Chientao)
5) Ch'onggunbu (Ch'oe Chin-dong, Hŏ Kŭn)
6) Kungmin Kundae (An Mu, Chŏng Il-mu)
7) Tongnipkun Kundae (Hong Bŏm-do, Yi Ch'ŏng-ch'ŏn)
8) Kunjŏngsŏ Kundae (Sŏ Il, Pak Tu-hŭi)

Note [ ] are names of commanders.
Sources Kim Kyu-myŏn, *Nobyŏng Kim Kyu-myŏn ŭi pimangnok esŏ,* pp. 34-35; Yi In-sŏp, *Mang-myŏngja ŭi sugŭi*, pp. 95-96; "Chae-Ro Koryŏ hyŏngmyŏng kundae yŏnhyŏk," p. 13; Kim Chŏng-ju [Kin Sei-tsū] ed., *Chōsen tōchi shiryō*, vol. 7, pp. 31-35.

Although Yi Kwang-su oversimplified the idea that Yi Tong-hwi proposed to declare war against Japan,[230] Yi Tong-hwi's advocacy of the "immediate advancement" was closely related to the urgent situation in Manchuria and the Primorye. He and other Korean leaders, who were from Chientao and the Primorye in Shanghai, felt more urgency to take over the political, military and financial arrangements for the Korean military troops, which were forced to move to the Amur region. The troops had relocated there where they were safe from the attacks of the Japanese military thanks to the prevalence of the Russian revolutionary forces (See Table 5. 3). Furthermore, the Korean National Council which had declared itself as the official government was endeavoring to incorporate the Korean independence armies, which were on the way from Manchuria and the Primorye to Svobodnyi City (Alekseyevsk in Tsarist period) in Amur Province, under its control by dispatching key members to those troops and by negotiating with the Second Corps of the People's Revolutionary Army of the Far Eastern Republic in Khabarovsk.[231]

In the political turmoil caused by the Kando Incident, An Ch'ang-ho criticized the advocates of "the immediate advancement" in his address at the Korean Residents' Association in Shanghai on November 27, 1920. Yi Kwang-su, in his long editorial titled "the Kando Incident and the Future Plans for the Independence Movement" (published in the *Tongnip Sinmun* in a series of six articles from December 18 through February 5 1921, criticized advocates of the "immediate advancement strategy" by comparing them with those who "urged the crippled to run."[232] Yi Kwang-su also criticized political and military organizations such as the Korean National Council in Blagoveshchensk, the Korean National Association and the Military Government in North Chientao and the Korean Association in West Chientao for spending funds on military activities: the establishment of military schools and military quarters, purchase of weapons and organization of military troops. Yi Kwang-su even accused the organizations in North Chientao of imposing excessive burden on Koreans and of provoking the tragic incident (Chientao Incident). Yi Kwang-su, instead, emphasized the importance of industry and education, the traditional theme of the "gradual advancement party."[233]

When the Shanghai Provisional Government was facing internal and external political difficulties after the Kando Incident, Yi Sŭng-man came to Shanghai on December 8, 1920. Yi Sŭng-man's visit to Shanghai was in response to the frequent requests of the Shanghai Provisional Government. His visit, however, intensified the political disputes among Korean patriots in Shanghai. Wŏn Se-hun, in his letter dated January 12 1921 to Yi Hae-ch'ŏng in Blagoveshchensk,

Amur Province, wrote that "since the so-called President Yi Sŭng-man arrived here, public struggles and hidden conflicts intensified further, and after the Incident in Yanji and Hunchun (Kando Incident), 10,000 mouths are talking."[234]

Three consecutive Cabinet meetings, which Yi Sŭng-man attended for the first time after the establishment of the "unified" Provisional Government, were held from January 5, 1921. At the first meeting, Yi Tong-hwi proposed to take appropriate measures for the internal and external problems caused by Yi Sŭng-man's petition for mandated American rule. Yi Tong-hwi pointed out that Yi Sŭng-man's petition and Chŏng Han-gyŏng's [Henry Chung] advocacy of self-rule were great diplomatic failure because they completely disregarded the popular demands of Koreans for "complete independence." Yi Tong-hwi also raised criticism that Yi Sŭng-man's petition for mandate rule caused confusion among the Korean people and that the petition provided anti-Provisional Government force with ammunition to attack the Shanghai Provisional Government. Yi Sŭng-man retorted that "although the petition for mandate rule was not intended to deny the independence of Korea, it is already a matter of the past and no longer relevant to the current international situation." The majority of the Cabinet members suggested issuing a statement based on what Yi Sŭng-man said in order to clear the suspicions of the general population, but Yi Sŭng-man strongly refused to compromise.[235]

Secondly, Yi Tong-hwi pointed out that the President had been staying in America and did not understand administrative affairs of the government in Shanghai. Accordingly, the Cabinet frequently failed in gaining approval of the President mainly because of misunderstanding resulting from the geographic distance. Yi Tong-hwi proposed to abolish the Presidential system and instead to adopt the system of Ministers' Council, which would have all decisive political power. Yi Sŭng-man rejected Yi Tong-hwi's proposal, arguing that a system of Ministers' Council, conflicted with the principle of the Hansŏng Government.[236] Yi Tong-hwi's proposal, in fact, would have meant the complete transformation of the Shanghai Provisional Government into a "Korean Revolutionary Committee," which would be organized by the Korean revolutionaries representing various organizations and regions.[237] Other Ministers except Nam Hyŏng-u, however, desired to maintain the status quo, and did not agree with Yi Tong-hwi's proposal.[238] They instead proposed a compromise that Yi Sŭng-man come to Shanghai and take charge of the government; that Yi Sŭng-man entrust the Premier with the decision-making power [*kyŏlchaekwŏn*] on the administrative matters and that the President receive a monthly report from the Premier. Yi Sŭng-man rejected the compromise saying that "diplomacy in Washington is crucial" and "it is not necessary to entrust the decision-making power."[239]

Yi Tong-hwi failed in realizing his idea to reform the Shanghai Provisional Government in the face of the strong opposition of Yi Sŭng-man and other Ministers who supported him. On January 24, 1921, Yi Tong-hwi at last withdrew from the Provisional Government by issuing a statement: "The Cabinet meeting did not discuss my proposal at all and it is beyond my capability to overcome the difficult situation."[240] O Yŏng-sŏn (Cabinet Chief Secretary), Yun Hyŏn-jin (Vice-Minster of Finance) and An Pyŏng-ch'an (Vice-Minister of Justice) resigned from the government and some Provisional Assembly members such as Kye Pong-u, Yu Ye-gyun, Wang Sam-dŏk and Hong To either resigned or refused to attend the Provisional Assembly.[241]

By the resignation of Yi Tong-hwi and his followers, the "unified"

Provisional Government, which had existed more than one year, finally ended in failure. Furthermore, Yi Tong-hwi's resignation reinforced the stance and activities of the anti-Provisional Government groups in Shanghai and Beijing, who started movements for convening the People's Congress [*Kungmin Taehoe*] to deal with the reform and reorganization of the government. In Shanghai, the members of the Union of Iron and Blood and the Our Club [Oin Kurakpu], who had worked for the destruction of the Provisional Government, had demonstrated in front of the Provisional Assembly, and condemned Yi Sŭng-man and the Provisional Government. Thirteen influential Korean nationalists such as Pak Ŭn-sik, Wŏn Se-hun, Yu Ye-gyun and Wang Sam-dŏk, who had previously supported the Provisional Government, organized the Preparatory Committee for the People's Congress and distributed printed materials attacking Yi Sŭng-man and the Provisional Government.[242]

In Beijing, the Committee for Promoting the Unification of Military Organizations [Pukkyŏng Kunsa T'ongil Ch'okchinhoe] which was organized for uniting the Korean military organizations in Manchuria by Pak Yong-man, Sin Suk and Nam Kong-sŏn, proposed the Preparatory Committee for the People's Congress in Shanghai to cooperate in convening the People's Congress. They distributed a statement entitled "the manifesto for denouncing Yi Sŭng-man," which criticized Yi Sŭng-man's petition for America's mandated rule of Korea and demanded the dissolution of the Provisional Government.[243] Kim Kyu-sik and No Paek-rin, who had come to Shanghai at the end of January and early February respectively, requested that Yi Sŭng-man resign, arguing that the current disorder originated from Yi's petition for the mandate rule.[244]

On March 5, 1921, Yi Sŭng-man made his 35 followers organize a pro-government organization, the Cooperation Association [Hyŏpsŏnghoe] with programs of "absolute support of the Provisional Government" and "confidence in the President and Cabinet members."[245] On April 27, the Committee for Promoting the Unification of Military Organizations in Beijing sent a resolution requesting dissolution of the Provisional Government and Assembly within three days.[246] In this situation, the Shanghai Provisional Government could not overcome the political turmoil intensified by Yi Tong-hwi's resignation. At the end of April, Nam Hyŏng-u (Minister of Communication) and Kim Kyu-sik (Minister of Education and Chairman of the Korean Commission in Europe and America) resigned.[247]

At last, on May 7, An Ch'ang-ho, who had played key role in establishing the "unified" Provisional Government and tried to overcome the political crisis by keeping Yi Sŭng-man as the President, finally resigned from the government, and proposed to convene the People's Congress as the anti-Provisional Government groups were suggesting. In the end, only Yi Sŭng-man's supporters who were from the central regions [*Kiho*] of Korea remained in the Provisional Government. Following these events, Yi Sŭng-man abruptly left Shanghai for Honolulu on May 19, 1921.[248]

2. Bloody Defeat at the Communist Front

The withdrawal of the Korean Socialist Party from the Shanghai Provisional Government meant the collapse of the first "united front" between the nationalists and socialists, and between and the "American Group of Nationalists" and the "Siberian Manchurian Group."[249]

The Korean Socialist Party had discarded its previous strategy to utilize the Provisional Government to represent the Korean revolu-

Table 5. 4

Korean Communist Organizations as of May 1921

(1)	(2)	(3)	(4)	(5)
Primorye Province				
1. Solbakkwan	Prov. Com.	Jul. 1920	500	1,000
2. Tizinkhe	Party	Oct. 1920	33	-
3. Suchan	Party	Sep. 1920	168	284
Priamur Province				
4. Khabarovsk	Prov. Com.	Jul. 1920	57	5
5. Novonikolaevsk	Section	Nov. 1920	26	35
6. Osipovka	Party	Aug. 1920	?	?
Amur Province				
7. Blagoveshchensk	Prov. Com.	Apr. 1920	73	42
8. KNC	Sell	Jan. 1921	22	-
9. Svobodnyi	Comsomol	Jan. 1921	77	19
10. Zeia	Party	Sep. 1920	36	-
Siberia				
11. Irkutsk	Section	Jan. 1920	98	47
12. Tiumen	Section	Dec. 1920	?	5
13. Omsk	Section	*1919, Mar. 1921	8	5
14. Semipalatinsk	Section	June 1919	13	62
15. Moscow	Section	Aug. 1920	20	47
PRA				
16. 1st Comp. (PRA)	Cell	Jan. 1921	105	-
17. 2nd Comp. (PRA)	Cell	Jan. 1921	97	11
18. 4th Comp. (PRA)	Cell	Feb. 1921	117	37
19. 5th Comp. (PRA)	Cell	Nov. 1920	139	-
Manchuria				
20. Yehho	Party	Jul. 1920	27	2
21. Harbin	Party	Dec. 1919	27	5
China				
22. Beijing	Party	?	?	?
23. Shanghai	Party	Sep. 1920	25	14
Korea				
24. Seoul	Party	Oct. 1919	85	5,000
	Total		1,753	6,624

Notes (1) Regions

KNC: Korean National Council, **PRA:** People's Revolutionary Army.

(2) Form of Organization

Prov. Com.: Provincial Committee, **Party**: Communist Party Hanin Kongsandang, **Section**: Korean Section of the Russian Communist Party, **Cell**: Communist Cell in the military or mass organizations.

(3) Date of Organization.

(4) Number of Regular Members.

(5) Number of Candidates.

* This table is based on the reports of the representatives at the Constituent Congress of the Korean Communist Party in Irkutsk (May 1921).

Source "Uchreditel'nyi S'ezd Koreiskoi Kommunisticheskoi partii," *Narody Dal'nego Vostoka*, 2 (23 June 1921), pp. 212-17.

tionary movement for obtaining financial and military support from the Soviet government. From the end of 1920, the Korean Socialist Party instead put all its efforts into establishing a unified "All-Korea Communist Party" which would have political and military leadership over various Korean Communist groups rising through 1920 in Russia and China (see Table 5. 4) and Korean military forces gathering in Svobodnyi City in Amur Province, Russia.

In close cooperation with Yi Tong-hwi and Kim Rip in Shanghai, five key leaders of the Korean Socialist Party (Pak Ae, Kye Pong-u, Kim Chin, Chang To-jŏng and Pak Ch'ang-ŭn), who were representing Korean Communist organizations in Chita, Shanghai, Za-Baikal, Priamur and Amur respectively, organized the Haninbu (Korean Section) under the Far Eastern Bureau of the Russian Communist Party [Dal'biuro] in Chita.[250] The Haninbu claimed temporarily to have authority over the Korean Communist organizations in Korea, Japan, China, Manchuria and the Russian Far East until the establishment of the "unified national Korean Communist Party."[251] On March 3, 1920, the Russian Communist Party established the Far Eastern Bureau [Dal'biuro] to lead the Russian Communist parties in the territory of the Far Eastern Republic. The Bureau was led by Krasnoshchekov, a moderate Bolshevik in the Far East and a driving force for establishing the Far Eastern Republic with the support of

Lenin.[252] He was also a long-time supporter of the Korean Socialist Party and had shared close comradeship in the partisan struggles with Pak Ae, key leader of the Haninbu since 1917.[253]

With the full support of Krasnoshchekov, the Haninbu also resolved to take responsibility for organizing the "unified national Korean Communist Party and incorporating various Korean military forces in Svobodnyi City under one single unified commander.[254] At the same time, the Haninbu decided to advise the "Irkutsk Group" and Korean Communist Party Committee in the Primorye [Yŏnhaeju Hanjok Kongsandang Wiwŏnhoe] — both of which were claiming to be the central committee of the Korean Communist Groups — call themselves a regional committee.[255] This way, the Korean Socialist Party planned to put Korean Communist groups and military forces under its political and military leadership and get financial and military support from the Russian Bolsheviks. The Korean Socialist Party and its supporting forces, which was called the "Shanghai Group," also had enough funds which Pak Chin-sun and Han Hyŏng-gwŏn had obtained from the Soviet government.[256]

This group, which was called at that time the "Shanghai Group," however, had to face the challenge of the "Irkutsk Group." The "Irkutsk Group" also claimed to be the central organ of the Korean Communist organizations and had the support of Boris Zakharovich Shumiatsky, head of the Far Eastern Secretariat of the Comintern in Irkutsk, which succeeded the Section of the Eastern Peoples of the *Sibbiuro* (Sibeiran Bureau of the Russian Communist Party). It was established in January 1921 in Irkutsk with the purpose of leading the revolutionary movement in the Far East.[257] Shumiatsky was one of the most influential hard-liner Bolsheviks in Sovietized Siberia who was opposed to the conclusion of the Brest-Litovsk Treaty and

Krasnoshchekov's plan of the Far Eastern Republic.[258] In May 1920, the Central Committee of the Russian Communist Party appointed him a member of the Far Eastern Bureau in Chita in order to strengthen the Party's control over the Bureau; he also became the Prime Minister and Minister of Foreign Affairs of the Far Eastern Republic. In January 1921, Shumiatsky was appointed head of the Far Eastern Secretariat of the Comintern and the Political commissar of the Fifth Army in Siberia. At the same time, Shumiatsky served plenipotentiary of the Ministry of Foreign Affairs of the Soviet government.[259]

The first half of 1921 was a crucial period when the two rival factions of the Korean Communist movement, the "Shanghai Group" and the "Irkutsk Group," were competing for hegemony over the Korean Communist movement and military forces in Siberia and the Russian Far East. Shumiatsky, the patron of the "Irkutsk Group," was called the "king in the east of the Urals." He reportedly seized "absolute power" over party, military and government in Siberia and the Russian Far East.[260] The "Irkutsk Group," which had functioned as the Korean Section of the Eastern Peoples, now became the Korean Section [Koryŏbu] of the Bureau for the Far Eastern Secretariat of the Comintern. As the key members of the Korean National Council such as Kim Ch'ŏl-hun, Han Myŏng-se [Andrei Avramovich], Kim Ha-sŏk and Ch'oe Ko-ryŏ joined the "Irkutsk Group," the rivalry between the Provisional Government and the Korean National Council was now transferred to the Korean Communist movement in the form of factional struggle between the "Shanghai Group" and the "Irkutsk Group."[261]

The outcome of this struggle was already determined when the Comintern, in January 1921, decided to transfer power over the Korean Communist organizations and military forces in the Far East from the Far Eastern Bureau in Chita to the Far Eastern Secretariat of the Comintern in Irkutsk.[262] On February 8, 1921, Shumiatsky notified the Haninbu in Chita that both the Constituent Congress of the Korean Communist Party and the Congress of representatives of the Korean military organizations should be held in Irkutsk and ordered the Haninbu to move to Irkutsk.[263] Although the Haninbu resisted the order of Shumiatsky by proceeding with its own plan of convening the two congresses, it rather greatly intensified Shumiatsky's negative attitude toward the "Shanghai Group," against whom the members of the "Irkutsk Group" constantly complained to Shumiatsky.[264]

Concurrently, with the rise of Shumiatsky, Krasnoshchekov, a strong patron of the "Shanghai Group," was losing his political power in the Far Eastern Republic. Shumiatsky, together with other Bolshevik hardliners, disliked the policies of Krasnoshchekov and had continually worked to decrease his influence in the Far Eastern Republic after he was dispatched by the *Sibbiuro* to the Far Eastern Bureau in Chita. At last, in April 1921, six Bolshevik leaders of the Far Eastern Republic inflicted serious political damage on Krasnoshchekov, who was at that time suffering from an illness, by sending a telegram criticizing him to the Central Committee of the Russian Communist Party.[265]

With the one-sided support of Shumiatsky, the "Irkutsk Group" dominated the preparatory committee for the Constituent Congress of the Korean Communist Party, which would be held in Irkutsk in May 1921.[266] The Far Eastern Secretariat and the "Irkutsk Group" eventually dissolved the Haninbu in Chita and Korean Communist organizations in Blagoveshchensk and Khabarovsk, all which were under the control of the "Shanghai Group." They also suspended the *Sin Segye* (New World) which was the organ of the Korean

Communist Committee in Blagoveshchensk.[267] The "Irkutsk Group" also arrested and imprisoned in Irkutsk Pak Ae, Kye Pong-u, Chang To-jŏng and Kim Chin, key leaders of the "Shanghai Group" in Chita and member of the Haninbu, on charges of "stirring the Korean revolutionary troops to bring about division and conflict" as well as "opposing the Korean Revolutionary Military Council which was organized by the Far Eastern Secretariat."[268] They issued an order to arrest key leaders of the "Shanghai Group" including Pak Chin-sun and also attempted to arrest 13 military leaders of the "Shanghai Group" in Mazanovo, Amur Province including Kim Kyu-myŏn and Han Un-yong, but failed because of the interference of members of the Russian Political Security Bureau who were favorable toward the "Shanghai Group."[269]

Under the leadership of Shumiatsky, the "Irkutsk Group" held its Constituent Congress of the Korean Communist Party from May 4 to May 15, 1921 in Irkutsk.[270] The congress organized the Korean Communist Party with 11 members of the Central Committee headed by An Pyŏng-ch'an and Han Kyu-sŏn[271] and elected five members of the delegation to the third Congress of the Comintern which would be held from June 22 to July 12, 1921.[272] The congress also organized the Korean Revolutionary Military Council [Koryŏ Hyŏngmyŏng Kunjŏng Ŭihoe], which would seize command of the Korean military forces in Siberia and the Russian Far East, and established a military tribunal for punishing the arrested party and military leaders of the "Shanghai Group."[273] Five leaders of the "Shanghai Group," including Chang Ki-yŏng, Afanasii Kim [Kim Sŏng-u], and Kim Tong-han, who had attended the congress, were accused of "rejecting the theoretical guidance of the Far Eastern Secretariat," and punished.[274] The Central Executive Committee of the Korean Communist Party in Irkutsk expelled Yi Tong-hwi, Kim Rip, Pak Chin-sun, Kim Ha-gu, Yi Han-yŏng, and Kim Kyu-myŏn from the Party.[275]

Throughout 1921, Shumiatsky and the "Irkutsk Group" were arresting all the "leading figures of the Korean Communists who had competed with the Korean National Council." For the members of the "Shanghai Group," it was "impossible to go out to the Far East and to go to Moscow."[276] This precarious situation continued until the end of 1921 when the delegation of the "Shanghai Group," composed of Yi Tong-hwi, Pak Chin-sun and Hong To, succeeded in obtaining official decisions of the Comintern, which brought about the release of the imprisoned members and removed the threat in Siberia.

From May 20 to 23, 1921, in response to the exclusive congress of the "Irkutsk Group," the "Shanghai Group" convened the third Congress of the Korean Socialist Party in Shanghai and created the Korean Communist Party. Several Communist and labor organizations also participated as well as the Korean Social Revolutionary Party [Sahoe Hyŏngmyŏngdang],[277] which had been organized by Kim Ch'ŏl-su, Yi Pong-su, Chu Chong-gŏn in Seoul, Korea in June 1920.[278] The congress elected the Central Executive Committee with Yi Tong-hwi as its Chairman and Kim Ch'ŏl-su as its Secretary-General. It also appointed a delegation composed of Yi Tong-hwi, Pak Chin-sun and Hong To to the Third Comintern Congress.[279]

On June 28, 1921, bloody military conflicts occurred in Svobodnyi City, Amur Province, when the Korean Revolutionary Military Council, which was organized by and under the control of the "Irkutsk Group," attempted to disarm resisting military troops which were supporting the "Shanghai Group." In this incident, which Koreans called "*Chayusi Ch'ambyŏn*" ("Disaster in Free City"), hundreds of Korean soldier were killed or injured.[280] Shortly after the incident, the Korean Military Council investigated the arrested Koreans. The soldiers who belonged to the military troops from Chientao led by Ch'oe Chin-dong and Hŏ Kŭn were found "not-guilty" and were incorporated into the Korean Revolutionary Military Council. However, 72 officers and soldiers of the 500 who had supported the "Shanghai Group" were charged with having committed "serious crimes," and were transferred to Irkutsk for imprisonment. Another 428 were handed over to the 2nd Battalion of the Russian People's Revolutionary Army and were immediately sent to forced labor in Ushumun along the Amur River.[281] The Russian Bolsheviks recognized only one group in Irkutsk among the Korean Communist organizations and excluded by force the group critical of the Far Eastern Secretariat of the Comintern.

Bolshevik agents such as Georgy Safarov and Gregory Voitinsky, who were in charge of the Korean Communist movement in the 1920s, followed the policies of Shumiatsky, who had allowed just one group to monopolize the power to organize the "legitimate" Korean Communist Party, instead of attempting to unify the diverse Communist groups.[282] The aftermath of these internecine struggles in 1921 continued to affect the development of the Korean Communist movement. As influence of the Korean Communists increased in the anti-Japanese liberation movement, the previous dissensions among Korean Communists had negative impacts even on the Korean liberation movement in general.

Chapter Six

CONCLUSION

After 1905, patriotic activities began to flourish among Koreans in North Chientao and the Primorye initially thorough leadership of the loyalist Koreans such as Yi Yong-ik and Yi Pŏm-yun. In particular, Korean residents in the Primorye, at first, welcomed and supported the anti-Japanese *ŭibyŏng* movement led by Yi Pŏm-yun (former Administrator of Northern Border and Chientao of the Korean government). However, *ŭibyŏng* movement declined after the failed attack on North Korea in the summer of 1908. In addition to the Russian authorities' prohibitive policies against *ŭibyŏng* activities, the loss of support from the Korean communities was a chief cause of its decline in the Primorye.

Previous study has pointed out that following threats of Japanese authorities to prohibit commercial activities in Korea, wealthy Koreans appealed to Russian authorities to expel Yi Pŏm-yun and other *ŭibyŏng* leaders.[1] Those appeals, however, clearly show that Yi Pŏm-yun's untrustworthy behavior (he did not keep his promise to carry out military attacks on North Korea) and extravagant life style were enough to arouse resentment among Koreans. Yi Pŏm-yun accumulated military materials and manpower by appealing to the patriotism of Koreans and asserting his authority as the former Administrator of Northern Border and Chientao. But his authoritarian and high-handed attitude brought about internal conflicts among the *ŭibyŏng* leaders such as Ch'oe Chae-hyŏng who had provided facilities for the *ŭibyŏng* movement; these conflicts continued to affect later anti-Japanese activities of Korea nationalists in the Primorye. Unless Koreans, particularly the *wŏnhoin* (old settlers) Koreans who had already acquired relative economic security in Russia, were directly threatened by Japanese authorities, they were very hesitant to get involved in the anti-Japanese movement. They were particularly wary of military activities which might have threatened their life in Russia. Even after the February Revolution, the *wŏnhoin* Koreans were more concerned with improving their social, political and economic status in Russian society. It was only after the Siberian Intervention when Japanese military forces occupied the Russian Far East and threatened the basic life of the Koreans that some wealthy *wŏnhoin* Korean leaders became active in the anti-Japanese movement.

Another group which contributed significantly to nationalism among Koreans in the Russian Far East, was the Kongnip Hyŏphoe and the Kungminhoe, which had headquarters in San Francisco. Unlike the loyalist leaders of the *ŭibyŏng* movement, they emphasized education, industry, and religion (Christianity) and their influence swept through Korean communities in the Russian Far East, Siberia and Manchuria. Their gradual and peaceful approach was seen as acceptable to both the local Russian authorities and the Korean communities as well. However, factional struggles based on regionalism and ideological differences among members of the Kungminhoe — between the "Seoul faction" and the "Western faction" — aroused resentment from the Koreans in the Primorye, whose majority were from the northeastern part of Korea (Hamgyŏng Provinces). More importantly, their republican political ideology and affiliation with American missionaries served as a source of suspicion for local Russian authorities in the Primorye. Therefore, the leaders of the Kungminhoe, mostly from the northwestern part of Korea (P'yŏngan Provinces), had to move to Chita in the middle of 1911 and concentrated their activities among Koreans in Za-Baikal and Siberia.

From 1911 to 1914, the Kwŏnŏphoe (1911-1914) in the Primorye, and Korean Educational Association [Kyoyukhoe] (1910-1912) and the Kanminhoe (1913-1914) in North Chientao were leading Korean nationalist organizations. The core group of these nationalist organizations in North Chientao and the Primorye, who had frequently come to and from these two regions, was composed of the followers of Yi Tong-hwi, one of the most influential nationalists in 1910s and the founder of the Korean Socialist Party. This group both in North Chientao and the Primorye had basically same strategies. Firstly, in order to preclude any Japanese interference, they endeavored to obtain recognition and patronage of the Chinese and local Russian authorities. At the same time, they proceeded with projects such as campaigns for naturalization and peaceful patriotic activities in education, industry and religion while publicly refraining from any anti-Japanese activities which might incite strong protest from the Japanese government and create diplomatic issues with China and Russia. This strategy was also necessary to obtain the support of the *wŏnhoin* Korean leaders, who were opposed to any activities which might weaken their position in Russia by violating the policies of the Russian government. While utilizing legal and peaceful activities such as publication of newspapers and books and establishment of schools, libraries, churches, *yŏboin* (new settlers) Korean nationalists, however, had secretly carried out military training and purchased weapons in preparation for possible military actions against the Japanese when China or Russia would enter a war with Japan.

In North Chientao, new cultural and educational activities (Western knowledge and science) and campaigns for adopting Chinese citizenship of the Educational Association and the Kanminhoe (1913-1914) were strongly opposed by Confucian Koreans and old settled Korean farmers. Most leaders of Educational Association and Kanminhoe were Christians and followers of Yi Tong-hwi from Hamgyŏng Provinces, as were most of the Korean population in the two regions.

Opposition to the new education and campaign for naturalization by the Kwŏnŏphoe in the Primorye was not as strong as in North Chientao. However, one of the most serious internal problems in the Korean nationalist movement in the Primorye was regional factional struggles. In the process of establishing the Kwŏnŏphoe, the three regional factions (Northern, Seoul and Western) were in constant competition demonstrating Korean unity only when the Kwŏnŏphoe was officially established with legal recognition of local Russian authorities. Korean nationalist leaders of other factions were frequently accused as Japanese agents and arrested by Russian authorities. Upset that leadership of the Kwŏnŏphoe was held by the Northern faction, the Seoul faction finally withdrew from all its activities.

Japanese diplomatic pressure on Russian authorities also threatened the Korean nationalists. Although the local Russian authorities in the Primorye had favorable policies toward the Korean nationalist movement, they frequently controlled activities of the Korean nationalists in observation of treaties with Japan. Although the local Russian authorities in the Primorye never turned over Korean nationalists to the Japanese government, they arrested or exiled them to the inner part of Siberia shortly after the Japanese annexation of Korea and the outbreak of World War I. However, the local Russian authorities in Harbin turned over arrested Korean nationalists to the Japanese Government-General in Korea at the time of former Prime Minister Katsura Tarō's visit to Russia in the summer of 1912.

At the end of 1913, the *yŏhoin* nationalists including Yi Tong-hwi, Yi Chong-ho, Yi Sang-sŏl, Chŏng Chae-gwan and Yi Tong-nyŏng, secretly organized the Korean Restoration Military Government in preparation for the possible "second Russo-Japanese War" in 1914, the tenth anniversary of the first Russo-Japanese War. Their plan was frustrated by the outbreak of the World War I and the resulting suppressive actions of the Russian government against Korean nationalists. In early 1915, expecting the "second Sino-Japanese war" as a result of the diplomatic stalemate over the issue of the "Twenty-One Demand," those who had fled to Manchuria, together with their comrades in North Chientao, planned to launch cooperative military campaigns with China against Japan. However, they faced suppression from local Chinese authorities under Japanese diplomatic pressure. World War I created a terrible situation for the Korean nationalist movement, both in North Chientao and the Primorye. Korean nationalist leaders had to stop their activities or hide in the inner regions of Manchuria and the Primorye. Yi Chong-ho, Kye Pong-u and Kim Ha-sŏk were arrested and transferred to Korea by the Japanese police while Yi Tong-hwi and Kim Rip were imprisoned in Russia and charged as German agents. Other key leaders such as Yi Sang-sŏl, Kim To-yŏ and Yi Kap died shortly before and after the Russian February Revolution.

In the democratic political mood created by the Russian February Revolution, the *wŏnhoin* Koreans organized the Central Executive Committee of the Korean Associations in Russia [Koryŏjok Chungang Ch'onghoe] as the "unified and central organ" of Koreans at the Congress of the Delegates of Koreans in Russia in June 1917. More concerned about the improvement of their social and political status in Russian society and expressing support for the policies of the Russian Provisional Government, the Congress excluded from the agenda the issues of anti-Japanese activities and the release of the anti-Japanese Korean leaders like Yi Tong-hwi.

Relying on the new political environment after the Bolshevik Revolution, pro-Bolshevik Koreans led by Alexandra Kim and the anti-Japanese national revolutionary group led by Yi Tong-hwi, attempted to organize their own "central organ" of Koreans in Russia [Hanjok Chungang Ch'onghoe] representing the *yŏhoin* Koreans, mainly poor peasants, and based on the ties made with the Russian Bolsheviks in January 1918. Although the leaders of the latter group agreed to establish a unified central organ of Koreans (Central Executive Committee of the Korean Associations in All Russia, Chŏllo Hanjok Chungang Ch'onghoe), with the Koryŏjok Ch'onghoe, they secretly organized the Korean Socialist Party after the model of the Russian Social Democratic Party in addition to more active anti-Japanese programs.

At the Second Special Congress of the Delegates of the Koreans in All Russia held in Nikol'sk-Ussurisk in June 1918, the Korean Socialist Party opposed the *wŏnhoin* Koreans, who composed the majority of the Congress and had close relations with the Russian Socialist Revolutionary Party (SRs), over major issues of politics, land and labor. The Siberian Intervention of the Allies, occurring shortly after the Congress, forced the Korean Socialist Party to go underground and the Central Executive Committee of the Korean Associations in All Russia as a result could barely maintain its legal existence.

With the explosive upsurge of anti-Japanese patriotism among Koreans in early March 1919 after the March First Movement, the Central Executive Committee of the Korean Associations in All Russia transformed itself into the Korean National Council, with the joining of the nationalist forces not only in the Primorye, but also in North and West Chientao, and claimed itself as the central organ of all Koreans. The Korean National Council competed for leadership of the Korean nationalist movement with the Shanghai Provisional Government, which the Seoul faction member of the Korean National Council and the Korean nationalists in Shanghai organized in April 1919.

At its 2nd Congress in April 1919, the Korean Socialist Party also reinforced its organization and activities by merging with the New People's Union [Sinmindan] and promoted its pro-Bolshevik platform by reinforcing its propaganda activities among the nationalistic Koreans and military organizations. According to its Moscow-oriented policy, the congress decided to dispatch a delegation to the Comintern and boycott the Versailles-oriented policies of the Korean National Council.

Because of the unfavorable political environment in the Primorye under the White regime supported by the Japanese, the Korean National Council faced difficulties in enforcing its influence. The delegation to Paris also failed to arrive on time for the Conference.

After the Paris Peace Conference, it became clear that the Shanghai Provisional Government was on the winning side in the power struggle with the Korean National Council, in part due to the comparatively favorable political freedom in the French Leased Territory in Shanghai, the joining of key Korean nationalists from various regions, and the propaganda activities of its delegation in Paris.

In August 1919, the Shanghai Provisional Government and the Korean National Council agreed to dissolve themselves into a new "unified" Shanghai Provisional Government organized in line with the composition of the Cabinet of the Hansŏng Government declared at the end of April 1919 in Seoul. In its April Congress, the Korean Socialist Party also decided to join the "unified" Provisional Government. The Korean National Council, however, refused to join the Shanghai Provisional Government, arguing that "restructuring" without its dissolution to change the title of "Chief Executive" of the Hansŏng Government into "President" were violations of the agreement for the unification of Shanghai and Vladivostok. In this political turmoil, the Korean Socialist Party joined the Shanghai Provisional Government, with expectation to utilize the authority of the "unified" Provisional Government. This move led to the deterioration of its relationship with the Korean National Council, which in turn launched retaliatory anti-Shanghai Provisional Government and anti-Korean Socialist Party actions.

Expectations of the Korean Socialist Party soon proved too optimistic. The "unified" Shanghai Provisional Government allocated too much political power to the President, Yi Sŭng-man, who monopolized the funds from Koreans in the United States. These funds had been the only financial source for the Shanghai Provisional Government which Yi spent only on his own diplomatic activities in America.

Due to disagreements on key issues such as Yŏ Un-hyŏng's visit to Tokyo and dispatch of the government delegation to Moscow, Yi Tong-hwi (Chairman of the Korean Socialist Party and Premier of the Provisional Government) found himself completely isolated from other Ministers including An Ch'ang-ho, his long-time comrade since 1907 as cofounder of the New People's Association. Yi Tong-hwi's and Kim Rip's movement for expelling Yi Sŭng-man in cooperation with five Vice-Ministers in the spring of 1920 was also frustrated by the stubborn opposition of An Ch'ang-ho and other Ministers who did not want a change to the status quo.

Although Yi Tong-hwi canceled his resignation from the Premiership at the end of July 1920, he and his comrades began to redirect all efforts toward reinforcing the Korean Socialist Party whose key members, Pak Chin-sun and Han Hyŏng-gwŏn, were winning diplomatic success in Moscow in the summer of 1920. Pak Chin-sun became an executive member of the Comintern in charge of the Far East and Han Hyŏng-gwŏn obtained 400,000 gold rubles (among promised 2 million gold rubles) from the Soviet government.

When the Japanese military brutally killed thousands of Koreans and destroyed Korean communities in West and North Chientao at the end of 1920, criticism against the Provisional Government intensified. The Provisional Government needed to take urgent action in order to provide a single and unified command and financial and military support for the military forces which were gathering in the Amur Province from Manchuria and the Primorye. In this context, Yi Tong-hwi strongly urged transformation of the Provisional Government into "the revolutionary committee" which would include all anti-Japanese organizations both inside and outside Korea and would lead the anti-Japanese activities. Yi Sŭng-man, who hurried from

America to Shanghai at repeated requests of the Cabinet, however, rejected the proposal, emphasizing the crucial importance of diplomacy in America. The majority of other ministers, who wanted the status quo maintained, rejected Yi Tong-hwi's proposal as well.

With breakdown of the "united front," the Shanghai Provisional Government lost its authority as the central organ of the Korean independence movement. Thereafter, the Provisional Government degraded into no more than an organization controlled by Yi Sŭng-man's supporters, who were mainly from the central part of Korea. From that time until the end of the World War II, the Provisional Government never regained support from the Korean military and revolutionary forces in Manchuria and Russia.

The Korean Socialist Party (Shanghai Group) which withdrew from the Provisional Government had to compete with the "Irkutsk Group" composed of the Korean Communists who had joined the Russian Communist Party and were under the direct control of the Far Eastern Secretariat of the Comintern headed by Boris Zakharovich Shumiatsky. If the cabinet members of the Provisional Government had more seriously considered about Yi Tong-hwi's proposal and succeeded in retaining him and his followers in the government, the situation might have been quite different. The Provisional Government would not only have enhanced its authority and influence with the diplomatic success in Moscow, but through this authority would have been able to prevent the bloody military clashes in Svobodnyi City.

Yi Sŭng-man would eventually be impeached and discharged by the Provisional Assembly in March 1925 for "inviolability of the state law and degrading the authority of the government by arbitrarily violating the Constitution and making disorder in state administration" and "destroying the spirit of democracy" "by attempting to stay as permanent President."[2]

This study demonstrated five major characteristics of the Korean nationalist movement in the Russian Far East and North Chientao during the early period of the Japanese colonial rule (1905-1921). These characteristics remained common to nationalists and Communists alike in the Korean anti-Japanese movement through the whole period of Japanese colonial rule.

First, in North Chientao and the Russian Far East, nationalists endeavored to inspire patriotism and unite Koreans by publishing newspapers and magazines, establishing schools and churches, and organizing lectures. The Korean nationalists, however, could not express and communicate their political ideas considering the political system of their benefactor countries. Prior to the Russian Revolution, for example, Tsarist authorities inhibited the expression of republican political ideas. Furthermore, in articles published in newspapers or magazines, Korean nationalists frequently used pseudonyms in order to avoid the possible interferences of the Japanese authorities.

Second, despite the efforts to inspire unity, internecine factional struggles erupted between Koreans based on their various regional origins. The lack of common political ideas and expression impeded the progress of Korean nationalism and thwarted the development of authoritative central leadership. In the turmoil of factional struggles, Korean nationalists sometimes appealed to Chinese and Russian authorities in order to restrain their rivals. The frequent arrests of Korean leaders by the foreign authorities were in many cases caused by false accusations submitted by rival groups and leaders.

Third, the geographical distance among Korean leaders largely hindered communications among Korean leaders and sometimes deepened misunderstandings and dissensions among them as well. Frequent intercepts of letters between the Korean national activists by the Japanese authorities aggravated the difficulties.

Fourth, political or military interference from the outside, that is, the authorities of Japan, China and Russia inflicted the most critical wounds on the Korean liberation movement. Although Korean revolutionaries committed great effort to obtain favors from the Chinese and Russian authorities, their diplomatic relations were frequently interfered by Japan in opposition to the goals of the Korean liberation movement. Also, the peaceful diplomatic pressures and even military interference of the Japanese authorities created a dangerous situation for Korean nationalists. The outbreak of World War I (1914), the Allied Intervention (1918), the April Disaster (1920) and Kando Incident (1920) completely destroyed what Korean nationalists had accomplished to that point. Even the Russian Bolsheviks in Siberia and the Russian Far East intensified the internal factional struggles by unilaterally supporting one group ("Irkutsk Group") and suppressing other competing groups ("Shanghai Group").

Fifth, regardless of all these internal and external difficulties, it can be seen that the Korean nationalist movement endured. Popular participation and explosive patriotic demonstrations during and after the March First Movement in 1919, both in Korea and abroad, clearly proved the durability of Korean nationalism.

Ch'ŏlhyŏl Kwangboktan (鐵血光復團): Union of Iron and Blood Restoration

Ch'ŏlhyŏltan (鐵血團): Union of Iron and Blood

Chŏllo Hanjok Chungang Ch'onghoe (全露韓族中央總會): Central Executive Committee of the Korean Associations in All Russia

Ch'ŏndogyo (天道教): Religion of Heavenly Way

Ch'ŏngnyŏn Ch'inmokhoe (青年親睦會): Youth Friendship Association

Ch'ŏngnyŏn Kŭnŏphoe (青年勤業會): Youth Association for Diligence and Industry

Ch'ŏngnyŏn Kurakpu (青年구락부): Youth Club

Ch'ŏnhan Kongsandang (全韓共產黨): All-Korea Communist Party

Chunghan Yŏnhap Chŏndohoe (中韓聯合傳道會): Chinese-Korean Joint Christian Mission

Hambuk Ch'ŏngnyŏnhoe (咸北青年會): North Hamgyŏng Province Youth Association

Hangugin Kongjehoe (韓國人共濟會): Korean Mutual Assistance Association

Haninbu (韓人部): Korean Section

Haninhoe (韓人會): Korean Association

Hanin Kongsandang (韓人共產黨): Korean Communist Party

Hanin Kŏryuminhoe (韓人居留民會): Korean Residents' Association

Hanin Kuninhoe (韓人軍人會): Korean Soldiers' Association

Hanin Sahoedang (韓人社會黨): Korean Socialist Party

Hanjok Chungang Ch'onghoe (韓族中央總會): Central Executive Committee of the Korean Associations (in All Russia)

Hanjok Tongnip Kisŏnghoe (韓族獨立期成會): Korean Association for Achieving Independence

Hanjokhoe (韓族會): Korean Association

Hanmin Chach'ihoe (韓民自治會): Korean Self-Administrative Association

Hanminhoe (韓民會): Korean Association

Hanmin Kyoyukhoe (韓民教育會): Korean Educational Association

Hansŏng Chŏngbu (漢城政府): Hansŏng Government

Hapsŏng Hyŏphoe (合成協會): United Korean Association

Hŭngsadan (興士團): Young Korean Academy

Hyŏpsŏnghoe (協成會): Cooperation Association

Hyŏptonghoe (協同會): Association for Cooperation

Ilchinhoe (一進會): One Advancement Association

Ilsedang (一世黨): One World Party

Kanminhoe (墾民會): Korean Association in Chientao

Kanmin Kyoyukhoe (墾民教育會): Korean Educational Association in Chientao

Kanmin Yŏnguhoe (墾民研究會): Research Association of the Koreans in Chientao

Kilim Kunjŏngsa (吉林軍政司): Military Government in Jilin

Konggyohoe (孔教會): Association of Confucians

Kongnip Hyŏphoe (共立協會): United Korean Association

Koryŏbu (高麗部): Korean Section

Koryŏ Hyŏngmyŏng Kunjŏng Ŭihoe (高麗革命軍政議會): Korean Revolutionary Military Council

Koryŏjok Chungang Ch'onghoe (高麗族中央總會): Central Executive Committee of the Korean Associations (in All Russia)

Koryŏ Kongsan Tanch'e Chungang Kanbu (高麗共產團體中央幹部): Central Executive Committee of the Korean Communist Organizations within the Russian Communist Parties

Koryŏ Kongsandang (高麗共産黨): Korean Communist Party

Kunbidan (軍備團): Union for Military Preparation

Kumi Chuch'a Hanguk Wiwŏnbu(歐美駐箚韓國委員部): Korean Commission in America and Europe

Kungmin Taep'yohoeŭi (國民代表會議): Conference of the National Representatives

Kungminhoe (國民會): Korean National Association

Kwangboktan (光復團): Restoration Union

Kwangŭidan (光義團): Union of Restoration and Righteousness

Kwŏnŏphoe (勸業會): Work Promotion Association

Nongmugye (農務契): Agricultural Community Compact

Noindan (老人團): Union of Elderly Men

Oin Kurakbu (吾人俱樂部): Our Club

Puin Tongnipan (婦人獨立團): Women's Union for Independence

Pukkando Kyoyuktan (北間島教育團): North Chientao Education Group

Pukkyŏkng Kunsa T'ongil Ch'okchinhoe (北京軍事統一促進會): Committee for Promoting Unification of Military Organizations in Beijing

Pungno Kunjŏngsŏ (北路軍政署): Military Government in North Chientao

Pungno Tokkunbu (北路督軍府): Korean Military Command in North Chientao

Rŏsia Kongsandang nae Koryŏ Kongsan Tanch'e Taep'yojahoe (러시아共産黨內高麗共産團體代表者會): Congress of the Representatives from the Korean Communist Sections within Russian Communist Parties

Sahoe Hyŏngmyŏngdang (社會革命黨): Social Revolutionary Party

Sahoejuŭi Yŏnguso (社會主義硏究所): Institute for Study of Socialism

Sasuk Kaeryanghoe (私塾改良會): Association for Private Village School Reform

Saugye (士友契): Confucian-Scholars' Compact

Shanghae Imsi Chŏngbu (上海臨時政府): Korean Provisional Government in Shanghai

Sich'ŏngyo (侍天教): Religion of Serving the Heaven

Sinmindan (新民團): New People's Union

Sinminhoe (新民會): New People's Association

Sipsamdo Ŭigun (十三道義軍): Righteous Army of Thirteen Provinces of Korea

Sŏbuk Hakhoe (西北學會): Northwestern Educational Association

Sŏngmyŏnghoe (聲明會): Manifesto Association

Sŏngnigyo (聖理敎): Holy Truth Religion

Sŏro Kunjŏngsŏ (西路軍政署): Military Government in West Chientao

Taedong Hyŏpsinhoe (大東協新會): Association for Cooperation and Renewal of the Great East

Taedong Kyoyukhoe (大東敎育會): Korean Educational Association

Taedong Pogukhoe (大東保國會): Korean Association for Protecting Nation

Taehan Kungmin Ŭihoe (大韓國民議會): Korean National Council

Taehan Kungminhoe (大韓國民會, 北間島): Korean National Association in North Chientao

Taehan Kungminhoe Chungangch'onghoe (大韓國民會中央總會): Central Executive Committee of Korean National Associations in Russia

Taehan Kwangbokkun Chŏngbu (大韓光復軍政府): Korean Restoration Military Government

Taehan Kunmu Todokpu (大韓軍務都督府): Headquarters of Korean Military Command

Taehan Tongnipkun (大韓獨立軍): Korean Independence Army

Taehanin Kungminhoe Chungang Ch'onghoe (大韓人國民會中央總會): Central Executive Committee of Korean National Associations in America

Taejonggyo (大倧敎): Religion of Tangun Worship

Tongnip Hyŏphoe (獨立協會): Independence Club

Tongnipkunbu (獨立軍府): Korean Independence Army Headquarters

Tongŭihoe (同義會): Comrades' Association

Tongniptan (獨立團): Independence Union

Ŭigunbu (義軍府): Headquarters of Righteous Army

Ŭigundan (義軍團): Union of the Righteous Army Corps

Ural Nodongja Tongmaeng (우랄勞動者同盟): Workers' Union in the Urals

Yŏnhaeju Hanjok Kongsandang Wiwŏnhoe (沿海洲韓族共産黨委員會): Korean Communist Party Committee in the Primorye

■ NOTES

Preface

1. Cho Tong-gŏl, "Imsi chŏngbu surip ŭl wihan ilch'ŏn gubaek sipch'il nyŏn ŭi 'Taedong tangyŏl ŭi sŏnŏn'" [The 1917 declaration for the establishment of the provisional government], in *Hangukhak nonch'ong*, 9 [Seoul: Kukmin Taehak Hangukhak Yŏnguso (the Center for Korean Studies of Kumin University), 1987], pp. 123-52.
2. In May 1921, two Korean Communist Parties [Koryŏ Kongsandang] with the same name were organized by two competing Korean Communist groups in Shanghai and Irkutsk. In order to differentiate between the two parties, Korean nationalists and Russian Bolsheviks referred to the two parties by the name of the places where they were organized: the "Shanghai Group" and "Irkutsk Group." The "Shanghai Group" was the Korean Communist Party organized by the Korean Socialist Party together with the Korean Social Revolutionary Party [Sahoe Hyŏngmyŏngdang] in Shanghai.
3. The Commission on the Korean Question was established at a session of the plenum of the Executive Committee of Comintern held on November 2, 1921. At the session, Bela Kun (Hungary), Safarov (Russia), and Kuusinen (Finland) were appointed as members of the Commission, which was entrusted with working out an adequate draft by consulting with Korean comrades. See Kommunistischen Internationale, *Die Tätigkeit der Exekitives und des Präsidiums des E. K. der Kommunistischen Internationale vom 13 Juli 1921 bis 1. Februar 1922* [Activities of the Executive and the Presidium of the Executive Committee of the Communist International: Petrograd 1922] (Feltrinello Reprint, 1967), p. 248.
4. Kim Chŏng-ju [Kin Sei-tsū] ed., *Chōsen tōchi shiryō* [Historical Sources on the

Administration of Korea], vol. 7 (Tokyo: Kankoku Shiryō Kenkyūshō, 1970), pp. 194-95.

Chapter One

1. Din'shun' Pak [Pak Chin-sun], "Koreiskaia emigratsiia v Rossii" [Korean Emigration to Russia], *Zhizn' Natsionalostei*, 18 Apr. 1920, p. 2; Kye Pong-u, *Kkum sog ŭi kkum* [A Dream in a Dream], vol. 1, ms. (Kzyl Orda, Kazakstan, 1944), p. 163.
2. Kim Chŏng-ju [Kin Sei-tsū] ed., *Chōsen tōchi shiryō*, vol. 1, pp. 5-6; Lee Hoon-ku [Yi Hun-gu], *Manchu wa Chosŏnin* [Manchuria and Koreans] (P'yŏngyang: Union Christian College Press, 1932), pp. 92-95; Ki-hoon Kim, "Japanese Policy for Korean Rural Immigration to Manchuria, 1932-1945," diss. University of Hawai'i (1992), pp. 30-31. A copy of the epitaph of the demarcation stone can be seen in Hyŏn Kyu-hwan, *Hanguk yuiminsa* [A History of Korean Wanderers and Emigrants] (Seoul: Ŏmungak, 1976), vol. 1, p. 47. English translation is included in Ki-hoon Kim, "Japanese Policy for Korean Rural Immigration to Manchuria, 1932-1945," p. 31: "Muketung, the Governor of the Ula region, on orders from His Majesty the Great Emperor of Great Qing, arrived here on a survey tour to determine the border. The west stream becomes the Yalu River and the east stream forms the Tumen (土門) River. Upon this watershed, therefore, the stone tablet is hereby erected in memory of the settlement of the boundary between the two countries." As we will see later, how to locate the "Tumen" (土門) in the epitaph became the source of the territorial disputes between China and Korea at the turn of the century. The Japanese officials assumed that the Kangxi Emperor and Chinese officials must have confused the Tumen (土門) River which flows to the northeast, into the Sungari River, with the Tuman (豆滿) River which flows to the southeast and finally into the Sea of Japan (Tonghae in Korean, Eastern Sea). See Kim Chŏng-ju [Kin Sei-tsū] ed., *Chōsen tōchi shiryō*, vol. 1, p. 5.
3. Ko Sŭng-je, *Hanguk iminsa yŏngu* [Studies on History of Korean Emigration] (Seoul: Changmungak, 1973), p. 17.
4. Hyŏn Kyu-hwan, *Hanguk yuiminsa*, p. 135.
5. The Chinese call the region "Yanbian," which means "extended edge area."
6. Yun Pyŏng-sŏk, "Yun Chŏng-hŭi chŏ 'Kando kaech'ŏksa' pu 'Yŏngsin hakkyo yŏnhyŏk" [Bibliographical Introduction to Yun Chŏng-hŭi's 'History of the Chientao Development' and its Appendix 'History of Yŏngsin School'], *Hangukhak Yŏngu*, 3, Mar. 1991, p. 5.
7. Kye Pong-u, *Kkum sog ŭi kkum*, vol. 1, p. 141.
8. Din'shun' Pak, "Koreiskaia emigratsiia v Rossii."
9. Yun Chŏng-hŭi, "Kando kaech'ŏksa," *Hangukhak Yŏngu*, 3, Mar. 1991, p. 14; Kye Pong-u, *Kkum sog ŭi kkum*, vol. 1, p. 141.

10. Nagano Akira, *Manshū mondai no jissō* [The True Picture of the Problems in Manchuria] (Tokyo: Shina Mondai Kenkyusho, 1928), pp. 54-55.
11. Yun Chŏng-hŭi, "Kando kaech'ŏksa," pp. 15-16.
12. Kim Chŏng-ju [Kin Sei-tsū] ed., *Chōsen tōchi shiryō*, vol. 1, p. 33.
13. I-shou Wang, "Chinese Migration and Population Change in Manchuria, 1900-1940" (diss. University of Minnesota, 1971), pp. 40-41.
14. Kim Chŏng-ju [Kin Sei-tsū] ed., *Chōsen tōchi shiryō*, vol. 1, p. 9.
15. Ibid., vol. 1, pp. 9-10, 57, 275.
16. Lee Hoon-ku, *Manchu wa Chosŏnin*, p. 94.
17. Robert H. G. Lee, *The Manchurian Frontier in Ch'ing History* (Cambridge: Harvard UP, 1970), p. 134; "Kukkyŏng chibang sich'al pongmyŏngsŏ" [Report on the On-site Inspection of the Border Regions Following Order], *Paeksan Hakpo*, 9, Dec. 1970, p. 189.
18. Hyŏn Kyu-hwan, *Hanguk yuiminsa*, 138.
19. Kim Chŏng-ju [Kin Sei-tsū] ed., *Chōsen tōchi shiryō*, vol. 1, p. 276; Hyŏn Kyu-hwan, *Hanguk yuiminsa,* pp. 41-42, 137-38.
20. Ibid., vol. 1, pp. 513-14.
21. Kim Chŏng-ju [Kin Sei-tsū] ed., *Chōsen tōchi shiryō*, vol. 1, pp. 12, 276-77.
22. Ki-hoon Kim, "Japanese Policy for Korean Rural Immigration to Manchuria, 1932-1945," p. 35; Hyŏn Kyu-hwan, *Hanguk yuiminsa,* p. 137.
23. The "Ch'ŏnji" [Heavenly Pool] has been widely referred to a pool on the top of Mt. Paektu, which was formed as a result of volcanic explosion. However, in the late 19th century, "Yongwangdam" ("Longwangdan in Chinese") or "Taedam" ("Big Pond") had been used for calling the pool. See Murchison James Henry Evans, *Long White Mountain: A Journal in Manchuria* (London and New York: Longmans, Green and Co., 1888), frontispiece; Yun Pyŏng-sŏk, "Yun Chŏng-hŭi chŏ 'Kando kaech'ŏksa' pu 'Yŏngsin hakkyo yŏnhyŏk," p. 16.
24. Kim Chŏng-ju [Kin Sei-tsū] ed., *Chōsen tōchi shiryō*, vol. 1, pp. 12-18, 276-77, 513-14; Ko Sŭng-je, *Hanguk iminsa yŏngu*, pp. 20-21.
25. Kim Chŏng-ju [Kin Sei-tsū] ed., *Chōsen tōchi shiryō*, vol. 1, pp. 13, 15, 54-57. At the time of second negotiation, a commissioner of the Qing China threatened the Korean commissioner Yi Chung-ha to agree to China's argument, but Yi resisted saying, "after you cut my head, then you can curtail our territory."
26. Kim Chŏng-ju [Kin Sei-tsū] ed., *Chōsen tōchi shiryō*, vol. 1, pp. 15-16.
27. Nagano Akira, *Manshū mondai no jissō*, p. 54.
28. Robert H. G. Lee, *The Manchurian Frontier in Ch'ing History*, p. 134.
29. Kim Chŏng-ju [Kin Sei-tsū] ed., *Chōsen tōchi shiryō*, vol. 1, pp. 18-19; Japanese government-General Office of Korea [Chōsen Sōtokufu], Department of Social Affairs,

Manshū kyū Shiberia chihō ni okeru Chōsenjin jijō [Situation of Koreans in Manchuria and Siberia] (Seoul: 1923), pp. 3-4.

30. Yun Chŏng-hŭi, "Kando kaech'ŏksa," p. 17.
31. Ibid., 17.
32. "Chosŏn oe esŏ ŭi Chosŏnin sanghwang ilban" [General Situation of Koreans outside Korea], *Sindonga* (Feb. 1967), p. 474.
33. Yun Chŏng-hŭi, "Kando kaech'ŏksa," pp. 17-18.
34. Ko Sŭng-je, *Hanguk iminsa yŏngu*, p. 21. The following report by Japanese officials tells the truth of the situation of Koreans in Chientao: "The residents of Chientao are mixed by Chinese and Koreans. . . . most of them are peasants. . . . Chinese are mostly landowners and most of the Koreans are tenants. The cultivation of Chientao was launched first by Koreans, but their rights were not enhanced because of the lack of government protection, and eventually degenerated into the condition of slaves. In contrast, the Chinese became landowners by occupying vast lands appropriate for cultivation under the protection of their government officials, and employed Koreans for cultivating and renting those lands. . . . There are Koreans who bought and cultivated lands, but the number of those Koreans is few. . . . Many Koreans are laboring as tenants." See Kim Chŏng-ju [Kin Sei-tsū] ed., *Chōsen tōchi shiryō*, vol. 1, pp. 298-99.
35. Robert H. G. Lee, *The Manchurian Frontier in Ch'ing History*, p. 134.
36. Japanese Government-General Office of Korea, *Manshū Shiberia chihō ni okeru Chōsenjin jijō*, p. 4.
37. Yun Chŏng-hŭi, "Kando kaech'ŏksa," pp. 18-19.
38. Kim Chŏng-ju [Kin Sei-tsū] ed., *Chōsen tōchi shiryō*, vol. 1, p. 19.
39. Ibid., vol. 1, p. 150.
40. Kim Chŏng-ju [Kin Sei-tsū] ed., *Chōsen tōchi shiryō*, vol. 1, pp. 19, 513-14.
41. Ibid., vol. 1, p. 20.
42. Yun Chŏng-hŭi, "Kando kaech'ŏksa," p. 20.
43. Kim Chŏng-ju [Kin Sei-tsū] ed., *Chōsen tōchi shiryō*, vol. 1, pp. 20-22; Yun Chŏng-hŭi, "Kando kaech'ŏksa," p. 20.
44. Ibid., vol. 1, pp. 22; Yun Chŏng-hŭi, "Kando kaech'ŏksa," p. 20.
45. Kye Pong-u, *Kkum sog ŭi kkum*, vol. 1, pp. 143-44.
46. Kim Chŏng-ju [Kin Sei-tsū] ed., *Chōsen tōchi shiryō*, vol. 1, pp. 23-24.
47. Ibid., vol. 1, pp. 37, 296. The administrative Department for Appeasing People and Administration (*Lishiting*) was established in 1903 and generally called *Yanjiting* (Office in Yanji).
48. Kim Chŏng-ju [Kin Sei-tsū] ed., *Chōsen tōchi shiryō*, vol. 1, pp. 396-400.
49. Ibid., vol. 1, pp. 105-106, 412.
50. Yun Chŏng-hŭi, "Kando kaech'ŏksa," p. 21; Kim Chŏng-ju [Kin Sei-tsū] ed., *Chōsen*

tōchi shiryō, vol. 1, pp. 92-91.

51. Kim Chŏng-ju [Kin Sei-tsū] ed., *Chōsen tōchi shiryō*, vol. 1, pp. 96-97.

52. Ibid., pp. 98, 308-10. Those local Korean community leaders were appointed by local Qing authorities and were required to wear Manchu hair and dress. See Kim Chŏng-ju [Kin Sei-tsū] ed., *Chōsen tōchi shiryō*, vol. 1, pp. 37, 296 and "Kukkyŏng chibang sich'al pongmyŏngsŏ," p. 197.

53. Ibid., pp. 99-104.

54. The Ilchinhoe was organized in November of 1904 in Seoul by merging two organizations, the Chinbohoe (Progressive Association) and the Ilchinhoe (One Advancement Association). Based on the followers of the Tonghak (Eastern Learning), the Chinbohoe was organized after the outbreak of the Russo-Japanese War by Son Pyŏng-hŭi, a leader of the Tonghak Peasant Rebellion of 1894 and now the third head of the Tonghak Learning. The Chinbohoe had four platforms to reform the government and administration: 1) to respect the royal family and to consolidate a foundation for the independence of Korea; 2) to reform the government; 3) to readjust military and financial administration; 4) to protect the lives and property of the people. Son Pyŏng-hŭi was in exile in Japan and assigned the leadership of the Chinbohoe to Yi Yong-gu. The number of Chinbohoe members was said to reach one million who cut their long hair and wore black. However, when the Chinbohoe was merged with the Ilchinhoe, a political organization under the protection of the Japanese army in Korea, Yi Yong-gu, in cooperation with Song Pyŏng-jun, an interpreter working for the Japanese army information agency, took active pro-Japanese stances. Just before the conclusion of the Protectorate Treaty (November 1905), the Ilchinhoe suggested that Korean be put under the Japan's protectorate rule and mobilized Tonghak followers for supporting the Japanese military operations such as construction of the Seoul-Sinŭiju Railroad and transportation of the Japanese military supplies. In order to separate from the pro-Japanese Ilchinhoe, Son Pyŏng-hŭi created the Ch'ŏndogyo (Religion of Heavenly Way) in December 1905. Son immediately returned to Korea, and expelled Yi Yong-gu and sixty other leaders of the Ilchinhoe from his organization. Responding to Song's action, Yi Yong-gu and Song Pyŏng-jun created their own religious organization, the Sich'ŏn-gyo (Religion of Serving the Heaven). Although the Ilchinhoe contributed to the Japanese annexation of Korea, it was dissolved by the Japanese shortly after the annexation. See Kim Pyŏng-je, "Chinbohoe wa Ilchinhoe ŭi pihwa" ("Secret Story of the Chinbohoe and Ilchinhoe"), *Hyesŏng*, Jan. 1932, pp. 132-35 and *Tonga Ilbo*, 2 Jan. 1928, p. 3. The members of the Ilchinhoe helped the Japanese military policemen as guides and intelligence agents. In this context, the members of the Ilchinhoe were called the "running dog" ["*chugu*"] of the Japanese and became targets of anti-Japanese Korean patriots and *ŭibyŏng* fighters. See Kye Pong-u,

Kkum sog ŭi kkum, vol. 1, p. 130.

55. Kim Chŏng-ju [Kin Sei-tsū] ed., *Chōsen tōchi shiryō*, vol. 1, pp. 110, 312-14.

56. "Kukkyŏng chibang sich'al pongmyŏngsŏ," p. 225.

57. Kim Chŏng-ju [Kin Sei-tsū] ed., *Chōsen tōchi shiryō*, vol. 1, pp. 110, 312-14; Yun Chŏng-hŭi, "Kando kaech'ŏksa," pp. 21-22.

58. Ibid., pp. 155-56, 159-63.

59. Kim Chŏng-ju [Kin Sei-tsū] ed., *Chōsen tōchi shiryō*, vol. 1, vol. 1, pp. 164-65.

60. "Kukkyŏng chibang pongmyŏng sich'al pogosŏ," p. 234.

61. Kye Pong-u, *Kkum sog ŭi kkum*, vol. 1, pp. 143-44.

62. Kim Chŏng-ju [Kin Sei-tsū] ed., *Chōsen tōchi shiryō*, vol. 1, p. 117.

63. Ibid., pp. 117-19, 315-18, 414-15. Hyŏn was released by a special pardon after the Japanese annexation of Korea in September 1910, and resumed anti-Japanese activities with Chinese support.

64. Kim Chŏng-ju [Kin Sei-tsū] ed., *Chōsen tōchi shiryō*, vol. 1, pp. 150-53.

65. Lee Hoon-ku, *Manchu wa Chosŏnin*, pp. 95-96; Kim Chŏng-ju [Kin Sei-tsū] ed., *Chōsen tōchi shiryō*, vol. 1, pp. 177-228.

66. Kim Chŏng-ju [Kin Sei-tsū] ed., *Chōsen tōchi shiryō*, vol. 1, p. 387.

67. Ko Sŭng-je, *Hanguk iminsa yŏngu*, p. 26.

68. Kim Chŏng-ju [Kin Sei-tsū] ed., *Chōsen tōchi shiryō*, vol. 1, p. 348; Ki-hoon Kim, "Japanese Policy for Korean Rural Immigration to Manchuria, 1932-1945," p. 39.

69. Kim Chŏng-ju [Kin Sei-tsū] ed., *Chōsen tōchi shiryō*, vol. 1, p. 387.

70. Lee Hoon-ku, *Manchu wa Chosŏnin*, pp. 95-96; Ki-hoon Kim, "Japanese Policy for Korean Rural Immigration to Manchuria, 1932-1945," pp. 39-40. An English translation of the Agreement related to the Chientao region (September 4, 1909) can be found in John MacMurray's book, *Treaties and Agreements with and Concerning China, 1894-1919*, vol. 1 (New York and London: Oxford UP, 1921), pp. 796-97. The following description is based on John MacMurray's book.

71. Kim Chŏng-ju [Kin Sei-tsū] ed., *Chōsen tōchi shiryō*, vol. 1, p. 254.

72. Ki-hoon Kim, "Japanese Policy for Korean Rural Immigration to Manchuria, 1932-1945," pp. 40-41.

73. Japanese Government-General Office of Korea, *Chōsen no hogo kyū heigō [Protection and Annexation of Korea]*(Seoul: 1918), pp. 357-58; Nagano Akira, *Manshū mondai no jissō*, p. 76.

74. Department of State, *The Korean Minority in Manchuria* (Washington: Office of Intelligence Coordination and Liaison, 1946), pp. iii-iv.

75. "Extraterritoriality," Lasker Bruno ed., *Problems of the Pacific 1931: Proceedings of the Fourth Conference of the Institute of Pacific Relations, Hangchow and Shanghai, China*, October 21 to November 2 (Chicago: University of Chicago Press, 1932), pp. 287-88;

Nagano Akira, *Manshū mondai no jissō*, p. 76.

76. Department of State, *The Korean minority in Manchuria*, p. 12.

77. Pak Kyŏng-sik, *Nippon Teikokushūgi no Chōsen shihai* [The Rule of Japanese Imperialism in Korea], vol. 1 (Tokyo: Aoki Shoten, 1973), pp. 57-59. Accoring to Chong-sik Lee, the number of Japanese in Korea was as follows. 1905 — 42,460, 1910 — 171,543, 1918 — 336,812. See Chong-sik Lee, *The Politics of Korean Nationalism* (Berkeley and Los Angeles: U of California, 1965), p. 95.

78. Pak Kyŏng-sik, *Nippon Teikokushūgi no Chōsen shihai*, pp. 92-99.

79. Tokōkai, *Chōsen minjō shisatsu hōkoku* [Report of Observations on the Condition of Korean People] (Tokyo: 1923), 10. Quoted from Pak Kyŏng-sik, *Nippon Teikokushūgi no Chōsen shihai*, p. 91.

80. A Japanese report recorded that all 17,779 anti-Japanese *ŭibyŏng* fighters were killed, 3,706 were injured and 2,139 were arrested by the Japanese army during the period from 1906 to the end of 1909. See Pak Kyŏng-sik, *Nippon Teikokushūgi no Chōsen shihai*, p. 166. According to another source, during the 6 year period from 1906 through 1911, the total number of battles between Korean *ŭibyŏng* troops and the Japanese regular army reached 2,800 with the participation of about 140,000 *ŭibyŏng* fighters. Among them, about 50,000 were killed or injured. See Kang Man-gil, *Koch'ŏssŭn Hanguk Kŭndaesa* [Revised Modern History of Korea] (Seoul: Ch'angjak kwa Pip'yŏngsa, 1994), p. 230.

81. Ki-hoon Kim, "Japanese Policy for Korean Rural Immigration to Manchuria, 1932-1945," p. 44.

82. According to a report of the Department of State in 1946, half of the Koreans were living in Chientao and the other half were scattered throughout other parts of Manchuria. Koreans formed only about 3 percent of the total population in Manchuria, but in Chientao, they constituted almost three-quarters of the population in this province. See Department of State, *The Korean Minority in Manchuria*, p. iii.

83. Department of State, *The Korean Minority in Manchuria*, p. 6.

84. Hyŏn Kyu-hwan, *Hanguk yuiminsa,* pp. 776-77.

85. Edward D. Sokol, "Ussuri Cossack Host," Joseph L. Wieczynski ed., *The Modern Encyclopedia of Russian and Soviet History* (Academic International Press, 1978), vol. 41, p. 135; Haruki Wada, "Koreans in the Soviet Far East, 1917-1937," *Koreans in the Soviet Union*, Dae-sook Suh ed., (Honolulu: Center for Korean Studies, University of Hawaii at Manoa, 1987), p. 25. At the time of the Aihun and Beijing Treaties, there were 105,000 Chinese, in the Amur and 2,000-3,000 in the Primorye. See V. V. Grave, *Kitaitsy, Koreitsy i Iapontsy v Priamur'e* [Chinese, Koreans and Japanese in the Priamur] (St. Petersburg: V. F. Grishbaum, 1912), p. 5.

86. V. V. Grave, *Koreitsy i Iapontsy v Priamur'e*, p. 128. Based on the report of Russian

Lieutenant Rezanov, all Russian historical materials recorded that for the first time in 1863 thirteen Korean families emigrated to Tizinkhe region. An article dated February 26, 1908, of the *Haejo Sinmun*, a Korean newspaper published in Vladivostok, also agreed with those records. However, the author of the article certainly confused the date by saying "The year of 1863 in the Western Calendar is the year of *kapcha* in the lunar calendar. At this time, more than ten families of our brethren, for the first time, crossed to Tizinkhe in Russia and cultivated the wild lands. . . ." The year of Kapcha is 1864. See Ch'oe Pong-jun, "Palganhanŭn mal" ("Words for Publishing") in *Haejo Sinmun*, 26 Feb. 1908. Since then, Koreans in Russia came to memorize the year of *kapcha* as the year of the first Korean emigration to Russia. Accordingly, as we will see in Chapter 2, in 1914, the Koreans in the Primorye prepared an unsuccessful ceremony for the fiftieth anniversary of Korean emigration to Korea. Later, based on materials prepared for the 50th anniversary of Korean emigration to Russia in 1914, Kye Pong-u in his article, wrote that Korean emigration started with two Koreans, Ch'oe Un-bo (from Musan) and Yang Ŭng-bŏm (from Kyŏnghŭng) who colonized the land in Tizinkhe in the winter of 1864. Kye Pong-u's argument is now widely accepted by South Korean scholars. See Twibabo [Kye Pong-u], "Aryŏng silgi (1)" [Real Record of (Koreans) in Russian Territory], *Tongnip Sinmun*, 1 Mar. 1920, p. 8 and *Kwŏnŏp Sinmun*, 2 Aug. 1914, p. 3. A Japanese official report wrote that thirteen Korean families crossed Tumen River for the first time in 1862. See Japanese government, Ministry of Foreign Affairs, *Archives in the Japanese Ministry of Foreign Affairs* (hereafter cited as AJMFA), MT1148, 3.

87. Twibabo, "Aryŏng silgi (1)," *Tongnip Sinmun*, 1 Mar. 1920, p. 8.
88. Boris Dmitrievich Pak, *Koreitsy v Rossiiskoi imperii: Dal'nevostochnyi period* [*Koreans in the Russian Empire (Far Eastern Period)*] (Moscow: Mezhdunarodnyi Tsentr Koreevedeniia Moskovskogo Gosudarstvennogo Universiteta, 1983), pp. 19-20.
89. Boris Dmitrievich Pak, *Koreitsy v Rossiiskoi imperii*, pp. 19-20.
90. Twibabo, "Aryŏng silgi (1)," *Tongnip Sinmun*, 1 Mar. 1920, p. 8. In the conflict, a soldier was killed and a old woman and a girl were arrested.
91. Ibid., p. 8. Ch'oe Un-bo was one of the two Koreans who had led the first group of Korean farmers to Tizinkhe in 1863.
92. V. V. Grave, *Kitaitsy, Koreitsy i Iapontsy v Priamur'e*, p. 129; *Sinhan Minbo*, 9 Jun. 1909, p. 1.
93. AJMFA, MT1148, 4. According to V. V. Grave, 165 families settled in Pos'et region. See Ibid., p. 128.
94. The Korean government decapitated four of the border-crossing criminals and displayed their heads to the public two times in 1864 and 1867. See Hyŏn Kyu-hwan, *Hanguk yuiminsa,* p. 777.
95. Semen Davidovich Anosov, *Koreitsy v Ussuriiskom krae* [Koreans in the Ussurisk

Region] (Khabarovsk and Vladivostok: Knizhnoe Delo, 1928), p. 9.

96. Twibabo, "Aryŏng silgi (1)," *Tongnip Sinmun*, 1 Mar. 1920, p. 8.

97. Ibid., p. 8. Particularly in Kyŏnghŭng, 96 families decided to cross the river in fear of the rumor that local officials would investigate the people in Kyŏnghŭng who had privately taken commodities from an American ship which had been wrecked in Ungi Bay, North Hamgyŏng Province.

98. AJMFA, MT1148, 5. According to Boris Pak, 6,543 persons (3,533 males and 3,010 females) crossed the border to Ussurisk *krai* in 1869. See Boris Dmitrievich Pak, *Koreitsy v Rossiiskoi imperii*, p. 30.

99. Boris Dmitrievich Pak, *Koreitsy v Rossiiskoi imperii*, p. 30.

100. J. F. Bishop [Isabella L. Bird], *Korea and Her Neighbors: A Narrative of Travel, with an Account of the Recent Vicissitudes and Present Position of the Country*, vol. 2 (London: John Murray, 1898), p. 14.

101. Ch'oe Pong-jun, "Palganhanŭn mal," *Haejo Sinmun*, 26 Feb. 1908, p. 2. In 1870, Russian authorities helped new Korean emigrants survive by delivering three baskets per person. Although the Russian authorities in August of that year retrieved the grain which they had delivered to Koreans, thanks to a rich harvest the first year, the Koreans were able to survive. See "Pon saju Ch'oe Pong-jun kong yŏksa" [History of the Owner of This Company, Honorable Ch'oe Pong-jun], *Haejo Sinmun*, 26 Mar. 1908, p. 1.

102. Syn Khva Kim, *Ocherki po istorii sovetskikh koreitsev* [Essays on the History of Soviet Koreans] (Alma Ata: Nauka, 1965), pp. 29-30; Boris Dmitrievich Pak, *Koreitsy v Rossiiskoi imperii*, pp. 32-33.

103. Boris Dmitrievich Pak, *Koreitsy v Rossiiskoi imperii*, p. 34.

104. AJMFA, MT1148, 5-6; Syn Khva Kim, *Ocherki po istorii sovetskikh koreitsev*, p. 30; Boris Dmitrievich Pak, *Koreitsy v Rossiiskoi imperii*, p. 30.

105. Semen Davidovich Anosov, *Koreitsy v Ussuriiskom krae*, p. 9; Boris Dmitrievich Pak, *Koreitsy v Rossiiskoi imperii*, p. 44.

106. V. V. Grave, *Kitaitsy, Koreitsy i Iapontsy v Priamur'e*, p. 129; AJMFA, MT1148, 6-7; Semen Davidovich Anosov, *Koreitsy v Ussuriiskom krae*, p. 9; Kim Se-yong, "Sŏbaengnia ŭi Chosŏnin hwaltong" [The Activities of Koreans in Siberia], *Samchŏlli* Oct. 1930, p. 3; Boris Dmitrievich Pak, *Koreitsy v Rossiiskoi imperii*, p. 39; Syn Khva Kim, *Ocherki po istorii sovetskikh koreitsev*, p. 31. Because of the expense, this experiment was not repeated later. See Semen Davidovich Anosov, *Koreitsy v Ussuriiskom krae*, p. 9.

107. V. V. Grave, *Kitaitsy, Koreitsy i Iapontsy v Priamur'e*, p. 129.

108. Boris Dmitrievich Pak, *Koreitsy v Rossiiskoi imperii*, p. 29.

109. Ibid., pp. 44, 47-48. Koreans named geographic places in the Far East and Siberia using Korean characters similar to the Russian pronunciation or borrowed Chinese names. For example, Tizinkhe: Chisinhŏ, Pos'et: Mokhŏu, Vladivostok: Haesamwi, Suifen:

Ch'up'ung or Songwangnyŏng, Suchan: Such'ŏng, Khabarovsk: Hwabalp'o, Blagoslovennoe: Samalli, Blagoveshchensk: Bulgaemisk, Chita: Chŏkt'ap, Tomsk: Toumch'i etc.

110. Din'shun' Pak, "Koreiskaia emigratsiia v Rossii"; AJMFA, MT1148, 3-4.

111. Andrew Malozemoff, *Russian Far Eastern Policy 1881-1904: with Special Emphasis on the Cause of the Russo-Japanese War* (New York: Octagon Books, 1977), pp. 1-10.

112. Semen Davidovich Anosov, *Koreitsy v Ussuriiskom krae*, pp. 5-6.

113. John J. Stephan, *The Russian Far East: A History* (Stanford: Stanford UP, 1994), p. 73; Andrew Malozemoff, *Russian Far Eastern Policy 1881-1904*, p. 5.

114. The Geographical Section of the Naval Intelligence Division, Naval Staff, Admiralty, *A Handbook of Siberia and Arctic Russia*, vol. 1 (London: His Majesty's Stationary Office, 1914), p. 210.

115. Semen Davidovich Anosov, *Koreitsy v Ussuriiskom krae*, p. 7.

116. Andrew Malozemoff, *Russian Far Eastern Policy 1881-1904*, pp. 22-26.

117. The Geographical Section of the Naval Intelligence Division, *A Handbook of Siberia and Arctic Russia*, p. 211.

118. P. F. Unterberger, *Primorskaia Oblast'. 1856-1898 gg.* [Primore Oblast, 1856-1898] (St. Petersburg: V. F. Kirshbauma, 1900), p. 265.

119. The Geographical Section of the Naval Intelligence Division, *A Handbook of Siberia and Arctic Russia*, pp. 204-205; Andrew Malozemoff, *Russian Far Eastern Policy 1881-1904*, p. 13; John J. Stephan, *The Russian Far East: A History*, p. 65.

120. John J. Stephan, *The Russian Far East: A History*, p. 65; Semen Davidovich Anosov, *Koreitsy v Ussuriiskom krae*, p. 6.

121. Derber Petr Iakovlevich and Sher M. L., *Ocherki Khazaistvennoi Zhizni Dal'nego Vostoka* [Essays on Agricultural Life of the Far East] (Moscow and Leningrad: Gosudarstvennoe Izdatel'stvo, 1927), p. 30.

122. V. V. Grave, *Kitaitsy, Koreitsy i Iapontsy v Priamur'e*, pp. 129-30.

123. Andrew Malozemoff, *Russian Far Eastern Policy 1881-1904*, p. 25.

124. Semen Davidovich Anosov, *Koreitsy v Ussuriiskom krae*, p. 10.

125. "Kangdong swinhae" [Fifty Years (of Koreans) in the Primorye], *Hanin Sinbo*, 23, Sep. 1917, p. 3. All the Koreans were opposed to the order of Russian authorities to leave their village, but they were beaten and their houses were set on fire by Russian police. 2,600 Koreans from 270 households were immediately relocated to uncultivated lands in the Taubikhe (currently Anuchino) region. The name of the village, "Nasŏn" originates from the amalgamation of the names of two pre-modern Korean kingdoms, "Silla" (BCE 57-CE 935) and "Chosŏn" (CE 1392-1910).

126. AJMFA, MT1148, 12.

127. "Kangdong swinhae," *Hanin Sinbo*, 23 Sep. 1917, p. 3.

128. Ibid., p. 3; Ibid., 30 Sep. 1917, p. 3. According to a Japanese report, 8,514 of the total Korean population of 13,880 were living in the Pos'et region. See AJMFA, MT1148, 17.

129. Twibabo, "Aryŏng silgi (8)," *Tongnip Sinmun*, 25 Mar. 1920, p. 1; J. F. Bishop, *Korea and Her Neighbors: A Narrative of Travel, with an Account of the Recent Vicissitudes and Present Position of the Country*, vol. 1, p. 15.

130. Twibabo, "Aryŏng silgi (8)," *Tongnip Sinmun*, 25 Mar. 1920, p. 1; Hwang Uk, "Chae oe kak chibang sanghwang: Sojaha chibang chŏnghwang" [Situation of Every Region Abroad: Sojaha Region], *Tongnip Sinmun*, 4 Apr. 1923, p. 4.

131. Boris Dmitrievich Pak, *Koreitsy v Rossiiskoi imperii*, pp. 72-74. An English translation of the Regulations can be seen in Great Britain Foreign Office ed., *British and Foreign State Papers*, vol. LXXIX (1887-1888) (London), pp. 634-41.

132. Great Britain Foreign Office ed., *British and Foreign State Papers*, vol. LXXIX (1887-1888), p. 636.

133. Semen Davidovich Anosov, *Koreitsy v Ussuriiskom krae*, p. 10; Boris Dmitrievich Pak, *Koreitsy v Rossiiskoi imperii*, p. 78.

134. Semen Davidovich Anosov, *Koreitsy v Ussuriiskom krae*, p. 11.

135. V. V. Grave, *Kitaitsy, Koreitsy i Iapontsy v Priamur'e*, pp. 131-32.

136. The Geographical Section of the Naval Intelligence Division, *A Handbook of Siberia and Arctic Russia*, p. 211.

137. V. V. Grave, *Kitaitsy, Koreitsy i Iapontsy v Priamur'e*, p. 131; Boris Dmitrievich Pak, *Koreitsy v Rossiiskoi imperii*, p. 76.

138. V. V. Grave, *Kitaitsy, Koreitsy i Iapontsy v Priamur'e*, p. 131; Semen Davidovich Anosov, *Koreitsy v Ussuriiskom krae*, pp. 9-10; AJMFA, MT1148, 7-10. Many records and studies incorrectly wrote that the rule for the three well-known categories regarding Korean migrants in Russia was agreed upon between Russia and Korea in the Treaty of 1884. See Hyŏn Kyu-hwan, *Hanguk yuiminsa,* pp. 779-80; Mazolemoff; AJMFA, MT1148, 7-10; The Geographical Section of the Naval Intelligence Division, *A Handbook of Siberia and Arctic Russia*, p. 211.

139. *Taedong Kongbo*, 24 Mar. 1909, p. 3.

140. Boris Dmitrievich Pak, *Koreitsy v Rossiiskoi imperii*, pp. 78-79.

141. V. V. Grave, *Kitaitsy, Koreitsy i Iapontsy v Priamur'e*, p. 132.

142. Ibid., p. 132; Din'shun' Pak, "Koreiskaia emigratsiia v Rossii"; Semen Davidovich Anosov, *Koreitsy v Ussuriiskom krae*, p. 10.

143. Ch'oe Pong-jun, "Palganhanŭn mal," *Haejo Sinmun*, 26 Feb. 1908, p. 2; "Kangdong swinhae," *Hanin Sinbo*, 30 Sep. 1917, p. 3; *Taedong Kongbo*, 20 Mar. 1909, p. 3. According to the census of 1895, number of the Koreans in the Primore was as follows: first category — 11,311; second category — 2,400; third category — 3,000. See

Boris Dmitrievich Pak, *Koreitsy v Rossiiskoi imperii*, p. 83 and Haruki Wada, "Koreans in the Soviet Far East, 1917-1937," p. 27.

144. AJMFA, MT1148, 10; Semen Davidovich Anosov, *Koreitsy v Ussuriiskom krae*, p. 10. A male Russian received 100 *desiatins* until 1901 when the Russian government reduced the allotment of land to 15 *desiatins* per male. See *Taedong Kongbo*, 24 Mar. 1909, p. 3.

145. V. V. Grave, *Kitaitsy, Koreitsy i Iapontsy v Priamur'e*, p. 132; AJMFA, MT1148, 14; Semen Davidovich Anosov, *Koreitsy v Ussuriiskom krae*, p. 10.

146. Davidovich Anosov, *Koreitsy v Ussuriiskom krae*, p. 10.

147. V. V. Grave, *Kitaitsy, Koreitsy i Iapontsy v Priamur'e*, p. 132; AJMFA, MT1148, 17; Davidovich Anosov, *Koreitsy v Ussuriiskom krae*, p. 10.

148. AJMFA, MT1148, 19-20.

149. Kim Se-yong, "Sŏbaengnia ŭi Chosŏnin hwaltong," p. 3.

150. As we will see later, Koreans who obtained Russian citizenship thanks to the policy of Governor-General Gondatti in the early 1910s were not called *wŏnhoin*, but *yŏhoin*. *Wŏnhoin* and *yŏhoin* [yuhoin] seem to have been borrowed from the Russian words (Starozhily, long time settler) and *novosyoly* (new settler). According to a new law decreed on June 22, 1900, the Russian government abolished the allotment of 100 *desiatin*s for Russian migrator and after 1901, 15 *desiatin*s of land were allotted to Russian males. These new types of Russian settlers were called *novosyoly*. See V. V. Grave, *Kitaitsy, Koreitsy i Iapontsy v Priamur'e*, p. 7; Haruki Wada, "Koreans in the Soviet Far East, 1917-1937," p. 28 and Syn Khva Kim, *Ocherki po istorii sovetskikh koreitsev*, p. 44.

151. Kye Pong-u, *Kkum sog ŭi kkum*, vol. 1, p. 166; "Chosŏn oe esŏ ŭi Chosŏnin sanghwang ilban," p. 483. The *yŏhoin* paid 40-60% of the harvest to landowners, the same as Korean tenants in Korea, but the fertile land and land availability provided better lives than in Korea. See Kim Se-yong, "Sŏbaengnia ŭi Chosŏnin hwaltong," pp. 3-4.

152. KHM, "Noryŏng Chosŏnin nongch'on chŏnghyŏng ŭi kŭmsŏk [Present and Past of the Situation of Korean Agricultural Villages in Russian Territory], *Kaebyŏk*, 61, Jul. 1925, p. 100.

153. Pak Yŏng-gap, "Aryŏng Osori Such'ŏng yangnon (2)" [Brief Review of Suchan in Ussurisk, Russian Territory], *Sinhan Minbo*, 20 July 1910, p. 3; Chi Kŏn, "Na ŭi ilgŭi (2)" [My Diary], *Hanin Sinbo*, 13 Jan. 1918, p. 3; Kang Ho-yŏ, "Such'ŏng ŭibyŏngdae ŭi yŏnhyŏk" [The History of the Partisan Unit in Suchan], Yi In-sŏp ed., *Nŭrgŭn ppalchisan dŭl ŭi hoesanggi* [Recollections of the Old Partisans] ms., 1964-1965, p. 16.

154. Bishop, *Korea and Her Neighbors: A Narrative of Travel, with an Account of the Recent Vicissitudes and Present Position of the Country*, vol. 2, pp. 4-10, 15-19, 137.

155. "Kangdong swinhae," *Hanin Sinbo*, 23 Sep. 1917, p. 3; 30 Sep. 1917, p. 3: 7 Oct. 1917, p. 3; *Sinhan Minbo*, 11 Jul. 1918, p. 4; Twibabo, "Aryŏng silgi (5)," *Tongnip Sinmun*, 13 Mar. 1920, p. 3. Well-known Korean *podriadchiks* were Han Ik-sŏng in Tizinkhe, Ch'ae Tu-sŏng in Pos'et, Mun Ch'ang-bŏm in Nikol'sk-Ussurisk, Ch'oe Pong-jun and Kim Pyŏng-hak in Vladivostok, Kim Tu-sŏ, Chŏn T'ae-guk, and Yi In-baek in Khabarovsk.

156. "Kandong swinhae," *Hanin Sinbo*, 30 Sep. 1917, p. 3. All 52 Koreans went to Seoul as interpreters for Russians. Among them, Kim Hong-nyuk was a well-known figure who started his career as an interpreter for the Russian Consulate and later became the Minister of the Privy Council.

157. "Kandong swinhae," *Hanin Sinbo*, 30 Sep. 1917, p. 3.

158. AJMFA, MT1148, 17-19, 28.

159. Ibid., 28.

160. Derber Petr Iakovlevich and Sher M. L., *Ocherki Khazaistvennoi Zhizni Dal'nego Vostoka*, pp. 30-31.

161. Derber and Sher 30-31. The number of the Russian migrants to Priamur from 1909 to 1914 were as follows: 1909 — 37,081; 1910 — 39,903; 1911 — 20,894; 1912 — 20,658; 1913 — 18,200; 1914 — 26,076.

162. AJMFA, MT1148, 30-32.

163. Unterberger, *Primorskaia oblast' 1856-1898*, pp. 114-15. See also Semen Davidovich Anosov, *Koreitsy v Ussuriiskom krae*, p. 12; V. V. Grave, *Kitaitsy, Koreitsy i Iapontsy v Priamur'e*, p. 135; Haruki Wada, "Koreans in the Soviet Far East, 1917-1937," p. 29.

164. Semen Davidovich Anosov, *Koreitsy v Ussuriiskom krae*, p. 12; V. V. Grave, *Kitaitsy, Koreitsy i Iapontsy v Priamur'e*, pp. 134-35; Haruki Wada, "Koreans in the Soviet Far East, 1917-1937," p. 29.

165. Semen Davidovich Anosov, *Koreitsy v Ussuriiskom krae*, p. 13; V. V. Grave, *Kitaitsy, Koreitsy i Iapontsy v Priamur'e*, p. 136.

166. *Sinhan Minbo*, 9 Jun. 1909, p. 1; AJMFA, MT1148, 32.

167. Din'shun' Pak, "Koreiskaia emigratsiia v Rossii."

168. AJMFA, MT1148, 33, 58.

169. Ibid., 76.

170. AJMFA, MT1148, 148; G. A. Tkachev, "Immigratsiia na Dal'nem Vostoke Rossii v 20-e-30e gody" [Immigrations in the Russian Far East in the 1920-30s] (Unpublished paper, 1994), p. 1.

171. AJMFA, MT1148, 66-67.

172. John J. Stephan, *The Russian Far East: A History*, p. 318.

173. Semen Davidovich Anosov, *Koreitsy v Ussuriiskom krae*, p. 10.

174. Governor-General Gondatti told Japanese Consul-General Otori Fujitarō in Vladivostok on October 31, 1911: "Originally, Koreans are mild people and good peasants. In addition, there are extremely few crimes. In comparison, there are many criminals among the Chinese. I will expel Chinese laborers and will recruit Koreans instead, and I will soon provide Koreans with lands near gold mines." See AJMFA, MT1148, 194-197.

175. AJMFA, MT1148, 123-124.

176. Ibid., 127-128.

177. AJMFA, MT1148, 127-128; 162-163.

178. Ibid., 126-127.

179. AJMFA, MT1148, 122.

180. Ibid., 148.

181. AJMFA, MT1148, 143-146.

182. Responding to the inquiries of the Japanese Consul-General in Vladivostok, the Russian Governor-General Office of the Priamur, in October of 1912, replied, "After the annexation, there is no revision or abolishment in laws with regard to the Koreans." See AJMFA, MT1148, 215-216 and Hara Teruyuki, "The Korean Movement in the Russian Maritime Province, 1905-1922," Dae-sook Suh ed., *Koreans in the Soviet Union* (Honolulu: Center for Korean Studies, University of Hawai'i at Manoa, 1987), p. 5.

183. Hara Teruyuki, "The Korean Movement in the Russian Maritime Province, 1905-1922," p. 5.

184. Ivan Gozhenskii, "Uchastie Koreiskii emigratsii v revoliutsionnom dvizhenii na Dal'nem Vostoke" [The Participation of the Koreans in the Revolutionary Movement in the Far East], Kommissiia po Istorii Oktiabryskoi Revoliutsii i R. K. P ed., *Revoliutsiia na Dal'em Vostoke*, vol. 1 (Moscow and Petrograd: Gosudarstvennoe Izdatel'stvo, 1923), p. 359.

185. AJMFA, MT1148, 207-208.

186. Ibid., 192-193. Through the appeals of the Korean nationalist organization, the Kwŏnŏphoe, the Russian authorities stopped expelling the Koreans in the Pos'et emigration area until after the Koreans finished the harvest that year. See *Kwŏnŏp Sinmun*, 21 Jul. 1912, p. 3.

187. *Kwŏnŏp Sinmun*, 4 Aug. 1912, p. 3.

188. "Kangdong swinhae," *Hanin Sinbo*, 7 Oct. 1917, p. 3.

189. "Chosŏn oe esŏ ŭi Chosŏnin sanghwang ilban," p. 474.

190. AJMFA, MT1148, 23-24.

191. Ibid., 22-24.

192. Kim Se-yong, "Sŏbaengnia ŭi Chosŏnin hwaltong," p. 3.

193. Din'shun' Pak, "Koreiskaia emigratsiia v Rossii."

194. Boris Dmitrievich Pak, *Koreitsy v Rossiiskoi imperii*, pp. 104-105.
195. "Chosŏn oe esŏ ŭi Chosŏnin sanghwang ilban," pp. 474-75, 481.
196. Ibid., p. 478.
197. G. A. Tkachev, "Immigratsiia na Dal'nem Vostoke Rossii v 20-e-30e gody," p. 3.
198. Ibid.

Chapter Two

1. Pak Ŭn-sik, *Hanguk tongnip undong chi hyŏlsa* [Bloody History of Korean Independence Movement] (Seoul: Seoul Sinmunsa Ch'ulp'anguk, 1946), p. 3.
2. Chong-sik Lee, *The Politics of Korean Nationalism* (Berkeley and Los Angeles: University of California, 1965), p. 16.
3. Most Korean scholars have explained these Korean nationalist movements in late 19th century by dividing them into three movements of *wijŏng ch'ŏksa* (defend orthodoxy, ban heterodoxy) led by Confucian scholars, the *kaehwa* (enlightenment) led by enlightened government officials and peasants' Tonghak (Eastern Learning). For a summary of ideologies of these movements, see Li Kwang-rin, "The Rise of Nationalism in Korea," *Korean Studies*, 10, 1986, pp. 1-12.
4. *Sunjong kukchannok* [Record of the National Funeral for King Sunjong] (Seoul: n. p., 1926), pp. 56-57.
5. *Sinhan Minbo*, 6 Sep. 1917, p. 1. Kang Chae-ŏn's article provides a good reference for the theories on "base for Korean independence movement" elaborated by Yu In-sŏk and Yi Sang-yong, leaders of *ŭibyŏng* military units and cultural-educational movement respectively. See Kang Chae-ŏn, "Chōsen dokuritsu undō no konkyochi mondai" [The Question of Bases for Korean Independence Movement], *Chōsen Minjoku Dokuritsu Undōshi Kenkyū*, 1, Jan. 1984, pp. 9-68.
6. Ch'osa, "Ilse rŭl kyŏngdong sikidŭn k'woegŏl Yi Yong-ik ŭi kusim man wŏn sakŏn" [Nine Hundred Thousand Wŏn Case of Unusual Hero, Yi Yong-ik Who Had Startled a World], *Samch'ŏlli*, Sep. 1930, pp. 18-20; Yu Cha-hu, *Chosŏn hwap'ye go* [Study on the Currency of Korea] (Seoul: Hagyesa, 1940), pp. 782-88.
7. Hirose Teizō, "Li Yoyok no seiji katsudō (1904-7) ni tsuite: sono gaikō katsudō o tsūsin ni" [Concerning Political Activities of Yi Yong-ik (1904-7): Focusing on His Diplomatic Activities], *Chōsenshi Kenkyūkai Ronbunshū*, 25, Mar. 1988, pp. 83-86.
8. Ch'osa, "Ilse rŭl kyŏngdong sikidŭn k'woegŏl Yi Yong-ik ŭi kusim man wŏn sakŏn," p. 20; Kuksa P'yŏnch'an Wiwŏnhoe ed., *Han'guk tongnip undongsa charyo* [The History of the Korean Independence Movement: Source Materials], vol. 8 (Seoul: Kuksa P'yŏnch'an Wiwŏnhoe, 1983), p. 74 (hereafter will be cited as *Kukp'yŏn charyo*).
9. Yu Cha-hu, *Yi Chun sŏngsaeng chŏn* [Biography of Mr. Yi Chu] (Seoul: Tongbang Munhwasa, 1957), p. 290.

10. Kye Pong-u, *Kkum sog ŭi kkum*, vol. 1, p. 150; *Zaigai hainichi Senjin yuryokusha meibo* [Register of Influential Anti-Japanese Koreans] ms., 1919, p. 16.

11. AJMFA, MT16116, 211-223.

12. Ibid., 224-226; Hirose Teizō, "Li Yoyok no seiji katsudō (1904-7) ni tsuite: sono gaikō katsudō o tsūssin ni," p. 98.

13. AJMFA, MT16116, 234; Hirose Teizō, "Li Yoyok no seiji katsudō (1904-7) ni tsuite: sono gaiko katsudō o tsūssin ni," p. 98.

14. AJMFA, MT16116, 235-236; Hirose Teizō, "Li Yoyok no seiji katsudō (1904-7) ni tsuite: sono gaikō katsudō o tsūssin ni," p. 98.

15. Yu Cha-hu, *Yi Chun sŏnsaeng chŏn*, pp. 263-30.

16. Hirose Teizō, "Li Yoyok no seiji katsudō (1904-7) ni tsuite: sono gaikō katsudō o tsūssin ni," p. 100.

17. Yun Pyŏng-sŏk, *Yi Sang-sŏl chŏn* [Biography of Yi Sang-sŏl] (Seoul: Ilchogak, 1984) p. 57.

18. Yun Chŏng-hŭi, "Kando kaech'ŏksa," pp. 20-21.

19. "Yi Chun kong i p'ihŭlin nal" [The Day When Honorable Yi Chun Bled], *Kwŏnŏp Sinmun*, 19 Jul. 1914, p. 1.

20. Yu Cha-hu, *Yi Chun sŏnsaeng chŏn*, pp. 345-46.

21. "Kangdong swinhae," *Hanin Sinbo*, 7, Oct. 1917, p. 3.

22. *Sunjong kukchangnok*, pp. 57-60.

23. *Kongnip Sinbo*, 16 Aug. 1907, p. 1.

24. *Zaigai hainichi Senjin yuryokusha meibo*, p. 23; "Kangdong swinhae," *Hanin Sinbo*, 7 Oct. 1917, p. 3; Boris Dmitrievich Pak, *Koreitsy v Rossiiskoi imperii*, p. 165.

25. Boris Dmitrievich Pak, *Koreitsy v Rossiiskoi imperii*, p. 165.

26. *Zaigai hainichi Senjin yuryokusha meibo*, p. 23.

27. *Kukp'yŏn charyo*, vol. 7, p. 281.

28. *Zaigai hainichi Senjin yuryokusha meibo*, 25; *Kukp'yŏn charyo*, vol. 7, p. 280. A Korean word, "Pijikkae" is thought to come from "Petia," the pet name of Ch'oe Chae-hyŏng' [Pyotr Semyniovich]. "Pijikkae" means "the match." There is another view that "pijikkae" is the Korean pronunciation of "pechka," a Russian brick stove. "Match" or "Pechka" implied that Ch'oe Chae-hyŏng was a warm and inclusive figure who enjoyed wide popularity among Koreans.

29. *Kukp'yŏn charyo*, vol. 13, pp. 467-68.

30. "Zaiavlenie" [Statement], Boris Dmitrievich Pak, *Koreitsy v Rossiiskoi imperii*, pp. 198-99; *Kukp'yŏn charyo*, vol. 12, p. 258. About 10,000 rubles were collected only in the Suchan region in 1907. See Boris Dmitrievich Pak, *Koreitsy v Rossiiskoi imperii*, p. 166.

31. *Kukp'yŏn charyo*, vol. 12, p. 258; "Li Pŏm-yun kwa *ŭibyŏng*" [Yi Pŏm-yun and

Righteous Soldier], *Sinhan Minbo*, 25 May 1910, p. 1. In the summer of 1907, Yi Pŏm-yun dispatched two of his associates to Seoul in order to get King Kojong's authorization to lead the anti-Japanese activities among Koreans residing in the Primorye. We cannot confirm whether Yi Pŏm-yun got King Kojong's authorization, but Yi continuously utilized the authority King Kojong had given to him previously.

32. Yi Chun died shortly after the Conference as a result of frustration over the failure his delegation's mission in the Hague.
33. "Kangdong swinhae," *Hanin Sinbo*, 7 Oct. 1917, p. 3.
34. Tansŏn [Kye Pong-u], "Mango ŭisa An Chung-gŭn chŏn (10)" [Biography of Permanent Righteous Person, An Chung-gŭn], *Kwŏnŏp Sinmun*, 29 Aug. 1914, p. 3.
35. Tansŏn, "Mango ŭisa An Chung-gŭn chŏn (10)," *Kwŏnŏp Sinmun*, 29 Aug. 1914, p. 3; *Kukp'yŏn charyo*, vol. 7, pp. 225, 437; Boris Dmitrievich Pak, *Koreitsy v Rossiiskoi imperii*, p. 167.
36. *Kukp'yŏn charyo*, vol. 7, p. 437.
37. "Tongŭihoe ch'wijisŏ" [Prospectus of the Tongŭihoe], *Haejo Sinmun*, 10 May 1908, p. 1; *Kukp'yŏn charyo*, vol. 7, p. 257; Tansŏn, "Mango ŭisa An Chung-gŭn chŏn (10)," *Kwŏnŏp Sinmun*, 29 Aug. 1914, p. 3: Pak Min-yŏng, "Kuhanmal sŏbuk pyŏngyŏng chiyŏk ŭi ŭibyŏng yŏngu" [Study on the Righteous Army in Northwestern Border Region in Late Chosŏn Dynasty] (diss. Hanguk Chŏngsin Munhwa Yŏnguwŏn Hangukhak Taehakwŏn, 1995), pp. 280-82.
38. *Kukp'yŏn charyo*, vol. 7, pp. 257, 280, 285.
39. Kuksa P'yŏnch'an Wiwŏnhoe, *Hanguk tongnip undongsa*, 2nd ed., vol. 1 (Seoul: Chŏngŭm Munhwasa, 1983), p. 982.
40. *Kukp'yŏn charyo*, vol. 7, p. 281.
41. *Haejo sinmun*, 10 May 1908: 19 May 1908: 23 May 1908.
42. *Zaigai hainichi Senjin yuryokusha meibo*, p. 25.
43. *Kukp'yŏn charyo*, vol. 18, p. 418.
44. Ibid., vol. 7, p. 257.
45. *Kukp'yŏn charyo*, vol. 7, p. 437.
46. Ibid., p. 222.
47. Boris Dmitrievich Pak, *Koreitsy v Rossiiskoi imperii*, p. 167.
48. *Kukp'yŏn charyo*, vol. 11, p. 180.
49. Boris Dmitrievich Pak, *Koreitsy v Rossiiskoi imperii*, pp. 167-70.
50. *Kukp'yŏn charyo*, vol. 12, pp. 638-39.
51. Ibid., vol. 11, pp. 460-61.
52. *Kukp'yŏn charyo*, vol. 11, p. 461.
53. Tansŏn, "Mango ŭisa An Chung-gŭn chŏn (10)," *Kwŏnŏp Sinmun*, 29 Aug. 1914, p. 3

54. *Kukp'yŏn charyo*, vol. 7, pp. 434-36; Kim Chŏng-ju [Kin Sei-tsū] ed., *Chōsen tōchi shiryō*, vol. 1, pp. 119-20.

55. Boris Dmitrievich Pak, *Koreitsy v Rossiiskoi imperii*, p. 169; Pak Min-yŏng, "Kuhanmal sŏbuk pyŏngyŏng chiyŏk ŭi ŭibyŏng yŏngu," pp. 256-61.

56. Boris Dmitrievich Pak, *Koreitsy v Rossiiskoi imperii*, p. 169.

57. *Kongnip Sinbo*, 9 Sep. 1908, p. 1; S. S. Grigortsevich, "Uchastie koreitsev russkogo Dal'nevo Vostoka v antiiaponskoi natsional'no-osvoboditel'noi bor'be (1906-1916)" [Participation of Koreans in the Russian Far East in the Anti-Japanese National Liberation Struggle (1906-1916)], *Voprosy Istorii*, 10 (1958), pp. 144-45; Boris Dmitrievich Pak, *Koreitsy v Rossiiskoi imperii*, p. 170.

58. *Kukp'yŏn charyo*, vol. 12, p. 259.

59. Ibid., vol. 13, p. 193.

60. Grigortsevich, "Uchastie koreitsev russkogo Dal'nevo Vostoka v antiiaponskoi natsional'no-osvoboditel'noi bor'be (1906-1916)," p. 145.

61. *Kukp'yŏn charyo*, vol. 12, p. 636.

62. Ibid., vol. 7, pp. 222, 225, 437.

63. *Kukp'yŏn charyo*, vol. 12, pp. 633-34.

64. Quoted from "Zaiavlenie" in Boris Dmitrievich Pak, *Koreitsy v Rossiiskoi imperii*, p. 199.

65. *Kukp'yŏn charyo*, vol. 13, p. 799.

66. "Pon saju Ch'oe Pong-jun kong yŏksa nonp'yŏng" [Comment on the History of This Company's Owner, the Honorable Ch'oe Pong-jun], *Haejo Sinmun*, 27 Mar. 1908, p. 1.

67. "Pon saju Ch'oe Pong-jun kong yksa," *Haejo Sinmun*, 26 Mar. 1908, p. 1; "Kangdong swinhae," *Hanin Sinbo*, 7 Oct. 1917, p. 3; *Sinhan Minbo*, 11 July 1918, p. 4.

68. Kuksa P'yŏnch'an Wiwŏnhoe, *Hanguk tongnip undongsa*, 2nd ed., vol. 1 (Seoul: Chŏngŭm Munhwasa, 1983), p. 546; Pak Hwan, *Rŏsia Hanin minjok undongsa* [Korean National Movement in Russia] (Seoul: T'amgudang, 1995), pp. 62-63.

69. *Kukp'yŏn charyo*, vol. 12, pp. 497, 633; Ibid., vol. 13, p. 201.

70. Ibid., vol. 13, pp. 466-67.

71. *Kukp'yŏn charyo*, vol. 13, p. 201.

72. Ibid., vol. 13, pp. 466-67, 809.

73. *Kukp'yŏn charyo*, vol. 15, p. 167. Ch'oe Pong-jun's criticism went so far as to appraise the policies of the Japanese in Korea. According to a Japanese information report, Ch'oe Pong-jun delivered an address on June 12, 1909, to the people in a Korean village called Hyangsan-dong in the border area. "In Suchan, Vladivostok, and Pos'et, there are people who are calling themselves *ŭibyŏng* (righteous soldiers), but they are, in fact, bandits. I can give evidence for their being bandits, from last year, they collected

aid funds from every village and extorted sweat and blood from people, but there is nothing to increase the interest of state and happiness of the people. Furthermore, it is not entirely clear how they spent the funds. In the incident in Sŏsura (*ŭibyŏyng* attacked Sŏsura region, in July 1908), the massacred people were actually stupid and belonged to a low class. We have to suppress the so-called *ŭibyŏng* and discuss measures for suppression with the Korean authorities. See *Kukp'yŏn charyo*, vol. 15, pp. 160-61.

74. *Kukp'yŏn charyo*, vol. 12, p. 258.

75. Ibid., vol. 13, p. 469. An Chung-gŭn, to a Japanese investigator, also confirmed the demise of Yi Pŏm-yun as follows. "Yi Pŏm-yun is hiding now. . . . Yi collected a lot of money for military funds. If he does not organize *ŭibyŏng* and perform, he will be killed by the people, or if he organizes the *ŭibyŏng*, then will be arrested by the Russian authorities." See *Kukp'yŏn charyo*, vol. 7, pp. 436-37.

76. Ch'oe Chae-hyŏng, "Kwanggo" [Announcement], *Taedong Kongbo*, 20 Jan. 1909, p. 3.

77. *Kukp'yŏn charyo*, vol. 13, p. 803.

78. *Taedong Kongbo*, 3 Mar. 1909, p. 1.

79. *Kukp'yŏn charyo*, vol. 13, p. 467.

80. Ibid., vol. 15, p. 160.

81. Pak Hwan, *Rŏsia Hanin minjok undongsa*, p. 81.

82. Concerning An Ch'ang-ho's earlier life experience, educational, political activities, see Arthur Leslie Gardner, "The Korean Nationalist Movement and An Ch'ang-ho, Advocate of Gradualism," diss. University of Hawai'i (1979), pp. 5-28.

83. Arthur Leslie Gardner, "The Korean Nationalist Movement and An Ch'ang-ho, Advocate of Gradualism," p. 31; "Tosan ŏnhaeng sŭpyu" [Collections of Behaviors and Words of Tosan], Yun Pyŏng-sŏk and Yun Kyŏng-no ed., *An Ch'ang-ho iltaegi* [Biography of An Ch'ang-ho] (Seoul: Yŏkminsa, 1995), pp. 174-77.

84. *Sinhan Minbo*, 24 Nov. 1909, p. 1; "Kungmihoe yŏksa" [History of the Kungminhoe], *Sinhan Minbo*, 5 Feb. 1914, p. 1; Kim Wŏn-yong [Kim Warren Y.], *Chaemi hanin osimnyŏnsa*, p. 88; Arthur Leslie Gardner, "The Korean Nationalist Movement and An Ch'ang-ho, Advocate of Gradualism," pp. 35-36.

85. "Kungmihoe yŏksa," *Sinhan Minbo*, 5 Feb. 1914, p. 1; Kim Wŏn-yong [Kim Warren Y.], *Chaemi hanin osimnyŏnsa*, p. 88; Arthur Leslie Gardner, "The Korean Nationalist Movement and An Ch'ang-ho, Advocate of Gradualism," p. 37.

86. "Kungmihoe yŏksa," *Sinhan Minbo*, 5 Feb. 1914, p. 1. In August, the Kongnip Hyŏphoe included seven or eight hundred of the 1,000 Koreans in America. See *Kongnip Sinbo*, 16 Aug. 1907, p. 3.

87. "Taehan Sinminhoe ch'wijisŏ gŭp tonghoe changjŏng" [Korean New People's Association's Prospectus and its Platform], *Hanguk Tongnip undongsa*, vol. 1 (Seoul: Chŏngŭm Munhwasa, 1983), p. 1027.

88. Yun Pyŏng-sŏk and Yun Kyŏng-no ed., *An Ch'ang-ho iltaegi*, p. 238; Arthur Leslie Gardner, "The Korean Nationalist Movement and An Ch'ang-ho, Advocate of Gradualism," pp. 89-90; Kim To-hun, "Kongnip Hyŏphoe (1905-1909) ŭi minjok undong yŏngu" [Study on National Movement of the Kongnip Hyŏphoe (1905-1909)], *Hanguk Minjok Undongsa Yŏngu*, 4, 1989, pp. 17-26.

89. Yun Pyŏng-sŏk and Yun Kyŏng-no ed., *An Ch'ang-ho iltaegi*, pp. 238-39.

90. *Kongnip Sinbo*, 27 Dec. 1907, p. 3; "Kungminhoe yŏksa," *Sinhan Minbo*, 5 Feb. 1914, p. 1.

91. *Kongnip Sinbo*, 13 Dec. 1907, p. 4.

92. Ibid., 11 Mar. 1908, p. 2.

93. *Sinhan Minbo*, 12 May 1909, p. 3.

94. *Haejo Sinmun*, 29 Mar. 1908, p. 1: 2 Apr. 1908, p. 3: 23 Apr. 1908, p. 1.

95. "Kangdong swinhae," *Hanin sinbo*, 22 Oct. 1917, p. 3.

96. *Sinhan Minbo*, 17 Feb. 1909, p. 2.

97. *Kongnip Sinbo*, 18 Nov. 1908, p. 2; *Taedong Kongbo*, 4 Apr. 1909, p. 3; 31 Mar. 1909, p. 3; *Kongnip Sinbo*, 17 Feb. 1909, p. 1.

98. *Kongnip Sinbo*, 18 Nov. 1908, p. 2; 28 Oct. 1908, p. 3; "Kungminhoe yŏksa," *Sinhan Minbo*, 26 Feb. 1914, p. 1.

99. *Taedong Kongbo*, 7 Mar. 1909, p. 3; *Sinhan Minbo*, 17 Feb. 1909, p. 1.

100. Ibid.

101. As of March of 1908, there were eleven elementary schools in Korean communities in Vladivostok, Suifen, Nikol'sk-Ussurisk, Pos'et and Suchan mainly supported by *wŏnhoin* Koreans including Ch'oe Chae-hyŏng (Pos'et), Mun Ch'ang-bŏm (Suifen), Ch'oe Pong-jun, Kim Hak-man, Ch'oe Man-hak (Vladivostok), Kim Ki-ok, Kim Sŏk-yŏng (Suchan) and Yi In-baek (Khabarovsk). See *Kongnip Sinbo*, 10 June 1908, p. 3; *Haejo Sinmun*, 20 Mar. 1908, p. 2: 30 Apr. 1908, p. 3: 20 Apr. 1908, p. 3: 8 May 1908, p. 3.

102. *Taedong Kongbo*, 10 Mar. 1909, p. 1; "Kangdong swinhae," *Hanin Sinbo*, 14 Oct. 1917, p. 3.

103. *Hanguk tongnip undongsa*, vol. 1, p. 981.

104. *Kukp'yŏn charyo*, vol. 7, pp. 224, 248.

105. *Taedong Kongbo*, 3 Mar. 1909, p. 1.

106. *Kongnip Sinbo*, 13 Jan. 1909, p. 1; "Kungminhoe yŏksa," *Sinhan Minbo*, 26 Feb. 1914, pp. 1-2. The Hapsŏng Hyŏphoe was organized on September 2, 1907 by unifying 24 Korean associations in various places in Hawaii. The Hapsŏng Hyŏphoe had 47 branches and began to publish its official organ, the *Hapsŏng Sinbo* on October 22, 1907. See *Haejo Sinmun*, 20 Mar. 1908, p. 1; "Kungminhoe yŏksa," *Sinhan Minbo*, 5 Feb. 1914, p. 1.

107. *Sinhan Minbo*, 26 Feb. 1914, p. 2. On February 1910, the Kungminhoe changed its name into the Taehanin Kungminhoe (Korean National Association) when it was merged with the Taedong Pogukhoe (Korean Association for Protecting Nation), which was a monarchist anti-Japanese organization in San Francisco and was developed from the Taedong Kyoyukhoe (Korean Educational Association).

108. *Sinhan Minbo*, 17 Feb. 1909, p. 1.

109. "Kungminhoe yŏksa," *Sinhan Minbo*, 26 Feb. 1914, pp. 1-2. A branch had to have more than 15 enrolled members. See *Sinhan Minbo*, 24 Mar. 1909, p. 1.

110. "Ponbo ŭi myŏngch'ing" [The Title of This Newspaper], *Sinhan Minbo*, 10 Feb. 1909, p. 1.

111. *Sinhan Minbo*, 10 Feb. 1909, p. 1.

112. Ibid., 25 May 1910, p. 1.

113. *Sinhan Minbo*, 26 Apr. 1911, p. 4.

114. Yun Pyŏng-sŏk, *Kugoe Hanin sahoe wa minjok undong* [Korean Communities Abroad and the National Movement] (Seoul: Ilchogak, 1990), p. 366.

115. *Sinhan Minbo*, 17 Feb. 1909, p. 1.

116. Ibid., 2 June 1909, p. 3.

117. *Kongnip Sinbo*, 13 Jan. 1909, p. 1: 20 Jan. 1909, p. 2; *Kukp'yŏn charyo*, vol. 7, pp. 254-55.

118. *Sinhan Minbo*, 18 Aug. 1909, p. 2; *Taedong Kongbo*, 22 July 1909, p. 3.

119. *Sinhan Minbo,* 17 Feb. 1909, p. 1: 12 Oct. 1910, p. 2: 2 Nov. 1910, p. 3: 23 Nov. 1910.

120. *Sinhan Minbo*, 7 July 1909, p. 3: 15 Sep. 1909, p. 2: 27 Oct. 1909, p. 1: 27 Oct. 1909, p. 2: 8 Dec. 1909, p. 2: 22 Dec. 1909, p. 4.

121. *Sinhan Minbo*, 30 Mar. 1910, p. 2: 20 July 1910, p. 3: 10 Aug. 1910, p. 3: 12 Oct. 1910, p. 2: 2 Nov. 1910, p. 3: 25 Jan. 1911, p. 3: 1 Feb. 1911, p. 3: 22 Feb. 1911, p. 3: 8 Mar. 1911, p. 2: 10 May 1911: 17 May 1911, p. 2: 31 May 1911, p. 3: 19 July 1911, p. 2.

122. *Sinhan Minbo*, 1 Nov. 1911, p. 3: 18 Oct. 1912, p. 3: 4 Nov. 1912, p. 2.

123. In February 1911, enrolled membership was more than 3,000: 1,000 in Hawaii, 800 in North America and more than 1,000 in Russia. See *Sinhan Minbo*, 10 Feb. 1909, p. 1.

124. Yi Kwang-su, "Na ŭi kobaek" [My Confession], *Yi Kwang-su chŏnjip*, vol. 13 (Seoul: Samjungdang, 1964), p. 216.

125. The Vladivostok branch had 30 members and the executive and ordinary members were as follows: O Chu-hyŏk (president), Chŏng Sun-man (vice-president), Yi Hong-gi (secretary), Yun Nŭng-hyo (treasurer), Han Hyŏng-gwŏn (education), Yang Sŏng-ch'un (reception), T'ae Wŏn-sŏn (reception), Yi Ch'i-gwŏn, Ham Tong-ch'ŏl, Sŏ Sang-gu, Sŏ Sŏng-hae, Ki San-do, Yi Chong-sŭng [Yi Yong], Chŏn Wŏn-gyu, Kim Ŏn-

sang, Hong Kŭn-p'yo, Yun Uk [Yun Il-byŏng], Pak Kŭn-ch'an, Ch'ae Sŏng-ha, U Si-ha, Han Chin-t'aek, Chŏn Ch'ang-sik, Ŏm Un-sŏp (probably Ŏm In-sŏp), Yu Wan-mu, Kim Chong-ch'ŏl, Kim Ch'ŏl-hun, Cho Yŏng-rae, Ch'oe Ku-dong, Yi Chong-hwan, P'yo Hŭng-sik. See *Sinhan Minbo*, 17 Feb. 1909, p. 1.

126. Pak Hwan, *Rsia Hanin minjok undongsa*, p. 197.
127. *Kukp'yŏn charyo*, vol. 7, p. 248; Yi Kwang-su, "Na ŭi kobaek," p. 20.
128. Sin Yong-ha, *Hanguk minjok tongnip undongsa yŏngu* [Study on the History of Korean National Independence Movement] (Seoul: Ŭlyu Munhwasa, 1985), p. 201; *Kukp'yŏn charyo*, vol. 7, p. 265. The assassination of Durnham White Stevens, advisor to Japanese Residency-General of Korea, by a Korean nationalists in San Francisco in March 1908 obviously contributed to enhancing their optimistic expectations. Thanks to the support of the Kungminhoe and the Taehan Pogukhoe, Chŏn Myŏng-un who attempted to shoot Stevens was acquitted and Chang In-hwan who shot Stevens was sentenced to 25 years-in prison. See Yun Pyŏng-sŏk, *Kugoe Hanin sahoe wa minjok undong*, pp. 368-88.
129. *Taedong Kongbo*, 1 Nov. 1909, p. 1.
130. Sin Yong-ha 202. An Chung-gŭn was persecuted on March 26, 1910. See "Kangdong swinhae," *Hanin Sinbo*, 14 Oct. 1917, p. 3.
131. "Osu pulmang" [Do not Forget Our Enemy], *Hanguk tongnip undongsa*, vol. 2, p. 623; *Taehan Maeil Sinbo*, 2 Nov. 1909: 9 Nov. 1909: 30 Nov. 1909: 1 Jan. 1910: 9 Jan. 1910: 11 Jan. 1910: 13 Jan. 1910: 22 Jan. 1910: 29 Jan. 1910: 22 Feb. 1910: 5 Mar. 1910.
132. *Taedong Kongbo*, 21 Nov. 1909, p. 1.
133. *Kukp'yŏn charyo*, vol. 7, pp. 210-91.
134. *Sinhan Minbo*, 2 Mar. 1910, p. 1: 1 Jun. 190, p. 1.
135. Ibid., 17 Feb. 1909, p. 1.
136. *Taedong Kongbo*, 5 May 1909, p. 4.
137. *Sinhan Minbo*, 2 Mar. 1910, p. 1.
138. *Taedong Kongbo*, 24 Apr. 1910, p. 3.
139. Yi In-sŏp, "Ch'oe Ko-ryŏ chasŏjŏn ŭl yŏnguhadaga na ŭi sogam" [My Impressions while Studying the Autobiography of Ch'oe Ko-ryŏ] ms., 1961, p. 45.
140. Yi Kwang-su, "Na ŭi kobaek," p. 220.
141. There is a record that Chŏng Chae-gwan was born in Chaeryŏng, Hwanghae Province. See Kim Kyu-myŏn, *Nobyŏng Kim Kyu-myŏn ŭi pimangnok esŏ* [From the Memoirs of the Old Soldier Kim Kyu-myŏn], ms., n. d., p. 79.
142. Kim Kyu-myŏn, *Nobyŏng Kim Kyu-myŏn ŭi pimangnok esŏ*, pp. 79-80.
143. Yun Pyŏng-sŏk's *Yi Sang-sŏl chŏn* is the only and detailed biography of Yi Sang-sŏl.
144. *Taedong Kongbo*, 5 May 1909, p. 4; Dae-sook Suh ed., and trans., *The Writings of Henry*

Cu Kim: Autobiography with Commentaries on Syngman Rhee, Pak Yong-man, and Chŏng Sun-man (Honolulu: U of Hawai'i Press, 1987), pp. 278-85.

145. Among the young Koreans, Han Hyŏng-gwŏn and Ham Tong-ch'ŏl were Kungminhoe members and the other leaders were Kim Kyu-sŏp, Nikolai Kim, Vasilii O and Ham Se-in.

146. *Taedong Kongbo*, 24 Apr. 1910, p. 4. The chief editor, Yi Kang resigned the post and was hiding, for a letter signed by An Chung-gŭn and U Tŏk-sun was sent to Yi Kang. See *Sinhan Minbo*, 16 Mar. 1910, p. 2. Chŏng Chae-gwan wanted to succeed Yi Kang's the chief-editorship, but because of opposition, probably by Yun Il-byŏng, he instead became a guest-editor. See *Kukp'yŏn charyo*, vol. 18, pp. 418-19.

147. *Taedong Kongbo*, 28 Apr. 1910, p. 1.

148. Ibid., 28 Apr. 1910, p. 2.

149. *Taedong Kongbo*, 15 May 1910, p. 2.

150. Kim Chŏng-gyu, *Yongyŏn Kim Chŏng-gyu ilgi* [Diary of Kim Chŏng-gyu], vol. 1 (Seoul: Tongnip Kinyŏmgwan, 1994), p. 476.

151. *Kukp'yŏn charyo*, vol. 7, pp. 280-81.

152. In April 1910, Ch'oe Pong-jun also resigned from the chairmanship of the Korean Residents' Association in Vladivostok. See *Kukp'yŏn charyo*, vol. 18, p. 419.

153. Pak Min-yŏng, "Kuhanmal sŏbuk pyŏngyŏng chiyŏk ŭi ŭibyŏng yŏngu," pp. 62-63.

154. Yu In-sŏk, *Ŭiamjip* [*Collection of* Yu In-sŏk*'s Writings*], vol. 1 (Seoul: Kyŏngin Munhwasa, 1973), pp. 304, 308.

155. *Kukp'yŏn charyo*, vol. 17, pp. 98-101.

156. Ibid., vol. 17, pp. 127-31.

157. *Taedong Kongbo*, 26 May 1910, p. 1.

158. *Sinhan Minbo*, 25 May 1910, p. 1.

159. "Zaiavlenie," Boris Dmitrievich Pak, *Koreitsy v Rossiiskoi imperii*, p. 199.

160. An Chung-gŭn, an assassin of Ito Hirobumi, in an investigation by the Japanese evaluated Hong Pŏm-do as follows: "His age is about 40 and brave and has vital force, but is uneducated, so has no knowledge about the trends of the time. He was a miner and killed any person with short-cut hair. . . . It is barbarious to kill any short-haired person. . . . Short-haired persons are not necessarily traitors. . . . [Hong Pŏm-do] does not have much knowledge about the situation, but his loyalty to the monarch is the deepest. He is clean-handed and does not violate the property of innocent people and wore very modest clothes. See *Kukp'yŏn charyo*, vol. 7, p. 406.

161. Hong Pŏm-do, "Hong Pŏm-do ŭi ilchi" [Diary of Hong Pŏm-do], Pak Sŏng-su ed., *Hanguk tongnip undongsa charyojip: Hong Pŏm-do p'yŏn* [Materials on Korean Independence Movement: Part for Hong Pŏm-do] (Seoul: Hanguk Chŏngsin Munhwa Yŏnguwŏn, 1995), pp. 3-20; *Taedong Kongbo*, 29 June 1910, p. 2.

162. *Sinhan Minbo*, 13 July 1910, p. 1.

163. *Taedong Kongbo*, 26 May 1910, p. 1.

164. Yu In-sŏk, *Ŭiamjip*, vol. 1, p. 366.

165. Yun Pyŏng-sŏk, *Kugoe hanin sahoe wa minjok undong*, pp. 177-78; Boris Pak, *Koreitsy v Rossiiskoi imperii*, p. 181; S. S. Grigortsevich, "Uchastie koreitsev russkogo Dal'nevo Vostoka v antiiaponskoi natsional'no-osvoboditel'noi bor'be (1906-1916)," p. 146; Pak Min-yŏng, "Kuhanmal sŏbuk pyŏngyŏng chiyŏk ŭi ŭibyŏng yŏngu," pp. 329-34.

166. Yun Pyŏng-sŏk, *Kugoe hanin sahoe wa minjok undong*, p. 178.

167. Ibid., pp. 178-79.

168. *Taedong Kongbo*, 11 Aug. 1910, p. 1; Boris Dmitrievich Pak, *Koreitsy v Rossiiskoi imperii*, p. 184.

169. Yun Pyŏng-sŏk, *Yi Sang-sŏl chŏn*, p. 133.

170. Japanese Government-General Office of Korea, *Chōsen no hogo kyū heigō*, pp. 357-58.

171. Yun Pyŏng-sŏk, *Yi Sang-sŏl chŏn*, p. 137.

172. Ibid., pp. 134-37.

173. Yun Pyŏng-sŏk, *Yi Sang-sŏl chŏn*, pp. 137-45; Boris Dmitrievich Pak, *Koreitsy v Rossiiskoi imperii*, p. 186.

174. Japanese Government-General of Korea, *Chōsen no hogo kyū heigō*, p. 356.

175. *Sinhan Minbo*, 26 Oct. 1910, p. 2.

176. Boris Dmitrievich Pak, *Koreitsy v Rossiiskoi imperii*, p. 187.

177. *Sinhan Minbo*, 19 Oct. 1910, p. 2; Boris Dmitrievich Pak, *Koreitsy v Rossiiskoi imperii*, p. 187.

178. Yu Hyo-jong, "Kyokutō Roshia ni okeru Chōsen mizoku undō: Kangoku Heigo kara dai nichi sekai taisen no hotpatsu made" [Korean National Movement in the Russian Far East: From the Annexation of Korea through the World War I], *Chōsenshi Kenkūyshi Nonshū*, 22 (1985), p. 142; Song Sang-do, *Kiro sup'il* [Donkey-Riding Tour Essays] (Seoul: Kuksa P'yŏnch'an Wiwŏnhoe, 1955), p. 116.

179. AJMFA MT. 1148, 49-50; *Sinhan Minbo*, 12 Oct. 1910, p. 3; Boris Dmitrievich Pak, *Koreitsy v Rossiiskoi imperii*, pp. 185-86.

180. Boris Dmitrievich Pak, *Koreitsy v Rossiiskoi imperii*, p. 188.

181. Ibid., pp. 199-200.

182. Yu Hyo-jong, "Kyokutō Roshia ni okeru Chōsen mizoku undō," p. 142.

183. *Sinhan Minbo*, 23 Nov. 1910, p. 2; Boris Dmitrievich Pak, *Koreitsy v Rossiiskoi imperii*, p. 189; Yu Hyo-jong, "Kyokutō Roshia ni okeru Chōsen mizoku undō," p. 142. At first, the Japanese government asked the Russian authorities to hand Yi Pŏm-yun over to Tokyo. See *Sinhan Minbo*, 7 Dec. 1910, p. 3.

184. Boris Dmitrievich Pak, *Koreitsy v Rossiiskoi imperii*, pp. 190-91; Yu Hyo-jong, "Kyokutō Roshia ni okeru Chōsen mizoku undō," p. 142.

185. Yi Hong-guk, "Pukkando Sŏjŏn Hakkyo wasan silok" [The Real Story of the Closure of the Sŏjŏn School], *Haejo Sinmun*, 26 May 1908, p. 3; Sabangja [Kye Pong-u], "Pukkando kŭ kwagŏ wa hyŏnjae" [North Chientao, its Past and Present], *Tongnip Sinmun*, 1 Jan. 1920, p. 5; Yun Chŏng-hŭi, "Kando kaech'ŏksa," p. 20.

186. Yun Pyŏng-sŏk, *Yi Sang-sŏl chŏn*, pp. 50-53; Yun Chŏng-hŭi, "Kando kaech'ŏksa," pp. 20-21.

187. Yi Hong-guk, *Haejo Sinmun*, 26 May 1908, p. 3; Yun Chŏng-hŭi, "Kando kaech'ŏksa," p. 2.

188. Sabangja, "Pukkando kŭ kwagŏ wa hyŏnjae," *Tongnip Sinmun*, 1 Jan. 1920, p. 5; Kye Pong-u, *Kkum sog ŭi kkum*, vol. 1, p. 144; Yun Pyŏng-sŏk, *Yi Sang-sŏl chŏn*, pp. 54-55.

189. Mun Chae-rin, "Myŏngdong ŭn Kando ŭi Oryongch'on" [Myŏngdong is the Five Dragon Village in Chientao], Sŏ Kwoeng-il and Tongam ed., *Kandosa sillon*, vol. 1 (Seoul: Uridŭl ŭi P'yŏnjisa, 1993), p. 81.

190. Pak Kye-ju, "Taeji ŭi sŏngjwa" [Constellation in the Great Earth], *Pak Kye-ju chŏnjip* [Collections of Pak Kye-ju's Works], vol. 6 (Seoul: Samyŏng Ch'ulp'ansa, 1957), p. 318.

191. Kim Chŏng-gyu, *Yongyŏn Kim Chŏng-gyu ilgi*, vol. 1, pp. 353-54.

192. AJMFA MT. 11259, 163-164; *Kukp'yŏn charyo*, vol. 18, p. 408.

193. Yun Chŏng-hŭi, "Kando kaech'ŏksa," p. 22.

194. AJMFA MT. 11259, 163-164; *Kukp'yŏn charyo*, vol. 18, p. 408; Kim Chŏng-gyu, *Yongyŏn Kim Chŏng-gyu ilgi*, pp. 323-24.

195. AJMFA M. 11259, 164, 175.

196. Im Sang-ch'o, Kim Ha-sŏk etc., Letter to the Governor Office of the Jilin Dongnanlu, 26 Mar. 1914, Tongnip Kinyŏmgwan (Korean Independence Hall Archive, hereafter cited as KIHA), Document no. 6393-31.

197. AJMFA MT. 11259, 163-164.

198. *Hanguk tongnip undongsa*, vol. 2, pp. 544-45; AJMFA MT. 11259, 56-59, 164-165. Yun Hae majored in law at Posŏng College, which Yi Yong-ik had established in 1904, and had been actively involved in patriotic educational and cultural activities in Korea. Yun Hae is said to have inspired patriotism in Yi Tong-ch'un who was a Sinicized Korean and had encouraged him to join anti-Japanese activities in North Chientao. Yun Hae was a key figure who played a role comparable to that of Kim Rip, a key organizer of the Kwŏnŏphoe in Vladivostok in 1911, as we will see later. See Kye Pong-u, *Kkum sog ŭi kkum*, vol. 1, pp. 145-46.

199. AJMFA MT11259, 160.

200. Owen Lattimore, *Manchuria: Cradle of Conflict* (New York: The Macmillan Company, 1931), pp. 241-42.

201. AJMFA MT11259, 166-169.

202. Ibid., 176, 207.

203. *Taehanin Chŏnggyobo*, 1 Aug. 1912, p. 21; *Kwŏnŏp Sinmun*, 6 July 1913, p. 3; *Sinhan Minbo*, 15 Aug. 1913, p. 3; AJMFA MT11259, 160.

204. Im Sang-ch'o, Kim Ha-sŏk etc., KIHA, Document no. 6393-31; Sabangja, "Pukkando kŭ kwagŏ wa hyŏnjae," *Tongnip Sinmun*, 1 Jan. 1920, p. 5.

205. *Sinhan Minbo*, 26 Oct. 1910, p. 2; Sabangja, "Pukkando kŭ kwagŏ wa hyŏnjae," *Tongnip Sinmun*, 1 Jan. 1920, p. 5.

206. AJMFA MT11259, 56-59, 175-176.

207. Ibid., 160-162.

208. *Hanguk tongnip undongsa*, vol. 2, p. 544; Kye Pong-u, *Kkum sog ŭi kkum*, vol. 1, p. 146.

209. Pak Kye-ju, "Taeji ŭi sŏngjwa," p. 324.

210. Kye Pong-u, *Kkum sog ŭi kkum*, vol. 1, p. 145; Pak Kye-ju, "Taeji ŭi sŏngjwa," pp. 324-25.

211. Im Sang-ch'o, Kim Ha-sŏk etc., KIHA, Document no. 6393-31.

212. Kim Chŏng-gyu, *Yongyŏn Kim Chŏng-gyu ilgi*, vol. 2, pp. 381-82, p. 406.

213. Kye Pong-u, *Kkum sog ŭi kkum*, vol. 1, pp. 133-34.

214. Robert Grierson, *Episodes on a Long, Long Trail* (ts., 1957), p. 45.

215. *Hanguk tongnip undongsa*, vol. 2, pp. 544-45. Those "disciples of Yi Tong-hwi" were Kim Rip, Yun Hae, Kye Pong-u, Chang Ki-yŏng, Kim Ha-sŏk, Kim Ha-gu, O Yŏng-sŏn, Chŏng Ch'ang-bin, Yu Ye-gyun, Ma Chin, Sŏ Sang-yong, To Yong-ho, Ko Myŏng-su, Kim Pyŏng-hŭp, Yi Pin, Ch'oe Pin, Nam Kong-sŏn, Yu Il-po, Yi Hong-jun, Kang Pong-u, Cho P'il-u, Chang Sŏk-ham. See Pak Kye-ju, "Taeji ŭi sŏngjwa," p. 323 and *Tongnip Sinmun*, 10 Apr. 1920, p. 2.

216. According to a survey of the Japanese Consulate General in 1915, there were 429 Protestant families with 2,140 believers in North Chientao and 1,000 in Hunchun. There were 268 Catholic families with 1,340 in Chientao and 49 in Hunchun. See "Kukkyŏng chibang sich'al pongmyŏngsŏ," pp. 224-27.

217. "Yi Tong-hwi tongmu ŭi ilsaeng" [A Whole Life of Comrade Yi Tong-hwi], *Sŏnbong*, 4 Feb. 1935, p. 4; Koreits [Pak Chin-sun], "Probuzhdenie Korei" [Awakening of Korea], *Zhizn' Natsional'nostei*, 7 Mar. 1920, p. 3.

218. For a biographical review of Yi Tong-hwi, see Ban Byung Yool, "Yi Tong-hwi wa Hanmal minjok undong" [Yi Tong-hwi and the National Movement in late Chosŏn Dynasty], *Hanguksa Yŏngu*, 87, Dec. 1994, pp. 147-91.

219. *Kwŏnŏp Sinmun*, 12 Apr. 1914, p. 1; Pak Kye-ju, "Taeji ŭi sŏngjwa," p. 325.

220. Pak Kye-ju, "Taeji ŭi sŏngjwa," p. 325.

221. Ibid., 325.

222. Kye Pong-u, *Kkum sog ŭi kkum*, vol. 1, pp. 148-49; "Kukkyŏng chibang sich'al

pongmyŏngsŏ," pp. 236-40.

223. *Taehanin Chŏnggyobo*, 1 Dec. 1912, p. 11. Other schools such as the Ch'angdong School, the Chŏngdong School in Yanji and the Myŏngdong School in Helong were also prominent Korean schools managed by members of the Educational Association.

224. The Kwangsŏng School had courses for elementary, intermediate, teacher training and girls. Kim Rip and Yun Hae, graduates of Posŏng College taught law and politics, and Mun Kyŏng was in charge of military training. At the time of establishment, the administrators and teachers were: Yi Tong-ch'un (superintendent), Kim Rip (vice-superintendent), Chŏng Hyŏn-sŏl (finance), Ku Ch'un-sŏn, Yi Pong-u, Yi Nam-wŏn, Hwang Wŏn-ho (managers), Pak Ch'un-sŏ (dining room) and Yun Hae, Kye Pong-u, Chang Ki-yŏng, Kim Ha-sŏk, O Yŏng-sŏn, Kye Pong-u and Mun Kyŏng (teachers). See Kye Pong-u, *Kkum sog ŭi kkum*, vol. 1, pp. 148-57; Pak Kye-ju, "Taeji ŭi sŏngjwa," p. 324.

225. Sabangja, "Pukkando kŭ kwagŏ wa hyŏnjae," *Tongnip Sinmun*, 1 Jan. 1920, p. 5; Kye Pong-u, *Kkum sog ŭi kkum*, vol. 1, p. 147.

226. Yun Pyŏng-sŏk, "Yongyŏn Kim Chŏng-gyu ŭi saengae wa yasa" [The Life of Kim Chŏng-gyu and *Unauthorized History*], *Hanguk Tongnip Undongsa Yŏngu*, 5 (1991), pp. 2-7; Pak Min-yŏng, "Kuhanmal sŏbuk pyŏngyŏng chiyŏk ŭi ŭibyŏng yŏngu," pp. 220-72.

227. Kim Chŏng-gyu, *Yongyŏn Kim Chŏng-gyu ilgi*, vol. 1, pp. 362-63.

228. Ibid., vol. 1, pp. 362-63, p. 477. Kim's letter was not delivered to Wu.

229. Kim Chŏng-gyu, *Yongyŏn Kim Chŏng-gyu ilgi*, vol. 2, pp. 402-404.

230. Ibid., vol. 2, p. 406.

231. Im Sang-ch'o, Kim Ha-sŏk etc., KIHA, Document no. 6393-31; Kim Chŏng-gyu, *Yongyŏn Kim Chŏng-gyu ilgi*, vol. 2, p. 406.

232. Kim Chŏng-gyu, *Yongyŏn Kim Chŏng-gyu ilgi*, vol. 2, p. 410.

233. Ibid., p. 517.

234. *Kwŏnŏp Sinmun*, 9 Nov. 1913, p. 3: 1 Feb. 1914, p. 1; *Taehanin Chŏnggyobo*, 1 May 1912, p. 13; Ibid., 1 Aug. 1912; Japanese Government-General Office of Korea, Department of Social Affairs, *Manshū kyū Shiberia chihō ni okeru Chōsenjin jijō*, p. 94.

235. Paek Wŏn-bo, letter to An Ch'ang-ho, 1 Sep. 1911, *Tosan An Ch'ang-ho charyojip* [*Collections of An Ch'ang-ho*], comp. Tongnip Kinyŏmgwan Tongnip Undongsa Yŏnguso, vol. 1 (Ch'ŏnan: Tongnip Kinyŏmgwan, 1990), pp. 152-53; Chang To-bin, letter to An Ch'ang-ho, 1 Nov. 1912, *Tosan An Ch'ang-ho charyojip*, vol. 3, p. 43.

236. Pak Kye-ju, "Taeji ŭi sŏngjwa," p. 325. According to a reporter who visited North Chientao and contributed an article August 1, 1912, to the *Taehanin Chŏnggyobo* in Chita, the Educational Association was already dissolved.

237. "Kanminhoe chojik ch'onghoe sojip t'ongjisŏ" [Notice of an Organizational General Meeting for the Kanminhoe], ms., 13 Jan. 1913.

238. "Jilin Doudu jian minzheng changguan pi" [Instruction of the Military-Governor and Government-General in Jilin], KIHA, Document no. 5437-1; "Qingyuanshu" [Application], KIHA, Document no. 6393-36.

239. Sabangja, "Pukkando kŭ kwagŏ wa hyŏnjae," *Tongnip Sinmun*, 1 Jan. 1910, p. 5.

240. "Jilin Dongnanlu zaju guyu kenminhui" [Korean Association in the Mixed Residence District of the Jilin East-South Route], KIHA, Document 5437-1, 30 Mar. 1913.

241. As of November 1913, Korean and Chinese Population in three prefectures of North Chientao was as follows:

	Yanji	Wangqing	Helong	(Total)	Hunchun
Koreans	98,777	9,605	40,405	(148,787)	6,973
Chinese	10,371	10,644	1,786	(22,801)	10,281
	109,148	20,249	42,191	(171,588)	17,254

Source "Kukkyŏng chibang sich'al pongmyŏngsŏ," p. 168.

242. "Baogaoshu dierhao" [Report no. 2], KIHA, Document no. 6393-37, Dec. Apr. 1913.

243. *Kwŏnŏp Sinmun*, 8 June 1913, p. 3.

244. KIHA, Document no. 5437-1: 55437-3.

245. *Sinhan Minbo*, 5 Sep. 1913, p. 3.

246. "Baogao diwuhao" [Report no. 5], KIHA, Document no. 5437-1, 24 July 1913.

247. Chŏng Chae-myŏn, letter to An Ch'ang-ho, 25 Nov. 1913, *Tosan An Ch'ang-ho charyojip*, vol. 2, p. 303; Kye Pong-u, *Kkum sog ŭi kkum*, vol. 1, p. 172; Pae Ryŏng, letter to An Ch'ang-ho, 23 Nov. 1913, *Tosan An Ch'ang-ho charyojip*, vol. 2, p. 327.

248. Yi Tong-hwi had been released from exile in July of 1912, escaped Japanese surveillance and finally arrived at North Chientao through Changbai Prefecture in June 1913. See Yi Tong-hwi, letter to An Ch'ang-ho, 19 June 1917, *Tosan An Ch'ang-ho charyojip*, vol. 2, p. 292.

249. "Chosŏn oe esŏ ŭi Chosŏnin sanghwang ilban," *Sindonga*, Feb. 1967, p. 489; *Sinhan Minbo*, 5 Sep. 1913, p. 3.

250. Chŏng Pyŏk, letter to An Ch'ang-ho, 28 July 1911, *Tosan An Ch'ang-ho charyojip*, vol. 2, p. 221.

251. Pak Kye-ju, "Taeji ŭi sŏngjwa," pp. 325-26.

252. *Sinhan Minbo*, 30 June 1913, p. 3.

253. Kim Chŏng-gyu, *Yongyŏn Kim Chŏng-gyu ilgi*, vol. 2, pp. 492-93.

254. Kye Pong-u, *Kkum sog ŭi kkum*, vol. 1, pp. 146-47. As far as Koreans in North Chientao were concerned, Owen Lattimore's following observation hit the mark: "On the other hand the Koreans have thus far shown, even when naturalized as Chinese, great resistance to absorption by the Chinese, and no tendency at all to consider themselves

truly Chinese. While they are glad to reside in China, they have no desire to be anything but Korean in race, language and culture. Few of them even learn to speak Chinese well, many of them speak practically no Chinese at all, and they tend to settle in strong enough groups to prevent modification of this attitude even in the second generation." See Owen Lattimore, *Manchuria: Cradle of Conflict*, p. 241.

255. Kim Chŏng-gyu, *Yongyŏn Kim Chŏng-gyu ilgi*, vol. 2, p. 497.
256. *Kwŏnŏp Sinmun*, 21 Sep. 1913, p. 2; KIHA, Document no. 5437-3, 13 Nov. 1913.
257. KIHA, Document no. 5437-3, 13 Nov. 1913.
258. KIHA, Document no. 6393-57.
259. Im Sang-ch'o, Kim Ha-sŏk etc., KIHA, Document no. 6393-31, 26 Mar. 1914; KIHA, Document no. 6393-2, 8 Jan. 1914; KIHA, Document no. 5437-3, 13 Nov. 1913.
260. KIHA, Document no. 5437-3, 13 Nov. 1913.
261. Ibid.
262. KIHA, Document no. 5437-3, 13 Nov. 1913.
263. Ibid.
264. Kim Chŏng-gyu, *Yongyŏn Kim Chŏng-gyu ilgi*, vol. 2, pp. 503, 508-10, 523; KIHA, Document no. 5437-3, 20 Dec. 1913; *Kwŏnŏp Sinmun*, 25 Jan. 1914, p. 2.
265. "Jilin Dongnan Guanchashi disan hao" [Directive no. 3 of the Jilin East-South Governor], KIHA, Document no. 5437-3.
266. Kye Pong-u, *Kkum sog ŭi kkum*, vol. 1, pp. 171-72.
267. *Kwŏnŏp Sinmun*, 25 Jan. 1914, p. 2; Pak Kye-ju, "Taeji ŭi sŏngjwa," pp. 327-28.
268. Im Sang-ch'o, Kim Ha-sŏk etc., KIHA, Document no. 6393-31, 26 Mar. 1914.
269. *The Writings of Henry Cu Kim*, 279; Zaigai hainichi Senjin yuryokusha meibo," p. 29; Pak Kye-ju, "Taeji ŭi sŏngjwa," p. 327.
270. Pak Kye-ju, "Taeji ŭi sŏngjwa," pp. 327-28.
271. KIHA, Document, no. 5437-3, 5 Nov. 1913.
272. "Jianbaian dierhao" [Proposal no. 2], KIHA, Document no. 5437-3, 21 Nov. 1913. The prohibition of the sale and purchase of lands would cause economic damage to Koreans peasants. The Kanminhoe proposed the Chinese authorities grant the Kanminhoe power to issue warranties to those Koreans who would purchase land after a careful investigation of the backgrounds of the applicants.
273. *Kwŏnŏp Sinmun*, 7 Dec. 1913, p. 3; Chŏng Chae-myŏn, letter to An Ch'ang-ho, 25 Nov. 1913, *Tosan An Ch'ang-ho charyojip*, vol. 2, p. 303.
274. Kim Chŏng-gyu, *Yongyŏn Kim Chŏng-gyu ilgi*, vol. 2, p. 547; *Kwŏnŏp Sinmun*, 25 Jan. 1914, p. 2.
275. "Qingyuanshu" [Petition], KIHA, Document no. 5437-3, 17 Dec. 1913; Document no. 6393-2, 8 Dec. 1913; Kim Chŏng-gyu, *Yongyŏn Kim Chŏng-gyu ilgi*, vol. 2, pp.

548-52; Im Sang-ch'o, Kim Ha-sŏk etc., KIHA, document no. 6393-31, 26 Mar. 1914; KIHA, Document no. 5437-3, 12 Nov. 1913.

276. Hwang Yong-guk [Huang Long-guo] ed., *Chosŏnjok hyŏngmyŏng t'ujaengsa* [History of the Revolutionary Struggles of Koreans] (Liaoning: Ryonyŏng minjok ch'ulp'ansa, 1988), p. 28.

277. KIHA, Document no. 6393-2, 9 Jan. 1914; Document no. 6393-79, 9 Jan. 1914; *Kwŏnŏp Sinmun*, 25 Jan. 1914, p. 2. 300 Koreans except for 20 key leaders were released on January 10, 1914.

278. "Baogao disihao" [Report no. 4], KIHA, Docement no. 6393-11, 2 Feb. 1914; *Kwŏnŏp Sinmun*, 8 Mar. 1914, p. 2.

279. *Sinhan Minbo*, 7 May 1914, p. 2.

280. KIHA, Document no. 6393-57, 2 June 1914; Document no. 6393-87, 1 Apr. 1914.

281. *Kwŏnŏp Sinmun*, 15 Feb. 1914, p. 2.

282. AJMFA, SP. 128, 16; *Kwŏnŏp Sinmun*, 5 Apr. 1914, p. 2; *Sinhan Minbo*, 28 May 1914, p. 2.

283. KIHA, Document no. 6393-87, 1 Apr. 1914; Document no. 6393-61, 12 May 1914.

284. Im Sang-ch'o, Kim Ha-sŏk etc., KIHA, Document no. 6393-31, 26 Mar. 1914.

285. KIHA, Document no. 6393-29, 17 May 1914.

286. Ibid., no. 6393-57.

287. KIHA, Document no. 6393-57.

288. Hara Teruyuki, "The Korean Movement in the Russian Maritime Province, 1905-1922," p. 4. The Russo-Japanese Treaty of Extradition was signed on June 1, 1911, by Malevskii-Malevich, Russian Ambassador to Japan, and Komura Toshitarō, Japanese Minister of Foreign Affairs in Tokyo. The ratification of the treaty was exchanged on August 26 and publicized September 15, 1911. For more detailed information about the treaty, see Wada Haruki, "Nichiro tōbō hanzainin hikiwatashi jōyaku fuzoku himitsu sengensho" [Secret Declaration Appended to the Russo-Japanese Treaty of Extradition], *Shakai Kagaku Kenkyū*, 27, no. 4 (1976), pp. 86-116.

289. S. S. Grigortsevich, *Dal'nevostochnaia politika imperialisticheskikh derzhav v 1906-1917 gg.* [Far Eastern Politics of the Imperial Power, 1906-1917] (Tomsk: Izatel'stvo Tomskogo Universiteta, 1965), pp. 254-55.

290. The naturalization movement was widely advocated by most Korean patriots abroad, except for Confucian conservatives, since shortly after the Japanese annexation of Korea. For example, the *Sinhan Minbo*, in its comment on the Japanese arrest of Korean patriots after the annexation of Korea in China and Russia, concluded as follows: "Facing this difficult time, the way to save patriots and carry on activities by our will and to seek a future task is for each of us to be naturalized in our respective countries.

Koreans in Chinese territory can get the protection of China and Koreans in Russian territory can get the protection of Russia. . . . [We can] eliminate the infiltration of the officials of our enemy, Japan." See *Sinhan Minbo*, 30 Nov. 1910, p. 1.

291. Pauline Tompkins, *American-Russian Relations in the Far East* (New York: The Macmillan Company, 1949), pp. 26-27.

292. Yun Pyŏng-sŏk and Yun Kyŏng-no ed., *An Ch'ang-ho iltaegi*, pp. 195-96. Yi Kang recollected the name of the Russian *gendarme* head as Mirikov.

293. Boris Dmitrievich Pak, *Koreitsy v Rossiiskoi imperii*, p. 209; Yu Hyo-jong, "Kyokutō Roshia ni okeru Chōsen mizoku undō," pp. 152-53.

294. This faction was also called *Namp'a* (Southern faction).

295. Kim Kyu-myŏn, *Sŏngjae yakchŏn e kwanhan hoesanggi* [Recollection on the Biography of Yi Tong-hwi], ms., pp. 2-3.

296. Kye Pong-u, *Kkum sŭog ŭi kkum*, vol. 1, p. 170; *Kukp'yŏn charyo*, vol. 7, pp. 280-81.

297. Kuksa P'yŏnch'an Wiwŏnhoe, *Hanguk tongnip undongsa*, vol. 1, p. 981; *Kukp'yŏn charyo*, vol. 7, pp. 224, 252; Paek Wŏn-bo, letter to An Ch'ang-ho, 1 Sep. 1911, *An Ch'ang-ho charyojip*, vol. 1, p. 150; Paek Wŏn-bo, letter to An Ch'ang-ho, 23 Sep. 1912, *An Ch'ang-ho charyojip*, vol. 1, pp. 190-91.

298. Chang To-bin, letter to An Ch'ang-ho, 1 Nov. 1912, *Tosan An Ch'ang-ho charyojip*, vol. 3, p. 43.

299. The full name of the Kŭnŏphoe was the Ch'ŏngnyŏn Kŭnŏphoe (Youth Association for Diligence and Industry).

300. *Sinhan Minbo*, 26 July 1911, p. 3.

301. "Kangdong swinhae," *Hanin Sinbo*, 22 Oct. 1917, p. 3; Paek Wŏn-bo, letter to An Ch'ang-ho, 30 June 1911, *Tosan An Ch'ang-ho charyojip*, vol. 1, pp. 118-19.

302. AJMFA, SP. 205-6, 22389-22390.

303. *Taedong Kongbo*, 23 June 1910, p. 3.

304. Yun Pyŏng-sŏk and Yun Kyŏng-no ed., *An Ch'ang-ho iltaegi*, pp. 196-97; Arthur Leslie Gardner, "The Korean Nationalist Movement and An Ch'ang-ho, Advocate of Gradualism," pp. 132-40. Yi Kang's recollection is inaccurate. Yun Hae was in North Chientao working as a key leader of the Korean Educational Association and it was in the middle of 1912 that he came to Vladivostok.

305. *Sinhan Minbo*, 22 June 1910, p. 3.

306. Yi Kap, letter to An Ch'ang-ho, 3 Apr. 1911, *Tosan An Ch'ang-ho charyojip*, vol. 1, pp. 235-36; Yu Hyo-jong, "Kyokutō Roshia ni okeru Chōsen mizoku undō," pp. 150-51.

307. Kim Rip (1880-1922) was born in Myŏngch'ŏn, North Hamgyŏng Province, the same hometown as Yi Chong-ho. Kim Rip studied law and politics at Posŏng College in Seoul and got deeply involved in new educational activities as a member of the New

People's Association and the Northwestern Educational Association [Sŏbuk Hakhoe]. See Kim Kyu-myŏn, *Nobyŏng Kim Kyu-myŏn ŭi pimangnok esŏ*, p. 112. Kim Rip came to Vladivostok in early 1910. Kim Rip's political capability was so prominent that a Japanese official reported in 1919 that Kim Rip's "talent and knowledge is the best among the anti-Japanese Koreans." See "Zaigai hainichi Senjin yuryokusha meibo," p. 17. Yi Kwang-su who met Kim Rip in 1913 in Vladivostok evaluated him as a "schemer" ["*ch'aeksa*"] and key figure of the Kwŏnŏphoe and Kye Pong-u, Kim Rip's close friend also commented that in 1920, there was no one comparable to Kim Rip among Korean patriots in Shanghai. See Yi Kwang-su, "Na ŭi kobaek," p. 215 and Kye Pong-u *Kkum sog ŭi kkum*, vol. 2, p. 671. In Febrauary 1922, Kim Rip was assassinated in Shanghai by two young Koreans sent by Kim Ku, a key figure of the Korean Provisional Government.

308. Yu Hyo-jong, "Kyokutō Roshia ni okeru Chōsen mizoku undō," pp. 150-51; Hwang Kong-do, letter to An Ch'ang-ho, 18 July 1911, *Tosan An Ch'ang-ho charyojip*, vol. 1, p. 375.

309. Yu Chin-yul, letter to An Ch'ang-ho, 23 Aug. 1911, *Tosan An Ch'ang-ho charyojip*, vol. 3, p. 18; Paek Wŏn-bo, letter to An Ch'ang-ho, 30 June 1911, *Tosan An Ch'ang-ho charyojip*, vol. 1, p. 120. According to Paek Wŏn-bo, the *Taeyangbo* group decided to hand over the management of the newspaper to Yi Chong-ho in order to prevent the suspension of the newspaper.

310. Hwang Kong-do, letter to An Ch'ang-ho, 18 July 1911, *Tosan An Ch'ang-ho charyojip*, vol. 1, pp. 372-73. According to a Japanese report, the commercial company's name was Yanggunho (Shop for Training Soldiers, which was involved in preparing military activities. See Yun Pyŏng-sŏk, *Kugoe Hanin sahoe wa minjok undong*, 208.

311. Twibabo, "Aryŏng silgi," *Tongnip Sinmun*, Apr. 3 1920, p. 1; "Kangdong swinhae," *Hanin Sinbo*, 22 Oct. 1917, p. 3. Before he committed suicide, Yi Pŏm-jin donated 1,000 ruble to the school. The New Korean Village was formed when the Russian authorities ordered all Korean residents in Vladivostok to move to the region near Pervaia Rechka, the New Korean Village [Sinhanch'on] in March 1911. In spite of economic burden, Koreans could live in clean and improved environment and more importantly, the New Korean Village became the center of Korean patriotic activities. In 1911, there lived about 300 naturalized Korean households in the New Korean Village. See *Sinhan Minbo*, 3 May 1911, p. 3; AJMFA, MT1148, 203; 242.

312. Hwang Kong-do, letter to An Ch'ang-ho, 18 July 1911, *Tosan An Ch'ang-ho charyojip*, vol. 1, pp. 372-73.

313. Yi Kang and Chŏng Chae-gwan, letter to An Ch'ang-ho, 7 Aug. 1911, *Tosan An Ch'ang-ho charyojip*, vol. 1, p. 10.

314. *Sinhan Minbo*, 15 Mar. 1911, p. 3.

315. Ibid., 26 July 1911, p. 3; 9 Aug. 1911, p. 3; "Kangdong swinhae," *Hanin Sinbo*, 14 Oct. 1917, p. 3.

316. Yi Kang and Chŏng Chae-gwan, letter to An Ch'ang-ho, 7 Aug. 1911, *Tosan An Ch'ang-ho charyojip*, vol. 1, p. 10.

317. Paek Wŏn-bo, letter to An Ch'ang-ho, 30 June 1912, *Tosan An Ch'ang-ho charyojip*, vol. 1, p. 119; *Sinhan Minbo*, 9 Aug. 1911, p. 3.

318. Yi Kang and Chŏng Chae-gwan, letter to An Ch'ang-ho, 7 Aug. 1911, *Tosan An Ch'ang-ho charyojip*, vol. 1, p. 10; *Sinhan Minbo*, 23 Aug. 1911, p. 2; Yu Hyo-jong, "Kyokutō Roshia ni okeru Chōsen mizoku undō," p. 148; Song Sang-do, *Kiro sup'il*, p. 116.

319. Yi Kang and Chŏng Chae-gwan, letter to An Ch'ang-ho, 7 Aug. 1911, *Tosan An Ch'ang-ho charyojip*, vol. 1, p. 10.

320. Ibid., vol. 1, p. 10; Hwang Kong-do, letter to An Ch'ang-ho, 18 July 1911, *Tosan An Ch'ang-ho charyojip*, vol. 1, pp. 372-75.

321. Hwang Kong-do, letter to An Ch'ang-ho, 18 July 1911, *Tosan An Ch'ang-ho charyojip*, vol. 1, pp. 372-75.

322. Ibid., p. 372; Yu Chin-yul, letter to An Ch'ang-ho, 23 Aug. 1911, *Tosan An Ch'ang-ho charyojip*, vol. 3, pp. 18-20.

323. Pak Hwan, *Rŏsia Hanin minjok undongsa*, p. 146. It was Ŏm In-sŏp, An Chung-gŭn's oath brother that stole the printing types under orders of the Japanese Consulate General in Vladivostok.

324. Kim Sŏng-mu, letter to An Ch'ang-ho, n. d. 1912, *Tosan An Ch'ang-ho charyojip*, vol. 1, p. 300; Ch'oe Pong-jun, letter to An Ch'ang-ho, 18 Aug. 1911, *Tosan An Ch'ang-ho charyojip*, vol. 3, p. 38.

325. Paek Wŏn-bo, letter to An Ch'ang-ho, 16 Sep. 1911, *Tosan An Ch'ang-ho charyojip*, vol. 1, p. 163.

326. Ibid., pp. 172-73; Yun Chin-yul, letter to Yi Kap, 23 Aug. 1911, *Tosan An Ch'ang-ho charyojip*, vol. 1, pp. 379-80.

327. *Kwŏnŏp Sinmun*, 19 Dec. 1912, p. 3.

328. Pak Hwan, *Rŏsia Hanin minjok undongsa*, p. 123; "Izvlechenie iz Otcheta obshchestva Razvitiia Truda / Kuön-ön-khoi / za 1911 i 1912 g. g. / s 6-go Dekabria 1911 goda po 1-oe Ianvaria 1913 goda" [Excerpts from the Report of the Work Promotion Association / Kwŏnŏphoe / for 1911 and 1912 / from December 6, 1911 to January 1, 1913] (St. Petersburg Central State Historical Archives).

329. Paek Wŏn-bo, letter to An Ch'ang-ho, 29 Dec. 1911, *Tosan An Ch'ang-ho charyojip*, vol. 1, pp. 172-73; Yi Kang, letter to An Ch'ang-ho, 12 Feb. 1912, *Tosan An Ch'ang-ho charyojip*, vol. 1, pp. 56-57; Paek Wŏn-bo, letter to An Ch'ang-ho, 9 Mar. 1912, *Tosan An Ch'ang-ho charyojip*, vol. 1, pp. 175-76. Chŏng Chae-gwan arrived at Vladivostok

in January and the Kwŏnŏphoe leaders resolved to persuade Yu Chin-yul, Kim Kyu-sŏp, Ch'a Sŏk-po, and Ch'oe Pong-jun, four main figures rejecting the Kwŏnŏphoe, to join. Among these four, all except Yu Chin-yul joined the association.

330. *Kwŏnŏp Sinmun*, 19 Dec. 1912, p. 3.
331. Boris Dmitrievich Pak, *Koreitsy v Rossiiskoi imperii*, pp. 212-13.
332. Ibid., pp. 212-13.
333. Twibabo, "Aryŏng silgi," *Tongnip Sinmun*, 3 Apr. 1920, p. 1; Kye Pong-u, *Kkum sog ŭi kkum*, vol. 1, p. 162.
334. Din'shun' Pak, "Koreiskaia emigratsiia v Rossii."
335. *Sinhan Minbo*, 23 Aug. 1911, p. 1.
336. *Taehanin Chŏnggyobo*, 3, 1 May 1912, p. 27.
337. *Kwŏnŏp Sinmun*, 8 Feb. 1914, p. 1.
338. Ibid., 19 Dec. 1912; 3. Polianovsky was the drafter of the Kwŏnŏphoe regulations.
339. *Kwŏnŏp Sinmun*, 19 Dec. 1912, p. 3; 22 Dec. 1912, p. 2.
340. Ibid., 29 Dec. 1912, p. 3; AJMFA, MT1148, 255.
341. "Izvlechenie iz Otcheta obshchestva Razvitiia Truda."
342. Ibid.; "Svedeniia o Koreiskoi ezhenedel'noi gazete 'Kuon-op-sim-mun'" (Information about the Korean Weekly Newspaper *Kwŏnŏp Sinmun*], Tomsk Far Eastern State Central Archives, 30 Aug. 1914.
343. Yun Pyŏng-sŏk, *Kugoe Hanin sahoe was minjok undong*, pp. 194-95; Pak Hwan, *Rŏsia Hanin minjok undongsa*, pp. 156-79.
344. *Kwŏnŏp Sinmun*, 19 Dec. 1912, p. 3.
345. Ibid., p. 3; 3 Nov. 1912, p. 3; 7 Dec. 1913, p. 3; 9 Feb. 1913, p. 2; 20 Apr. 1913, p. 3; 1 Feb. 1914, p. 2; 15 Feb. 1914, p. 2; 26 Apr. 1914, p. 2; 3 May 1914, p. 2; 31 May 1914, p. 2; 9 May 1914, p. 2; 14 June 1914, p. 2; 21 June 1914, p. 3; 26 July 1914, p. 2.
346. *Kwŏnŏp Sinmun*, 26 July 1914, p. 1.
347. Ibid., 23 Nov. 1913, p. 3.
348. *Kwŏnŏp Sinmun*, 8 Feb. 1914, p. 1.
349. "Izvlechenie iz Otcheta obshchestva Razvitiia Truda."
350. *Kwŏnŏp Sinmun*, 22 Mar. 1914, p. 2.
351. Ibid., 1 Dec. 1912, p. 4.
352. *Kwŏnŏp Sinmun*, 30 Mar. 1913, p. 2.
353. Ibid., 19 Dec. 1912, p. 3.
354. "Izvlechenie iz Otcheta obshchestva Razvitiia Truda."
355. *Kwŏnŏp Sinmun*, 20 Apr. 1913, p. 2-3; 14 Dec. 1913, p. 3; 11 Jan. 1914, p. 3; 11 Jan. 1914, p. 3; 18 Jan. 1914, p. 1. Limited qualification (only for naturalized Koreans), lack of financial support, and the misunderstanding of Koreans were pointed to as the main causes for the failure. See *Kwŏnŏp Sinmun*, 2 Aug. 1914.

356. Ibid., 25 Jan. 1913, p. 3; 26 Jan. 1913, p. 3.

357. *Kwŏnŏp Sinmun*, 31 Aug. 1913, p. 1.

358. Ibid., 2 Mar. 1913, p. 3.

359. *Kwŏnŏp Sinmun*, 11 Jan. 1914, p. 1.

360. Ibid., 8 Feb. 1914, p. 2; Boris Dmitrievich Pak, *Koreitsy v Rossiiskoi imperii*, p. 214.

361. *Kwŏnŏp Sinmun*, 5 Apr. 1914, p. 2; Boris Dmitrievich Pak, *Koreitsy v Rossiiskoi imperii*, p. 215.

362. Ibid., 12 Apr. 1914, p. 1; 26 Apr. 1914, p. 3; Boris Dmitrievich Pak, *Koreitsy v Rossiiskoi imperii*, p. 214. The executive members of the committee were Ch'oe Chae-hyŏng (President), Elisei Lukich Han (Vice-President), Kim Ki-ryong (Secretary) and Ham Se-in.

363. *Kwŏnŏp Sinmun*, 26 Apr. 1914, p. 3.

364. Yu Hyo-jong, "Kyokutō Roshia ni okeru Chōsen mizoku undō," p. 155.

365. Kye Pong-u, *Kkum sog ŭi kkum*, vol. 1, p. 169; Twibabo, "Aryŏng silgi (9)," *Tongnip Sinmun*, 30 Mar. 1920, p. 1.

366. Yi Tong-hwi, letter to An Ch'ang-ho, 3 Feb. 1914, *Tosan An Ch'ang-ho charyojip*, vol. 2, p. 298.

367. Yi Tong-hwi, letter to An Ch'ang-ho, 7 Jan. 1914, *Tosan An Ch'ang-ho charyojip*, vol. 1, pp. 398-99.

368. Twibabo, "Aryŏng silgi (9)," *Tongnip Sinmun*, 30 Mar. 1920, p. 1; Kye Pong-u, "Riryŏksŏ," [Resume], ms., Jan. 1936; Kye Pong-u, *Kkum sog ŭi kkum*, vol. 1, pp. 169-71.

369. Yi Hong-jik, *Kuksa taesajŏn* [Korean History Encyclopedia] (Seoul: Chimungak, 1968), p. 1337.

370. Hwang Uk, "Chae oe kak chibang sanghwang: Sojaha chibang chŏnghwang [Situation of Every Region Abroad: Sojaha Region]; *Tongnip Sinmun*, 4 Apr. 1923, p. 4.

371. Yi Kang, letter to An Ch'ang-ho, 5 Mar. 1914, *Tosan An Ch'ang-ho charyojip*, vol. 1, p. 92; Kye Pong-u, *Kkum sog ŭi kkum*, vol. 1, p. 169.

372. Kye Pong-u, *Kkum sog ŭi kkum*, vol. 1, p. 169.

373. Twibabo, "Aryŏng silgi (9)" *Tongnip Sinmun*, 30 Mar. 1920, p. 1; Kye Pong-u, *Kkum sog ŭi kkum*, vol. 1, pp. 169-70.

374. *Zaigai hainichi Senjin yuryokusha meibo*, 28.

375. Twibabo, "Aryŏng silgi (9)" *Tongnip Sinmun*, 30 Mar. 1920, p. 1. Local Russian officials were worried that anti-Japanese Koreans might utilize the ceremony of the fiftieth anniversary of Korean immigration to Russia for radical purposes, presumably military activities. When Ch'oe Chae-hyŏng visited Gondatti on May 30, 1914, in order to report on the ceremony project, Gondatti raised such concerns of Russians. See *Kwŏnŏp Sinmun*, 31 May 1914, p. 3.

376. For example, the Military-Governor ordered the cancellation of founding ceremony of the Kwŏnŏphoe scheduled for January 27, 1912. *Kwŏnŏp Sinmun*, 19 Dec. 1912, p. 3.

377. Kim Chŏng-ju [Kin Sei-tsū] ed., *Chōsen tōchi shiryō*, vol. 1, p. 618. As we saw, Gondatti did not keep his promise and became an honorary member of the Kwŏnŏphoe.

378. Boris Dmitrievich Pak, *Koreitsy v Rossiiskoi imperii*, p. 217.

379. Ibid., pp. 221-22.

380. *Kwŏnŏp Sinmun*, 21 July 1912, p. 2; *Zaigai hainichi Senjin yuryokusha meibo*, pp. 5, 9-11.

381. Yi Kang, letter to An Ch'ang-ho, 1 Aug. 1912, *Tosan An Ch'ang-ho charyojip*, vol. 1, p. 63.

382. *Kwŏnŏp Sinmun*, 28 July 1912, p. 3; 1 Sep. 1912, p. 2; Paek Wŏn-bo, letter to An Ch'ang-ho, 22 July 1912, *Tosan An Ch'ang-ho charyojip*, vol. 1, p. 184; Paek Wŏn-bo, letter to An Ch'ang-ho, 22 Sep. 1912, *Tosan An Ch'ang-ho charyojip*, vol. 1, pp. 187-88; Wada Haruki, "Nichiro tōbō hanzainin hikiwatashi jōyaku fuzoku himitsu sengensho," pp. 113-14. Ch'oe Kwan-hŭl, a Presbyterian pastor dispatched from Korea, was arrested in Harbin, but was released by the help of Vasilii O, a Russian Orthodox priest in Vladivostok. After his release, Ch'oe immediately became a Russian Orthodox missionary. See "Kangdong swinhae," *Hanin Sinbo*, 22 Oct. 1917, p. 3.

383. *Kwŏnŏp Sinmun*, 25 Aug. 1912, p. 2; Ibid., 1 Sep., 1912, p. 2; *Zaigai hainichi Senjin yuryokusha meibo*, p. 48.

384. *Kwŏnŏp Sinmun*, 21 Dec. 1913, p. 3; 3 Nov. 1912, p. 2.

385. Wada, "Nichiro tōbō hanzainin hikiwatashi jōyaku fuzoku himitsu sengensho," p. 114.

386. Boris Dmitrievich Pak, *Koreitsy v Rossiiskoi imperii*, p. 192.

387. Ibid., pp. 216-17. As we saw earlier, the Kwŏnŏphoe was entrusted with the census by the Military-Governor of the Primorye.

388. Paek Wŏn-bo, letter to An Ch'ang-ho, 22 Sep. 1912, *Tosan An ch'ang-ho charyojip*, vol. 1, pp. 186-87; *Sinhan Minbo*, 18 Mar. 1915, p. 1.

389. Paek Wŏn-bo, letter to An Ch'ang-ho, 22 Sep. 1912, *Tosan An ch'ang-ho charyojip*, vol. 1, pp. 186-87; 21 Jan. 1913, vol. 1, pp. 190-91.

390. Yi Kang, letter to An Ch'ang-ho, 27 Nov. 1913, *Tosan An ch'ang-ho charyojip*, vol. 1, pp. 186-87: AJMFA SP. 128, 11.

391. AJMFA SP. 128, 11. The Seoul faction and Western faction complained of Yi Chong-ho's strong influence in the Kwŏnŏphoe. Most of the expenses for the activities of the Kwŏnŏphoe and the *Kwŏnŏp Sinmun*, particularly in the first year (1912) relied heavily on the financial support of Yi Chong-ho. Although membership fees and donations from other members increased, Yi Chong-ho's financial contribution was crucial factor for the Kwŏnŏphoe. See *Kwŏnŏp Sinmun*, 8 Feb. 1914, p. 1; "Kangdong

swinhae" *Hanin Sinbo*, 22 Oct. 1917, p. 3; Yi Kang, letter to An Ch'ang-ho, 1 Aug. 1912, *Tosan An Ch'ang-ho charyojip*, vol. 1, p. 64. Yi Chong-ho's financial support contributed to various kinds of anti-Japanese activities not only in the Primorye, but also in North Chientao. For example, of the total reported annual expenses for the Kwŏnŏphoe (3141 rubles), two thirds (2133 rubles) was donated by Yi Chong-ho. See "Izvlechenie iz Otcheta obshchestva Razvitiia Truda."

392. Yi Kap, letter to Ch'oe Chŏng-ik etc., 24 Nov. 1911, *Tosan An Ch'ang-ho charyojip*, vol. 1, pp. 263-64.

393. Yi Kap, letter to An Ch'ang-ho, 9 Nov. 1911, *Tosan An Ch'ang-ho charyojip*, vol. 1, 259. As of August 1914, about 370 copies of the *Sinhan Minbo* were distributed in the Far East. See *Sinhan Minbo*, 6 Aug. 1914, p. 2.

394. *Sinhan Minbo*, 9 Dec. 1912, p. 3.

395. Paek Wŏng-bo, letter to An Ch'ang-ho, 16 Sep. 1911, *Tosan An Ch'ang-ho charyojip*, vol. 1, pp. 162-64.

396. Yi Kang and Chŏng Chae-gwan, letter to An Ch'ang-ho, 12 Sep. 1911, *Tosan An Ch'ang-ho charyojip*, vol. 1, p. 17.

397. Ibid., 17.

398. Yi Kang, letter to An Ch'ang-ho, 12 Feb. 1912, *Tosan An Ch'ang-ho charyojip*, vol. 1, p. 57.

399. Yi Kang and Chŏng Chae-gwan, letter to An Ch'ang-ho, 12 Sep. 1911, *Tosan An Ch'ang-ho charyojip*, vol. 1, p. 14.

400. *Sinhan Minbo*, 12 July 1911, p. 3.

401. Yi Kang, letter to An Ch'ang-ho, 21 Sep. 1913, *Tosan An Ch'ang-ho charyojip*, vol. 1, p. 73.

402. *Sinhan Minbo*, 7 June 1911, p. 2; 19 July 1911, p. 2.

403. Yi Kang and Chŏng Chae-gwan, letter to An Ch'ang-ho, 20 Dec. 1911, *Tosan An Ch'ang-ho charyojip*, vol. 1, p. 51.

404. *Sinhan Minbo*, 12 July 1911, p. 3. Other executive members were Kwŏn Hwa-sun (Vice-President) and Ko Sŏng-sam (Chief of General Affairs) who were all from Hamgyŏng Provinces.

405. Yi Kang and Chŏng Chae-gwan, letter to Ch'oe Chŏng-ik, 23 Sep. 1911, *Tosan An Ch'ang-ho charyojip*, vol. 1, p. 19.

406. *Taehanin Chŏnggyobo* 1, 2 Jan. 1912, p. 33.

407. Ibid., p. 2.

408. *Taehanin Chŏnggyobo* 1, 2 Jan. 1912; Ibid 2, 3 Feb. 1912; Ibid 3, 1 May 1912.

409. Boris Dmitrievich Pak, *Koreitsy v Rossiiskoi imperii*, p. 228.

410. Yi Kang and Chŏng Chae-gwan, letter to An Ch'ang-ho, 16 Nov. 1911, *Tosan An Ch'ang-ho charyojip*, vol. 1, pp. 47-48.

411. Yi Kang, letter to An Ch'ang-ho, 20 Dec. 1911, *Tosan An Ch'ang-ho charyojip*, vol. 1, p. 51.

412. *Sinhan Minbo*, 18 Oct. 1912, p. 3. Twelve branches in the Suchan region were put under the control of the Suchan Regional Central Committee and five other branches in Nikol'sk-Ussurisk, Perm', Osoriman (Ussuri Bay region), Koryŏ, and Tiumen were under the direct control of the Central Committee.

413. Yi Kang, letter to An Ch'ang-ho, 12 Feb. 1912, *Tosan An Ch'ang-ho charyojip*, vol. 1, pp. 56-57.

414. The report on the two congresses can be seen in *Tosan An Ch'ang-ho charyojip*, vol. 3, pp. 103-32.

415. *Tosan An Ch'ang-ho charyojip*, vol. 3, p. 112.

416. Ibid., p. 118.

417. *Tosan An Ch'ang-ho charyojip*, vol. 3, pp. 114-15.

418. *Sinhan Minbo*, 11 Nov. 1915, p. 3.

419. Paek Wŏn-bo, letter to An Ch'ang-ho, 21 Jan. 1913, *Tosan An Ch'ang-ho charyojip*, vol. 1, pp. 190-91; Chŏng Kyŏng-o, letter to An Ch'ang-ho, 28 Nov. 1912, *Tosan An Ch'ang-ho charyojip*, vol. 1, p. 394.

420. *Kwŏnŏp Sinmun*, 16 Aug. 1914, p. 1.

421. Ibid., 23 Aug. 1914, p. 1.

422. *Kwŏnŏp Sinmun*, 16 Aug. 1914, p. 2.

423. Boris Dmitrievich Pak, *Koreitsy v Rossiiskoi imperii*, p. 217; "Kangdong swinhae," *Hanin Sinbo*, 22 Oct. 1917, p. 3; Kye Pong-u, *Kkum sog ŭi kkum*, vol. 1, pp. 169-70; Kim Chŏng-ju [Kin Sei-tsū] ed., *Chōsen tōchi shiryō*, vol. 7, p. 619; Pak Hwan, *Rŏsia Hanin minjok undongsa*, p. 179. At the end of 1914, all non-naturalized Koreans were expelled from Pos'et region. See Kim Chŏng-ju [Kin Sei-tsū] ed., *Chōsen tōchi shiryō*, vol. 7, p. 619.

424. Twibabo, "Aryŏng silgi (9)" *Tongnip Sinmun*, 30 Mar. 1920, p. 1.

425. Nomura (Japanese Consul General in Vladivostok), letter to the Military-Governor of the Primorye, 20 Aug. 1914 (Far Eastern Central State Archives in Tomsk, F. 1, O. 12, E. 581).

426. Boris Dmitrievich Pak, *Koreitsy v Rossiiskoi imperii*, p. 230. Yi Sang-sŏl, at that time, resigned from all activities related to the Kwŏnŏphoe and the Korean Restoration Military Government as a result of dissatisfaction with Yi Chong-ho at the end of 1913.

427. Nomura, letter to the Military-Governor of the Primorye.

428. *Zaigai hainichi Senjin yuryokusha meibo*, p. 5.

429. Boris Dmitrievich Pak, *Koreitsy v Rossiiskoi imperii*, p. 218.

430. *Zaigai hainichi Senjin yuryokusha meibo*, p. 13; Boris Dmitrievich Pak, *Koreitsy v Rossiiskoi imperii*, p. 230.

431. Yi Kang, letter to An Ch'ang-ho, 11 Mar. 1915, *Tosan An Ch'ang-ho charyojip*, vol. 1, p. 4.

432. *Sinhan Minbo*, 11 Nov. 1915, p. 3; Kim Chŏng-ju [Kin Sei-tsū] ed., *Chōsen tōchi shiryō*, vol. 7, p. 619. According to Boris Dmitrievich Pak, 15 Koreans were arrested at that time. See Boris Dmitrievich Pak, *Koreitsy v Rossiiskoi imperii*, p. 226. While Kungminhoe leaders were still on bail, Nam Ch'ang-sŏk's group convened their own congress of representatives on July 15, 1915, and attempted to organize their own "Kungminhoe" by destroying the Kungminhoe led by Yi Kang and Chŏng Chae-gwan. Only three of more than 20 branches dispatched representatives to the congress.

433. Kim Chŏng-ju [Kin Sei-tsū] ed., *Chōsen tōchi shiryō*, vol. 7, p. 619.

434. Ibid., p. 619.

435. *Sinhan Minbo*, 22, Feb. 1916, p. 1.

436. Boris Dmitrievich Pak, *Koreitsy v Rossiiskoi imperii*, pp. 223-24; Pak Hwan, *Rŏsia Hanin minjok undongsa*, p. 239.

437. Ibid., pp. 224-25.

438. Boris Dmitrievich Pak, *Koreitsy v Rossiiskoi imperii*, p. 233.

439. Ibid., p. 228.

440. Yi Yŏng-il, "Yi Tong-hwi Sŏngjae sŏnsaeng" [Mr. Yi Tong-hwi], *Hangukhak Yŏngu*, 5, July 1993 (Inch'ŏn: Center for Korean Studies, Inha University), p. 204.

441. "Yi Tong-hwi tongmu i ilsaeng," *Sŏnbong*, 4 Feb. 1935, p. 4; Yi Yŏng-il, "Yi Tong-hwi Sŏngjae sŏnsaeng," p. 201.

442. Sabangja, *Tongnip Sinmun*, 1 Jan. 1920, p. 5; Twibabo, "Kim Alneksandra chŏn" [Biography of Alexandra Kim], *Tongnip Sinmun*, 20 Apr. 1920, p. 3; Kim Chŏng-myŏng [Kin Seimei] ed., *Chōsen dokuritsu undō* [Korean Independence Movement], vol. 5, p. 292.

443. Kim Kyu-myŏn, *Sŏngjae yakchŏn e kwanhan hoesanggi*, p. 3.

444. Kim Chŏng-myŏng [Kin Seimei] ed., *Chōsen dokuritsu undō [Korean Independence Movement]*, vol. 3, pp. 425-27. Confucianist Konggyohoe members such as Kim Chŏng-gyu, Ch'a Ho-gyun and Chi Chang-hoe also had great expectations of a Sino-Japanese war, but were deeply disappointed with the conclusion of the Twenty-one Demands. The Japanese Consulate held a big party in celebration of the diplomatic agreement. See Kim Chŏng-gyu, *Yongyŏn Kim Chŏng-gyu ilgi*, vol. 3, pp. 117-20, 211.

445. Kim Chŏng-myŏng [Kin Seimei] ed., *Chōsen dokuritsu undō* [Korean Independence Movement], vol. 3, p. 427.

446. Ibid., p. 427.

447. Yi Yŏng-il, "Yi Tong-hwi Sŏngjae sŏnsaeng," p. 203.

448. Twibabo, "Kim Alneksandra chŏn," *Tongnip Sinmun*, 20 Apr. 1920, p. 3.

449. Kye Pong-u, *Kkum sog ŭi kkum*, vol. 1, p. 173; *Sinhan Minbo*, 12 July 1917, p. 2.

450. *Zaigai hainichi Senjin yuryokusha meibo* [Register of Influential Anti-Japanese Koreans], ms., 1919, p. 37.

451. Kye Pong-u, *Kkum sog ŭi kkum*, vol. 1, pp. 173-76.

452. AJMFA MT11259, 292-297.

453. AJMFA, MT52254, 1126-1130; MT52255, 365-368; *The Manchurian Daily News*, 5 Apr. 1915; Boris Dmitrievich Pak, *Koreitsy v Rossiiskoi imperii*, p. 234.

454. AJMFA, MT52254, 272.

455. Boris Dmitrievich Pak, *Koreitsy v Rossiiskoi imperii*, p. 234.

456. Ibid., pp. 234-35.

457. *Sinhan Minbo*, 8 Sep. 1916, p. 2; 21 Sep. 1916, p. 2.

458. Kim Kyu-myŏn, *Sŏngjae yakchŏn e kwanhan hoesanggi*, p. 3; Kye Pong-u, *Kkum sog ŭi kkum*, vol. 1, p. 170.

459. *Sinhan Minbo*, 8 Sep. 1916.

460. Kim Chŏng-ju [Kin Sei-tsū] ed., *Chōsen tōchi shiryō*, vol. 10, p. 44.

461. *Sinhan Minbo*, 15 Feb. 1917.

462. Ibid., 24 May 1917, p. 3; 16 July 1917, p. 3.

463. *Sinhan Minbo*, 12 July 1917, p. 2.

464. Ibid., 4 Oct. 1917, p. 3; Yi Yŏng-il, "Yi Tong-hwi Sŏngjae sŏnsaeng," pp. 207, 209; Paek Wŏn-bo, letter to An Ch'ang-ho, *Tosan An Ch'ang-ho charyojip*, vol. 1, p. 221.

465. *Sinhan Minbo*, 16 Aug. 1917; 3; AJMFA, SP. 205-6, 22388; Kim Chŏng-myŏng [Kin Seimei] ed., *Chōsen dokuritsu undō* [Korean Independence Movement], vol. 10, p. 44.

Chapter Three

1. Paek Wŏn-bo, letter to An Ch'ang-ho, 23 July 1917, *Tosan An Ch'ang-ho charyojip*, vol. 1, p. 219.

2. "Japanization of Korea: General Ichibana Interviewed," *Japan Chronicle*, 17 Apr. 1916.

3. Din'shun Pak, "Koreiskaia emigratsiia v Rossii."

4. Pak Ŭn-sik, *Hanguk tongnip undong chi hyŏlsa*, p. 164.

5. Walter Kolarz, *The Peoples of the Soviet Far East* (New York: Frederick A. Praeger, 1954), p. 34.

6. *Sinhan Minbo*, 23 Aug. 1917, p. 3: 15 Nov. 1917, p. 3.

7. Ivan Gozhenskii, "Uchastie Koreiskii emigratsii v revoliutsionnom dvizhenii na Dal'nem Vostoke," p. 360.

8. Kolarz, *The Peoples of the Soviet Far East*, 34.

9. Boris Dmitrievich Pak, *Koreitsy v Rossiiskoi imperii*, p. 248.

10. Kim Chŏng-ju [Kin Sei-tsū] ed., *Chōsen tōchi shiryō*, vol. 10, p. 45.

11. Ibid., vol. 10, p. 45.
12. Paek Wŏn-bo, letter to An Ch'ang-ho, *Tosan An Ch'ang-ho charyojip*, vol. 1, pp. 220-21.
13. Din'shun' Pak, "Koreiskaia emigratsiia v Rossii."
14. Ivan Gozhenskii, "Uchastie Koreiskii emigratsii v revoliutsionnom dvizhenii na Dal'nem Vostoke," p. 360; Din'shun Pak', "Koreiskaia emigratsiia v Rossii."
15. Kim Chŏng-ju [Kin Sei-tsū] ed., *Chōsen tōchi shiryō*, vol. 10, p. 45.
16. Ivan Gozhenskii, "Uchastie Koreiskii emigratsii v revoliutsionnom dvizhenii na Dal'nem Vostoke," p. 360; Din'shun' Pak, "Koreiskaia emigratsiia v Rossii."
17. Kim Chŏng-ju [Kin Sei-tsū] ed., *Chōsen tōchi shiryō*, vol. 10, p. 34.
18. Ivan Gozhenskii, "Uchastie Koreiskii emigratsii v revoliutsionnom dvizhenii na Dal'nem Vostoke," p. 360; Din'shun Pak, "Koreiskaia emigratsiia v Rossii."
19. Semen Davidovich Anosov, *Koreitsy v Ussuriiskom krae*, p. 19; Boris Dmitrievich Pak, *Koreitsy v Rossiiskoi imperii*, p. 249.
20. Kim Chŏng-ju [Kin Sei-tsū] ed., *Chōsen tōchi shiryō*, vol. 10, pp. 45-46; Ivan Gozhenskii, "Uchastie Koreiskii emigratsii v revoliutsionnom dvizhenii na Dal'nem Vostoke," p. 360.
21. Ivan Gozhenskii, "Uchastie Koreiskii emigratsii v revoliutsionnom dvizhenii na Dal'nem Vostoke," p. 361.
22. Paek Wŏn-po, letter to An Ch'ang-ho, *Tosan An Ch'ang-ho charyojip*, vol. 1, p. 221; Ivan Gozhenskii, "Uchastie Koreiskii emigratsii v revoliutsionnom dvizhenii na Dal'nem Vostoke," p. 361.
23. Paek Wŏn-bo, letter to An Ch'ang-ho, *Tosan An Ch'ang-ho charyojip*, vol. 1, p. 221.
24. Ivan Gozhenskii, "Uchastie Koreiskii emigratsii v revoliutsionnom dvizhenii na Dal'nem Vostoke," p. 361; Yu Hyo-jong, "Kyokutō Roshia ni okeru jiūgatsu kakumei to Chōsenjin shyakai" [The October Revolution and the Korean communities in the Russian Far East], *Roshiashi Kenkyū*, 45, 1987, p. 24.
25. *Sinhan Minbo*, 16 Aug. 1917; 3. AJMFA, SP. 205-6, 22388. The Japanese agent in Russia reported to Government-General Hosegawa, in February 1918, and also pointed out that the main anti-Japanese Korean nationalists died or were in prison, and "the figures, who belong to the second class, lack both power and finance, so although they once voiced anti-Japanese arguments, now there is no one who sympathizes with those arguments." See Kim Chŏng-ju [Kin Sei-tsū] ed., *Chōsen tōchi shiryō*, vol. 10, p. 44.
26. *Sinhan Minbo*, 21 Sep. 1916, p. 3; Paek Wŏn-bo, letter to An Ch'ang-ho, in *Tosan An Ch'ang-ho charyojip*, vol. 1, p. 221. Kim Rip was released on 23 May 1917, about two months after the February Revolution.
27. *Sinhan Minbo*, 4 Oct. 1917, p. 3; Paek Wŏn-bo, letter to An Ch'ang-ho, *Tosan An*

Ch'ang-ho charyojip, vol. 1, p. 221; Yi Yŏng-il, "Yi Tong-hwi Sŏngjae sŏnsaeng," p. 209; *Sinhan Minbo*, 4 Oct. 1917, p. 3.

28. *Sinhan Minbo*, 13 Sep. 1917, p. 3.
29. Kim Chŏng-ju [Kin Sei-tsū] ed., *Chōsen tōchi shiryō*, vol. 10, pp. 45-46.
30. Yu Hyo-jong, "Kyokutō Roshia ni okeru jūgatsu kakumei to Chōsenjin shakai," p. 24.
31. John J. Stephan, *The Russian Far East: A History*, p. 113; Sugimori Kouji and Fujimoto Wakio, *Nichi-Ro Nisso kankei '200-nenshi': Nichi-ro no dei kara Shiberia kansho senso made* [Two Hundred Japanese-Russian and Japanese-Soviet Relations from the Encounter of Japan and Russia through the Siberian Intervention War] (Tokyo: Shinjidaisha, 1983), pp. 191-94.
32. *Sinhan Minbo*, 4 Oct. 1917, p. 3.
33. Paek Wŏn-bo, letter to An Ch'ang-ho, *Tosan An Ch'ang-ho charyojip*, vol. 1, p. 221.
34. *Hanin Sinbo*, 7 Oct. 1917; *Sinhan Minbo*, 21 Sep. 1916, p. 3; 12 July 1917, p. 3.
35. *Sinhan Minbo*, 8 Nov. 1917, p. 3; 13 Dec. 1917, p. 3.
36. Paek Wŏn-bo, letter to An Ch'ang-ho, *Tosan An Ch'ang-ho charyojip*, vol. 1, p. 221.
37. *Hanin Sinbo*, 4 Nov. 1917, p. 2; *Sinhan Minbo*, 13 Dec. 1917, p. 3.
38. Ibid, 4 Nov. 1917, p. 2; *Ch'ŏnggu Sinbo*, 18 Nov. 1917, p. 3.
39. Yi In-sŏp, "Ch'oe Ko-ryŏ chasŏjŏn ŭl yŏnguhadaga na ŭi sogam," p. 45. The Bolshevik government later reviewed the documents titled "Delo Li Donkhi" [The Case of Yi Tong-hwi] filed in the documents of the Kolchak government, and found out that Kerensky's Russian Provisional Government and the Kolchak government regarded Yi Tong-hwi as "the most dangerous figure" among the Koreans. It is said that this contributed to enhance the confidence of Bolshevik leaders in Yi Tong-hwi.
40. Yi In-sŏp, "Aleksandra Kim ŭi chŏngi (1)" [A Biography of Alexandra Kim], *Sisa Journal*, 216, 16 Dec. 1993, p. 76.
41. Ivan Gozhenskii, "Uchastie Koreiskii emigratsii v revoliutsionnom dvizhenii na Dal'nem Vostoke," p. 361.
42. Yi Yŏng-il, "Yi Tong-hwi Sŏngjae sŏnsaeng," pp. 209-10.
43. Inseb Li [Yi In-sŏp], "Vospominania o godakh interventsii i grazhdanskoi voiny na Dal'nem Vostoke, 1918-1922 gg." [Recollections on the Years of Intervention and Civil War in the Far East, 1918-1922], ts., 1962, p. 2.
44. Twibabo, "Kim Alneksandra chŏn," *Tongnip Sinmun*, 20 Apr. 1920, p. 3; Twibabo, "Aryŏng silgi (1)," *Tongnip Sinmun*, 1 Mar. 1920, p. 8.
45. Inseb Li, "Biografiya Aleksandry Petrovny Kim-Stankevich" [Biography of Alexandra Petrovna Kim Stankevich], ts., 1963, p. 1; Twibabo, "Kim Alneksandra chŏn," *Tongnip Sinmun*, 20 Apr. 1920, p. 3; Syn Khva Kim, *Ocherki po istorii sovetskikh koreitsev*, p. 91.
46. "Kangdong swinhae," *Hanin Sinbo*, 30 Sep. 1917, p. 3; Twibabo, "Aryŏng silgi (5),"

Tongnip Sinmun, 13 Mar. 1920, p. 3; Matvei Timofeevich Kim, *Koreiskie internatsionalisty v bor'be za vlast' sovetov na Dal'nem Vostoke, 1918-1922* [The Korean Internationalists Who Fought for Soviet Power in the Far East] (Moscow: Nauka, 1979), p. 49.

47. Yi In-sŏp, "Aleksandra Kim ŭi chŏngi (1)," p. 73.

48. Inseb Li, "Biografiya Aleksandry Petrovny Kim-Stankevich," p. 1.

49. Yi In-sŏp, "Aleksandra Kim ŭi chŏngi (1)," pp. 73-74.

50. Ibid., p. 74; M. T. Kim, *Koreiskie internatsionalisty v bor'be za vlasti sovetov na Dal'nem Vostoke (1918-1922)*, p. 50.

51. Inseb Li, "Biografiya Aleksandry Petrovny Kim-Stankevich," p. 1.

52. Yi In-sŏp, "Aleksandra Kim ŭi chŏngi (1)," p. 74.

53. Ibid., p. 74; *Taedong Kongbo*, 21 Aug. 1910, 14 Aug. 1910: 11 Aug. 1910: 4 Aug. 1910: 30 Jun. 1910; *Hanin Sinbo*, 14 Oct. 1917.

54. Yi In-sŏp, "Aleksandra Kim ŭi chŏngi (1)," p. 74.

55. Ibid., p. 74. According to Twibabo, Alexandra Kim had already worked as an underground revolutionary in 1914, and was expelled by Russian authorities from the Vladivostok fortress area to the Urals. The Russian authorities were concerned over the possibility that Russian revolutionaries might take advantage of the situation caused by the outbreak of World War I. See Twibabo, "Kim Alneksandra chŏn," *Tongnip Sinmun*, 20 Apr. 1920, p. 3.

56. Yi In-sŏp, "Aleksandra Kim ŭi chŏngi (1)," p. 74; Twibabo, "Kim Alneksandra chŏn," *Tongnip Sinmun*, 20 Apr. 1920, p. 3; M. T. Kim, *Koreiskie internatsionalisty v bor'be za vlast, sovetov na Dal'nem Vostoke (1918-1922)*, p. 73.

57. "Kangdong swinhae," *Hanin Sinbo*, 30 Sep. 1917, p. 3.

58. Kim Pyŏng-hak received 10,000 rubles from the Russian authorities in advance and gathered thousands of Korean workers and sent them to the Urals. Kim Pyŏng-hak was born in Russia and made money as a *podriadchik* during the construction of the Trans-Siberian Railroad. He was listed as one of the wealthiest persons among the Koreans in the Russian Far East together with Ch'oe Pong-jun who became wealthy by operating a military supply business during the Russo-Japanese War. About 3,000-4,000 Chinese workers were also sent from Harbin to the Urals. See Twibabo, "Kim Alneksandra chŏn," *Tongnip Sinmun*, 20 Apr. 1920.

59. Twibabo, "Kim Alneksandra chŏn," *Tongnip Sinmun*, 20 Apr. 1920, p. 3; H. M, "Chosŏn ŭi yŏryujuŭija ko Kim Sttankkebi yŏsa yakchŏn" [A Short History of Korean Feminist, the Late Mrs. Stankevich Kim], *Kaebyŏk*, 57, Mar. 1925, pp. 27-28; Yi In-sŏp, "Aleksandra Kim ŭi chŏngi (1)," p. 74; M. T. Kim, *Koreiskie internatsionalisty v bor'be za vlasti sovetov na Dal'nem Vostoke (1918-1922)*, p. 73.

60. In order to avoid possible conflicts with the Japanese government, the Chinese

government arrested some Korean activists and abolished private schools managed by Koreans. The military Academy at Luozigou, Wangqing Prefecture in North Chientao was apparently forced to close by the Chinese government. See Kim Chŏng-myŏng [Kin Seimei] ed., *Chōsen dokuritsu undō* [Korean Independence Movement], vol. 3, pp. 425-27.

61. Twibabo, "Kim Alneksandra chŏn," *Tongnip Sinmun*, 20 Apr. 1920; H. M 28; Kim Chŏng-myŏng [Kin Seimei] ed., *Chōsen dokuritsu undō* [Korean Independence Movement], vol. 3, p. 292; Kang Tŏk-sang, *Gendaishi shiryō* [*Sources on Contemporary History*], vol. 27 (Tokyo: Misuzu Shobō, 1970), p. 156.

62. Yi In-sŏp, "Aleksandra Kim ŭi chŏngi (1)," p. 75; Yi In-sŏp, "Aleksandra Kim ŭi chŏngi (2)," p. 73.

63. Yi In-sŏp, "Aleksandra Kim ŭi chŏngi (1)," p. 75. According to Yi In-sŏp, "there was no one who did not know Alexandra Kim in the Urals at that time."

64. H. M, "Chosŏn ŭi yŏryujuŭija ko Kim Sttankkebi yŏsa yakchŏn," pp. 27-28.

65. *Hanin Sinbo*, 7 Oct. 1917.

66. H. M, "Chosŏn ŭi yŏryujuŭija ko Kim Sttankkebi yŏsa yakchŏn," pp. 27-28; M. T. Kim, *Koreiskie internatsionalisty v bor'be za vlasti sovetov na Dal'nem Vostoke (1918-1922)*, p. 51.

67. Yi In-sŏp, "Aleksandra Kim ŭi chŏngi (1)," p. 75.

68. Twibabo, "Kim Alneksandra chŏn," *Tongnip Sinmun*, 20 Apr. 1920, p. 3.

69. Yi In-sŏp, "Aleksandra Kim ŭi chŏngi (1)," pp. 74-75.

70. Ibid., p. 75; In-sep Li, "Vospominania o godakh interventsii i grazhdanskoi voiny na Dal'nem Vostoke, 1918-1922 gg.," p. 3; Syn Khva Kim, *Ocherki po istorii sovetskikh koreitsev*, p. 91.

71. Yi In-sŏp, *Mangmyŏngja ŭi sugŭi* [The Handwriting of an Exile], ms., n. d., pp. 37, 84, 124-25, 132, 152-53. Like other Korean national revolutionaries in Russia, most of the seven came from northern part of Korea. Yi In-sŏp (from P'yŏngyang), Kim Yong-hwan (from Anbyŏn), and Yim Ch'i-hak (from Kanggye) were from Northwestern part of Korea and Sim Paek-wŏn was from the northeastern area [Tanch'ŏn]. Only Yi Chae-hyŏng came from the southern part of Korea (Kyŏngsang Province). The birthplace of An Kyŏng-ŏk and Ch'oe Yŏng-hun cannot be identified.

72. *Hanin Sinbo*, 28 Oct. 1917, p. 2: 9 Dec. 1917, p. 2.

73. M. T. Kim, *Koreiskie internatsionalisty v bor'be za vlasti sovetov na Dal'nem Vostoke (1918-1922)*, pp. 75-76; Yi In-sŏp, "Aleksandra Kim ŭi chŏngi (1)," pp. 75-76; Inseb Li, "Vospominania o godakh interventsii i grazhdanskoi voiny na Dal'nem Vostoke, 1918-1922 gg.," p. 2.

74. M. T. Kim, *Koreiskie internatsionalisty v bor'be za vlasti sovetov na Dal'nem Vostoke (1918-1922)*, pp. 73-75; Yi In-sŏp, *Mangmyŏngja ŭi sugŭi*, pp. 152-53; *Hanin Sinbo*,

9 Dec. 1917.

75. Twibabo, "Kim Alneksandra chŏn," *Tongnip Sinmun*, 20 Apr. 1920, p. 3; Yi In-sŏp, *Mangmyŏngja ŭi sugŭi*, p. 37.

76. Inseb Li, "Vospominania o godakh interventsii i grazhdanskoi voiny na Dal'nem Vostoke, 1918-1922 gg.," p. 3; Syn Khva Kim, *Ocherki po istorii sovetskikh koreitsev*, pp. 91-92; M. T. Kim, *Koreiskie internatsionalisty v bor'be za vlasti sovetov na Dal'nem Vostoke (1918-1922)*, p. 51.

77. Yi In-sŏp, "Aleksandra Kim ŭi chŏngi (1)," p. 76.

78. Hara Teruyuki, "Shiberia. Kyokutō Roshia ni okeru jūgatsukakumei" [The October Revolution in Siberia and the Russian Far East], *Surabu Kenkyū*, 24, 1979, pp. 89-90. According to Neibut (the chairman of the Far East Committee of the Russian Social Democratic Party from 1917-1919), fifteen Bolshevik leaders gathered at this conference: six delegates from Vladivostok (Neibut, Lyubarsky, Grossman, Antonov, Koval'chuk and I. P. Nikiforov), three from Nikol'sk-Ussurisk (Gelerson, Krasnoshchekov, Svidersky), one from Khabarovsk (Boshaev), from Suchan (Allilyev), one from Murav'ev-Amursk (Alexandra Kim), Blagoveshchensk (Kunarev), one from Harbin, and one from Stekol'no. See also Yi In-sŏp, "Vospominania o godakh interventsii i grazhdanskoi voiny na Dal'nem Vostoke, 1918-1922 gg.," p. 1.

79. Hara Teruyuki, "Shiberia. Kyokutō Roshia ni okeru jūgatsukakumei," p. 107.

80. Alexandr Mikhailovich Krasnoshchekov (1880-1937) was born of Jewish parents in Chernobyl, a small town near Kiev, on December 19, 1880. He became involved in radical activities and joined the Russian Social Democratic Party in 1896. After being arrested twice, he emigrated to Chicago and participated in labor movements under the pseudonym, A. S. Tobelson. He also joined the American Socialist Party. After the Russian Revolution broke out, he returned to Vladivostok. At first, he served the Vladivostok Soviet, but soon was sent by the Party to Nikol'sk-Ussurisk to strengthen its position there. He became the first chairman of the Far Eastern People's Commission. When the Far Eastern Republic was established as a buffer state between Soviet Russia and Japanese intervention troops, he became the first Prime Minister and the Minister of Foreign Affairs. Krasnoshchekov's death, while not publicized, probably resulted from imprisonment or execution during the purges in 1937. See Canfield F. Smith, "Krasnoshchekov, Alexandr Mikhailovich (1880-1937?)," Joseph L. Wieczynski ed., *The Modern Encyclopedia of Russia and Soviet History*, vol. 18 (Academic International Press, 1980), pp. 41-46 and Khromov, S. S. etc. ed., *Grazhdanskaia voina i voennaia interventsia v SSSR* [Civil War and Military Intervention in the USSR] (Moscow: Sovetskaia Entsiklopediia, 1987), p. 305. Krasnoshchekov had been a strong sponsor of the Korean Socialist Party and later the "Shanghai Group" of the Korean Communist Party.

81. Hara Teruyuki, "Shiberia. Kyokutō Roshia ni okeru jūgatsukakumei," pp. 108-109; Hara Teryuyuki, *Shiberia shuppei: kakumei to kanshō, 1917-1922* [The Siberian Expedition: Revolution and Intervention, 1917-1922] (Tokyo: Chikuma shobō, 1989), pp. 156-57.

82. M. T. Kim, *Koreiskie internatsionalisty v bor'be za vlasti sovetov na Dal'nem Vostoke (1918-1922)*, p. 52.

83. Inseb Li, "Vospominania o godakh interventsii i grazhdanskoi voiny na Dal'nem Vostoke, 1918-1022 gg.," p. 3.

84. Sipwŏl Hyŏngmyŏng Sipchunyŏn Wŏndong Kinyŏm Chunbi Wiwŏnhoe, *Sipwŏl hyŏngmyŏng sipchunyŏn kwa Ssobet Koryŏ minjok* [The Tenth Anniversary of the October Revolution and Koreans] (Vladivostok: Haesamwi Tosŏ Chusik Hoesa, 1927), pp. 47-48; Ivan Gozhenskii, "Uchastie Koreiskii emigratsii v revoliutsionnom dvizhenii na Dal'nem Vostoke," p. 366; John J. Stephan, *The Russian Far East: A History*, p. 321; Yi In-sŏp, "Aleksandra Kim ŭi chŏngi (1)," p. 76; M. T. Kim, *Koreiskie internatsionalisty v bor'be za vlasti sovetov na Dal'nem Vostoke (1918-1922)*, p. 52.

85. Yi In-sŏp, "Aleksandra Kim ŭi chŏngi (1)," p. 76.

86. Yu Hyo-jong, "Kyokutō Roshia ni okeru jiūgatsu kakumei to Chōsenjin shyakai," p. 26; *Ch'ŏnggu Sinbo*, 30 Dec. 1917, p. 3.

87. Ivan Gozhenskii, "Uchastie Koreiskii emigratsii v revoliutsionnom dvizhenii na Dal'nem Vostoke," p. 360; *Ch'ŏnggu Sinbo*, 18 Nov. 1917. One seat to the Constituent Assembly was given to every 200,000 people, but the Korean population was about 140,000.

88. *Ch'ŏnggu Sinbo*, 18 Nov. 1917.

89. The long-standing conflict between radicals in Vladivostok and defencists in Khabarovsk and Blagoveshchensk had disturbed the Socialist Revolutionary Party in the Amur Region. As a result, the peasants' Soviet refused to be associated with a party and appointed its candidates to the Constituent Assembly. See Oliver Henry Radkey, *The Sickle under the Hammer: the Russian Socialist Revolutionaries in the Early Months of Soviet Rule* (New York and London: Columbia University Press, 1963), p. 127.

90. *Hanin Sinbo*, 23 Dec. 1917, p. 3.

91. *Ch'ŏnggu Sinbo*, 18 Nov. 1917, p. 2. The Koryŏjok Chungang Ch'onghoe and the *Ch'ŏnggu Sinbo* advised to vote in the election according to the following order: 1) the Primorye Soviet of the Peasant Deputies (slate no. 2), 2) Socialist Revolutionary Party of Primorye (slate no. 1), 3) Soviet of the Peasant Deputies of Primorye (slate no. 7), 4) Socialist Revolutionary Party of Vladivostok, Nikol'sk-Ussurisk and Spaask (slate no. 8), 5) Russian Social Democratic Party (Menshevik) (slate no. 4), 6) Russian Social Democratic Party (Bolshevik) (slate no. 5). They also listed Constitutional Democrat, Cossacks and Small Russian Nationalist as "parties which have no relations with" the

Koreans.

92. *Hanin Sinbo*, 17 Nov. 1917, p. 2.

93. Ibid., 23 Dec. 1917, p. 3; *Ch'ŏnggu Sinbo*, 30 Dec. 1917, p. 3.

94. *Chŏnggu Sinbo*, 30 Dec. 1917, p. 3.

95. Ibid., p. 3.

96. *Sinhan Minbo*, 28 Feb. 1918, p. 3.

97. Hara Teruyuki, "Roshia kakumei, Shiberi sensō to Chōsen dokuritsu undō" [Russian Revolution, Siberian War and Korean Independence Movement], Kikuchi Masanori ed., *Roshia kakumeiron: rekishi no fukken* (Tokyo: Tabata Shoten, 1977), pp. 184-85; Hara Teruyuki, "Shiberia. Kyokutō Roshia ni okeru jūgatsukakumei," pp. 177-79; *Sinhan Minbo*, 14 Feb. 1918, p. 3: 28 Feb. 1918, p. 3.

98. Din'shun Pak, "Koreiskaia emigratsiia v Rossii." According to Pak Chin-sun, while the oblast and district councils allowed seats to Koreans, and the Siberian Duma also provided two seats to the Koreans, the executive committee of the Soviets did not allow any seats to the Koreans. Furthermore, the Soviet Power's anti-*kulak* policy made Korean *wŏnhoin* unfavorable to the Bolsheviks. Utilizing this situation, the supporters of *zemstvo*s agitated against the Soviet Power and made the Korean intelligentsia support *zemstvo*s.

99. Yu Hyo-jong, "Kyokutō Roshia ni okeru jūgatsu kakumei to Chōsenjin shakai," p. 24; *Sinhan Minbo*, 7 Feb. 1918, p. 3; 11 Apr. 1918, p. 3.

100. *Hanin Sinbo*, 23 Sep. 1917, p. 3; 23 Dec. 1917: 3; *Ch'ŏnggu Sinbo*, 18 Nov. 1917, p. 2; Twibabo, "Aryŏng silgi (11)," *Tongnip Sinmun*, 3 Apr. 1920. Kim Rip and Yi Han-yŏng took the post of chief editor and Chief of General Affairs respectively.

101. *Taedong Kongbo*, 18 Apr. 1909, p. 4; *Hanin Sinbo*, 30 Sep. 1919, p. 4; Twibabo, "Aryŏng silgi (11)," *Tongnip Sinmun*, 3 Apr. 1920, p. 1. The name "Mundŏk" was borrowed from a great general of the Koguryŏ Kingdom who defeated the troops of the Chinese Sui dynasty in 612.

102. Yi In-sŏp, letter to Kim Se-il, 5 Feb. 1969.

103. *Sinhan Minbo*, 7 Feb. 1918, p. 3; 11 Apr. 1918, p. 3.

104. Ibid., 11 Apr. 1918, p. 3.

105. *Sinhan Minbo*, 28 Feb. 1918, p. 3.

106. Twibabo, "Aryŏng silgi (5)," *Tongnip Sinmun*, 13 Mar. 1920, p. 3.

107. Kim Chŏng-ju [Kin Sei-tsū] ed., *Chōsen tōchi shiryō*, vol. 10, pp. 45-46.

108. *Sinhan Minbo*, 28 Feb. 1918, p. 3; Yu Hyo-jong, "Kyokutō Roshia ni okeru jūgatsu kakumei to Chōsenjin shakai," p. 27.

109. Ivan Gozhenskii, "Uchastie Koreiskii emigratsii v revoliutsionnom dvizhenii na Dal'nem Vostoke," p. 361.

110. Din'shun Pak, "Koreiskaia emigratsiia v Rossii."

111. Yu Hyo-jong, "Kyokutō Roshia ni okeru jiūgatsu kakumei to Chōsenjin shyakai," pp. 28-29.

112. Yi Yŏng-il, "Yi Tong-hwi Sŏngjae sŏnsaeng," p. 210.

113. Quoted from Yu Hyo-jong, "Kyokutō Roshia ni okeru jūgatsu kakumei to Chōsenjin shakai," p. 30.

114. Yi Yŏng-il, "Yi Tong-hwi Sŏngjae sŏnsaeng," pp. 212-13.

115. Ibid., pp. 215-16.

116. Yi In-sŏp, "Aleksandra Kim ŭi chŏngi (1)," p. 76.

117. Ibid., p. 76.

118. *Purgŭn Kunsa*, 24 Dec. 1921; *Sipwŏl hyŏngmyŏng sipchunyŏn kwa Ssobet Koryŏ minjok*, p. 46; Kim Kyu-myŏn, *Nobyŏng Kim Kyu-myŏn ŭi pimangnok esŏ*, pp. 2-3; Yi In-sŏp, "Aleksandra Kim ŭi chŏngi (1)," p. 76; Semen Davidovich Anosov, *Koreitsy v Ussuriiskom krae*, p. 19; Syn Khva Kim, *Ocherki po istorii sovetskikh koreitsev*, p. 92.

119. *Purgŭn Kunsa*, 24 Dec. 1921.

120. Chin-sun Pak, "The Socialist Movement in Korea," Dae-sook Suh ed., *Documents of Korean Communism 1918-1948* (Princeton: Princeton UP, 1970), p. 46; Dzhinshun Pak, "Sotsialisiticheskoe dvizhenie v Koree" [Socialist Movement in Korea], *Kommunisticheskii Internatsional*, 7-8 (Nov.– Dec., 1919), pp. 1171-76.

121. Hen Kuon Han [Han Hyŏng-gwŏn], "La Situation en Asie Orientale," *L'Internationale Communiste*, 13 (1920), p. 2558; R., "The Situation in Eastern Asia," *Communist International*, 13 (August 1920), p. 2548. "The Union of Serene Liberation" in the English version is correctly written as the "Union of Liberation" (Restoration Union) in the French version. The Union of Serene Liberation (Union of Iron and Blood Restoration, Ch'ŏlhyŏl Kwangboktan) was the unified organization of the two revolutionary unions, the Kwangboktan (Restoration Union) in Manchuria and the Ch'ŏlhyŏltan (Union of Iron and Blood) in the Russian Maritime Province at the end of 1918. See *See Sipwŏl hyŏngmyŏng sipchunyŏn kwa Ssovet Koryŏ minjok*, p. 50.

122. Kim Kyu-myŏn, *Nobyŏng Kim Kyu-myŏn ŭi pimangnok esŏ*, pp. 2-3; *Purgŭn Kunsa*, 24 Dec. 1921; *Sipwŏl hyŏngmyŏng sipchunyŏn kwa Ssobet Koryŏ minjok*, p. 46.

123. On the day after the Japanese landing, the Koreans Soldiers' Association [*Hanin Kuninhoe*] had an urgent meeting and organized the Security Guards [*Kyŏngbidan*] with returned Koreans soldiers for the purpose of guarding against possible Japanese attacks. See Yu Hyo-jong, "Kyokutō Roshia ni okeru jiūgatsu kakumei to Chōsenjin shyakai," p. 30.

124. Alexandr Krasnoshchekov had been arrested together with Mukhin when the Cossacks, led by Gamov attacked the headquarters of the Bolsheviks with the help of the Japanese and Chinese on March 6, 1918. He and Mukhin were released on 12 March when rescue squads composed of Red Guards, Austro-Hungarian and German

"internationalists" and Amur Flotilla sailors recovered Blagoveshchensk from the "counterrevolutionaries." See John J. Stephan, *The Russian Far East: A History*, pp. 119-20; Japan Rikugun Sanbō Hombu, *Shiberia shuppei* [Siberian Expedition], vol. 1 (Tokyo: Shinjidaishi, 1972), p. 207; Hara, *Shiberiya Shuppei*, pp. 194-201.

125. Yu Hyo-jong, "Kyokutō Roshia ni okeru jūgatsu kakumei to Chōsenjin shakai," p. 32.

126. Kim Kyu-myŏn, *Nobyŏng Kim Kyu-myŏn ŭi pimangnok esŏ*, p. 3; *Sipwŏl hyŏngmyŏng sipchunyŏn kwa Ssobet Koryŏ minjok*, p. 46.

127. Chun Cholkhun, "Uchastie Koreiskogo naseleniia v revoliutsionnom dvizhenii na Dal'nem Vostoke, 1917-1919 gg.: na Primore zhizni deiatel'nosti A. P. Kim-Stankevich" [Participation of the Korean Population in the Revolutionary Activities in the Far East, 1917-1919: On Primore Activities of A. P. Kim-Stankevich], diss. Diplomaticheskaia Akademiia Mid Rossii Institut Aktual'nykh Mezhdunardnykh Problem (Moscow, 1994), pp. 132-34.

128. Chun Cholkhun, "Uchastie Koreiskogo naseleniia v revoliutsionnom dvizhenii na Dal'nem Vostoke, 1917-1919 gg.: na Primore zhizni deiatel'nosti A. P. Kim-Stankevich," pp. 132-34.

129. Yi In-sŏp, "Aleksandra Kim ŭi chŏngi (1)," p. 76; Yi Yŏng-il, "Yi Tong-hwi Sŏngjae sŏnsaeng," pp. 216-17; Yi In-sŏp, letter to Kim Se-il, 7 Mar. 1968; Chun Cholkhun, "Uchastie Koreiskogo naseleniia v revoliutsionnom dvizhenii na Dal'nem Vostoke, 1917-1919 gg.: na Primore zhizni deiatel'nosti A. P. Kim-Stankevich," pp. 134-35; *Sŏnbong*, 11 Aug. 1923, p. 1.

130. Yi In-sŏp, letter to Kim Se-il, 7 Mar. 1968.

131. Semen Davidovich Anosov, *Koreitsy v Ussuriiskom krae*, pp. 19-20; Syn Khva Kim, *Ocherki po istorii sovetskikh koreitsev*, pp. 92-93.

132. Yi Yŏng-il, "Yi Tong-hwi Sŏngjae sŏnsaeng," p. 217.

133. Twibabo, "Aryŏng silgi (11), (12)" *Tongnip Sinmun*, 3 Apr. 1920, p. 1; 8 Apr. 1920, p. 3.

134. "Dai ni zen Ro Kanzoku daihyoshakai kaigiroku" [The Minutes of the Second Congress of the Korean Representatives in All Russia], AJMFA, MT16324.17 (File 4), 4-5.

135. "Dai ni zen Ro Kanzoku daihyoshakai kaigiroku," pp. 4-5.

136. Quoted from Yu Hyo-jong, "Kyokutō Roshia ni okeru jūgatsu kakumei to Chōsenjin shakai," p. 43.

137. Ibid., p. 43.

138. Semen Davidovich Anosov, *Koreitsy v Ussuriiskom krae*, p. 20; "Dai ni zen Ro Kanzoku daihyoshyakai kaigiroku," p. 6; Yu Hyo-jong, "Kyokutō Roshia ni okeru jūgatsu kakumei to Chōsenjin shakai," pp. 43-44.

139. Ivan Gozhenskii, "Uchastie Koreiskii emigratsii v revoliutsionnom dvizhenii na Dal'nem Vostoke," pp. 363-64.

140. "Dai ni zen Ro Kanzoku daihyoshakai kaigiroku," p. 6.

141. Walter Kolarz, *The Peoples of the Soviet Far East*, p. 34; Hara, "The Korean Movement in the Russian Maritime Province, 1905-1922," p. 9; Ivan Gozhenskii, "Uchastie Koreiskii emigratsii v revoliutsionnom dvizhenii na Dal'nem Vostoke," p. 364; Semen Davidovich Anosov, *Koreitsy v Ussuriiskom krae*, p. 20.

142. Ivan Gozhenskii, "Uchastie Koreiskii emigratsii v revoliutsionnom dvizhenii na Dal'nem Vostoke," p. 367.

143. *Sinhan Minbo*, 8 Aug. 1918, p. 3.

144. Ivan Gozhenskii, "Uchastie Koreiskii emigratsii v revoliutsionnom dvizhenii na Dal'nem Vostoke," p. 364.

145. "Dai ni zen Ro Kanzoku daihyoshakai kaigiroku," pp. 6-7.

146. Ibid., pp. 6-7.

147. "Dai ni zen Ro Kanzoku daihyoshakai kaigiroku," pp. 8-9. The "compensation" seemed to refer to financial redemption for damages which occurred when the Russian landlords retrieved rented lands from the Korean tenants. See Yu Hyo-jong, "Kyokutō Roshia ni okeru jūgatsu kakumei to Chōsenjin shakai," p. 37.

148. Ivan Gozhenskii, "Uchastie Koreiskii emigratsii v revoliutsionnom dvizhenii na Dal'nem Vostoke," p. 364.

149. Semen Davidovich Anosov, *Koreitsy v Ussuriiskom krae*, p. 20; Yi Yŏng-il, "Yi Tong-hwi Sŏngjae sŏnsaeng," pp. 56-57. Vasilii O returned his certificate of mandate and withdrew from the Congress on the first day. Chŏn T'ae-guk, who did not have voting rights, was also expelled from the Congress because of his "extreme talk" on the second day. According to Yi Yŏng-il, Yi Tong-hwi and his followers also left the Congress when the Congress discussed the question of the current situation.

150. Chang To-jŏng to Katayama Sen, "Korai kyōsantō no enkaku" [The History of Koryŏ (Korean) Communist Party], ms., n. d., 3.

151. Ivan Gozhenskii, "Uchastie Koreiskii emigratsii v revoliutsionnom dvizhenii na Dal'nem Vostoke," p. 364.

152. "Dai ni zen Ro Kanzoku daihyoshakai kaigiroku," pp. 9-10.

153. Semen Davidovich Anosov, *Koreitsy v Ussuriiskom krae*, p. 20; Syn Khva Kim, *Ocherki po istorii sovetskikh koreitsev*, p. 93.

154. "Dai ni zen Ro Kanzoku daihyoshakai kaigiroku," pp. 17-18. Among the members of the new Committee, only Yun Hae and Wŏn Se-hun were political exiles. Kim Ki-ryong had praised the "victory of Semenov" and was warned of his arrest by Krasnoshchekov's secretary Pak during the discussion on the political situation on the second day. See Yu Hyo-jong, "Kyokutō Roshia ni okeru jūgatsu kakumei to Chōsenjin shakai," p. 44.

155. Chang To-jŏng to Katayama Sen, "Korai kyōsantō no enkaku," p. 3.

156. *Sŏnbong*, 2 Sep. 1923.

157. Ivan Gozhenskii, "Uchastie Koreiskii emigratsii v revoliutsionnom dvizhenii na Dal'nem Vostoke," p. 367.

158. Chang To-jŏng to Katayama Sen, "Korai kyōsantō no enkaku," p. 5.

159. Japanese Government-General Office of Korea, Department of Colonization, "Chosŏn oe esŏ ŭi Chosŏn sanghwang ilban" [The General Situation of the Koreans Outside Korea], *Sindonga*, Feb. 1967, pp. 494-95.

160. Ivan Gozhenskii, "Uchastie Koreiskii emigratsii v revoliutsionnom dvizhenii na Dal'nem Vostoke," p. 368; Semen Davidovich Anosov, *Koreitsy v Ussuriiskom krae*, p. 21.

161. *Sipwŏl hyŏngmyŏng sipchunyŏn kwa Ssovet Koryŏ minjok*, p. 47; "Heitan kanbu chōhō junpō (Chōsenjin no jokyo)" ["Military Headquarters, the Kwantung Army (the Situation of the Koreans), December 21-31, 1918"], Selected Archives of the Japanese Army-Navy, 1868-1945, (VA)AA(F) no. 1042 (NA 14249)

162. Inseb Li, "Vospominania o godakh interventsii i grazhdanskoi voiny na Dal'nem Vostoke, 1918-1022 gg.," p. 4.

163. Walter Kolarz, *The Peoples of the Soviet Far East*, p. 35.

164. Pak No-sun, "1918-1922 nyŏn kungmin chŏnjaeng tangsi e kwanhayŏ" [Concerning the Civil War, 1918-1922], ms., n. d., pp. 2-5.

165. Yi Yŏng-il, "Yi Tong-hwi Sŏngjae sŏnsaeng," pp. 58-59; *Sipwŏl hyŏngmyŏng sipchunyŏn kwa Ssovet Koryŏ minjok*, p. 47; Kim Kyu-myŏn, *Nobyŏng Kim Kyu-myŏn ŭi pimangnok esŏ*, p. 26.

166. Yi In-sŏp, "Aleksandra Kim ŭi chŏngi (2)," p. 69.

167. Inseb Li, "Vospominania o godakh interventsii i grazhdanskoi voiny na Dal'nem Vostoke / 1918-1922 gg." p. 4.

168. Syn Khva Kim, *Ocherki po istorii sovetskikh koreitsev*, pp. 94-95; Semen Davidovich Anosov, *Koreitsy v Ussuriiskom krae*, p. 21.

169. Yi In-sŏp, "Aleksandra Kim ŭi chŏngi (2)," p. 69.

170. Ibid., pp. 70-71.

171. Yi In-sŏp, *Mangmyŏngja ŭi sugŭi*, pp. 74-75.

172. Yi In-sŏp, "Aleksandra Kim ŭi chŏngi (2)," pp. 70-72; M. T. Kim, *Koreiskie internatsionalisty v bor'be za vlasti sovetov na Dal'nem Vostoke (1918-1922)*, pp. 54-55. Among the Bolsheviks who were executed by the Whites headed by Kalmykov were the Hungarian "internationalist" G. Ballo, Krai military staff member Ermak, *krai* Commissar for the Waterway Karpenko, Perov, Pugachevsky, Roshchin, Krivoruchko, Kuksov and ten other Russian revolutionaries. See A. K. Chernyi ed., *Ocherkii Khabarovskoi kraevoi organizatsii KPSS (1900-1978 gody)* [Essays on Khabaorvsk krai Organizations of the Soviet Union Communist Party, 1900-1978] (Khabarovsk:

Khabarovskoe Knizhnoe Izdaltel'stvo, 1979), pp. 53-54.

173. Yi In-sŏp, "Aleksandra Kim ŭi chŏngi (2)," p. 71.

174. Kim Kyu-myŏn, *Nobyŏng Kim Kyu-myŏn ŭi pimangnok esŏ*, p. 6.

Chapter Four

1. Hosoi Hajime, *Sen-Man no keiei: Chōsen mondai no konpon kaiketsu* [Management of Korea and Manchuria: The Fundamental Solution of the Korea Question], vol. 2 (Tokyo: Jiyu Tokyusha, 1921), pp. 155-56; Yu Hyo-jong, "Kyokutō Roshia ni okeru jūgatsu kakumei to Chōsenjin shakai," p. 46.

2. Ivan Gozhenskii, "Uchastie Koreiskii emigratsii v revoliutsionnom dvizhenii na Dal'nem Vostoke," p. 368; Semen Davidovich Anosov, *Koreitsy v Ussuriiskom krae*, p. 21.

3. *Tonga Ilbo*, 26 May 1921; Kukhoe Tosŏgwan, *Hanguk minjok undongsa saryo: Chungguk p'yŏn* [Historical Materials on the Korean National Movement: China Part] (Seoul: Library of Korean National Assembly, 1976), p. 272.

4. *Gendaishi shiryō*, vol. 26, pp. 82-86: vol. 27, p. 205. The Koreans in America decided to dispatch Yi Sŭng-man, Chŏng Han-gyŏng [Henry Chung], and Min Ch'an-ho to Paris. However, they could not get visas from the American government. See Kim Pyŏng-jo, *Hanguk Tongnip undong saryak* [Brief History of Korean Independence Movement] (Seoul: Asea Munhwasa, 1977), pp. 14-15.

5. Yi Man-gyu, *Yŏ Un-hyŏng t'ujaengsa* [History of Yŏ Un-hyŏng's Struggle] (Seoul: Ch'ongmungak, 1946), p. 25. The New Korean Youth Party was organized by Korean nationalists in Shanghai following the model of the Turkish Youth Party at the end of August 1918, with the purpose of carrying out the Korean independence movement. The party dispatched Kim Kyu-sik to Paris as the representative of Korea at the beginning of January 1919, and Yŏ Un-hyŏng to Manchuria and Russia and Chang Tŏk-su to Korea at the end of January 1919, with the purpose of gathering funds for publishing English periodicals which would introduce Korea to the world. The plan of the New Korean Youth Party was initiated on the advice of Charles Crane who was dispatched by W. Wilson to China. See Yi Man-gyu, *Yŏ Un-hyŏng t'ujaengsa*, pp. 21-23 and "Yŏ Un-hyŏng chosŏ" [Protocol of Yŏ Un-hyŏng], *Hanguk kongsanchuŭi undongsa: charyo p'yŏn* [The History of Korean Communist Movement: Source Materials], Kim Chun-yŏp and Kim Ch'ang-sun ed., vol. 1 (Seoul: Koryŏ Taehakkyo Asea Munje Yŏnguso, 1979), pp. 365-67 (hereafter cited as "Yŏ Un-hyŏng chosŏ").

6. *Gendaishi shiryō*, vol. 27, p. 205.

7. Kukhoe Tosŏgwan, *Hanguk minjok undongsa saryo, 3. 1 undong p'yŏn* [*Historical Materials on the Korean National Movement: The March First Movement*], vol. 3 (Seoul: Library of Korean National Assembly, 1979), p. 108 (hereafter cited as *3. 1 undong*).

8. *Gendaishi shiryō*, vol. 26, pp. 82-86; *3. 1 undong*, vol. 3, p. 28.
9. *Narody Dal'nego Vostoka*, 3, 1 August 1921, p. 406; *Gendaishi shiryō*, vol. 26, pp. 30-31.
10. *3. 1 undong*, vol. 3, p. 28.
11. Kim Pyŏng-jo, "Hanguk tongnip undong saryak," in *Tongnip undongsa charyojip*, vol. 6 (Seoul: Tongnip Undongsa P'yŏnch'an Wiwŏnhoe, 1977), p. 242.
12. Yi In-sŏp, letter to Kim Se-il, 5 Feb. 1968; Ivan Gozhenskii, "Uchastie Koreiskii emigratsii v revoliutsionnom dvizhenii na Dal'nem Vostoke," p. 368.
13. Ban Byung Yool, "Taehan Kungmin Ŭihoe ŭi sŏngnip kwa chojik" [The Establishment and Organization of the Korean National Council], *Han'guk Hakpo*, 13, Spring, 1987, pp. 149-50. The Korean National Council, in its manifesto, declared the independence of Korea, "in the name of two hundred million Koreans," to the world and demanded Japan return independence, sovereignty and treasures to Korea. See *Kukp'yŏn charyo*, vol. 4, p. 305. A Japanese translation is included in *Gendaishi shiryō*, vol. 26, p. 44.
14. Yi Tong-hwi, "Sŭbbŭrapkka" (Reference), *Sŏnbong*, 17 Dec. 1929, p. 4.
15. Twibabo, "Aryŏng silgi (12)," *Tongnip Sinmun*, 8 Apr. 1920, p. 3. "Chae-Ro Koryŏ hyŏngmyŏng kundae yŏnhyŏk" [The History of the Korean Revolutionary Army in Russia], *Hanguk kongsanjuŭi undongsa charyo p'yŏn* [The History of Korean Communist Movement: Source materials]. Kim Chun-yŏp and Kim Ch'ang-sun ed., vol. 2 (Seoul: Koryŏ Taehakkyo Asea Munje Yŏnguso, 1980), p. 8.
16. Ibid., 8 Feb. 1930, p. 4.
17. Kim Ha-sŏk, "Yi Tong-hwi tongmu ŭi ssŭbbŭrapkka rŭl puinhanda" [I Deny the Reference of Comrade Yi Tong-hwi], *Sŏnbong*, 8 Feb. 1930, p. 4.
18. *Gendaishi shiryō*, vol. 26, p. 174.
19. Ibid., p. 96.
20. *Gendaishi shiryō*, vol. 27, p. 205; Ibid., vol. 26, pp. 42-45, 171-72. Kim Ha-sŏk, leader of the Korean National Council said: "Although, the uprising within Korea generally was widespread in every region and was the big one, it was basically no more than a riot of the masses without any weapons. When seen from foreign countries, it was no more than something to be acknowledged as a domestic disturbance and the result, that it got, was no more than evoking the attention of the Paris Peace Conference. With such a degree, the way to restore independence at which we aim is still far away. Therefore, from now, we have to seize weapons in a larger scale, fight against Japan and advance to the extent that the Powers recognize us as belligerent. Then, we can say that more than half our goal is accomplished." See *Gendaishi shiryō*, vol. 27, pp. 171-72.
21. *Gendaishi shiryō*, vol. 26, pp. 90, 93, 108.

22. Ch'oe Nam-sŏn, *Chosŏn tongnip undong sosa* [Short History of the Korean Independence Movement] (Seoul: Tongmyŏngsa, 1946), p. 40; Kim Pyŏng-jo, "Hanguk tongnip undong saryak," p. 242; *Gendaishi shiryō*, vol. 26, pp. 42-45, 91-92; A. N. Iaremenko, "Dnevnik kommunista" [Diary of a Communist], *Revoliutsiia na Dal'nem Vostoke* [Revolution in the Far East], vol. 1 (Moscow, Leningrad: Gosudarskvennoe Izdatel'stvo, 1923), pp. 216-17.

23. *Gendaishi shiryō*, vol. 26, pp. 91-192.

24. Ibid., p. 92.

25. M. T. Kim, *Koreiskie internatsionalisty v bor'be za vlasti sovetov na Dal'nem Vostoke (1918-1922)*, pp. 71, 74.

26. *Tongnip Sinmun*, 9 Sep. 1919, p. 4; *Gendaishi shiryō*, vol. 28, 92; vol. 26, p. 94; Ch'oe Nam-sŏn, *Chosŏn tongnip undong sosa*, p. 40; *Hanguk tongnip undongsa*, vol. 3, p. 276; *3. 1 undong*, vol. 3, p. 616.

27. *Gendaishi shiryō*, vol. 26, pp. 104-105.

28. John J. Stephan, *The Russian Far East: A History*, p. 319.

29. Kim Ha-sŏk, "Yi Tong-hwi tongmu ŭi ssŭbbŭrapkka rŭl puinhanda."

30. Yi Sŭng [Hong P'a], "Kwagŏ 50-nyŏn ŭl tolna pomyŏn" [When I Recollect the Past Fifty Years], Kho Song-mu ed., *News on Korean Studies in Kazakstan and Central Asia*, 4, July 1993 (Alma-Ata, Kazakstan: Department of Korean Studies Centre of Oriental Studies of Kazakstan Academy of Science), p. 66.

31. Ch'oe Ke-rip, letter to Kim Se-il, n. d.

32. Twibabo, "Aryŏng silgi (12)," *Tongnip Sinmun*, 8 Apr. 1920, p. 3; Semen Davidovich Anosov, *Koreitsy v Ussuriiskom krae*, p. 21; *3. 1 undong*, vol. 3, pp. 383-84, 532; Kim Chŏng-myŏng [Kin Seimei] ed., *Chōsen dokuritsu undō*, vol. 3, p. 877. In August 1918, the Korean Russian officer Mikhail Wŏn organized the Korean Independent National Battalion in Harbin with the support of Radola [Rudolf] Gaida, Commander-in-Chief of the Czech armies and Horvath. Ch'oe Chae-hyŏng, the leader of the *wŏnhoin* supported the recruitment of the unit. In February 1919, the number of soldiers under the command of Wŏn was about one hundred and twenty with eight officers. Wŏn was suspected as a pro-Japanese by the Korean National Council because of his ambiguous attitude toward Japan. In opposition to Wŏn, Pyotr Ivanovich Kim organized the second Korean Independent National Battalion with cooperation and support from the Korean National Council. See "Chosŏn oe esŏ ŭi Chosŏnin sanghwang ilban," p. 495; *3. 1 undong*, vol. 3, p. 532.

33. Yi Tong-hwi, "Sŭbbŭrapkka."

34. Representatives of the Korean Delegation to the First Congress of the Communist and Revolutionary Parties of the Far East, Moscow, to the Executive Committee III. *Communist International*, 5 Apr. 1922, ts., 7.

35. Yi Yŏng-il, "Yi Tong-hwi Sŏngjae sŏnsaeng," pp. 210-11.

36. *Gendaishi shiryō*, vol. 26, p. 94.

37. Ibid., vol. 27, pp. 185-86; "Yi Tong-hwi tongmu ŭi ilsaeng," *Sŏnbong*, 4 Feb. 1935, p. 4; Chŏng T'ae, letter to Kim Se-il, n. d. . In his book, *The Truth about Korea* published in San Francisco, in July 1919, C. W. Kendall also wrote: "A National Council was called at Nikolskoe, on the Ussuri River in Siberia, and a provisional government established, with a temporary capitol in Manchuria. . . . The portfolio of the Secretary of War was given to General Lee Dong Whui, who immediately began the organization of an army." See C. W. Kendall, *The Truth about Korea* (San Francisco: The Korean National Association, 1919), pp. 34-35.

38. *Gendaishi shiryō*, vol. 27, p. 171; Ivan Gozhenskii, "Uchastie Koreiskii emigratsii v revoliutsionnom dvizhenii na Dal'nem Vostoke," p. 359. According to Ivan Gozhenskii, only 4-5% of the Koreans who received Russian citizenship under Gondatti and were mobilized, appeared and the rest of them emigrated with their families to Manchuria escaping the mobilization.

39. *Gendaishi shiryō*, vol. 27, p. 171.

40. Twibabo, "Aryŏng silgi (12)," *Tongnip Sinmun*, 8 Apr. 1920, p. 3; *Gendaishi shiryō*, vol. 27, pp. 171, 175.

41. *Gendaishi shiryō*, vol. 27, pp. 172-73.

42. Ibid., p. 172. The Japanese agent in Vladivostok reported the situation as follows: "During the period of the 'maximalists' [rule] after the Revolution, the army was dissolved and the dismissed soldiers were allowed to return to their place with military weapons and clothes and were supposed to report the holding of the weapons to the village offices. However, social order was so disturbed that there were very few who reported and turned in their weapons and most of the returned soldiers hid the weapons without permission. After the overthrow of the 'maximalist' regime, the Siberian Government ordered that every person turned in all weapons and sought to confiscate the weapons after searching the houses of the people who did not turn in weapons. However, very few of the people, who got the order to turn in weapons, responded and most of them avoided it and hid the weapons. These weapons were moved into the hands of the 'maximalists,' or sold secretly to others. Accordingly, if there were funds, it is not very difficult to get one gun with one hundred bullets. It is what the person, who is familiar with the issue, is saying. The situation is like this, so it seems to be still closer to the truth that there are a considerable number of weapons in the hands of Yi Tong-hwi's followers."

43. Yi Tong-hwi, "Sŭbbŭrapkka."

44. Kim Ha-sŏk, "Yi Tong-hwi Tongmu ŭi ssŭbbŭrapkka rŭl puinhanda."

45. The Japanese officials in Vladivostok also regarded Yi Tong-hwi as the Minister of the

War Declaration. See *Gendaishi shiryō*, vol. 27, p. 204.

46. *Gendaishi shiryō*, vol. 26, pp. 159-61. "Chae-Ro Koryŏ hyŏngmyŏng kundae yŏnhyŏk," p. 8.

47. *Gendaishi shiryō*, vol. 27, pp. 173-75.

48. Ibid., p. 173.

49. Kim Chŏng-myŏng [Kin Seimei] ed., *Chōsen dokuritsu undō*, vol. 3, p. 877.

50. *Gendaishi shiryō*, vol. 27, p. 175.

51. *Sŏnbong*, 11 Aug. 1923, p. 1.

52. *Gendaishi shiryō*, vol. 26, p. 197; Ibid., vol. 27, pp. 171, 175.

53. Chin-sun Pak, "The Socialist Movement in Korea," p. 47.

54. Ibid., p. 47; Kim Kyu-myŏn, *Nobyŏng Kim Kyu-myŏn ŭi pimangnok esŏ*, p. 6.

55. Chin-sun Pak, "The Socialist Movement in Korea," p. 47.

56. Ibid., p. 49.

57. Chin-sun Pak, "The Socialist Movement in Korea," p. 47. The full official name of the New People's Union was "The New People's Union for the Korean Independence [Taehan Tongnip Sinmindan]." See *Gendaishi shiryō*, vol. 26, pp. 251, 255.

58. Kye Pong-u, *Kkum sog ŭi kkum*, vol. 2, p. 72.

59. Kim Yong-hae, *Taehan kidokkyo ch'imnye kyohoesa* [*History of Korean Baptist Churches*] (Seoul: Taehan Kidokkyo Ch'imnye Kyohoe Ch'onghoe, 1964), p. 28; Kim Kyu-myŏn, *Nobyŏng Kim Kyu-myŏn ŭi pimangnok esŏ*, pp. 114-15; "Who is Who of the Korean National Council," p. 2; *Sinmindapo*, no. 1, July 1919 in *Gendaishi shiryō*, vol. 26, pp. 235, 251-53.

60. *Gendaishi shiryō*, vol. 26, p. 255.

61. Ibid., pp. 208-209.

62. R [Han Hyŏng-gwŏn], "The Situation in Eastern Asia," *Communist International*, 13, Aug. 192), p. 2546.

63. *Gendaishi shiryō*, vol. 26, p. 209.

64. Chin-sun Pak, "The Socialist Movement in Korea," p. 48.

65. Ibid., pp. 47-48.

66. Chin-sun Pak, "The Socialist Movement in Korea," p. 49.

67. Ibid., pp. 48-49; Koreits, "Probuzhdenie Korei."

68. Chin-sun Pak, "The Socialist Movement in Korea," p. 49.

69. Ibid., p. 49.

70. The Union of Iron and Blood Restoration [Ch'ŏlhyŏl Gwangboktan] was called by Korean nationalists "the Chŏlgwangtan" using its initials. The two secret revolutionary organizations, the Union of Iron and Blood [Ch'ŏlhyŏltan] and the Restoration Union [Kwangboktan] were unified into a single organization at the end of 1918 under the name of the Union of Iron and Blood Restoration. The Union of Iron

and Blood was organized in 1914 in the Primorye with the goal of achieving the liberation of Korea. The Restoration Union was organized in early 1911 in North Chientao, with the same goal by Yi Tong-hwi and his followers. See *Sipwŏl hyŏngmyŏng sipchunyŏn kwa koryŏ minjok*, p. 50; "Chosŏn oe esŏ ŭi Chosŏnin sanghwang ilban," p. 489.

71. Semen Davidovich Anosov, *Koreitsy v Ussuriiskom krae*, p. 22; *Gendaishi shiryō*, vol. 26, p. 193.

72. Kim Kyu-myŏn, *Sŏngjae yakchŏn e kwanhan hoesanggi*, p. 17. The Central Committee was composed of 15 regular members and 7 candiate members: one chairman, two vice-chairmen, one secretary-general and three secretaries.

73. Kim Kyu-myŏn, *Nobyŏng Kim Kyu-myŏn ŭi pimangnok esŏ*, p. 7; "Korai kyosanto oyobi Zenro kyosanto ni kansuru chiyosasho" [Investigation Report on the Koryŏ Communist Party and All Russian Communist Party], *Chotokuho*, 12, 6 Mar. 1923 (Seoul: Chōsengun Sambobu), p. 7; *Gendaishi shiryō*, vol. 29, p. 454.

74. Semen Davidovich Anosov, *Koreitsy v Ussuriiskom krae*, p. 22.

75. Dinshun' Pak, "Revoliutsionnoe dvizhenie v Koree" [Revolutionary Movement in Korea], *Izvestiia*, 22 Aug. 1920, p. 1.

76. Dinshun Pak [Pak Chin-sun] and Khun Te [Cho Hun], "Brief Review of Modern Korea," ts., Sep. 1924, p. 4.

77. Chin-sun Pak, "The Socialist Movement in Korea," pp. 50-51.

78. According to Dae-sook Suh, the Congress also adopted a resolution prohibiting the members of the Korean Socialist Party from joining the Shanghai Provisional Government. See Dae-sook Suh, *The Korean Communist Movement, 1918-1948* (Princeton: Princeton UP, 1967), p. 8.

79. Semen Davidovich Anosov, *Koreitsy v Ussuriiskom krae*, p. 22.

80. The Provisional Government in Shanghai was organized and declared on April 11, 1919. The Military Government in Jilin was organized after the March First Movement in Jilin, Manchuria and was widely known as the Kilim [Jilin] Government by Korean nationalists. The Military Government in Jilin claimed to be the Government of Korea competing with the Shanghai Provisional Government and the Korean National Council. The head of the Military Government in Jilin was Yu Tong-yŏl, who used to be a member of the Korean Socialist Party. However, it gradually lost its influence among Koreans. See *Gendaishi shiryō*, vol. 25, pp. 630-31; vol. 27, pp. 204-205.

81. Semen Davidovich Anosov, *Koreitsy v Ussuriiskom krae*, p. 22. It is clear that the members of the Korean Socialist Party did not get any information about the Hansŏng Government which was declared a few days prior.

82. Chin-sun Pak, "The Socialist Movement in Korea," p. 49.

83. Sogong, "Yi Sung-man gun ŭige irŏn ŭl chunora" [A Word to Mr. Yi sŭng-man]

Tongnip Sinmun, 31 Mar. 1925, p. 2. According to Sogong, three "governments" were declared in Korea, one in Chientao, and one in Russia (the Korean National Council), and the Provisional Government in Shanghai.

84. For example, Yi Tong-nyŏng was the speaker of the Provisional Assembly.

85. *Gendaishi shiryō*, vol. 27, p. 173; Pak Kye-ju, "Taeji ŭi sŏngjwa," pp. 329-30. Referring to this context, Han Hyŏng-gwŏn, in an article submitted to *The Communist International*, August 1920 said that "In Shanghai, the Right Wing opposition of the Korean National Council formed a Provisional Government, which was afterwards named the "Shanghai Government." See R., "The Situation in Eastern Asia," p. 2546.

86. "Hanil kwangye saryojip" [Collection of Materials on the Relations between Korea and Japan], *Kukp'yŏn charyo*, vol. 4, pp. 208-209; "Chōsen minjoku undō nenkan" [Yearbook of Korean National Movement], Kim Chŏng-myŏng [Kin Seimei] ed., *Chōsen dokuritsu undō*, vol. 2, p. 91.

87. *Gendaishi shiryō*, vol. 26, p. 152.

88. Ibid., p. 152.

89. R., "The Situation in Eastern Asia," p. 2546; Hanguk Komunhŏn Yŏnguhoe, *Yesim chonggyŏl kyŏlchŏlp'an* [*Final Decision of the Preparatory Trial*] (Seoul: Hanguk komunhŏn Yŏnguhoe, 1968), p. 56.

90. Hanguk Komunhŏn Yŏnguhoe, *Yesim chonggyŏl kyŏlchŏlp'an*, pp. 62-63; "Taehan tongnip hyŏlchŏngi" [The Records of the Bloody Struggle of Korea], 15 Aug. 1919, *Kukp'yŏn charyo*, vol. 4, pp. 323-26; "Hanil kwangye saryojip," p. 207; No Chae-yŏn, "Chae-Mi Hanin saryak" [A Short History of the Koreans in America], *Tongnip undongsa charyojip*, vol. 8 (Seoul: Tongnip undongsa P'yŏnch'an Wiwŏnhoe), pp. 514-15.

91. R., "The Situation in Eastern Asia," p. 2546.

92. *Gendaishi shiryō*, vol. 26, pp. 166-67; Soon Hyun [Hyŏn Sun], *My Autobiography*, ts., p. 83; "Hanil kwangye saryojip," p. 207.

93. *Sinhan Minbo*, 2 Apr. 1920. The authority and legitimacy of the Hansŏng Government originated from the fact that it was "established by the blood inside" Korea. See *Sinhan Minbo*, 11 Oct. 1923.

94. "Imsi ŭijŏngwŏn kisarok, 1 hoe-6 hoe" [The Minutes of the Provisional Legislature, from the First Session through the Sixth Session], *Kukp'yŏn charyo*, vol. 2, pp. 388-99.

95. "Imsi ŭijŏngwŏn kisarok che sahoejip" [The Minutes of the Provisional Assembly's Fourth Session], *Kukp'yŏn charyo*, vol. 2, p. 397.

96. Chu Yo-han, *An Tosan chŏnsŏ* [*The Complete Writings of An Tosan*] (Seoul: Samjungdang, 1963), p. 201; Arthur Leslie Gardner, "The Korean Nationalist Movement and An Ch'ang-ho, Advocate of Gradualism," pp. 210-11.

97. *Gendaishi shiryō*, vol. 26, p. 236.

98. *Kukp'yŏn charyo*, vol. 2, pp. 401-402.

99. Pak Ŭn-sik, *Hanguk tongnip undong chi hyŏlsa*, pp. 108-109; *Gendaishi shiryō*, vol. 26, pp. 235-36; Ibid., vol. 27, p. 204.

100. Sogong, *Tongnip Sinmun*, 31 Mar, p. 2. 1925; Pak Ŭn-sik, *Hanguk tongnip undong chi hyŏlsa*, pp. 108-109. Pak Ŭn-sik, who came from Vladivostok to Shanghai in the fall of 1919, and became the second President of the Shanghai Provisional Government succeeding impeached Yi Sŭng-man in 1925, said: "Any place inside Korea was not occupied [by any organization for the independent of Korean]. The Eastern Three Provinces [Manchuria] in China and Siberia in Russia are the regions where the most of the Koreans [among in foreign countries] are living, but the Japanese armies are stationed there, so these regions are not safe. The several regions in America are isolated far from the mainland [Korea] and also are not proper locations. Only Shanghai in China is an important place for transportation in the Orient. Although Shanghai is not satisfactorily safe, it is better compared to other places. Accordingly, our independence movement activists have gathered at this place since the end of March."

101. *Tongnip Sinmun*, 21 May 1921, p. 3.

102. *Gendaishi shiryō*, vol. 26, p. 169; *Kukp'yŏn charyo*, vol. 2, p. 397; *3. 1 undong*, vol. 3, pp. 520-21.

103. Kim Wŏn-yong [Kim Warren Y.], *Chaemi hanin osimnyŏnsa* [The Fifty-Year History of Koreans in America] (Reedley, California, 1959), p. 459.

104. Arthur Leslie Gardner, "The Korean Nationalist Movement and An Ch'ang-ho, Advocate of Gradualism," pp. 201-202: "Hanil kwangye saryojip," *Kukp'yŏn charyo*, vol. 4, p. 209.

105. Chang To-jŏng to Katayama Sen, "Korai kyōsantō no enkaku," p. 3.

106. Yi In-sŏp, letter to Kim Se-il, 5 Feb. 1969.

107. Ibid., 7 Mar. 1968.

108. *Gendaishi shiryō*, vol. 26, pp. 243-44. The Japanese information sources reported incorrectly that the "Korean Maximalist organization" named "senitozev" was established in Nikolsk-Ussurisk, but it correctly mentioned Yi Tong-hwi and Kim Rip among the four key leaders of the organization and the organization was working for the Bolsheviks on the orders of Alexandr Krasnoshchekov.

109. Kim Sŭng-bin, letter to Kim Se-il, 2 Mar. 1970.

110. Yi In-sŏp, letter to Kim Se-il, 7 Mar. 1968.

111. Ibid., 7 Mar. 1968: 5 Feb. 1969; Kim Kyu-myŏn, *Nobyŏng Kim Kyu-myŏn ŭi pimangnok esŏ*, pp. 88-90.

112. Yi In-sŏp, letter to Kim Se-il, 18 Jan. 1968; 7 Mar. 1968; Ch'oe Kye-rip, letter to Kim Se-il; Kim Kyu-myŏn, *Nobyŏng Kim Kyu-myŏn ŭi pimangnok esŏ*, pp. 88-90; Kim Chŏng-myŏng [Kin Seimei] ed., *Chōsen dokuritsu undō*, vol. 3, p. 877.

113. Kye Pong-u, *Kkum sog ŭi kkum*, vol. 2, p. 61.
114. *Gendaishi shiryō*, vol. 26, p. 235; vol. 27, pp. 175-76.
115. Ibid., vol. 26, pp. 254-55; Ibid., vol. 27, p. 175.
116. *Gendaishi shiryō*, vol. 26, p. 254; Ibid., vol. 27, pp. 175-76.
117. Ibid., vol. 27, p. 175.
118. Yi Yŏng-il, "Yi Tong-hwi Sŏngjae sŏnsaeng," p. 240.
119. Kim Ch'ŏl-su, "Kim Ch'ŏl-su ch'inp'il yugo" [Posthumous Personal Manuscripts of Kim Ch'ŏl-su], *Yŏksa Pip'yŏng* 5, Summer 1989, p. 368.
120. *Purgŭn Kunsa*, Dec 24. 1921.
121. Kye Pong-u, *Kkum sog ŭi kkum*, vol. 2, p. 72.
122. *Gendaishi shiryō*, vol. 27, p. 177.
123. Ibid., vol. 26, p. 251.
124. Kye Pong-u, *Kkum sog ŭi kkum*, vol. 2, p. 60.
125. *Gendaishi shiryō*, vol. 27, pp. 102-103; Kim Chŏng-myŏng [Kin Seimei] ed., *Chōsen dokuritsu undō*, vol. 3, pp. 440-41. Shortly after the Paris Peace Conference, on July 19, the Shanghai Provisional Government appointed Yi Sŭng-man, Kim Kyu-sik and Sŏ Chae-p'il as members of the delegation to the League of Nations, which, Korean Nationalists believed, would be held in October and discuss the question of Korea. See Kim Chŏng-myŏng [Kin Seimei] ed., *Chōsen dokuritsu undō*, vol. 2, p. 200.
126. "Chōsen minzoku undō nenkan," Ibid., vol. 2, pp. 202-203.
127. *3. 1 undong*, vol. 2, pp. 743-44; Kim Wŏn-yong [Kim Warren Y.], *Chaemi hanin osimnyŏnsa*, pp. 457-58.
128. Kim Wŏn-yong [Kim Warren Y.], *Chaemi hanin osimnyŏnsa*, p. 458.
129. Chu Yo-han, *An Tosan chŏnsŏ*, p. 211; *Kukp'yŏn charyo*, vol. 2, pp. 462-63.
130. "Wŏn Se-hun sŏnsaeng ŭi tongnip t'ujaeng yaksa" [The Brief History of the Struggle of Mr. Wŏn Se-hun for the Independence]. ms., 1950. Mr. Song Nam-hŏn, who was a close associate of Wŏn Se-hun and accompanied Kim Kyu-sik to P'yŏngyang in April 1948, recalled that this document was an election pamphlet which Wŏn Se-hun distributed for the Assembly election in South Korea held on May 30 in 1950.
131. Kim Wŏn-yong [Kim Warren Y.], *Chaemi hanin osimnyŏnsa*, pp. 457-58.
132. *Tongnip Sinmun*, 2 Sep. 1919, p. 2.
133. "Chōsen minzoku undō nenkan," p. 202. Pae, Sŏ and Chŏng were Korean nationalists working in North Chientao, and came to Shanghai after the Provisional Government was established.
134. Soon Hyun 85; *Kukp'yŏn charyo*, vol. 2, p. 463; *Tongnip Sinmun*, 25 Mar. 1920, p. 2.
135. Chu Yo-han, *An Tosan chŏnsŏ*, p. 214.
136. Soon Hyun, *My Autobiography*, p. 85.
137. Kim Chŏng-myŏng [Kin Seimei] ed., *Chōsen dokuritsu undō*, vol. 2, p. 202; Chang To-

jŏng to Katayama Sen, "Korai kyōsantō no enkaku," p. 4.

138. *Gendaishi shiryō*, vol. 27, pp. 13-14.
139. Chu Yo-han, *An Tosan chŏnsŏ*, pp. 214-15.
140. *Kukp'yŏn charyo*, vol. 2, p. 13.
141. R., "The Situation in Eastern Asia," p. 2546.
142. Chu Yo-han, *An Tosan chŏnsŏ*, p. 21; Soon Hyun, *My Autobiography*, p. 86.
143. Kim Kyu-myŏn, *Sŏngjae yakchŏn e kwanhan hoesanggi*, p. 9.
144. *Tongnip Sinmun*, 20 Sep. 1919, p. 3; 23 Sep. 1919, p. 3.

Chapter Five

1. Kim Wŏn-yong [Kim Warren Y.], *Chaemi hanin osimnyŏnsa*, p. 459.
2. Ibid., pp. 459-60.
3. Kim Wŏn-yong [Kim Warren Y.], *Chaemi hanin osimnyŏnsa*, p. 460.
4. *Tongnip Sinmun*, 25 Mar. 1920, p. 2.
5. Ibid., p. 2.
6. Ibid., 9 Sep. 1919, pp. 1-2.
7. C. W. Kendall, *The Truth about Korea*, pp. 66-67; Ko Chŏng-hyu, "Taehan Minguk Imsi Chŏngbu Kumi Wiwŏnbu (1919-1925) yŏngu" [Study on the Committee on European and American Affairs of the Korean Provisional Government] (diss. Korea University, 1992), pp. 24-26, 61. Yi Sŭng-man was born in P'yŏngsan, Hwanghae Province, but he grew up and studied in Seoul and accordingly, he was considered as a person of Seoul.
8. Sogong, *Tongnip Sinmun*, 31 Mar. 1925, p. 2.
9. *Tongnip Sinmun*, 28 Oct. 1919, pp. 2-3; *Tongnip Sinmun*, 1 Nov. 1919, p. 1.
10. "Wŏn Se-hun sŏnsaeng ŭi tongnip t'ujaengsa yaksa."
11. *Gendaishi shiryō*, vol. 27, pp. 13-14.
12. Kim Wŏn-yong, *Chaemi hanin osimnyŏnsa*, p. 461.
13. *Tongnip Sinmun*, 4 Nov. 1919, p. 2; Ibid., 25 Mar. 1920, p. 2.
14. Kim Chŏng-myŏng [Kin Seimei] ed., *Chōsen dokuritsu undō,* vol. 3, p. 442. Commenting on the Japanese attempt to arrest Yi Tong-hwi, Kim Rip and Yi Kang in Vladivostok on September 14, shortly after Kang U-gyu's failed attempt to assassinate Saitō, the third Government-General of Korea, Ch'oe Chae-hyŏng said: "the credibility of these guys [Yi Tong-hwi, Kim Rip and Yi Kang] fell to the ground and they are not qualified to do anything. Even though [the Japanese] do something to these guys, there will be no harm." See *Gendaishi shiryō*, vol. 27, p. 177.
15. This one-sidedness of the regional backgrounds of the members of the Provisional Assembly had been repeatedly pointed out later as one of the factors which contributed to the lack of the legitimacy of the Shanghai Provisional Government.

16. An article dated 25 January 1914 of the *Kwŏnŏp Sinmun* in Vladivostok pointed out that the *T'aep'yŏngyang Chapchi* had criticized anti-Japanese activities and called the Japanese Emperor "His Majesty" ["*Ch'ŏnhwang P'yeha*"] and said that Yi Sŭng-man's followers had attended the ceremony for the birthday of the Japanese Emperor held by the Japanese Consulate General in Honolulu. See *Kwŏnŏp Sinmun*, 25 Jan. 1914, p. 1. Yi Kang, editor of the *Taehanin Chŏnggyobo* in Chita also had same attitude with the *Kwŏnŏp Sinmun* and urged editors of the *Sinhan Minbo* to criticize *T'aep'yŏngyang Chapchi*. See *Taehanin Chŏnggyobo*, 9, Mar. 1914, p. 25.
17. *Tongnip Sinmun*, 28 Oct. 1919, pp. 1-2.
18. Ibid., 8 Nov. 1919, p. 2: 20 Nov. 1919, p. 2: 17 Jan. 1920, p. 4: 30 Jan. 1920, p. 4: 17 Feb. 1920, p. 4.
19. *Hanguk tongnip undongsa*, vol. 3, p. 399.
20. Kim Chŏng-myŏng [Kin Seimei] ed., *Chōsen dokuritsu undō*, vol. 3, p. 452.
21. Ibid., pp. 455, 494.
22. *Gendaishi shiryō*, vol. 27, pp. 13-14, 264.
23. *Tongnip Sinmun*, 1 Nov. 1919, p. 1. Yi Tong-nyŏng and Yi Si-yŏng came to Shanghai from Beijing by the request of Hyŏn Sun who was Vice-Minister of Internal Affairs and was dispatched by the Provisional Government. See Hyun Soon, *My Autobiography*, p. 86.
24. *Tongnip Sinmun*, 4 Nov. 1919, p. 2.
25. Ibid., 4 Nov. 1919, p. 2.
26. Yun Pyŏng-sŏk and Yun Kyŏng-no ed., *An Ch'ang-ho iltaegi*, pp. 210-11.
27. *Tongnip Sinmun*, 4 Nov. 1919, p. 1.
28. Ibid., 11 Nov. 1919, p. 3: 25 Dec. 1919, p. 1.
29. R., "The Situation in Eastern Asia," p. 2548.
30. *Gendaishi shiryō*, vol. 27, p. 190.
31. R., "The Situation in Eastern Asia," p. 2547.
32. Ibid., pp. 2547-48.
33. R., "The Situation in Eastern Asia," pp. 2548.
34. Chu Yo-han, *An Tosan chŏnsŏ*, p. 214.
35. Ban Byung Yool, "Taehan Kungmin Ŭihoe wa Sanghae Imjŏng ŭi t'onghap chŏngbu surip undong" [The Movement for the Unification between the Korean National Council and the Shanghai Provisional Government], *Hanguk Minjok Undongsa Yŏngu*, 2, Mar. 1988, p. 113-114.
36. Kim Chŏng-myŏng [Kin Seimei] ed., *Chōsen dokuritsu undō*, vol. 3, p. 452.
37. "Ilgi" [Diary], 25 Jan. 1920, Chu Yo-han ed., *An Tosan chŏnsŏ* (Seoul: Samjungdang, 1963), p. 634 (hereafter cited as "Tosan Ilgi").
38. Kim Chŏng-myŏng [Kin Seimei] ed., *Chōsen dokuritsu undō*, vol. 2, pp. 213-23.

39. "Chae-Ro Koryŏ hyŏngmyŏng kundae yŏnhyŏk," pp. 8-9.

40. Ibid., pp. 8-9.

41. Kukhoe Tosŏgwan, *Hanguk minjok undongsa saryo: Chungguk p'yŏn*, 355.

42. For reference on Yŏ Un-hyŏng's life and activities, see biographies written by Yi Man-gyu, Yŏ's close associate and Yŏ Un-hong, Yŏ Un-hyŏng's younger brother. Yi Man-gyu, *Yŏ Un-hyŏng t'ujaengsa* [History of Yŏ Un-hyŏng's Struggle] (Seoul: Ch'ongmungak, 1946) and Yŏ Un-hong, *Mongyang Yŏ Un-hyŏng* (Seoul: Ch'ŏng-hagak, 1967).

43. Kang Tŏk-sang, "Shōkai Rinji Seifu to Ryo Un-kyō" [The Shanghai Provisional Government and Yŏ Un-hyŏng], *Sansenri* 40 (Winter 1984), pp. 166-68.

44. *Tongnip Sinmun*, 15 Nov. 1911, p. 2; 2 Feb. 1920, p. 1; Yi Man-gyu, *Yŏ Un-hyŏng t'ujaengsa*, pp. 32-33.

45. *Tongnip Sinmun*, 15 Nov. 1919, p. 2: 20 Feb. 1920; Yi Man-gyu, *Yŏ Un-hyŏng t'ujaengsa*, p. 34.

46. *Tongnip Sinmun*, 20 Feb. 1920, p. 2.

47. Ibid., 15 Nov. 1919, p. 2.

48. *Tongnip Sinmun*, 1 Jan. 1920, p. 6; 11 Jan. 1920, p. 4: 17 Jan. 1910, p. 4: 3 Feb. 1920, p. 4: Yi Man-gyu, *Yŏ Un-hyŏng t'ujaengsa*, pp. 38-58.

49. Ibid., 27 Dec. 1919, p. 1; Yi Man-gyu, *Yŏ Un-hyŏng t'ujaengsa*, pp. 58-59.

50. *Tongnip Sinmun*, 25 Dec. 1919, p. 3.

51. Ibid., 2 Dec. 1919, p. 2.

52. *Tongnip Sinmun*, 25 Dec. 1919, p. 3.

53. Kang Tŏk-sang, "Yonjūni teikoku gikai to Ryo Un-kyō" [The Forty-second Imperial Diet and Yŏ Un-hyŏng], *Sansenri*, 43, Fall 1985, p. 214; Arthur Leslie Gardner, "The Korean Nationalist Movement and An Ch'ang-ho, Advocate of Gradualism," p. 239.

54. Yi Man-gyu, *Yŏ Un-hyŏng t'ujaengsa*, pp. 60-61. According to Yi Man-gyu, Yŏ Un-hyŏng had planned to organize anti-Japanese demonstrations and was ready to risk being imprisoned.

55. *Tongnip Sinmun*, 27 Dec. 1919, p. 1.

56. Ibid., 20 Nov. 1919, p. 2; 10 Jan. 1920, p. 2; Yi Man-gyu, *Yŏ Un-hyŏng t'ujaengsa*, p. 33.

57. Kang Tŏk-sang, "Shōkai Rinji Seifu to Ryo Un-kyō," p. 168.

58. *Tongnip Sinmun*, 20 Nov. 1919, p. 2.

59. "Yŏ Un-hyŏng chosŏ (2)," p. 375.

60. *Tongnip Sinmun*, 10 Jan. 1920, p. 2.

61. Korean scholars considered the *Tongnip Sinmun* as the official organ of the Shanghai Provisional Government, mainly based on the memoirs of An Ch'ang-ho and An's associates. However, Yŏ Un-hyŏng, in his statement to Japanese policemen, the official

organ of the Shanghai Provisional Government was not the *Tongnip Sinmun*, but the *Imsi Chŏngbu Kongbo* [Official Report of the Provisional Government]. See "Yŏ Unhyŏng chosŏ (2)," p. 295. Kye Pong-u, who came to Shanghai at the end of 1919, also recollected that the *Tongnip Sinmun* was the organ of the Hŭngsadan (Young Korean Academy) which An Ch'ang-ho organized in 1913 in America. See Kye Pong-u, *Kkum sog ŭi kkum*, vol. 2, p. 67.

62. *Tongnip Sinmun*, 20 Nov. 1919, p. 2.
63. Ibid., p. 2.
64. *Tongnip Sinmun*, 20 Nov. 1919, p. 2.
65. Ibid., p. 2.
66. *Tongnip Sinmun*, 27 Nov. 1919, p. 2; 2 Dec. 1919, p. 2; 25 Dec. 1919, pp. 2-3.
67. Ibid., 25 Dec. 1919, p. 2-3.
68. *Tongnip Sinmun*, 1 Jan. 1920, p. 6; 11 Jan. 1920, p. 4: 17 Jan. 1920, p. 4: 3 Feb. 1920, p. 4.
69. Ibid., 10 Jan. 1920, p. 2.
70. "Tosan ilgi," 17 Jan. 1920; 18 Jan. 1920. 19 Jan. 1920.
71. Kye Pong-u, *Kkum sog ŭi kkum*, vol. 2, p. 67; *Tongnip Sinmun*, 1 Nov. 1919, p. 4. The chief editor of the *Sin Taehan* was Kim Tu-bong who was from South Kyŏngsang Province and a student of Chu Si-gyŏng, the most prominent Korean linguist. See *Tongnip Sinmun*, 8 Jan. 1920, p. 2.
72. Yi Yŏng-il, "Yi Tong-hwi Sŏngjae sŏnsaeng," p. 240.
73. Yi In-sŏp, letter to Kim Se-il, 5 Feb. 1968: Kim Kyu-myŏn, *Nobyŏng Kim Kyu-myŏn ŭi pimangnok esŏ*, p. 8.
74. *Tongnip Sinmun*, 27 Nov. 1919, p. 2.
75. *Gendaishi shiryō*, vol. 29, p. 454; Chin-sun Pak, "The Socialist Movement in Korea," p. 44.
76. *Gendaishi siryŏ*, vol. 27, pp. 11, 242-43.
77. Kim Kyu-myŏn, *Nobyŏng Kim Kyu-myŏn ŭi pimangnok esŏ*, p. 12.
78. *Tongnip Sinmun*, 29 Apr. 1920, p. 2. For short biographies of Pak Chin-sun, refer to M. T. Kim, *Koreiskie internatsionalisty v bor'be za vlasti sovetov na Dal'nem Vostoke (1918-1922)*, pp. 63-65 and Kwŏn Hŭi-yŏng, "Koryŏ Kongsandang ironga Pak Chin-sun ŭi saengae wa sasang" [The Life and Thoughts of Pak Chin-sun, Theoretician of the Korean Communist Party], *Yŏksa Pip'yŏng*, 4, Spring, 1989, pp. 285-94.
79. *Gendaishi shiryō*, vol. 27, pp. 183-84.
80. Kim Chŏng-ju [Kin Sei-tsū] ed., *Chōsen tōchi shiryō*, vol. 8, p. 235.
81. Din'shun Pak, "Sotsialisticheskoe dvizhenie v Koree," pp. 1171-76.
82. Din'shun Pak, "Reforma v Koree i Koreiskaia sotsialisticheskaia partiia," *Izvestiia*, 12 Feb. 1920, p. 1.

83. Din'shun Pak, "Osvoboditel'noe dvizhenie narodov Vostoka in Sovetskaia Rossia," *Zhizn' Natsionalostei*, 64, 29 Feb. 1920.
84. Koreits [Pak Chin-sun], "Probuzhdenie Korei," *Zhizn' Natsionalostei*, 65, 7 Mar. 1920.
85. Din'shun Pak, "Koreiskaia emigratsiia v Rossii," *Zhizn' Natsionalostei*, 68, 18 Apr. 1920.
86. Din'shun Pak, "Revoliutsionyi Vostok i ocheredhaia zadacha Kommunisticheskogo Internatsionala," *Kommunisticheskii Internatsional*, 12 July 1920), pp. 2315-20.
87. Din'shun Pak, "Revoliutsionnoe dvizhenie v Koree," *Izvestiia*, Aug. 22, 1920.
88. Din'shun Pak, "Zhenskoe dvizhenie v Koree," *Zhizn' Natsionalostei*, 86, 24 Sep. 1920.
89. E. H. Carr, *The Bolshevik Revolution 1917-1923*, vol. 3 (New York and London: Norton, 1953), p. 496.
90. *Tongnip Sinmun*, 12 Feb. 1920, p. 2; *Kukp'yŏn charyo*, vol. 2, p. 212. Accordingly, the Soviet government asked Koreans in Russia to have passport issued by the Provisional Government.
91. *Tongnip Sinmun*, 1 Mar. 1920, p. 1.
92. Han Hyŏng-gwŏn, "Hyŏngmyŏngga ŭi hoesangnok: Lenin kwa tamp'an, tongnip chagŭm isipŏk wŏn hoektŭk" [Recollections of a Revolutionary: Negotiation with Lenin, Obtaining Two Billion Wŏn as the Funds for Independence Movement], *Samch'ŏlli*, 6, Oct. 1948, p. 10.
93. Han Hyŏng-gwŏn, "Hyŏngmyŏngga ŭi hoesangnok," p. 10.
94. Kim Chŏng-myŏng, vol. 2, pp. 244-45; Han Hyŏng-gwŏn, "Hyŏngmyŏngga ŭi hoesangnok," p. 10; "Tosan ilgi," 14 Jan. 1920: 15 Jan. 1920: 22 Jan. 1920.
95. Han Hyŏng-gwŏn, "Hyŏngmyŏngga ŭi hoesangnok," p. 10.
96. "Tosan ilgi," 26 Jan. 1920: 31 Jan. 1920.
97. "Yŏ Un-hyŏng chosŏ (2)," p. 345.
98. "Tosan Ilgi," 1 Feb. 1910.
99. Ibid., 31 Jan. 1910.
100. "Tosan ilgi," 28 Feb. 1920.
101. Kim Ch'ŏl-su, "Kim Ch'ŏl-su ch'inp'il yugo," p. 351.
102. Ibid., p. 351. Available materials do not provide the exact date of Han Hyŏng-gwŏn's departure. Here, the author assumed the date as "the end of April," based on following three facts: 1) The Far Eastern Republic was established on April 6, 1920; 2) According to a Japanese source which was based on confiscated materials from the Provisional Government, Han Hyŏng-gwŏn applied for his travel funds to the Ministry of Foreign Affairs on April 25, 1920, p. 3 [see Kim Chŏng-myŏng [Kin Seimei] ed., *Chōsen dokuritsu undō*, vol. 2, p. 238] In a letter dated May 11, 1920, sent to Ku Ch'un-sŏn, Yi Tong-hwi, Kim Rip and Kye Pong-u said, "Han Hyŏng-gwŏn will arrive in Moscow

in the near future as well." (see Kim Chŏng-ju ed., *Chōsen tōchi shiryō*, vol. 8, p. 236). According to Han Hyŏng-gwŏn, it took about forty or fifty days to reach Moscow from Shanghai.

103. Kim Ch'ŏl-su, "Kim Ch'ŏl-su ch'inp'il yugo," p. 351; Yi Yŏng-il, "Yi Tong-hwi Sŏngjae sŏnsaeng," p. 340.

104. Han Hyŏng-gwŏn, "Hyŏngmyŏngga ŭi hoesangnok," pp. 10-11. Han Hyŏng-gwŏn's travel is introduced by Chong-sik Lee based on Han's recollection. See Robert A. Scalapino and Chong-sik Lee, *Communism in Korea*, vol. 1 (Berkeley, Los Angeles and London: U of California P, 1972), pp. 17-19.

105. Kim Ch'ŏl-su, "Kim Ch'ŏl-su ch'inp'il yugo," p. 351.

106. Han Hyŏng-gwŏn, "Hyŏngmyŏngga ŭi hoesangnok," p. 11. English translation was quoted from Robert A. Scalapino and Chong-sik Lee, *Communism in Korea*, p. 19.

107. Ibid., p. 11; Robert A. Scalapino and Chong-sik Lee, *Communism in Korea*, p. 18.

108. Han Hyŏng-gwŏn, "Hyŏngmyŏngga ŭi hoesangnok," p. 11.

109. Dinshun' Pak, "V presidium krestinterna: dokladnaia zapiska" [To the Presidium of the Peasant International: Report] (ts., Jan. 1926), 1.

110. *The 2nd Congress of the Communist International: As Reported and Interpreted by the Official Newspapers of Soviet Russia* (Washington: Government Printing Office, 1920), p. 133.

111. *Gendaishi shiryō*, vol. 27, p. 73; "Chae-Ro Koryŏ hyŏngmyŏng kundae yŏnhyŏk," p. 9.

112. Kim Kyu-myŏn, *Nobyŏng Kim Kyu-myŏn ŭi pimangnok esŏ*, p. 116.

113. Vladimir Dmitrievich Kim ed., *Tumangan: Pogranichnaia Reka* [Tuman River: Border River] (Tashkent: Uzbekistan, 1994), p. 59.

114. *The Report of the Executive Committee of the Communist International: A Speech Delivered by G. Zinoviev at the III Congress of the Communist International, at Moscow, on June 25th, 1921* (Moscow: The Press Bureau of the Communist International, 1921), p. 6.

115. *Vtoroi kongress Kominterna, iul'-avgust 1920 g.* [The Second Congress of the Comintern, July-August 1920] (Moscow: Partiinoe Izdatel'stvo, 1934), pp. 619-25; *Der Zweite Kongress der Kommunistischen Internationale: Protokoll der Verhandlungen vom 19. Juli in Petrograd und vom 23. Juli bis 7. August 1920 in Moskau* [The Second Congress of the Communist International: Protocol of Proceedings of July 19 in Petersburg and from July 23 till August 7, 1920 in Moscow] (Hamburg: Carl Hoym Nacht. Louis Chahnbley, 1921), p. 780. According to the list of the delegates, Pak Chin-sun was listed as no. 78 of all 218 delegates as the delegate of the "Communist Party" of Korea and An Yong-hak and Liu Shao-zhou were listed as nos. 79 and 80 with consultative rights as the delegates of "the Central Bureau of the Chinese Workers' Party."

116. *Vtoroi kongress Kominterna, iul'-avgust 1920 g.*, p. 627.

117. Kim Ch'ŏl-su, "Kim Ch'ŏl-su ch'inp'il yugo," p. 351: M. T. Kim, *Koreiskie internatsionalisty v bor'be za vlasti sovetov na Dal'nem Vostoke (1918-1922)*, pp. 64-65.

118. *Zhizn' Natsionalostei*, 82, M1 Aug. 1920, p. 1.

119. *Vtoroi kongress Kominterna, iul'-avgust 1920 g.*, pp. 125-27.

120. Din'shun Pak, "Revoliutsionyi Vostok i ocheredhaia zadacha Kommunisticheskogo Internatsionala," *Kommunisticheskii International*, 12, July 1920, pp. 2315-20. An English translation is included in Dae-sook Suh ed., *Documents of Korean Communism 1918-1948*, pp. 53-59.

121. *Vtoroi kongress Kominterna, iul'-avgust 1920 g.*, p. 457; *The 2nd Congress of the Communist International: As Reported and Interpreted by the Official Newspapers of Soviet Russia*, p. 74.

122. Murata Yōichi ed., *Kominterun shiryōshū*, vol. 1 (Tokyo: Taogatsu Shoten, 1979), p. 195; Kim Kyu-myŏn, *Nobyŏng Kim Kyu-myŏn ŭi pimangnok esŏ*, p. 116.

123. Han Hyŏng-gwŏn, "Hyŏngmyŏngga ŭi hoesangnok," p. 11.

124. Dinshun' Pak, "V presidium krestinterna: dokladnaia zapiska," p. 1.

125. "Tosan ilgi," 21 Feb. 1920.

126. Kye Pong-u, *Kkum sog ŭi kkum*, vol. 2, p. 67.

127. "Tosan ilgi," 5 Feb. 1920: 21 Feb. 1920: 21 Apr. 1920.

128. Sogong, *Tongnip Sinmun*, 31 Mar. 1925, p. 3.

129. Ibid., p. 3; Ko Chŏng-hyu, "Taehan Minguk Imsi Chŏngbu Kumi Wiwŏnbu (1919-1925) yŏngu," pp. 137-39.

130. According to Ko Chŏng-hyu's study, of approximately 45,000 dollars collected by the Korean Commission from September 1919 to May 1920, no funds were sent to the Shanghai Provisional Government. See the Table 2 and Table 3 in Ko Chŏng-hyu, "Taehan Minguk Imsi Chŏngbu Kumi Wiwŏnbu (1919-1925) yŏngu," pp. 129, 131-32.

131. Kim Wŏn-yong, *Chaemi hanin osimnyŏnsa*, pp. 374-75.

132. Ibid., pp. 474-75.

133. Yu Cha-hu, *Yi Chun sŏnsaeng chŏn*, pp. 103-10.

134. "Tosan ilgi," 26 Feb. 1920.

135. Ibid., 21 Feb. 1920: 12 Mar. 1920: 21 Apr. 1920.

136. *Tongnip Sinmun*, 23 Mar. 1920, p. 3.

137. Kim Wŏn-yong, *Chaemi hanin osimnyŏnsa*, pp. 175-76.

138. "Tosan ilgi," 21 Feb. 1920.

139. Ibid., 12 Mar. 1920.

140. "Tosan ilgi," 21 Apr. 1920: 23 Apr. 1920: 24 Apr. 1920.

141. Ibid., 6 May 1920. Yi Tong-hwi secretly ordered Korean armed forces in West

Chientao to gather and discuss military actions against Japan.

142. "Tosan ilgi," 6 May 1920: 10 May 1920.

143. Ibid., 13 May 1920: 14 May 1920: 15 May 1920.

144. "Tosan ilgi," 14 May 1920.

145. Ibid., 17 May 1920.

146. "Tosan ilgi," 11 May 1920: 13 May 1920: 14 May 1920: 15 May 1920: 16 May 1920.

147. Ibid., 16 May 1920.

148. As we saw earlier, these four Vice-Ministers (Kim Rip, Yun Hyŏn-jin, Kim Ch'ŏl and Yi Kyu-hong) helped Yi Tong-hwi dispatch Han Hyŏng-gwŏn to Moscow.

149. "Tosan ilgi," 17 May 1920: 7 June 1920.

150. Yun Hyŏn-jin proposed two alternatives to An Ch'ang-ho after removing Yi Sŭngman from the Government: 1) Yi Tong-hwi as President and An Ch'ang-ho as Premier, or 2) An Ch'ang-ho as President, Yi Tong-hwi as Vice-President and Yi Tong-nyŏng as Premier. See "Tosan ilgi," 5 June 1920.

151. "Tosan ilgi," 7 June 1920: 8 June 1920.

152. "Tosan ilgi," 12 June 1920; Japanese Government-General Office of Korea, the Police Department, *Kōtō kankei nenpyō* [High-Level Police Related Chronology] (Seoul, 1929), p. 29.

153. "Tosan ilgi," 20 May 1920: 30 May 1920.

154. Ibid., 16 June 1920.

155. "Tosan ilgi," 12 July 1920.

156. Ibid., 16 July 1920.

157. "Tosan ilgi," 18 June 1920: 23 June 1920.

158. According to a Japanese investigation, as of April 1920, the 150,000 Koreans, 20,000 Chinese and 3,000 Japanese were "infected with radical thoughts." See Kim Chŏng-ju [Kin Sei-tsū] ed., *Chōsen tōchi shiryō*, vol. 8, p. 235.

159. *Gendaishi shiryō*, vol. 27, pp. 290-91, 299.

160. *Izvestiia*, 15 Aug. 1919.

161. Ibid. At this meeting, A. Voznesenskii, representing the Eastern Department of the Ministry of Foreign Affairs, read the following appeal of the Soviet government to the Korean people, which was declared on 26 July 1919: "To the Korean Revolutionary Organization, Kun-Min-khe [Kungminhoe] and all Korean people. Victorious troops of the Workers' and Peasants' Government in Russia, after a two-year struggle against the Tsarist generals in Siberia, entered the Siberian plains, (giving) all aid and freedom to the peasants and workers of Siberia and the Koreans. At this moment, the Soviet government appeals to all Korean revolutionaries who are fighting against their oppressors, the Japanese, with the following words: Already for fifteen years, Korean people have fought with the Japanese robbers who took from them land and robbed

their independence, executed and separated the best of her sons to prison. Korean revolutionaries had to take refuge in foreign countries, in Russia, America, Australia and China. However, Japan, from 1914 concluded an alliance with these countries, at the head of which were as well as Japan, the government of the Tsar, king, the rich and other predators and all these governments, according to the agreement with the Japanese deprived the Korean revolutionaries of refuge and the Tsarist government and its serfs, Kolchak, Horvath even began to hand over Korean revolutionaries to the Japanese for persecution and execution. Now, Moscow became the only refuge for the Koreans. In Soviet Russia, the Korean National Union was established with a goal of revolution in Korea and the restoration of Korean independence. Korean revolutionaries joined the ranks of our Red Army and formed their regiments which now help Korean workers in Russia, they joined the Third International in Moscow, that is, to the whole-world Union of workers and toilers against capitalists and oppressors, and work hand in hand with the oppressed classes of other countries. While the Red Army and Korean soldiers will fight the Japanese from the side of the Urals, the Korean people must revolt in their country and make every effort to establish relations with the Workers' and Peasants' Government in Russia. Then with cooperative force, we can force out the Japanese from Vladivostok and from the country of the Morning Calm. Time of liberation is near. Korean revolutionaries, exert your last effort."

162. *Gendaishi shiryō*, vol. 27, pp. 290-91, 299. A Japanese police report said that Yi Wi-jong mobilized about 7,800 Koreans and twenty Korean officers were training them. Another Japanese report said that Yi was commanding Korean troops composed of 4,000 soldiers in the Red Army in the region west of Irkutsk.

163. *Izvestiia*, 6 Sep. 1919. In its application to a city district committee of the Russian Communist Party, the Korean Communist cell defined its task, "to lead propaganda and agitation among the Korean workers in Russia and Siberia for the establishment of a Soviet regime in Korea" and "to form Korean detachments for the liberation of Korea," and to participate in a world socialist revolution. The Korean Communist cell asked the district committee to accept the Korean Communists in the Russian Communist Party. This first Korean Communist cell in Russia was headed by Kang Sang-ju. See *Gendaishi shiryō*, vol. 27, p. 74. Kang Sang-ju participated at the First Congress of the Comintern as representative of the Korean Workers' Union [Taedongdan] with consultative rights. See *Pervy Kongress Kominterna: Marta 1919 g.* [The First Congress of the Comintern: March 1919] (Moscow: Partiinoe Izdatel'stvo, 1933), pp. 131, 161, 249, 251; M. T. Kim, *Koreiskie internatsionalisty v bor'be za vlasti sovetov na Dal'nem Vostoke (1918-1922)*, pp. 65-66.

164. *Gendaishi shiryō*, vol. 27, p. 74. Japanese sources mistakenly recorded Sŏnu Chŏng as

Ch'oe Chong-ho.

165. Yi In-sŏp, *Mangmyŏngja ŭi sugui*, pp. 84-85; *Gendaishi shiryō*, vol. 27, pp. 291, 299.

166. Yamaguchi Hōsuke, *Shiberiya hishi* [*Secret History of Siberia*] (Tokyo: Nippon Hyōronsha, 1923), p. 312. Yanson went to Moscow in order to be in charge of the Eastern Section of the Commisaritat of Foreign Affairs in June 1920. Later, Yanson became the Minister of Foreign Affairs of the Far Eastern Republic.

167. *Gendaishi shiryō*, vol. 27, p. 74; Yi In-sŏp, *Mangmyŏngja ŭi sugŭi*, pp. 27-28. According to Yi In-sŏp, the director of the Bureau was Gapon and the other members were Ch'ae Sŏng-yong (secretary, Korea), Yi In-sŏp (Korea), Choibalsan (Mongolia) and Liu Liao (China). Yi In-sŏp was also in charge of the Japanese section. See Yi In-sŏp, letter to Kim Se-il, 5 Feb. 1968 and V. D. Kim 67.

168. *Gendaishi shiryō*, vol. 27, pp. 290-92; Kim Chŏng-ju [Kin Sei-tsū] ed., *Chōsen tōchi shiryō*, vol. 7, p. 164.

169. Canfield F. Smith, *Vladivostok under Red and White Rule: Revolution and Counterrevolution in the Russian Far East, 1920-1922* (Seattle and London: University of Washington Press, 1975), p. 40; *Tongnip Sinmun*, 20 Apr. 1920, pp. 1-2; *Gendaishi shiryō*, vol. 27, pp. 325-26.

170. Canfield F. Smith, *Vladivostok under Red and White Rule: Revolution and Counterrevolution in the Russian Far East, 1920-1922*, p. 41. The *Tongnip Sinmun* in Shanghai also reported that all 380 Koreans were arrested in the Primorye. See *Tongnip Sinmun*, 13 Apr. 1920, p. 3; 17 Apr. 1920, p. 2; 20 Apr. 1920, pp. 1-2; 22 Apr. 1920, p. 2.

171. *Gendaishi shiryō*, vol. 27, pp. 327-34.

172. Ibid., p. 333; *Tongnip Sinmun*, 15 May 1920, pp. 1-2.

173. *Gendaishi shiryō*, vol. 27, pp. 252, 331.

174. Ibid., pp. 252, 329-35.

175. Kim Chŏng-ju [Kin Sei-tsū] ed., *Chōsen tōchi shiryō*, vol. 7, p. 164.

176. *Gendaishi shiryō*, vol. 27, pp. 291, 299; Kim Chŏng-ju [Kin Sei-tsū] ed., *Chōsen tōchi shiryō*, vol. 7, p. 402.

177. M. T. Kim, *Koreiskie internatsionalisty v bor'be za vlasti sovetov na Dal'nem Vostoke (1918-1922)*, p. 94; Wieczynski Joseph L. *The Modern Encyclopedia of Russian and Soviet History*, vol. 42, p. 219.

178. Kim Chŏng-ju [Kin Sei-tsū] ed., *Chōsen tōchi shiryō*, vol. 8, p. 235.

179. As we saw in Chapter 2, Kye Pong-u was arrested in November 1916 in North Chientao and transferred to Korea. After one year exile, Kye was put under house arrest in Yŏnghŭng, his hometown in South Hamgyŏng Province. Kye went to Vladivostok after the March First Movement and joined the Union of Iron and Blood Restoration [Ch'ŏlgwangdan]. At the end of 1919, Kye was elected Chairman of the Union and was also dispatched by the Korean National Association in North Chientao together with

Yu Ye-gyun, as representatives to the Shanghai Provisional Assembly. In April 1920, Kye joined the Korean Socialist Party on Kim Rip's strong encouragement. See Kye Pong-u, *Kkum sog ŭi kkum*, vol. 2, pp. 60-72.

180. Yi Tong-hwi, Kim Rip and Kye Pong-u, letter to Ku Ch'un-sŏn (11 May 1920); Kim Chŏng-ju [Kin Sei-tsū] ed., *Chōsen tōchi shiryō*, vol. 8, pp. 236-39; *Gendaishi shiryō*, vol. 27, pp. 195-96.

181. Kim Chŏng-ju [Kin Sei-tsū] ed., *Chōsen tōchi shiryō*, vol. 8, pp. 239-40. This information was based on Kye Pong-u's letter to Ku Ch'un-sŏn dated May 14, 1920, which was secretly intercepted by the Japanese authorities.

182. *Gendaishi shiryō*, vol. 27, pp. 291, 299.

183. "Tosan ilgi," 23 June 1920.

184. Kim Chŏng-ju [Kin Sei-tsū] ed., *Chōsen tōchi shiryō*, vol. 7, p. 402.

185. Kye Pong-u, *Kkum sog ŭi kkum*, vol. 2, pp. 71-72.

186. "Tosan ilgi," 23 June 1920; 29 June 1920. Yi T'ak suggested that An Ch'ang-ho make Sin Tu-sik enter the Party of Yi Tong-hwi and Kim Rip in order to get inside information on the Party. An Ch'ang-ho, however, rejected the idea. See "Tosan ilgi," 23 June 1920.

187. "Tosan ilgi," 24 June 1920.

188. Ibid., 27 June 1920: 28 June 1920: 29 June 1920; Kim Chŏng-ju [Kin Sei-tsū] ed., *Chōsen tōchi shiryō*, vol. 7, p. 165.

189. "Tosan ilgi," 17 July 1920: 21 July 1920: 22 July 1920: 24 July 1920.

190. Ibid., 22 July 1920: 23 July 1920: 24 July 1920.

191. "Chae-Ro Koryŏ hyŏngmyŏng kundae yŏnhyŏk," p. 9; Kim Chŏng-myŏng [Kin Seimei] ed., *Chōsen dokuritsu undō*, vol. 2, p. 241.

192. "Tosan ilgi," 9 July 1920; Kim Chŏng-ju [Kin Sei-tsū] ed., *Chōsen tōchi shiryō*, vol. 7, p. 403.

193. "Chae-Ro Koryŏ hyŏngmyŏng kundae yŏnhyŏk," p. 9; Kye Pong-u, *Kkum sog ŭi kkum*, vol. 2, p. 72.

194. Kye Pong-u, *Kkum sog ŭi kkum*, vol. 2, p. 72.

195. *Gendaishi shiryō*, vol. 27, p. 73.

196. "Chae-Ro Koryŏ hyŏngmyŏng kundae yŏnhyŏk," p. 23; *Tonga Kongsan*, 3, 25 Sep. 1920, pp. 3-4; *Narody Dal'nego Vostoka*, 2, 23 June 1921, p. 157.

197. *Tonga Kongsan* 5, 25 Oct. 1920, p. 2.

198. "Chae-Ro Koryŏ hyŏngmyŏng kundae yŏnhyŏk," p. 9.

199. "Uchreditel'nyi S'ezd Koreiskoi Kommunisticheskoi partii" ["Constituent Congress of the Korean Communist Party"], *Narody Dal'nego Vostoka*, 2, 23 June 1921, p. 214; "Chae-Ro Koryŏ hyŏngmyŏng kundae yŏnhyŏk," p. 9; Yi Yŏng-il, "Yi Tong-hwi Sŏngjae sŏnsaeng," p. 252; Yi In-sŏp, letter to Kim Se-il, 7 Mar. 1968.

200. Yi Yŏng-il, "Yi Tong-hwi Sŏngjae sŏnsaeng," p. 252; Yi In-sŏp, letter to Kim Se-il, 7 Mar. 1968.

201. *Tonga Kongsan*, 14, 10 May 1921; Kim Kyu-myŏn, *Nobyŏng Kim Kyu-myŏn ŭi pimangnok esŏ*, p. 38.

202. *The 2nd Congress of the Communist International*, 46; *Gendaishi shiryō*, vol. 27, p. 183.

203. *Vtoroi kongress Kominterna, iul'-avgust 1920 g.*, 621.

204. "Yŏ Un-hyŏng chosŏ (2)," p. 248. Yŏ Un-hyŏng joined the Korean Communist Party after he met Voitinsky.

205. Ibid., p. 317.

206. "Uchreditel'nyi S'ezd Koreiskoi Kommunisticheskoi partii," p. 214; "Doklad Koreiskoi Kommunisticheskoi partii III-mu Kongressu Kominterna" [Report of the Korean Communist Party to the Third Congress of the Comintern], *Narody Dal'nego Vostoka*, 2, 23 June 1921, p. 258.

207. "Uchreditel'nyi S'ezd Koreiskoi Kommunisticheskoi partii," p. 215.

208. "Chae-Ro Koryŏ hyŏngmyŏng kundae yŏnhyŏk," p. 9.

209. Kye Pong-u, *Kkum sog ŭi kkum*, vol. 2, pp. 72-73, 81-84.

210. "Chae-Ro Koryŏ hyŏngmyŏng kundae yŏnhyŏk," p. 9.

211. Han Hyŏng-gwŏn, "Hyŏngmyŏngga ŭi hoesangnok," p. 11.

212. Kim Chŏng-ju [Kin Sei-tsū] ed., *Chōsen tōchi shiryō*, vol. 7, p. 403.

213. *Tongnip Sinmun*, 25 Dec. 1920, p. 1; Kim Chŏng-myŏng [Kin Seimei] ed., *Chōsen dokuritsu undō*, vol. 2, pp. 243-44.

214. "Chae-Ro Koryŏ hyŏngmyŏng kundae yŏnhyŏk," p. 9.

215. Kye Pong-u, *Kkum sog ŭi kkum*, vol. 2, pp. 83-84.

216. "Chae-Ro Koryŏ hyŏngmyŏng kundae yŏnhyŏk," p. 9. The detailed story of the travels of Kim Rip and Kye Pong-u can be seen in Kye Pong-u's *Kkum sog ŭi kkum*, vol. 2, pp. 74-97. However, Kye Pong-u's description unfortunately stops in Mongolia.

217. *Gendaishi shiryō*, vol. 27, p. 270. Han Kun-myŏng said in his address at the ceremony: "In the past, [we] were opposed to the Shanghai Government, but from now [we] will retain connections [with the Government] and wait for orders [from the Government] and will work and cooperate in harmony with other organizations and associations."

218. *Gendaishi shiryō*, vol. 27, pp. 30-31, 296-97.

219. Ibid., vol. 27, pp. 30-31; "Doklad Koreiskoi Kommunisticheskoi partii III-mu Kongressu Kominterna," p. 253.

220. Kuksa P'yŏnch'an Wiwŏnhoe, *Hanguk tongnip undongsa*, vol. 3, pp. 632-33; *Gendaishi shiryō*, vol. 27, pp. 80-81. The Military Government in North Chientao [Pungno Kunjŏngsŏ] led by the believers of the nationalist religion, the Taejonggyo (Religion of Tangun Worship), did not join the Military Command in North Chientao [Pungno Tokkunbu].

221. *Hanguk tongnip undongsa*, vol. 3, pp. 707-12.

222. *Tongnip Sinmun*, 22 June 1920, p. 2; 25 Dec. 1920, p. 2; *Hanguk tongnip undongsa*, vol. 3, p. 717.

223. *Hanguk tongnip undongsa*, vol. 3, p. 644.

224. Ibid., pp. 666-706.

225. *Tongnip Sinmun*, 18 Dec. 1920, p. 2. According to the investigation of the Japanese 19th division, 522 Koreans were killed and one was injured and 534 Korean houses were burnt down. See *Gendaishi shiryō*, vol. 26, pp. 520-71.

226. *Tongnip Sinmun*, 25 Dec. 1920, p. 2; *Hanguk tongnip undongsa*, vol. 3, pp. 720-29.

227. Yi Kwang-su, "Na ŭi kobaek," pp. 246-47.

228. *Tongnip Sinmun*, 18 Dec. 1920, p. 1.

229. Kim San and Nym Wales, *Song of Ariran* (New York: The John Day Company, 1941), p. 52.

230. According to Yi Kwang-su, Yi Tong-hwi failed to pass his proposal to declare "immediate full-scale war" against Japan. See Yi Kwang-su, "Na ŭi kobaek," p. 247.

231. "Chae-Ro Koryŏ hyŏngmyŏng kundae yŏnhyŏk," p. 13. The Korean partisan troops in the Primorye and Priamur regions moved to Svobodnyi City in November 1920 and Korean military troops in Manchuria also arrived at Svobodnyi City from the end of January to the middle of March 1921. The number of soldiers is not available and even the total number is different according to sources, ranging from 1,800 to 3,000. The "Shanghai Group" led by Yi Tong-hwi and the combined faction of the "Irkutsk Group" and the Korean National Council competed over these Korean military forces during the period from the end of 1920 to the middle of 1921, and the factional struggle over the military hegemony led to the tragic "Svobodnyi Incident" at the end of June 1921.

232. *Tongnip Sinmun*, 18 Dec. 1920, p. 1.

233. Ibid, 25 Dec. 1920, p. 1.

234. *Gendaishi shiryō*, vol. 27, p. 199.

235. Kim Wŏn-yong, *Chaemi hanin osimnyŏnsa*, pp. 478-79.

236. Ibid., p. 480; Kim Chŏng-ju [Kin Sei-tsū] ed., *Chōsen tōchi shiryō*, vol. 7, p. 411.

237. Kim Kyu-myŏn, *Sŏngjae yakchŏn e kwanhan hoesanggi*, p. 12. According to Kim Kyu-myŏn, Yi Tong-hwi suggested that the "Korean revolutionary committee" would convene the representatives of various organizations from all regions including all provinces in Korea and organize the "central revolutionary committee" and regional revolutionary committees by representatives. The regional revolutionary committees would be organized both inside and outside Korea to the provincial and county levels.

238. Kim Chŏng-ju [Kin Sei-tsū] ed., *Chōsen tōchi shiryō*, vol. pp. 7, 411. Yi Tong-nyŏng, Yi Si-yŏng and Sin Kyu-sik did not want to change the government system. Although

An Ch'ang-ho proposed reducing the number of government officials, he basically supported the status quo. Kim Kyu-sik suggested changing the title of President [*Taet'ongnyŏng*] to Chief Executive [*Chipchŏnggwan*]. Only Nam Hyŏng-u wanted to reform the government system. See "Tosan ilgi," 6 Feb. 1921: 7 Feb. 1921: 9 Feb. 1921: 28 Feb. 1921.

239. Kim Wŏn-yong, *Chaemi hanin osimnyŏnsa*, pp. 479-80. According to Kwak Im-dae, a close associate of An Ch'ang-ho, Yi Sŭng-man failed to present any plan for the independence movement and only emphasized the importance of diplomacy in America. Yi Tong-hwi criticized Yi Sŭng-man saying, "I do not want to hear your talk about the all-round capability of diplomacy. It is not an independence movement to advocate the mandated rule without doing anything. You had better stop such diplomatic activity. See Kwak Im-dae, "An To-san" [An Ch'ang-ho], 1968, *Hangukhak Yŏngu*, 4, Mar. 1992 (Center for Korean Studies, Inha University), p. 241.

240. Kim Chŏng-myŏng [Kin Seimei] ed., *Chōsen dokuritsu undō*, vol. 2, pp. 266-67.

241. Ibid., vol. 2, pp. 266-68; *Tongnip Sinmun*, 17 Feb. 1921, p. 1; 19 Mar. 1921, p. 1.

242. Kim Chŏng-ju [Kin Sei-tsū] ed., *Chōsen tōchi shiryō*, vol. 7, pp. 411-12; Kim Chŏng-myŏng [Kin Seimei] ed., *Chōsen dokuritsu undō*, vol. 2, p. 268; Sin Suk, *Na ŭi ilsaeng* [May Life] (Seoul: Ilsinsa, 1956), pp. 61-63; "Tosan ilgi," 3 Feb. 1921: 4 Feb. 1921: 6 Feb. 1921.

243. Sin Suk, *Na ŭi ilsaeng*, pp. 61-63.

244. Kim Chŏng-ju [Kin Sei-tsū] ed., *Chōsen tōchi shiryō*, vol. 7, p. 412.

245. Kim Chŏng-myŏng [Kin Sei-tsū] ed., *Chōsen dokuritsu undō*, vol. 2, p. 269; Kim Chŏng-ju [Kin Sei-tsū] ed., *Chōsen tōchi shiryō*, vol. 7, p. 412.

246. Kim Chŏng-myŏng [Kin Sei-tsū] ed., *Chōsen dokuritsu undō*, vol. 2, pp. 275-76.

247. Ibid., p. 272.

248. Kim Chŏng-myŏng [Kin Sei-tsū] ed., *Chōsen dokuritsu undō*, vol. 2, p. 273; Kim Chŏng-ju [Kin Sei-tsū] ed., *Chōsen tōchi shiryō*, vol. 7, p. 413.

249. Kim San and Nym Wales, *Song of Ariran*, p. 52.

250. "Chae-Ro Koryŏ hyŏngmyŏng kundae yŏnhyŏk," p. 8; Kyŏngjae, "Hŭkha sabyŏn ŭi chinsang" [The Real Facts of the Amur Incident], *Tongnip Sinmun*, 6 May 1922, p. 1; Im Kyŏng-sŏk, "Koryŏ kongsandang *Yŏngu*" [Study on the Korean Communist Party] (diss. Sŏnggyungwan University, 1993), pp. 185-87.

251. "Tongaguk Haninbu chojikpu ilchi" [Daily Record of the Korean Section of the Far Eastern Bureau], ms., Jan. 1921.

252. Canfield F. Smith, "Krasnoshchekov, Alexandr Mikhailovich (1880-1937?)," p. 42.

253. Kyŏngjae, *Tongnip Sinmun*, 6 May 1922, p. 1.

254. "Chae-Ro Koryŏ hyŏngmyŏng kundae yŏnhyŏk," pp. 8-11; 18-19; Kyŏngjae, *Tongnip Sinmun*, 6 May 1922, p. 1.

255. Im Kyŏng-sŏk, "Koryŏ kongsandang *Yŏngu,*" pp. 188-89.

256. Kim Rip and Kye Pong-u, who had been dispatched by the Korean Communist Party in Shanghai, met Pak Chin-sun and Han Hyŏng-gwŏn who brought 400,000 gold rubles from Moscow. Han Hyŏng-gwŏn went to Chita and gave 40,000 rubles to Kim Kyu-myŏn and Yi Yong, who were in charge of unifying Korean military forces in Svobodnyi City, and returned to Moscow. Kim Rip transferred the other 340,000 rubles through Mongolia to Shanghai. See Dinshun' Pak, "V presidium krestinterna: dokladnaia zapiska" [To the Presidium of the Peasant International: Report], ts. Jan. 1926, 1; Kim Kyu-myŏn, *Nobyŏng Kim Kyu-myŏn ŭi pimangnok esŏ*, pp. 37-38; Kim Chŏng-ju [Kin Sei-tsū] ed., *Chōsen tōchi shiryō*, vol. 7, p. 192.

257. M. A. Persits, "Eastern Internationalists in Russia and Some Questions of the National Liberation Movement (1918 – July 1920)," R. A. Ulyanovsky ed., *The Comintern and the East* (Moscow: Progress Press, 1979), p. 87.

258. Canfield F. Smith, "Krasnoshchekov, Alexandr Mikhailovich (1880-1937?)," p. 44.

259. Canfield F. Smith, "Shumiatskii, Boris Zakharovich (1886-1943?)," Wieczynski Joseph L. ed., *The Modern Encyclopedia of Russia and Soviet History*, vol. 35 (Academic International Press, 1983), pp. 74-75; Khromov, S. S. etc. ed., *Grazhdanskaia voina i voennaia interventsia v SSSR* [Civil War and Military Intervention in the USSR], (Moscow: Sovetskaia Entsiklopediia, 1987), p. 684.

260. Kim Tan-ya, "Lenin hoegyŏn insanggi" [Impressive Memoirs on the Meeting with Lenin], *Chosŏn Ilbo*, 30 Jan. 1925.

261. "Uchreditel'nyi S'ezd Koreiskoi Kommunisticheskoi partii," p. 217; "Chae-Ro Koryŏ hyŏngmyŏng kundae yŏnhyŏk," p. 8; *Gendaishi shiryō*, vol. 27, p. 199.

262. "Tongaguk Haninbu ilchi," 16 Jan. 1921.

263. Ibid., 8 Feb. 1921.

264. Chang To-jŏng to Katayama Sen, "Korai kyōsantō no enkaku," p. 12.

265. Canfield F. Smith, "Krasnoshchekov, Alexandr Mikhailovich (1880-1937?)," p. 44. Krasnoshchekov was finally recalled to Moscow in July 1921.

266. Kim Hong-il, "Chayusi ch'ambyŏn chŏnhu" [All the Details of the Free City Tragic Incident], *Sasanggye*, Feb. 1965, p. 221; Yi Sŏk-t'ae ed., *Sahoe kwahak taesajŏn* [Encyclopedia on Social Science] (Seoul: Munu Insŏgwan, 1948), pp. 599-600.

267. Yi In-sŏp, letter to Kim Se-il, 5 Feb. 1968.

268. "Chae-Ro Koryŏ hyŏngmyŏng kundae yŏnhyŏk," pp. 20-21. These arrested leaders of the "Shanghai-Chita Group" were sentenced guilty from three years to five years of imprisonment.

269. "Chae-Ro Koryŏ hyŏngmyŏng kundae yŏnhyŏk," p. 34; Kim Kyu-myŏn, *Nobyŏng Kim Kyu-myŏn ŭi pimangnok esŏ*, pp. 39-42.

270. Detailed reports about the Congress are found in "Uchreditel'nyi S'ezd Koreiskoi

Kommunisticheskoi partii," pp. 187-48 and "Doklad Koreiskoi Kommunisticheskoi partii III-mu Kongressu Kominterna," pp. 249-60.

271. Yi Sŏk-t'ae, Sahoe kwahak taesajŏn, p, 600; "Chŏng Chae-dal, Yi Chae-bok chosŏ" [Protocol of Chŏng Chae-dal and Yi Chae-bok], Kim Chun-yŏp and Kim Ch'ang-sun ed., *Hanguk kongsanchuŭi undongsa: charyo p'yŏn*, vol. 1 (Seoul: Koryŏ Taehakkyo Asea Munje Yŏnguso, 1979), pp. 103-104; M. T. Kim, *Koreiskie internatsionalisty v bor'be za vlasti sovetov na Dal'nem Vostoke (1918-1922)*, p. 92; Kim Kyu-myŏn, *Nobyŏng Kim Kyu-myŏn ŭi pimangnok esŏ*, p. 40.

272. Yi Sŏk-t'ae ed., *Sahoe kwahak taesajŏn*, p. 600.

273. "Chae-Ro Koryŏ hyŏngmyŏng kundae yŏnhyŏk," p. 54.

274. "Doklad Koreiskoi Kommunisticheskoi partii III-mu Kongressu Kominterna," p. 256. Chang Ki-yŏng and Afanasii Kim were exiled to Krasnoiarsk and Kim Tong-han was exiled to Tiumen. See Kim Kyu-myŏn, *Nobyŏng Kim Kyu-myŏn ŭi pimangnok esŏ*, pp. 39-40.

275. "Uchreditel'nyi S'ezd Koreiskoi Kommunisticheskoi partii," p. 229. At the congress, Yi Tong-hwi was not included in the list of the "Shanghai Group" leaders who would be expelled from the Party, but later the Central Executive Committe of the Korean Communist Party ("Irkutsk Group") expelled Yi Tong-hwi from the Party, obviously by the order of Shumiatsky.

276. Kim Ch'ŏl-su, "Kim Ch'ŏl-su ch'inp'il yugo," p. 354; Kim Chŏng-myŏng [Kin Seimei] ed., *Chōsen dokuritsu undō*, vol. 5, p. 294; Dinshun' Pak, "V Prezidium Krestinterna. Dokladnaya zapiska Pak Dinshun," p. 2; Kim Kyu-myŏn, *Nobyŏng Kim Kyu-myŏn ŭi pimangnok esŏ*, pp. 39-40.

277. Kim Chŏng-ju [Kin Sei-tsū] ed., *Chōsen tōchi shiryō*, vol. 7, p. 171.

278. Kim Ch'ŏl-su, "Kim Ch'ŏl-su ch'inp'il yugo," pp. 349-50; *Purgŭn Kunsa* 24 Dec. 1921.

279. Kim Kyu-myŏn, *Sŏngjae yakchŏn e kwanhan hoesanggi*, 14; Kim Ch'ŏl-su, "Kim Ch'ŏl-su ch'inp'il yugo," pp. 350-51; Kim Chŏng-myŏng [Kin Seimei] ed., *Chōsen dokuritsu undō*, vol. 5, p. 294; Dinshun' Pak, "V presidium krestinterna: dokladnaia zapiska," p. 3; Yi Yŏng-il, "Yi Tong-hwi Sŏngjae sŏnsaeng," p. 93.

280. The documents of the two sides provided different numbers of victims. "Shanghai-Chita Group" — shot: 72; drowned: 37; chased by horse cavalry: more than 200; missing: more than 250; arrested: 917. "Irkutsk Group" — killed: 37; injured: 4; ran away: more than 50; arrested: more than 900. See Kim Chŏng-ju [Kin Sei-tsū] ed., *Chōsen tōchi shiryō*, vol. 7, pp. 31-37.

281. "Chae-Ro Koryŏ hyŏngmyŏng kundae yŏnhyŏk," p. 43.

282. Kim Enman [Kim Yŏng-man], "Zaiavlenie v Politisecretariat IKKI" [Report to the Executive Committee of the Comintern], 6 Mar. 1928.

Chapter Six

1. Boris Dmitrievich Pak, *Koreitsy v Rossiiskoi imperii*, p. 188.
2. Kim Wŏn-yong, *Chaemi hanin osimnyŏnsa*, pp. 498-501.

I. Primary Sources

1. Korean

An, Ch'ang-ho. "Ilgi" [Diary]. In Chu Yo-han ed. *An Tosan chŏnsŏ*. pp. 621-787.

"Chae-Ro Koryŏ hyŏngmyŏng kundae yŏnhyŏk" [The History of the Korean Revolutionary Army in Russia]. In Kim Chun-yŏp and Kim Ch'ang-sun ed. Hanguk *kongsanjuŭi undongsa charyo p'yŏn*, vol. 2. pp. 1-54.

Chi, Kŏn. "Na ŭi ilgŭi" [My Diary]. *Hanin Sinbo*, 6, Jan. 1918. p. 3: 13 Jan. 1918. p. 3.

Ch'oe, Chae-hyŏng. "Kwanggo" [Announcement]. *Taedong Kongbo*, 20 Jan. 1909. p. 3.

Ch'oe, Kye-rip. Letter to Kim Se-il. n.d.

Ch'oe, Nam-sŏn. *Chosŏn tongnip undong sosa* [A Short History of the Korean Independence Movement]. Seoul: Tongmyŏngsa. 1946.

Ch'oe, Pong-jun. "Palganhanŭn mal" [Words for Publication]. *Haejo Sinmun*, 26 Feb. 1908. p. 2.

Chŏng, T'ae. Letter to Kim Se-il. n.d.

Ch'ŏnggu Sinbo [Green Hills Newspaper]. Vladivostok. Reprinted by Asea Munhwa Yŏnguso, Hallim University. Ch'unch'ŏn: 1995. Oct. 1917-Dec. 1919.

Ch'osa. "Ilse rŭl kyŏngdong sikidŭn k'oegŏl Yi Yong-ik ŭi kusim man wŏn sakŏn"

[Nine Hundred Thousand Wŏn Case of Unusual Hero, Yi Yong-ik Who Had Startled a World]. *Samch'ŏlli*, Sep. 1930. pp. 18-21.

Chosŏn Ch'ongtokpu [Japanese Government-General Office of Korea]. "Chosŏn oe esŏ ŭi Chosŏnin sanghwang ilban" [General Situation of Koreans outside Korea]. *Sindonga*, Feb. 1967. pp. 474-98.

Chu, Yo-han. *An Tosan chŏnsŏ* [The Complete Writings of An Tosan]. Seoul: Samjungdang. 1963.

H. M. "Chosŏn ŭi yŏryujuŭija ko Kim Sttankkebi yŏsa yakchŏn" [A Short History of Korean Feminist, the Late Mrs. Stankevich Kim]. *Kaebyŏk*, 57, Mar. 1925. pp. 25-32.

Haejo Sinmun [The Vladivostok Korean Gazette]. Vladivostok. Feb.-May 1908.

Han, Hyŏng-gwŏn. "Hyŏngmyŏngga ŭi hoesangnok: Lenin kwa tamp'an, tongnip chagŭm isipŏk wŏn hoektŭk" [Recollections of a Revolutionary: Negotiation with Lenin, Obtaining Two Billion Wŏn as the Funds for Independence Movement]. *Samchŏlli*, 6, Oct. 1948. pp. 10-11.

Hanin Sinbo [The Korean Newspaper]. Vladivostok. Reprinted by Asea Munhwa Yŏnguso, Hallim University. Ch'unch'ŏn: 1995. Sep. 1917-Jan. 1918.

Hong, Pŏm-do. "Hong Pŏm-do ŭi ilchi" [Diary of Hong Pŏm-do]. Pak Sŏng-su ed. *Hanguk tongnip undongsa charyojip: Hong Pŏm-do p'yŏn* [Materials on Korean Independence Movement: Part for Hong Pŏm-do]. Seoul: Hanguk Chŏngsin Munhwa Yŏnguwŏn. 1995. pp. 3-20.

Huang, Long-guo ed. 1988. *Chosŏnjok hyŏngmyŏng t'ujaengsa* [History of the Revolutionary Struggles of Koreans]. Liaoning: Ryonyŏng Minjok Ch'ulp'nasa.

Hwang, Uk. "Chae oe kak chibang sanghwang — Sojaha chibang chŏnghwang" [Situation of Every Region Abroad — Sojaha Region]. *Tongnip Sinmun*, 4 Apr. 1923. p. 4: 2 May 1920. p. 4: 21 July 1920. p. 4.

Kang, Ho-yŏ, "Such'ŏng ŭibyŏngdae ŭi yŏnhyŏk" [The History of the Partisan Unit in Such'an]. Yi In-sŏp ed. *Nŭrgŭn ppalchisan dŭl ŭi hoesanggi* [Recollections of the Old Partisans]. ms. 1964-1965.

"Kangdong swinhae" [Fifty Years (of Koreans) in the Primorye]. *Hanin Sinbo*, 23 Sep. 1917: p. 3, 30 Sep. 1917. p. 3: 7 Oct. 1917. p. 3: 14 Oct. 1917. p. 3: 22 Oct. 1917. p. 3.

"Kanminhoe chojik ch'onghoe sojip t'ongjisŏ" [Notice of an Organizational General Meeting for the Kanminhoe]. ms. 13 Jan. 1913.

KHM. "Noryŏng Chosŏnin nongch'on chŏnghyŏng ŭi kŭmsŏk" [Present and Past of the Situation of the Korean Agricultural Village in Russian Territory]. *Kaebyŏk*, 61, July 1925. pp. 100-104.

Kim, Ch'ŏl-su. "Kim Ch'ŏl-su ch'inp'il yugo" [Posthumous Personal Manuscripts of Kim Ch'ŏl-su]. *Yŏksa Pip'yŏng*, 5, Summer 1989. pp. 348-74.

Kim, Chŏng-gyu. *Yongyŏn Kim Chŏng-gyuilgi* [Diary of Kim Chŏng-gyu], 3 vols. Seoul: Tongnip Kinyŏmgwan. 1994.

Kim Chun-yŏp and Kim Ch'ang-sun. ed. *Hanguk kongsanjuŭi undongsa: charyop'yŏn* [The History of Korean Communist Movement: Source Materials], 2 vols. Seoul: Koryŏ Taehakkyo Asea Munje Yŏnguso. 1979-1980.

Kim, Ha-sŏk. "Yi Tong-hwi tongmu ŭi ssŭbbŭrapkka rŭl puinhanda" [I Deny the Reference of Comrade Yi Tong-hwi]. *Sŏnbong*, 8 Feb. 1930. p. 4.

Kim, Hu-gyŏng. *Taehan Minguk tongnip undong konghunsa* [History of the Meritorious Figures Who Contributed to the Independence of the Republic of Korea]. Seoul: Kwangbok Ch'ulp'ansa. 1983.

Kim, Kyu-myŏn. *Nobyŏng Kim Kyu-myŏn ŭi pimangnok esŏ* [From the Memoirs of the Old Soldier Kim Kyu-myŏn]. ms. n. d.

_______. *Sŏngjae yakchŏn e kwanhan hoesanggi* [Recollection on the Biography of Yi Tong-hwi]. ms. n. d.

Kim, Pyŏng-je. "Chinbohoe wa Ilchinhoe ŭi pihwa" [Secret Story of the Chinbohoe and Ilchinhoe]. *Hyesŏng*, Jan. 1932. pp. 130-35.

Kim, Pyŏng-jo. *Hanguk tongnip undong saryak* [Brief History of Korean Independence Movement]. Seoul: Asea Munhwasa. 1977.

Kim, Se-yong. "Sŏbaengnia ŭi Chosŏnin hwaltong" [The Activities of Koreans in Siberia]. *Samchŏlli*, Oct. 1930. pp. 2-9.

Kim, Sŭng-bin. Letter to Kim Se-il, 2 Mar. 1970.

Kim, Wŏn-yong [Kim Warren Y.]. *Chaemi hanin osimnyŏnsa* [The Fifty Year History of Koreans in America]. Reedley, California: 1959.

Kongnip Sinbo [The United Korean]. San Francisco: 1907-1909.

Kukhoe Tosŏgwan. *Hanguk minjok undongsa saryo: chunggukp'yŏn* [Historical Materials on the Korean National Movement: China Part]. Seoul: Library of Korean National Assembly. 1976.

"Kukkyŏng chibang sich'al pongmyŏngsŏ (1)" [Report on the On-site Inspection of the Border Regions Following Order]. *Paeksan Hakpo*, 9, Dec. 1970. pp. 168-246.

Kuksa P'yŏnch'an Wiwŏnhoe comp. *Hanguk tongnip undongsa* [The History of the

Korean Independence Movement]. 1968. 5 vols. Seoul: Chŏngŭm Munhwasa. 1983.

_______. *Hanguk tongnip undongsa charyo* [The History of the Korean Independence Movement: Sources], 27 vols. Seoul: Kuksa P'yŏnch'an Wiwŏnhoe. 1983-.

Kwak, Im-dae. "An To-san" [An Ch'ang-ho]. 1968. *Hangukhak Yŏngu*, 4, Mar. 1992. Center for Korean Studies of Inha University. pp. 167-273.

Kwŏnŏp Sinmun [Work Promotion Gazette]. Vladivostok. Reprinted by Asea Munhwa Yŏnguso. Hallim University, Ch'unch'ŏn: 1995. May 1912-Aug. 1914.

Kye, Pong-u. *Kkum sog ŭi kkum* [A Dream in a Dream]. ms. 2 vols. Kzyl Orda [Kazakstan]. 1944.

_______. "Osu pulmang" [Do not Forget Our Enemy]. In Kuksa P'yŏnch'an Wiwŏnhoe, comp. *Hanguk tongnip undongsa*, vol. 2. pp. 607-37.

Mun, Chae-rin. "Myŏngdong ŭn Kando ŭi Oryongch'on" [Myŏngdong was the Sŏ Kwoeng-il and Tongam ed. Five Dragon Village in Chientao]. *Kandosa sillon*, vol. 1. Seoul: Uridŭl ŭi P'yŏnjisa. 1993.

No, Chae-yŏn. "Chae-Mi Hanin saryak" [A Short History of the Koreans in America]. *Tongnip undongsa charyojip*, vol. 8. Seoul: Tongnip Undongsa P'yŏnch'an Wiwŏnhoe. 1963.

Pak, Kye-ju. "Taeji ŭi sŏngjwa" [Constellation in the Great Earth]. *Pak Kye-ju chŏnjip*, vol. 6. Seoul: Samyŏng Ch'ulp'ansa. 1957.

Pak, No-sun. "1918-1922 nyŏn kungmin chŏnjaeng tangsi e kwanhayŏ" [Concerning the Civil War, 1918-1922]. ms. n.d.

Pak, Ŭn-sik. *Hanguk tongnip undong chi hyŏlsa* [Bloody History of Korean Independence Movement]. Seoul: Seoul Sinmunsa Ch'ulp'anguk. 1946.

Pak, Yŏng-gap. "Aryŏng Osori Such'ŏng yangnon" [Brief Review of Such'an in Ussurisk, Russian Territory]. *Sinhan Minbo*, 20 July 1910. p. 3.

"Pon saju Ch'oe Pong-jun kong yŏksa" [History of the Owner of This Company, Honorable Ch'oe Pong-jun]. *Haejo Sinmun*, 26 Mar. 1908. p. 1.

"Pon saju Ch'oe Pong-jun kong yŏksa nonp'yŏng" [Comment on the History of This Company's Owner, the Honorable Ch'oe Pong-jun]. *Haejo Sinmun*, 27 Mar. 1908. p. 1.

Purgŭn Kunsa [Red Soldiers]. 24 Dec. 1921. Irkutsk.

Sabangja [Kye Pong-u]. "Pukkando kŭ kwagŏ wa hyŏnjae" [North Chientao, its Past and Present]. *Tongnip Sinmun*, 1 Jan. 1920. p. 5: 10 Jan. 1920. p. 2: 13 Jan. 1920. p. 3: 22 Jan. 1920. p. 2.

Sin, Suk. *Na ŭi ilsaeng* [My Life]. Seoul: Ilsinsa. 1956.

Sinhan Minbo [The New Korea]. San Francisco and Los Angeles. Mar. 1909-.

Sin Tonga P'yŏnjipsil. *Hanguk kŭndae inmul paeginsŏn* [Selected One Hundred Persons of Modern Korea]. Seoul: Tonga Ilbosa. 1985.

Sipwŏl hyŏngmyŏng sipchunyŏn wŏndong kinyŏm chunbi wiwŏnhoe. *Sipwŏl hyŏngmyŏng sipchunyŏn kwa Ssobet Koryŏ minjok* [The Tenth Anniversary of the October Revolution and Koreans]. Vladivostok: Haesamwi Tosŏ Chusik Hoesa. 1927.

Sogong. "Yi Sung-man gun ŭige irŏn ŭl chunora" [A Word to Mr. Rhee Syngman]. *Tongnip Sinmun*, 31 Mar. 1925. pp. 2-4.

Sŏnbong [The Vanguard]. Vladivostok. 1923-1937 (Reprinted by Koryŏ Sŏrim, Seoul: 1994).

Song Sang-do, *Kiro sup'il* [Donkey-Riding Tour Essays]. Seoul: Kuksa P'yŏnch'an Wiwŏnhoe. 1955.

Sunjong kukchannok [Record of the National Funeral for King Sunjong]. Seoul: n. p. 1926.

Taedong Kongbo [The Great East Gazette]. Vladivostok. 17 Jan.1909-14 Aug. 1910 (Reprinted by Ministry of Patriots and Veterans Affairs, Korea: 1993).

Taedong Sinbo [The Great East Newspaper]. Vladivostok. 18 Aug. 1910-1 Sep. 1910 (Reprinted by Ministry of Patriots and Veterans Affairs, Korea: 1993).

Taehain Chŏnggyobo [Bulletin of the Russian Orthodoxy for Koreans]. Chita: 1912-1914 (Reprinted by Asea Munhwa Yŏnguso, Hallim University, Ch'unch'ŏn, Korea, 1995).

"Taehan Minguk Imsi Chŏngbu kwanryŏn yosich'alin myŏngbu" [List of the Persons Related to the Korean Provisional Government Who Need to be Observed]. Seoul: Kukka Pohunch'ŏ. 1996.

Tansŏn [Kye Pong-u]. "Mango ŭisa An Chung-gŭn chŏn" [Biography of Permanent Righteous Person, An Chung-gŭn]. *Kwŏnŏp Sinmun*, 28 June 1914. p. 3: 5 July 1914. p. 3: 12 July 1914. p. 3: 19 July 1914. p. 3: 26 July 1924. p. 3: 2 Aug. 1914. p. 3: 9 Aug. 1914. p. 3: 16 Aug. 1914. p. 3: 23 Aug. 1914. p. 3: 29 Aug. 1914. p. 3.

Tonga Kongsan [East Asian Commune]. Irkutsk. no.1 (14 Aug. 1920)-no. 4 (10 May 1921).

Tonga Ilbo, 2 Jan. 1928: 26 May 1921.

Tongnip Kinyŏmgwan Tongnip Undongsa Yŏnguso [Korean Independence Hall].

comp. *Tosan An Ch'ang-ho charyojip* [Collections of An Ch'ang-ho], 3 vols. Ch'ŏnan: Tongnip Kinyŏmgwan. 1990.

Tongnip Sinmun [The Independence Newspaper]. Shanghai and Nanjing. 21 Aug. 1919-11 Nov. 1925 (Reprinted by the Korean Independence Hall, 1985).

"Tosan ŏnhaeng sŭpyu" [Collections of Behaviors and Words of Tosan]. Yun Pyŏng-sŏk and Yun Kyŏng-no ed. *An Ch'ang-ho iltaegi* [Biography of An Ch'ang-ho]. Seoul: Yŏkminsa. 1995. pp. 155-226.

Twibabo [Kye Pong-u]. "Aryŏng silgi" [Real Record of (Koreans) in Russian Territory]. *Tongnip Sinmun*, 26 Feb. 1920. p. 1, 1 Mar. 1920. p. 8: 4 Mar. 1920. p. 3: 13 Mar. 1920. p. 3: 18 Mar. 1920. p. 1: 20 Mar. 1920. p. 2: 25 Mar. 1920. p. 1: 30 Mar. 1920. p. 1: 1 Apr. 1920. p. 1: 3 Apr. 1920. p. 1: 8 Apr. 1920. p. 3.

_______. "Kim Alneksandra chŏn" [Biography of Alexandra Kim]. *Tongnip Sinmun*, 17 Apr. 1920. p. 3: 20 Apr. 1920. p. 3: 20 Apr. 1920. p. 3.

"Wŏn Se-hun Sŏnsaeng ŭi tongnip t'ujaeng yaksa" [The Brief History of the Struggle of Mr. Wŏn Se-hun for the Independence]. ms. 1950.

"Yi Chun kong i p'ihŭlin nal" [The Day When Honorable Yi Chun Bled]. *Kwŏnŏp Sinmun*, 19 July 1914. p. 1.

Yi, Hong-guk. "Pukkando Sŏjŏn Hakkyo wasan silok" [The Real Story of the Closure of the Sŏjŏn School]. *Haejo Sinmun*, 26 May 1908. p. 3.

Yi, In-sŏp. "Ch'oe Ko-ryŏ chasŏjŏn ŭl yŏnguhadaga na ŭi sogam" [My Impressions while Studying the Autobiography of Ch'oe Ko-ryŏ]. ms. 1961.

_______. "Aleksandra Kim ŭi chŏngi" [Biography of Alexandra Kim]. *Sisa Journal*, 216, 16 Dec. 1993. pp. 70-76: *Sisa Journal*, 217, 23 Dec. 1993. pp. 68-73.

_______. *Mangmyŏngja ŭi sugŭi* [The Handwriting of an Exile]. ms. n. d.

_______. Letter to Kim Se-il. 18 Jan. 1968.

_______. Letter to Kim Se-il. 5 Feb. 1968.

_______. Letter to Kim Se-il. 7 Mar. 1968.

Yi, Kwang-su. "Na ŭi kobaek" [My Confession]. *Yi Kwang-su chŏnjip*, vol. 13. Seoul: Samjungdang. 1964.

Yi, Man-gyu. *Yŏ Un-hyŏng t'ujaengsa* [History of Yŏ Un-hyŏng's Struggle]. Seoul: Ch'ongmungak. 1946.

"Yi Pŏm-yun kwa *ŭibyŏng*" [Yi Pŏm-yun and Righteous Soldier]. *Sinhan Minbo*, 25 May 1910. p. 1.

Yi Sŏk-t'ae. *Sahoe kwahak taesajŏn* [Social Science Encyclopedia]. Seoul: Munu Insŏgwan. 1948.

Yi, Sŭng [Hong, P'a]. "Kwagŏ 50-nyŏn ŭl tolna pomyŏn" [When I Recollect the Past of Fifty Years]. Kho Song-mu ed. *News on Korean Studies in Kazakstan and Central Asia*, 4, July 1993 (Alma-Ata, Kazakstan: Department of Korean Studies Centre of Oriental Studies of Kazakstan Academy of Science). pp. 56-67.

Yi, Tong-hwi. "Sŭbbŭrapkka" [Reference]. *Sŏnbong*, 17 Dec. 1929. p. 4.

"Yi Tong-hwi tongmu ŭi ilsaeng" [A Whole Life of Comrade Yi Tong-hwi]. *Sŏnbong*, 4 Feb. 1935. p. 4.

Yi, Yŏng-il. "Yi Tong-hwi Sŏngjae sŏnsaeng" [Mr. Yi Tong-hwi]. *Hangukhak Yŏngu*, 5, Jul. 1993 (Center for Korean Studies of Inha University). pp. 167-333.

Yŏ, Un-hong. *Mongyang Yŏ Un-hyŏng* [Yŏ Un-hyŏng]. Seoul: Ch'ŏnghagak. 1967.

Yu, Cha-hu. *Chosŏn hwap'ye go* [Study on the Currency of Korea]. Seoul: Hagyesa. 1940.

_______. *Yi Chun sŏngsaeng chŏn* [Biography of Mr. Yi Chun]. Seoul: Tongbang Munhwasa. 1957.

Yu, In-sŏk. *Ŭiamjip* [Collection of Yu In-sŏk's Writings], 2 vols. Seoul: Kyŏnin Munhwasa. 1973.

Yun, Chŏng-hŭi. "Kando kaech'ŏksa" [History of the Chientao Development]. *Hangukhak Yŏngu*, 3, Mar. 1991. Center for Korean Studies of Inha University. pp. 13-28.

2. Japanese

Archives in the Japanese Ministry of Foreign Affairs.

Chang, To-jŏng. "Korai kyōsantō no enkaku" [The History of Koryŏ (Korean) Communist Party]. ms. n.d.

Chōsen sōtokufu [Japanese Government-General Office of Korea]. *Chōsen no hogo kyū heigō* [Protection and Annexation of Korea]. Seoul: 1918.

Chōsen sōtokufu [Department of Social Affairs]. *Manshū Shiberia chihō ni okeru Chōsenjin jijō* [Situation of Koreans in Manchuria and Siberia]. Seoul: 1923.

Chōsen sōtokufu [Police Department]. *Kōtō kankei nenpyō* [High-Level Police Related Chronology]. Seoul: 1929.

"Dai ni zen Ro Kanzoku daihyōshakai kaigiroku" [The Minutes of the Second

Congress of the Korean Representatives in All Russia]. AJMFA, MT16324.17 (File 4).

Hanguk Komunhŏn Yŏnguhoe. *Yesim chonggyŏl kyŏlchŏlp'an* [Final Decision of the Preparatory Trial]. Seoul: Komunhŏn Yŏnguhoe. 1968.

"Heitan kanbu chōhō junpō (Chōsenjin no jokyo)" [Military Headquarters, the Kwantung Army, the Situation of the Koreans]. December 21-31, 1918. *Selected Archives of the Japanese Army-Navy, 1868-1945*. (VA)AA (F) no.1042 (NA14249).

Hosoi, Hajime. *Sen-Man no keiei: Chōsen mondai no konpon kaiketsu* [Management of Korea and Manchuria: The Fundamental Solution of the Korea Question], vol. 2. Tokyo: Jiyu Tokyusha. 1921.

Kang, Tŏk-sang. *Gendaishi shiryō* [Sources on Contemporary History], 6 vols (25-30). Tokyo: Misuzu Shobō. 1967-1972.

Kim, Chŏng-ju ed. *Chōsen tōchi shiryō* [Historical Sources on the Administration of Korea], 10 vols. Tokyo: Kankoku Shiryō Kenkyūshō, 1970-1971.

Kim Chŏng-myŏng [Kin Seimei] ed. *Chōsen dokuritsu undō* [Korean Independence Movement], 5 vols. Tokyo: Hara Shohō, 1966-1967.

"Kora kyōsantō oyobi Zenro kyōsantō ni kansuru chiyosasho" [Investigation Report on the Koryŏ Communist Party and All Russian Communist Party]. *Chotokuho*. Seoul: Chosengun Sambobu. 12, 6 Mar. 1923.

Murata, Yōichi ed. *Kominterun shiryōshū* [Collections on the Comintern], vol. 1. Tokyo: Taogatsu Shoten. 1979.

Nagano, Akira. *Manshū mondai no jissō* [The True Picture of the Problems in Manchuria]. Tokyo: Mondai Kenkyūshō. 1928.

Nippon Rikugun Sambō Hombu. *Shiberia shuppei* [Siberian Expedition], vol. 1. Tokyo: Shinjidaishi. 1972.

Yamaguchi, Hōsuke. *Shiberiya hishi* [Secret History of Siberia]. Tokyo: Nippon Hyōronsha. 1923.

"Yŏ Un-hyŏng chosŏ" [Protocol of Yŏ Un-hyŏng]. In Kim Chun-yŏp and Kim Ch'ang-sun ed. *Hanguk kongsanchuŭi undongsa: charyop'yŏn*, vol. 1. pp. 227-435.

Zaigai hainichi Senjin yūryokusha meibo [Register of Influential Anti-Japanese Koreans]. ms., 1919.

3. Chinese

Chungguk Tangangwan charyo [Documents from the Chinese Government Archives in Yanji, Helong and Wangqing Prefectures]. Tongnip Kinyŏmgwan Charyosil [Korean Independence Hall Archive].

4. English

Bishop J. F. [Isabella L. Bird]. *Korea and Her Neighbors: A Narrative of Travel, with an Account of the Recent Vicissitudes and Present Position of the Country*, 2 vols. London: John Murray. 1898.

Department of State. *The Korean Minority in Manchuria*. Washington: Office of Intelligence Coordination and Liaison. 1946.

Eudin, X. J. and R. C. North. *Soviet Russia and the East, 1920-1927: A Documentary Survey*. Stanford: Stanford UP. 1957.

Evans, Murchison James Henry. *Long White Mountain: A Journal in Manchuria*. London and New York: Longmans, Greenand Co. 1888.

"Extraterritoriality." Lasker Bruno ed. *Problems of the Pacific 1931: Proceedings of the Fourth Conference of the Institute of Pacific Relations, Hangchow and Shanghai, China, October 21 to November*, 2 (Chicago: U of Chicago P. 1932). pp. 169-315.

Grierson, Robert. *Episodes on a Long, Long Trail*. ts. 1957.

Hyun, Soon [Hyŏn, Sun]. *My Autobiography*. ts. n. d.

"Japanization of Korea: General Ichibana Interviewed." *Japan Chronicle*, 17 Apr. 1916.

Kendall, C. W. *The Truth about Korea: Facts about the New Korean Republic and Japanese Military Autocracy*. San Francisco: The Korean National Association. 1919.

MacMurray, John. *Treaties and Agreements with and Concerning China, 1894-1919*, 2 vols. New York and London: Oxford UP. 1921.

Pak, Chin-sun, "The Socialist Movement in Korea." In Suh ed. *Documents of Korean Communism 1918-1948*. Princeton: Princeton UP. 1970.

R [Han Hyŏng-gwŏn]. "The Situation in Eastern Asia." *Communist International*, 13 (Aug. 1920). pp. 2541-50.

Representatives of the Korean Delegation to the First Congress of the Communist and Revolutionary Parties of the Far East, Moscow, to The Executive

Committee III Communist International, Moscow. ts. 5 Apr. 1922.
Suh, Dae-sook ed. *Documents of Korean Communism 1918-1948*. Princeton: Princeton UP. 1970.
Suh, Dae-sook ed. and trans. *The Writings of Henry Cu Kim: Autobiography with Commentaries on Syngman Rhee, Pak Yong-man, and Chŏng Sun-man*. Honolulu: U of Hawaii P. 1987.
The Geographical Section of the Naval Intelligence Division [Naval Staff, Admiralty]. *A Handbook of Siberia and Arctic Russia*, vol. 1. London: His Majesty's Stationary Office. 1914.
The Manchurian Daily News. 5 Apr. 1915.
The Report of the Executive Committee of the Communist International: A Speech Delivered by G. Zinoviev at the III Congress of the Communist International, at Moscow, on June 25th, 1921. Moscow: The Press Bureau of the Communist International. 1921.
The 2nd Congress of the Communist International: As Reported and Interpreted by the Official Newspapers of Soviet Russia. Washington: Government Printing Office. 1920.
"Who is Who of the Korean National Council." ts. 1923.

5. Russian

Anosov, Semen Davidovich. *Koreitsy v Ussuriiskom krae* [Koreans in the Ussurisk Region]. Khabarovsk and Vladivostok: Knizhnoe Delo. 1928.
"Doklad Koreiskoi Kommunisticheskoi partii III-mu Kongressu Kominterna" [Report of the Korean Communist Party to the Third Congress of the Comintern]. *Narody Dal'nego Vostoka*, 2, 23 June 1921. pp. 249-60.
Gozhenskii, Ivan. "Uchastie Koreiskii emigratsii v revoliutsionnom dvizhenii na Dal'nem Vostoke" [The Participation of the Koreans in the Revolutionary Movement in the Far East]. Kommissia po Istoriii Oktiabr'skoi Revoliutsii R. K. P. ed. *Revoliutsiia na Dal'nem Vostoke*, vol. 1. Moscow and Leningrad: Gosudarskvennoe Izdatel'stvo. 1923. pp. 357-74.
Grave, V. V. *Kitaitsy, Koreitsy i Iapontsy v Priamur'e* [Chinese, Koreans and Japanese in the Priamur]. St. Petersburg: V. F. Grishbaum. 1912.
Iakovlevich, Derber Petr and M. L. Sher. *Ocherki Khazaistvenno i Zhizni Dal'nego Vostoka* [Essays on Agricultural Life of the Far East]. Moscow and Leningrad:

Gosudarstvennoe Izdatel'stvo. 1927.

Iaremenko, A. N. "Dnevnik kommunista" [Diary of a Communist]. Kommissia po Istoriii Oktiabr'skoi Revoliutsii R. K. P. ed. *Revoliutsiia na Dal'nem Vostoke*, vol. 1. Moscow and Leningrad: Gosudarskvennoe Izdatel'stvo. 1923. pp. 131-279.

Izvestiia. 1919-1920.

"Izvlechenie iz Otcheta obshchestva Razvitiia Truda / Kuön-öp-khoi / za 1911 i 1912 g.g. / s 6-go Dekabria 1911 goda po 1-oe Ianvaria 1913 goda" [Excerpts from the Report of the Work Promotion Association/ Kwŏnŏphoe/ for 1911 and 1912/ from December 6, 1911 to January 1, 1913]. St. Petersburg Central State Historical Archives.

Kim, Vladimir Dmitrievich ed. *Tumangan: Pogranichnaia Reka* [Tuman River: Border River]. Tashkent: Uzbekiston. 1994.

Kommissia po Istoriii Oktiabr'skoi Revoliutsii R. K. P. Bolshevikov] ed. *Revoliutsiia na Dal'nem Vostoke*, 2 vols. Moscow-Leningrad: Gosudarskvennoe Izdatel'stvo. 1923.

Kommunisticheskii International.

Koreits [Pak Chin-sun]. "Probuzhdenie Korei" [Awakening of Korea]. *Zhizn' Natsional'nostei*, 7 Mar. 1920. p. 3.

Li, Inseb [Yi In-sŏp]. "Biografiya Aleksandry Petrovny Kim-Stankevich" [Biography of Alexandra Petrovna Kim Stankevich]. ts. 1963.

_______. "Vospominania o godakh interventsii i grazhdanskoi voiny na Dal'nem Vostoke, 1918-1922 gg." [Recollections on the Years of Intervention and Civil War in the Far East, 1918-1922]. ts. 1962.

Narody Dal'nego Vostoka [Peoples of the Far East], no. 1, n. d.; no. 2, June 1921; no. 3, Aug. 1921; no. 4, Oct. 1921; no. 5, Dec. 1921.

Nomura [Japanese Consul General in Vladivostok]. letter to the Military-Governor of the Primorye. 20 Aug. 1914. Far Eastern Central State Archives in Tomsk, F.1, O.12, E. 581.

Pak, Din'shun' [Pak Chin-sun]. "Koreiskaia emigratsiia v Rossii" [Korean Emigration to Russia]. *Zhizn' Natsionalostei*, 18, Apr. 1920. p. 2.

_______. "Osvoboditel'noe dvizhenie narodov Vostoka in Sovetskaia Rossia" [Liberation Movement of the Peoples of the East in Soviet Russia]. *Zhizn' Natsionalostei*, 64, 29 Feb. 1920.

_______. "Reforma v Koree i Koreiskaia sotsialisticheskaia partiia" [Reform in Korea

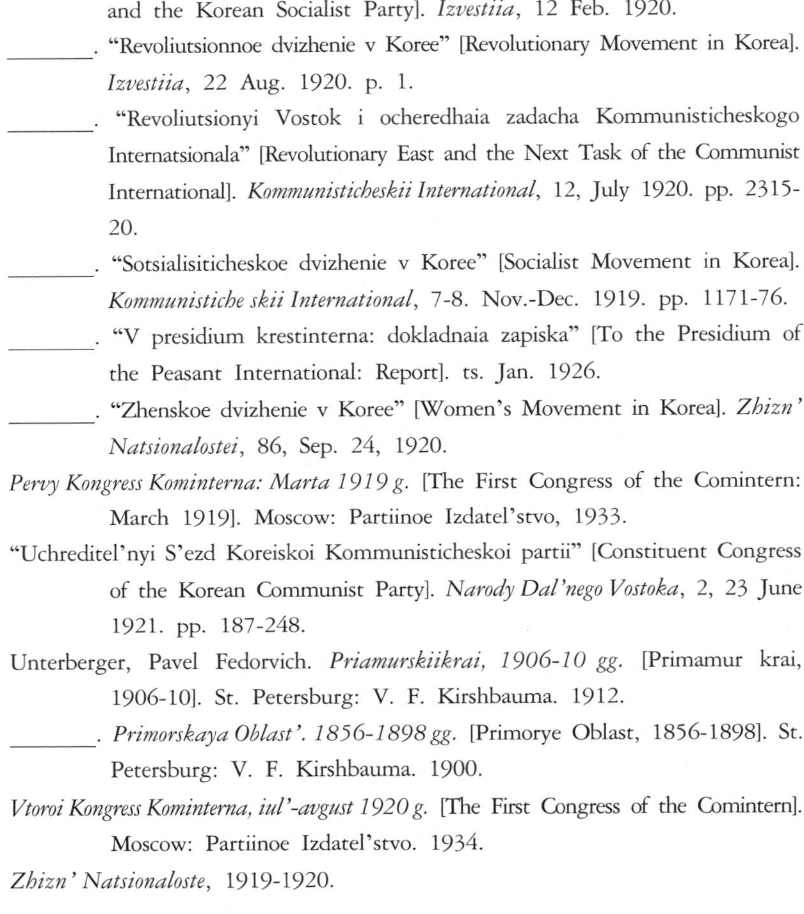

and the Korean Socialist Party]. *Izvestiia*, 12 Feb. 1920.

_______. "Revoliutsionnoe dvizhenie v Koree" [Revolutionary Movement in Korea]. *Izvestiia*, 22 Aug. 1920. p. 1.

_______. "Revoliutsionyi Vostok i ocheredhaia zadacha Kommunisticheskogo Internatsionala" [Revolutionary East and the Next Task of the Communist International]. *Kommunisticheskii International*, 12, July 1920. pp. 2315-20.

_______. "Sotsialisiticheskoe dvizhenie v Koree" [Socialist Movement in Korea]. *Kommunistiche skii International*, 7-8. Nov.-Dec. 1919. pp. 1171-76.

_______. "V presidium krestinterna: dokladnaia zapiska" [To the Presidium of the Peasant International: Report]. ts. Jan. 1926.

_______. "Zhenskoe dvizhenie v Koree" [Women's Movement in Korea]. *Zhizn' Natsionalostei*, 86, Sep. 24, 1920.

Pervy Kongress Kominterna: Marta 1919 g. [The First Congress of the Comintern: March 1919]. Moscow: Partiinoe Izdatel'stvo, 1933.

"Uchreditel'nyi S'ezd Koreiskoi Kommunisticheskoi partii" [Constituent Congress of the Korean Communist Party]. *Narody Dal'nego Vostoka*, 2, 23 June 1921. pp. 187-248.

Unterberger, Pavel Fedorvich. *Priamurskiikrai, 1906-10 gg.* [Primamur krai, 1906-10]. St. Petersburg: V. F. Kirshbauma. 1912.

_______. *Primorskaya Oblast'. 1856-1898 gg.* [Primorye Oblast, 1856-1898]. St. Petersburg: V. F. Kirshbauma. 1900.

Vtoroi Kongress Kominterna, iul'-avgust 1920 g. [The First Congress of the Comintern]. Moscow: Partiinoe Izdatel'stvo. 1934.

Zhizn' Natsionaloste, 1919-1920.

6. German

Der Zweite Kongress der Kommunistischen Internationale: Protokoll der Verhandlungen vom 19. Juli in Petrograd und vom 23. Juli bis 7. August 1920 in Moskau [The Second Congress of the Communist International: Protocol of Proceedings of July 19 in Petersburg and from July 23 till August 7, 1920 in Moscow]. Hamburg: Carl Hoym Nacht. Louis Chahnbley. 1921.

Kommunistischen Internationale. *Die Tätigkeit der Exekitives und des Präsidiums des E. K der Kommunistischen Internationale vom 13 Juli 1921 bis 1. Februar*

1922 [Activities of the Executive and the Presidium of the Executive Committee of the Communist International] from 13 July 1921 till 1 February 1922. Petrograd: Feltrinello Reprint. 1967.

7. French

Han, Hen Kuon [Han Hyŏng-gwŏn]. "La Situation en Asie Orientale" [The Situation in East Asia]. *L'Internationale Communiste*, 13. 1920. pp. 2551-60.

II. Secondary Sources

1. Korean

Ban, Byung Yool. "Taehan Kungmin Ŭihoe ŭi sŏngnip kwa chojik" [The Establishment and Organization of the Korean National Council]. *Han'guk Hakpo*, 13, Spring 1987. pp. 123-67.

_______. "Taehan Kungmin Ŭihoe wa Sanghae Imjŏng ŭi t'onghap chŏngbu surip undong" [The Movement for the Unification between the Korean National Council and the Shanghai Provisional Government]. *Hanguk Minjok Undongsa Yŏngu*, 2, Mar. 1988. pp. 89-129.

_______. "Yi Tong-hwi wa Hanmal minjok undong" [Yi Tong-hwi and the National Movement in late Chosŏn Dynasty]. *Hanguksa Yŏngu*, 87, Dec. 1994. pp. 147-91.

Cho, Tong-gŏl. "Imsi chŏngbu surip ŭl wihan ilch'ŏn gubaek sipch'il nyŏn ŭi 'Taedong tangyŏl ŭi sŏnŏn'" [The Declaration of 1917 for the Establishment of the Provisional Government]. *Hangukhak Nonch'ong*, 9. 1987. pp. 123-52.

Hyŏn, Kyu-hwan. *Hanguk yuiminsa* [A History of Korean Wanderers and Emigrants], vol. 1. Seoul: Omungak. 1976.

Im Kyŏng-sŏk. "Koryŏ kongsandang *yŏngu*" [Study on the Korean Communist Party]. Unpublished Ph. D. Diss. Sŏnggyungwan U. 1993.

Kang, Man-gil. *Koch'ŏssŭn Hanguk Kŭndaesa* [Revised Modern History of Korea]. Seoul: Ch'angjak kwa Pip'yŏngsa. 1994.

Kim To-hun. "Kongnip Hyŏphoe (1905-1909) ŭi minjok undong yŏngu" [Study on National Movement of the Kongnip Hyŏphoe (1905-1909)]. *Hanguk Minjok Undongsa Yŏngu*, 4. 1989. pp. 15-51.

Kim, Yong-hae. *Taehan kidokkyo ch'imnye kyohoesa* [History of Korean Baptist Churches]. Seoul: Taehan Kidokkyo Ch'imnye Kyohoe Ch'onghoe. 1964.

Ko, Chŏng-hyu. "Taehan Minguk Imsi Chŏngbu Kumi Wiwŏnbu (1919-1925) yŏngu" [Study on the Committee on European and American Affairs of the Korean Provisional Government]. Unpublished Ph. D. Diss. Korea U. 1992.

Ko, Sŭng-je. *Hanguk iminsa yŏngu* [Studies on History of Korean Emigration]. Seoul: Changmungak. 1973.

Kuksa P'yŏnch'an Wiwŏnhoe comp. *Han'guk tongnip undongsa* [The History of the Korean Independence Movement], 5 vols. 1968 (Seoul: Chŏngŭm Munhwasa. 1983).

Kwŏn, Hŭi-yŏng. "Koryŏ Kongsandang ironga Pak Chin-sun ŭi saengae wa sasang" [The Life and Thoughts of Pak Chin-sun, Theoretician of Korean Communist Party]. *Yŏksa Pip'yŏng*, 4, Spring, 1989. pp. 285-94.

Lee, Hoon-ku [Yi Hun-gu]. *Manchuwa Chosŏnin* [Manchuriaand Koreans]. P'yŏngyang: Union Christian College Press. 1932.

Pak, Hwan. *Rŏsia Hanin minjok undongsa* [Korean National Movement in Russia]. Seoul: T'amgudang. 1995.

Pak, Min-yŏng. "Kuhanmal sŏbuk pyŏngyŏng chiyŏk ŭi ŭibyŏng yŏngu" [Study on the Righteous Army in Northwestern Border Region in Late Chosŏn Dynasty]. Unpublished Ph. D. Diss. Hanguk Chŏngsin Munhwa Yŏnguwŏn Hangukhak Taehakwŏn. 1995.

Sin, Yong-ha. *Hanguk minjok tongnip undongsa yŏngu* [Study on the History of Korean National Independence Movement]. Seoul: Ŭlyu Munhwasa. 1985.

Sŏ, Kwoeng-il and Tongam ed. *Kandosa sillon* [New Essayson Chientao], 2 vols. Seoul: Uridŭl ŭi P'yŏnjisa. 1993.

Yi, Hong-jik. *Kuksa taesajŏn* [Korean History Encyclopedia]. Seoul: Chimungak. 1968.

Yun, Pyŏng-sŏk. *Yi Sang-sŏl chŏn* [Biography of Yi Sang-sŏl]. Seoul: Ilchogak. 1984.

_______. *Kukoe Hanin sahoe wa minjok undong* [Korean Communities Abroad and the National Movement]. Seoul: Ilchogak. 1990.

_______. "Yun Chŏng-hŭi chŏ 'Kando kaech'ŏksa' pu 'Yŏngsin hakkyo yŏnhyŏk' haeje" [Bibliographical Introduction to Yun Chŏng-hŭi's *History of the*

Chientao Development and its Appendix 'History of Yŏngsin School'].
Hangukhak Yŏngu, 3, Mar. 1991. pp. 5-11.

_______. "Yongyŏn Kim Chŏng-gyu ŭi saengae wa ≪yasa≫" [The Life of Kim Chŏng-gyu and ≪Unauthorized History≫]. *Hanguk Tongnip Undongsa Yŏngu*, 5, 1991. pp. 113-41.

2. Japanese

Hara, Teruyuki. "Roshia kakumei, Shiberi sensō to Chōsen dokuritsu undō" [Russian Revolution, Siberian War and Korean Independence Movement]. Kikuchi Masanori. ed. *Roshia kakumeiron: rekishi no fukken*. Tokyo: Tabata Shoten. 1977. pp. 171-216.

_______. "Shiberia.Kyokuto Roshia ni okeru jūgatsukakumei" [The October Revolution in Siberia and the Russian Far East]. *Surabu Kenkyū*, 24. 1979. pp. 75-125.

_______. *Shiberia shuppei: kakumei to kanshō, 1917-1922* [The Siberian Expedition: Revolution and Intervention, 1917-1922]. Tokyo: Chikumashobō. 1989.

Kang, Chae-ŏn. "Chōsen dokuritsu undō no konkyochi mondai" [The Question of Bases for Korean Independence Movement]. *Chōsen Minjoku Dokuritsu Undōshi Kenkyū*, 1, Jan. 1984. pp. 9-68.

Kang, Tŏk-sang. "Shōkai Rinji Seifu to Ryo Un-kyō" [The Shanghai Provisional Government and Yō un-hyŏng]. *Sansenri*, 40, Winter 1984. pp. 154-70.

_______. "Yonjūni teikoku gikai to Ryo Un-kyō" [The Forty Second Imperial Diet and Yō un-hyŏng]. *Sansenri*, 43, Fall 1985. pp. 214-27.

_______. "Kaigai ni okeru Chōsen dokuritsu undō no hattatsu" [Development of Korean Independence Movement Abroad]. *Chōsen Minzoku Undōshi Kenkyū*, 2. 1985. pp. 7-62.

Pak, Kyŏng-sik. *Nippon Teikokushūgi no Chōsenshihai* [The Rule of Japanese Imperialism in Korea], 2 vols. Tokyo: Aoki Shoten. 1973.

Sugimori, Kōji and Fujimoto Wakio. *Nichi-Ro Nisso kankei '200-nenshi': Nichi-ro no dei kara Shiberia kansho senso made* [Two Hundred Japanese-Russian and Japanese-Soviet Relations from the Encounter of Japan and Russia through the Siberian Intervention War]. Tokyo: Shinjidaisha. 1983.

Teizō, Hirose. "Li Yoyok no seiji katsudō (1904-7) ni tsuite—sono gaikō katsudō o tsūsin ni" [Concerning Political Activities of Yi Yong-ik (1904-7)—

Focusing on His Diplomatic Activities]. *Chōsen Minjoku Dokuritsu Undōshi Kenkyū*, 25, Mar. 1988. pp. 83-109.

Wada, Haruki. "Nichiro tōbō hanzainin hikiwatashi jōyaku fuzoku himitsu sengen-sho" [Secret Declaration Appended to the Russo-Japanese Treaty of Extradition]. *Shakai Kagaku Kenkyū*, 27, no. 4. 1976. pp. 86-116.

Yu, Hyo-jong. "Kyokutō Roshia ni okeru Chōsen mizoku undō: Kangoku Heigo kara dai nichi sekai taisen no hotpatsu made" [Korean National Movement in the Russian Far East — From the Annexation of Korea through the World War I]. *Chōsenshi Kenkyūshi Nonshū*, 22. 1985. pp. 135-66.

_______. "Kyokutō Roshia ni okeru jūgatsu kakumei to Chōsenjin shakai" [The October Revolution and the Korean Communities in the Russian Far East]. *Roshiashi Kenkyū*, 45. 1987. pp. 23-51.

_______. "Nigatsu kakumei to Kyokutō Roshia no Chōsenjin shakai" [The February Revolution and the Korean Communities in the Russian Far East]. *Roshia to Nihon*, 3. 1992. pp. 61-82.

3. English

Carr, Edward Hallet. *The Bolshevik Revolution 1917-1923*, 3 vols. 1953 (New York and London: Norton & Company. 1980-1981).

Gardner, Arthur Leslie. "The Korean Nationalist Movement and An Ch'ang-ho, Advocate of Gradualism." Unpublished Ph. D. Diss. U of Hawaii. 1979.

Ginsberg, George. "The Citizenship Status of Koreans in Pre-Revolutionary Russia and the Early Years of the Soviet Regime." *Journal of Korean Affairs*, 5, 2 July 1975. pp. 1-19.

Kho, Song-moo. *Koreans in Soviet Central Asia*. Helsinki: Finnish Oriental Society. 1987.

Kim, Ki-hoon. "Japanese Policy for Korean Rural Immigration." Unpublished Ph. D. Diss. U of Hawaii. 1992.

Kolarz, Walter. *The Peoples of the Soviet Far East*. New York: Frederick A. Praeger. 1954.

Lattimore, Owen. *Manchuria: Cradle of Conflict*. New York: The Macmillan Company. 1931.

Lee, Chong-sik. *The Politics of Korean Nationalism*. Berkeley and Los Angeles: U of California. 1965.

Lee, Robert H. G. *The Manchurian Frontier in Ch'ing History*. Cambridge: Harvard UP. 1970.

Li, Kwang-rin. "The Rise of Nationalism in Korea." *Korean Studies*, 10. 1986.

Malozemoff, Andrew. *Russian Far Eastern Policy 1881-1904: with Special Emphasis on the Cause of the Russo-Japanese War*. New York: Octagon Books. 1977.

Persits, M. A. "Eastern Internationalists in Russia and Some Questions of the National Liberation Movement (1918 – July 1920)." R. A. Ulyanovsky ed. *The Comintern and the East*. Moscow: Progress Press. 1979.

Radkey, Oliver Henry. *The Sickle under the Hammer: the Russian Socialist Revolutionaries in the Early Months of Soviet Rule*. New York and London: Columbia UP. 1963.

Scalapino, Robert A. and Chong-sik Lee. *Communism in Korea*, 2 vols. Berkeley, Los Angeles and London: U of California P. 1972.

Shin, Paul Hobom. "The Korean Colony in Chientao: A Study of Japanese Imperialism and Militant Korean Nationalism, 1905-1932." Unpublished Ph. D. Diss. U of Washington. 1980.

Smith, Canfield F. *Vladivostok under Red and White Rule: Revolution and Counterrevolution in the Russian Far East, 1920-1922*. Seattle and London: U of Washington P. 1975.

_______. "Krasnoshchekov, Alexandr Mikhailovich (1880-1937?)." Wieczynski Joseph L. ed. *The Modern Encyclopedia of Russia and Soviet History*, vol. 18. Academic International Press. 1980. pp. 41-46.

_______. "Shumiatskii, Boris Zakharovich (1886-1943?)." Wieczynski Joseph L. ed. *The Modern Encyclopedia of Russia and Soviet History*, vol. 35. Academic International Press. 1983. pp. 70-76.

Sokol, Edward D. "Ussuri Cossack Host." Wieczynski Joseph L ed. *The Modern Encyclopedia of Russian and Soviet History*, vol. 41. Academic International Press. 1978. pp. 135-40.

Stephan, John J. *The Russian Far East: A History*. Stanford: Stanford UP. 1994.

_______. "The Korean Minority in the Soviet Union." *Mizan,* 13, 3 Dec. 1971. pp. 138-50.

Suh, Dae-sook ed. *The Korean Communist Movement, 1918-1948*. Princeton: Princeton UP. 1967.

_______. *Koreans in the Soviet Union*. Honolulu: Center for Korean Studies. U of Hawaii. 1987.

Suh, Dae-sook and Edward J. Schultz ed. *Koreans in China*. Honolulu: The Center for Korean Studies. U of Hawaii. 1990.

Tompkins, Pauline. *American-Russian Relations in the Far East*. New York: The Macmillan Company. 1949.

Wada, Haruki. "Koreans in the Soviet Far East, 1917-1937." In Suh ed. *Koreans in the Soviet Union*. 1987. pp. 24-59.

Wang, I-shou. "Chinese Migration and Population Change in Manchuria, 1900-1940." Unpublished Ph. D Diss. U of Minnesota. 1971.

4. Russian

Chernyi, A. K. *Ocherkii Khabarovskoi kraevoi organizatsii KPSS (1900-1978 gody)* [Essay on Khabarovsk krai Organizations of the Soviet Union Communist Party (1900-1978)]. Khabarovsk: Khabarovskoe Knizhnoe Izdaltel'stvo. 1979.

Chun, Cholkhun. "Uchastie Koreiskogo naseleniia v revoliutsionnom dvizhenii na Dal'nem Vostoke (1917-1919 gg.: na Primore zhizni deiatel'nosti A. P. Kim-Stankevich)" [Participation of the Korean Population in the Revolutionary Activities in the Far East (1917-1919): On Primorye Activities of A. P. Kim-Stankevich]. Diss. Diplomaticheskaia Akademiia Mid Rossii Institut Aktual'nykh Mezhdunardnykh Problem. Moscow: 1994.

Grigortsevich, S. S. "Uchastie koreitsev russkogo Dal'nevo Vostoka v antiiaponskoi natsional'no-osvoboditel'noi bor'be (1906-1916)" [Participation of Koreans in the Russian Far East in the Anti-Japanese National Liberation Struggle]. *Voprosy Istorii*, 10. 1958. pp. 139-51.

_______. *Dal'nevostochnaia politika imperialisticheskikh derzhavv 1906-1917 gg.* [Far Eastern Policy of the Imperial Power, 1906-1917]. Tomsk: Izdatel'stvo Tomskogo Universiteta. 1965.

Khromov, S. S. etc. ed. *Grazhdanskaia voina i voennaia interventsia v SSSR* [Civil War and Military Intervention in the USSR]. Moscow: Sovetskaia Entsiklopediia. 1987.

Kim, Matvei Timofeevich. *Koreiski in ternatsionalisty v bor'be za vlast' sovetov na Dal'nem Vostoke (1918-1922)* [The Korean Internationalists Who Fought for Soviet Power in the Far East]. Moscow: Nauka. 1979.

Kim, Syn Khva. *Ocherki po istorii sovetskikh koreitsev* [Essays on the History of Soviet Koreans]. Alma Ata: Nauka. 1965.

Pak, Boris Dmitrievich. *Osvoboditel'naia bor'ba koreiskogo naroda nakanune pervoi mirovoi voiny* [The Liberation Struggle of the Koreans on the Eve of the First World War]. Moscow: Nauka. 1967.

_______. *Rossia i Koreia* [Russia and Korea]. Moscow: Nauka. 1979.

_______. *Koreitsy v Rossiiskoi imperii: Dal'nevostochnyi period* [Koreans in the Russian Empire: Far Eastern Period]. Moscow: Mezhdynarodnyi Tsentr Koreevedeniya Moskovskogo Gosudarstvennogo Universiteta. 1983.

Tkachev, G. A. "Immigratsiia na Dal'nem Vostoke Rossii v 20-e-30e gody" [Immigrations in the Russian Far East in the 1920-30s]. Unpublished Paper. 1994.

■ Author

Byung Yool Ban (Pyŏng-nyul Pan) is a Professor of History at the Hankuk University of Foreign Studies in the Republic of Korea.
Dr. Ban is an expert in the history of the Korean independence movement and of Korean minorities in Russia, China and the United States on which Dr. Ban has published numerous articles and authored several books.

한울아카데미 1818

THE RISE OF THE KOREAN SOCIALIST MOVEMENT

Nationalist Activities in Russia and China, 1905-1921

지은이 | Byung Yool Ban(반병률)
펴낸이 | 김종수
펴낸곳 | 한울엠플러스(주)

책임편집 | 양혜영

초판 1쇄 인쇄 | 2016년 3월 25일
초판 1쇄 발행 | 2016년 3월 31일

주소 | 10881 경기도 파주시 광인사길 153 한울시소빌딩 3층
전화 | 031-955-0655
팩스 | 031-955-0656
홈페이지 | www.hanulmplus.kr
등록번호 | 제406-2015-000143호

Printed in Korea.
ISBN 978-89-460-5818-7 93910(양장)
978-89-460-6041-8 93910(반양장)